W9-AZO-458

# PUBLIC
## POLICY

# PUBLIC POLICY

## Politics, Analysis, and Alternatives

**MICHAEL E. KRAFT**
AND **SCOTT R. FURLONG**
UNIVERSITY OF WISCONSIN–GREEN BAY

CQ PRESS

A Division of Congressional Quarterly Inc.
WASHINGTON, D.C.

CQ Press
1255 22nd St., N.W., Suite 400
Washington, D.C. 20037

Phone, 202-729-1900
Toll-free, 1-866-4CQ-PRESS (1-866-427-7737)

www.cqpress.com

Copyright © 2004 by CQ Press, a division of Congressional Quarterly Inc.

All rights reserved. No part of this publication may be reproduced or transmitted in any form or by any means, electronic or mechanical, including photocopy, recording, or any information storage and retrieval system, without permission in writing from the publisher.

∞ The paper used in this publication exceeds the requirements of the American National Standard for Information Sciences—Permanence of Paper for Printed Library Materials, ANSI Z39.48-1992.

Cover design: Kimberly Glyder
Composition: MidAtlantic

Printed and bound in the United States of America

07   06   05   04        5   4   3   2

**Library of Congress Cataloging-in-Publication Data**

Kraft, Michael E.
    Public policy : politics, analysis, and alternatives / Michael E. Kraft and Scott R. Furlong.
        p.   cm.
Includes bibliographical references and index.
    ISBN 1-56802-484-3 (alk. paper)
    1. Policy sciences—Evaluation.   2. Political planning—Citizen participation.   3. Political planning—United States—Evaluation.   4. Public administation—United States—Evaluation.
4. Public administration—United States—Evaluation.   5. Evaluation research (Social action programs)—United States   I. Furlong, Scott R.   II. Title.
    H97.K73 2004
    320'.6'0973—dc21

                                                                        2003012116

FOR

SANDY, SASHA, AND JESSIE

AND

DEBBIE, KYLE, AND DARCY

## PART III  ISSUES AND CONTROVERSIES IN PUBLIC POLICY

Health care costs are certain to soar in the coming decades as the baby boom generation ages and begins to demand an array of increasingly expensive medical services. In 2001 spending on health care rose a full 8.7 percent for a total of $1.4 trillion, or about 14 percent of the U.S. economy. This translates into more than $5,000 for each person in the nation each year. Prescription drug costs alone totaled approximately $140 billion in 2001, with some widely used newer drugs priced at hundreds of dollars. What is the best way to deal with these rising costs? How should we protect the solvency of the Social Security system as the baby boomers threaten to bankrupt it and jeopardize benefits for future generations? Indeed, what form of health care and social security will be available to the generation of citizens now in their teens and twenties? What will the alternatives be?

Such public policy decisions touch nearly every aspect of daily life in the United States, although many people fail to recognize or fully understand their impact. Social Security reform, for example, may not seem terribly urgent to most young people today, but it undoubtedly will shape the quality of their lives decades down the road. This is why citizens need to understand not only how governments make policy choices but also how to evaluate those choices. We believe the reason to be politically aware is simple: policymakers are more responsive to the public's preferences and needs and, in some cases, more effective when citizens take a greater interest in public affairs and play a more active role in the policymaking process. We hope this new text stimulates interest and concern while equipping readers with the skills they need to think critically and creatively about policy problems.

The subtitle of this book—politics, analysis, and alternatives—explicitly expresses what we are trying to accomplish. Different from typical policy texts, this text integrates three aspects of public policy study: government institutions and the policymaking process, the concepts and methods of policy analysis, and the choices that we make collectively about substantive public policies at all levels of government. Throughout, we focus on the interrelationship of government institutions, the interests and motivations of policy actors both inside and outside of government, and the role of policy analysis in clarifying public problems and helping citizens and policymakers choose among policy alternatives. These central themes are reinforced by providing students with the tools they need—how to find key information, how to use specific evaluative criteria, how to apply policy analysis methods, and how to assess the politics of policymaking—to investigate issues and carry out policy analysis on their own. We believe that this hands-on approach is the best way to teach the skills of analysis and give students not only an understanding of the conduct of public policy but also a way *into* the process.

## A FOCUS ON POLICY ANALYSIS

By emphasizing the pervasiveness of public policy, we make its study a vital activity for students. They can better appreciate the power they wield to effect change in the system once they are armed with the tools of policy analysis. However, the logic of public policy and its study must be addressed before students encounter these powerful tools of the trade. In Part I we demonstrate that public policy choices are not made in a vacuum. Social, economic, political, and cultural contexts matter, as do the distinguishing characteristics of the U.S. government and the rationales behind government intervention. An understanding of the structure of institutions, the motivation of policy actors (both formal and informal), and the unique political nature of the U.S. system will allow students to comprehend the complexity of government while discovering opportunities for engagement with the process. We present multiple perspectives on the policymaking process, from elite theory to rational choice theory, but concentrate on the policy process model—a portrayal of policymaking as a sequence of key activities from agenda setting to policy implementation—that is used in the rest of the book. We hope these chapters encourage students to ask how decisions are made as well as why they are made in one way and not another.

Part II gets to the heart of the book and explains the approaches and methods of policy analysis, laying a foundation for dissecting and understanding public problems and policy choices. With careful application of the tools of policy analysis, students can interpret complex and conflicting data and arguments, evaluate alternative courses of action, and anticipate the consequences of policy choices. Specific cases—from tax cuts and criminal justice to urban traffic congestion—illustrate both the difficulty of policy analysis and its value in policymaking. Students learn how to find and interpret policy-relevant information, and acquire an understanding of the limitations to what government can do about public problems. The evaluative criteria at the book's core—a focus on effectiveness, efficiency, and equity—train students to think clearly about policy alternatives. Ethical considerations necessarily receive considerable attention as well. Case studies involving family planning, profiling in relation to homeland security goals, national energy policy, and the morality of stem cell research give students the opportunity to grapple controversial issues for which no policymaker has *the* answer.

Part III consists of five substantive policy chapters designed to illustrate and apply the concepts and methods introduced in the first two sections of the book. The five core policy areas—economics and budgeting, health care, welfare and Social Security, education, and energy and the environment—represent a substantial part of contemporary U.S. policymaking and also present a diversity of economic, political, and ethical issues for analysis. This part of the text offers a clear picture of the issues that beginning analysts would encounter in policymaking or in the evaluation of all areas of public policy. For readers who want to probe more deeply into those policy areas that we discuss peripherally—for instance, criminal justice, civil rights and liberties, or foreign and defense policy—we recommend *Issues for Debate in American Public Policy,* which offers selections from the *CQ Researcher* and abundant references to current policy debates.

Consistent with the text's emphasis on analysis, we begin each policy area chapter with a brief illustration of a policy scenario (budget surpluses and deficits, the promise of school vouchers, the rising cost of health care, Social Security reform, and the risks of climate change) to spark student interest. A background section describes the public problems faced and the solutions chosen to date. We briefly summarize major policies and programs, discuss when and how they came into effect, review available policy evaluations, and suggest how students can investigate policy alternatives. At the end of each chapter, we offer a focused discussion of policy reform in terms of economic, political, and ethical issues. These discussions link closely to the kind of questions that can be asked about any proposal for policy change and how it might be addressed. At the end of Part III, a concluding chapter brings together the arguments of the text and looks to future challenges in public policy.

## SPECIAL FEATURES

To underscore the importance we place on active learning and critical engagement, we developed two unique text boxes to guide students as they research policy problems: "Working with Sources" and "Steps to Analysis." The first type of feature identifies important sources of information and how to utilize them, providing step-by-step suggestions on how to make good (and critical) use of the information found on Internet sites—among other resources—that offer important data sources and policy perspectives. The "Steps to Analysis" features invite critical thinking about specific policy problems. They demonstrate how to ask the urgent questions that drive policy analysis, and then present ways to narrow and refine these questions into feasible projects. To further direct students to the information they need, discussion questions at the end of each chapter get at, for instance, the "best" way to deal with health care concerns, environmental problems, and education issues. These questions are followed by annotated suggested readings, suggested Web sites, and a list of keywords. Students will find chapter notes and a reference list at the end of book as well.

A variety of ancillaries accompany this text. A companion Web site at www.cqpress.com/college/publicpolicy offers students concise chapter summaries, practice quiz questions (modeled on the test bank questions), exercises that further the book's goals, annotated links that allow easy access to the sites found in the text, and much more. All of these features are keyed to each of the twelve chapters in the text, and they will be updated regularly. Instructors should note that the exercises on the Web site, as well as those in the text itself, provide the basis for potential assignments for students. These can be used as models that instructors can adjust as necessary to concentrate on other areas of public policy. An instructor CD, free to adopters, includes a full test bank of approximately 250 questions that have been fully class tested. Included also is test generation software—*CQP Test Writer*—that can generate multiple forms of customized tests. To assist in classroom preparation, PowerPoint lecture outlines for all twelve chapters are also available.

We have tried to make this text a distinctive and appealing introduction to the study of public policy while also maintaining a commitment to scholarly rigor. Our experience with students in many years of teaching tells us that they can handle demanding reading and exercises if these are linked firmly to concrete issues affecting society and students' personal lives.

Above all, the text emphasizes the urgency of making government more responsive to citizen concerns and equips students with the skills they need to understand policy controversies. Thus we hope the text inspires students to take a serious interest in government, politics, and public policy, and to participate enthusiastically in policy debates and decision making throughout their lives.

## ACKNOWLEDGMENTS

Preparation of this text reflects contributions from many individuals and institutions. We are particularly grateful for support from the University of Wisconsin, Green Bay and our colleagues in the Department of Public and Environmental Affairs. Our students in Introduction to Public Policy, Public Policy Analysis, and other courses have taught us much over the years, especially about what they need to know to become informed citizens and effective policy professionals. We are also grateful to them for allowing the liberty of asking them to read drafts of the chapters.

We also appreciate the efforts of hundreds of creative public policy scholars whose work makes a book like this possible. Our citation of their publications is a modest way of acknowledging our dependence on their research and insights into policy analysis and policymaking. We thank Christopher Borick at Muhlenberg College, Ross Cheit at Brown University, John Cranor at Ball State University, Kenneth Godwin at University of North Carolina, Charlotte, Deborah Orth at Grand Valley State University, and Gerry Riposa at California State University, Long Beach, as well as the anonymous reviewers of the manuscript for their critical appraisals and perceptive, helpful suggestions. Special thanks are also due to the skilled and conscientious staff at CQ Press: Brenda Carter, Charisse Kiino, Elise Frasier, Carolyn Goldinger, Belinda Josey, and Lorna Notsch. As always any remaining errors and omissions rest on our shoulders. We hope readers will alert us to any such defects and suggest changes they would like to see in future editions. Contact us at kraftm@uwgb.edu or furlongs@uwgb.edu.

MICHAEL E. KRAFT
SCOTT R. FURLONG

# PUBLIC
## POLICY

IN OCTOBER 2002 THE FIRST U.S. NATIONAL STANDARDS FOR labeling food as *organic* went into effect. The U.S. Department of Agriculture (USDA) spent more than ten years developing the rules to govern which foods merit the label *organic* and which must be marketed without such a designation, presumably at a disadvantage to their producers because the demand for cleaner, safer food is growing. In fact, the U.S. market for organic food has been increasing at 20 percent annually since the early 1990s, reaching nearly $9 billion in sales in 2002. An act of Congress, the Organic Foods Production Act of 1990, mandated the USDA action, which the department's Agricultural Marketing Service implemented. The law requires the establishment of national **standards** and seeks to assure consumers that certain agricultural products, whether produced domestically or imported, meet the standards.

Fearing a potential loss of business, traditional farming and ranching interests, particularly large agribusinesses, lobbied fiercely for a weak definition of what qualifies as organic. They wanted to be able to market many conventionally raised and processed foods with the organic label. On the other side of this dispute, the Organic Trade Association fought for a strict definition to protect what it regards as purer sources of food. At stake in the battle over the standards was nothing less than the nation's food dollars.

In December 1997 the Clinton administration's USDA released a draft of the proposed standards, but they were not nearly as strong as the final guidelines the agency adopted in 2002 during the Bush administration. The USDA agreed to tougher language after it was subjected to intense criticism; it had received some 280,000 public comments on the draft rule, many of them protesting the initial standards. After all the battles were fought, the new rule is anything but simple. It runs to about five hundred pages and, like most other laws and **regulations**, reflects compromises designed to meet the demands of opposing interests.[1]

As this example of organic food labeling requirements illustrates, public policies do not appear out of thin air; rather, they are arrived at after long hours of research and debate from many sources, including the public. In addition, a policy deals with a particular slice of American life, although it also may be important to the public's general health and well-being. Pub-

President George W. Bush signs into law the No Child Left Behind Act of 2001, a sweeping federal education bill. The act mandates that states administer a national assessment test every year to determine how well public schools are performing and to ensure that students are promoted based on demonstrated mastery of the subject matter. Schools that fail to meet the new standards are eligible to receive federal funds to help them improve, but at the same time parents with children in those schools can choose to move them to different schools. The education initiative illustrates how the federal government and the states often share power, as well as the emphasis given at both levels to the use of new policy approaches that promise greater effectiveness in resolving public problems.

lic policy, however, deals with just about everything, affecting life in ways that are obvious and sometimes ways that are difficult to recognize.

## WHAT IS PUBLIC POLICY?

Public policy can be defined in many different ways, but basically it is a course of government action (or inaction) taken in response to social problems. Social problems are conditions the public widely perceives to be unacceptable and therefore requiring intervention. Problems such as environmental degradation, workplace safety, or access to health care services can be addressed either through government action; private action, meaning that individuals or corporations take the responsibility; or a combination of the two. What actually happens depends on how the public defines the problem and on prevailing societal attitudes about private action in relation to the government's role.

For the organic food labeling law, it was the public's perception of inadequate food safety and concern about pesticides and other contaminants in meats, produce, and processed food that prompted Congress to act and the USDA to issue the regulations. In contrast, Congress in 2001 chose to reject proposed workplace safety regulations and allow the private marketplace to resolve the problem. The Occupational Safety and Health Administration had sought to impose Clinton administration ergonomics rules in an effort to reduce repetitive motion injuries, but Congress concluded that the mandatory rules were too burdensome and costly for U.S. businesses. It preferred to allow each business to decide on its own how to deal with the safety of its employees.

Any level of government, whether federal, state, or local, may be involved in a particular policy effort because social problems, and the public demand for action on them, manifest themselves from the local to the national level. At the local level, failing public schools, high crime rates, or urban sprawl might attract enough attention to spur the school board, mayor, or city council to find remedies. At the national level, concern about inequitable access to health care or the country's heavy reliance on imported oil may galvanize policymakers and lead to policy development.

Whatever the level of government, proponents of policy actions seek a multitude of **goals**. For laws that govern personal conduct, such as speed limits, policies aim to restrict individual behavior as a way to protect lives or prevent injuries and property damage; that is, the goal is to promote the public's welfare or common good. After government enacts the laws, public policies also affect how the mandated services, such as police protection, public education, or national defense, are provided. Another form of public policy is the direct government payment. **Social Security** checks for senior citizens, agricultural subsidies for farmers, and research grants to universities sustain long-term individual and collective well-being.

Public policies reflect not only society's most important values but also the conflict between values. How do policymakers deal with the urgency of fighting crime or terrorism and the protection of citizens' civil liberties? What about the need to protect the environment and individual or corporate property rights? Policies therefore reflect which of many different values are given the highest priority in any given decision. David Easton (1965) captured this view in his frequently quoted observation that politics is "the authoritative allocation of values for a society."

What Easton means is that the actions of policymakers can determine definitively and with the force of law which of society's different and sometimes conflicting values will prevail. Should the federal government raise auto fuel efficiency standards to reduce emissions of greenhouse gases and cut U.S. dependence on imported oil, even if doing so raises the cost of buying a car? Or should such decisions be left to the marketplace and individual choice? Should government continue to recognize a woman's right to choose to have an abortion or restrict the choice and instead promote the rights of the fetus?

Because public policy almost always deals with tough questions—the fundamental issues of human values—the resulting policies are going to affect people's lives. For these reasons, this book was designed with several goals in mind. One is to help readers develop a fuller understanding of public policy and the way governments make policy decisions. The second goal is to encourage readers to look ahead to the implications of policy choices. The third is to foster critical thinking about public policy and possible alternative courses of action. For this reason, basic concepts related to policy analysis are introduced throughout the text. Here, the aim is to equip readers with essential skills in analytical thinking that will enhance their understanding of policy issues and make possible more effective participation in the policy process.

Developing a critical, analytical approach to policy issues has many advantages over simply learning the details of policy history, the present legal requirements in various programs, or an overview of current policy debates. Such knowledge is important, but it is inherently limited, in part because public policies and debates over them continually change, making earlier accounts less useful. In contrast, those who learn the basic principles of policymaking and policy analysis will have a better grasp of *why* governments make the decisions they do and be better able to identify the strengths and weaknesses in present policies as well as in proposals to change them. Individuals can apply these skills to the wide range of problems everyone faces as citizens and in their personal lives and careers.

## CLARIFYING BASIC CONCEPTS

Several fundamental concepts in the study of public policy require clarification. These include government, politics, public policy, and policy analysis. Although these terms are in common usage, no universal definition exists for any of them. Even a quick look at American government or public policy textbooks reveals substantial variation in the way political scientists and other students of public policy use them. Most analysts, however, employ these concepts in roughly comparable ways.

Government refers to the institutions and political processes through which public policy choices are made. These institutions and processes represent the legal authority to govern or rule a group of people. In the United States, the federal Constitution describes the government's institutions, which include Congress, the president, the various agencies of the executive branch, and the federal court system. Each is granted specific but overlapping legal authority to act under a **separation of powers** system. At state and local levels, parallel government institutions develop policy for citizens within their jurisdictions, guided by the authority granted in state constitutions and in state and local statutes and ordinances. The

American system of governance adheres to the principle of **federalism,** in which the national government shares authority with the states and local governments in many areas of public policy. Quite often, national policies, such as those dealing with environmental protection, are implemented chiefly by the states through an elaborate system of **intergovernmental relations** in which the federal government grants legal authority to the states to carry out national policies. In other policy areas, such as education, crime control, and land use regulation, state and local governments play the dominant role.

Politics refers to the processes by which government structures and authority are established and maintained and how public policies are formulated and adopted. Politics can also be thought of as the processes used to resolve conflicts in society. As Harold Lasswell (1958) expressed it, politics is about "who gets what, when, and how." So, if politics is about power and influence in society and in the processes of policymaking, it therefore concerns who participates in and who shapes the decisions that governments make and who gains and who loses as a result.

In the United States and most other democracies, politics is also related to the **electoral processes** by which citizens select the policymakers who represent them. In this sense, politics concerns political parties and their agendas and the political ideologies, philosophies, and beliefs held by candidates for office, their supporters, and their campaign contributors. The precise relationship of politics to public policy may not always be clear, however. Defenders and critics of specific policy actions may offer arguments based in economics, ethics, or other concepts of the public interest, but no one doubts that electoral politics is a major component of the policymaking process.

Politics exerts this strong influence on policymaking in part because elected officials necessarily must try to anticipate how their policy statements and actions might affect their chances for reelection. Policymakers are therefore sensitive to the views of the groups and individuals who helped them win office in the first place and whose support may be essential to keeping them there. These political incentives motivate public officials to pay particular attention to the policy preferences of their core constituencies, especially the activists, while also trying to appeal to the general electorate. For Republicans, the core constituencies include business interests, political conservatives, farmers, and suburban and rural residents, among others. For Democrats, the core constituencies are labor interests, environmentalists, African Americans, political liberals, residents of urban areas, and others.

Politics is also one of the principal reasons public policy is so riddled with conflict and why it can be so difficult to analyze. The debate over smoking is a perfect example. In recent years the government has stepped up its efforts to establish policies regarding smoking and tobacco (Derthick 2002; Fritschler 1995). A number of government agencies, such as the Office of the Surgeon General, the Food and Drug Administration (FDA), and the Federal Trade Commission (FTC), have been promoting policies to reduce smoking in the United States, while, at the same time, the USDA has been giving subsidies to tobacco farmers, a policy that seems to be in conflict with the spirit of the policies to discourage smoking. In addition, for years the military sold cigarettes at discount prices in military commissaries, sometimes at 30 percent to 60 percent less than the price available to civilians. When the Pentagon tried in 1996 to end the subsidy of tobacco products to discourage troops from using them, the tobacco industry lobbied Congress to block the plan.[2]

Clearly, tobacco policy today—whether higher cigarette taxes meant to curtail smoking, public ad campaigns to warn children and teenagers about the dangers of smoking, or actions to regulate tobacco as a drug—is influenced by conflicting sources such as **public opinion**, the actions of interest groups that represent the industry, and public health studies. All of these points of view are parts of the contentious process of setting new policy directions.

It would be wrong to assume, however, that such conflicts merely reflect inconsistencies in government policies, or worse, that they demonstrate bad faith. In fact, the process of resolving conflicts helps to determine where the public interest lies. It is also true that the conflicts are myriad: for example, should the nation rely less on fossil fuels or nuclear power and more on renewable sources of energy such as wind and solar power? Should it maintain a strong public school system or switch to a voucher system that gives students public money to attend private schools? Should students pay a greater percentage of the cost of attending public colleges and universities through higher tuition levels or should state taxpayers cover more of the bill to increase student access to higher education?

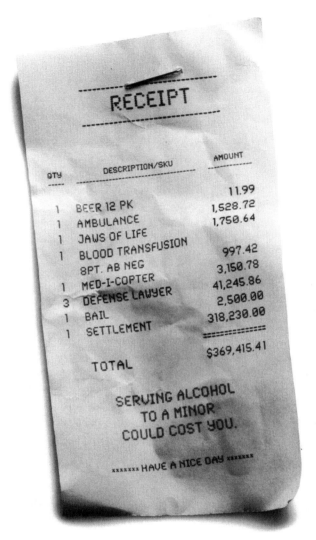

According to two Minnesota laws, you can be held financially liable and charged with a felony if you give alcohol to minors.

Mothers Against Drunk Driving   MN Department of Public Safety   Office of Juvenile Justice and Delinquency Prevention   Minnesota Join Together   Hennepin County Community Health Department   **Minnesota Prevention Resource Center**

This ad, cosponsored by Mothers Against Drunk Driving (MADD), uses dark humor to present a serious argument about drinking and driving: restaurants, bars, convenience stores, and other establishments that knowingly serve or sell alcohol to minors may be held liable for the consequences. A nonprofit, grassroots organization with more than six hundred chapters nationwide, MADD provides information on the dangers of drunk driving; works to prevent underage drinking; and supports victims of alcohol-related incidents. It also lobbies to change state and local laws so that those injured can seek payment of monetary damages. Posters, pamphlets, bumper stickers, school visits, and multimedia advertisements are just some of the methods used to promote the group's message. Such public education campaigns are common among citizen groups.

On these topics and countless others, government officials, interest groups, and active citizens promote their views about what to do, and they bring all kinds of information to bear on the decisions. Naturally, individual **policy actors** can and do disagree vigorously about the kinds of public policies that are needed and the proper role of government in addressing the problems.

The policymaking process within government provides abundant, although not necessarily equal, opportunities for all of these policy actors to discuss problems, formulate and promote possible policy solutions to them, and press for formal adoption by legislatures at the national, state, and local levels. Ultimately, executive agencies and departments, such as the Environmental Protection Agency (EPA), the Department of Defense, or a local police or public health department are responsible for implementing and evaluating what the legislators enact and, therefore, they are responsible for the success or failure of those policies.

We use the term *policy actors* throughout the text to refer to the many different players in the policymaking process. Formal policy actors include elected officials, such as city council members, governors, state legislators, members of Congress, and the president, as well as political appointees and career personnel in government agencies. Informal policy actors include organized interest groups, journalists, citizens, and policy analysts, among others. It is often difficult to determine whether the informal or formal policy actors are the most influential on a particular issue. Because the U.S. political system is perhaps the most open in the world, it provides many opportunities for nongovernmental policy actors to exert considerable influence over the direction and content of public policy.

The term *policy* refers in general to a purposive course of action that an individual or group consistently follows in dealing with a problem (Anderson 2003). In a more formal definition, a policy is a "standing decision characterized by behavioral consistency and repetitiveness on the part of both those who make it and those who abide by it" (Eulau and Prewitt 1973, 465). Whether in the public or private sector, policies also can be thought of as the instruments through which societies regulate themselves and attempt to channel human behavior in acceptable directions (Schneider and Ingram 1997). This book focuses on public policy, or what governments and public officials and the citizens they represent, choose to do or not to do about public problems. Such policies represent a settled course of action or pattern of activity over time, not a single or discrete decision.

Many students of public policy also distinguish between the intention to achieve certain defined goals and objectives through policy actions and their consequences, not all of which may be intended. For example, health care policies designed to reduce costs may succeed in saving money, but result in less adequate care for patients. Analysts also refer to **nonpolicies,** instances of governments either ignoring a problem or choosing not to deal with it, and instead allowing private or market forces to determine events. Urban sprawl is a prime example.

The language used to discuss public policy is sometimes confusing. Charles O. Jones (1984, 27) suggests separating the various elements of public policies, which include **intentions** (the purposes of government action), goals (the stated ends to be achieved), **plans** or **proposals** (the means for achieving goals), **programs** (the authorized means for pursuing goals), **decisions** or **choices** (specific actions that are taken to set goals, develop plans, and implement and evaluate programs), and **effects** (the effects that programs have on society, whether intended or unintended). One also needs to recognize the legal expressions of policy, such as laws, statutes, legislation, executive orders, regulations, and judicial rulings. All may constitute public policy or at least a portion of it. In addition, this text distinguishes between **policy outputs** (the formal actions that governments take to pursue their goals) and **policy outcomes** (the effects such actions have on society).

The following definition may help to integrate the various perspectives: *public policy is a course of government action or inaction in response to public problems. It is associated with formally approved policy goals and means, as well as the regulations and practices of agencies that implement programs.* This definition emphasizes the actual behavior of implementing agencies and officials, not merely the formal statements of policy goals and means found in statutes, executive orders, judicial opinions, and other expressions of government policy.

Consistent with this view, scholars have long argued that, ultimately, policy must be defined by students of public policy themselves (Jones 1984; Hogwood and Gunn 1984). That is, policy is not something that one discovers by looking at a statute, law textbook, or a government document, although it is possible to find a summary of policy goals or policy-maker intentions that way. Sometimes, more is needed, and then individuals need to research and understand the defining features of the policy. The point is that each person must learn how to look for information about policy commitments and actions and to **draw conclusions** about what the policy really is and what difference it is making in his or her life. For this reason, the text emphasizes basic principles of public policy and the research skills needed to find and evaluate such information, which leads to the subject of **public policy analysis.**

Analysis means deconstructing an object of study, that is, breaking it down into its basic elements to understand it better. Policy analysis is the examination of components of public policy, the policy process, or both. Put another way, it is the study of the causes and consequences of policy decisions. Duncan MacRae and James Wilde (1979, 4) have called policy analysis "the use of reason and evidence to choose the best policy among a number of alternatives." Policy analysis uses many different methods of inquiry and draws from various disciplines to obtain the information needed to assess a problem and think clearly about alternative ways to resolve it. The same information also shapes public debate and deliberation over what actions to take. At heart, policy analysis encourages deliberate critical thinking about the causes of public problems, the various ways governments and/or the private sector might act on them, and which policy choices make the most sense. Doing so requires not only knowledge of government and politics but also the ability to evaluate the policy actions. Chapter 6 discusses the major evaluative criteria used to make such judgments.

## WHY STUDY PUBLIC POLICY?

The study of public policy occurs in many different institutions and for diverse reasons. Policy analysts both in and outside of government have a professional concern for public policy. Scholars at universities and research institutions share some of the same interests as policy analysts, but scholars are more often concerned with building general knowledge of the policy process. For citizens with no professional concerns, but strong personal interests in government and public policy, the U.S. political system affords numerous opportunities to become

## WORKING WITH SOURCES

## INTEREST GROUPS ON THE WEB

Interest group Web sites are treasure troves of policy information, but a word of warning is in order. Visitors to these sites need to be cautious about how they approach the materials and policy recommendations they find. Information on these sites is always selective; it may be limited in scope and biased in ways that a naïve reader may not discern. Policy briefings and reports made available by such groups therefore merit careful and critical reading, and our goal here is to teach you how to be alert to the general political orientation of the group sponsoring the site. We start by asking about the credibility of the studies and reports you find there.

Visit the Web site of the American Petroleum Institute (http://api-ep.api.org)*, the major trade association for the oil industry, and access reports and data regarding its positions on energy issues by selecting the link for Issues and Advocacy. Then click on the Energy Policy link. From there, select the link for National Energy Strategy to read the group's position on the Bush administration's proposals to Congress in 2001. Note especially the language the API uses to support its position that the nation should expand its use of fossil fuels. It emphasizes "responsible

development" of energy sources "without compromising the environment" and speaks of the need to have "reliable and affordable energy supplies." Look also at the link for Increased Production and examine the API's statement on the need to drill for oil in the Arctic National Wildlife Refuge (ANWR).

For a contrasting view, visit the Natural Resources Defense Council's Web site (www.nrdc.org) and follow the link to clean air and energy, and then to energy. You will find brief fact sheets and more in-depth discussions of the NRDC's position on drilling in ANWR and energy policy in general.

How credible is the information you found on the two Web sites? Does either supply references to authoritative sources for the information presented, such as government reports or studies published in scientific or scholarly journals? How else can you judge the facts and issue positions on these pages? By comparing the different positions and the language used to defend them, can you determine which group offers the most defensible stance on energy production and the most convincing case for either drilling or not drilling for oil in ANWR?

*Note: Web sites are changed and upgraded frequently. The sites provided throughout this text are meant to be current; however, design changes may require you to investigate a site more thoroughly then originally assigned.

involved. Interest alone is a good reason to study public policy, but it is not the only one. Studying public policy may help citizens sharpen their analytic skills, decide what political positions and policies to support, and evaluate democratic governance. It may encourage students to consider careers in public policy, law, or government. Two additional reasons are presented here: the citizens' ability to participate in policy processes and make choices and their ability to influence policy decisions.

## Citizens' Ability to Participate and Make Choices

The United States is a representative democracy. Its citizens elect delegates to act for them, but that is not necessarily the end of citizen participation. Within democracies, citizens may speak out on policy development and government actions. Lack of knowledge about public problems, policies, government decisions, or politics does not normally keep people from acting in this way, but they can participate more effectively and have greater leverage by improving their understanding of the issues. During political campaigns, candidates for public office state their positions on the issues through speeches and advertisements in hopes of persuading voters to support them. Voters who study public policy are better equipped to understand the candidates' policy ideas and to evaluate them—that is, to determine what impacts they are likely to have and whether they are desirable. If elections are to turn on informed assessments of the issues rather than how good the candidate looks on camera, policy knowledge of this kind is essential.

Citizens can also join with others in an **interest group** to learn more about public policy. Scholars often observe that the **logic of collective action** suggests that a single individual would be irrational to join an interest group when almost no personal gain follows (Olson 1971). The enormous growth of citizen lobbies over the last several decades, however, clearly indicates that agreement with a group's goals persuades many people to sign up and participate (Berry 1997, 1999). Interest groups operate at all levels of government, and one of their roles is to educate policymakers and citizens about public policy issues. For example, many of them—from the National Rifle Association to the Sierra Club—commission policy studies and use them in the political process to advance their views (Wolpe and Levine 1998; Cigler and Loomis 2002). Nearly all of the major groups maintain Web sites that offer issue briefings and facilitate communication with public officials. The box "Working with Sources: Interest Groups on the Web" addresses the role of such groups in shaping public policy.

At state and local levels citizens may have the opportunity to get more directly involved in policymaking through **referendums**, **initiatives**, or participation in public hearings and meetings (Cronin 1989). A referendum is a law proposed by a state or locality for voters to approve or reject. An initiative is much the same, but a group of citizens organizes the effort to place it on the ballot. About half the states allow citizen-generated initiatives. Naturally, the voters can better determine whether to support or oppose a ballot measure if they understand the proposal and its possible effects. Obtaining that information and developing a sound position on the issues is often a challenge for the average voter and one reason critics argue that many initiatives lead to bad public policy, especially when insufficient thought goes into the drafting of the proposals or the public acts emotionally or in response to misleading media advertisements (Ellis 2002).

Although it was not a misleading initiative, a measure on the ballot in California in 1996 illustrates the problems of relying on this process for making public policy. Proposition 215, the California Medical Marijuana Initiative, won voter approval 56 percent to 44 percent. The new law did not legalize marijuana; rather, it allowed physicians to recommend marijuana use in medical treatment. The idea was to establish a legal exemption from existing drug laws and safeguard patients from criminal prosecution. The patient has the burden of proof to show that his or her medical condition justifies using an otherwise illegal substance. Most observers agree that the California legislature would never have approved the policy. But was the proposition a good idea? Shortly after the voters approved it, the federal government challenged the initiative, saying the government would use its authority under the national Controlled Substances Act to revoke the license of any doctor who recommended marijuana to a patient. A group of doctors and patients sued the federal government in an attempt to reverse its position and in late 2002 they won in a

## WORKING WITH SOURCES

## THE PUBLIC'S POLITICAL KNOWLEDGE

As indicated throughout the text, the enormous amount of information available through Web sites makes citizen activism more feasible than ever before. After all, the potential for activism is facilitated by information as well as by individual motivation to get involved. Reliance on Web sources, however, also presents a challenge: how to manage the huge amount of information.

In 2000 the federal government launched FirstGov (www.firstgov.gov), an official portal to U.S. government Web sites. Its mission was to make government more accessible and seamless and to make it easier for citizens to find the services they seek and to complete transactions online. A new search engine developed specifically for accessing such material is capable of sifting through about fifty-one million pages of information from national, state, and local governments in a fraction of a second.

A simple exercise indicates how useful First-Gov can be. Go to the site, look under the Citizens list of links, and select Volunteer. Once on this page, select a particular field of interest, such as Civic and Community. Type in your zip code to find a list of organizations in your community that are seeking volunteers.

A more challenging illustration of how to navigate through FirstGov involves a different kind of citizen participation: voting. Once again, look under the Citizens links and select the link for "and much more." Then, under Information by Topic, choose Voting and Elections. Under U.S. Congress select the Learn About Candidates heading and type in your zip code to see information about candidates from your congressional district. Click on one or more of the candidates to find information about voting records (for the incumbent), campaign contributions, and personal background. At this level, you can also send an e-mail message to the candidate or visit the candidate's Web site. The Web sites typically list candidate positions on the issues. Incumbents, not surprisingly, usually have more elaborate statements on the issues than challengers do. Note that candidate or campaign Web pages also may invite citizens to volunteer in the next campaign.

---

unanimous decision by a three-judge panel of the Ninth U.S. Circuit Court of Appeals in San Francisco, but that decision may not be the end of the dispute.

Public meetings afford perhaps the greatest opportunity to participate directly with other citizens and public officials to learn more about local problems and decide what to do about them. Notices of such meetings and hearings are posted in the local newspaper or on pertinent Web sites. The box "Working with Sources: The Public's Political Knowledge" is an introduction to a primary government source.

## Citizens' Ability to Influence Policy Decisions

Policymakers and others involved in the policy process need information to understand the dynamics of a particular problem and develop options for action. When examining **policy**

**alternatives**, they turn to studies that use methods of analysis such as **cost-benefit analysis or risk assessment**. The studies may use economic analysis to determine which of three options will provide society with the most efficient way of improving access to quality education or to health care—that is, to achieve policy objectives with the least expenditure of resources.

An awareness of the politics of the situation is also critical to deciding what action to take. Those who seek to reform the Social Security system, for example, must recognize the interests of the AARP (formerly known as the Association for the Advancement of Retired Persons), an interest group with more than thirty million members over the age of fifty. AARP members have strong views on Social Security, can easily be mobilized to contact policymakers, and they vote at a higher rate than other segments of the population. Members of Congress and other policymakers tend to pay attention to the AARP and take the group's positions on the Social Security system seriously.

Understanding the policymaking process provides citizens with opportunities to make their views known. To influence **environmental policy**, for example, one should know who the major players are and how they interact with one another. Although most people recognize the importance of Congress in making laws, those with a deeper understanding of the U.S. political system recognize that bureaucratic agencies, such as the EPA, play a central role in implementing the laws. At the state and local levels, knowledge of these governments and their operations equips citizens to play an active role and influence policy decisions.

## THE CONTEXTS OF PUBLIC POLICY

Public policy is not made in a vacuum. It is affected by social and economic conditions, prevailing political values and the public mood at any given time, the structure of government, and national and local cultural norms, among other variables. Taken together, this environment determines which problems rise to prominence, which policy alternatives receive serious consideration, and what actions are viewed as most economically and politically feasible. Some aspects of the environment, such as the U.S. system of separation of powers and the free-market economy, are relatively stable. Others, such as which party controls the White House and Congress, the public mood or political climate, and media coverage of policy-related developments, can vary considerably over time. To underscore how these variables shape the policymaking process, we offer a brief description of the social, economic, political, governing, and cultural contexts of public policy.

### Social Context

Social conditions affect policy decisions in myriad ways, as is evident in controversies over phenomena as diverse as urban sprawl, inner-city crime rates, and immigration. Moreover, social conditions are dynamic, not static. The population changes because of immigration, growth in nontraditional households, and lower or higher birth rates. These social changes in turn alter how the public and policymakers view and act on problems ranging from crime to the rising cost of health care. Today, for example, the elderly make up the fastest growing segment of the U.S. population. Their needs differ from those in other cohorts of the population, and they are more likely than younger citizens to demand that government pay attention to them. One critical concern is Social Security. As the elderly population continues to increase, policymakers face difficult challenges, particularly how they can ensure the system's solvency as greater numbers of people begin to draw benefits. Fifty years ago, Social Security was a government program that posed no special risk to budgetary resources. Now, however, public officials recognize that they must find politically and economically realistic ways to deal with an aging population and the imminent retirement of the baby boom generation, those Americans born between 1946 and 1964.

The growth of two-income families is another significant social change. It is now commonplace for both parents in a traditional two-parent household to have full-time jobs. Indeed, the Census Bureau reported in 2000 that two-income families have become the majority (Lewin 2000). No single explanation for this shift in employment patterns is apparent, but the policy implications are clear. One of the more obvious is child care. Should government help parents pay for it? Regulate day care centers to ensure quality? Another set of issues stems from the increase of women in the workplace, especially in professions and positions previously held by men. Affirmative action is one example: To what extent should governments intervene to guarantee equality of opportunity and pay?

How citizens relate to one another in their communities also influences public policymaking. People tend to place a high value on having homes and private spaces where they and their families feel secure. In some areas, the desire for security has led to the rise of "gated communities." Do the gates create a mental barrier as well as a physical one? Even without gates, suburban growth, often at the expense of older urban cores, continues almost unabated, creating economic and social tensions between cities and their suburbs. Some of these trends have prompted public officials at all levels of government to think more about the "livability" of their communities over the next few decades. One solution is **sustainable development**— communities in which social, economic, and environmental concerns are approached in an integrated and comprehensive manner. President Bill Clinton established the Office of Sustainable Development to develop "bold, new approaches to achieve our economic, environmental, and equity goals" (President's Council on Sustainable Development 1996). Even without the help of the White House, however, public officials and local leaders in communities across the nation are searching for innovative approaches to bring about sustainability. In the process, they are looking at public policies designed to affect urban growth, transportation, air and water quality, recreational opportunities, and the location of new industry and businesses, housing, and schools (Mazmanian and Kraft 1999; Paehlke 2003; Portney 2003).

## Economic Context

The state of the economy has a major impact on the policies governments adopt and implement. Economic policy deals with **inflation** and **unemployment**, but the economy itself affects the development of many other programs. For example, a strong economy often leads to lower unemployment, which, in turn, reduces the need for welfare and comparable assistance programs. The federal and state governments all claimed credit for reform policies that reduced the welfare rolls in the late 1990s, but could this change have occurred without a strong economy and near record low rates of unemployment? The welfare reform example illustrates how a change in economic conditions can affect the dynamics of public policymaking. As the United States shifts from a traditional industrial economy to one based on providing information and services, many similar impacts on public policy will become apparent.

Another way to appreciate the influence of the economic context is to consider budgetary politics. For years the United States operated in the red. The government was spending more money than it was collecting in taxes and other revenues. Congress tried many ways to reduce the deficit, including the Balanced Budget and Emergency Deficit Control Act of 1985 and a proposed constitutional amendment mandating a balanced budget. Policymakers were particularly concerned because the continuing deficits meant they could not enact any new policy initiatives since no money was available to pay for them. Nor could they continue to fund programs without increasing taxes, always a politically unattractive option.

This situation changed in 1998 when President Clinton announced a federal budget **surplus** for the fiscal year and projected surpluses for years to follow. In 1992 the federal government had registered a record deficit of $290 billion, but by fiscal 2000 it had a record surplus of $237 billion, a result of the expanding economy and tax revenues. The dynamics of the policymaking process changed dramatically. Rather than thinking about how to save money to reduce the deficit, by 2000 members of Congress and candidates for federal office were preoccupied with various proposals for how to spend the surplus or to reduce taxes.

The economic context shifted once more early in the Bush administration. In 2001 the president proposed and Congress approved a massive tax cut that greatly reduced government revenues. The tax cut, combined with a broad economic slowdown in 2001 and 2002, the economic toll of the September 11, 2001, attacks and the subsequent war on terrorism, and a large increase in defense spending, plunged the U.S. government back into deficit. Many state governments also found themselves dealing with unexpected deficits as a result of the economic slowdown. At the federal and state level, policymakers struggled once more with tough decisions on program priorities and budget cuts.[3]

## Political Context

It is impossible to understand public policy without considering politics, which affects public policy choices at every step, from the selection of policymakers in elections to shaping how conflicts among different groups are resolved. To appreciate the political context, one must be aware of the relative strength of the two major parties; the influence of minor parties; ideological differences among the public, especially the more **attentive publics** such as committed liberals and conservatives; and the ability of organized interest groups to exert pressure. Democrats and Republicans, liberals and conservatives, often hold sharply different views about the legitimacy of government action and which policies are acceptable. During the 1990s partisan differences widened, and on many policy issues ideological polarization between the parties made government action difficult. Chapter 2 discusses these and other reasons for policy stalemate.

The student of public policy also needs to recognize, however, that political labels such as liberal and conservative are not always a reliable guide to predicting specific policy positions. That is, it is simplistic to think that conservatives always want a smaller government and that liberals favor the opposite. Most conservatives argue for less government intrusion into the economy and decision making within business and industry, but often favor a strong government role to achieve certain social goals, such as reducing crime or banning abortions and gay marriages. Liberals, on the other hand, rally against government threats to civil liberties and individual rights, but are among the first to call for government regulation of business activity to protect consumers and workers or to control air and water pollution.

Party labels, therefore, may be a poor indicator of positions taken on policy issues. Within the major political parties one can find ideological differences among members; some Democrats, particularly southerners, are conservative, and some Republicans are moderate to liberal, although many fewer today than several decades ago. The same is true within the minor or "third" party organizations such as the Green Party or the Reform Party, which has served as a vehicle to promote the divergent views of H. Ross Perot, former Minnesota governor Jesse Ventura, and conservative Patrick Buchanan.

Because the United States has a weak party system, individual politicians not only run their own campaigns for office but also promote their own ideas. Many feel little obligation to support the official party position on policy issues, especially when electoral forces in their constituencies differ from those influencing the national party. In the same vein, the political context can vary greatly from one state to another, or even from one community in a state to another. Some states and cities tend to favor conservative policies, while others support liberal policies. Much depends on the alignment of party and ideological forces in the particular jurisdiction, in addition to the social and economic contexts.

Among the policy implications of the prevailing political context in the United States is the continual challenge of reconciling partisan and ideological differences. Policy actors who cannot agree on what to do may decide to do nothing, allowing social problems to continue unchanged. Or policy actors might reach a temporary compromise that falls short of an ideal solution. It is not at all unusual in the U.S. political system to see enactment of such policy compromises, which may contain broad or vaguely worded components. The details, where the greatest conflicts often occur, are worked out later, typically by the rulemakers and managers in the executive branch agencies.

## Governing Context

The U.S. government is highly complex, and its structure has a major impact on public policymaking. The authority to act is dispersed among many actors. As a result, the time needed to resolve differences among the policy actors can be lengthy. In addition, the inevitable compromises lead to policies that may be less focused or coherent than many would wish.

The separation of powers mandated by the Constitution requires that any policy developed at the national level be acceptable to a majority of Congress and to the president. Policymakers in both institutions must therefore find common ground. In recent decades, the search for consensus has been difficult because of **divided government**, with one political party in control of the White House and the other in control of one or both houses of Congress. Strong philosophical differences among policymakers over the role of government and the need to satisfy differing political constituencies often make them unwilling to compromise. If policymakers dig in their heels and do nothing, outdated, ineffective policies continue in force, and consideration of new, and possibly more effective, policies does not progress.

Under the U.S. political system, the federal government and the states share governing responsibilities. Prior to the New Deal, these institutions had defined areas of governance. The situation is less clear today, and, more often than not, state and federal government responsibilities overlap. For example, state governments traditionally were responsible for education policy, but since 1960 the federal government has become more involved in education. It provides billions of dollars in education grants to state and local governments and subsidizes student loan programs in higher education, but the funds can come with many strings attached. For example, the federal government is pushing for evaluation of success in the nation's schools, including setting standards for what students know.

In addition to overlapping responsibilities, the states and the federal government face other problems of divided authority that arise when federal and state agencies try to determine what they need to do to put a policy into effect. Sometimes, the federal government is willing to share governing responsibility, but not money. For example, the federal government has granted authority to the states to implement many environmental programs, such as those falling under the Clean Water Act, but the states say that the funds from Washington are insufficient to cover the costs of their new duties. Throughout the 1990s, states frequently grumbled about these so-called **unfunded mandates**. Congress made some efforts to limit the practice in regard to future mandates, but did little about the previously approved mandates.

Americans sometimes complain that "government can't get anything done." In light of the complexity of the U.S. governance structure, with its overlapping responsibilities and political disagreements, a more accurate statement might be that it is a minor miracle that policies get enacted and implemented at all.

## Cultural Context

**Political culture** refers to widely held values, beliefs, and attitudes, such as trust and confidence in government and the political process, or the lack of it. Political culture also includes commitment to individualism, property rights, freedom, pragmatism or practicality, equality, and similar values, some of which are distinctly American. These values are acquired through a process of political socialization that takes place in families, schools, and society in general, and that at times seems to reflect popular culture and television (Putnam 1995, 2000). Scholars have found that such political cultures not only vary from nation to nation but from state to state within the United States, and even from one community to another, as one might expect in a diverse society. These cultural differences help to explain the variation in state (and local) public policies across the nation (Elazar 1984; Lieske 1993). Some states routinely enact progressive policies, such as California's medical marijuana initiative and stringent environmental policies, while other states are reliably conservative in their policy enactments.

Antiabortion protesters march in front of the U.S. Supreme Court in Washington on January 22, 2003, the thirtieth anniversary of the Court's *Roe v Wade* decision. In that historic case the Court overturned state restrictions on a woman's right to choose to have an abortion. It established guidelines for permissible state intervention to regulate abortion but stated that a woman's right to privacy, including the personal choice to terminate a pregnancy, was paramount. The persistent controversies over abortion rights illustrate the striking way in which deeply held cultural values can affect citizen attitudes, public involvement in politics, and the direction of public policy. Given the cultural context of abortion politics, it is no surprise that the members of Congress are often subject to intense pressure on the issue, as they were in 2003 when the Senate voted to ban so-called partial birth abortions.

At times, the policies under consideration are linked directly to cultural perspectives. For example, writers such as William Bennett and James Q. Wilson have connected what they see as a decline in morality to crime, abortion, and education. Those who believe that the ideals of right and wrong have not been given sufficient weight in U.S. society tend to promote stricter punishments for convicted criminals. Those who believe in deterrence feel that education and opportunity can reduce crime. Recurring battles over family planning programs, abortion rights, and international population policy reflect cultural conflicts, especially over the role of women in society, that have yet to be resolved.

In one interesting case in 1999, the Kansas State Board of Education voted six to four to eliminate evolution, or anything that hinted at the age of the Earth, from statewide standards for science teaching in deference to the teaching of creationism. The governor denounced the decision, as did six Kansas college and university presidents and numerous editorials in the nation's newspapers. In the next election the voters threw out three of the board members who had approved eliminating evolution from the tests, and in 2001 the board reversed its position by a seven to three vote. The effort in Kansas, while not the only attempt to promote creationism in public schools, is a clear example of the ongoing battle over the relative roles of science and religion in modern life. A recent assessment of such cultural conflict in U.S. politics traces its roots to a "values divide" that reflects the reexamination of Americans' personal values in a time of rapid change (White 2002).

Cultural conflicts also affect public judgments about government officials and their conduct and may influence the policymaking process. President Clinton's impeachment by the House of Representatives in 1998 and his subsequent trial in the Senate clearly demonstrated the differences of opinion over his fate. Many conservatives wanted to punish Clinton for what they saw as his immoral behavior as well as violations of law, such as lying to a grand jury. In contrast, many liberals were willing to overlook Clinton's sexual misconduct and attempts to hide it because they placed a higher value on his contributions to government and public policy, which they believed substantially enhanced the nation's well-being. The conflicts between the two sides significantly affected the policy process during the investigation, impeachment, and trial and for months after by deflecting attention from policy proposals and by weakening support for White House initiatives. These conflicts also show that, for many political and policy issues, citizens and policymakers must decide how much weight to give to competing social values, such as the relative importance of personal and professional behavior.

## RATIONALES FOR GOVERNMENT INTERVENTION

When the public and policymakers believe that government needs to intervene to correct a social problem, they create or alter policies. But this does not mean the matter is settled permanently. The rationales offered for government involvement were highly contested in the past, they are today, and they will likely cause disagreements in the future. The arguments for and against government intervention in the economy and in people's lives draw from political philosophies and ideologies, specific beliefs about public policy, and the positions that each of the major political parties has staked out. These arguments often are advanced during the processes of **agenda setting** (to discourage or encourage action), **policy formulation** (where the form of intervention is designed), or **policy legitimation** (where the rationale for intervention may be debated). The three leading, and somewhat overlapping, rationales for government intervention are: political reasons, moral or ethical reasons, and economics or market failure. The last of these rationales warrants a longer discussion than the others because it is often thought to be more complex.

### Political Reasons

The public and policymakers may decide that government should intervene to solve a problem for political reasons. These reasons may vary, but often they reflect a notable shift in public opinion or the rise of a social movement pressing for action. After the 1954 Supreme Court decision on public school segregation and the rise of the civil rights movement, for example, the federal government began to act on civil rights. President Lyndon Johnson persuaded Congress to adopt new policies to prevent discrimination against minorities, including the Civil Rights Act of 1964. In the 1960s the federal government began the Medicare program after more than twenty years of public debate in which critics argued that such actions constituted a step toward "socialized medicine." The federal government also increased its involvement in consumer protection, automobile safety, and the environment because of rising public concern about those issues.

### Moral or Ethical Reasons

In addition to the power of public opinion or a social movement, certain problems and circumstances may dictate that government should be involved for moral or ethical reasons.

In other words, the government action is seen as the right thing to do even without public pressure. Some portion of the population or members of an organized interest group may be unwilling to witness suffering from poverty, hunger, or human rights abuses, either at home or abroad, and want the government to do something about it. They may join groups to lobby policymakers or contact them directly to persuade them to take action. One might argue that the development of the Social Security program falls into this category. To ensure that the elderly, disabled, and the minor children of deceased or disabled workers had a regular income, the government created the program, which is financed by payroll taxes. The debate over the future of the Social Security system continues this moral argument.

Another example is farm support policies, a subject addressed in Chapter 3. For years the federal government has provided financial support to farmers to make sure they can continue farming. In a purely competitive market, such supports would not exist. Farmers would simply be on their own and take their chances with the weather, crop yields, and prices on the open market. Yet government continues to intervene to protect farmers from bankruptcy. One reason for the intervention is the public's perceptions about family farmers and their importance to the development of our country. The public is willing to support such policies even when only a small percentage of the population farms the land and large agribusiness corporations such as Archer Daniels Midland, Cargill, and ConAgra control much of the nation's agricultural acreage.

## Economics and Market Failures

In a pure capitalist or market system, most economists would not consider the family farmers' plight a legitimate reason for government intervention. They would argue that government intrusion into the marketplace distorts the **efficiency** with which a competitive market economy can allocate society's resources. In such a market, voluntary and informed exchanges between buyers and sellers allow them to meet their needs efficiently, especially when large numbers of people are involved so that the market operates fairly. In this world, competition sets the fair market value on houses, cars, and other goods.

Economists acknowledge, however, that a situation known as **market failure** warrants government intervention. A market failure occurs when the private market is not efficient. Market failures fall into four types: the existence of monopolies and oligopolies, externalities, information failures, and the inability to provide public or collective goods.

A **monopoly** or **oligopoly** exists when one or several persons or companies dominate the market and can control the price of a product or service. Examples abound. It is a rare community that has more than one cable television operator or power company. Monopolies of this sort are called natural or technical because they are essentially unavoidable. There would be little sense in having multiple cable TV operators or power companies in an average size city if greater efficiency can be achieved by having a single company invest in the necessary infrastructure. Governments usually accept this kind of monopoly but institute regulations to ensure that the public is treated fairly, yet the balance between government regulation and economic freedom for the monopoly is the subject of ongoing debate.

Externalities are the decisions and actions of those involved in the market exchange that affect other parties, either negatively or positively. A **negative externality** occurs when two parties interact in a market and, as a result of that interaction, a third party is harmed and does not get compensated for harm. Pollution is a negative externality. For example, consumers enter into an agreement with the utility to provide electricity. In the absence of government regulation, the utility may decide to use the least expensive fuel, most likely, coal. When coal is burned, it sends pollutants into the atmosphere, which settle downwind and may cause health problems to a third party. The third party, not the two parties interacting in the electricity market, pays the costs of those health problems. Ideally, the health care costs associated with electricity production would be considered part of the cost of production, and government intervention ensures that this happens. Through environmental regulation, the government requires utilities to install pollution control technology on their plants to limit the amount of pollutants emitted.

A **positive externality** occurs the same way as a negative externality, but the third party gains something from the two-party interaction and does not have to pay for it. Higher education is an example of a positive externality. Some policymakers argue that because society benefits from a well-educated population, it should be willing to provide financial support to encourage people to continue their education. Many state governments subsidize higher education tuition for their local institutions. For example, Georgia recently began the Hope Scholarship program. It provides tuition for students who graduate high school with a 3.0 average within a certain core curriculum and maintain that average in college (Georgia Student Finance Commission 1999). In essence, this benefit increases students' incomes and enables them to afford more schooling.

**Information failure** is the third kind of market failure. According to the theories of market operation, to have perfect competition, buyers and sellers must have all of the information needed to enter into a transaction or exchange. When the information is not fully or easily available, a market failure may occur. At times, the consumers' lack of complete information about a product or service does not present a major problem: consumers can adjust their buying behavior if they believe there is something wrong with the goods or services purchased. When the lack of information leads the consumer to suffer significant financial or personal loss, the government may step in. A clear example of such government intervention is its regulation of prescription and over-the-counter pharmaceuticals. Without government, consumers would find it impossible to figure out whether medical drugs are safe and effective. Federal law established the Food and Drug Administration (FDA) and authorized it to test proposed drugs to ensure their safety and efficacy. Chapter 8 discusses how well the FDA does its job.

A fourth kind of market failure occurs when markets cannot provide for the **public good,** also called the **collective good.** A public or collective good is defined by two criteria: the ability to exclude someone from getting the good and the ability to jointly consume the good. Exclusion within the U.S. economy typically occurs through pricing. If an individual can charge for a good or service, then he or she can exclude someone from getting it. Goods that can be jointly consumed are those in which one person's consumption does not prevent another from also consuming it. The two criteria can be displayed as a typology (Table 1-1) of private goods and public goods that clarifies the range of what analysts call collective goods.

| TABLE 1-1 | Private Goods and Public Goods | |
|---|---|---|
| | No Joint Consumption | Joint Consumption |
| Exclusion Is Feasible | 1<br>Pure private goods<br>Examples: DVD players, automobiles, houses | 2<br>Toll goods<br>Examples: cable TV services, electrical utilities |
| Exclusion Is Not Feasible | 3<br>Common pool resources<br>Examples: air, water, grazing land, oceans, fisheries, wildlife | 4<br>Pure public goods<br>Examples: national defense, public parks |

Text block 1 in the table refers to goods that are private and for which there is no market failure. It represents the normal day-to-day interactions between the private sector and consumers. The other three boxes refer to nonprivate or public goods, and they signal conditions that may require government intervention to alleviate the market failure.

Text block 2 represents what some call **toll goods.** These goods can be jointly consumed, and exclusion is feasible. An obvious example is a utility such as electricity or cable services. One person's use of cable services does not preclude another person's use, but a cable company's charges may exclude low-income individuals. Earlier, we identified such goods as natural monopolies. To keep essential services affordable, government intervenes by regulating prices. For years public utility commissions (PUCs) regulated prices that electric companies could charge their consumers. Experiments in electricity market deregulation have tried to create more competition and choices for consumers, but they have not always succeeded. California's energy crisis in 2000 and 2001, when electricity was in short supply, was widely attributed to its failed experiment with such deregulation and to fraudulent action by some power companies.

Text block 3 shows **common pool resources,** goods that cannot be jointly consumed and for which exclusion is not feasible. For example, environmental scientists write about a "tragedy of the commons," which comes about from use of natural resources such as air, water, grazing land, fisheries, and the like. The tragedy is that each individual seeks to maximize his or her use of the common pool resources without regard to their degradation or depletion because no one owns them. Such individual behavior may lead to the loss of the resources even when each person would benefit from their continued use. To ensure the preservation of these shared goods, government intervenes. The government requires individuals to have a license to fish, which may preclude some from partaking in the good, but the funds raised through the licensing fee can be used to restock the fishery. Government may also set catch limits on different species to prevent overfishing. The government requires ranchers to pay a fee to allow their cattle to feed on public grazing land. For common pool resources, the government's role is to develop policies to ensure their continuance or sustainability. Without government, the public would likely deplete these goods.

Text block 4 represents a category of goods called **pure public goods.** These are goods that can be jointly consumed and for which exclusion is not feasible. They would not be provided at all without government intervention because the private sector has no incentive to provide them. National defense and public parks are examples. For these kinds of goods government intervention is necessary to ensure the general public has them.

These three reasons for government intervention—political, moral and ethical, and economic or market failures—are not exhaustive. Other reasons may present themselves, and these three may not be mutually exclusive; that is, policymakers may favor government action for one or more reasons at the same time. The reasons also may change over time: policies are adopted and changed in a continuous cycle, which is part of society's response to public problems and efforts to find solutions. Government intervention is simply one of these options. When such intervention no longer works or no longer makes sense, policies may be changed in favor of private action or free markets once again. Much of the movement toward deregulation of financial markets in the 1980s and of energy markets in the late 1990s reflected such views. The adverse consequences of deregulation prompted a new round of public debate over what kind of government intervention best serves the public interest.

## PERSPECTIVES ON THE STUDY OF PUBLIC POLICY

An earlier section of the chapter discussed the reasons why students and other citizens might want to study public policy, emphasizing the enhancement of people's understanding and influence over the policymaking process. Here, the chapter shifts to the reasons professional policy analysts and academics study public policy. No single purpose motivates academics, policy analysts, and advocacy organizations. Instead, many interests move individuals and organizations to deal with public policy, and distinct aspects of its study reflect their interests. One way to describe this diversity is to say there are scientific, professional, and political reasons to study and act on public policy. Chapter 4 covers these distinctions more fully, but a brief overview here introduces the role that policy analysis plays in contemporary policymaking processes at all levels of government.

Some individuals, particularly academics, study public policy for scientific purposes, that is, to build general understanding of public problems and the policymaking process. They seek "truth" through scientific methods, regardless of whether the knowledge is relevant or useful in some immediate way. Their goal is to explain the causes and consequences of public policies, quite apart from what governments *ought* to do. For example, university-based social scientists try to develop theories of the policy process and of political behavior, such as how policy agendas are set, how policies are formulated and adopted, and how they are implemented in a bureaucracy (Weimer and Vining 1999, 30). Chapter 3 examines how models and theories of the policy process can show the forces at work in shaping public policy and the opportunities for influence or change.

Some people study public policy for professional reasons, such as conducting policy analyses for government agencies, think tanks, or interest groups. Their objective is to examine public problems and policy alternatives and produce usable knowledge that can help policymakers, interest groups, or citizens choose those policies that are likely to achieve a desired outcome (MacRae and Wilde 1979; Patton and Sawicki 1993). Many policy analysts, both in and out of government, are committed to producing the best analysis possible, and they adhere to strong professional norms for economic analysis, modeling of complex situations, and **program evaluation**. Chapter 4 discusses the professional study of policy and the contributions of independent think tanks such as the American Enterprise Institute, the Urban Institute, and the Brookings Institution. Readers might want to visit the Web sites of one or more of the leading think tanks and determine for themselves if the studies presented are objective or show bias. Selected Web addresses are listed at the end of Chapter 4, and they can easily be found by using Google or a comparable search engine.

Some analysts may be as rigorous in the methods they use as the professionals, but they are also committed to specific policy values and goals and sometimes to ideological and partisan agendas. Not surprisingly, they try to emphasize the studies and findings that help to advance those values and goals. This kind of policy study can be described as political, rather than professional or scientific. Analysts who work for interest groups or activist organizations, such as Common Cause, the National Organization for Women, the Christian Coalition, or the National Rifle Association, are especially likely to have this orientation, as are those who work for political parties and ideological groups. It may be difficult to distinguish this kind of politically oriented policy study from policy advocacy, but, as Deborah Stone (2002) argues, it is also impossible to completely separate even rigorous policy studies from the political processes in which they are imbedded. Analysis, she asserts, is itself "a creature of politics" and often it is "strategically crafted argument" designed to advance particular policy values.

Even if such arguments are persuasive, readers need to keep in mind their distinct perspectives and appreciate the differences among the studies and arguments. As is often true in human affairs, critical judgment is needed to assess what organizations and analysts say about public policy. Some studies will present stronger scientific evidence than others, and some positions will demonstrate more passion than others, but everyone needs to determine how credible the information is and its implications for public policy.

## POLICY ANALYSIS

Policy analysis is usually described as a systematic and organized way to evaluate public policy alternatives or existing government programs. Often it involves applying economic tools and other **quantitative methods** or **measures**. Policy analysis may therefore seem to some students of public policy to hold little relevance to anyone except policy specialists, but in reality everyone uses policy analysis in many day-to-day activities. Buying a car, selecting a particular college course, or deciding on a restaurant for dinner all require thinking about the pros and cons associated with the available choices, including how to spend money.

Policy analysis can be used throughout the policy process, but it becomes especially important in the formulation of policies and evaluation of programs after they are implemented. In assessing a public problem, policy analysis may assist in describing its scope, such as the percentage of public schools that are failing. When developing alternatives and choosing a direction, a decision maker can use analysis to assess the feasibility of the choices based on economic, administrative, political, and ethical criteria. The same methods can be used to evaluate a program to determine its **effectiveness**, or whether it has achieved its expected results.

In short, policy analysis represents an attempt to dissect problems and solutions in what is usually described as a rational manner. By this, practitioners mean that they bring information and systematic analysis to bear on policy issues and try to show how a given set of goals and objectives might be achieved most efficiently. Public policy goals and objectives are usually determined in a political process—for example, how much can the government pay for health care services for the elderly—but analysis can help policymakers weigh competing ideas about how best to deliver such services.

Policy analysts argue that their systematic analyses should be given serious consideration as a counterweight to the tendency of public officials to make policy choices based on their partisan positions, ideology, or support for important constituencies and interest groups. They point to inconsistencies in public policy or to what some would describe as unwarranted or inefficient policy actions. For example, why does the federal government give subsidies to farmers growing tobacco while it also tries to reduce smoking? Why does Congress continue to subsidize mining and timber harvesting on public lands that causes environmental damage and costs taxpayers more than the revenues these activities earn? Why do members of Congress vote to spend public money on particular projects they favor and at the same time complain about the government's wasteful spending? The answers lie mostly in interest group and constituency pressures that elected officials find difficult to resist, particularly when the general public fails to take an interest in such decisions.

Ordinary citizens and organizations also can benefit from policy analysis. Citizens with an interest in public policy or the political system may make decisions based on their general political views; for example, liberals usually favor government regulation to improve the environment. But most people would understand the benefit of a focused study of a particular program or proposal that put aside personal political views. Perhaps the liberal environmentalist will come to question whether regulation is the best way to achieve environmental goals. A conservative might be moved to reassess whether stringent laws that put first-time drug offenders in prison for years makes sense.

It is not unusual for individuals or interest groups to use information developed through policy analysis to reinforce the arguments they make to government policymakers. An organization will often dangle its latest research or analysis to convince policymakers that the group is correct in its beliefs. For example, the following information was gathered from the Sierra Club's Web site, www.sierraclub.org, advocating policies for cleaner air. The quotations come from a *Washington Post* article summarizing recent studies that the group included to reinforce its position on maintaining stringent clean air standards.

- "A study published in today's issue of the *Journal of the American Medical Association* concludes that people living in the most heavily polluted metropolitan areas have a 12 percent increased risk of dying of lung cancer than people in the least polluted areas."
- "Air pollution levels have declined significantly during the past 20 years because of stepped-up enforcement of clean air laws, yet levels of fine particle emissions in New

York, Los Angeles, Chicago and Washington are at or exceed limits set by the Environmental Protection Agency."
- "Previous research by Harvard University and the American Cancer Society strongly linked these fine particles to high mortality rates from cardiopulmonary diseases such as heart attacks, strokes and asthma. Until now, however, scientists lacked sufficient statistical evidence to directly link those emissions to elevated lung cancer death rates."

By citing these analytical, presumably objective, studies, the Sierra Club hopes to move the direction of clean air policy toward stronger air quality standards.

The Sierra Club's opponents in the business community will circulate information, sometimes from the same studies, that bolsters their arguments about the **uncertainty** inherent in such health assessments and the high costs imposed on society if environmental policies and regulations are overly restrictive. For example, in 2002 the U.S. Chamber of Commerce made the following statement on its Web page, www.uschamber.com, dealing with environmental and energy issues: "The U.S. Chamber's objective is to ensure that air quality standards are based on: a market-based approach rather than the out-dated command-and-control structure; sound, publicly available science; and a balancing of environmental protection and the needs of communities and business." Note in particular the emphasis given to "sound science" and to the need to balance environmental protection against the needs of communities and business. In this usage, "sound" is a buzzword signaling a distrust of the kind of science often used to support clean air and other environmental standards. Business groups contend that such scientific studies use methods that are frequently flawed and lead to unjustified regulations.

Presented with conflicting assumptions and **interpretations**, students of public policy need to be aware of the sources of information and judge for themselves which argument is strongest. This book provides the tools and techniques to help students make informed judgments. In particular, Chapters 4 through 6 cover the major approaches to policy analysis and some of the methods, such as cost-benefit analysis and risk assessment, that make clear what the studies say and how the findings relate to policy choice.

For policymakers, policy analysis is an essential tool for the development of public policy and its evaluation. For citizens interested in public affairs, it provides a way to organize thoughts and information to be able to better understand the alternatives presented and the possible implications of these choices. Individuals do not have to know how to conduct complex economic analysis to recognize the importance of using a wide range of information when making decisions; they just need to be able to think about problems and solutions from different perspectives. The box "Steps to Analysis: How to Interpret Policy Studies" offers some suggestions for how to interpret the policy studies you encounter.

At least four criteria, effectiveness, efficiency, equity, and political feasibility, can be used to judge the acceptability of policy ideas. Effectiveness refers to the likely achievement of the policy's goals and objectives. For policy areas such as the environment, the technical and administrative feasibility of a proposed solution often influences effectiveness. Program evaluation is an important tool for examining this criterion. Efficiency is the consideration of economic feasibility. To determine economic feasibility, an analyst compares the costs of a policy alternative to the benefits expected from its adoption. In other words, efficiency means the desire

| | STEPS |
|---|---|
| HOW TO INTERPRET POLICY STUDIES | TO |
| | ANALYSIS |

Policy analysis is pervasive and critically important for the policymaking process at all levels of government. To determine which studies are credible and which are not, and which might be used as a basis for making policy decisions, students of public policy need to hone their analytical skills. How to do this? One way is to ask questions such as the following:

- What is the purpose of the study, and who conducted it?
- Does it seek and present objective information on the nature of the problem and possible solutions?
- Does the information seem to be valid, and what standard should you use to determine that?

- Is the report's argument logical and convincing?
- Does the report omit important subject matter?
- Does the study lay out the policy implications clearly and persuasively?

We will address these kinds of questions throughout the book when summarizing particular studies.

to realize the greatest possible benefit out of the dollars spent. **Equity** means that government officials need to consider what constitutes a fair proposal or how a program's costs and benefits are distributed among citizens. This criterion is especially important to Americans, given the nation's political and cultural background. Policymakers also need to decide how to balance equity concerns against other demands—protection from unsafe consumer products or freedom for businesses to operate. The question is how much government intrusion into daily life are citizens willing to accept, and is the reduction in personal (or corporate) freedom worth the benefits that the policy provides to society? **Political feasibility** concerns how government officials appraise the acceptability of a proposal. Of necessity in a democracy, policymakers must consider the preferences and potential reactions of the public, interest groups, and other government officials when developing policies.

These criteria are not meant to be exhaustive. Others, such as the flexibility of a policy, the extent of public participation during policy formulation and adoption, ethical considerations, or the responsiveness of government action to citizen needs and concerns, may also be relevant, depending on the issue at hand. In addition, these criteria may not have equal weight in the decision-making process. Public officials acting on national defense and foreign policy issues, for example, rarely consider economic costs as paramount in reaching decisions. Personal freedom might be the primary consideration for some when considering policies in areas such as abortion rights, gun control, crime, and the privacy of e-mail and cellular telephone communications. Chapters 4 through 6 examine these criteria and the tools used to evaluate them more fully.

## POLICY INITIATIVES FOR THE TWENTY-FIRST CENTURY

The arrival of the new century has inspired mixed commentary on the future of government, politics, and public policy. Some observers look at the problems that governments will face, the predominant style of politics in the United States, and the public policy solutions likely to be adopted and see a continuity. Others anticipate a rapidly changing world that will create quite different kinds of problems and call for innovative policy solutions. The world population is expected to increase substantially in the decades ahead, bringing new pressures on global resources such as fresh water, arable land, fisheries, and forests. Many scholars expect the demands on scarce natural resources to exacerbate social instability and ethnic, religious, and national tensions that are already a source of violent conflict in the world (Homer-Dixon 1999). At home, the retirement of the baby boomers will place unprecedented pressures on the health care system, Medicare, and Social Security. Policymakers will need to figure out how to cover the rising costs without placing unfair burdens on younger generations.

Institutional inertia, the tendency of organizations to maintain their behavior over time, probably guarantees that much public policy will continue largely unchanged over the next few decades. It is equally likely, however, that the public and policymakers will demand fresh approaches to public policy that offer better opportunities to deal with existing problems and those that will arise as the world experiences economic, technological, environmental, and social change.

One important domestic change is the larger role for states in the development and **implementation** of public policy. Contrary to the widespread belief that government is growing, the number of federal employees has shrunk in recent years, but the responsibilities of government have not. State and local governments have been forced to step in to fill the gap. With the passage of welfare reform in 1996, state governments took on additional responsibilities for the provision of services to the poor. Although the results of welfare reform are still being examined, states are using their new authority to implement a wide range of initiatives to get people off the welfare rolls. For example, some states provide child care subsidies to low-income families to alleviate one of their major concerns. As states seek more authority in policymaking in a variety of areas, they also develop and implement new initiatives. This **devolution** of authority to the states, however, may also produce a "race to the bottom" as states compete with one another to save money. The evidence on the effects of such devolution is mixed to date (Donahue 1997; Rabe 2003).

Another major opportunity for policy development, lost for now, was the federal budget surplus. During the 1980s and 1990s, as the U.S. budget deficit grew, policymakers had to limit development of new programs and watch their spending on existing programs. They had to play a **zero-sum game**—to increase spending in one area, they had to decrease it in another. In fact, the Budget Enforcement Act of 1990 dictated these terms. From a policymaking perspective, the budget surplus changed the equation, and policymakers were beginning to think about how to use the excess revenues coming into the Treasury. The development of new programs, increased funding of existing programs, tax cuts, or paying down the national debt were all possibilities. The Bush administration tax cut of 2001 consumed a major portion of this surplus, putting an end to new spending, and, after that, changes in the economy, the war on terrorism, and the situation in Iraq intensified the debate over the wisdom of the tax cuts.

One of the major constraints on policymaking is not new, but is particularly problematic today. Partisanship is more apparent than before at both the state and national level. Retiring members of Congress have observed that partisan rancor, ideological disputes, and a decreased willingness to compromise on policy issues has made policymaking far more difficult than it was only a decade ago (Bond and Fleisher 2000). As a result, government often finds itself deadlocked, completely unable to deal effectively with issues. The inability to solve public problems further erodes the public's trust in government and diminishes its willingness to get involved in the political process.

**Entitlement programs,** such as Social Security, **Medicare**, and **Medicaid**, will place constraints on policy initiatives for the foreseeable future. These programs are legal obligations of funding to eligible individuals, and they represent a massive budgetary commitment. President George W. Bush's fiscal 2003 budget projected entitlements, or mandatory spending, to be about 54 percent of the entire federal budget, compared to 28 percent in 1968 (Pianin and Berry 1999), and this percentage will continue to increase.[4] These obligations mean that **discretionary spending** for defense, foreign aid, environmental protection, and education may have to be reduced. Unless these entitlements are dealt with in some way, the situation will only get worse. To date, discussions have begun about Medicare and Social Security, but the political resistance to making changes in these programs is fierce, and public officials are loath to incur the wrath of those who benefit from existing programs.

## CONCLUSIONS

This chapter introduces the basic concepts of the study of public policy and policy analysis. It lays out the reasons for citizens, policymakers, and scholars to study both the policymaking process and the substance of public policy. It describes the contexts in which public policy debate and decisions take place: social, economic, political, governing, and cultural. And it reviews the major justifications or rationales for intervention by government in the form of public policy. The chapter explains the role of policy analysis in government policymaking processes and the need for citizens to think critically about the sources of information that are used to justify or to challenge policy action. Understanding the most frequently used criteria for evaluating public policy proposals—such as effectiveness, efficiency, and equity—is a good place to begin. Students of public policy also need to learn how to distinguish objective analysis from biased analysis. The suggestions on this point made here are augmented by many in the chapters to come.

The remainder of Section I continues an analysis of the big picture: the institutions involved, and ways to approach public policy. Chapter 2 introduces the government institutions and actors involved in policymaking and how they interact. Chapter 3 explains the prevailing models and theories used to study public policy, focusing on the policy process.

Section II is a departure from other policy texts in its thorough coverage of policy analysis. In addition to an overview of policy analysis, Chapter 4 presents the many different ways practitioners carry it out. Chapter 5 stresses problem analysis or understanding the nature of public problems, their causes, and solutions. It also considers the various policy tools available to governments and how to think creatively about policy alternatives. Chapters 6 describes the leading methods of policy analysis and summarizes the most frequently used criteria to judge the acceptability of policy proposals.

The five chapters of Section III combine the material from the first two sections to delve into substantive policy topics. Each chapter follows the same format to illustrate how to think critically and constructively about public policy. These chapters highlight the nature of the problem, provide background on policy development, discuss different perspectives on policy change, and indicate how students might think about and assess the issues. Chapter 12 is a brief conclusion that emphasizes the role of citizen participation in policy choices.

The material at the end of each chapter includes discussion questions to assist students in examining the implications of the material and short lists of suggested readings and useful Web sites. Because the nature of the Internet, readers should expect that some Web addresses will need to be updated. At the end of the book is a reference list for all of the works cited in the individual chapters.

## DISCUSSION QUESTIONS

How can the study of public policy enhance citizens' ability to participate in government processes and to make policy choices?

How would you go about determining whether the information you find on a public policy Web site is valid?

Of the various evaluative criteria discussed in the chapter, which do you think are the most important for judging public policy proposals or programs? Why?

Looking ahead several decades, either for the United States or the whole world, which challenges facing government and public policy do you believe are most critical?

## SUGGESTED READINGS

James E. Anderson, *Public Policymaking: An Introduction,* 5th ed. (Boston: Houghton Mifflin, 2003). A leading text on the policy process that describes multiple perspectives on politics and policymaking.

Charles O. Jones, *An Introduction to the Study of Public Policy,* 3d ed. (Monterey, Calif.: Brooks/Cole Publishing Company, 1984). An older but still useful text on politics and policymaking.

Deborah Stone, *Policy Paradox: The Art of Political Decision Making,* rev. ed. (New York: W. W. Norton, 2002). An original and provocative assessment of the role of policy analysis in the political process.

Carl E. Van Horn, Donald C. Baumer, and William T. Gormley Jr., *Politics and Public Policy,* 3d ed. (Washington, D.C.: CQ Press, 2001). A unique, perceptive analysis of politics and policymaking in the U.S. system.

## SUGGESTED WEB SITES

**www.apsanet.org.** Home page for the American Political Science Association, with information on academic study of public policy and related fields in the discipline.

**http://apsapolicysection.org/index.html.** Public policy section of the American Political Science Association. Has useful links to policy organizations, journals, and political science research on public policy issues.

**www.firstgov.gov.** The federal government's portal to government sites.

**www.ipsonet.org/page.cgi.** Policy Studies Organization home page.

**www.policylibrary.com/index.html.** Policy Library home page, with links to worldwide policy studies.

**www.publicagenda.org.** A guide to diverse policy issues and public opinion surveys.

## KEYWORDS

agenda setting   19
attentive publics   15
choices   8
collective good   21
common pool resources   22
cost-benefit analysis   13
decisions   8
devolution   28
discretionary spending   29
divided government   16
draw conclusions   9
effectiveness   25
effects   8
efficiency   20
electoral processes   6
entitlement programs   29
environmental policy   13
equity   27
federalism   6
goals   4
implementation   28
inflation   14

information failure   21
initiatives   11
intentions   8
interest group   11
intergovernmental relations   6
interpretations   26
logic of collective action   11
market failure   20
Medicaid   29
Medicare   29
monopoly   20
negative externality   21
nonpolicies   8
oligopoly   20
plans   8
policy actors   8
policy alternatives   12
policy evaluation   26
policy formulation   19
policy legitimation   19
policy outcomes   9
policy outputs   9
political culture   17

political feasibility   27
positive externality   21
program evaluation   24
programs   8
proposals   8
public good   21
public opinion   7
public policy analysis   9
pure public goods   23
quantitative methods or measures   24
referendum   11
regulations   3
risk assessment   13
separation of powers   5
Social Security   4
standards   3
surplus   15
sustainable development   14
toll goods   22
uncertainty   26
unemployment   14
unfounded mandates   17
zero-sum game   28

# 2

# GOVERNMENT INSTITUTIONS AND POLICY ACTORS

IN AN ACCOUNT THAT WOULD FUNDAMENTALLY ALTER national policy on cleaning up toxic waste sites around the nation, the *New York Times* on August 2, 1978, carried a front-page story on the now infamous Love Canal, near Niagara Falls, New York. The paper reported that twenty-five years after the Hooker Chemical Company stopped using a local canal as an industrial dump, "82 different compounds, 11 of them suspected carcinogens, have been percolating upward through the soil, their drum containers rotting and leaching their contents into the backyards and basements of 100 homes and a public school built on the banks of the canal."[1] Once Americans became aware of the dangers posed by toxic and hazardous wastes such as those found at Love Canal and many other locations, their concern was instrumental in the enactment of federal policies to reduce the risks.

At times since then, however, the leading federal program for controlling the most serious of the nation's abandoned or uncontrolled hazardous waste sites, the Comprehensive Environmental Response, Compensation, and Liability Act (CERCLA) popularly known as Superfund, has been at a standstill. Critics condemn the law for the slow and costly cleanup of those sites and claim some of its provisions stimulate more **litigation** than cleanup. For the critics, including many in industry, Superfund is a poster child for what is wrong with complex, inflexible environmental regulatory programs. Environmentalists, however, view Superfund as a critically important program that correctly imposes demanding standards for the cleanup of chemical waste sites to protect the public's health. They also applaud the law's stringent liability standards that force polluters to pay for the cost of cleanup. Largely because the critics and defenders of the law see the issues so differently and are so determined to have their respective way, Congress has been unable to agree on how to modify Superfund so that it can achieve its goals more effectively and efficiently (Kraft 2003; Portney and Stavins 2000).

The policy impasse evident in the case of Superfund can be found in other national environmental policies, such as the Endangered Species Act, and in other policy areas. For example, Congress was also divided over dealing with **health care policy** during the Clinton administration in the early 1990s and about prescription drug coverage and other

Traffic heads toward downtown Los Angeles in June 2002 as a curtain of smog shrouds the skyline. National policies to improve air quality involve both cooperation and conflict between the federal government and the states. The states are responsible for most policy implementation, and California has long led the nation in imposing stringent clean air standards to deal with its severe pollution problems. As one sign of conflict over clean air goals, in late 2002 the Bush administration sided with automobile manufacturers in seeking to overturn the state's innovative policy mandating the sale of zero-emission and hybrid vehicles. Opponents of the policy charged that it usurped federal authority for setting fuel efficiency standards.

health policy issues in 2002. Members of Congress were unable to reach agreement in 2001 and 2002 on a national energy policy, despite recognition that the nation was becoming dangerously dependent on imported oil and the attendant economic and national security risks. In all of these policy areas, conflict was simply too great to permit members of Congress to act.

When political decision makers are unable or unwilling to compromise in a way that permits public policy action, the result is **gridlock.** It occurs for many reasons: high levels of partisanship and ideological conflict, disagreements among policymakers and influential interest groups over policy goals and means, a lack of consensus among the public, and the complexity of the problems. Whether the public is worse off or better off because of gridlock depends on the particular policy conflict, but few doubt that the public views a government stalemate negatively or that it is a source of political cynicism about a political process in which leaders often appear unwilling to act (Hibbing and Theiss-Morse 1995, 2002).

Most people see policy gridlock of this kind as a failure of government, and in many ways it is. But it is also true that U.S. political institutions were designed with the clear intention of making actions on public policy—and therefore the expansion of government authority—difficult. The chosen institutional structure reflected the prevailing political values and culture of late eighteenth century America. At that time only about 4 million people lived in the United States, most of them in rural areas and small towns. In 2003 the population was about 290 million, with the overwhelming majority of people living in large metropolitan areas and their suburbs. At its founding, the nation faced relatively few public problems, and most people believed that it was more important to maintain their freedoms than to create a powerful government that could act swiftly in response to national problems. Many critics of the U.S. system wonder whether its political institutions are even capable of responding effectively to the highly complex and interdependent problems the United States faces at home and abroad (Chubb and Peterson 1989; Ophuls and Boyan 1992; Sundquist 1986).

Understanding this system of government and how policy actors maneuver within it is essential for students of public policy. It enables students to assess the constraints on policy development and the many opportunities that nevertheless exist within the U.S. political system for solving public problems through creative policy action. The complexity of so many contemporary problems, from urban sprawl to failing public school systems, also hints at the crucial role that policy analysis plays, or can play, in designing effective, economically feasible, and fair solutions.

This chapter surveys the major actors and institutions involved in making public policy in the United States. It looks at the interrelationship of policy actors and their institutions, and how political incentives as well as constitutional and legal constraints affect their behavior. Of particular interest are the resources they have (or can develop) to address the myriad challenges of the twenty-first century discussed in Chapter 1. The next chapter deals with the policymaking process and how policy analysis can clarify issues and choices.

# GOVERNMENT INSTITUTIONS AND POLICY CAPACITY

The nation's Founders created a system of checks and balances to ensure that the institutions of government could not tyrannize the population. The formal structure of government they established more than two hundred years ago remains much the same today. The U.S. system is based on a tripartite division of authority among legislative, executive, and judicial institutions, and a federal system in which the national government and the states have both separate and overlapping authority. Each branch of the federal government has distinct responsibilities under the Constitution, but also shares authority with the other two. This system of separated institutions sharing power had the noble intention of limiting government authority over citizens and protecting their liberty, but the fragmentation of government power also has a significant impact on policymaking processes and the policies that result.

Fragmented power does not prevent policy action, as the array of current national policies and programs clearly attests. When conditions are right, U.S. policymaking institutions can act, sometimes quickly, to approve major policy advances. Often they do so with broad bipartisan support (Jones 1999; Mayhew 1991). Enactment of the demanding Clean Air Act Amendments of 1990 is an example. Passage of a comprehensive welfare reform package in 1996 and a new federal education policy in 2001 are others. What conditions lead to such major **policy changes** in a system that generally poses significant barriers to such action? It is an intriguing question to ponder, and one that this chapter explores.

Despite policy successes, the fragmented U.S. political system generally makes it difficult for policymakers to respond to most public problems in a timely, coherent manner. The same can be said about the constitutional mandate for a federal system in which the states share power with the national government. The fifty states and about eighty thousand local governments chart their own policy courses within the limits set by the Constitution and national law. State policies, such as California's stringent air quality laws, sometimes result in significant advantages for their citizens that people living in other states do not have. In addition, serious conflicts can develop between the federal government and the states. For example, in the 1950s and 1960s the federal government enacted legislation banning segregation in response to state Jim Crow laws that denied African Americans equal rights. But, even passage of the federal Civil Rights Act of 1964, which ended legally sanctioned discrimination, did not resolve all of the conflicts (Williams 1987).

Even if students are already familiar with the major U.S. government institutions, a brief review of their most notable features and the implications for public policymaking may be useful. The reason is that the way institutions are designed and structured is critical to how they function, as are the rules they adopt for decision making. Both affect their **policy capacity,** which is their ability to identify, analyze, and respond to public problems while also bearing in mind the diverse interests in society.

It should be said, however, that the way government institutions are structured and how they make decisions are not immutable. They can be changed, and occasionally they are, as citizens and policymakers seek to improve government performance or try new approaches to decision making. The Clinton administration sought to "reinvent" government through new management techniques. The Bush administration attempted to substitute market-based and voluntary approaches for government regulation. In response to the September 11 terrorist attacks, President Bush proposed creation of a new cabinet department to prevent future terrorist attacks. The new Department of Homeland Security represents the largest reorganization of the executive branch since World War II. It brought together twenty-two agencies and their approximately 170,000 employees, and it has an estimated budget of $36 billion for fiscal 2004.[2]

Figure 2-1 provides an overview of the U.S. political structure, with a focus on its proactive elements—Congress and the president and the rest of the executive branch. State governments are organized in a similar manner. The figure illustrates the different institutions and policy actors who play a role in public policy development and implementation. It can be read in two somewhat different ways. First, it serves as a reminder that the U.S. system imposes substantial barriers to a top-down, unilateral approach to making public policy. Second, it shows the many different points of access the system affords to policy advocates. State and local governments dominate in many policy areas, such as education and crime control. They also sometimes intervene when the federal government chooses not to act. For example, faced with federal inaction, many states have adopted climate change policies that try to reduce use of fossil fuels (Rabe 2002).

The next section discusses the major features of the U.S. government system, beginning with federalism and followed by the institutions of the federal government. The chapter continues with "informal" policy actors, those outside of government who shape public policy, including the general public and organized interest groups. The purpose is twofold: first, to reacquaint readers with the basic components of government and, second, to encourage readers to think about the choices that are represented in these arrangements. Why is government structured one way and not another? What difference does the structure of government make for public policymaking and the substance of public policy? What changes in government might be desirable in terms of improving performance, especially the effectiveness, efficiency, and equity of policies? Or in improving the responsiveness of government to the U.S. public?

## FEDERALISM

The Constitution of the United States designed a system of government in which power is divided between the national government and the states (and for some purposes, Indian tribes).[3] National and state governments have the ability to make laws and public policies. This section begins with a brief discussion of the history of federalism, the federal-state relationship; the continuing controversies over the proper allocation of responsibility between the federal government and the states; and the variation among the states in their capacity for public policy innovation.

# Federal, State, and Local Agents of Policymaking and Avenues of Policy Formation

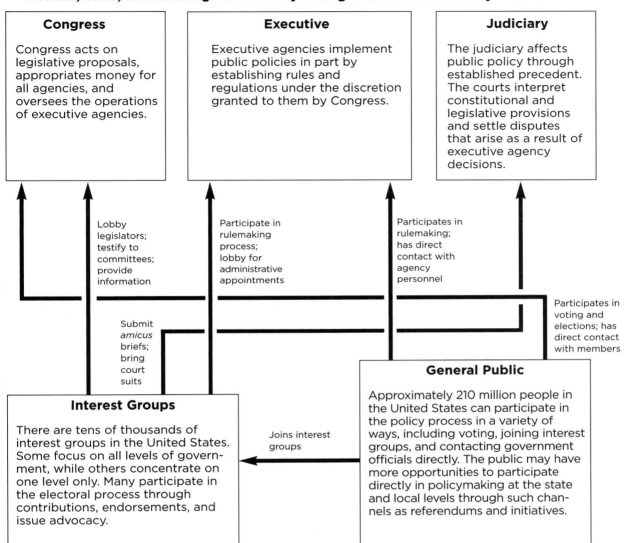

**Congress**

Congress acts on legislative proposals, appropriates money for all agencies, and oversees the operations of executive agencies.

**Executive**

Executive agencies implement public policies in part by establishing rules and regulations under the discretion granted to them by Congress.

**Judiciary**

The judiciary affects public policy through established precedent. The courts interpret constitutional and legislative provisions and settle disputes that arise as a result of executive agency decisions.

Lobby legislators; testify to committees; provide information

Participate in rulemaking process; lobby for administrative appointments

Participates in rulemaking; has direct contact with agency personnel

Participates in voting and elections; has direct contact with members

Submit *amicus* briefs; bring court suits

**Interest Groups**

There are tens of thousands of interest groups in the United States. Some focus on all levels of government, while others concentrate on one level only. Many participate in the electoral process through contributions, endorsements, and issue advocacy.

Joins interest groups

**General Public**

Approximately 210 million people in the United States can participate in the policy process in a variety of ways, including voting, joining interest groups, and contacting government officials directly. The public may have more opportunities to participate directly in policymaking at the state and local levels through such channels as referendums and initiatives.

**FIGURE 2-1** The U.S. government is a highly complex system with multiple actors at all levels and multiple interactions among these different levels. But the system is also fragmented; public policy decisions can often be made within any of the units described. Because of this dispersal of power, the general public and interest groups alike have numerous points of access to decision-making organizations and thus may be able to influence policy decisions. This diagram illustrates these connections for the national level of government. It is also important to recognize that similar points of access occur at the state and local government levels. All state governments have a similar tripartite separation of powers with legislative committees and state level agencies. Local governments also disperse power in a variety of ways that provide opportunities for groups and citizens to access policymakers.

### The Evolution of Federal-State Relations

The relationship between national and state governments in policymaking has changed since the nation's founding. In the late eighteenth century the functions or responsibilities of each level of government were quite distinct. State governments, for example, were responsible for education and transportation policies. The national government limited itself to larger issues such as national defense and international trade. Little integration of the two levels of government existed. This state of affairs is often referred to as **dual federalism,** and it persisted throughout the nineteenth century, in part because the federal government's activities remained fairly modest. This is not to say that the relationship between the national and state governments was always serene. During the early history of the United States, disputes arose over how much power the national government should have and what should be left to the states. As the national government attempted to assert itself on issues such as the establishment of a national bank and the rules of interstate commerce, its authority was challenged. The Supreme Court, led by Chief Justice John Marshall, supported an expanded role of the national government. Yet, as disagreement over the spread of slavery to new states and the subsequent Civil War showed, major conflicts persisted over interpretation of the national government's powers.

In the twentieth century federal-state relations changed significantly, especially in response to the Great Depression of the 1930s. President Franklin Roosevelt's legislative program, known as the New Deal, was an expansive economic recovery program that began to break down the imaginary barriers between national and state policy. It was not unusual to see the national government become involved in what were traditionally considered state responsibilities. Thus dual federalism over time evolved into **cooperative federalism,** as collaboration on policymaking between the national and state governments increased. Many large scale federal programs begun in the 1960s and 1970s, another period of government growth, relied on such a model. The federal clean air and clean water programs, for example, involved a mix of national and state responsibilities, with the national government setting environmental protection standards and the states carrying out most implementation actions.

Much of the cooperation that occurred between the national and state governments was a result of additional monies being provided to the states through block grants and categorical grants. States were grateful for the federal funds, but also concerned about the expectations that such funding carried. Did the money have to be spent in a certain way? On certain programs? How would such stipulations affect the states' autonomy in designing and managing their own policies?

### Continuing Controversies over the Allocation of Power

During the 1970s and 1980s critics of federalism urged the states to retake some of their policymaking responsibilities. President Richard Nixon's "new federalism" initiatives in the early 1970s were designed to move away from categorical grants and toward block grants of money that would allow the states more discretion in how they used the funds. The devolution of policy to the states continued under President Ronald Reagan. His conservative philosophy and political rhetoric gave a significant boost to the trend already under way to restore greater authority to the states. Although many states welcomed this change, they also worried about the subsequent decrease in federal dollars coming into their treasuries. In addition, the national government had discovered a new way to enact popular policies without paying for them: it gave implementation responsibilities to the states. Federal policymakers received political credit for the new programs without spending federal tax dollars. These unfunded mandates—federal requirements placed upon the state governments without funds for implementation—added stress to the relationship between the national and state governments.

That relationship continues to evolve. In 1995 Congress enacted the Unfunded Mandates Reform Act to limit future financial impacts on the states, but conflict over policymaking in a federal system did not vanish as a result. For one thing, the legislation Congress passed was not implemented very effectively. Congress continued to approve new mandates for which insufficient money was made available. For another, the act did not remove the extensive mandates for state action that were already in place. Continued conflict between the federal government and the states could be seen in 2001 over federal education policy, specifically, the No Child Left Behind program. Debate focused on the impact on the states of mandatory national standards for promoting primary and secondary school students to the next grade. Supporters of the standards want to ensure that students have the skills and knowledge to compete nationally and internationally. Few question the goal of improving the quality of the nation's schools, but many are concerned about the imposition of federal standards in a policy area that has traditionally been a state responsibility. According to the Department of Education, $387 million was authorized for the states to develop and implement the tests, but many state officials complained that the federal funds were insufficient to meet their responsibilities under the act.

## State Variation in Policy Capacity

Both of the major political parties seem interested in continuing the **decentralization** of power to the states. The focus, however, has shifted to asking whether the states have the capacity to handle additional responsibilities. The issues that arise in this debate parallel the book's main evaluative criteria. For example, critics of decentralization are concerned about the implications for program effectiveness, efficiency, and equity because they recognize that the fifty states are quite different from one another both in their capacity to act on policy issues and in the kinds of policies they enact.

The states also differ in fundamental ways such as physical size, population, extent of industrialization, and affluence. Moreover, each state and region has a distinctive history and culture that shape policy actions (Elazar 1984; Lieske 1993). What may work well and be acceptable to residents of Wisconsin or Minnesota might not be appropriate or feasible in Texas or Mississippi. Some states have extensive state parks and other recreational facilities, while others have strict vehicle inspection programs to promote highway safety. California, Vermont, Maine, and Utah, and perhaps other states, do not permit smoking in restaurants.[4]

Arkansas governor Mike Huckabee poses with graduates of that state's Welfare-to-Work program. State governments are often at the forefront of policy development and implementation. In certain policy domains, state governments have the capacity to be innovative in dealing with public problems. A good example is the level of autonomy that states have in implementing policies associated with the national welfare reform law enacted in 1996. The law made major changes in the program, requiring states to reduce their welfare caseloads. States used a wide range of actions to meet the law's requirements, and the Welfare-to-Work program, has proven to be relatively successful in moving individuals off of the welfare rolls even if less successful in other respects.

There is nothing inherently negative about such policy variation among the states; indeed, throughout the nation's history Americans have celebrated the rich diversity of state cultures and policy preferences. When a state's policies are so different from others that its residents may be deprived of essential human needs or federally protected rights, however, the federal government is likely to intervene.

Those who favor increasing state authority tend to believe that the states are capable of handling additional responsibilities and are better equipped than the federal government at defining their citizens' needs. Indeed, for some, the states are the "new heroes" of American federalism, with greater capacity for policy innovation and closer ties to citizens than a national government in which many have lost faith. Studies show that over the past several decades state legislatures and bureaucracies have become more skilled than they were before at dealing with policy issues (Hedge 1998). Their new capacity comes from growth in their professional staffs and expertise, including the ability to appraise policy needs and evaluate programs with greater accuracy. Until an economic downturn in 2001 reduced state revenues, the states also could act on public problems because they had sufficient funds, from federal transfer dollars and state taxation, to do so (Bowman and Kearney 1999). The best evidence in support of

## WORKING WITH SOURCES

### STATE PUBLIC POLICIES

One way to become familiar with public policy variation among the fifty states is to explore what several of them have done in a particular policy area, such as education, health care, environmental protection, economic development, or criminal justice. The Web site for the Council of State Governments (www.csg.org) provides links to all fifty state government home pages, which in turn have links to major policy areas. The council also has extensive news reports on policy activities that affect the states, including policy innovation. Reading about different policy actions within the states is one of the best ways to become informed about state capacity for policy development and to see how the states differ from one another.

Visit the council's Web page and click on States at the top of the page and then select State Pages. From the list of the fifty states, select California, and then Environment and Natural Resources. Select the link to Safeguarding California's Environment, and then the link to Clean Air, which is located under the heading of Protecting Air and Water Quality. Clicking on the Clean Air link takes you to the California Air Resources Board home page. Here, you can read about several state programs, such as the stringent mandate for Zero-Emission Vehicles (ZEV—located on the links listed on the right of the page), and the state's new Fuel Cell Partnership program. The Cleaner Cars Buyer's Guide lists and ranks new model cars that qualify for credit under ZEV program.

To compare California's actions on clean air to those in other states, follow comparable links. For example, go to the Texas state Web page, select Environment and Natural Resources, and then Pollution. What conclusions can you draw about the differences between the two states? For another example, select the Minnesota state Web page and select Environment, and then Pollution. How would you compare Minnesota's efforts on pollution control to those of Texas and California?

Try selecting a different policy area, such as criminal justice, health care, education, or welfare. Compare two or more states in the same way. Can you discover enough information to discern the differences between states on the topic?

these arguments can be found in the many innovative and effective measures states have taken over the past several decades in areas as diverse as highway safety, antismoking programs, energy conservation, criminal justice, and environmental protection (Borins 1998; Rabe 2003). The box "Working with Sources: State Public Policies" indicates where readers can locate information about variation among the states in public policy.

Nevertheless, analysts have several reasons to remain skeptical of how much more decentralization of federal power to the states is desirable. First, policy performance varies from state to state, and citizens may suffer the consequences.[5] For example, some states fail to fully test drinking water or to enforce clean air and clean water laws, even though they are violating federal environmental laws (Rabe 2003). Second, the states with more money and greater expertise than others can design better programs and offer more services to their citizens. Third, business and industry interest groups may exert more influence at the state level than at the national level because of the states' eagerness to attract businesses and jobs. Fourth, decisions may be less open and less visible at the state level, despite the closer proximity of government to citizens. Fifth, many public problems, such as air and water pollution, cross state boundaries, suggesting that a higher level of government is needed to address them adequately. Finally, only the federal government has sufficient resources to support policy activities such as scientific research for environmental protection and health care.

It seems likely that public debate over the proper distribution of authority between the states and the federal government will continue. The question at the heart of the controversy is which level of government is best suited to address different kinds of public policies. That question has no automatic answer, however, and each person's position is likely to be influenced by his or her basic beliefs about the role of government in society, particularly the national government. As public policy students become acquainted with **evaluative criteria** and how they apply to public policy questions, the appropriate level of government to address them may become apparent.

## SEPARATION OF POWERS

One of the distinguishing characteristics of the U.S. Constitution is the separation of powers. Governing power is shared among the three branches of government: legislative, executive, and judicial. This arrangement reflected the Founders' experience of living under what they saw as the tyranny of the British monarch. They feared that unrestrained government authority could abuse citizens' rights, and they believed that the checks and balances built into a system of separated powers would ensure that no one branch of government would have enough power to threaten liberty. In fact, under this system, the legislative and executive branches must cooperate to accomplish almost anything, and such cooperation is not always easy to achieve (Jones 1999). Most people would agree that the goal of preventing tyranny is a worthy one, but the separation of powers also has added to the **complexity** and difficulty of policymaking and to gridlock.

The number of policy actors and their overlapping responsibilities contribute to the complexity, making it difficult to figure out who has responsibility for any particular government action. Think about oversight of financial markets and the collapse of the Enron Corporation in 2001 because of its extensive accounting irregularities that went undetected for years. It seems clear that the Securities and Exchange Commission (SEC) was remiss, but why? Did Congress fail to provide adequate financial support for the agency to exercise oversight or fail to urge it to use its oversight authority? Or consider the investigations of terrorist threats to the nation prior to September 11 and the seeming inability (or unwillingness, which is a policy decision) of the Federal Bureau of Investigation (FBI) and other intelligence agencies to share information and cooperate (Sanger 2002; Van Natta and Johnston 2002).

Difficulty in policymaking is a reflection of the government's capacity to respond to public problems in light of divided institutions and authority and the political conflicts that inevitably arise over how best to deal with those problems. In other words, it is not easy to identify and define problems, develop suitable solutions, and approve these solutions in such a fragmented governing system. The next sections explore the branches of the national government, each branch's major characteristics, and the implications of these characteristics for policymaking. In general, all state governments have similar systems and must also deal with comparable complexity and difficulty within their own policy processes.

## Legislative Branch

The legislative branch of the United States is a **bicameral** (two-house) Congress, consisting of the House of Representatives and the Senate. The two chambers differ from one another in their composition and operating style. The House, with members elected every two years from separate districts within each state, is the more representative or democratic chamber of the two. It has 435 voting members, each representing about 650,000 constituents.[6] Senators serve six-year terms, giving them more independence than House members. Moreover, with only one-third of its members up for reelection every two years, the Senate is also more insulated than the House from short-term political forces. Each state, regardless of its size, elects two senators, so that the one hundred members serve quite different constituencies. California's senators, for example, represent more than 35 million people, while the senators from Delaware represent about 800,000. The Senate also allows its members more freedom than the House to debate issues. Senators have the right to **filibuster,** or to talk for an extended period of time in hope of delaying, modifying, or defeating a proposal. Threats of a filibuster can force policy compromises as members try to prevent having all other business grind to a halt.

Article I of the Constitution spells out Congress's powers, but the most important today are its lawmaking and budgetary responsibilities. In addition to passing legislation, Congress each year must appropriate the funds necessary to run government programs. To accomplish these tasks, both chambers operate under a system that allows for division of labor and policy specialization. Policy development is concentrated within this elaborate system of **committees** and **subcommittees,** each of which is chaired by the party holding a majority of seats in Congress.

Each of the close to two hundred committees and subcommittees has specific jurisdiction over certain public policies and the executive agencies that administer them. Each has a substantial staff that can bring experience and expertise to bear on lawmaking and on oversight and investigations of the executive agencies. Bills introduced into either chamber are referred to a committee for consideration. If the committee chooses to move ahead on the legislation, it typically conducts public hearings to acquire information on the advantages and disadvantages of the proposed law. Executive branch officials and experts from academia, think tanks, and interest groups may be invited to Capitol Hill to testify. (It is easy to find verbatim accounts of testimony through services available at most college libraries.) Eventually, the committees accept, modify, or reject the legislation. For bills that are to move forward, the committees submit reports on their findings and recommendations to the full chamber for consideration. To become law, a bill must pass both chambers in identical form and be signed by the president. Presidents may **veto** or reject a bill approved by Congress, and Congress in turn may override the president's veto with a two-thirds vote in both houses. Normally, Congress has a difficult time overriding a presidential veto.

The fragmentation of authority among the committees can pose an obstacle to policymaking, but there is an upside as well. The large number of committees and subcommittees

## WORKING WITH SOURCES

### CONGRESS

Most members of Congress have a personal Web page, which they use to discuss state or district policy issues and their positions on them. Access their Web pages from the Library of Congress portal (http://thomas.loc.gov) by clicking on either the House of Representatives or Senate link in Quick Links at the top of the page. Visit the site for your own representative or one of your senators to see what issues are featured. Go a step further and examine a specific policy area to identify and evaluate the representative's or senator's position.

For example, look for the member's position on Social Security, use of school vouchers, national energy policy and drilling in the Arctic National Wildlife Refuge, or prescription drug coverage for Medicare recipients. Try comparing your representative or senator with others to determine how reasonable or defensible his or her position is. Or look for specific arguments and supportive evidence used to defend the positions you find on these issues. Based on the logic of the argument or the evidence presented, do you find the position to be well supported and convincing or not?

creates multiple venues for highlighting public problems and considering policy proposals. In this way, almost any issue, from energy conservation to child care, can gain attention on Capitol Hill and possibly media coverage as well. During 2002, for example, Rep. Ed Markey, D-Mass., introduced legislation to create a national G-force standard to make roller coasters and other amusement park rides safer after reports of brain injuries and deaths attributed to some rides were made public. Increased visibility can pave the way for legislative action, whether at the time a proposal is first considered or when public demand may be greater or supporting data stronger.

Often the committees, or the full House and Senate, fail to agree on policy proposals, and gridlock results. It is easy to fault members of Congress for inaction, but the causes of policy disagreement and stalemate are legion. It is not too far off the mark to say that when Congress is divided on public policy, so is the nation, and, as a representative political institution, Congress reflects the larger society for better or worse. In a sense, Congress struggles continuously with its dual roles of representation and lawmaking (Davidson and Oleszek 2002).

That tension is evident in the policy behavior of members of Congress. Incumbent members usually seek reelection and are overwhelmingly successful. As David Mayhew (1974) has argued, because of their **electoral incentive,** members are strongly motivated to stay in the spotlight; take positions on the issues, even if they do nothing about them; and claim credit for public policy actions, particularly those that materially benefit the district or state. These pressures mean that members often introduce bills, make speeches, and issue press releases on many issues, even when the legislation has no chance of moving forward. In many ways, Congress is a loosely connected assembly of 535 elected officials who, because of the electoral incentive, often go their own way. If they do not act as teammates, policy action that requires agreement may be stymied.

To rein in this natural tendency toward political individualism, Congress relies on the elected leadership within each house, which is organized by political parties. The majority party dominates the House and Senate agendas and decision-making processes to a substantial degree. Historically, the party leadership has been instrumental in overcoming ideological and regional divisions within Congress and forging consensus; it also negotiates with the president on potentially divisive policy issues (Jones 1999; Sinclair 2000). As parties have weakened, however, the leadership role is less evident, and individual members of Congress rely on their substantial personal staffs to develop policy. Policy development of this kind is particularly likely in the Senate where members have larger staffs and attract greater media coverage than do House members. The box "Working with Sources: Congress" explains how to access congressional Web pages and see what senators and representatives have to say on many issues.

In recent years both the House and the Senate have been closely divided in party membership, which forces the two major parties to work together to fashion legislative compromises. Party control of each chamber remains highly important, however, as demonstrated vividly in 2001 when Sen. James Jeffords of Vermont left the Republican Party to become an independent and voted with the Democrats. His action gave the Democrats majority control of the Senate, which in turn meant that President Bush faced more difficulty securing the approval of Congress for his legislative initiatives and budget proposals.

## Executive Branch

The federal executive branch is responsible for carrying out the laws enacted by Congress. It is made up of the president, the vice president, the White House staff, and the federal bureaucracy. Although presidents do not make laws, they are actively involved in agenda setting, policy formulation and adoption, and implementation (Jones 1999). Other than the vice president, the president is the only federal official who is elected nationally. In effect, the president embodies the U.S. government, symbolizes U.S. culture and values, and speaks for the nation abroad. As such he commands enormous public and media attention that gives him unequaled influence in agenda setting and policy leadership. For example, President George H. W. Bush got discussions started on amending the Clean Air Act. His interest in amending the law and being an active player in its development broke a decade-long logjam and in 1990 eventually led to one of the most sweeping environmental laws ever enacted (Vig and Kraft 2003). His son, George W. Bush, played a comparable role in redefining domestic security after the September 11 attacks.

In addition to the president, the entire White House staff and the **Executive Office of the President** (EOP) are intimately involved in policy development. The EOP consists of the White House offices and agencies that assist the president in the development and implementation of public policy. Among other offices, these include the Office of Management and Budget (OMB), the Council of Economic Advisers, the National Security Council, the Council on Environmental Quality, and the Office of Science and Technology Policy. Together these offices constitute a "mini-bureaucracy" that provides the president and his staff with vital information and policy ideas in their respective areas. The EOP keeps the president informed about the plethora of policies under consideration in Congress or being implement-

## WORKING WITH SOURCES

## EXECUTIVE DEPARTMENTS AND AGENCIES

One way to become better acquainted with how executive departments and agencies contribute to public policy is to visit several of their Web sites. Begin with the federal portal, www.first-gov.gov, and select a cabinet department or agency. The cabinet departments are Agriculture, Commerce, Defense, Education, Energy, Health and Human Services, Homeland Security, Housing and Urban Development, Interior, Justice, Labor, State, Transportation, Treasury, and Veterans Affairs.

You might look at the Department of Health and Human Services. Within HHS, you could select the Food and Drug Administration (FDA). Consider looking at the Department of Justice and the FBI. Or you could look at one of the independent agencies such as the Central Intelligence Agency (CIA) or the EPA. To get an idea of what the agency does, look for links to current issues. The FDA site, for example, has a box listing "FDA Activities" and another box called "Products FDA Regulates," which includes foods, drugs, medical devices, and cosmetics. Click on any one of these links to see full descriptions of what the FDA does in these areas and the issues and controversies that arise.

ed in the federal bureaucracy, giving him opportunities to influence policy direction. In most policy areas, the president's agenda and his positions, particularly on domestic issues, reflect his party affiliation, political ideology, and the constellation of constituencies most important to his party and, if he is in his first term, to his reelection. Democratic and Republican presidents tend to adopt distinctive policy positions on most issues because of their differing philosophies of governance and the particular array of interests the parties represent.

The federal bureaucracy constitutes the bulk of the executive branch. It includes all of the agencies and offices that fall under each of the cabinet departments and other offices and agencies whose mission is to develop and implement policy in specialized areas. The best known of these are the fifteen **cabinet-level departments,** each of which is managed by a secretary appointed by the president and confirmed by the Senate.

Each cabinet department includes subsidiary agencies, some of which may be better known than their home departments. For example, the Federal Aviation Administration (FAA), which has primary responsibility for aviation safety, is part of the Transportation Department. The Food and Drug Administration (FDA), responsible for ensuring the safety of food and medicines, is part of Health and Human Services, and the FBI is located in the Justice Department. The bureaucratic agencies issue reports and studies that enable the public to follow the agencies' activities in their special policy areas. A great deal of this information can be found on agency Web sites. See the box "Working with Sources: Executive Departments and Agencies."

Each agency makes policy within its specialized area through the interpretation of legislative language and development of regulations that are essential to policy implementation. Career federal officials in the agencies have considerable authority to shape public policy, even though ultimate responsibility for policymaking rests with the president's appointees at the top of each agency and department. These career officials work closely with the White House to ensure that agency and department policy decisions are consistent with the president's programs and priorities, at least where the decisions are not strictly limited by statutory specifications. As a result, the U.S. bureaucracy is more politicized than bureaucracies in many other developed nations, and its policies can change significantly from one administration to the next.

The shift from President Clinton to President Bush provides illustration. Bush's appointees to executive agencies and his administration's policies were decidedly more conservative than his predecessor's. Such differences were notable even in the selection of individuals to serve in a voluntary capacity on scientific advisory committees to executive agencies such as the FDA and the Centers for Disease Control and Prevention (CDC). Such advisory committees are intended to help inform government decisions in public health and other policy areas. The Department of Health and Human Services alone has more than 250 advisory committees of this kind. Because their interpretation of scientific evidence can push policy decisions one way or another, presidents and cabinet officials take a keen interest in who serves on these committees.[7]

Such a shift in political ideology also makes it difficult for the administration to fill important agency positions. For the first two years of the Bush administration, the FDA had no commissioner because Democrats and Republicans in Congress could not agree on the appropriate qualifications for the head of the agency. Democrats said they would oppose candidates with close ties to industries the FDA regulates, including those associated with drugs, medical devices, food, and cosmetics. Republicans reportedly insisted that the nominee support conservative positions, for example, on halting sale of RU-486, the so-called abortion pill. In October 2002 Bush nominated Mark McClellan, an internist and associate professor at Stanford University, who had bipartisan credentials and a pragmatic rather than ideological approach to FDA issues.

Outside of the cabinet departments are the numerous independent executive and regulatory agencies. One of the best known is the Environmental Protection Agency (EPA), an **independent executive agency** with an appointed administrator who has major policymaking and implementation responsibilities for environmental policy. Independent agencies differ from cabinet-level departments chiefly in their responsibilities for a more focused policy area. Other examples include the National Aeronautics and Space Administration (NASA), the Central Intelligence Agency (CIA) and the Nuclear Regulatory Commission (NRC), which oversees the civilian use of nuclear energy, including power plants and the high-level waste they produce.

The **independent regulatory commission** (IRC) is yet another breed of executive agency. Like cabinet secretaries, the commissioners are appointed by the president and confirmed by the Senate, but for fixed and staggered terms. These fixed terms are intended to insulate IRC decision making from political pressure from the president or Congress. In addition, most IRCs are responsible for the economic regulation of certain industries. For example, the Federal Communication Commission (FCC) regulates the broadcasting industry, and the SEC regulates the financial markets. An IRC focuses on one industry, and therefore its scope of authority tends to be narrow. Although each agency operates within its own area of expertise, what it does can be in conflict with another agency. For example, the EPA, intent on its mission to reduce pollution, for years wanted automobiles to have onboard pollution controls to cut emissions coming from engines. The National Highway Traffic Safety Administration (part of the Transportation Department), concerned with its mission of safe automobile travel, believed that such a mechanism would make cars more susceptible to explosion.

Addressing a news conference on Capitol Hill in March 2003, Rep. Charlie Gonzales, D-Texas, right, speaks against President George W. Bush's nomination of Miguel Estrada to a federal appeals court. Linda Chavez-Thompson, executive vice president of the AFL-CIO, left, looks on. Republicans stressed Estrada's Hispanic heritage in the battle over his appointment to the federal judiciary. Democrats tried to counter the action by mounting a filibuster against Estrada's nomination, raising concerns about the conservative lawyer's likely rulings on the appeals court, his possible nomination later to the Supreme Court, and his reluctance during confirmation hearings to answer questions about his judicial philosophy.

## Judicial Branch

The federal judiciary is made up of the nine-member Supreme Court, thirteen **circuit courts of appeals,** and ninety-four **federal district courts,** as well as special courts such as bankruptcy courts, a court of appeals for the armed services, and a court of federal claims. Although many would not think of them as policymakers, the courts play a vital role by interpreting the policy decisions made by others; indeed, the courts often have the last word on policy. The major distinction between the judiciary and the other two branches is that the courts' policymaking is *reactive* rather than *proactive.* Unlike Congress and the executive branch, which can initiate policy, the federal courts offer rulings and opinions only on cases brought before them. Yet these rulings may dictate policy far beyond the actual cases. Consider the Supreme Court ruling in *Brown v. Board of Education of Topeka* (1954), which overruled the precedent of "separate but equal" public schools, thereby ending legally sanctioned segregation. Or the Court's decision in *Roe v. Wade* (1973), which struck down state laws that made abortion a crime. Although each was an important case in its own right, the Court's ruling in each had greater policy implications than perhaps initially anticipated.

The court's functions shape public policy in many ways. The courts serve as gatekeepers by deciding who has standing to sue or the right to appeal to the federal courts or whether a dispute is "ripe," or ready for review. The courts also set standards for review, including whether they will defer to the expert judgment of administrative agencies or review an agency's decisions more critically. Courts interpret the Con-

**WORKING WITH SOURCES**

**THE FEDERAL JUDICIARY**

To learn more about how the courts affect public policy, visit the U.S. courts Web portal at www.uscourts.gov. The site has links to the Supreme Court, the courts of appeals, and the district courts as well as to all the administrative offices. The Supreme Court page (www. supremecourtus. gov) offers access to details about what is on the Court's docket, or the cases up for review; the current schedule of cases being heard; oral arguments made before the Court and briefs submitted; Court rulings; and the full text of opinions.

stitution, statutory language, administrative rules, regulations, executive orders, treaties, and prior court decisions regarded as precedent. The policy language in these various documents may be ambiguous or vague, or new situations may arise that the architects of the language failed to anticipate. The courts have the final say on what the law means, unless Congress revises the law to make its meaning clearer. Finally, courts also have some discretion in choosing a judicial remedy, such as imposition of fines, probation, or incarceration (O'Leary 2003).

The federal courts, therefore, are more constrained in their policymaking roles than Congress and the executive branch. In addition to having to wait for a suitable case, judges must anchor their rulings in law or precedent, not personal beliefs or **interest group politics** as elected officials are free to do. The legitimacy of the courts depends upon the public's willingness to abide by judicial rulings. If judges deviate too far from acceptable legal rationales for their decisions, they risk losing citizens' confidence. Still, judges clearly differ in their judicial philosophies, or the bases they use for decision making. Some are more conservative or liberal than others, and analysts tend to describe the federal courts, especially the Supreme Court, in terms of the justices' ideological or philosophical leanings.

Federal judges are nominated by the president and confirmed by the Senate, but their jobs are for life, if they choose to stay in them. For that reason, the senators, along with interest groups and the public, scrutinize their views on public policy issues when they are nominated. Presidents usually get the judges they want appointed to office, but the Senate sometimes blocks nominees it finds unacceptable, often for ideological reasons. Given the typical lengthy service of a federal judge, a president's influence on public policy continues for decades after he leaves office. The box "Working with Sources: The Federal Judiciary" provides links to Web sites that offer detailed coverage of the organization and operation of the federal courts.

Under the U.S. system of separated powers, it is essential that the three branches of government cooperate to ensure policy enactment and effective implementation. Indeed, policy results from the interaction of the branches rather than their separate actions. Constitutionally, the legislature may be the branch responsible for policymaking, but many other policy actors must also be involved. It is clear that each branch has a strong capacity to analyze public problems and devise solutions to them, but equally clear that building consensus among diverse policy actors with different political incentives and constituencies, although necessary, is rarely easy.

## POLICY SUBGOVERNMENTS AND ISSUE NETWORKS

So far, this chapter has dealt with the formal government institutions involved in making public policy. It is easy for citizens to understand these institutions and the people who work in them. Yet much policymaking occurs in less formal settings or venues and involves policy actors within particular issue areas, such as agriculture, forestry, or energy. Political scientists refer to these informal arrangements as **subgovernments** or **issue networks** (Heclo 1978; Lowi 1979; McConnell 1966; McCool 1990). They used to be called **iron triangles** because of the supposed power and autonomy of their three components: congressional subcommittees, an executive agency, and an outside economic interest group, such as cotton farmers or oil companies. These subgovernments usually operate under the radar of most citizens, and they may not be influenced as much by citizen values or policy preferences as the more formal institutions are.

The reality is that decision making about many programs and policies tends to be highly specialized. Because of the complexity of public problems and policies, and the often detailed knowledge required to understand them, specialization will no doubt continue to be the norm. One group of policy actors specializes in health care policy; another quite different group acts in the area of defense policy or environmental protection. Each develops its own distinctive channels of communication, and even terminology, to discuss policy issues. The areas of specialization, and the people and institutions active in them, are known as issue networks, subgovernments, or subsystems to reflect the fact that decision making takes place below the level of the full system of government (Freeman 1965; Thurber 1996a). For example, defense procurement decision making (how much to spend on weapons systems and which ones to buy) involves the congressional armed services committees, the Department of Defense, and private defense contractors—those who build the weapons. All tend to favor increased spending for defense, and they work together toward provision of defense systems, usually without much involvement, oversight, or criticism by those who are not part of the subgovernment or network.

Historically, the subgovernments have been exceptionally powerful in setting U.S. policy, particularly in areas of limited interest to the general public, such as agricultural subsidies, mining and forestry, weapons procurement, and highway and dam construction. Today, however, the subgovernments are less autonomous and generally operate with more visibility and "outside" participation. More policy actors are involved, sometimes hundreds of different institutions and individuals. Use of the term *issue network* rather than *subgovernment* reflects this evolution in U.S. policymaking (Heclo 1978). Nevertheless, these networks or subsystems are still important. To varying degrees, their participants remain preoccupied with narrow economic interests; they may afford limited participation beyond the core members; and they may be able to resist external influences (Anderson 2003). If nothing else, it is clear that much U.S. policymaking involves informal networks of communication in which prevailing policy ideas and the evaluation of new studies and information shape what is likely to be acceptable to the major policy actors (Kingdon 1995). Fortunately for students of public policy, it is much easier today to gain access to those networks and to see what the specialized policy communities are thinking about and where change may be possible.

## PUBLIC OPINION AND POLICYMAKING

As one would expect in a democracy, public opinion is a major force in policymaking. It influences what elected officials try to do, especially on issues that are highly salient, or of great importance to voters, or on those that elicit strong opinions, such as abortion rights or gun control. Although public opinion is rarely the determinative influence on policymaking, it sets boundaries for public policy actions. Policymakers cross those boundaries at their own risk. The broad direction of public policies therefore tends to reflect the concerns, fears, and preferences of the U.S. public (Page 1992; Manza, Cook, and Page 2002).

The common definition of public opinion is what the public thinks about a particular issue or set of issues at any point in time (O'Connor and Sabato 2002), but what is meant by "the public" is not always clear. The attentive public can be distinguished from the general public. The attentive public, typically less than 10 percent of the public, includes those who are apt to take an interest in a particular problem or policy. They are more likely than other people to become informed about the issues and to get involved in some way. Actions and communication from either of these publics may influence policy development, but the general public's opinions tend to shape only the overall direction of policy, while the views of the attentive public, especially of organized interests, tend to have a greater impact. This influence can be especially pronounced for policies with low salience for the general public.

Americans have numerous ways and opportunities to voice their opinions, so policymakers at all levels of government need to be aware of the shifting beliefs of the population. Beyond answering **polls** or **surveys**, people can express their opinions through their political participation, which may include not just voting, but attending meetings, writing or speaking to government officials, joining interest groups, and backing referendums and initiatives placed on state or local ballots. These are forms of direct citizen involvement in policymaking, and many states permit their use. The medical marijuana initiative mentioned in Chapter 1 is one example. Another is California's Proposition 65, which the state's voters adopted by a two-to-one margin in 1986. The measure requires companies to provide "clear and reasonable warning" whenever the public is exposed to cancer-causing chemicals, or substances that are toxic to the reproductive system. The initiative is one of the first examples of what are called **information disclosure** policies, where the public's "right to know" is the basis of policy action (Graham 2002; Hadden 1989).

It makes sense intuitively that public opinion should be important in a democracy, even if in a less direct way than a ballot initiative. The truth is, however, that most citizens pay relatively little attention to government, politics, and public policy. They are preoccupied with their families, jobs, homes, and other matters that are important to them on a day-to-day basis. As a result, they may not be well informed on policy issues, and they may have few strong opinions about them. Such opinions are often characterized as being low in **saliency** and **intensity.** Both qualities are important for predicting whether and how likely people are to act on their opinions. For example, most people express views sympathetic to environmental protection, but they do not act like environmentalists in their energy use, consumer purchases, and so forth. Because environmental policy is a low salience issue, it is also not as likely as other issues to shape people's votes during election years (Bosso and Guber 2003).

**Stability** is the continuation of an opinion over time. Public opinion can be fleeting and change quickly, and it can be influenced by current events and the way issues are presented in the media and by public officials. A good example is what public opinion analysts call the "rally-around-the-flag" effect, which often occurs when an international crisis prompts citizens to emphasize patriotic feelings and to support the president and other national leaders

## STEPS TO ANALYSIS

## PUBLIC OPINION

An enormous amount of contemporary poll data can be found on the Web. Several specific examples illustrate the kind of material you can find and how you might evaluate it. If the particular poll data we discuss here are not available when you access the site, try to find comparable information in the newer polls that appear regularly.

Go to the Public Agenda Web site (www. publicagenda.org) and select the abortion topic. Under the public opinion category, select the link People's Chief Concerns. Then select the link to one of the findings reported on the site: "Only one-third of Americans say they want abortion's current legal status changed." The site refers to a 1999 poll sponsored by the *Wall Street Journal* and NBC News that asked the following question: "Which position do you tend to side with more? Government should pass more laws that restrict the availability of abortions, or, government should not interfere with a woman's access to abortion?" The results were as follows: 65 percent of the sample chose the "no government interference" position, and 30

percent chose the "more government restrictions" option. Five percent said they were not sure. What conclusions would you draw from these data about public opinion on abortion? Do you think the question asked was fairly worded?

Next, go back to the People's Chief Concerns page and click on the link headed: "Americans are almost evenly divided on whether they are pro-choice or pro-life." Poll results here are from a Fox News /Opinion Dynamics poll of January 2002. That survey reported that 47 percent of the U.S. population is "pro-choice" and 41 percent is "pro-life," with 7 percent not sure, and 5 percent saying they fall in between the two choices. The question was: "On the issue of abortion, would you say that you are more pro-choice or pro-life?" The sample in this case was "900 registered voters" interviewed by telephone. This second survey suggests that the public is more closely divided on the subject of abortion than the first. Why do you think the results differ so much? Which of the two sets of results do you think is more valid?

more than they normally would. President Bush clearly benefited from the effect following the September 11 attacks; the evidence could be seen in his soaring approval ratings. As this discussion indicates, it is often difficult to figure out just what citizens want from government and what policy proposals they are prepared to endorse. Yet, the more stable public opinion is on an issue, the more likely policymakers are to pay attention and consider the public's views when making decisions.

Partly because so few Americans approach government and public policy with a clear, strong political ideology, they find it easy to hold inconsistent views on the role of government. Ideologically, a majority of Americans tend to be somewhat conservative; that is, they prefer limited government and, when offered the choice, less bureaucracy and regulation, at least in the abstract. This same majority, however, is likely to demand that government provide a great many services, from regulation of foods and drugs and environmental quality to provision of public education and police protection. The way people react to any given policy proposal depends greatly on *how* it is presented to them. When pollsters ask people about concrete policy programs, they generally find considerable public support for them. At the same time, politicians can elicit public sympathy if they attack government, bureaucracy, regulation, and taxation in a very general or abstract manner.

Public opinion is usually expressed as the aggregate or sum of the individual attitudes and opinions of the adult population. Polltakers measure it through interviews, typically conducted over the telephone, with a random sample of the adult population. (In a random sample, each person in the population has an equal chance of being selected.) If standard opinion research methods are followed, a typical survey or poll of about a thousand to twelve hundred adults will be accurate to within about three percentage points, meaning that the result is only three percentage points higher or lower than it would be if the entire U.S. population had been interviewed. Before accepting a poll's results as accurate, however, the public policy student needs to ascertain whether the survey followed proper methods. For example, were the questions objective or did they lead those responding to a particular position? Was a random sample used (Asher 2001)? Internet polls and other self-selected surveys almost always fail to meet these standards, as do many polls commissioned by interest groups, where leading questions are common. The box "Steps to Analysis: Public Opinion" highlights some sources of public opinion data and shows how one might critically examine the questions and other methods used in surveys.

Despite the public's often weak grasp of policy issues, there are reasons to believe that, given the opportunity, citizens can take a keen interest in public affairs, inform themselves on the issues, voice their opinions, and influence public policies. Especially at the local level, citizens can and do get involved, and they can have a major voice in public policy (Berry, Portney, and Thomson 1993). Even in highly technical areas such as nuclear power and nuclear waste policy, studies suggest a substantial potential for citizen involvement and influence (Hill 1992; Dunlap, Kraft, and Rosa 1993). Moreover, governments have ways to encourage a greater level of citizen involvement if they want to do so (Ingram and Smith 1993). Local communities that are trying to become more sustainable, for example, have created numerous opportunities for citizens to play a central role in the process (John and Mlay 1999; Mazmanian and Kraft 1999; Portney 2003).

Interest groups can take many forms, including individual businesses and the people they employ. Arthur Andersen employees rally in March 2001 in support of their embattled company in the wake of public anger and government investigations into questionable accounting practices that contributed to the collapse of the Enron Corporation. Executives of accounting companies also lobbied to weaken proposed new regulations of their business practices. Interest groups use a variety of techniques in their attempts to influence policymaking and public opinion. Grassroots mobilization and the organization of rallies are considered indirect lobbying methods. Groups often use these strategies to mobilize the rank-and-file of an organization in an effort to show policymakers the sheer numbers of people supporting (or opposing) a policy action. In contrast, communication with policymakers, such as speaking to members of Congress, testifying in front of a congressional committee, or submitting comments in response to agency rulemaking, is referred to as direct lobbying. Such communication usually involves the professional staff of an interest group or a firm specializing in lobbying.

## INTEREST GROUPS AND PUBLIC POLICY

Organized interest groups are a major influence on public policy, and by most measures their numbers and activities have soared since the 1960s (Berry 1997; Cigler and Loomis 2002). The number of citizen groups, or so-called public interest groups, such as the Sierra Club, the National Rifle Association, the Christian Coalition, or Mothers Against Drunk Driving, has risen significantly during this period, but so has the number of what are usually termed "special interest" groups, those with a direct economic stake in public policy, such as organized labor, business groups, and professional groups. Most groups are involved in direct lobbying of policymakers, indirect or grassroots lobbying aimed at mobilizing the public or the group's supporters, public education campaigns, electioneering, and litigation.

**Lobbying** is probably the most visible group activity, but it is not what people often suspect—illegal pressure of some kind. Groups lobby legislators mainly by supplying information on their policy views or summaries of policy-related studies they have conducted. They may testify in legislative committee hearings, meet with individual members or their staffs, and urge their members and supporters to write or call legislators (Wolpe and Levine 1996). All of this activity generally is intended to support policy proposals the group favors, oppose those it does not favor, or keep certain issues or policy alternatives off the legislative agenda. Groups also lobby executive branch agencies by submitting studies and recommendations during formal public comment periods on proposed regulations, as well as through frequent and informal communication with agency officials. In both the legislative and executive arenas a great deal of interest group activity consists of trying to block proposals (Kingdon 1995). A good example is the intense efforts by accounting companies during 2002 to water down proposed new regulatory oversight of the industry. The proposed regulations came about because the public was outraged over the behavior of the Arthur Andersen accounting firm in the Enron debacle, among other accounting scandals of 2001 and 2002 (Spinner 2002).[8]

Many groups issue studies, reports, and news releases. They sometimes produce commercials that air on television and radio or appear in newspapers and are intended to educate the public. That is, groups provide information and perspectives on public policy issues and try to win the public to their side. For example, the Nuclear Energy Institute, representing the nuclear energy industry, issues frequent reports and publishes newspaper and magazine advertisements touting the benefits of nuclear power and its safety.

Many interest groups participate actively in the electoral process. They openly endorse candidates for office, contribute money and other resources to their campaigns, and sponsor issue advocacy advertisements that are intended to affect voter opinion on the issues and, the groups hope, their votes. These efforts are aimed at getting people who are sympathetic to the particular group's positions elected or reelected and defeating those who oppose its positions. Groups also use litigation as a **policy tool**. They may file a suit against an agency because of a ruling or regulation and try to get the courts to change the policy. In the late 1990s, for example, the American Trucking Association sued the EPA over its proposed higher standards for ozone and particulate matter, which the association charged would adversely affect the trucking industry. The case went all the way to the Supreme Court, and the justices affirmed the EPA's regulations.

The lobbying directed at executive agencies is often intense; after all, the businesses and other groups have a great deal at stake. When administrative agencies implement policy, they write rules and regulations, including specific standards, that affect business operations. These rules can have a major impact on business and industry, as well as on ordinary citizens. The federal Administrative Procedure Act requires that the rulemaking process follow due process of law and be open and fair. Because of the importance of these administrative decisions, interest groups often discuss the issues informally with agency officials. For example, television executives talk to officials at the FCC about requirements for digital television broadcasting standards and the schedule for their implementation. Chemical company officials are in close contact with the EPA over any proposed changes in regulations pertaining to toxic air emissions. In the late 1990s labor union representatives were keenly interested in the ergonomics regulations to promote worker safety that the Occupational Safety and Health Administration was developing.

## WORKING WITH SOURCES

## INTEREST GROUP POLICY STRATEGIES

Organized interest groups are pervasive in the policy process. To find out what they do, visit a group's Web site and look for information on the organization's policy goals and political orientation, the issue positions it takes, and the strategies and tools it uses to lobby government officials and to spur its members and the general public to become active. Select several from the lists to see different points of view.

### PUBLIC INTEREST GROUPS

Population Connection (www.population connection. org)
Mothers Against Drunk Driving (www.madd. org)
National Organization for Women (www.now. org)
U.S. Public Interest Research Groups (www.uspirg. org)
Natural Resources Defense Council (www.nrdc. org)

### PROFESSIONAL ASSOCIATIONS

National Education Association (www.nea.org)
American Medical Association (www.ama-assn. org)
American Bar Association (www.abanet.org)

### BUSINESS GROUPS

National Association of Manufacturers (www. nam.org)
National Federation of Independent Businesses (www.nfib.com)
Recording Industry Association of America (www.riaa.org)
Nuclear Energy Institute (www.nei.org)

### LABOR GROUPS

AFL/CIO (www.aflcio.org)
United Auto Workers (www.uaw.org)
Teamsters (www.teamsters.org)

Business, labor, and other interests act more formally through the rulemaking process as well, particularly when a proposed rule or regulation is open to public comment. Although anyone may provide comments to administrative agencies, in reality most comments come from the interest groups that are directly affected by the agency's policy. So, if the FAA wants to require that all children under the age of two be seated in a child safety seat on airplanes, one would expect the airlines, and perhaps groups representing consumers, to provide a majority of the public comment.

Chapter 3 introduces several models of politics and public policy. One model, **pluralism,** deals with the role of interest groups and asserts that many (plural) sources of political power exist in society and that no one source of power or single interest group is dominant across the range of public policy decisions. The reason is that interest groups specialize in certain policy areas, so groups having influence in one area, such as health care, are not necessarily involved in or influence another policy arena, such as national security. This view of politics contrasts with **elite theory,** which states that certain powerful organizations (elites) have power and authority over all policy arenas (Dye 2001; Dye and Zeigler 1999).

Since the 1950s debate has raged over whether pluralism is an accurate depiction of U.S. politics and policy (Connolly 1969; Dahl 1966; Polsby 1980). Does the theory correctly describe politics and policymaking, or does elitism come closer to the mark? From a **normative dimension** or **perspective**, which would look at this question in terms of political values, should pluralism be a preferred way of developing policy because it encourages citizen and group involvement and government accountability? Or does such a system provide certain groups and segments of the population, such as corporate interests and the wealthy, privileged access at the expense of others? The box "Working with Sources: Interest Group Policy Strategies" provides some tools for thinking about these questions. It lists a number of leading interest groups and provides their Web addresses. One of the best ways to learn about the goals and values of the groups is to visit their sites and read about their activities.

## GROWTH OF GOVERNMENT

Most people recognize that government today is much larger and in many ways more intrusive than it was at the nation's founding. The First Congress, representing thirteen states, had sixty-five representatives and twenty-six senators. The bureaucracy consisted of three cabinet-level departments (War, Treasury, Foreign Affairs, to which one more, the Justice Department, was added) compared with fifteen departments, numerous bureaus and agencies, and more than 2.5 million federal employees in modern times (Office of Personnel Management 2002). Despite widespread belief to the contrary, the federal government's size, measured by employees and not budgets, has been stable since the 1970s, and indeed it decreased during the 1990s.[9] In fact, most of the recent growth in government employees has been in the states. Still, viewed in the broad sweep of history, it is important to understand why government has grown to its present size.

Obviously, part of the growth of government results from the expansion of the United States in area and population. The population increased seventyfold from 4 million at the time of the first census (1790) to 281 million in the 2000 census. The population today is heavily urban and well educated, compared to that of 1790, and occupies land from coast to coast as well as Alaska and Hawaii. Demographics and geography, however, cannot fully explain the growth of government, which has more to do with the changing nature of public problems and citizen expectations than the nation's size.

One major reason for the growth in government is that American society is more complex than in earlier days. This added complexity, which comes in part from advances in science and technology, has led to all kinds of government intervention, from regulation of television, radio, and satellite communications to airline safety, none of which was a reason for concern a hundred years ago. Few people today would argue that government should not be in the business of air safety regulation, or regulation of food and drug safety, or automobile safety, or environmental protection, all for similar reasons. Indeed, as scientific knowledge increases about the technological risks posed by nuclear power or toxic chemicals, the more likely the public is to demand government policies that protect everyone from unacceptable dangers (Andrews 2003; Lowrance 1976).

Another reason for the growth of government is the public's acceptance of business regulation. Even though politicians still like to talk about the free-market economy, the United States has moved away from it to a regulated, or mixed, economy. Nowhere does the Constitution mention the power to prevent monopolies, ensure a cleaner environment, provide for safe food and drugs, or require limits on child labor, but all of these policies are in effect, to varying degrees, today. They resulted not only from legislation but also from the Supreme Court's expansive interpretations of the Commerce Clause and the Necessary and Proper Clause of the Constitution.

Viewed from a historical perspective, policy change on government regulation has been astonishing. Congress has enacted regulatory statutes that, prior to the Progressive Era of the late nineteenth and early twentieth centuries, would have been considered improper exercises of government authority. By then, however, social pressure for reform was sufficiently strong that government had the backing to correct some of the excesses that resulted from the rapid industrialization of the 1800s. These included unsafe food and drugs, dangerous working conditions, and the domination of entire industries by monopolies. These social pressures also spurred major changes in business regulation during President Roosevelt's New Deal (Harris and Milkis 1996). At first resistant to New Deal legislation, the Supreme Court eventually ruled many of these acts constitutional. In doing so, the Court reflected society's endorsement of these new powers of government.

Attitudes have also changed about government's role in **social welfare.** Again, under the New Deal the federal government signified its responsibility to provide a minimal level of support for certain individuals, including the poor, farmers, and the elderly. By that time many states had already developed such social programs for certain categories of individuals (Skocpol 1995). President Lyndon Johnson's Great Society agenda expanded those commitments in the 1960s. As government moved into the area of social welfare support, it also grew to administer these programs. For example, Social Security today is the single largest government program and requires an organization of more than sixty thousand people to administer it (Social Security Administration 1999).

America's role in the world has also contributed to government growth. After Word War II (1941–1945) the United States emerged as a superpower and took a larger role in world affairs. The government had to grow to keep up with the new responsibilities in foreign affairs and national defense, which has meant not only an increase in the budget and personnel of the Departments of Defense and State, but also in agencies with peripheral connections to international affairs, such as the EPA and the Departments of Commerce and Agriculture.

In addition, the size, scope, and cost of certain projects mean that only the government can undertake them. They may come about because of a market failure, as discussed in Chapter 1, or changes in public expectations of government. Some individuals and organized groups therefore argue that for social or economic progress to occur, government needs to become involved. No other entity, they say, can perform the functions of government, especially space exploration and other scientific research and development, including work in the areas of defense, energy, and health.

Finally, Americans must accept some responsibility for the growth of government. Citizen demands for government action continue to rise. Americans tend to be ideologically conservative but liberal in practice with respect to provision of government services, from police protection to health care for the elderly. One can see the evidence throughout the federal rulemaking process, which is a good indicator of government growth.

> [T]he American people have developed a habit that is the ultimate cause of rulemaking. To reduce significantly the number of rules written by agencies, someone or something must persuade the American people to stop turning to government as a means of achieving their aspirations or solving their problems. (Kerwin 1999, 276)

The Tenth Amendment of the Constitution declares: "The powers not delegated to the United States by the Constitution, nor prohibited by it to the States are reserved to the States respectively, or to the people." These powers are often referred to as the reserve powers of the states and are the basis for their right to legislate in many areas. Despite the federal government's involvement in public policy issues that were formerly the states' exclusive domain, state and local governments also have grown substantially over the past fifty years. Moreover, the trend since 1980 toward devolution to the states, the new federalism, has meant that many of these governments now are often at the leading edge of policy development (and many are not). The potential for policy innovation at the state and local levels is explored in later chapters.

The effects of government growth are many. First, government policies affect most of what people do every day. Second, government growth has led to an entire occupational sector. Not only are governments at all levels major employers, but also their buying power has a substantial impact on numerous economic sectors that rely on government programs and spending. Third, the scope of government increases the likelihood of conflicting public policies and greater difficulty in addressing society's problems. Fourth, policymaking in a large, complex government organization takes more time and effort—to analyze problems, discuss alternatives, decide on solutions, and implement programs—than in a smaller entity. When such efforts cannot succeed, the result is policy stalemate or gridlock, a phenomenon that has become common over the past twenty years, and students of public policy should understand its causes and consequences.

## POLICY STALEMATE AND POLICY CAPACITY

This chapter's review of major policymaking institutions and policy actors pointed out the difficulty of designing, approving, and implementing solutions to complex twenty-first century problems. Regulating financial markets, provisioning high quality public education, ensuring access to health care services, and dealing with global climate change are just a few of the

A teacher leads a group of pre-kindergarteners through a lesson at a school participating in the Head Start program. Head Start is geared toward children from low-income families to increase school readiness. Launched in 1965, the program has continued with only minor changes throughout its history. These changes have been at the margin, such as expanding the number of participants and increasing the budget over time; the original mission and goals of the program remain the same. Incremental changes to existing programs are common in public policy, especially if programs are seen as successful or if the political environment makes it difficult to enact or implement more fundamental changes.

challenges the United States faces. Government gridlock in the face of serious problems is a reminder that the Framers intended the government to make decisions not in haste, but deliberately. But it is also a reminder that the partisan and ideological differences that characterize contemporary politics have consequences for policymaking (Bond and Fleisher 2000). Nevertheless, government and the political process have proven not only capable of policymaking on complex issues but also able to design innovative policies that fully meet the criteria of effectiveness, efficiency, and equity. In fact, most of the time, policymaking involves action that falls between gridlock and innovation. The norm in U.S. politics is **incremental policymaking,** especially for relatively noncontroversial policies. Incremental policy changes are small steps, often taken slowly. They are adjustments made at the margins of existing policies through minor amendments or the gradual extension of a program's mandate or the groups it serves. The Head Start preschool program is a good example of incremental change, made possible because the program is seen as a success.

Nevertheless, the reasons for policy gridlock need to be understood. Among the most important are constitutional design and divided government; the intractable nature of many public problems; a lack of consensus in the U.S. public; the power of organized interests; ineffective political leadership; and the personal relationship among policy actors.

## Constitutional Design and Divided Government

By its very nature, the complex and fragmented system of government in the United States increases the likelihood of stalemate in the policy process because of the number of institutions and individuals involved in policymaking, review, and concurrence (Mezey 1989; Thurber 1991). In one, perhaps extreme, example of what can happen in a local government, Jeffrey Pressman and Aaron Wildavsky (1979) found a minimum of seventy clearance points necessary before the Economic Development Administration in Oakland, California, could successfully implement a policy. The probability of achieving agreement at each point was low, and the probability of success across all of the potential veto points was practically nil. Stalemate occurs in organizations such as this because of constitutional design and government structure. Fortunately, the situation is not so dire in most local governments. They find ways to move programs along.

Stalemate within the constitutional system usually increases during periods of divided government, when one political party controls the presidency and the other at least one house of Congress (Thurber 1991; Ripley and Franklin 1991). The reasons are clear. Members of the same political party tend to have similar beliefs concerning the scope of government and the direction of policies, but the two major parties often hold strongly conflicting views on these matters. Although divided government makes agreement and cooperation difficult, even in these circumstances policymaking can proceed. In fact, David Mayhew (1991) argues that divided government has a limited impact on the enactment of major public policies at the national level. A good illustration is one of the most expansive laws ever written, the Clean Air Act Amendments of 1990, approved in a period of split party control of the White House and Congress. During the Carter administration, on the other hand, Democrats controlled both the White House and Congress, but President Carter was ineffective at getting his priority legislation through Congress. Still, it is worth remembering that between 1970 and 2002 the national government was unified for only six years.

## Complex and Intractable Public Problems

The nature of the problems government must address also contributes to gridlock. Some problems are so complex technically or economically that policy actors cannot easily find feasible and effective solutions, even if they are motivated to do so. Global climate change is a good example. Scientists may disagree about the seriousness of the challenge faced; at what point the consequences, such as rising temperatures or a greater frequency of storms, may become severe; and the cost of taking action, such as cutting back on the use of fossil fuels. The scientists base their predictions on computer models, and these models are subject to dispute. The scientific uncertainty and disagreement exacerbate the search for policy consensus in this and many other policy areas, such as the feasibility of a space-based missile defense system. The more complex the issue and the weaker the consensus among scientists and other experts on causes and solutions, the more likely gridlock is to occur. When scientific consensus reigns, Congress and other policymaking bodies are likely to reach agreement on what to do.

## Public Opinion and Policy Consensus

In a democratic nation, public opinion is another variable that affects the policy process. But what happens when the public is divided in its views of public policy, as it has been on abortion rights, support for **school vouchers**, and crime control measures? The more the public disagrees over basic policy directions, the more likely it is that members of Congress or state or local legislators will reflect that diversity of opinion, with policy stalemate the only result. When the public reaches a consensus on what to do about a policy issue, such as conservation of public lands and protection of open space, which were popular initiatives in the late 1990s, policymakers are able to overcome stalemate. Indeed, policymakers may fight over who has the strongest or most generous package of proposals in their eagerness to respond to public opinion.

Public opinion is often difficult to determine, however, and people may hold contradictory views on some subjects. For example, almost everyone would say they want better health care, but they also would prefer that somebody else pay for it. People tend to oppose increases in taxes, but want to continue or expand government services to which they have become accustomed. Policy stalemate often reflects the inconsistency in public opinion, as different policymakers emphasize one or another of the public's apparent preferences and then argue over whose interpretation of the public's views is correct.

## The Power of Organized Interests: Group-Based Politics

Another reason for conflict and stalemate is pluralism. Interest groups are omnipresent and highly influential in the policy process (Berry 1997; Cigler and Loomis 2002). Interest group participation at all levels, and within all branches, of government often slows the policy process and contributes to gridlock. If opposing interest groups cannot reconcile their positions, they may prefer to block policy initiatives with which they disagree.

Another complication is that the president and the members of Congress serve different constituencies (Thurber 1996a). The president is elected by the nation as a whole and is typically concerned with national policies, but each senator represents a state, and each House member a particular congressional district. Members of Congress tend to be more concerned with meeting the interests of the citizens who elected them—and the interest groups on whose financial and electoral support they depend for reelection. The differing perspectives between executives and legislators also extend to the state and local levels of government. For example, with states facing sizable budget deficits in 2002, some governors proposed budget cuts that the legislators could not accept. They feared the wrath of organized groups and their voters. Many states, including California, New Jersey, and Wisconsin, found it enormously difficult to resolve these differences.

## Ineffective Political Leadership

In the fragmented U.S. political system, strong political leadership, either in the White House or in Congress, is needed to overcome policy gridlock. Scholars have argued for years that presidential leadership is one of the most effective ways to overcome institutional fragmentation, but strong leadership in Congress, at the committee level and in the party leadership, also may help to forge the majorities needed for enacting legislation. For example, in the

104th Congress (1995–1996), Speaker Newt Gingrich, R-Ga., and his principal deputy, Majority Leader Dick Armey, R-Texas, were able to quickly push the Contract With America agenda through the House (Davidson and Oleszek 2002). Without effective leadership in the White House or on Capitol Hill, however, building consensus among highly disparate interests is often impossible. Here again, a parallel situation exists at the state and local level. Policy stalemate is less likely when a governor, a mayor, or a strong legislator can help to reconcile policy conflicts and bring together policy actors with different views.

## Personal Relationships among Policy Actors

According to Randall Ripley and Grace Franklin (1991), the personal relationships among policy actors can lead to either cooperation or conflict. If the actors involved in policy development cannot get along, stalemate is likely to result. Cooperative relationships need to be formed within the legislature, between the legislature and the executive branch, and with pertinent interest groups. In recent years, observers have noted that these relationships have soured. For example, Democrats and Republicans in the 104th and 105th Congresses (1995–1999) clashed repeatedly over environmental protection, regulatory reform, and many other issues. Journalists and scholars frequently mentioned the new level of poisonous rhetoric and partisan rancor that had come to dominate political dialogue on Capitol Hill. Relations between congressional leaders and the Clinton White House were also strained, and opportunities to cooperate in many policy areas were lost because of personal and partisan conflict (Bond and Fleisher 2000; Kraft 2003).

Even if personal relationships are amiable, the working relationship among the actors may not be. Congress, as the lawmaking branch, demands to be involved in policy development, and members will be offended if the president ignores them during policy formulation. Full and meaningful participation by Congress decreases conflict because members can have their say on the issues they consider important. The failure to include powerful members of Congress doomed President Clinton's comprehensive health care reform proposal in 1993. When President Carter pushed Congress in the 1970s to enact a national energy policy, he failed to win the support he might have gained from earlier and more extensive consultation with leading legislators (Kraft 1981).

Sometimes policymakers consider gridlock preferable to making compromises that could hurt them politically. Moreover, they may believe they have a better chance to fashion a suitable policy in the future (Gilmore 1995). A case in point was the partisan standoff in Congress over national energy policy in 2002. Neither party was willing to compromise on auto fuel efficiency standards or on drilling for oil in the Arctic National Wildlife Refuge for fear of alienating its core constituencies on whom it relied for reelection (Adams 2002). Dependence on those constituencies also pushes members toward ideological rigidity rather than moderation and a willingness to seek policy compromises. That pattern has been evident in recent years on a range of issues, from Social Security and Medicare prescription drug coverage to family planning programs (Foerstel 2002).

## IMPROVING POLICY CAPACITY

This chapter demonstrates that the design of U.S. government institutions and the conflicting demands of the nation's citizens make governing a difficult task. Still, the history of U.S. public policy development also indicates a robust capacity for policy formulation, adoption, and implementation. The proof is in the extensive collection of public policies in operation today. Much the same can be said about the policy capacity of state and local governments. Although some are clearly more capable than others, considerable policy innovation and successful implementation is apparent at this level as well (Borins 1998; Hedge 1998).

Does policy capacity need to be improved? If so, what measures will work? The institutions of government might be altered or the decision-making process changed, and more opportunities for citizen participation might be offered. Policy analysis could assist in determining what particular changes are needed. For example, is it a good idea to create more state and local referendums to allow **direct citizen participation** in lawmaking? What has been the result of referendums and initiatives at the state and local level that could inform that choice (Cronin 1989; Ellis 2002)? What about term limits for legislators? The idea gained popularity in the late 1980s and early 1990s, but in 1994 the Supreme Court said it was unconstitutional at the federal level. If states continue to impose term limits, would the loss of experienced and knowledgeable legislators hurt state policymaking? Would term limits increase the power of special interests, whose expertise might be in greater demand under such conditions?

It seems clear that additional citizen participation enhances policy capacity at the state and local level, but some programs designed to involve citizens in the policy process are more effective than others. Most scholars today recognize the desirability of going beyond the conventional hearings and public meetings to offer more direct and meaningful citizen access to policymaking. Citizen advisory committees, citizen panels, and similar mechanisms foster a more intense citizen engagement with the issues (Beierle and Cayford 2002). Governments at all levels continue to endorse **collaborative decision making** with local and regional stakeholders, especially on issues of urban planning and management, natural resource use, and the like. In many states smart growth planning, watershed management, and ecosystem restoration are heavily dependent on citizen councils of this kind (John and Mlay 1999; Paehlke 2003; Weber 2003).

Whatever the form of public involvement, its effectiveness needs to be considered. Increasing citizens' voices in policymaking can come at some cost in terms of the expediency of policy development and implementation. In other words, it can slow down the policy process and make it more difficult to resolve conflicts. Even with these qualifications, however, the successful involvement of the public in local and regional problem-solving processes is encouraging for the future. Enhancing civic engagement in these ways might even help to reverse a long pattern of citizen withdrawal, not only from politics but also from their communities (Bok 2001; Putnam 2000; Skocpol and Fiorina 1999).

## CONCLUSIONS

This chapter covers a lot of ground, from the constitutional design for U.S. government to the way policy actors within the major institutions interrelate when dealing with public problems and policymaking. It stresses not only the difficulty of governing and the potential for policy gridlock but also the many strengths of the U.S. political system. These strengths are found at all levels of government, but especially in the states' growing policy capacity and their efforts at policy innovation in recent years.

Knowing how government is organized and makes decisions is the foundation for the study of public policy, but equally important is understanding the political incentives that motivate and influence how policy actors relate to each other. Armed with these tools, students of public policy can see why government sometimes works and sometimes does not, and what needs to be done to improve government's capacity for analyzing public problems and developing solutions to them. In the same vein, the chapter suggests that few changes would do more to enhance democracy than finding ways for U.S. citizens to become better informed about public policy and more engaged with government and the policy process.

## DISCUSSION QUESTIONS

What do you see as the most significant strengths and weaknesses of the U.S. system of government?

Do states have sufficient capabilities in policymaking to assume a greater role in the federal system of government? Or is the present balance of power between the national government and the states about right?

What conditions do you think foster policy innovation at the national, state, or local levels of government?

Is the American public capable of playing a more active role in the policymaking process than it does at present? Or would greater public involvement in policymaking pose risks to the quality of decision making? Why do you think so?

What are the advantages and disadvantages of extensive interest group participation in the U.S. policymaking process?

## SUGGESTED READINGS

Sandford Borins, *Innovating with Integrity: How Local Heroes Are Transforming American Government* (Washington, D.C.: Georgetown University Press, 1998). An analysis of the potential for state and local government policy innovation with examples of successful innovation.

Allan J. Cigler and Burdett A. Loomis, eds., *Interest Group Politics,* 6th ed. (Washington, D.C.: CQ Press, 2002). A leading volume on interest group activity in U.S. politics. Includes some of the best current work in the field.

Roger H. Davidson and Walter J. Oleszek, *Congress and Its Members,* 8th ed. (Washington, D.C.: CQ Press, 2002). The leading text on Congress and a treasure trove of information on the role of Congress in policymaking.

David M. Hedge, *Governance and the Changing American States* (Boulder: Westview, 1998). A leading text on state government and recent changes in state policy capacity.

Charles O. Jones, *Separate but Equal Branches: Congress and the Presidency,* 2d ed. (New York: Chatham House Publishers, 1999). A valuable assessment of the relationship between Congress and the presidency.

## SUGGESTED WEB SITES

**http://thomas.loc.gov.** The Library of Congress's Thomas search engine for locating congressional documents.

**www.ciser.cornell.edu/info/polls.html.** Cornell University Web site that lists all major public opinion companies, with links to the Gallup Organization, Roper Center, New York Times/CBS, Washington Post, National Opinion Research Center at the University of Chicago, and National Election Studies at the University of Michigan. Includes the major state and regional polling organizations.

**www.csg.org.** Council of State Governments, with links to all fifty states as well as public policy issues, think tanks, and suggested state legislation.

**www.firstgov.gov.** Federal government Web portal, with links for online services for citizens, businesses, and governments and links to federal, state, local, and tribal government agencies. Includes links to all fifty state government home pages and national associations dealing with state and local issues.

**www.publicagenda.org.** A nonpartisan opinion research organization Web site that includes reports from national firms on public policy issues such as race, health care, privacy, drug abuse, crime, the economy, poverty, welfare, the environment, immigration, and others. Has a good collection of colorful graphs and tables and advice on how to read public opinion polls.

**www.uscourts.gov.** Portal to U.S. judiciary system.

**www.whitehouse.gov.** White House home page, with links to president's stand on various policy issues, news, appointments, speeches, and more.

## KEYWORDS

bicameral   43

cabinet-level departments   46

circuit courts of appeals   48

collaborative decision making   64

committees   43

cooperative federalism   38

Council for Environmental Quality   45

decentralization   39

direct citizen participation   64

dual federalism   38

electoral incentive   44

elite theory   57

evaluative criteria   39

Executive Office of the President (EOP)   45

federal district courts   48

filibuster   43

Food and Drug Administration (FDA)   46

gridlock   34

health care policy   33

incremental policymaking   60

# CHAPTER 3

# UNDERSTANDING THE POLITICS OF PUBLIC POLICY

**National Parks Pass**

EXPERIENCE
YOUR
AMERICA

JANE HATHAWAY
PARTNER SINCE 2000

003 6487 1100

IN JUNE 2001 CONGRESS ENACTED, AND PRESIDENT GEORGE W. BUSH signed, the Economic Growth and Tax Relief Reconciliation Act of 2001. The legislation, better known as the Tax Relief Act, was a ten-year, $1.35 trillion tax reduction measure, the biggest tax cut in twenty years and the most sweeping change in the tax laws in fifteen years. Its supporters asserted that the nation could easily afford this steep drop in tax revenues because of the rising federal budget surplus. The surplus resulted from the economic expansion of the 1990s, which had produced enormous tax revenues.[1]

Opponents of the Bush tax cut, including many Democrats, were skeptical of the economic assumptions behind it and worried about the impact on government programs. They also questioned the wisdom of giving a large share of the benefits to the wealthy. Writing in *Business Week,* former Clinton economic adviser Laura D'Andrea Tyson said, "Fuzzy math and fuzzier economic logic have prevailed over fiscal responsibility and fairness." She warned that Congress and the president would soon face the need to curtail government spending, dip into Social Security or Medicare trust funds, or scale back the tax cut in future years. Otherwise, she claimed, the nation would face yet another round of soaring budget deficits, much as it did during the 1980s and 1990s (Tyson 2001).

In spring 2002, just one year later, government revenues were dropping sharply as a result of an economic slowdown, and the Bush White House and the Congressional Budget Office (CBO) were projecting deficits rather than surpluses.[2] In hindsight, the tax cut's proponents relied on economic **projections** that were unrealistically optimistic. What is surprising, in light of new **forecasts** of impending budgetary woes, is that business as usual prevailed on Capitol Hill. Members of Congress were prepared to spend record sums on national defense and domestic programs without retreating on the previously approved tax cuts.

In May 2002, for example, Congress approved, and the president signed, a six-year, $249 billion farm bill that increased agricultural spending by $45 billion, an 18 percent rise over existing law. With this bill, Congress reversed its decision of six years earlier to phase out costly agricultural subsidies, most of which go to the nation's largest grain and cotton agribusinesses. In an election year, with the major parties battling for control of the closely divided

In 2000 the National Park Service began selling $50 credit-card-style passes like the one shown here. Good toward admission to national parks nationwide, the agency hopes the passes will raise millions of extra dollars for the Park Service. Recent park budgets have been insufficient to meet basic needs, much less to address long deferred maintenance and facility upgrades. Understandably then, park service officials are pursuing new revenue sources, such as these pre-paid cards, in order to improve services and better meet public expectations. The National Parks Pass program also illustrates one of the policy options available to governments—provide services directly to the public in a manner similar to private enterprise.

Senate, neither wanted to risk losing the farm states of the Midwest. But the spending did not stop with the farmers. To ensure the farm bill's passage, Congress also approved a record $17 billion over ten years for significant conservation and environmental programs such as farmland and wetland preservation. Even the **food stamp program** portion of the bill was generous at $137 billion over six years. To secure the votes of members from urban areas, the measure raised benefits for working families and children and reinstated the right of legal immigrants to receive food stamps (Martinez 2002a, 2002b).[3]

Such measures may prompt one to ask, "What were they thinking?" This chapter offers some answers. Chapter 2 showed how the structure and rules of U.S. government institutions create certain political incentives that push policymakers toward the kinds of decisions reflected in the tax cut and agricultural policies. This chapter introduces several models and theories that further explain why policymakers reach decisions like these. After a brief consideration of five competing approaches, the chapter focuses on the policy process model, which is widely used in the study of public policy. It is particularly helpful for clarifying the role of policy analysis in the design and formulation of the most appropriate policy actions government can take, and in evaluating how well those policies work once they are implemented.

As Chapter 2 argued, policymaking in the U.S. political system is inherently difficult because of the institutional dispersal of power, the multiplicity of policy actors, and the sharp conflicts that often arise over what policy actions to take. Policy analysis can help to resolve the conflicts by clarifying the issues and bringing reliable information to bear on the decision-making process. It is especially useful when dealing with complex public problems, such as economic forecasts, that are not easy to understand, and when policymakers need to make the best estimates they can about a proposal's likely effectiveness, costs, and fairness.

## MODELS AND THEORIES OF POLITICS AND PUBLIC POLICY

Social scientists use models and theories, abstract representations of the real world, to understand the way things work. Models and theories can create meaning out of what otherwise might seem to be a complicated and chaotic world in which nothing makes sense and all acts are random. The models and theories discussed here pertain to the world of government, politics, and public policy, and they provide the concepts and language that facilitate communication with others about these subjects. They also help to focus people's attention on the most important factors that affect government decision making.

Political scientists use several different models and theories to explain the nature of policymaking and the policies that result. Among the most common are elite theory, group theory, institutional theory, rational choice theory, political systems theory, and the policy process model (Anderson 2003; McCool 1995). Each offers a different perspective on the principal determinants of decision making within government and therefore on what people might regard as the major forces that shape the direction and content of public policies. If the public asks why the United States has one kind of economic, agricultural, health care, or education policy and not another, the answer depends in part on which theory or model is used.

## Elite Theory

Elite theory emphasizes how the values and preferences of governing elites, which differ from those of the public at large, affect public policy development. The primary assumption of elite theory is that the values and preferences of the general public are less influential in shaping public policy than those of a smaller, unrepresentative group of people, or elites (Dye 2001; Dye and Zeigler 2003). These policy actors may be economic elites—foundations, wealthy people, corporate executives, and professionals such as physicians or attorneys. They may be cultural elites, such as actors, filmmakers, and recording artists, or media stars. Elected officials constitute an elite, as do other influential policy actors, such as scientists and policy analysts. Elite theory, then, focuses on the role of leaders and leadership in the development of public policy.

A single power elite or establishment is seldom at the center of policy decisions because different elites tend to dominate in different policy areas. For example, one elite may be influential in foreign policy, another in defense policy, and others in areas as diverse as health care, agriculture, education, energy, and the environment. One elite may compete with another to win attention for its concerns or to secure a superior level of funding for the programs it favors. Still, by emphasizing the power of these groups, elite theory demonstrates that the U.S. policymaking process may not be as democratic as many believe it to be. Critics of President Bush's 2001 tax cut measure were convinced that it was shaped with the interests of a wealthy elite in mind (Krugman 2002). At the same time, conservatives often blame the liberal cultural elite of Hollywood and New York for what they see as lax moral standards in today's society.

The role of different elites is particularly evident in the subgovernments or issue networks described in Chapter 2 (Baumgartner and Jones 1993; Kingdon 1995). This kind of elite dominance is in part a function of the low salience of policymaking within subgovernments or issue networks. Most people outside of the narrow circles that are concerned about a matter, such as Federal Communications Commission regulation of the television and telecommunication industries, would have little reason to pay attention to the issues or to participate in policy decisions. In fact, most members of Congress tend to defer to their colleagues who work regularly on these issues. Much the same can be said for the influence of agribusiness on U.S. farm policy, the defense industry on weapons procurement policy, Wall Street investment bankers on regulation of financial markets, and pharmaceutical companies on health care policy. Parallels to these kinds of subgovernments or narrow policy communities also exist at the state and local levels.

Elites can sometimes exert their influence through a process of **symbolic politics**. As Murray Edelman (1964) argued, policymakers often formulate public policies that appear to meet public needs but actually serve the material needs of a narrow elite. The benefits conveyed to the public are largely symbolic. This situation is particularly likely, Edelman said, in the area of regulatory policy. For example, the government adopts a clean air act that requires industries to clean up their facilities. The public thinks the air will be free of pollutants. Certain industries, such as coal-fired power plants, however, are exempted from the act, and many others receive generous air quality permits that allow them to continue polluting. Although one might think that people could easily see that the air in many urban areas was still polluted, the

President George W. Bush waves to Navy personnel near the Aegis Cruiser USS Philippine Sea. Speaking at Mayport Naval Station in Jacksonville, Florida, on February 13, 2003, Bush expressed his confidence in the troops and voiced his desire for UN support of possible U.S. efforts against Iraq and Saddam Hussein. He also took the opportunity to push his plan to further cut the federal income tax, a move opposed by many congressional Democrats and moderate Republicans for economic and equity reasons. They believe the plan favors the wealthy and provides little relief to middle- and low-income taxpayers. Public officials can help set the political agenda through the use of powerful symbols—such as the president appearing with U.S. troops next to a massive U.S. military ship. This public appearance and Bush's subsequent statements promoted the idea that both the war and the tax plan are patriotic acts in the public's best interest.

public is placated by the symbolic side of politics and permits the policies to continue. This outcome is especially likely when the issues are not very salient to the average person. Because so much of politics and public policy involve highly value-laden symbols such as freedom, privacy, individualism, justice, equality, and morality, it is easy to see how policy actors might be able to manipulate the symbols to their advantage.

## Group Theory

**Group theory,** closely associated with pluralism, sees public policy as the product of a continuous struggle among organized interest groups (Baumgartner and Leech 1998; Cigler and Loomis 2002). In contrast to elite theory, pluralists believe that power in the U.S. political system is widely shared among interest groups, each of which seeks access to the policymaking process. In this view, some groups provide countervailing power to others—for example, labor unions versus manufacturing interests—as they lobby legislators and executive officials and appeal to the broader public through issue advocacy campaigns. This balance helps to ensure that no one group dominates the policy process, although it is logical to assume that the groups with greater financial resources, recognition, access to policymakers, and prestige are likely to have more influence than others. At the opposite end of the spectrum are those people, such as the poor and homeless, who are not well organized, lack significant political resources, and are poorly represented in the policy process. When people speak of "special interests" influencing government decisions, they are using the concepts of group theory. Examples include the influence of agribusiness and lobbyists from farm states in the 2002 agriculture bill and the influence of the music recording industry in protecting copyrights by restricting Internet access to MP3 music files.

A modern variant of interest group theory, the **advocacy coalition framework** (ACF),

When specific industries decide to lobby for or against a particular policy, they often become critical actors in the policymaking process. A recent example is the music industry's effort to gain copyright protection in the face of access to free downloadable music online. Not all industry members share this opposition, however. Singer Courtney Love has been an outspoken critic of the way musicians and artists are treated by the industry and has questioned the extent to which the new technology that permits music downloads is a threat to copyright guarantees.

focuses on the "interactions of competing advocacy coalitions," particularly within a policy sub-system such as agriculture, telecommunications, or environmental protection (Sabatier and Jenkins-Smith 1993). Each coalition consists of policy actors from different public and private institutions and different levels of government who share a particular set of beliefs about the policies that government should promote. In the clash between environmentalists and industry representatives, for example, each coalition tries to manipulate government processes to achieve its goals over time. Whether and to what degree the coalitions reach their objectives depends on forces in the rest of the political system and the larger society and economy that either provide opportunities or throw up obstacles. The ACF framework posits that policy change can occur over time, as each coalition uses its resources to change the views or policy beliefs of leading policy actors. For example, environmentalists to some extent have persuaded the business community to think about long-term goals of sustainable development. The business community in turn has been able to persuade many actors in this policy arena that new policy approaches such as **market incentives**, collaboration, and information provision are more attractive than conventional regulation, which they view as burdensome and ineffective (Mazmanian and Kraft 1999).

Many students of public policy argue that group theory tends to exaggerate the role and influence of organized interest groups in policymaking and to underestimate the leadership of public officials and the considerable discretion they have in making policy choices. It is easy to believe that lurking behind every policy decision is a special interest group eager to have its way, but assigning too much power to organized groups oversimplifies a more complex dynamic in policymaking. Public officials also frequently use organized interest groups to promote their own political agendas and to build support for policy initiatives. The relationship between groups and policymakers is often a subtle, two-way exercise of influence.

## Institutional Theory

**Institutional theory** or institutionalism emphasizes the formal and legal aspects of government structure. Institutional models look at the way governments are arranged, their legal powers, and their rules for procedure. Those rules include basic characteristics such as the degree of access to decision making provided to the public, the availability of information from government agencies, and the sharing of authority between the national and state governments under federalism. A major tenet of institutionalism is that the structures and rules make a big difference in the kind of policy process that occurs and which policy actors are likely to be influential in it. The farm bill example illustrates the power in the Senate of less populous agricultural states such as Iowa and South Dakota. Because the Constitution provides that each state has two senators, these less populous states have as much voting power in the Senate as the more populous New York and California.

The term *institution* can have many meanings. It refers to "both the organizations and the rules used to structure patterns of interaction within and across organizations" (Ostrom 1999, 36). Therefore, in addition to a focus on organizations such as legislatures, courts, or bureaucracies, the term encompasses how people within organizations relate to one another and to those in other organizations—that is, the rules that govern their behavior. Many kinds of institutions can influence public policy: markets; individual firms or corporations; national, state, and local governments; voluntary associations such as political parties and interest groups; and foreign political regimes. Analysts use institutional theory to study how these different entities perform in the policymaking process as well as the rules, norms, and strategies used by individuals who operate within particular organizations, such as the U.S. Congress or the federal court system.

Although formal institutional analysis can become quite complex, institutional theory is a simple reminder that certain aspects of government structure and the procedural rules can empower or obstruct political interests. A common axiom is that there is no such thing as a neutral rule. Rules have real consequences for the way decisions are made, helping some and hurting others. They can make some groups more influential than others and some policy outcomes more likely than others. For example, the Nuclear Waste Policy Act of 1982 set out a formal, detailed process for selecting the nation's first repository for the radioactive wastes produced at nuclear power plants. Among the act's stipulations was that public hearings be held near any site under serious consideration. That legislative provision resulted in extensive opportunities for public comment on the plan, which was widely condemned across the country. Congress was forced to revise the act in 1987 to focus on a single site at Yucca Mountain, Nevada (Dunlap, Kraft, and Rosa 1993).

## Rational Choice Theory

**Rational choice theory,** also called public choice and formal theory, draws heavily from economics, especially microeconomic theory, and often uses elaborate mathematical modeling. A highly developed and rigorous theory, rational choice theory has been widely applied to questions of public policy (Ostrom 1998, 1999; Schneider and Ingram 1997). Analysts have used it to explain actions as diverse as individual voter decisions and the calculations of public officials as they face national security threats. It assumes that in making decisions, individuals are rational actors; that is, they seek to maximize attainment of their preferences or further their self-interest. The theory suggests that analysts consider what individuals value, how they perceive a given situation, the information they have about it, various uncertainties that might affect the outcome, and how a particular context or the expectations of others—for example, rules and norms—might affect their actions. The goal is to deduce or predict how individuals will behave under a variety of conditions.

Public choice theory tries to explain public policy in terms of the actions of self-interested individual policy actors, whether they are voters, corporate lobbyists, agency officials, or legislators. David Mayhew (1974) provided a simple illustration in his classic *Congress: The Electoral Connection.* Mayhew asked what kind of behavior one might expect from members of Congress if their only incentive was reelection. He found that this simple assumption about individual motivation could reveal a great deal about the way members behaved and even about what kinds of public policy actions such a Congress was likely to produce. Mayhew found that the "electoral incentive" caused members to advertise themselves, claim credit, and take positions on the issues. This is not to imply that members of Congress and other politicians do not have many concerns other than getting reelected, including a genuine desire to promote the public welfare. Mayhew's example simply highlights the explanatory power of rational choice theory. It forces people to think about the core motivation of individual political actors and the consequences of such motivation for the larger political system and for public policy. Analysis of this kind is used throughout the text.

The critics of public choice theory argue that individuals are not always single-minded pursuers of their own self-interest. The critics also question the narrow and rigid assumptions that underlie the theory, such as the ability of individuals to behave rationally when they may lack pertinent information or when decision makers have different and unequal information—a condition called **information asymmetry** (Green and Shapiro 1994; Shepsle and Bonchek 1997). Some say that the theory gives too little emphasis to the willingness of individuals to engage in collective action pursuits, such as joining public interest groups or participating in community organizations (Stone 1997).

Even so, rational choice theory provides useful insights into political behavior that can affect the design of public policies. It is especially useful to formulate predictions of how agency officials and those who are the object or target of the policy action are likely to respond to policy initiatives (Schneider and Ingram 1997). For example, economists say that to persuade individuals to significantly reduce their fuel consumption would take a hike in the gasoline tax of 50 cents or more per gallon. Anything less would likely not alter the consumers' behavior because they would see the incentive as too small to make a difference in their personal welfare.

## Political Systems Theory

**Political systems theory** is more comprehensive, but also more general, than the other models and theories. It stresses the way the political system (the institutions and activities of government) responds to demands that arise from its environment, such as public opinion and interest group pressures (Easton 1965). Systems theory emphasizes the larger social, economic, and cultural context in which political decisions and policy choices are made. Examples include a general preference for limited government, low taxes, and individual freedom. How these contexts affect the motivations and behavior of policy actors is apparent in the farm bill and tax cut measures discussed earlier in this chapter.

Systems theory is a more formal way to think about the interrelationships of institutions and policy actors and the role of the larger environment. Systems theory also supplies some useful terms, such as *input, demands, support, policy outputs, policy outcomes,* and *feedback.* In systems theory, input into the political system comes from demands and support. Demands are the claims individuals and groups seeking to further their interests and values make on the political system. For example, a union calls for safety regulations in the workplace. Support signifies the acceptance by individuals and groups of the actions of government as well as the actions' legitimacy. Support is evident when people obey the law and respect the system's rules and procedures and when they vote in elections and express trust and confidence in institutions and leaders. For workplace safety regulations, support was established when the

AFL-CIO made it a legislative priority and President Nixon agreed to back legislation on the subject (Kelman 1980).

In this theory, the political system responds to demands and support in the process of policymaking and produces outputs (decisions, law, policies) that over time may create changes (policy outcomes) in the situations that prompted the demands and support in the first place. Systems models incorporate yet another element—feedback from these kinds of outputs and outcomes, which can alter the environment and create new demands or support. An example is strong public support for additional policies to protect nonsmokers, such as bans on smoking in restaurants, which followed other antismoking policies over the past four decades.

Systems theory is a simple way to portray how governments respond to society's demands on them. It proposes an almost biological model of politics suggesting that governments and public officials react to the political climate much as organisms respond to environmental stimuli. As the environment changes—for example, the economy deteriorates or the public becomes distressed with crime rates or corporate malfeasance—individuals and groups are moved to make demands on government to deal with the situation. Once government acts, the system readjusts in light of the particular decisions and their effects. Like the other models, systems theory is useful for thinking about the forces that impinge on government and public officials and how their actions in turn affect the public.

Each of these theories is helpful. Each offers a distinct conceptual lens through which to view politics and public policy, highlighting particular features of the political and institutional landscape, but none by itself is completely satisfactory. We believe another approach, the policy process model, is more useful than the others, in part because it can incorporate the most valuable elements of the others. It also has the advantage of portraying the activities of government and policymaking more clearly than the others and using language that most people can understand intuitively. This chapter and the rest of the book makes extensive use of the policy process model, also called the policy cycle model (Anderson 2003; Jones 1984).[4]

## THE POLICY PROCESS MODEL

The policy process model posits a logical sequence of activities affecting the development of public policies. It depicts the policymaking process and the broad relationships among policy actors within each stage of it. The model can also be helpful to understand the flow of events and decisions in different cultures and institutional settings; in other words, the concepts and language are general enough to fit any political system and its policy processes.

Table 3-1 presents the model as a set of six distinct, if not entirely separate, stages in policymaking, in keeping with the way the model is discussed in most textbooks. Sometimes the phrase **policy cycle** is used to make clear that the process is cyclical or continuous rather than a one-time set of actions. Instead of a top-down listing of each stage, it could be presented as a series of stages linked in a circle because no policy decision or solution is ever final. Changing conditions, new information, formal evaluations, and shifting opinions often stimulate reconsideration and revision of established policies. In addition, in the real world these stages can and do overlap or are sometimes skipped. In other words, policies might be formulated

| TABLE 3-1 | The Policy Process Model | |
|---|---|---|
| **Stage of the Process** | **What It Means** | **Illustrations** |
| Agenda setting | How problems are perceived and defined, command attention, and get onto the political agenda. | Energy problems rose sharply on the agenda in 2001. The Bush administration defined them in terms of an insufficient supply requiring more oil and gas drilling rather than conservation to reduce demand. |
| Policy formulation | The design and drafting of policy goals and strategies for achieving them. Often involves the use of policy analysis. | The 2001 tax cut reflected conflicting economic assumptions and forecasts and differing estimates of future impacts on domestic programs. |
| Policy legitimation | The mobilization of political support and formal enactment of policies. Includes justification or rationales for the policy action. | The 2002 farm bill reflected intense lobbying by farming interests and environmentalists to build a compromise bill all could support. |
| Policy implementation | Provision of institutional resources for putting the programs into effect within a bureaucracy. | Implementation of the federal Endangered Species Act has lagged for years because of insufficient funding, which reduced its effectiveness. |
| Policy and program evaluation | Measurement and assessment of policy and program effects, including success or failure. | Efforts to measure the effectiveness of the 1996 welfare reform policy and of the experimental use of vouchers to improve public education have produced mixed results. |
| Policy change | Modification of policy goals and means in light of new information or shifting political environment. | Adoption of new national security, airport security, and immigration reforms following the terrorist attacks of 2001. |

Sources: Drawn primarily from Charles O. Jones, *An Introduction to the Study of Public Policy*, 3d ed. (Monterey, Calif.: Brooks/Cole, 1984); and Garry D. Brewer and Peter deLeon, *The Foundation of Policy Analysis* (Homewood, Ill.: Dorsey Press, 1983). The original policy process model can be traced to Harold Lasswell's early work on the policy sciences, "The Policy Orientation," in Daniel Lerner and Harold D. Lasswell, eds., *The Policy Sciences* (Stanford: Stanford University Press, 1950).

before they are high on the political agenda, or it may be impossible to differentiate policy formulation from legitimation. At times, policy evaluations begin before the policies are fully implemented.

Despite these complications, the policy process model captures important aspects of policymaking that correspond to political reality, as the review of the six components, or stages, of the model makes clear. Moreover, policy analysis can potentially affect each of the stages; that is, methods of policy analysis can provide knowledge and insights that might influence every stage of policymaking, from how the agenda is set and policies are formulated to how existing programs are evaluated and changed. For example, economic forecasts had a powerful influence on the 2001 tax cut decision. If more realistic assumptions had been used, some legislators might have questioned the wisdom of adopting such generous cuts as the economy was weakening. Even with that knowledge, another possibility is that the members were so eager to cut taxes that no forecast or other policy analyses would have dissuaded them from doing so. Even in 2002, when many officials thought those tax cuts went too far and would lead to rising federal budget deficits, legislators were not willing to consider repealing some of them for fear of voter retaliation. That politics sometimes trumps even the best policy analysis is a truth that must be faced.

## Problem Definition and Agenda Setting

Governments at all levels in the United States deal with many different public problems and policies each year. But how do the problems generate interest to begin with? That is, why do people pay attention to them, or why are they considered important enough to solve? And why do some problems, such as crime, command so much attention while others, such as population growth, tend to be ignored? If a problem does rise to a level of visibility, as energy issues did in 2001, who determines that it is the government's responsibility to address it rather than to leave it to individuals and the private sector? These questions are at the center of the problem-definition and agenda-setting stage of the policy process. In many ways, this step is the most critical of all. If a problem is not well-defined, and if the public, the media, and policymakers cannot be persuaded to pay attention to it, it may go unresolved, even if society continues to suffer the ill effects.

***Defining a Problem.*** It might seem relatively easy to define a problem, that it can be done objectively, and that politics would not enter into the equation. One might think that everyone can easily recognize a problem and there would be no arguments over it. If the issue is juvenile violence and school killings, for example, who would not agree that these are serious problems and that society should do everything possible to prevent them? Are the causes of the problem equally clear? Perhaps they include easy access to firearms and the media's tendency to emphasize violence. But analysts may need to look for other causes as well. What about the rise of bullying in school? The effect of two-income and single-parent homes? Or what some see as the moral decay in society, which they blame on the ban of prayer in school?

As the example illustrates, defining a problem and determining its causes are not always simple tasks, and the search for answers usually reflects a number of different perspectives. How one defines a problem also goes a long way toward shaping the solution offered. As John Kingdon (1995, 110) stated, "Problem definition and struggles over definition turn out to have important consequences." **Problem definition** may also come with some distinct biases. As Deborah Stone (2002, 133) put it:

> Problem definition is a matter of representation because every description of a situation is a portrayal from only one of many points of view. Problem definition is strategic because groups, individuals, and government agencies deliberately and consciously fashion portrayals so as to promote their favored course of action.

In other words, "Where you stand depends on where you sit." A person's perspective and background determine how he or she defines a problem and relates to it. Personal ideology and values are likely to influence how the problem is defined or even if the individual considers a situation to be a problem at all. The issue of Internet pornography, for example, could be defined as one of protecting children or of protecting basic civil liberties, with very different implications. Family planning might be thought of as a simple public health issue, or defined in moral terms and associated with abortion, or seen as a matter of women's rights and privacy.

Making comparisons is part of problem definition (Kingdon 1995). Americans might think gasoline prices and taxes are too high and therefore resist proposals to raise them. But if they compared the price of gasoline in the United States to that in Europe and Japan, where it is three to four times higher because of government taxes, they might conclude that U.S. prices are in fact quite low (Parry 2002). In a comparison of test scores with students in other countries, American students lag behind in math and science. This finding has raised concerns about the quality of education in the United States. As these examples suggest, the way problems are defined and measured is not a neutral activity. Nor is it without important implications for whether and how public policies are formulated and implemented.

The different actors and institutions (formal and informal) reviewed in Chapter 2 are almost always deeply involved in problem definition (Rochefort and Cobb 1994). Reports by executive agencies are crucial in supplying information on a problem and how it is changing over time. Congressional committees frequently hold hearings on public problems and invite testimony from various experts. Congressional advisory bodies, such as the General Accounting Office, issue authoritative reports on nearly all public problems, from oil imports to public education and health care. Even interest groups get involved. Most interest groups work hard not only to interpret the policy studies but also to supply other information that portrays a problem as they prefer to see it. For example, Common Cause, a public interest group concerned with honest and accountable government, has for years highlighted the implications of election campaign financing as a problem and called for its reform; the group celebrated its success when President Bush signed the Bipartisan Campaign Reform Act of 2002. The private sector also defines public problems. In the early years of radio, broadcasters became concerned about the anarchy of the airwaves, a problem they believed needed a solution. It eventually led to the government's licensing of airwave frequencies.

By supplying new, and often objective, information on the nature of a problem and its implications, policy analysts can help to steer political debate toward a **rational assessment** of the scope of the problem, its causes, and possible solutions. A study of urban sprawl, for example, might highlight the adverse impacts on highway congestion, land use, and water supplies and suggest how better growth management could minimize those effects. The findings and recommendations of such a study would no doubt differ significantly from the arguments of real estate developers and pro-growth public officials, as Atlanta, Georgia, and other high-growth metropolitan areas have learned in recent years (Jehl 2002; Murray 2002).

**Setting the Agenda.** Defining a problem is not enough; the public and policymakers must recognize it as a problem, and it must rise high enough on the agenda that action becomes likely. At that point, the search for solutions, or policy formulation, begins. Yet it is by no means easy for societal problems to reach agenda status because at any given moment so many problems are competing for social and political attention. Some make it onto the agenda and some do not (Birkland 1997; Cobb and Elder 1983).

Because of the competition for agenda space, many problems that government could potentially address never capture its attention and are neglected. Energy issues are a prime example. Only rarely do they rise on the political agenda, but the underlying problems remain from year to year, including heavy reliance on oil imported from the Middle East, the economic impacts of rising energy prices, and the environmental effects of burning fossil fuels. Another example is population. The United States is growing as fast or faster than any other industrialized nation. Its growth rate, about 1 percent a year, is ten times that of most European nations, partly because of its generous immigration policies. The Census Bureau projects that the U.S. population of 290 million in 2003 is likely to rise to 420 million by 2050, for a gain of 130 million people (Kent and Mather 2002). That is the equivalent of adding about four states the size of California to the nation. Except for a few cities and regions, however, population growth has never been an issue that commanded much attention from either the U.S. public or its elected officials.

The implications are plain. The mere existence of a problem is no guarantee that it will attract government attention or be acted on. Indeed, the term *nonissues* best distinguishes those problems that fail to gain attention from those that do. Some issues are intentionally kept off the agenda by those who oppose acting on them, as was true of civil rights in much of the South in the 1950s and 1960s. Others, such as population growth and energy use, are ignored by an indifferent public and policymakers. For the former, what some scholars call agenda denial, E. E. Schattschneider (1960, 71) explained the phenomenon:

> All forms of political organization have a bias in favor of the exploitation of some kinds of conflicts and the suppression of others because *organization* is the *mobilization of bias*. Some issues are organized into politics while others are organized out.[5]

When policymakers begin active discussions about a problem and potential solutions, the issue is said to be "on the agenda." Scholars distinguish between a **systemic agenda**, of which the public is aware and may be discussing, and an **institutional agenda** or **government agenda**, which are issues to which policymakers give active and serious consideration (Cobb and Elder 1983). John Kingdon's (1995, 3) definition of the agenda captures the meaning of the institutional agenda. It is, he said, "the list of subjects or problems to which governmental officials, and people outside of government closely associated with those officials, are paying some serious attention at any given time." The term *agenda,* therefore, means the subjects that gain such attention and become possible objects of policy action. There is no official or formal listing of such an agenda; rather, it becomes evident in the subjects elected officials choose to talk about, the media cover prominently, and interest groups and other policy actors work on at any given time.

Agenda setting is central to the policy process: if an issue does not attract the appropriate attention, chances are it will languish without government response. Therefore, the public policy student needs to understand what facilitates the movement of certain issues onto the agenda. Obviously, the elites in government can define a problem and raise its visibility. Members of Congress or the president may highlight a particular concern or issue they want addressed, as President Lyndon Johnson did in the 1960s for civil rights and President Bush did with education reform in 2001. Governors or mayors do the same at the state or local level. Government agencies that deal with a particular problem can also raise awareness and move related issues onto the agenda. The media, by deciding which issues to report on and those to which they give less attention, also highlight public problems and may sway public opinion about them. Interest groups likewise emphasize those problems of greatest concern to them and try to define them as suits their own political values and goals. The box "Steps to

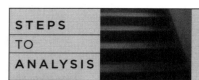

## STEPS TO ANALYSIS

## WHAT'S ON THE AGENDA?

How can you find out what is on the agenda or what is not? One way is to visit some government and media Web sites and look for the issues the sites emphasize and assign the most space. Starting at the national level, go to the White House site (www.whitehouse.gov) and see if you can determine what the president's agenda is. Visit your governor's site to do the same for your state or the mayor's or local government's site for your community. To reach your state government page, go to the Council of State Governments at www.csg.org. From that site, select the link to States at the top of the page and then click on State Pages. Either select the governor's office or look for a link to local government to find your city and then the mayor's office.

Next, sample one or more of the leading media sites to determine which issues their jour-

nalists believe merit the most coverage. Choose from CNN, CBS, NBC, ABC, and other television networks and the *New York Times, Washington Post,* or your city's newspaper. Here are the major links:

www.cnn.com
www.cbsnews.com
www.msnbc.com/news
www.abcnews.com
www.newyorktimes.com
www.washingtonpost.com

Do the government and media sites overlap, or do they cover different issues? Can you think of major problems—national, state, or local—that the media and elected officials are ignoring? What do you think are the reasons for this issue neglect?

Analysis: What's on the Agenda?" is an exercise in determining what issues are occupying the government's attention right now.

***Determinants of Agenda Setting.*** Some issues make it to the agenda automatically. They are mandated, or required, actions with which government must deal. Examples include the annual budget, legislation to reauthorize existing programs, and acting on a president's or governor's nominees for executive appointments. These issues alone probably take up most of the time that policymakers have available, leaving little to the discretionary issues. So what determines which of the optional issues receive attention and possibly policy action? In one of the best attempts to answer that question, Kingdon (1995) points to the intersection of three largely independent sets of activities in what he calls the problem, policy, and political "streams" that flow through society. When the streams converge, they create opportunities to consider certain issues. Whether they successfully move to the political agenda and are acted on is sometimes in the hands of influential **policy entrepreneurs**, or leaders who invest much of their time and resources in the issue.

The **problem stream** refers to the various bits of information available on the problem, whom it affects, and in what ways. Government reports and other studies are a valuable resource. They are released frequently and can assess the magnitude of the problem, both in terms of how serious it is and how widespread. Some issues, such as airline safety or the safety of nuclear power plants, warrant attention because of their potential harm to large numbers of people. Information about a problem or a possible solution works both ways: it may either help an issue make it to the agenda or prevent it. Acid rain and global warming did not become agenda items until an adequate amount of information had been collected to document the problems. Policymakers may not, however, spend time on a problem if the technology is not available for a solution. Sometimes the failure of the private sector to address an issue will get it on the agenda. Finally, government programs may have spillover effects that spur concern about another area.

A **focusing event**, such as a crisis, usually improves an issue's chance of getting on the agenda, in part because of the exceptional media coverage it receives. The terrorist attacks of September 11, 2001, clearly altered the agenda status of airport and airline security in extraordinary ways. Likewise, natural disasters focus attention on the risk to public well-being of hurricanes, floods, and earthquakes and may stimulate a government response. The nuclear power plant accidents at Chernobyl and Three Mile Island dramatically affected public opinion on the viability of nuclear energy (Dunlap, Kraft, and Rosa, 1993). These focusing events are sometimes linked to powerful national priorities, such as defense, public safety, and public health, that may spur government action.

The **policy stream** refers to what might be done about the problem—that is, the possible alternative policies. Legislators and their staffs, executive agency officials, interest groups, academics, or policy analysts all may develop policy proposals. Often, the ideas are floated as trial balloons to see how they are received. Some become the subject of speeches, press releases, legislative proposals, hearings, and study reports. The policy ideas tend to circulate within the specialist communities, or issue networks, of those most concerned about the problem, and with the public through books, magazines, the broadcast media, and the Internet. Kingdon (1995) compares this process to evolution because only the fittest ideas survive. Policy alternatives that are inconsistent with the current political climate, the "unfit," may be dropped from consideration temporarily and incubated until the climate improves. Those that fit better with the political climate may receive serious attention from policymakers and other policy actors. What Kingdon calls the "criteria for survival" are what this text refers to as evaluative criteria, such as economic feasibility and political acceptability. Chapter 6 addresses these criteria.

The **political stream** refers to this political climate or public mood. It is evident in public opinion surveys, the results of elections, and the activity and strength of interest groups. For example, Ronald Reagan's election in 1980 abruptly changed the political climate by greatly increasing the acceptability of conservative policy ideas. Bush's election in 2000 did much the same thing. Although it is never easy to decipher the political mood of the nation, and it changes quickly, elected officials have a well-developed ability to detect a shift in public attitudes, especially in their own constituencies.

When these three streams converge, policy entrepreneurs have their best chance to move problems and policy ideas onto the agenda and a step closer to approval. Moreover, policy entrepreneurs may help to bring about such a convergence. They may be inside government or outside; they may be official policymakers or one of the legions of unofficial policy actors, such as interest group leaders. The president holds a unique position as a powerful agenda setter, in part because of the enormous media attention the office receives. At the state or local level, the parallel would be a governor or mayor.

As Chapter 2 noted, however, one of the intriguing characteristics of the U.S. political system is the dispersal of power, meaning that policy leadership can come from many sources. At the national level, congressional committees and subcommittees are often hotbeds of innovative policy ideas precisely because members and their staffs are not only continually seeking ways to improve public policy but also to enhance their own visibility and compete with the other major party. Policy think tanks and interest groups are rich sources of policy proposals. Indeed, as the next three chapters explain, one of the major purposes of policy analysis is to conduct studies that evaluate the potential of new policy ideas. When the politically astute activist think tanks and interest groups put their weight behind these studies, influential policymakers and their staffs are likely to read them and take note of the results. Colleges and universities, professional associations, state and regional think tanks, citizens groups, and the business community are also sources of policy ideas.

Another way to think about why one issue may gain agenda status while another does not is to look to the particular issue's characteristics, especially its salience and conflict (Walker 1977). Salience is the issue's relative importance to the general public, and conflict refers to the level of disagreement over it. The logic here is that policymakers would rather deal with a problem the public believes is important than with an issue people are ignoring. In addition, policymakers prefer to avoid conflict and so will tend to shy away from contentious issues. Therefore, one would expect that the issue with the best chance of getting on the agenda would be one that is highly salient, but low in conflict, and the one with the worst chance would have low salience and high levels of conflict. Table 3-2 illustrates these differences. Why do the items fall into the text blocks as shown? Can you think of other illustrations of the salience-conflict view of agenda setting? What other examples of policy issues might fit into the text blocks shown in the table?

## Policy Formulation

Policy formulation is the development of proposed courses of action to help resolve a public problem. As noted, policy alternatives are continually being studied and advocated as part of

| TABLE 3-2 | Influences on Agenda Setting | |
|---|---|---|
| **Level of Conflict** | **Level of Issue Saliency** | |
| | HIGH | LOW |
| HIGH | Crime, gun control, abortion rights | **Worst chance** Population growth, energy issues, health care reform |
| LOW | **Best chance** Airline safety | Pork-barrel projects, such as research grants, water projects, agricultural subsidies |

the policy stream and constantly being evaluated against the prevailing standards for policy acceptance. Among the standards for policy acceptance are economic cost, social and political acceptability, and likely effectiveness in addressing the problem. Policy analysis is abundant at this stage of the policy process, as the leading policy actors (formal and informal) look for information and ideas that will allow them to pursue their goals. The next three chapters deal with policy analysis in depth, but here it is sufficient to note that formulation is a technical as well as a political process. Policies that are carelessly formulated—for example, by using inadequate data, questionable projections, or unreasonable assumptions—may fail. A recent case of failure is California's deregulation of its energy market. The state made a series of disastrous decisions in designing a policy that eventually cost California residents some $30 billion in excess electricity charges and forced one of the state's major utilities into bankruptcy (Brennan 2001).

Who is involved in policy formulation? Chapter 2 discussed the formal policy actors in government, such as legislators, chief executives, and agency officials, who are especially influential at this stage. In most policy areas the appointed and career officials in a bureaucracy are among the most experienced and knowledgeable policy actors. They have the technical information needed to develop policy and the political knowledge that comes from working in the policy arena. Their expertise can cut both ways, however. On the one hand, it can be enormously valuable in formulating new policy approaches. On the other hand, current officials who are strongly wedded to traditional policy approaches may be concerned about the implications of new policies for their offices, resources, and careers. In short, agency officials may be conservative about policy proposals and favor only incremental changes, while those outside the agency are willing to experiment with innovative policy designs.

In addition to agency expertise, legislators and executive branch officials have access to many other sources of information and advice as they formulate public policy proposals. The president, for example, draws not only from his White House staff but also from the Executive Office of the President (EOP), which includes specialized agencies such as the National Security Council, the Council of Economic Advisers, the Council on Environmental Quality, and the Office of Management and Budget. The last serves as a well-staffed, centralized policy clearinghouse for the White House. Legislators, particularly at the national level, also have sources of expertise and advice. Working for Congress are the General Accounting Office (a diversified program evaluation office), the Congressional Research Service (for policy research), and the Congressional Budget Office. These offices are supplemented by extensive staffs that serve the several hundred committees and subcommittees where policy formulation is concentrated. Executives and legislators at state and local levels have fewer resources for policy formulation, but the larger states and cities may nevertheless be well equipped to address the kinds of questions that arise during formulation.

Interest groups are active contributors to policy formulation. Like the bureaucracy, interest groups have a great deal of information at their disposal to provide background or specific solutions to problems. This information ranges from technical details about the problem to judgments about whether a proposal is likely to have political support. But interest groups also attempt to shape policy to serve their own economic or political needs. One example of self-serving economic lobbying came to light during consideration of President Bush's pro-

| STEPS |
| TO |
| ANALYSIS |

## APPRAISING POLICY FORMULATION

What steps would you take to determine whether a policy proposal was properly formulated in any area of concern, such as health care, education, national security, or the economy? You might start by examining the assessments of the problem to determine whether they were based on appropriate data and analysis. Next, try to find out who was involved in the formu-

lation process, who dominated it, and whether any serious conflicts of interest existed. You could also review the main assumptions made and forecasts that were used to determine whether they were valid. And always question whether other policy alternatives were fairly considered and evaluated. What else would you consider?

posed national energy policy. A secret task force, headed by Vice President Dick Cheney, formulated the energy plan, which strongly favored drilling for oil in the Arctic National Wildlife Refuge, among other locations. Environmentalists complained bitterly that the recommendations reflected what they saw as the undue influence of energy industry lobbyists, some of whom were among the top donors to the Bush election campaign. The evidence seemed to support the accusations. The Cheney task force was in close contact with energy industry officials, including executives from the Enron Corporation, and its final report strongly favored their positions (Van Natta and Banerjee 2002). The box "Steps to Analysis: Appraising Policy Formulation" suggests some questions that might be asked about the reliability and fairness of the process of formulation as it applies to any area of public policy.

### Policy Legitimation

Policy legitimation is defined as giving legal force to decisions or authorizing or justifying policy action. It may come from a majority vote in a legislature or a formal executive, bureaucratic, or judicial decision (Jones 1984). From some perspectives, the process of legitimation includes the legitimacy of the action taken, that is, whether it is thought to be a proper exercise of government authority and its broad acceptability to the public and/or other policy actors.

Legitimation as a step in the policy process is at once both simple and complex. It is simple when it merely means that a recognized authority considered and approved a policy proposal. A bill becomes a law at the national level if both houses of Congress approve it and the president signs it, but does that process necessarily imply that the measure was legitimated? This question may be especially pertinent for the large number of policy measures that are part of omnibus legislative packages, or the government's growing tendency to adopt budget riders, which are policy actions attached to mandatory **appropriations** bills. These riders often are buried deep within budget bills precisely to avoid legislative scrutiny and public criticism (Davidson and Oleszek 2002).

The complex view is that legitimation requires more than a majority vote or legal sanction by a recognized authority. Policy legitimacy or acceptability in this sense flows from several conditions: the action is consistent with the Constitution or existing law; it is compatible with U.S. political culture and values; and it has demonstrable popular support. Legitimation also may follow from a process of political interaction and debate that involves all major interests and a full and open airing of the issues and controversies (Lindblom and Woodhouse 1993). A careful assessment of any policy analyses or other technical studies might be part of this process of discussion and debate. So too might public participation through public meetings, hearings, and citizen advisory bodies, or endorsement by respected community or national leaders. Sometimes lawmakers call on actors, recording artists, athletes, and other celebrities to convince the public of the worthiness of the issue under consideration. During 2002, for example, congressional committees heard testimony from Michael J. Fox, Christie Brinkley, Julia Roberts, Kevin Richardson of the Backstreet Boys, and former heavyweight boxing champion Muhammad Ali.

Policies that are adopted without such legitimation face serious hurdles. They may well fail to command public support; affected interest groups may oppose them or even challenge them in court; and their implementation could be adversely affected. As discussed earlier, the Nuclear Waste Policy Act of 1982 is an example of a failed policy. Congressional proponents of the act seriously misjudged the public's willingness to accept high-level nuclear waste repositories, the spent fuel from nuclear power plants. They also misjudged the public's trust and confidence in the Department of Energy, the bureaucracy in charge of the program. The policy's backers were so determined to speed up the process of repository location and construction that they rejected the advice from Congress's own Office of Technology Assessment, which had warned that public concern and opposition would scuttle the program's success. Similar issues arose during revision of the act in 1987, when Congress voted to study only one possible site in the nation, at Yucca Mountain in Nevada, over the strenuous objections of the state (Kraft 1992). Fifteen years later the controversy over these decisions was continuing as Nevada fought the federal government's actions.

Policy formulation has both technical and political elements, but the process of policy legitimation is mostly political. Nevertheless, policy analysis is still applicable at this stage;

## STEPS TO ANALYSIS

### JUDGING POLICY LEGITIMATION

How would you determine whether a policy proposal has been fully legitimated during its process of approval? Would you look for supportive public opinion poll data? Whether sufficient consideration was given to the views of major interest groups? Whether sufficient time had been allocated for deliberation and debate by policymakers? Whether the legitimacy of government action was considered? Whether ethical issues were explicitly and thoughtfully addressed? Or, to turn the question around, if a proposal is not accepted, how would you determine whether its rejection was legitimate? Consider the two examples in the chapter: approval of the Bush tax cuts in 2001 and the reinstatement of generous agricultural policies in 2002. How sound were those decisions in light of the expectations for policy legitimation?

assessment of a policy's political feasibility and social acceptability remains relevant. Analysis of public opinion on the policy is also useful, as is measuring interest group support and opposition. **Ethical analysis** is both appropriate and helpful to determine what is fair and equitable in a policy decision or how it affects individual freedom or liberty. These kinds of questions arise frequently in public debates over welfare reform, access to higher education, patients' rights, family planning and abortion, fetal stem cell research, and many other issues. The box "Steps to Analysis: Judging Policy Legitimation" poses some questions that might be asked about the process of legitimation in any political venue.

### Policy Implementation

For many, the passing of a law by Congress, a state legislature, or a city council signals the end of the policy process. In reality, it is just the beginning of government activity that ultimately will affect most citizens and businesses more than they may realize. When Congress enacted the Clean Air Act Amendments of 1990, did industry automatically comply and stop polluting the air? When Congress lifted the federal highway speed limit of 55 miles per hour, were drivers immediately allowed to legally drive 70 miles per hour? The obvious answers to both of these questions is no. Once a policy is formulated and adopted, it must be implemented.

According to Charles Jones (1984), implementation is the "set of activities directed toward putting a program into effect." Three of these activities, organization, interpretation, and application, are particularly important to successful implementation. Organization is the establishment of resources, offices, and methods for administering a program. Interpretation means translating the program's language—the plans, directives, and regulatory requirements—typically found in a law or regulation into language that those affected can understand. Application is the "routine provision of services, payments, or other agreed upon program objectives or instruments" (Jones 1984, 166). In other words, implementation depends on the development of the program's details to ensure that policy goals and objectives will be attained. One of the primary mechanisms agencies use to implement the laws is regulation. A regulation, which has the force of law, is simply the rule that governs the operation of a particular government program.

Policy implementation is a crucial stage of the policy process because it is where one sees actual government intervention and real consequences for society (Mazmanian and Sabatier 1983; Goggin et al. 1990). For example, the Occupational Safety and Health Act (OSH) is a relatively short law that governs workplace health and safety in the United States. The law itself provides few details on how the Occupational Safety and Health Administration (OSHA) is to go about the business of protecting workers. It has been the implementation of the OSH Act, rather than its adoption, that has most directly affected workplace health and safety conditions.

Executive branch agencies implement most public policies within the United States. The traditional view of executive branch agencies was that they simply carried out the will of the legislature by following the established guidelines. This view regarded agencies and their personnel as nonpolitical administrators who had no say in the policy beyond its execution. This viewpoint, however, is unrealistic and fails to take into consideration how active agencies and their administrators are in formulating policy and how much discretion they have in its implementation.

Because of this degree of discretion, agency decisions often reflect the political philosophy and preferences of the chief executive who appointed the agencys' administrators. Chief executives try to place in the top agency jobs people who agree with them on matters such as how to interpret the law, agency priorities and budget allocations, and which policy tools to use. In addition, debates that occur during policy formulation often continue during implementation. A good example is the continuing conflict within the Environmental Protection Agency (EPA) over the costs of implementing the 1990 Clean Air Act Amendments. When these kinds of conflicts develop, agency officials have to work in close consultation with the chief executive, and no one was surprised to discover that clean air implementation in the Bush EPA differed significantly from that of the agency during the Clinton administration. At times, the executive's enthusiasm for the law, or lack thereof, becomes apparent when it comes time to write the rules. When the Federal Election Commission began to write the rules for implementing the controversial campaign finance reform law of 2002, the law's sponsors in Congress complained those rules "would severely undermine the new law" (Mitchell 2002).

All government agencies and programs depend on a continuing supply of money to operate and carry out the various activities of policy implementation. The federal government uses an annual budget process that begins with the president's budget recommendations to Congress and ends with Congress passing appropriations bills, without which, according to the Constitution, no money can be spent. In between these two steps, Congress decides whether to accept or modify the president's budget and in what ways. Some of those decisions depend on performance assessments, judgments about how well the agencies are implementing their programs. The programs that have proven successful probably have an easier time securing the same or larger budgets; those seen as less successful may have to get along with less money. State governments often use a biennial budget process rather than an annual one and usually make adjustments in the second year. The overall process is similar to what occurs at the national level. Ultimately, agency budgets reflect a compromise between what the chief executive wants and what the legislature is willing to give.

## Policy Evaluation and Change

The last two stages of the policy process are evaluation and change. Policy evaluation, or program evaluation, is an assessment of whether policies and programs are working well. In particular, analysts look for evidence that a program is achieving its stated goals and objectives. For example, did a welfare reform policy reduce the number of people on welfare? Do the students enrolled in Head Start do better in school than children who were not enrolled in the program? Do the programs have unanticipated consequences, particularly any that are viewed as harmful? Evaluation involves judging a program's success not only in terms of policy outcomes but also in terms of a program's legitimacy or need, regardless of how well it is working, especially for controversial programs such as family planning or affirmative action.

Of the many reasons governments engage in policy and program evaluation, costs may be among the most important. Government programs are usually expensive, and policymakers, who must be accountable to the voters, want to know if the results are worth the money, a question that lies at the heart of policy analysis. In addition to costs versus benefits, analysts have many other methods for evaluating policies and programs, but, as with policy formulation, legitimation, and implementation, evaluation is not merely about technical studies of program results. It also involves political judgments about a program's worth, decisions that are likely to be of great interest to all policy actors involved. In this sense, programs are continually, if often informally, evaluated by members of Congress, interest groups, think tanks, and others.

Should government expand a program or reduce its scope? Should the administrators try a different policy approach? Questions like these may follow the evaluations and lead to policy change. Termination of a policy or program is one of many kinds of changes that might be considered, although it is rare. Most often a policy or program undergoes incremental change in an attempt to make it more effective or to meet the objectives of its main constituencies and other policy actors. A clear illustration is Congress's decision in 2002 to expand agricultural crop subsidies, which was discussed at the beginning of the chapter. Just six years earlier, Congress had decided to phase out the same subsidies. This 1996 policy change failed to satisfy agribusiness interests, and they pressured Congress to reinstate, and substantially increase, the subsidies.

The farm bill demonstrates that the policy process never really ends. What is thought to be a resolution of a problem through policy adoption at one point is later evaluated and judged to be unacceptable. Interested parties then advocate changes. Another round of the policy cycle begins as the newly recognized needs reach the political agenda and a different policy is formulated and adopted. There is nothing wrong with this process. Indeed, all public policies can be considered to be experiments in which government and the public learn what works well and what does not. With the knowledge that comes from such learning (perhaps aided by formal evaluations), policymakers are in a better position to redesign programs and try again (Sabatier and Jenkins-Smith 1993). Becoming overly committed to existing policies and programs could be harmful, blocking the capacity to learn from experience and to improve government performance.

## INSTRUMENTS OF PUBLIC POLICY

In public policy, one of the first decisions to be made is whether government should intervene at all to deal with a problem or simply leave its resolution to individual action or the marketplace. Chapter 1 described the most common rationales for intervention, which included political reasons, moral reasons, and market failures. Complicating the decision about government action is that liberals and conservatives, with their differing perspectives, often disagree, sometimes heatedly, about it.

Should citizens and policymakers decide that government intervention is indeed necessary, they can choose from a diverse menu of possibilities. Policymakers consider many questions when deciding which **policy instrument** to use to address a particular issue or problem. The most obvious is whether the instrument will be effective in addressing the problem, but others include its political acceptability, technical feasibility, economic impact, and long-term effects. Chapter 5 examines policy alternatives in some detail. The next sections explain the most common policy tools that governments use.

## Regulation

One of the best known policy instruments, regulation, encompasses several different kinds of government actions, including the laws that legislatures enact and the rules bureaucracies adopt. Regulations are government decrees that require citizens to do something or prevent citizens from doing something. Particular requirements ensure compliance by individuals, corporations, and other units of government. Typically, the regulations impose sanctions, such as fines or imprisonment, for failure to comply. For the most part, citizens and corporations comply voluntarily with legal requirements, but the means are available to force compliance when necessary.

## Government Management

Governments use the **direct services** or **direct management** of resources as instruments of public policy. Education, defense, public parks, and most municipal services, such as police and fire protection, are examples of policies that governments implement by providing the

Seen here under construction in May 1999, the California City Correctional Center is a for-profit prison built to house maximum-security convicts. Its owner, Nashville-based Corrections Corporation of America, claims it runs prisons as well as the state corrections department and saves taxpayers money. The development of private prisons illustrates the increasing appeal of the privatization of services once considered exclusively functions of government. Assessments of the effectiveness and efficiency of privatization offer a mixed verdict. Some privatized programs have worked well; others have proven less effective and more costly than programs managed by government agencies.

service directly to citizens. Governments offer most of these services because they need to be provided in a specific way, such as making national park lands available to all for a modest fee. Today, it is not unusual for governments, especially at the local level, to contract out a wide variety of services and pay private companies to provide them.

The questions of which government services might be handled by private businesses and whether doing so is a good idea are the subjects of ongoing public policy debate. According to James Anderson (2003, 13), "**Privatization** supports transferring many government assets or programs to the private sector and contracting with private companies to handle many public services." Policymakers evaluate the options by using criteria such as effectiveness, cost, and accountability to the public, and the public sector remains responsible for ensuring the quality of the work, even though the private sector is providing the services. To date, many services and programs that were once part of the public sector have been privatized or contracted out, including solid waste collection, fire fighting, and the management of jails and prisons (Savas 2000). But even before the privatization movement, the government relied on the market to provide services. A clear example is national defense and the letting of contracts to the defense industry to build aircraft, tanks, ships, and missiles.

## Taxing and Spending

Governments also use their ability to **tax and spend** to achieve policy goals and objectives. One form of spending policy is the direct payment of money to citizens. Social Security is an obvious example: the federal government transfers money from people who are working to retirees or those who are otherwise covered by the system's rules. Governments also provide monetary payments as a way of promoting certain activities. For example, under welfare reform, the federal government provides money to the states to distribute as they see fit to those needing assistance, but the states must show that they have reduced the welfare rolls or risk losing some of this federal funding. Government spending policies affect a wide range of public activities, from scientific research to highway and mass transit construction and protection of public lands.

Governments also use tax policy to promote or discourage certain activities. For example, the federal government promotes home buying by allowing homeowners to deduct their mortgage interest from their taxable income. Many state governments have increased the tax on cigarettes not only to discourage smoking but also to raise revenue for other programs. California launched a two-pronged attack on teenage smoking in the 1990s. The state raised the cigarette tax and used the additional revenue for antismoking campaigns that lowered the rate of teenage smoking.

Environmentalists often urge governments to raise the taxes on gasoline to discourage inefficient use of fossil fuels and promote energy conservation. Although hardly popular with the public and policymakers, the proposal takes into account that U.S. energy prices are among the lowest in the industrialized world and contribute to the nation's dependence on imported oil, which raises national security and economic concerns. Using a strategy similar to fuel taxes, some communities tax their residents for the amount of solid waste they produce by requiring the purchase of special garbage bags that are the only containers collected. This pollution tax is implemented both to decrease the amount of solid waste produced and to increase the use of recycling in a community.

## Market Mechanisms

Governments can take advantage of **market mechanisms** as a form of public policy. Using the market may be an explicit decision by government not to intervene in any way but instead to allow the laws of supply and demand to work. For the most part, by 2002 the government had chosen not to regulate the rapidly developing electronic commerce on the Internet, or even to impose taxes on Internet purchases, much to the dismay of local merchants who found themselves losing market share to Amazon.com and other companies.

Governments also actively use market incentives rather than other approaches to achieve policy goals. For example, when Congress passed the 1990 Clean Air Act Amendments, it required a certain amount of reductions in sulfur dioxide and nitrogen oxides, which are precursors to acid rain. In the past, Congress may have used regulation as the tool to achieve these reductions, but under the 1990 act the government is using marketable permits to get the reductions. The permits, which are emission allowances, are provided to companies based on their previous emissions levels, but with the target of lower emissions over time. Companies then decide how to use these permits; they can buy, sell, trade, or bank the permits, using whatever strategy allows them to meet the emissions targets

Jeff Bezos, CEO and founder of Amazon.com, kisses a stuffed bear as John Eyler, CEO of Toys "R" Us Inc., looks on. At this August 2000 press conference in New York, Bezos and Eyler announced that Amazon.com and Toys "R" Us would be collaborating to set up online stores selling toys, video games, and baby products. Internet commerce continues to grow at an astonishing rate, in part because users do not pay sales taxes on online purchases. State and local officials complain that such a policy is inequitable. They argue that their inability to tax these sales significantly affects a major source of government revenue and that Internet sales translate into less business for conventional retail outlets—adversely affecting state and local economies. Despite such protests, government policymakers may decide not to address a perceived problem and allow the market to operate unencumbered in a survival-of-the-fittest manner.

at the least cost. If companies can emit less pollution than they have allowances for, they can sell their additional permits to companies for which emissions reductions are more difficult and more costly (Freeman 2003).

### Education, Information, and Persuasion

Another policy instrument the government can use is **citizen education** in an attempt to persuade people to behave in a certain way. Following a natural disaster in the United States, the president usually makes a personal appeal to Americans to support relief efforts. This type of message is called exhortation or a hortatory appeal (Schneider and Ingram 1997), and the bully pulpit can be an effective instrument of public policy under certain circumstances. Public opinion polls, however, have shown that trust in government and its leaders has decreased over the past thirty years (Nye, Zelikov, and King 1997), although the pattern was reversed temporarily following the September 11 terrorist attacks (Mackenzie and Labiner 2002). As trust decreases, the effectiveness of persuasion as a public policy instrument also decreases. People may not comply with a request of a public official if they question the official's justification or if they rate the government low in legitimacy.

Providing information to the public can be a powerful policy instrument. Anne Schneider and Helen Ingram (1997) call it a "capacity building" tool. It has the potential to inform, enlighten, and empower people through training, education, technical assistance, and making information available. Use of this instrument has increased in recent years and is common in the areas of health, safety, and environmental protection (Graham 2002). For example, the Food and Drug Administration requires nutritional labeling as a way of informing consumers about the substances in their food and allowing them to make decisions on healthy eating. The EPA each year collects and makes available on its Web site information about emissions of toxic chemicals from industries around the nation. In creating this policy in 1986, Congress hoped, with some success, that publicizing toxic emissions would give businesses an incentive to correct their pollution problems (Graham and Miller 2001).

## POLICY TYPOLOGIES

Policymakers are likely to think about policy options in terms of the tools at their disposal. For example, what will be more effective in reducing toxic chemical emissions, regulation or information provision approaches? Which instrument will work better to cut fuel consumption, regulation (raising vehicle fuel efficiency standards) or a market incentive (imposing a larger gasoline tax)? Public policy scholars think about the different kinds of policies that governments adopt and why they do so for a slightly different reason (McCool 1995). The goal is to understand the basic differences among policies and the political conditions that lead to one kind of policy rather than another. To that end, this chapter continues with a review of the best known and most often cited typology, developed by Theodore Lowi (1964), and with a related analysis of the politics of regulation by James Q. Wilson (1980).

According to Lowi (1964), all government functions can be classified into three types: distributive, redistributive, and regulatory. Individual programs or grants that a government provides without regard to limited resources or zero-sum situations (where one group's gain is another's loss) are characterized as **distributive policies**. Examples include college research grants, weapons procurement, agricultural subsidies, highways and bridges, and other public construction projects. Many people label these kinds of programs *pork barrel*. The term is used to describe the tendency of elected officials, such as members of Congress, to try to provide government programs and services that directly benefit their constituencies. Such politicians are said to excel at "bringing home the bacon." These kinds of policies are often noncontroversial because they tend to be visible only to those directly involved, and members usually do not seriously question each other's pet projects because to do so may jeopardize their own. One might expect these kinds of policies to be particularly attractive when spending limits and budget deficits are viewed as unimportant, because the potential exists for most members of Congress to get something out of this kind of spending. As the agriculture subsidies example illustrates, however, elected officials may continue to support costly distributive policies even in lean times. The direct electoral rewards of providing such benefits to their states and districts appear to override concern about the budget.

Conflict is what makes **redistributive policies** different from distributive policies. For every redistributive policy, winners and losers are associated with its approval, which makes such policies controversial and difficult to adopt. Because redistributive policies provide benefits to a category of individuals at the expense of another, they often reflect ideological or class conflict. Some examples include welfare, Social Security, affirmative action programs, and tax policy. A proposed tax cut may benefit chiefly upper-income taxpayers while eroding services that assist lower-income citizens because of reduced government revenue. If a company adopts an affirmative action policy in hiring women or racial minorities, these groups may benefit at the expense of others.

Lowi's final policy type is **regulatory policy**. According to Kenneth Meier, a leading scholar of regulation, "Regulatory policy is government restriction of individual choice to keep conduct from transcending acceptable bounds" (Meier 1993, 82). This definition covers a wide range of government activities, from consumer protection to ensuring environmental quality. The range is so broad that some scholars divide regulatory policies into two subcategories. The first is **competitive regulatory policies**, which are mostly associated with the regulation of specific industries and their practices, such as computer software and communications companies. The second is **protective**, or **social**, **regulation**, which protects the general public from activities that occur in the private sector (Ripley and Franklin 1991; Eisner, Worsham, and Ringquist 2000).

Competitive regulatory policy includes the licensing of radio and television broadcasting and antitrust actions, such as the Justice Department's suit against Microsoft Corporation in the late 1990s for monopolistic practices. Protective regulatory policies include consumer protection and workplace health and safety policies, such as those administered by the Consumer Product Safety Commission and the Occupational Safety and Health Administration. These kinds of policies are controversial because they require the government to intervene into the activities of private businesses, often leading to increased operating costs or restrictions on corporate behavior.

Lowi's policy typology provides a simple but helpful way to classify different kinds of government programs and policies. The characteristics associated with each type allow the student of public policy to understand the debate surrounding the issue, why policies may or may not gain approval, how they might be implemented, and the public's acceptance of them.

In a similar vein, James Wilson (1980) offers a persuasive explanation of how certain kinds of policies are enacted and maintained over time, despite an apparent lack of public support. He also explains how the nation decides to adopt regulatory policies in the face of industry opposition. In effect, Wilson urges analysts to look at the *distribution* of the costs and benefits of government action. The "perceived distribution of their costs and benefits" by policy actors, whether monetary or nonmonetary, creates incentives for different actors to participate in the policymaking process and especially to "form political organizations and to engage in collective action" (366). Wilson argues that the policy actors are constantly judging the equity of policy rewards and comparing the benefits and burdens in relation to what others gain or lose. Table 3-3 illustrates the four types of political interaction associated with the concentration or dispersal of costs and benefits. All four are very much in evidence in U.S. public policy and illustrated throughout the text.

Thinking about the likelihood of citizen or interest group action, when both the costs and benefits of expected government action are broadly distributed or diffuse, Wilson says we can expect **majoritarian politics.** Most people expect to gain and also to pay for the cost of public policies. These issues tend not to give rise to interest groups because no one can hope either to gain a disproportionate share of the benefits or be asked to bear a disproportionate share of the burden the policy places on society. Therefore, if proposals achieve sufficient agenda status, are considered to be legitimate exercises of government authority, and ideological objections can be overcome, they stand a good chance of being enacted. One example is the approval of the Social Security Act in 1935; another is the adoption of Medicare in 1964.

In contrast, when businesses such as automobile manufacturers, cable television operators, or mining companies face the possibility of new regulations, they have a material reason to organize and fight them. Not surprisingly, they often succeed. The public receiving the broadly dispersed benefits of automobile safety and pollution control requirements, for example, is not usually motivated to the same degree to rise in their defense. This scenario is what Mancur

| TABLE 3-3 | Policies Associated with Concentrated or Broadly Distributed Benefits and Costs | |
|---|---|---|
| **Costs** | **Benefits** | |
| | BROADLY DISTRIBUTED | CONCENTRATED |
| BROADLY DISTRIBUTED | **Majoritarian politics** Examples: Social Security; general tax benefits such as the deductibility of home mortgage and home equity interest payments | **Client politics** Examples: subsidies for mining, ranching, and agricultural interests; veterans benefits; subsidies for nuclear power and fossil fuels such as oil, gas, and coal |
| CONCENTRATED | **Entrepreneurial politics** Examples: environmental protection policies, consumer protection policies, food and drug regulation | **Interest group politics** Examples: cable television versus satellite companies; miners union versus mine owners; trucking companies versus railroads and airlines |

Source: Developed from James Q. Wilson, *The Politics of Regulation* (New York: Basic Books, 1980).

Olson (1971) calls the logic of collection action. Consumers or the public in general have little incentive to organize or actively support actions that benefit society as a whole. No one doing so would get any more than anyone else. Under some circumstances, however, what Wilson (1980) calls **entrepreneurial politics** may alter the outcome. Policy entrepreneurs are sometimes able to mobilize latent public sentiment on an issue. These policy activists may be able to capitalize on well-publicized crises and other catalytic events, attack their opponents for endangering the public's welfare, and associate proposed legislation with widely shared values, such as clean air and public health. Evidence that this strategy works is found in the extensive array of regulatory policies the nation enacted, particularly in the 1960s and 1970s.

A quite different situation exists when the benefits of public policies flow to narrow economic interests—for example, the nuclear power industry, the highway construction industry, or sugar cane growers in Florida—and the public at large bears the costs. In these situations, the economic beneficiaries organize and lobby fiercely to protect their interests, while public interest groups find it difficult to mobilize the general public, even though most people consider the subsidies or "give-aways" to be improper or at least unfair. Typically, however, these decisions are low-salience issues for the public, as they are for the media. The same is true for the policymakers who, as some say, "have no dog in this fight." Those with the affected interests in their districts or states are likely to take a strong interest and work to secure the benefits. With most people doing nothing about the situation, the beneficiaries are allowed to maintain their preferred status. Opponents of the programs may mount campaigns against what is known as "corporate welfare," but they face significant political obstacles to success. Therefore, whether what Wilson calls **client politics** prevails depends on how visible the policies are and the extent to which the public and organized groups are able to challenge the beneficiaries effectively. Decisions by Congress in the 1990s to deregulate commodity trading directly benefited the Enron Corporation and other businesses like it. As a result of the legislation, Enron was able to hide its risky energy trading activities and fraudulent accounting practices from government and shareholder scrutiny.

Finally, in what Wilson calls interest group politics the benefits and costs are both narrowly concentrated. A regulatory action or a government subsidy may benefit a small group at the expense of another group, but cause no particular harm to the public. For example, the trucking industry and the airlines compete for the business of shipping goods throughout the country, and each has a powerful incentive to organize to protect its interests. Cable television companies compete with home satellite services for customers, and labor unions and management disagree over contract terms in any number of economic sectors, such as auto manufacturing. The public at large is likely to be indifferent to the outcome of these kinds of battles because the overall economic impact is much the same and the issues are unlikely to be salient for the general public. The outcome therefore depends on the ability of each competing interest group to make its case and influence the policy process.

## CONCLUSIONS

This chapter describes the leading models and theories used to explain the politics of policymaking. It focuses primarily on the policy process model and explores each of its stages, noting the roles of different policy actors and the potential for policy analysis in each. We believe this model enables the public policy student to formulate effective questions about the policy process. It also aids in evaluating the information and arguments used to advance certain policy proposals or to criticize existing programs. The models and theories introduced here are the tools for figuring out what policy actors are doing at any given time and why they are doing it.

The next three chapters explore in more detail some of the themes touched on so far. They cover the nature of policy analysis and its growth over time, particularly through the rise of independent think tanks and the expansion in interest group analysis and policy promotion. They introduce concepts and methods for measuring and analyzing public problems and thinking creatively about possible policy alternatives for dealing with them. They elaborate on the leading criteria for evaluating policy proposals and the range of policy analysis methods that can provide information about the likely effects of those proposals.

## DISCUSSION QUESTIONS

What kind of evidence would support a conclusion that an elite dominates in a given policy area? What kind of evidence suggests the opposite?

What kind of evidence would suggest that the U.S. political system is fundamentally democratic, that, for example, public policy broadly reflects the demands of the American public?

What do you see as the strengths and weakness of the policy process model introduced in this chapter?

Think about a specific issue currently on the local, state, or national agenda. What factors propelled it onto the government agenda or keep it there?

Considering the various policy instruments discussed in the chapter, how would you determine whether one (for example, regulation, market incentives, or public education) is more appropriate in a given situation than another?

## SUGGESTED READINGS

Thomas A. Birkland, *An Introduction to the Policy Process: Theories, Concepts, and Models of Public Policy Making* (Armonk, N.Y.: M. E. Sharpe, 2001). A useful text that describes the U.S. policy process.

John W. Kingdon, *Agendas, Alternatives, and Public Policies*, 2d ed. (New York: HarperCollins College, 1995). A classic analysis of agenda setting in U.S. politics, with exceptional insight into the policy process, agenda setting in particular.

Charles E. Lindblom, *Inquiry and Change: The Troubled Attempt to Understand and Shape Society* (New Haven: Yale University Press and New York: Russell Sage Foundation, 1990). An original and perceptive treatment of the role of policy analysis in the process of problem solving and policymaking.

Charles E. Lindblom and Edward J. Woodhouse, *The Policy-Making Process*, 3d ed. (Upper Saddle River, N.J.: Prentice Hall, 1993). A unique text on the policymaking process that links it to policy analysis.

## SUGGESTED WEB SITES

The Web sites listed at the end of Chapter 1, especially those of major government institutions and public opinion surveys, are also useful here. Sites for the leading policy think tanks are listed at the end of Chapter 4. In addition, see the following for the study of public policy and policymaking.

**http://apsapolicysection.org/index.html.** Public policy section of the American Political Science Association. Has useful links to policy organizations, journals, and political science research on public policy issues.

**www.firstgov.gov/Citizen/Citizen_Gateway.shtml.** The citizen portal for FirstGov, with links to news, government studies and reports, consumer action, and government e-services.

**www.ipsonet.org/page.cgi.** Policy Studies Organization home page.

**www.napawash.org.** National Academy of Public Administration home page, with links to events and academy publications on government and public policy.

**www.polisci.com/web/web.htm.** A useful portal for government, politics, and journalism, with links to state legislatures, city governments, political parties, and interest groups.

## KEYWORDS

advocacy coalition framework   73
appropriations   86
citizen education   94
client politics   97
competitive regulatory policies   95
define the problem   79
direct management   91
direct services   91
distributive policies   95
entrepreneurial politics   97
ethical analysis   88
focusing event   83
food stamp program   70
forecasts   69
government agenda   81
group theory   73
information asymmetry   76
institutional agenda   81
institutional theory   74
majoritarian politics   96

market incentives   74
market mechanisms   93
policy cycle   77
policy entrepreneurs   82
policy instrument   91
policy stream   83
political stream   83
political systems theory   76
privatization   92
problem definition   79
problem stream   82
projections   69
protective or social regulation   95
rational assessment   80
rational choice theory   75
redistributive policies   95
regulatory policy   71
symbolic politics   71
systemic agenda   81
tax and spend   92

CHAPTER 4

# POLICY ANALYSIS: AN INTRODUCTION

AMERICANS ARE USING THEIR CELLULAR PHONES MORE THAN ever before and in places where they sometimes bother other people, such as restaurants and theaters. What has sparked the most controversy, however, is not a matter of bad manners, but one of safety. Some studies suggest that driver distraction while talking on a cell phone is a significant cause of highway accidents, with a risk equivalent to driving with a blood alcohol level at the legal maximum.[1] About twenty nations now ban the use of cell phones by drivers, and many states and communities are considering similar restrictions or the imposition of penalties for irresponsible use of phones by drivers (Clines 2001).

In fact, in 2001 New York became the first state to pass a law prohibiting drivers from using hand-held cell phones. "By requiring drivers to put down their cell phones and pay attention to the road, this new law will help make our roads safer and save lives," Gov. George Pataki said. As a rationale for the law, Pataki cited the number of families that had "suffered the tragedy of seeing a loved one injured—sometimes fatally—in an accident caused by someone who was driving and was using a cell phone." Those who violate the ban face a $100 fine for the first offense, a $200 fine for a second, and a $500 fine for every subsequent violation.[2]

Was this restriction a good idea? Was New York justified in passing the law and imposing the fines? Before attempting to answer these questions, policy analysts would probably ask a few of their own. Should the ban apply only to hand-held cell phones and not to phones that can be operated hands-free? Do the higher accident rates stem from holding the phone or from the distractions of talking on it? Are the anticipated gains in highway safety worth the sacrifice of individual freedom to use the phones? Clearly, New York decided it was, but other states and communities may come to a different conclusion.

Analysts could also ask about other distractions. Does it make sense, or is it fair, to restrict the use of cell phones while driving but not activities such as drinking coffee, eating snacks, tuning the radio, or sliding a compact disk into the player? What about electronic navigational maps in cars, Internet access and e-mail, faxes, or other visual services? All would seem to pose a similar risk of accidents. How do the risks of cell phones compare to these other sources of distraction?

A heavily armed police officer stood guard on the front steps of the Capitol in Washington, D.C., in March 2003 as the war with Iraq was about to begin. The federal government raised the national terror alert to orange, indicating a high risk of terrorism. The threat of terrorist attacks highlights an important dimension to policy analysis: the need to weigh competing criteria in making policy choices. How should analysts, citizens, and policymakers evaluate the expected gains in homeland security in relation to a possible loss of individual rights—for example, in access to public buildings, in freedom to travel, or in protection against false arrest? Is security so important that personal and civil liberties pale in comparison? Or is the nation so dedicated to protection of individual rights that it is prepared to accept a higher risk of terrorism?

A number of studies suggest that a variety of visual distractions, such as looking at pedestrians, animals, and road construction are among the major causes of highway accidents, followed by adjusting the radio or sound system. Talking on a cell phone was found to be less important, about the same as eating or drinking. A flaw with these studies, however, is that drivers involved in accidents are unlikely to admit they were talking on their cell phones. Some experimental studies found that accident risks are about four times greater when a driver is talking on a cell phone, and whether the phone is hand-held or hands-free appears to make little difference. Other studies, particularly in Japan, where the police keep better track of this kind of accident, showed that they decreased markedly after Japan in 1999 banned drivers from using hand-held cell phones (Brody 2002). At least one initial study by the Insurance Institute for Highway Safety found that New Yorkers were complying with the ban, cutting the practice in half.[3] Analysts and policymakers might also ask about other policy options that could work as well as a ban. For example, would a public education campaign be just as effective as sanctions? As drivers and citizens, everyone should ask how policymakers can ultimately reach decisions that are effective, fair, and reasonable. This chapter demonstrates that policy analysis can help.

Chapter 3 elaborated on the policy process model, which is particularly useful for understanding how policy analysis contributes to the process. Whether in the form of testimony before legislative committees, the release of studies and reports on the Internet, or the publication of articles and reports, policy analysis is usually performed at the policy formulation stage. Here, policymakers search for the proposals they believe hold promise for addressing public problems. But policy analysis is also used throughout the policymaking process, starting with defining the nature of the problem right through to implementing and evaluating policies within administrative agencies.

This chapter examines the nature and purposes of policy analysis, the different approaches analysts use, and basic steps in the policy analysis process. The next two chapters go into greater detail on these steps. No one expects these chapters to make students instant analysts; rather, their purpose is to convey the challenge of understanding and solving public problems and the need for clear, critical thinking about public policy. Readers should learn what policy analysis is all about, how to question the assumptions that analysts make about their work, and how analysis is used in support of political arguments. Also provided are some sources of information that can be useful in writing issue papers or policy analyses.

## THE NATURE OF POLICY ANALYSIS

As Chapter 1 discussed, the term *policy analysis* covers many different activities. It may mean examining the components of the policymaking process, such as policy formulation and implementation, or substantive public policy issues, or both. The process usually involves collecting and interpreting information that clarifies the causes and effects of public problems and the likely consequences of using one policy option or another to address them. Because public problems can be understood only through the insights of many disciplines, policy analysis draws from the ideas and methods of economics, political science, sociology, psychology, philosophy, and various technical fields (Anderson 2003; Weimer and Vining 1999).

Most often policy analysis refers to the assessment of policy alternatives. According to one expert, it is "the systematic investigation of alternative policy options and the assembly and integration of the evidence for and against each option" (Jacob Ukeles, quoted in Patton and Sawicki 1993, 22). Policy analysis is not intended to make policy decisions but to inform the process of public deliberation and debate. As in the case of cell phone use in cars, analysis can provide useful information and comparisons. Ultimately, however, the public and its elected officials must decide what course of action is desirable.

As should be clear, policy analysis is part science and part political judgment. Doing analysis often means bringing scientific knowledge to the political process or "speaking truth to power" (Wildavsky 1979). To put it in a slightly different way, policy analysis involves both descriptive (empirical) study, which tries to determine the facts of a given situation, and a normative or value-based assessment of the options (Fischer 1995; Tong 1986). Policy analysis can never be reduced to a formula for solving public problems, but, ideally, it is performed in a way that informs and involves the public in the policy process, and thereby enhances the democratic process (Ingram and Smith 1993). A good example is the effort in hundreds of communities in the United States to take sustainable development seriously and to implement "smart growth" policies (Mazmanian and Kraft 1999; Portney 2003).

By now, it should be clear that the study of public policy and the conduct of policy analysis are rarely simple matters. Public problems are usually complex and multifaceted, and people are bound to disagree intensely over how serious they are, what might be done about them, and the role of government in relation to the private sector. Some problems, such as global climate change or the challenge of terrorism, are monumental. Some, such as how best to provide for a high quality public school system or limit urban sprawl, may be a bit easier to grasp. But none are simple. If they were, the course of action would be clear and not very controversial—removing snow and collecting trash, for example. Unfortunately, dealing with most problems is not so straightforward.

So what exactly does policy analysis do? One of its primary functions is to satisfy the need for pertinent information and thoughtful, impartial assessments in the policy process. The information may not be widely available, or citizens and policymakers may not be able to understand it sufficiently, particularly when decisions must be made quickly because of impending deadlines or when the issues are politically controversial. Under these conditions, policy analysis can clarify the issues, the available alternatives, and the effects of decisions that citizens and policymakers might choose to make. Essentially, policy analysis involves looking ahead to anticipate the consequences of decisions and thinking seriously and critically about them. It is an alternative to "shooting from the hip" or making snap decisions based on ideology, personal experience, or limited or biased analysis of what should be done.[4]

The solution to a public problem, particularly if it is controversial, is rarely achieved by relying solely on government agency officials, policy analysts, or other experts. The "best" solution will always be a matter of judgment and political choice because inevitably questions arise about the likely effectiveness of the policies chosen, their costs, who gains and who loses as a result, or whether the action can be justified on ethical or moral grounds (Stone 2002; Tong 1986). As one student of public policy put it, policy analysis is an intellectual activity that takes place within a political setting. Its character and impact reflect that reality (Dunn 1994).

*"Are you just pissing and moaning, or can you verify what you're saying with data?"*

© 1999 *The New Yorker Collection,* Edward Koren from cartoonbank.com. All Rights Reserved.

People discuss government and public policy issues in many different settings: at home, in school, at work, and in bars and restaurants. In many cases the commentary is informal and can tend toward simplistic statements about, for instance, government proposals for some kind of policy change, from reducing crime rates to providing better health care services. In short, collectively, citizens often air their views about government, politics, and public policy—indeed, they hold strong opinions about what should be done about various problems—but they may not think systematically about why the problems exist in the first place or what kind of policy action is most appropriate. Policy analysts hope to raise the level of such discussions, even if it remains unlikely that bar conversations will be anchored in data analysis.

The politics are readily apparent in policy areas such as abortion rights, rights to privacy, or the use of public funds to support private school education; these issues touch on basic questions of values. But the political nature of policymaking is also evident in setting national or state health care priorities, regulating toxic chemicals, deciding whether to support alternative energy sources, reforming the welfare system, and almost every other major public policy decision. These kinds of policy choices reflect a combination of political preferences and an impartial assessment of the problem and possible solutions. In this context, policy analysis can pinpoint the nature of the problem, the policy choices available, and how each choice stands up against the different standards of judgment that might be used.

Think of it this way. Solving public problems must go beyond the all too human tendency to complain about a situation and express uninformed opinions. Rather, citizens, especially students of public policy, need to think seriously about why the problem exists, what might be done about it, and what kind of action makes the most sense. Armed with reliable information and the possible solutions, citizens should then try to determine which solutions are the most promising. The results will probably rest on more solid ground and be more persuasive to those with different political views than would otherwise be the case.

## TYPES OF POLICY ANALYSIS

No matter what kind of public problem needs a solution, from airline safety to urban air pollution, there is usually no shortage of policy studies that might apply. The abundance of policy studies reflects not only the dramatic rise in the number of think tanks since the 1970s but also the even more striking increase in the number of interest groups that seek to shape public opinion on the issues and affect the policy process. This shift in the political environment is most evident at the national level where policy researchers and interest groups pay rapt attention to the debates in Congress and the activities of administrative agencies. Policymakers at this level of government are the target of thousands of studies released each year. Even at state and local levels of government, particularly in the larger states and cities, policy studies and advocacy are common.

Prominent think tanks, interest groups, and policy-oriented law firms and consulting companies tend to establish their offices in Washington, D.C., or in state capitals, but organized interest groups are found all over the United States. Whether they are environmental activists, corporate trade associations, professional organizations, or unions, they all have a stake in policy decisions made by government, and most set up a public or governmental affairs office to monitor pending legislation or agency actions.

Scholars have noted the rise and influence of think tanks. Carol Weiss's study of these organizations attributes their dramatic growth and popularity to several trends and needs. First, government policymakers and the public need to understand and cope with complex problems. Second, policymakers find it useful in a time of political cynicism to demonstrate the reasonableness and rationality of their positions and actions, and policy analysis symbolizes an acceptable, or proper, procedure. Third, policy officials value independent research and analysis as supplements to the knowledge and skills within government and see the analyses as helping to persuade skeptical politicians and citizens. Fourth, certain interests believed they were underrepresented in government circles and sought to make their views known and promote their causes (Weiss 1992).

Whatever the reason for their rise, policy analysis organizations continue to thrive in the United States because of the character of government institutions and the political process. Fragmentation of government authority creates many opportunities for both interest group lobbying and policy analysis conducted outside of government. As political parties have weakened, interest group and think tank activity has strengthened. Forced to deal with intricate and interlinked problems, policymakers continually search for pertinent expertise, and the studies by think tanks and interest groups are often as influential as the analysis conducted within government agencies.

The leading think tanks, such as the Brookings Institution, the American Enterprise Institute, the Urban Institute, the Center for Strategic and International Studies, and the Heritage Foundation, are well endowed financially and can afford large professional staffs. Many of them

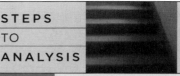

**STEPS TO ANALYSIS**

## THINK TANK POSITIONS ON POLICY ISSUES

All think tanks conduct analysis and advocate positions on public policy issues, but some of these groups are committed to political or ideological positions that affect their analyses and recommendations. Welfare reform is one issue that think tanks of varying political persuasions have studied. The federal welfare reform law, the Personal Responsibility and Work Opportunity Reconciliation Act of 1996, eliminated the Aid to Families with Dependent Children (AFDC) program and created a program called Temporary Aid for Needy Families (TANF). The new law had three primary goals: to reduce dependence on welfare and increase employment, to reduce poverty among children, and to strengthen marriages and reduce illegitimate births.

The various studies of welfare reform reached different conclusions about its success. But why? One reason is that the studies reflect the political slant of the think tanks. Another is that they sometimes addressed different questions. Are the welfare caseloads being reduced? Are the caseload reductions permanent? Are fewer people living in poverty? Are children better off as a result of welfare reform? The following summaries come from two think tanks that represent distinctive positions on the ideological spectrum: the conservative Heritage Foundation and the liberal Center on Budget and Policy Priorities. What conclusions can you draw about how these two policy research organizations evaluate welfare reform? What are the similarities and differences in their positions?

*(continues)*

receive significant and continuing support from foundations and industry or from government agencies for whom they conduct research under contract.[5] These research institutes are therefore generally well equipped to distribute their analyses throughout government, the Washington policy community, academia, and major media outlets nationwide (Ricci 1993; Weiss 1992). At the end of the chapter is a list of Web sites for think tanks and for other sources of policy studies. In the box "Steps to Analysis: Comparing Think Tank Positions on Policy Issues" is a comparison of the findings of two think tanks on welfare reform.

The large number of think tanks and active interest groups almost guarantees that the public and policymakers will suffer from information overload as they try to digest the surfeit of reports and studies available on any public policy topic. Hundreds of books and thousands of articles, papers, pamphlets, and seminar and workshop reports flood Washington and state capitals every year. Yet, as noted biologist E. O. Wilson (1998, 269) observed, we "are drowning in information, while starving for wisdom." The future, he said, will belong to those capable of synthesizing information to make it usable. They will be the people "able to put together the right information at the right time, think critically about it, and make important choices wisely." Another name for Wilson's synthesizers is policy analysts. Analysis, however, comes in a great many flavors, and policymakers and the public need to be able to differentiate the more worthy from the less worthy.

One way to do that is to understand the different kinds of policy studies or policy analyses available today, a matter addressed briefly in Chapter 1. As noted there, policy analyses fall into three broad categories: scientific, professional, and political. All serve valid purposes, but have

## THINK TANK POSITIONS ON POLICY ISSUES
### *(continued)*

STEPS TO ANALYSIS

### WHAT DOES THE HERITAGE FOUNDATION SAY ABOUT WELFARE REFORM?

- According to the Census Bureau, 3.5 million fewer people live in poverty today compared to 1995.
- Some 2.9 million fewer children live in poverty today than in 1995. The poverty rate for African American children has fallen to the lowest point in U.S. history.
- Hunger among children has been cut roughly in half according to the U.S. Department of Agriculture.
- Welfare caseloads have been cut in half and employment for the most disadvantaged single mothers has increased from 50 percent to 100 percent.
- The explosive growth of out-of-wedlock childbearing has come to a virtual halt.

Source: Robert Rector and Patrick F. Fagan, "The Continuing Good News about Welfare Reform," Heritage Foundation, February 6, 2003. Available at www.heritage.org/Research/Welfare/bg1620.cfm.

### WHAT DOES THE CENTER ON BUDGET AND POLICY PRIORITIES SAY ABOUT WELFARE REFORM?

- Overall, the number of single parents who now work has risen markedly.
- Those who work generally earn low wages and remain poor. The Center for Law and Social Policy found that former welfare recipients tended to earn between $6 and $8.50 per hour.
- Many families that left welfare do not receive Medicaid or Food Stamps even though they are eligible for these programs.
- Many people who left welfare did so not because they found a job, but because they were terminated from the program for failing to meet its requirements.
- Teen pregnancy and non-marital birth rates did fall in the 1990s, and the proportion of low-income children living in two-parent families rose. It is unclear how much, if at all, TANF policies affected these trends.

Source: Martha Coven, "An Introduction to TANF," Center on Budget and Policy Priorities, January 13, 2003. Available at www.cbpp.org/1-22-02tanf2.htm.

varying goals and objectives and use different methods. Table 4-1 provides a summary of the distinctions among the three perspectives, and offers illustrations of organizations associated with each approach. Students of public policy will find it useful to recognize their respective advantages and limitations.

For example, social science studies in the scientific category typically are not intended to influence public policy directly. Their purpose is, as one author put it, "to deepen, broaden, and extend the policy-maker's capacity for judgment—not to provide him with answers" (Millikin 1959, 167). In contrast, work that falls into the professional category, such as policy

| TABLE 4-1 | Orientations to Policy Analysis | | | |
|---|---|---|---|---|
| Type of Analysis | Objectives | Approaches | Limitations | Examples |
| Scientific | Search for "truth" and build theory about policy actions and effects | Use the scientific method to test hypotheses and theories; aim for objective and rigorous analysis; policy relevance less important than advancing knowledge | May be too theoretical and not adequately address information needs of decision makers | Academic social scientists and natural scientists, National Academy of Sciences, Intergovernmental Panel on Climate Change |
| Professional | Analyze policy alternatives for solving public problems | Synthesize research and theory to understand consequences of policy alternatives; evaluate current programs and their effects; aim for objectivity, but with goal of practical value in policy debate | Research and analysis may be too narrow due to time and resource constraints; may neglect fundamental causes of public problems | Brookings Institution, Urban Institute, American Enterprise Institute, General Accounting Office |
| Political | Advocate and support preferred policies | Use legal, economic, and political arguments consistent with value positions; level of objectivity and rigor varies; aim to influence policy debate to realize organizational goals and values | Often ideological or partisan and may not be credible; may lack analytic depth | Sierra Club, AFL-CIO, Chamber of Commerce, National Rifle Association, Heritage Foundation, CATO Institute |

Source: Drawn in part from Peter House, *The Art of Public Policy Analysis* (Beverly Hills, Calif.: Sage Publications, 1982); and David L. Weimer and Aidan R. Vining, *Policy Analysis: Concepts and Practice*, 3d ed. (Upper Saddle River, N.J.: Prentice Hall, 1999).

analysis from think tanks, is nearly always directed at policymakers with the clear intention of providing some answers to policy questions. Indeed, definitions of policy analysis refer explicitly to the practical purpose of helping policymakers and the public make decisions.

As Table 4-1 indicates, some think tanks should be placed in the political category because they have explicit ideological missions. For example, the Heritage Foundation Web site indicates that its purpose is to "formulate and promote conservative public policies based on the principles of free enterprise, limited government, individual freedom, traditional American values, and a strong national defense." It also calls itself a "research and educational institute—a think tank," but its mission statement makes clear that it is hardly neutral on political values.

Much the same can be said for the Cato Institute and the Competitive Enterprise Institute (CEI) and parallel think tanks on the left side of the political spectrum. The CEI Web page is more explicit than Heritage about its mission. The description says the organization "is not a traditional 'think tank." It is "not enough to simply identify and articulate solutions to public policy problems," the statement says. It is "also necessary to defend and promote those solutions. For that reason, we are actively engaged in many phases of the public policy debate." The box "Working with Sources: Comparing Think Tanks" describes the work of two prominent organizations, one conservative and one liberal.

## WHAT KIND OF ANALYSIS IS NEEDED?

No matter what policy area is involved, there is never a single correct way to conduct a policy study or one set of methods or tools to use. The next two chapters have more to say about appropriate methods and tools, but here it is worth emphasizing that, regardless of whether the policy research falls into the scientific, professional, or political category, analysts face important choices about the kind of assessment needed for a given study and what approaches to use.

### Root Causes or Pragmatic Adjustments?

One of the basic questions that all analysts must answer is whether they should focus on the **root causes** of public problems or examine policy actions that might ameliorate a pressing problem but do nothing about its underlying causes. Political scientist James Q. Wilson argued for the latter view in his influential book *Thinking about Crime* (1977, 55–59). The "ultimate causes cannot be the object of policy efforts," he said, because they cannot be changed. As he explained, criminologists, for example, know that men commit more crimes than women, and younger men more than older ones. It is a scientifically correct observation, Wilson said, but not very useful for policymakers concerned about reducing the crime rate. Why not? The answer is that society can do nothing to change the facts. So rather than address the root causes of crime, he suggested that policymakers concentrate on what governments can do to reduce the crime rate, or deal with what some call the **proximate causes**, or immediate causes, of the problem: "What is the condition one wants to bring into being, what measures do we have that will tells us when that condition exists, and what policy tools does a government (in our case, a democratic and libertarian government) possess that might, when applied, produce at reasonable cost a desired alteration in the present condition or progress toward the desired condition?" (59).

In contrast, the distinguished scholar Charles Lindblom (1972, 1) wrote that the kind of policy analysis illustrated by Wilson's statement can become a "conservative and superficial kind of social science" that fails to ask fundamental questions about the social and economic structures of society. It considers, according to Lindblom, "only those ways of dealing with policy that are close cousins of existing practices," and therefore reinforces a prevailing tendency to maintain current policies and practices even when they may be unsuccessful in

## WORKING WITH SOURCES

### COMPARING THINK TANKS

Policy research institutes, or think tanks, differ in many ways. Some are large and cover many policy issues, while others are small and highly specialized. Some aim for professional analysis of the issues, and others promote a policy or ideological agenda. Here, we highlight two prominent Washington think tanks that are well regarded for their analyses of policy issues. They also reflect different political philosophies: the Brookings Institution is usually characterized as slightly left of center, and the American Enterprise Institute as right of center.

### THE BROOKINGS INSTITUTION

Web site: www.brook.edu (contains about 25,000 separate items)

Founded: 1922

Orientation and mission: "committed to independent, factual and nonpartisan" research, analysis, education, and publication focusing on economics, foreign policy, and governance. "Brookings has dedicated itself to improving the equity of the American democratic process, the performance of the economy, the health of society, the effectiveness of diplomacy and defense, the quality of public discourse, and the workings of institutions." It emphasizes the use of "rigorous, innovative, clearly presented analysis" by scholars of diverse perspectives who try to identify realistic, constructive solutions. Says that "the remedies our scholars propose are rooted in open-minded inquiry, not in dogma or doctrine," and are written in language aimed at the general public.

Topics covered:

*Business and economics:* globalization, competition, international trade, fiscal and budget policy, health care financing, regulation, social security, tax policy, macroeconomic policy, labor, income distribution.

*Education:* quality and finance, research, elementary and secondary education, higher education, testing and assessment, school choice, urban and inner-city schools.

### AMERICAN ENTERPRISE INSTITUTE FOR PUBLIC POLICY RESEARCH

Web site: www.aei.org (large collection of studies and reports)

Founded: 1943

Orientation and mission: "dedicated to preserving and strengthening the foundations of freedom—limited government, private enterprise, vital cultural and political institutions, and a strong foreign policy and national defense—through scholarly research, open debate, and publications." Described as an independent organization that is "strictly nonpartisan and takes no institutional positions on pending legislation or other policy questions." AEI scholars, however, "testify frequently before congressional committees, provide expert consultation to all branches of government, and are cited and reprinted in the national media more often than those of any other think tank."

Topics covered:

*Economic policy studies:* U.S. and world economy (national budget, tax reform, monetary policy), health care, tax reform, social security reform (issues presented by the aging of the U.S. population, the adequacy of household savings, financial problems of the Social Security system, and major reform proposals), regulatory studies (proposals for improving regulatory policy through the use of cost-benefit analysis and private-market alternatives to government "command and control," the economic consequences

*(continues)*

*(continues)*

## WORKING WITH SOURCES

### COMPARING THINK TANKS *(continued)*

### THE BROOKINGS INSTITUTION *(continued)*

*Defense:* budget, strategy, weapons, military force and organization, homeland security, military technology, defense industry.

*Cities and suburbs:* poverty and welfare, transportation, housing, jobs, demographics, metropolitan growth, community development, public services.

*Social policy:* affirmative action, children and families, civil society, crime and law enforcement, health policy, immigration, poverty and inequality, religion, social norms and values.

*Science and technology:* energy, environment, medical research, arms control, military technology, telecommunications, information technology.

*Governance:* Congress, executive, judiciary, federalism, separation of powers, comparative politics, campaign finance.

*U.S. politics:* legislative politics, elections, parties, media and politics, term limits.

*Global politics:* terrorism, international organizations, European Union, area and country studies, human rights, weapons of mass destruction.

Sources of funding: Financed largely by an endowment and through support of philanthropic foundations, corporations, and private individuals. Also undertakes unclassified government contract studies.

### AMERICAN ENTERPRISE INSTITUTE FOR PUBLIC POLICY RESEARCH *(continued)*

of regulatory programs), environmental studies (designing environmental policies that seek to protect nature but also are compatible with democratic institutions and human liberty), financial markets, international trade and finance, telecommunications and information technology.

*Social and political studies:* American politics and political institutions, federalism, liability reform, constitutional studies, government programs and policy evaluations, social welfare, demography and immigration, culture and society, intellectual foundations and education (school financing and parental choice, the No Child Left Behind Act, curriculum and textbook-adoption standards, teacher education and certification, unionization, and the achievement gaps between white and minority students).

*Foreign and defense policy studies:* U.S. foreign policy, defense (emphasizing a strong and well-funded military, a streamlined force structure armed with cutting-edge technology, and robust intelligence policies), Middle East studies, new Atlantic initiative, Asian studies, other area studies, global governance and national sovereignty.

Sources of funding: Supported primarily by grants and contributions from foundations, corporations, and individuals.

addressing the problem. Analysts who favor Lindblom's perspective would examine the fundamental or root causes as well as the proximate causes of public problems; these analysts would not dismiss as fruitless idealism the possibility of taking action on the root causes of problems in some circumstances.

Even an incremental adjustment in policy, however, can make a big difference. Consider the imposition of a national minimum drinking age of twenty-one. In 1984 the federal government decided to deny a percentage of federal highway funds to states that refused to comply with this requirement. An assessment of the policy's results in Wisconsin showed that it had "immediate and conclusive effects on the number of teenagers involved in alcohol-related crashes." Accident rates declined by 26 percent for eighteen-year-olds and 19 percent for nineteen- and twenty-year-olds (Figlio 1995, 563).

## Comprehensive Analysis or Policy Relevance?

Should analysts use the most comprehensive and rigorous approaches available to ensure the credibility of their results, even though doing so may take longer and cost more? Or should they aim for a less comprehensive and less rigorous study that might provide pertinent results faster and cheaper, even at some risk of the credibility of the results? The answer depends on the nature of the problem under consideration. The most complex, controversial, and costly policy choices might require the most comprehensive analysis, while more limited studies might suffice in other situations.

Academic scientists (social and natural) tend to favor rigorous, comprehensive studies. They place a high value on methodological precision because they believe that only demanding scientific investigations produce knowledge that inspires confidence. Sometimes, however, a study can take so long to complete that it has less impact on policy decisions than it might have had if the results were known earlier. For example, the federal government sponsored a decade-long study of the causes and consequences of acid rain, at a cost of $500 million. It was widely viewed as first-rate scientific research, but also faulted for failing to address some critical topics in time to influence the major decision makers. By most accounts, the study had less impact than it should have had on adoption of the Clean Air Act Amendments of 1990, the first national effort to deal seriously with acid rain (Russell 1993). Chapter 10 discusses another example—the exhaustive studies carried out in selected cities of the impact of school voucher programs. Because of the different assumptions and methodologies, the studies offer conflicting conclusions. That complication aside, communities with problem school systems can use the studies to take action, even though the studies are still under way and some questions are unanswered.

Professional policy analysts are often distinguished from social science researchers in part because of the analysts' interest in applied policy research. The professionals are far more likely to aim their research at policymakers and other policy actors. Indeed, their studies often come with an "executive summary" that is designed to permit busy decision makers to quickly see the gist of the study's findings. The executive summary is typical of think tank studies and the more comprehensive studies and reports from special commissions or government agencies, such as the Environmental Protection Agency and the General Accounting Office.

Analysts associated with advocacy organizations in the "political" category shown in Table 4-1 are the most likely to emphasize short-term policy relevance. They also typically bring a strong commitment to the values embodied in the organization. It is not surprising that the studies by the Natural Resources Defense Council or the Sierra Club are unabashedly pro-environment, while those done by the National Rifle Association or the Nuclear Energy Institute support gun ownership and nuclear power, respectively. Such policy advocacy does not necessarily mean that the studies are invalid. Many are just as well done and valuable as those released by ostensibly more objective research institutes. Nevertheless, reports from advocacy organizations warrant a more critical reading because of possible bias.

## Consensual or Contentious Analysis?

Should analysts adhere closely to **consensual norms**, mainstream public values, or should they challenge them and propose new values or new ways of thinking about the problem under consideration? Political theorist Martin Rein (1976) argued for a **value critical approach** to policy research, urging analysts to be skeptical and distrust orthodoxy. He advocated approaches to policy study that made the analyst a "moral critic" who questions the value and belief assumptions behind policy research. He suggested three ways to engage in such research, with increasing degrees of critical inquiry: using consensual or mainstream approaches, using contentious or value critical approaches, and, the most radical, using **paradigm challenging approaches**. Most contemporary policy analyses fall into the first category, a much smaller number into the second, and a negligible number into the third. Yet one could argue that many public policies today are very much in need of bold new thinking and radical challenges, much as Rein suggested in the mid-1970s.

Most analyses are consistent with mainstream values because they are likely to be more socially and politically acceptable than radical studies. Indeed, because many government agencies, and outside groups under contract to an agency, conduct the analyses, the "client," who has specific and concrete expectations, may limit the scope of any inquiry. Academic studies, with analysts hired by a university or an independent research institute, are less likely to be constrained by short-term bureaucratic or corporate needs. The same can be said for studies by policy institutes or interest groups that fall toward the left and right ends of the political spectrum. These groups often favor actions that embody more radical changes in policy and public values. For example, the conservative Heritage Foundation was instrumental in shaping the policy agenda of Ronald Reagan's presidency, which broke with mainstream approaches in many areas such as environmental protection. Throughout the 1990s the libertarian Cato Institute released dozens of studies that supported its belief in individual rights and limited government.

## Rational Analysis or Democratic Politics?

Policy analysts are trained to engage in the rational assessment of public problems and their solutions, and they often use economic analysis and other quantitative methods to find the most logical, efficient, and, they hope, effective ways to deal with public problems. But should analysts also try to foster **democratic political processes**, such as citizen involvement (deLeon 1997; Gormley 1987; Jenkins-Smith 1990)? As noted, some advocates of policy analysis believe that public problems and policy choices are so complex that technical scientific analysis is essential to reach a defensible decision. These views sometimes conflict with the expectation that the public and elected officials are ultimately responsible for choosing the policy direction for the nation. In short, as citizens, we value rigorous analysis, but we also expect democracy to prevail.

Consider the case of nuclear waste disposal in terms of democratic ideals. Federal government analysts and most of those working for the nuclear industry and technical consulting companies focused on risk assessment, a form of policy analysis dealing with threats to health and the environment. Nearly all of the studies concluded that the risks from the radioactive waste are minor and manageable, even over the ten thousand years that the proposed repository at Yucca Mountain, Nevada, is to contain the waste without significant leakage. Critics of the government's position, however, including the state of Nevada and many environmental groups, countered that the scientific questions are far from settled and that the public's concerns about nuclear waste have not been satisfactorily addressed. They called for a decision-making process that allowed for greater citizen involvement and consultation, no matter how long it would take to build public trust (Dunlap, Kraft, and Rosa 1993; Wald 2002).

How can this kind of tension between analysis and democracy be resolved? The management of nuclear waste is by definition a serious issue: the United States produces it and must find a safe way to store it for thousands of years. That objective points strongly to the need for the best kinds of policy analysis before making a final decision. At the same time, these decisions affect millions of people, not only in Nevada, but all those who live along the transportation corridors across the nation. Tens of thousands of shipments of waste containers will have to cross the nation on highways and by rail, and the process will take several decades to complete. Critics charge that the Department of Energy has not given the transportation risks sufficient scrutiny to assure public safety. Environmentalists and other activists have mounted a campaign to protest those shipments should Yucca Mountain eventually receive full federal approval as a waste site. In light of the events of September 11, 2001, the possibility of terrorist attacks on the waste shipments raised a new concern. Given what is now an inevitable period of criticism and heightened public fear of waste shipments, would a decision-making process that was more open and democratic from the beginning have served the nation better?

## Other Aspects of Policy Analysis

The differences among the fundamental types of policy research is evident in the great variety of academic journals and other professional outlets, many of which are available on the Internet. Some publications, for example, the *Journal of Policy Analysis and Management,* emphasize the economic aspects of public policy, while others, such as the *Policy Studies Journal,* stress institutional and political factors. A few journals, such as *Philosophy and Public Affairs,* examine the ethical aspects of public policy, and nearly every law journal discusses the legal considerations of public policy. Public policy students are urged to browse the Web sites and to look at the journals in their campus libraries to see what information is available on different topics. Most think tanks and advocacy organizations publish their studies or summaries of them on the Internet as well as in journals, books, and reports.

The primary focus of this text is substantive policy analysis, which aims at answering real life questions, such as what are the effects of school voucher programs on the quality of education? Are market incentives more efficient at reducing air pollution than conventional regulation? But a great deal of work in the public policy field is descriptive and produces policy studies that explain a government agency's role in the policy process. For example, how does Congress make decisions on defense procurement? How does the White House influence agency regulatory decision making?

The perspectives and approaches of policy analysis apply to **institutional issues** as well as to substantive policy questions (Gormley 1987). This kind of analysis is especially helpful for examining proposals for institutional change. For example, institutional policy analysis might address a question such as what consequences could result if environmental protection policy was decentralized to the states? Or, in light of controversies over the 2000 presidential election, what kinds of ballots are most likely to minimize voter error and to be counted accurately?

**Ethical issues** in the conduct and use of policy studies deal with honesty and scruples. For example, what ethical obligations do analysts have to design and conduct their studies in a certain manner? To what extent are they influenced by the source of funding, particularly when the funds come from interest groups with a stake in the outcome, such as the tobacco companies that want to learn about the impact of antismoking initiatives? Does the analyst work primarily for the client who pays for the study, or does the analyst have a duty to represent the larger public interest? At a minimum, most analysts would agree that they are obliged to be open and transparent about their values and policy preferences, funding sources, the methods that are used, the data collected, and any critical assumptions made in the analysis of the data and the conclusions reached (Bowman and Elliston 1988; Tong 1986). Chapter 6 goes further into the criteria, including ethics, that can be used to evaluate policy alternatives.

## STEPS IN THE POLICY ANALYSIS PROCESS

The most common approach to policy analysis is to picture it as a series of analytical steps or stages, which are the elements in rational problem solving (Bardach, 2000; MacRae and Whittington 1997; Patton and Sawicki 1993; Starling 1988). According to models of **rational decision making,** one defines a problem, indicates the goals and objectives to be sought, considers a range of alternative solutions, evaluates each of the alternatives to clarify their consequences, and then recommends or chooses the alternative with the greatest potential for solving the problem. This process is similar to the way most people make everyday decisions, although they do it much more casually.

Often, the full-blown **rational-comprehensive approach** to analysis and decision making is not possible and the less demanding **incremental decision making** is substituted. Still,

| TABLE 4-2 | Steps in the Policy Analysis Process | |
|---|---|---|

| Steps | Type of Questions | Illustrations |
|---|---|---|
| Define and analyze the problem | What is the problem faced? Where does it exist? Who or what is affected? How did it develop? What are the major causes? How might the causes be affected by policy action? | How is cell phone use related to auto acidents? What is the potential to reduce accident rates through policy action? How does cell phone use compare to other distractions while driving? |
| Construct policy alternatives[a] | What policy options might be considered for dealing with the problem? | To reduce drivers' cell phone use, should state governments institute fines? Should states try to educate drivers on cell phone use? Is it technologically feasible to disable cell phones in a moving car? |
| Develop evaluative criteria | What criteria are most suitable for the problem and the alternatives? What are the costs of action? What is the likely effectiveness? Social and political feasibility? Equity? | What criteria are most important for regulation of cell phones? What options might be most effective in discouraging drivers from using phones? Will people find these options acceptable? Is it ethical to restrict individual behavior to achieve a social goal? |
| Assess the alternatives | Which alternatives are better than others? What kind of analysis might help to distinguish better and worse policy alternatives? Is the evidence available? If not, how can it be produced? | Are fines or education more likely to reduce drivers' cell phone use? How successful are the efforts of states and localities to regulate cell phone use? What evidence is needed to answer these questions? |
| Draw conclusions | Which policy option is the most desirable given the circumstances and the evaluative criteria? What other factors should be considered? | Should state governments impose stiff fines? Would fines be accepted as a legitimate action? How might the action be made more acceptable? |

[a]Most models of the policy analysis process place the task of developing policy alternatives after the stage of identifying evaluative criteria. See Carl V. Patton and David S. Sawicki, *Basic Methods of Policy Analysis and Planning*, 2d ed. (Englewood Cliffs, N.J.: Prentice Hall, 1993). The precise order may not matter because the two stages tend to occur together anyway, but we think most analysts would think about policy alternatives first and then about the criteria to use in judging their merits. Studies of the policymaking process, such as John Kingdon's book, *Agendas, Alternatives, and Public Policies*, 2d ed. (New York: HarperCollins College, 1995), suggest that alternative policies are discussed in various policy communities and then judged according to various criteria to determine their acceptability and which are likely to make it to a short list of ideas to be taken seriously.

essentially the same steps are involved. The only difference is that incremental decision making is more limited than the rational-comprehensive approach in the extent of analysis required. In political settings incremental decision making is a more realistic approach, given ideological and partisan constraints and the ever-present pressure from interest groups and other constituencies. All can restrict the range of policy options to be taken seriously (Anderson 2003; Lindblom and Woodhouse 1993).

Table 4-2 summarizes the major steps in policy analysis and the kinds of questions analysts pose. It also illustrates how each stage of analysis might apply to a particular policy problem. Each step is considered briefly here as a summary description of what policy analysis aspires to do. Chapters 5 and 6 examine each of these steps in greater detail.

## Define and Analyze the Problem

The first step in any kind of policy analysis is to define the problem. Everyone knows what the word *problem* means, but for policy analysts the term specifically refers to the existence of an unsatisfactory set of conditions for which relief is sought, either through private means or from government. Analysts therefore need to describe that set of conditions, usually through the collection of pertinent facts or data on its magnitude or extent. For example, who is affected by it and how seriously? How long has the situation existed and how might it change over the next several years or decades? How amenable is it to intervention through one means or another? The goals and objectives of such intervention, whether private or governmental, may not be clear to all concerned.

It may also be necessary to clarify what is meant by the set of conditions, to define it clearly, and to develop accurate measures of it. If the problem is homelessness in the United States, for example, an analyst would need to be clear about what is meant by homelessness, how to determine the extent of it, and who is affected by it. A great deal of information has been gathered on this problem: in 1999 federal officials estimated that nearly two million people within U.S. borders were homeless. About 40 percent of the homeless were African American, nearly four times their percentage in the population. Some 23 percent were veterans; 57 percent had suffered from mental illness at some point in their lives; 62 percent had problems with alcohol; and 58 percent with drugs.[6] For most public problems, analysts will want to develop quantitative measures of this kind. Many are readily available in government reports and other sources.

Beyond gathering basic information about the problem, analysts want to identify its causes, which is not always an easy task. Without a good idea of how and why the problem came about, however, it is difficult to think usefully about possible solutions to it. This kind of diagnosis of the problem is akin to what a physician does when a patient is ill or what a mechanic does when a car is not running properly. The importance of the diagnosis is clear if one looks at how policymakers are trying to cope with an issue as large as global terrorism. Without an understanding of the causes of terrorism—and they may be too numerous to deal with—policy actions are unlikely to be effective. To use a more concrete example, one has to first diagnose the reasons for failing public schools before a solution can be sought. Otherwise, there is little reason to believe that specific actions will improve the quality of schools.

A long-standing dispute over international development assistance illustrates the importance of careful measures and analysis of any public problem. Economic assistance to developing countries from twenty-two donor nations, including the United States, ran about $50 billion in 2002 or about 0.2 percent of the donor nations' combined gross national income. Although well below its level of 1990, this amount was nevertheless substantial. Donors believed that their assistance would spur **economic growth** in the receiving nations and save millions of lives through investment in health care services, education, and sanitation. But recent studies indicate that, despite $1 trillion in loans since the 1960s, the typical developing nation has shown no increase in per capita economic growth. The health and welfare of many people has actually worsened, due in large part to AIDS. How can that be? One answer appears to be that much of the aid was lost to corrupt and ineffective governments. So, now the question is: Should donor nations cease economic assistance because it has been misused? Some believe so, but just looking at the overall statistical portrait misses seeing the real success stories in economic assistance, which are abundant. One lesson would seem to be that economic aid is more likely to work when it comes in relatively small, well-targeted, and tightly controlled investments rather than in large sums delivered to a government that may waste it. One leading economist argues, for example, that a $25 billion investment in fighting malaria, tuberculosis, and other preventable diseases could save eight million lives a year in developing nations. The money would be spent on concrete measures such as vaccines, antibiotics, and AIDS prevention.[7]

As this example illustrates, analysts need to deal with the inevitable political disagreements that arise over how a problem is defined and measured and the consequences for society. Consider energy use and climate change and the argument over whether burning fossil fuels is the cause of global warming. Energy and automobile companies that resist changing their methods and products often put out studies that attempt to minimize the problem, for example, by emphasizing the scientific uncertainty on the climate change issue. They also lobby to ensure that scientists appointed to government study groups are sympathetic to their position. Environmental groups that favor action on climate change tend to release studies and reports saying that science has amassed enough information already and that not acting poses a dire risk for society. They also lobby to have scientists who support their position placed on groups such as the Intergovernmental Panel on Climate Change (Revkin 2002). As noted, it is sometimes difficult to distinguish a policy analyst from a lobbyist.

## Construct Policy Alternatives

Once analysts believe they know what the problem is, they begin to think about alternative ways of dealing with it. The policy typologies introduced in Chapter 3 suggest several different approaches, such as regulation, subsidies, taxing and spending, market incentives, and public education or information provision. The point is that government has a finite number of actions from which to choose. Based on the available inventory of possibilities, analysts could construct a set of policy options for further study and consideration, such as the relative advantages of regulation and market incentives for reducing the use of toxic chemicals. Chapter 5 introduces some useful ways to lay out a range of policy alternatives.

Constructing policy alternatives is perhaps the most important stage in the policy analysis process. If analysts and policymakers cannot think of creative ways of solving problems, conventional approaches that may no longer be appropriate will continue in use. Early in the process, therefore, analysts are called upon to think imaginatively and critically about how the problem might be addressed, both within government and outside it. One approach that has gained increasing acceptance is privatization, the transfer of public services from government to the private sector. Such private sector solutions, recommended by many policy analysts and organizations, and sometimes endorsed by government, are said to be more appealing, and perhaps more effective, than reliance on a government agency. Some communities have even turned over management of their public schools to private companies. Many people support a partial privatization of the Social Security system. Under this plan, workers would be allowed to manage a portion of their payroll taxes instead of having all of the money go into the general Social Security system where they have no control over the investment or rate of return. Neither idea was given much consideration a decade ago. These examples illustrate that the search for possible policy alternatives can produce new ideas that gain a measure of public acceptance. Chapter 5 also suggests some fruitful ways for students of public policy to think creatively about generating policy options.

## Choose the Evaluative Criteria

When the policy alternatives have been identified, the analysis shifts to assessing their potential. This task calls for deciding on suitable evaluation criteria. As Chapter 1 discussed, this text focuses on effectiveness or the likely success of proposals in solving the problem at hand, the economic costs and efficiency of proposals, and the implications for social equity. There are, however, other appropriate criteria, such as political feasibility, administrative feasibility, technical feasibility, environmental impacts, ethical considerations, and any number of political values, such as personal freedom, against which to assess policy proposals. They are further explored in Chapter 6 and summarized in Table 6-1.

No matter how long a list of potential evaluative criteria analysts might develop, some criteria will be more appropriate for a given problem than others. For example, for years the United States has been considering a missile defense system to protect against a missile attack. On what basis should analysts evaluate the proposal, particularly in relation to other national security issues? One criterion would have to be technical feasibility. Can the missile defense system, which is based on highly complex computer software and state-of-the art technology, do what it is supposed to do? What about the costs? The Pentagon spent more than $55 billion on the system between 1983 and 1999, and some $100 billion over four decades, with few positive results (Stevenson 1999). Moreover, the cost of a fully deployed system depends on how extensive a shield the government decides to construct. Estimates by the Congressional Budget Office in 2000 put the cost at between $30 and $60 billion through 2010, but the ultimate cost could easily be much higher (Dao 2001; Kitfield 2000). Indeed, some estimates put the total cost by the year 2025 at well over $200 billion. Is this outlay of money reasonable in light of the gains to the nation's defense and the risk that the technology might not work? How would an analyst go about determining the answer?

Plenty of information is available about the missile defense system, but a good deal of it is contradictory, and the analysts disagree heatedly about the core issues, such as technical feasibility. So any assessment of the desirability of creating and funding a system as technically complex as missile defense would be a demanding undertaking. Nevertheless, policymakers

The federal government's plan to store highly radio-active nuclear waste at Yucca Mountain, Nevada, has stirred strong public protests, particularly in Nevada. Deciding where to place such a waste repository rais-es important questions for citizens and policymakers. For example, how great is the risk to public health and the environment, both at the site of the facility and along the transportation corridors that will be used to send nuclear waste to Nevada? Is it fair to the citizens of Nevada to locate the repository at Yucca Mountain over their objections? Many argue that deci-sions about where to place such facilities should be made only after citizens are afforded abundant oppor-tunities to become informed and to participate in the process. Others believe such decisions should be left largely to technical experts and public officials. With either approach, policy analysis can help to inform deci-sion making by providing information about policy choices that are most acceptable to the public and also most likely to be effective, efficient, and fair.

and analysts need to ask the questions and try to find answers. Because multiple criteria for evaluat-ing such proposals exist (and for good reason), stu-dents of public policy need to be aware of them and be prepared to think about which criteria are best suited to making the correct choices for society.

For some policy actions, for example, whether and how to control gun ownership, the evaluative criteria would likely include political values. Person-al rights will be weighed against other needs, such as protecting the public's safety and well-being. As this example indicates, conflicts may arise between crite-ria. The war against terrorism that began after the September 11 attacks raises similar questions. On what basis should policy analysts, citizens, and poli-cymakers judge the suitability of policy options, such as military action against terrorist bases or eco-nomic development assistance to poor countries? Or the short-term national security implications of destroying terrorist operations versus the longer-term need to deal with the root causes of terrorism?

In some policy disputes, much of the battle between proponents and opponents of government action is over which criteria to use as well as which conclusions to draw. During 2001 and 2002, energy companies and environmentalists invoked numerous competing criteria to evaluate the proposal to drill for oil and natural gas in the Arctic National Wildlife Refuge. These included economic costs, national security, environmental protection, and technical feasibility. The two sides in this conflict also reached different conclusions as each of these criteria was considered. As this example shows, policy-makers, analysts, and lobbyists of one stripe or another bring their ideological biases to these debates. Those beliefs tend to frame their selection of evaluative criteria and therefore their assessment of the problem and the solutions they are willing to consider.

## Assess the Alternatives

With evaluative criteria at hand and a collection of possible courses of action to take, analysis turns to **assessing alternatives.** That is, the analysts ask which of the several alternatives that might be considered seriously is most likely to produce the outcome sought—whether it is to reduce the crime rate, improve the plight of the homeless, raise educational quality, or protect the environment. This exercise involves making judgments about how well each policy option fits in relation to the most relevant criteria. The analysts might rank the options in terms of overall desirability or consider the options in terms of each criterion, such as effectiveness, cost, and equity.

Some authors refer to this stage of the process as projecting the outcomes or assessing impacts (Patton and Sawicki 1993; Starling 1988). A number of different methods or tools are used to do this, and they are discussed fully in Chapter 6. They range from cost-benefit analysis to ethical analysis. Given their frequent use in policy studies and debates today, it is important even for the beginning student of public policy to understand these methods and their strengths and limitations.

Analysts have many ways to present the alternatives so that policymakers and other interested parties can understand the analysis and the choices they face. For example, if three policy options are offered for consideration, the analyst might present each in terms of its likely effectiveness, economic efficiency, and equity. Tradeoffs are inevitable in this kind of decision making. Only rarely does a given policy option rank highest on all of the evaluative criteria. It is far more likely that one option is judged to be most effective, but another cheaper or more equitable in its effects. Analysts, therefore, attach weight to each criterion. For example, is equity more important than efficiency in promoting cleanup of hazardous waste sites? Should governments clean up the most dangerous sites first or try to ameliorate the conditions at several sites at once? Or should the resources be directed to sites that have a disproportionate impact on poor and minority communities? Would doing so promote greater equity (Ringquist 2003)? As analysts consider more than a few conflicting bases for assessing policy options, the necessity for weighting criteria increases.

## Draw Conclusions

Most studies draw conclusions about what kind of policy action is desirable, and some strongly advocate a particular position on the issues. Many scientific and professional studies do not recommend a single policy action. Rather, the analysts summarize their findings and draw conclusions about the relative merits of competing policy proposals, but leave the choice of policy action to policymakers and the public.

Whichever approach is taken, one must bear in mind that all analysis is of necessity partial and limited. That is, analysis cannot ever be complete in the sense of covering every conceivable question that might be raised. It also cannot be free of limitations because every method or tool that might be used is subject to some constraints. Policy analysts need to develop a robust ability to deal with uncertainty, which comes with the territory.

The later chapters consider these challenges and how to deal with them. Students will become familiar with the range of methods used in the practice of public policy and how to use the different approaches and be better prepared to cope with the challenges. For example, the amount of information available might be so overwhelming that it seems impossible to find the desirable course of action, or so little information exists that no one can draw firm conclusions. Analysts may be faced with conflicting studies and interpretations that start with quite different definitions of the problem and evaluative criteria that render their conclusions and recommendations difficult to compare and judge.

At this stage, students are advised to learn to ask critical questions about the information they collect, especially regarding its validity. Where did the information come from, and how reliable is the source? Is there any way to double-check the facts and the interpretation of them? Does the information and analysis seem on its face to be believable? Are there any signs of bias that might affect the conclusions that the study offers? If two or more studies contradict one another, what are the reasons? Is it because of political ideologies, differences in the preferred policy actions, or differences in the way the problem is defined? Are the authors too selective in deciding what information should be presented and what can be left out? By gathering information from multiple sources and comparing different interpretations, students might find it easier to determine which of the studies is the most credible. Chapter 1 touched briefly on the need to develop these critical skills in appraising public policy information and studies, and the point is stressed throughout the book.

The best policy studies are those that are also sensitive to political reality. Their authors have made a special effort to understand the information needs of decision makers and the public, whether at the local, state, or national level. A common complaint within policy studies is that much analysis goes unread and unused either because it does not address the questions that decision makers think are important or because it is not communicated effectively to them so they can consider it. Analysis that is designed from the start to address these kinds of questions is far more likely to have an impact on the policy process (Lindblom and Cohen 1979; Weiss 1978).

## CONCLUSIONS

The example at the beginning of the chapter on drivers using their cell phones shows the challenge of making policy decisions when so many questions can be raised about the problem and the implications of taking action. Yet most students and practitioners of public policy are convinced that analysis can advance solutions by clarifying the problem, collecting information, and suggesting ways to make decisions. For that reason, this chapter surveyed the practice of policy analysis and showed how it relates to the policymaking process and to politics in general.

Today, analysis is ubiquitous, and it enters policy debate everywhere it occurs. Analysis is conducted in formal think tanks, interest groups, executive agencies, and legislative committees at all levels of government. Its thoroughness, objectivity, and purpose vary markedly, as might be expected. Students of public policy therefore need to be alert to the strengths and weaknesses of particular policy studies and prepared to question everything: the assumptions, the methods, and the conclusions. At the same time, however, students need to explore the many available sources of policy information and to think creatively about how to become engaged with contemporary policy problems.

## DISCUSSION QUESTIONS

To what extent can policy analysis be an objective activity rather than merely reflecting the biases of the analyst or the organization supporting a study? How would you go about determining which studies are valid and which are not?

Many students of public policy complain that policy analysis has not been very influential in the policymaking process. Why do you think that might be the case? What might be done to make analysis more useful to policymakers?

Should policy analysts try to deal with the fundamental causes of social problems such as crime or poverty, or aim for a more pragmatic and limited approach that may be more realistic and more politically acceptable?

How might policy analysis be conducted and disseminated in a way that enhances citizen capabilities for addressing policy controversies?

## SUGGESTED READINGS

James E. Anderson, *Public Policymaking,* 5th ed. (Boston: Houghton Mifflin, 2003). One of the best general treatments of the U.S. policymaking process.

Eugene Bardach, *A Practical Guide for Policy Analysis: The Eightfold Path to More Effective Problem Solving* (New York: Chatham House, 2000). A short but useful guide to the essentials of policy analysis, particularly for practitioners.

Carl V. Patton and David S. Sawicki, *Basic Methods of Policy Analysis and Planning,* 2d ed. (Englewood Cliffs, N.J.: Prentice Hall, 1993). One of the leading texts in policy analysis, with a focus on useful methods for basic or quick analysis.

Deborah Stone, *Policy Paradox: The Art of Political Decision Making,* rev. ed. (New York: W. W. Norton, 2002). An imaginative critique of conventional policymaking and policy analysis, with an emphasis on the role of politics and values in policymaking.

## SUGGESTED WEB SITES

**www.aei.org.** American Enterprise Institute.

**www.brook.edu.** Brookings Institution.

**www.cato.org.** Cato Institute, a libertarian think tank.

**www.cei.org.** Competitive Enterprise Institute, a conservative think tank and advocacy organization.

**www.heritage.org.** Heritage Foundation, a conservative think tank.

**www.hudson.org.** Hudson Institute, a conservative think tank.

**www.lib.umich.edu/govdocs/frames/psthinfr.html.** A comprehensive guide to think tanks and other political research centers.

**www.movingideas.org.** A guide to liberal think tanks and policy research.

**www.publicagenda.org.** Nonpartisan briefings on policy and polling; a digest of news, legislation, and studies; and research sources.

**www.public-policy.org.** Center for Public Policy, links to conservative policy organizations.

**www.rand.org.** RAND, Rand Corporation, the first organization to be called a think tank.

**www.rff.org.** Resources for the Future, a think tank specializing in economic analysis of environmental and natural resource issues.

**www.urban.org.** Urban Institute.


## LEADING GENERAL JOURNALS OF PUBLIC POLICY

*Journal of Policy Analysis and Management*
*Journal of Policy History*
*Journal of Public Policy*
*Policy Sciences*
*Policy Studies Journal*
*Review of Policy Research* (formerly *Policy Studies Review*)


## MAJOR PROFESSIONAL NEWS WEEKLIES WITH POLICY COVERAGE

*CQ Weekly*
*National Journal*


## KEYWORDS

assessing alternatives   120
consensual norms   113
democratic political processes   114
economic growth   118
ethical issues   115
incremental decision making   115
institutional issues   115

paradigm challenging approaches   113
proximate causes   109
rational-comprehensive approach   115
rational decision making   115
root causes   109
value critical approach   113

CHAPTER 5

# PUBLIC PROBLEMS AND POLICY ALTERNATIVES

TESTIMONY BEFORE CONGRESS IN 1997 AND 1998 ALLEGED THAT
Internal Revenue Service (IRS) agents had engaged in abusive behavior. The witnesses regaled
members of the oversight committees with horror stories about the unreasonable and harsh
actions the IRS took against ordinary taxpayers. Given widespread news coverage of the hearings, the conservative mood of Congress at the time, and the general dislike of the IRS, it was
not surprising that members of Congress lambasted the agency. After all, it was the politically
popular thing to do. Among other actions, Congress insisted that the IRS fire any agents who
were proven guilty of harassing citizens about tax collections.

Over the next two years taxpayers filed more than eight hundred complaints alleging the
IRS had harassed them. Upon investigation, however, neither the IRS nor its new congressional oversight body could substantiate any of these complaints. So was there in fact a problem of IRS harassment of taxpayers? If so, did Congress correctly diagnose the problem and
find a suitable solution? The evidence strongly suggests it did not. As one press account noted,
most of the original testimony was later determined to be false or misleading, or it was eventually disproved in court.[1]

It gets worse. Because of the allegations and the general unpopularity of the tax system,
during the 1990s Congress cut the agency's budget so deeply that it lacked sufficient staff to
enforce tax laws. Between 1995 and 2002 the auditing staff shrank by 29 percent, while the
number of tax returns rose by about 13 percent. The agency's enforcement data indicate that
it more or less gave up on trying to collect overdue payments from tax delinquent citizens. In
addition, the rate of tax return auditing plummeted by more than two-thirds from 1992 to
2000.[2] Some might think this was good news, but when people fail to pay their taxes, honest
taxpayers have to make up the difference. The only winners here are the tax cheats. Even from
a narrow economic perspective, the congressional action made little sense because the federal
government lost more money in revenue than it saved by cutting the agency's budget. In fact,
some estimates indicate that the government lost tens of billions of dollars a year in unpaid

Sometimes policymakers and analysts choose what are called "no-action"
options. Present policies and programs are maintained when, under different
circumstances, they might have been eliminated. Amtrak, the national rail system, is one example of the value of this approach. The system serves as an
alternative to highway and air travel—particularly in urban corridors such as
the one between Washington, D.C., and Boston where the sleek, high-speed
Acela trains are used. Despite its success in some service areas, however,
Amtrak has been unable to attract sufficient riders nationwide, and its federal
subsidy of about $500 million a year is only half of what it says it actually
needs to operate. Government reluctance to dissolve the railway in the face of
its poor financial return stems in part from the fear that should Amtrak be dis-
continued as a publicly supported rail system, it would be much more difficult
to reestablish in the future when environmental and economical factors may
make it a necessity.

taxes, which could have been recovered through fairly modest changes in the IRS budget and enforcement actions.[3]

Congress's IRS bashing illustrates some of the risks of ill-informed policymaking. Unfortunately, that kind of incident is not rare in American politics or, for that matter, in policymaking. When foolish decisions are made in any policy area, they serve as reminders of how difficult it is to adopt sensible policies that actually solve public problems. As was made clear in earlier chapters, policy analysis is no panacea for a political system vulnerable to short-sighted decision making, but it can, under the right conditions, help to counteract such tendencies and push the policy process toward more thoughtful and effective actions. This chapter focuses on two elements in policy analysis: how to define and analyze public problems and how to think about possible solutions. It also suggests some strategies for studying public problems and where to find useful information.

## PROBLEM ANALYSIS

The beginning of any policy study involves a description of a problem. Sometimes the problem, and perhaps even its causes, are obvious. For example, if the problem is teenage smoking and how to curtail it, one can find abundant information about the number of teenage smokers, why they choose to smoke, and the implications for lifelong smoking habits and the associated health problems. Some states, most notably California, have used that information to adopt educational programs aimed at prevention and other policies that have successfully reduced the rate of teenage smoking.

To consider another example, highway safety experts have known for some time that using seat belts greatly reduces deaths and injuries from traffic accidents. They also know that the extent of compliance depends on how stringently the states enforce the seat belt laws. In 2001 the national average for seat belt use in the United States was 71 percent, but the rate varied considerably from state to state. California, which strictly enforces its seat belt laws, had the highest rate of use, 90 percent. The rate was lowest in West Virginia, where fewer than half the drivers use seat belts. Compliance also varies by age. It is highest for children, presumably because every state requires that children use seat belts. It is lowest for young drivers. Based on this information, law enforcement agencies and highway safety councils concluded that one of the best ways to further reduce accident death rates was to make the seat belt laws tougher. The safety councils, in particular, believed that advertising campaigns, or persuasion, are ineffective policy strategies (Wald 2001). Nevertheless, in response to the low rate of seat belt use among young drivers, persuasion is still being tried, with advertisements designed to appeal to them, including the use of chat rooms on American Online and MTV.com.[4]

These examples show how simple some kinds of **problem analysis** can be. The problems are relatively straightforward, and the information needed to make a policy choice is at hand, thanks to national surveys that collect it. Evaluations of previous policy actions, such as the ineffectiveness of persuasion to achieve compliance, may also inform decision making. Although it is a rare public problem that is entirely without controversy, there are also many, such as the two examples here, about which reasonable people can agree on what actions to take and political ideology would not interfere. Such agreement is made easier when the facts about the problem are readily available and easily understood.

## The Nature of the Problem

Most public problems are not so simple nor the path to policy action so clear as trying to reduce smoking or increase seat belt use. Nevertheless, the first step in policymaking is the same whether the problem is straightforward or complicated: define and analyze the problem. Problem analysis involves trying to answer the basic questions about the nature of the problem, its extent or magnitude, how it came about, what its major causes are, and why it is important to deal with it as a matter of public policy. At heart, addressing these kinds of questions requires students of public policy to think critically and creatively about the problem. What does it entail? What is already known about it? What are the possible solutions? It also requires them to begin gathering the necessary information. The logic of information searches and useful strategies are discussed in this chapter.

DILBERT reprinted by permission of United Feature Syndicate, Inc.

Public problems are often difficult to understand. The challenge is even more daunting given that we are bombarded daily with limited, biased, and conflicting messages in numerous electronic and print formats. Whether the sources are journalists, interest groups, analysts, or policymakers, one of the most vexing issues is how to interpret information that comes to us without a meaningful context. The "contextual data," or background information, to which the cartoon refers is essential to make sense of a problem, to see how it compares to other concerns in our personal lives or in society, and to estimate what effects a proposal or action might have. One of the purposes of this text is to assist readers in building analytical skills so they are better able to understand policy information and learn how to ask pertinent questions.

***Definitions and Measures.*** An essential step in the policy process is to define the problem. The definitions enable those seeking a solution to communicate with one another with a degree of precision that otherwise might not be possible. For example, if analysts are studying the plight of the poor in the United States, they need to define what poverty means. Is being poor only a matter of having insufficient money or income, or does it include other characteristics, such as the lack of certain skills or abilities? Should poverty be defined in relative terms (richer or poorer than others) or in absolute terms (unable to meet essential human needs)? In 2002 the federal government placed the poverty line for a family of four at $18,100, and the number is important. It determines who is eligible for federal aid programs, including Head Start, food stamps, and children's health insurance, among others.[5] Real consequences for real people result from this particular definition. Analysts usually refer to this activity as clarifying the concept or seeing human needs clearly. Sometimes a quick literature search, discussed later in the chapter, will reveal both the usual definition of the concept and any debate that surrounds it.

Public policy arguments also turn on **operational measures** or **operational indicators** of problems. Rather than refer to poverty in the abstract, analysts want to know how many people live in poverty and their demographics. If discussing educational quality in the public schools, analysts want to see test scores and other student evaluations to determine if a problem exists in the schools and how one community's schools compare to another's. If the subject is violent crime, the analysts need statistics about the number of crimes committed nationally and in local communities, and whether the crime rate is increasing or decreasing.

Quantitative measures are abundant for most contemporary public problems (Miringoff and Miringoff 1999). How much statistical information needs to be provided is a matter of judgment, but, at a minimum, most issue papers or problem analyses would include some basic descriptive statistics. One descriptive type is the frequency count, such as the percentage of the population at different income levels or the number of people in a survey who respond one way or another. Another type is the mean (average) measure of a group or category, such as the average score on an examination. An alternative is the median of a variable, which is the point where one half of the group lies above and one half below. One example is the median price of homes sold in different regions of the nation. Some idea of the range of variation (the standard deviation) or the correlation or relationship between two variables, such as race and income, may be useful as well.

Statistical information can be displayed in many ways in a report. These include tables that show frequency counts or percentages of what is being studied, such as the percentage of different age groups in the population who smoke. Information can be superimposed on maps to show geographic variations such as rates of urban growth or the income levels for adjacent urban and suburban areas. Graphic figures—pie charts or bar charts—are common, as are line figures that show how the magnitude of a problem changes over time, such as the number of people without health care insurance from 1970 to 2000 (Ammons 2002; Berman 2002).

There is an art to choosing how best to display quantitative information. At a minimum, reports should aim for clarity. But some visual displays are also more likely to capture the reader's attention than others. The use of computer-generated color graphics allows a range of different formats, both in written form and in a PowerPoint or similar presentation. The best advice generally is to keep the audience and purpose clearly in mind when choosing the format of a report or presentation. The use of quantitative data also carries some risks. Analysts need to be alert to the possibility of inaccurate data in a report or an invalid measurement that does not truly capture the problem (Eberstadt 1995). For example, are the SAT or ACT scores of graduating seniors an appropriate gauge of school quality? Are they an accurate indicator of students' ability to do well academically in college? Critics have long charged that these so-called aptitude tests have built-in biases that significantly affect the results. They say that students who grow up in affluent homes with well-educated parents are likely to score higher than others because of personal experience rather than innate intelligence or academic abilities. Perhaps more important than SAT scores is that many other factors, such as personal ambition and hard work, affect performance and success in college, a fact that college admissions officers know well. In response to the criticism of the SAT test, it was modified in 2002.

Another example of a conventional indicator that has come under criticism is the gross domestic product (GDP), which measures the sum total of goods and services produced in the economy. Politicians use the GDP as an indicator of public well-being or the lack of it. They invariably applaud a rising GDP and vice versa, but many critics argue that the GDP is seriously flawed as a measurement. Environmentalists, for example, say it does not account for the use of natural resources. Cutting down old growth forests adds positively to the GDP because it is an economic activity, but the economists do not subtract the loss of irreplaceable old trees or for damage to forest ecosystems that depend on them. Some economists have proposed developing a new method called the GPI (genuine progress indicator) to substitute for the GDP and more accurately reflect human well-being (Cobb, Halsted, and Rowe 1995; see also www.rprogress.org). At least a few governments are beginning to think seriously about the use of this new and perhaps more accurate way to evaluate the economy.

Naturally, not all human concerns, such as happiness or the sense of well-being, can be reduced to quantitative measures. Analysts can, however, make use of surveys that ask people whether they are happy, enjoy living in their communities, believe the schools are doing a good job, and so forth. Where public problems cannot be measured directly, this kind of survey data may be a useful substitute. Economists also say that people can be asked to estimate the dollar value of many activities for which no market value exists. Their responses can help to calculate whether certain actions, such as preserving open space or planting trees, are justifiable uses of tax dollars.

An illustration of how to develop quantitative indicators is found in the effort of communities to become

Operating since 1986, Portland, Oregon's, light rail system has become a model for similar systems around the world. The system currently carries approximately eighty thousand riders daily over nearly forty miles of track; further expansions are under way. One of the few areas nationwide where public transit usage has grown faster than vehicle miles traveled, many Portlanders have cars but choose to use the light rail or bus instead. The light rail illustrates one creative solution communities are adopting to address serious problems such as traffic congestion and air pollution while enhancing residents' overall quality of life. As the photo indicates, such a system can be incorporated into a neighborhood much more organically than a multilane highway. Like Portland, many U.S. cities are turning to sustainable community initiatives in an effort to reduce the strains of population growth on local economies and ways of life.

## WORKING WITH SOURCES

## SUSTAINABLE DEVELOPMENT INDICATORS

Analysts and activists have developed a collection of indicators that allow a community, region, or nation to measure its progress toward sustainability. These indicators typically involve some common-sense measurements, such as the number of people and automobiles in the geographic area of concern, energy and water consumption, greenhouse gas emissions, and the like. Some not so obvious but useful social and economic indicators are the percentage of households that can afford to buy an average-priced house, high school graduation rates, and the extent of community involvement by citizens (Mazmanian and Kraft 1999). The availability of these kinds of statistics has allowed communities across the nation to convert the abstract concept of sustainable development into something that citizens and policymakers can easily understand. By developing quantitative measures, communities are able to compile a kind of sustainability status report and to track progress over time toward shared community goals. A number of Web sites compile sustainability statistics, as the following list indicates.

**www.sustainablemeasures.com.** Sustainable Measures. A database and perhaps the single most useful source for a description of sustainability indicators.

**www.sustainable.doe.gov.** Center for Excellence on Sustainable Development. A useful government site with multiple resources and links.

**www.moea.state.mn.us/sc/index.cfm.** State of Minnesota Sustainable Communities Program. Includes definitions and measures of sustainability and state policies through the Office of Environmental Assistance to encourage sustainable communities.

**www.rprogress.org.** Redefining Progress. An organization devoted to the use of new measurements of progress and environmental, social, and economic sustainability.

The best way to understand the kind of information collected at these sites is to visit one and look for particular indicators. For example, go to the Sustainable Measures site and select the link to Indicators of Sustainability to see a description of the qualities of indicators the site's analysts think are important. Read their description of a "sustainable community indicator check list" for a point-by-point review of what is important in selecting indicators to use for this purpose. For an example of a state's innovative approach to developing such indicators, see the Minnesota planning site. You can access it from the Sustainable Measures site list of "communities that are working on indicators" or directly at www.mnplan.state.mn.us/mm/index.html.

sustainable. Critics have derided the concept of sustainable development as a fuzzy if not meaningless term. Even so, communities around the country have adopted it as a goal, and many have selected quantitative indicators of sustainability to see whether they are making progress toward that goal over time (www.sustainablemeasures.com). The residents and policymakers are clear enough about what sustainability means—the integration of economic, social, and environmental goals—that they are able to engage the public and work cooperatively in thinking about the future of their communities (Mazmanian and Kraft 1999; Portney 2003). The box "Working with Sources: Sustainable Development Indicators" provides further information about sustainable communities and sources of information for various indicators of sustainability.

***The Politics of Problem Definition.*** Defining and measuring problems is not merely an exercise in analysis. People often disagree about a problem and what should be done about it. As Deborah Stone (2002, 133) says, there are "no fixed goals" in the policy process; instead, policy actors fight over "competing conceptions of abstract goals." Moreover, she says, "problem definition is never simply a matter of defining goals and measuring our distance from them. It is rather the strategic representation of situations." By this, she means a description of any given situation will vary, depending on a policy actor's perspective. The process becomes strategic, or political, because "groups, individuals, and government agencies deliberately and consciously fashion portrayals so as to promote their favored course of action."

One simple example of what Stone means concerns the irradiation of meat intended for human consumption, a process the federal government approved in 2000. The largest U.S. irradiator of ground beef lobbied members of Congress to define irradiated meat as "pasteurized." A farm state senator inserted the provision into a major agricultural bill at the last minute. Obviously, the meat processor believed that the word *pasteurized* would be more acceptable to the public than *irradiated*. At the time the legislative language was proposed, the U.S. Department of Agriculture and the Food and Drug Administration had yet to agree that meat that is irradiated would qualify as pasteurized (Becker 2002).

Similar political, or strategic, actions occur in nearly every major policy area. The Bush administration pressed Congress to adopt its energy policy proposal, heavy on energy production and light on conservation, by saying it was vital to national security, even though that argument was not used prior to the September 11, 2001, terrorist attacks. In one battle over that energy policy in 2002, the Big Three (DaimlerChrysler, Ford, and General Motors) auto-makers lobbied fiercely to defeat a proposal to raise auto fuel efficiency standards. They did so by redefining the issue in terms of the public's right to choose any vehicle desired, including SUVs, trucks, and vans, whose sales might be hurt by the proposal, rather than focus on what fuel economy gains could do to reduce the nation's dependence on imported oil (Rosenbaum 2002a).

The proponents of the nuclear waste repository at Yucca Mountain, Nevada, also argued that its approval had become more urgent than ever, given the vulnerability of nuclear waste to terrorist attacks. The waste has been stored near nuclear power plants around the nation, and it could continue to be stored there for decades to come. Opponents of the Yucca Mountain plan pointed to the even greater risk of terrorist attacks as the waste is moved by truck and rail across the country to Nevada. Each side in the dispute defined the problem its own way, and each cited studies to shore up its argument (Kriz 2001; Pianin 2002).

Some analysts might challenge Stone's view of the inherently political nature of problem analysis, but political scientists would probably agree with her. The evidence supports the observation that policymakers and interest groups will do whatever they can to set the policy agenda in their favor by defining problems their way. Political scientists have made thorough studies of such activities (Baumgartner and Jones 1993; Kingdon 1995; Rochefort and Cobb 1994). Still, most analysts would likely argue that resolution of a public problem—homelessness, crime, poor school quality, urban sprawl, energy needs, nuclear waste disposal—depends at least in part on the ability to clarify the nature of the problem, collect the most pertinent data, and foster a public debate over what might be done about it.

***Anticipating the Future.*** One other aspect of defining and measuring problems deserves mention. Any consideration of the present state of affairs must be grounded in an assessment of how it is likely to change over time. What will the problem look like in several years or decades? Forecasts, or projections, usually involve an extrapolation of current trends, but that is only one method for looking ahead.

Examples of forecasting include economic forecasting (will the nation have a surplus or deficit in five years?), population projections (how large will the U.S. population be by 2025 or 2050?), and energy needs (what kind, how much, and where?). Such projections are especially helpful if they reveal how that change will likely unfold with or without policy intervention. For example, if the nation adopted energy conservation measures, to what extent would that action reduce the otherwise increasing reliance on imported oil?

Such forecasting has become an integral part of the public debate over energy and environmental problems, the anticipated rise in Medicare and Social Security benefits as the baby boom generation ages, and economic policy, the assumptions made about government spending and taxation. As with other forms of policy analysis, it is always necessary to look at the assumptions that lie behind the forecasts to judge their validity. Circumstances also change, and a forecast made in one year may not be as useful in subsequent years.

## Thinking about Causes and Solutions

Any assessment of a public problem requires thinking about its **causes**, how it came about and why it continues. The answers make a big difference in whether and how public policy might resolve the problem. For example, if the question is why prison populations increased dramatically from 1970 to 2000, part of the answer is that states passed tougher sentencing laws and the public was willing to continue building prisons—often at the expense of funding for higher education. In many states, the growth in the prison population can be traced specifically to new laws that put even nonviolent drug offenders in jail and to the adoption of "three-strikes-and-you're-out" laws. These laws mandated long sentences, even life sentences, on conviction for a third felony offense, even for a relatively innocuous crime (Cannon 1998). In one case, a California shoplifter, who was charged with stealing $153 worth of videotapes, was sentenced to fifty years in prison because of his prior convictions. Many are questioning the wisdom of sentencing drug offenders to prison terms, both in terms of the justification for the harsh penalties and the costs of keeping them in prison. For example, Gov. Mike Huckabee of Arkansas captured the dilemma by noting that the long mandatory sentences were "good politics but bad public policy." He added that the system is locking up "people we are mad at but not afraid of."[6] Nearly half a million drug offenders were in prison in 2001, many on a first conviction for possession; the number represents a tenfold increase since 1980.[7]

How might this trend be reversed? One way is to change the laws that led to the growth of the prison population. In 2000, in California, where one in three prisoners in the state was incarcerated for a drug-related crime, the voters did just that. They approved a state referendum requiring that first- and second-time nonviolent drug offenders be put into treatment centers instead of prison, a move that is expected to reduce the prison population by about thirty-five thousand inmates a year (Nieves 2000).

As Chapter 4 discussed, most policy studies focus on what can be called proximate, or immediate, causes of public problems, such as the reasons for rising prison populations. The greater challenge is to deal with the root causes of problems. Taking policy action might be more difficult than it was in California because of long-standing public attitudes and habits that are resistant to change. Think about urban traffic congestion. Why does it exist? The obvious answer is that too many people are driving their cars on a limited number of roads at any given time. In addition, Americans are driving more miles per year—to work, to school, to shop, and for other purposes. Is the solution to build more highways? Or is it to think about ways to reduce the use of automobiles in urban areas where congestion is greatest? Some urban designers and environmentalists offer a more radical solution, at least for new communities. They suggest building cities with adequate mass transit and where people can live closer to where they work. Many states and communities are adopting "smart growth" policies with similar ambitions for managing anticipated growth over the next several decades.

Most public problems have multiple causes, and therefore people disagree over which is the most important and which ought to be the object of public policy. Liberals and conservatives may disagree about the causes of poor school performance, crime, environmental degradation, or anemic economic growth, and what might be done about them. The astute student of public policy learns how to deal with the politics and often overheated rhetoric that can sometimes cloud an objective review of the evidence.

Problem analysis can begin with making an explicit list of the goals and objectives of various policy actors and a determination of what might be done to reach them (Patton and Sawicki 1993). The objectives may include a specific measure of what is to be achieved, such as improving access to health care services or reducing the rate of teenage smoking. When analysts think of potential solutions to public problems, they try to identify the opportunities for policy intervention. They try to imagine how a change in public policy might affect the problem; for example, would raising the price of cigarettes reduce the rate of teenage smoking?

Finally, sometimes analysts want to describe the benefits and costs of trying to solve the problem. They look at how the consequences of policy action, positive or negative, are distributed across population subgroups, such as those in certain regions, occupations, or social groups—in other words, who gains and who loses if the problem is resolved. Politicians and other major policy actors are sometimes very clever about addressing these kinds of distributive concerns. They are almost always interested in knowing about them. They may speak about solving public problems as though the entire nation will benefit equally, but the reality is that some segments of the population are more likely than others to enjoy the benefits of acting on a problem, and some are more likely than others to pay the costs. So students of public policy would be wise to think about how to present such information in any studies they complete. The box "Steps to Analysis: Major Components of Problem Analysis" summarizes basic elements in problem analysis. The list can also be a guide to what questions might be addressed in preparing a problem analysis or issue paper.

## STEPS TO ANALYSIS

## MAJOR COMPONENTS OF PROBLEM ANALYSIS

**Define the problem.** If the problem is educational quality, what does that mean? In other words, what is the exact nature of the education problem under study? Has quality declined? Is it lower than many people believe it ought be? Is it lower in the United States than in other developed nations?

**Measure the problem.** Find a way to measure the problem that is consistent with the way it is defined. This step is sometimes called developing an operational definition. What kinds of quantitative indicators are available from reliable sources? What is the best measurement to use for educational quality? Student scores on standard examinations? Other measures of student learning? Indicators of the quality of a school's faculty?

**Determine the extent or magnitude of the problem.** Using indicators that are available, try to determine who is affected by the problem and by how much. Try to answer these kinds of questions: What groups in the population suffer from the problem being studied, how long have they been affected by it, and to what extent are they affected? For example, how does educational quality vary from one school district or state to another? From urban districts to suburban districts? From schools in less-affluent neighborhoods to those in more-affluent areas?

**Think about the problem's causes.** How did the problem come about, and why does it continue? What are the leading causes of the problem, and what other causes should be considered? Knowing the causes of a problem is critical to developing solutions to it. How has educational quality changed over the past several decades, and why?

**Set goals or objectives.** What should be done about the problem and why? Are certain goals and objectives of paramount importance, widely agreed upon, and economically or socially feasible? Over what period of time should the goals and objectives be sought? For educational quality, what goals or objectives are most appropriate? If quality is to be improved, how much progress should be expected for a given period of time?

**Determine what can be done.** What actions might work to solve the problem or to reach the specified goals and objectives? What policy efforts might be directed at the causes of the problem? What variables can be affected by such efforts? If the goal is improving educational quality to a certain extent, what needs to be done? Improving teacher quality? Reducing class sizes? Changing the curriculum?

Sources: Carl V. Patton and David S. Sawicki, *Basic Methods of Policy Analysis and Planning,* 2d ed. (Englewood Cliffs, N.J.: Prentice Hall, 1993). Patton and Sawicki devote a full chapter to steps in defining a problem. Other treatments of problem diagnosis can be found in Grover Starling's *Strategies for Policy Making* (Chicago: Dorsey Press, 1988).

## HOW TO FIND INFORMATION

To perform problem analysis and the other activities related to it, analysts need to collect reliable information. Indeed, good information is critical to successful analysis, but where to find it? This chapter provides some guidelines. The Web sites at the end of each chapter and those mentioned within the chapters are sources of extensive data on specific problems, as are articles in academic journals, books on the subject, and the better newspapers and professional news weeklies. Because the substantive policy chapters in the book provide many particular examples about using the data in policy studies and arguments, the information here is intended to be fairly general.

Most university libraries have a variety of Internet search tools available that can greatly simplify an information search. One of the best is Google (www.google.com), which can return many useful links for specific public policy inquiries. Online databases often contain full-text articles and can be searched by subject matter, titles, or authors. Card catalogs, generally online today, can be searched in the same way. Consider health care policy and the role of managed care organizations, which are addressed in Chapter 8. To identify articles or reports on public satisfaction or dissatisfaction with health maintenance organizations (HMOs), use Google or a similar search engine by typing in the keywords *HMOs, public, satisfaction,* and *complaints* to find a suitable list of studies and public opinion surveys. To vary the search, for example, to find material on whether patients believe it is difficult to obtain referrals to medical specialists, add or substitute keywords such as *cost, patients, referrals,* and *specialists.*

A good way to begin preparing issue papers and problem analyses is with an overview of a subject from sources such as the *New York Times,* the *Washington Post,* the *Wall Street Journal,* the *CQ Weekly,* or the *National Journal.* These and similar newspapers and news weeklies provide valuable information about current policy debates, particularly on a national level, and some background on the nature of the problem. For a broader historical perspective on public policy actions to address the problem, CQ's annual *Almanac* and its quadrennial volume *Congress and the Nation* are invaluable. Similar sources can be consulted for information at the state and local levels.

The main concern at this point of a search is to find enough information to understand the basics about a given policy problem. How much information is enough? If the initial search yields three or four high-quality articles that provide an idea of the history of the problem and policy efforts and recent controversies, and if they cover the different points of view about desirable policy actions, that may be enough to proceed. At this point, the researcher should be able to determine what else he or she needs to know to complete the assessment and then seek more detailed sources of information. An intense literature search could be profitable at this stage because the researcher knows what to look for and can focus on the best sources.

Most college and university libraries have access to online sources, such as LexisNexis, that include indexing and abstracting services. The most useful of these for public policy research are the congressional and statistical databases, or the separately published sources known as the Congressional Information Service (CIS) and the American Statistics Index (ASI). These two are exceptionally useful for public policy searches. The CIS includes an index to, and abstracts of, nearly all congressional documents, from testimony at committee hearings to committee reports on proposed policies. Those documents are excellent sources for the most current analyses of public problems and policy actions. For example, the records of testimony by policy experts at committee hearings may also offer excerpts from their latest research findings before they are available elsewhere. The ASI provides similar services for documents that include statistical data, but this database is by no means restricted to statistical analysis. Rather, it covers any description of a problem that includes numbers, such as population trends, crime rates, or the success of welfare reform. Many major university and college libraries are also government depository libraries and have many documents on paper if they are not available online.

Another way to locate pertinent information is to visit the Web site for the government agency most directly related to the issue. For example, the Department of Energy is the first place to look for nuclear waste controversies. For environmental issues, see the Environmental Protection Agency or the Department of the Interior, and for health and welfare issues, the Department of Health and Human Services. At the state and local levels, the same logic applies. Visit the Web sites of the local or state government agencies that deal with the subject matter. In addition, the Web sites for the major interest groups active in the policy area often have extensive reports and commentaries, as do the sites for policy think tanks. Many of those Web sites also incorporate search engines that allow you to quickly locate important documents. Comprehensive Web sites such as www.publicagenda.org and others listed at the end of Chapter 4 offer a portal to many of the most useful public policy sites.

Other indexing and abstracting services in addition to LexisNexis are also available to help locate articles, government reports, and other major documents. Which are most useful depends on the subject being studied. For most of these sites, users need to gain access through a library with a subscription to the service. Among the most helpful for public policy in general are the Public Affairs Information Service (PAIS), Academic Search Elite, Worldwide Political Science Abstracts, the Social Sciences Full Text, the Academic Universe online system (which covers state legislative activity), ProQuest Newspapers online (which covers local newspapers), the Index to Legal Periodicals, the Government Documents Catalog or the GPO Access for online services (www.access.gpo.gov), and the Library of Congress's Thomas Web site for legislative research (http://thomas.loc.gov). Most libraries have research guides that outline these services and discuss how best to use them.

If possible, students should arrange visits to government and other offices to obtain information and interview policy actors. At the local level especially, policymakers and other actors often welcome a visit by someone who is interested in what they are doing. Advance preparation is essential for this strategy. Students should know what information they are seeking and who is most likely to be able to provide it. Reading local newspaper coverage of the issue would be a good place to begin.[8]

Beyond conducting a search and locating the documents, one of the most challenging aspects of a literature review is the interpretation of the information gathered. As the text has emphasized throughout, policy analyses are of highly variable quality and are often prepared for use as ammunition in policy debates, with selective and sometimes misleading summaries and commentaries. Just because a statement appears in print or on the Web is no guarantee that it is true. It is always essential to find out the source of the information, the reliability of the author or organization, any critical assumptions that are made in a study or report (such as what is included and what is omitted), and any interpretations that might not be justified. At a minimum, the student researcher will want to determine whether the facts are current and accurate.

This description of how to find pertinent policy information is intended to be a general introduction to policy research. The real excitement in policy studies comes from having a strong interest in a particular policy area and learning where to find the information about it. For example, the student who is passionate about unequal pay for women in the workforce will find the search for appropriate data and studies exhilarating. For the researcher concerned about declining opportunities to download music and videos from the Internet, the hunt for information about copyright laws and restrictions on using downloaded files will be easy and a real learning experience.

## CONSTRUCTING ALTERNATIVES

After problem analysis has yielded a good sense of what the problem is, how extensive it is, why it occurs, and what the goals are for resolving it, the next step is to think about courses of action. Chapter 6 introduces a range of relevant criteria for evaluating policy options and some of the tools of analysis that can provide the requisite information to evaluate the policy alternatives. This section focuses on how to develop the list of alternatives that merit such further consideration. It emphasizes learning how to think creatively about public policy, particularly when ineffective policies and programs need to be replaced.

### What Governments Can Do

So how do analysts know which alternatives to consider? As Chapter 3 discussed, the starting point is to see what governments are doing or can do. Among their options, governments can regulate, subsidize, ration, tax and spend, contract out, use market incentives, privatize, charge fees for service, educate, create public trusts, and commission research (Patton and Sawicki 1993; Anderson 2003). Table 5-1 summarizes these activities and illustrates them with examples.

If current policies are not working well enough and a change is needed, analysts might suggest modifying the present policies or trying a different policy approach or strategy. Present policies could be strengthened; for example, the federal government could raise standards and penalties for clean air or water policies. Or policymakers could fund programs at a higher level, which might permit improved research, better enforcement, and better public information campaigns. Analysts and policymakers also consider alternatives to conventional regulatory policies, as was done for many environmental policies during the 1980s and 1990s (Mazmanian and Kraft 1999; Vig and Kraft 2003). These might include a combination of market-based incentives, public information campaigns, and various forms of what the Clinton administration called "regulatory reinvention," which are more flexible and efficient policy reforms.

For some policies and agencies, policymakers might try different institutional approaches, such as a new way to organize the bureaucracy in charge. A reorganization was proposed in 2002 for the much-maligned Immigration and Naturalization Service (INS), widely considered to be one of the least effective federal agencies. The Bush administration endorsed a plan to abolish the INS and create two new agencies, one for immigration services and the other for enforcement. As of March 2003 both new agencies were part of the new Department of Homeland Security. The first is now called the Bureau of Citizenship and Immigration Services, and the second is named the Directorate of Border and Transportation Security. Along with agency reorganization, the

| TABLE 5-1 | What Government Can Do |
|---|---|
| **Action** | **Illustrations** |
| Regulate | Licensing, inspection, enforcement of standards, application of sanctions.<br>Specific examples: environmental, health, and workplace safety regulation; corporate financial regulations. |
| Subsidize | Loans, direct payments or benefits, tax credits, price supports.<br>Specific examples: student loans; subsidies to farmers; dairy price supports; low interest loans for disaster recovery. |
| Ration | Limit access to scarce resources.<br>Specific examples: permits for backpacking in national parks; the Oregon Health Plan's limitations on coverage of health care services. |
| Tax and spend | Tax an activity at a level that encourages or discourages it.<br>Specific examples: allowing home mortgage deductions to encourage home ownership; imposing cigarette taxes to discourage smoking.<br><br>Spend money on preferred programs.<br>Specific examples: defense weapons, prisons, AmeriCorps, public higher education. |
| Contract out | Contract for government services from private sector or buy products for government agencies.<br>Specific examples: defense contracts for weapons procurement; purchase of computers and fleet vehicles for federal or state governments or public schools. |
| Use market incentives | A special category of taxation or imposition of fees that creates incentives to change behavior and achieve goals and objectives.<br>Specific examples: raising gasoline taxes to encourage conservation of fuel and reduce carbon dioxide emissions; tax rebates for purchasing hybrid vehicles. |
| Privatize | Transferring public services from government to the private sector.<br>Specific examples: turning over management of public schools to private companies; partially privatizing the Social Security system by allowing individuals to manage a portion of their retirement savings. |
| Charge fees | Fees for select services.<br>Specific examples: hunting and fishing licenses; requiring students to pay to ride the school bus. |
| Educate | Provide information to the public through formal programs or other actions.<br>Specific examples: formal public meetings; public education services; food safety labels; information on toxic chemical releases; automobile fuel efficiency labels. |
| Create public trusts | Holding public property in trust for citizens indefinitely.<br>Specific examples: local land conservation trusts; state and national parks and recreation areas. |
| Conduct research | Conduct or support research and development.<br>Specific examples: National Science Foundation support for academic studies; defense and environmental research; medical science research through the National Institutes of Health. |

present federal-state relationship, some form of which pervades most policy areas, can also be changed. For example, many policies during the 1980s and 1990s were further decentralized, giving the states greater authority to make decisions and allocate funds.

Many state and local governments are trying another interesting institutional reform option. They make routine government services available online, everything from providing tourist information to supplying government forms that people can fill out on their computers. Governments report improved efficiency, and the users say they are more satisfied with the result and think more highly of the agencies than before (Raney 2002). The federal government is also moving in this direction and has instituted an Internet portal for all federal information at FirstGov (www.firstgov.gov).

For many policy areas, actions are rooted in one of two views of the problem being confronted, what might be called **supply and demand perspectives**. If analysts believe a problem such as energy scarcity results from an insufficient supply of energy, they would likely recommend the policy alternative of increasing supply. They would consider actions to boost supplies of energy, whether from fossil fuels (oil, natural gas, and coal), nuclear energy, or alternative energy such as wind or solar power. The actions might include changes in rules that control exploration on public lands, various tax credits and incentives, and support for research that could speed up the introduction of new energy sources. The Bush administration took this position in its national energy policy proposal of 2001. But what if the problem is too much demand for energy rather than too little supply? Policymakers might consider energy conservation and efficiency measures, such as increasing fuel economy standards for cars or providing tax credits for high-mileage hybrid vehicles, which use a combination of electric batteries and a gasoline-powered engine. The most likely scenario would be a combination of the supply and demand perspectives.

In addition to considering which policy options will work best or be more efficient or fair, policymakers also have to think about the philosophical and ideological aspects. Conservatives and liberals, and Democrats and Republicans, differ significantly in the kinds of policy solutions they favor. On the Bush energy bill, for example, Republicans in Congress strongly favored a supply-side approach, while most Democrats supported conservation measures to reduce demand. On health care policy, Democrats want federal government programs to help pay the cost of prescription drugs, and Republicans reject that approach in favor of drug insurance policies offered by private companies and subsidized in part by the federal government.

The same kinds of philosophical differences pervade other areas of domestic policy. Early in the Bush administration in 2001 a debate took place over so-called ergonomics regulations for the workplace. The Clinton administration had proposed broad, mandatory rules, which organized labor favored, to reduce workplace injuries, such as neck strain and carpal tunnel syndrome, which result from repetitive motions such as lifting, bending, and typing.[9] A National Academy of Sciences report requested by Congress estimated that about one million of these injuries occur each year in the workplace, resulting in seventy million doctor visits annually and costing the nation's economy about $50 billion (Greenhouse 2001). The Bush administration and Republicans in Congress opposed the Clinton rules as excessively burdensome and costly, as did business interests. The business groups said the rules would cost $120 billion to put into effect, although the Clinton administration argued the cost would be only $4.5 billion. In 2001 Congress nullified the Clinton rules, and a year later the Bush adminis-

tration proposed a replacement policy based almost entirely on voluntary action by companies to reduce repetitive motion injuries on the job (Adams 2001a; Greenhouse 2002).

## Policy Typologies as Analytic Tools

Chapter 1 introduced several typologies that analysts can use to consider whether another
type of policy might be appropriate if the previously adopted policy or the one being given the
most attention proves to be unsuitable. For example, if a regulatory policy is not working or is
no longer politically feasible, the policymaker could consider either self-regulation or distributive policy actions, such as subsidies or incentives. Anne Schneider and Helen Ingram
(1997) developed an intriguing typology as part of their work on policy design.

**Policy design** refers to the careful consideration, during the policy formulation stage, of
the role of government "agents" and the "target population"—those who receive benefits or
who are the objects of government regulation. Schneider and Ingram argue that, for public
policies to stand a chance of working, they must be thoroughly grounded in an understanding
of the attitudes and motivations of the policy actors who will decide how the policies are
implemented and whether they have the desired effects. Underlying this view of policymaking
is a variation of rational choice theory: if policy actors are rational beings who respond to the
incentives and disincentives incorporated into a given policy, then the policymakers should be
able to design policies that encourage people to behave in the way that is needed.

Viewed from this perspective, policy tools, according to Schneider and Ingram, are "the elements in policy design that cause agents or targets to do something they would not otherwise
do with the intention of modifying behavior to solve public problems or attain policy goals"
(1997, 93). The choice of such tools, they say, reflects different views of how people behave and
what might lead them to change their behavior. They distinguish five such policy tools, which
are summarized in the box "Steps to Analysis: Policy Design Tools." Governments can invoke
their authority and ask for compliance, provide incentives or inducements to elicit compliance,
apply sanctions or penalties for noncompliance, try to inform and enlighten the public and
promote learning, and exhort people to change their behavior. The choice of which tools to use
and how depends on the analysis of a given case and the process of political deliberation and
debate that usually occurs at the stage of policy formulation and adoption.

Although it may seem an abstract exercise in rational choice theory, this policy design
approach is quite effective and offers many insights into human behavior that can help analysts
and policymakers figure out what kinds of policy action will likely succeed. Consider a situation
that was unfortunate for California in 2001. Electricity prices rose dramatically in 2000 and
2001 as a consequence of a poorly conceived state energy deregulation policy and a short-term
shortage of energy sources, which was brought about in part by the power companies' manipulation of the energy supply. As one solution, state policymakers adopted the nation's largest energy conservation program, with a strong focus on incentives for individuals to conserve energy.
For example, those who cut their previous electricity use by 20 percent or more would earn a
special rebate of 20 percent on their 2001 energy bills in addition to the direct savings they
enjoyed from using less electricity. The state called this a "pay-to-conserve" program.

## POLICY DESIGN TOOLS

Policy design is the consideration of a variety of possible approaches, instruments, or tools that may be appropriate for a given policy problem. The tools described here derive from anticipating how different policy actors are likely to respond to what governments attempt to do.

**Authority tools.** They assume people behave because someone in authority asks them to do so. The use of such tools, not always effective or democratic, is dependent on the perceived legitimacy of government. These tools may be particularly suitable during times of crisis when favorable responses by the public are more likely.

**Inducements and sanctions.** The assumption here is that people are rational actors who seek to maximize their self-interests. Inducements encourage people to act in a certain way because they will gain from doing so. Sanctions are negative incentives or penalties that are thought to discourage behavior that is inconsistent with policy goals.

**Capacity-building tools.** They provide training, education, information, and technical assistance, and they aim to inform or enlighten and thus empower people, either those in the target population or policy agents.

**Hortatory tools.** Governments invoke images and values through speeches, proclamations, and other communication to exhort people to behave in a certain way.

**Learning tools.** Policy agents and target populations are encouraged to participate and learn, for example, through citizen advisory panels and collaborative processes.

Source: Adapted from Anne Larason Schneider and Helen Ingram, *Policy Design for Democracy* (Lawrence: University Press of Kansas, 1997).

State policymakers were counting on individual incentives to alter consumer behavior that has proved difficult to change. California's policy is a good example of what Schneider and Ingram mean by offering inducements that persuade individuals to alter their behavior because they realize they will be better off by doing so. In this particular case, hortatory tools—the governor and news media urging people to conserve energy—probably also made a difference, as Californians were determined to break out of their energy crisis. The policymakers had calculated that 10 percent of the public would take advantage of the pay-to-conserve program, but by November 2001 more than one-third had done so. The financial inducement worked in part because rising energy prices provided a powerful financial incentive for individuals to save energy.[10]

Many other public policies are equally dependent on assumptions about how those affected by policy rules will behave. Traffic laws, for example, depend on drivers' willingness to stop at red lights and to abide by the posted speed limit. When people do not respond as expected, additional sanctions may be necessary. Jurisdictions impose substantial fines and other penalties for driving under the influence of alcohol as a way of discouraging this behavior. Some states maintain the death penalty for severe crimes in hope that it will deter criminals. Here too the assumption is that a person contemplating a criminal act would adjust his or her behavior with the understanding of the possible punishment.

This kind of thinking was illustrated at the beginning of the chapter, but the policy tool was directed at the agents of government rather than a target population among the public. Members of Congress were harsh in dealing with an allegedly abusive IRS. They imposed penalties on the agency by cutting its budget and staff and, by using hortatory and authority tools, tried to get the IRS to be less aggressive in its enforcement of the tax laws. The agency responded by cutting back severely on tax audits and prosecution of tax cheats. The IRS seizure of property to collect on back taxes plummeted in the late 1990s, as did the rate of audits of taxpayer returns. Congress succeeded in altering the behavior of IRS officials, although the legislative action had the perverse effect of reducing government revenues and placing a greater tax burden on honest taxpayers.[11]

These examples show that policy typologies, such as that proposed by Schneider and Ingram, can be useful when thinking about a government's possible courses of action. In conjunction with other analytic techniques, typologies like these can help analysts focus on the condition they are trying to bring about and what changes in human behavior may be necessary. Then they can consider various policy actions that may provide the necessary incentives.

## CREATIVE THINKING ABOUT POLICY ACTION

Beyond considering policy typologies or variations on existing policies, students of public policy can try other techniques to expand the list of alternatives. Carl Patton and David Sawicki's book *Basic Methods in Policy Analysis and Planning* (1993) offers an excellent discussion of how to apply **creative thinking** to policy action. Among other strategies, Patton and Sawicki suggest the following: **no-action analysis**, **quick surveys**, **literature reviews**, comparison to **real world situations**, **passive collection** and classification, use of **analogies** and metaphors, brainstorming, and comparison with an ideal.

No-action analysis begins with the status quo, or present policy, as a kind of baseline. It does not suggest that governments do nothing about a given problem, but that keeping present policies or programs, or defending them, may be a viable option. Many will favor this strategy during times of budget constraints when programs are vulnerable to cutbacks or elimination. A clear example is the idea of keeping Amtrak alive by continuing its government subsidies because the national passenger train system is an alternative to travel by car or airplane. Nearly every other developed nation subsidizes its railroads, but in the United States public and political support for passenger trains is limited. The level of support is so low that expanding Amtrak may not be viable, but keeping it going may prove to be an important decision because its demise would no doubt make it difficult to develop passenger rail systems in the future. The no-action option may also be a useful point of departure for considering other alternatives. One advantage of such alternatives is they are *not* the status quo, which may be unacceptable to those critical of the current program. The greater the dissatisfaction with the status quo option, the more likely policymakers and the public are to favor a search for alternatives and give them serious consideration.

Quick surveys involve talking with people in a particular policy network or searching through hearings transcripts, minutes of meetings, newspapers accounts, and the like for pertinent information about a problem and policy alternatives. The idea here is that people familiar with the issues have probably raised many alternatives, and interviewing them, distributing questionnaires to them, or reviewing what they have written or said on the issues should produce a short list of possible policy alternatives. This technique could be particularly useful at the local level where gaining access to principal policy actors is a real possibility.

A literature review is an examination of books, journal articles, Internet sites, and other sources. The purpose here is to look for policy alternatives that have been proposed or considered previously. This kind of search could extend to a survey of the options that policymakers have considered or adopted in other policy areas as well. For example, the National Environmental Policy Act required that government agencies conduct an environmental impact analysis, and make it public, before making a major decision such as building highways. Can an impact analysis be applied elsewhere? In other words, why not require that specific studies or reports be conducted and made public prior to reaching a final decision in many other areas of public policy?

Rather than think only about abstract ideas, analysts might ask what has worked well in specific, or real world situations, and therefore what might be considered an effective policy alternative for the present policy. Analysts would also want to know which alternatives have been tried elsewhere and found wanting. This kind of information is likely to be available because one of the great virtues of the U.S. federal system is that the fifty states and their approximately eighty thousand local governments often demonstrate great creativity in addressing public problems. As Supreme Court justice Louis D. Brandeis observed long ago, "A single courageous State may, if its citizens choose, serve as a laboratory; and try novel social and economic experiments without risk to the rest of the country."[12] Today, states frequently engage in innovative public policy actions. If several states have experimented with welfare reform, then other states or the federal government might look to them for ideas about what to consider. Indeed, the federal welfare reform measure of 1996 was based largely on what Wisconsin and a few other states were already doing. Many states and communities are taking action on global climate change in the face of the federal government's inaction. Many sources can be consulted for information on state or local policy innovation, including associations of state administrators and state legislative bodies, which often follow and evaluate state and local policy experiments. Analysts can also look to what other nations have tried to do about a particular problem and evaluate their success.

Similar to the quick survey approach, passive collection means finding out what others have suggested in a given policy area. Analysts might speak with a program's clients or administrators, advocates of various positions, and organizations that have taken a position on the issues. Do they offer creative ways of dealing with the problem that depart from present practices? Do those closely associated with a given policy area believe that some policy alternatives are politically infeasible because they have been raised and rejected earlier? Finding out these answers now can save analysts time and effort later.

Another approach is to look at parallel situations in other policy areas for ideas about what might be done. What seems to be a new problem may present much the same issues as an earlier problem. Analysts need to be alert to possible analogies. By listing and thinking about the attributes of the present problem, they may see its relationship to other problems. For example, measures to deal with the rights of the disabled have borrowed concepts and language from analogous civil rights legislation from the 1960s. Another approach to using analogies is to imagine oneself in the position of a client served by a given program. As a client, how do you respond to present policies? What would you like changed?

Another example concerns a problem peculiar to college towns. What might a city do about old couches that wind up on open-air porches, where inebriated students deliberately set them on fire during celebrations? Boulder, Colorado, home to the University of Colorado, borrowed from the practice in analogous areas of regulatory policy. It decided to ban the placement of upholstered furniture outside of a dwelling, much to the dismay of students who like the comfortable furniture on their porches. The measure applies only to the University Hill neighborhood of Boulder, a residential area near the campus that had been the scene of previous couch burnings. Other campus towns—including Fort Collins, Colorado; Normal, Illinois; and Blacksburg, Virginia—have adopted similar ordinances. The Boulder law carried penalties of ninety days in jail and fines of up to $1,000.

A popular technique to encourage creative thinking in public policy or in organizational change is **brainstorming**, which usually takes place in an informal meeting of people who share an interest in finding solutions to a given problem. In the brainstorming session the participants bounce ideas around with the goal of producing a list of possibilities. Ideas are offered and recorded as they are made, with no attempt to criticize or evaluate them. The freewheeling discussion of the issues should produce creative thinking and numerous suggestions. In the second phase of the meeting, the participants pare down the suggestions to come up with a shorter list of alternatives worthy of further consideration. Brainstorming can also take the form of written suggestions rather than an open meeting with verbal responses. Some variations on the brainstorming theme suggest that creativity is enhanced when some structure is introduced into the discussions (Goldenberg, Mazursky, and Solomon 1999).

Sometimes analysts compare policy alternatives with an **ideal situation**. For example, as part of smart growth planning or sustainability efforts, many communities hold "visioning" meetings in which residents are encouraged to think about the community they want for the future. What kind of residential neighborhoods, what kind of downtown, what kind of recreational opportunities? The goal is to envision an ideal future and use that vision to generate ideas for moving in the desired direction. Too often in public policy debates, the participants assume that an ideal situation is unattainable and therefore not worthy of serious consideration, but excluding the ideal guarantees that it will never come about. By encouraging the expression of an ideal, analysts can ensure that at least the more pragmatic ideas that do receive consideration are evaluated in terms of how close they come to the ideal.

Any one of these strategies for generating a list of policy alternatives should help an analyst to think clearly about how to solve a problem. At this point in the process, neither the cost nor the political feasibility of a particular option is the primary concern; rather, it is to think critically about the problem and try to imagine the various ways to address it. Chapter 6 suggests methods for evaluating the various policy options. In this chapter, however, the emphasis is on fostering the most creative thinking possible, especially if conventional policy action is thought not to be working well and alternatives are needed.

Consider this example. Studies have shown that the rate of obesity among children and teenagers is rising quickly, as are the rates of early-onset heart disease and Type 2 diabetes. Chapter 8 discusses the serious health consequences for the individuals and the significant costs to society if these conditions persist. So what might be done beyond encouraging people to eat healthier diets? Some states have thought about what public schools can do to reduce the availability of foods that contribute to the problem. They proposed restrictions on fast-food franchises in public schools and the imposition of a tax of several cents per can on soft drinks, which are loaded with sugar and calories. Predictably, soft drink makers opposed the initiatives and pointed instead to a sedentary lifestyle as the culprit. In 2001 California enacted legislation to eliminate junk food from schools by 2004, a move applauded by public health officials. Was this the right response? Would you favor such a move? If not this kind of action, what else do you think might reduce the high levels of obesity among children and teenagers?

Wesley Highland, a first grader at Pactolus Elementary School in Pactolus, North Carolina, enjoys several sweet potato pancakes as part of a Pitt County program to improve children's dietary habits. Taste Explorers offers healthy foods to elementary students as alternatives to high-calorie, high-fat selections, and exemplifies the creative thinking needed to deal with difficult social problems such as childhood obesity. As the obesity rate among children and teenagers continues to rise, more and more parents and school districts are considering how to improve children's diets and encourage healthier eating habits.

## CONCLUSIONS

John Gardner, the founder of the nonprofit organization Common Cause and a long-time political reformer, once said, "What we have before us are some breathtaking opportunities disguised as insoluble problems."[13] That is a fitting thought for this chapter on problem analysis and the creation of policy alternatives. It conveys a sense of optimism about how to face any public problem, from inadequate performance of public schools to an inability of local governments to deal with urban sprawl. Rather than complain, analysts, policymakers, and citizens could try to figure out just what the problem is and why it exists, gather some basic information about it, and then think about what might be done. As challenging as many public problems are, they are also opportunities to consider the role of government—and the private sector—in fresh ways and to imagine possibilities for changing unsatisfactory circumstances.

This chapter provides an overview of problem analysis. It discusses some of the perspectives and methods that can help analysts, whether professional or amateur, to identify, define, and measure problems. The chapter also notes some strategies for finding information about public problems. Finally, it offers some ways to generate alternative policy options that can later be evaluated against whatever standards or criteria apply. Problem analysis takes place within a political context that often leads to a proliferation of competing diagnoses and recommendations and sometimes to outright misleading and inaccurate portrayals of the problems faced. The skillful analysts learn to deal with the situation. They know how to conduct a critical review and appraisal of whatever studies and reports they find on a subject. Developing a healthy sense of skepticism, however, need not mean a loss of idealism or the willingness to think creatively about public policy change.

## DISCUSSION QUESTIONS

Early in the chapter, we presented an example about seat belt use to reduce injuries and deaths from automobile accidents. What kind of evidence would persuade you that more stringent seat belt laws would be more effective than a public education campaign?

Can public problems be described well by using quantitative measures? What are the limitations and advantages of quantitative measures? Consider two of the examples in the chapter: the use of seniors' SAT scores to measure school quality and the use of the GDP to measure a society's economic well-being. How valid are they?

How can one determine the causes of public problems? Is it useful to determine their root causes or only the immediate causes that are usually the focus of public policy? Consider some of the other examples in this chapter, such as overcrowded and expensive prisons or congested urban highways. What are the causes and what might governments do about them?

What is the best way to foster creativity in the consideration of policy alternatives? What factors inhibit creative thinking in an organization? In a policymaking body like Congress or a state legislature? How might these factors be overcome to allow unconventional policy alternatives to receive serious consideration?

## SUGGESTED READINGS

Frank R. Baumgartner and Bryan D. Jones, *Agendas and Instability in American Politics* (Chicago: University of Chicago Press, 1993). A major work on agenda setting, with many insights into the policymaking process and policy change.

Evan Berman, *Essential Statistics for Public Managers and Policy Analysts* (Washington, D.C.: CQ Press, 2002). A useful overview of basic statistics that can be applied in policy analysis.

Anne L. Schneider and Helen Ingram, "Policy Design: Elements, Premises, and Strategies," in *Policy Theory and Policy Evaluation,* ed. Stuart Nagel (Westport, Conn.: Greenwood, 1990). A shorter version of Schneider and Ingram's argument in *Policy Design for Democracy.* Not easy reading, but well worth it.

Anne Larason Schneider and Helen Ingram, *Policy Design for Democracy* (Lawrence: University Press of Kansas, 1997). One of the best treatments of policy design, with particular attention to incentives that policies provide to government officials and target populations to achieve policy success.

## SUGGESTED WEB SITES

**http://thomas.loc.gov.** The Library of Congress's Thomas search engines for locating congressional documents. Thomas is one of the most comprehensive public sites for legislative searches.

**www.access.gpo.gov.** Access to the federal government's printing office site for location of government documents.

**www.fedstats.gov.** A site that provides easy access to a vast amount of federal data on policy problems, organized by agency as well as substantive policy area.

**www.firstgov.gov.** Portal for federal government Web sites.

**www.gao.gov.** U.S. General Accounting Office, a treasure trove of reports on government agencies and programs, especially evaluation studies.

**www.lib.umich.edu/libhome/Documents.center/stats.html.** University of Michigan site that provides a comprehensive set of links to statistical resources on the Web organized by subject area—health, environment, education, energy, science, transportation, military, housing, economics, agriculture, business, and more. Links within each area lead the user to extensive lists of agencies and programs. The site is updated frequently.

**www.publicagenda.org.** Nonpartisan briefings on policy and polling; a digest of news, legislation, and studies; and research sources.

## KEYWORDS

analogies    144
brainstorming    146
causes    134
creative thinking    146
ideal situation    146
literature review    144
no-action analysis    144
operational indicators    130

operational measures    130
passive collection    145
policy design    142
problem analysis    128
quick surveys    144
real world situations    144
supply and demand perspectives    141

# CHAPTER 6

# ASSESSING POLICY ALTERNATIVES

ONE OF THE MOST CONTENTIOUS QUESTIONS BEFORE CONGRESS in 2002 was whether the federal government should permit drilling for oil and natural gas in the Arctic National Wildlife Refuge (ANWR). Proponents of drilling, which included energy companies, labor unions, the Bush administration, and most congressional Republicans, cited its feasibility and minimal environmental impact if properly designed and operated. They also argued that developing new sources of domestic oil was essential to reduce dependence on imported oil. Opponents, including environmentalists and most Democrats in Congress, questioned the wisdom of allowing possibly severe environmental damage to a pristine wilderness area, particularly when other options, such as energy conservation and improved automobile fuel efficiency, could reduce reliance on imported oil.

Each side pointed to policy studies that bolstered its position, and each challenged the other's assumptions and portrayals of the situation. It was a fairly typical policy debate, if more extended and better publicized than most. After the ANWR drilling amendment was defeated on the Senate floor in April 2002, the leading proponent of drilling, Sen. Frank Murkowski, R-Alaska, complained that the environmental groups had waged a war of misinformation. Environmentalists and other drilling opponents said much the same thing about Murkowski and his allies (Rosenbaum 2002b).

Throughout the debate nearly every major criterion for evaluating public policy proposals was addressed, although as Murkowski complained, not always with accuracy and fairness. The criteria included effectiveness (how likely drilling was to produce the large quantities of oil proponents expected), technical feasibility (the likelihood of reaching the oil with a minimal "footprint" from the necessary machinery and activity), and economic efficiency (the economic benefits of producing the oil compared to the costs). Also addressed were the national security implications in terms of reducing dependence on oil imported from the volatile Middle East, environmental impacts, and the social acceptability of massive oil and gas drilling in a prized wilderness area. Policy actors were also mindful of political feasibility, given that all the concerned parties were engaged in intensive lobbying, and the proposal had implications for the November 2002 elections, which would decide the makeup of a closely divided Congress.

The ten oil-drilling platforms shown here are all owned and operated by Unocal Alaska in Cook Inlet near Anchorage. The issue of oil and natural gas drilling in Alaska's Arctic National Wildlife Refuge (ANWR) has polarized Congress in recent years as the debate over the national energy policy rages. Proponents and opponents of drilling disagree on nearly every facet of the proposal—from the amount of oil that is likely to be extracted to the damage drilling may cause the local environment and animal life. The debate over energy policy and ANWR illustrates the need for students of public policy to be alert to the many ways in which such proposals may be evaluated, such as technical feasibility, economic benefits and costs, environmental impacts, ethical acceptability, and even national security.

For better or worse, the ANWR debate shows how policy studies are used—or misused—in the policymaking process. Politicians and their staffs eagerly seek out information and other justifications for the positions they hold. They cite policy studies, but not always to change minds; rather, they are more likely to use policy studies to reinforce and advocate existing positions and as ammunition against policy opponents (Sabatier and Jenkins-Smith 1993; Weiss 1978; Whiteman 1995). Policy analysts emphasize the objectivity and rigor of their work, but policy advocates tend to use whatever data are at hand to support their arguments, regardless of the methodological strengths or weaknesses of the study that produced the data. Whether policymakers use them fairly or not, policy analyses are integral to the modern policymaking process precisely because, as the ANWR example shows, the issues are complicated and often involve highly technical questions well beyond the expertise of elected officials. At the core of such analyses are a clear delineation of the criteria developed for judging policy alternatives and the application of available tools and methods to provide the information essential to decision making.

This chapter explores evaluative criteria and provides an overview of policy analysis methods. These methods range from cost-benefit analysis that addresses economic criteria to political and institutional assessments that estimate political or administrative feasibility. The combination of clear evaluative criteria and careful analysis should make it easier to determine whether one policy alternative is better than another. Is it likely to be more effective? Will it be cheaper? Will it be more equitable in the distribution of costs and benefits? It is the purpose of policy analysis to provide that kind of information; it is up to policymakers and the public to decide what to do with it.

## EVALUATIVE CRITERIA FOR JUDGING POLICY PROPOSALS

Evaluative criteria are the specific dimensions of policy objectives (what policy proposals seek to achieve) that can be used to weigh policy options and judge the merits of existing policies or programs. Evaluative criteria can also be thought of as justifications or rationales for a policy or government action. The use of explicit evaluative criteria establishes relatively clear standards that can keep policy analysis objective and focused on the issues of greatest concern to the analyst, the intended audience, or the client. Such standards also allow users to rank alternatives in order of their preferences. It makes sense to choose the criteria that fit a given policy area and set of circumstances. Obviously, some criteria make more sense for judging access to health care services than they would for determining whether Congress should cut agricultural subsidies. In addition, as Brian Hogwood and Lewis Gunn (1984) stated, policy analysis for the real world is always contingent on the political and institutional context of policy debate and is influenced by available resources and time.

The dimensions of policy objectives that are most often the target of inquiry and political argument include effectiveness, costs, benefits, risks, uncertainty, political feasibility, administrative feasibility, equity or fairness, liberty or freedom, legality, and (sometimes) constitutionality. This is a long list, and analysts seldom address all of these elements in any single project. Chapter 1 suggested the usefulness of focusing on three: effectiveness, efficiency, and equity. Concern about effectiveness, or how well a policy is working, is nearly universal. Because most public policies, from defense to education, spend public money, analysts consider efficiency—what clients get for their money—important. So too is equity, which concerns the fairness of government programs in considering the needs of different groups in the population. Of all the criteria discussed in the text, these three capture the most politically important standards used to judge policy proposals today.

Table 6-1 lists these three criteria along with five others often used in policy analysis and policy debate. The table gives the meaning of each criterion and the limitations in using it as a standard of judgment. It also indicates the type of public policies for which it is most apt. Critics such as Deborah Stone (2002) underscore the inherent ambiguities and problems of interpretation associated with such criteria. These qualities need not prevent their use in practical policy analysis, but suggest the need to be alert to their limits.

Typically, when these criteria are used, they must be expressed in terms of operational measurements or indicators, such as those discussed in Chapter 5. For example, analysts usually speak of efficiency in terms of dollar cost in relation to the value of benefits expected to be realized from a government action, such as improved workplace safety that might follow adoption of federal ergonomics standards. Effectiveness can be measured in terms of the likelihood of reaching a specific policy objective, such as reducing auto accident rates by 20 percent over a five-year period. For most of these criteria, multiple indicators are available, and analysts normally use several to compensate for the limitations of any one of them. Some criteria, however, involve making qualitative judgments rather than using such indicators, for example, when questions of equity arise or when the debate turns on the loss of personal liberty in furtherance of the larger public welfare. The personal liberty issues range from controversies over gun control and freedom of religious practice to fights over individual property rights in relation to government land use regulations.

Most policy debates resemble the battle over ANWR; they involve multiple and competing criteria. Policymakers and analysts want policy action to be effective, but they also want to minimize costs, or to promote the most equitable solution, or to maintain individual rights. It is a rare policy action that can maximize each of these criteria simultaneously. The analyst must therefore figure out which criteria are most important to the public or a client for the analysis and use those preferences to rank policy alternatives from best to worse. Another technique is to assign a different weight to each of the various criteria to reflect its relative importance. Then multiple criteria can be used at the same time to assess the attractiveness of different policy options. A brief discussion of the most frequently used criteria should clarify their meanings and suggest how they might be used in policy analysis.

## Effectiveness

The need for the effectiveness criterion is evident in the all too frequent complaints about the failure of government programs. Analysts and policymakers speak of what works and what does not work, about policy success and the lack of it. In a narrow sense, effectiveness refers to reaching the stated goals and objectives. For a program already in existence, evaluation of its

| TABLE 6-1 | Selected Criteria for Evaluating Public Policy Proposals | | |
|---|---|---|---|
| Criterion | Definition | Limits to Use | Where Most Likely Used |
| Effectiveness | Likelihood of achieving policy goals and objectives or demonstrated achievement of them. | Estimates involve uncertain projection of future events. | Virtually all policy proposals where concern exists over how well government programs work. |
| Efficiency | The achievement of program goals or benefits in relationship to the costs. Least cost for a given benefit or the largest benefit for a given cost. | Measuring all costs and benefits is not always possible. Policy decision making reflects political choices as much as efficiency. | Regulatory policies, such as workplace safety and environmental protection; consideration of market-based approaches. |
| Equity | Fairness or justice in the distribution of the policy's costs, benefits, and risks across population subgroups. | Difficulty in finding techniques to measure equity; disagreement over whether equity means a fair process or equal outcomes. | Civil rights, disability rights, tax equity, access to health services and higher education. |
| Liberty/Freedom | Extent to which public policy extends or restricts privacy and individual rights and choices. | Assessment of impacts on freedom are often clouded by ideological beliefs about the role of government. | Proposed national identification cards, restrictions on Internet use, property rights, abortion rights, regulatory actions that constrain choices of corporations and individuals. |
| Political feasibility | The extent to which elected officials accept and support a policy proposal. | Difficult to determine. Depends on perceptions of the issues and changing economic and political conditions. | Any controversial policy, such as gun control or changes in environmental regulations. |
| Social acceptability | The extent to which the public will accept and support a policy proposal. | Difficult to determine even when public support can be measured. Depends on saliency of the issues and level of public awareness. | Any controversial policy, such as crime control or abortion rights. |
| Administrative feasibility | The likelihood that a department or agency can implement the policy well. | Involves projection of available resources and agency behavior that can be difficult to estimate. | Expansion of agency duties, use of new policy approaches or new technologies, policies with complicated institutional structures. |
| Technical feasibility | The availability and reliability of technology needed for policy implementation. | Often difficult to anticipate technological change that would alter feasibility. | Science and technology policy, environmental and energy policies, telecommunications, defense policies. |

effectiveness usually turns on whether it has achieved the expected results or policy outcomes. For example, is the Clean Air Act improving air quality? Have public school students mastered the specified "learning outcomes"? Has a city's use of school vouchers raised the quality of education (see Chapter 10)? Assessments like these require that analysts develop suitable indicators or measurements for the specified outcomes. For a proposed policy, they try to estimate the likelihood that such goals and objectives would be attained if the proposal is adopted.

This view of effectiveness is rather narrow, however, because programs usually have multiple goals and objectives and may succeed at some and fall short on others. Moreover, some objectives may be attainable only over a long period of time, making assessment of short-term outcomes problematic. Another limitation is that estimating the probability that a proposal will be effective, or more effective than the present policy, requires a forecast of future conditions and events, an uncertain activity at best. In addition, analysts must learn to deal with a political environment in which politicians often exaggerate the weaknesses of current programs and tout the strengths of alternatives based more on ideological beliefs than any assessment of empirical evidence of program effectiveness.

On the plus side, the federal Government Performance and Results Act of 1993 requires regular evaluations of all existing programs and demonstrations of their performance or achievements. The act encourages agencies to focus on results, service quality, and public satisfaction, and it mandates annual performance plans and reports. The political mood in Washington, D.C., and across the nation creates a strong expectation that new policy proposals be able to meet the same standards of effectiveness as policies already in place or improve upon them. Analysts who evaluate policy proposals in terms of likely effectiveness or who try to measure the achievements of existing programs therefore find a ready audience for their assessments.

## Costs, Benefits, and Efficiency

If policy effectiveness is nearly universally expected in contemporary policymaking, the interest in keeping the cost of government programs within reason is universally desired. Whether efficiency is a specific measurement of costs in relation to benefits or gaining the most benefits for a fixed cost, the criterion amounts to the same thing. It strongly encourages analysts to think about the overall costs and benefits of existing programs and the various proposals to change them or substitute something different.

Essentially, efficiency is a way of justifying government action on the basis of economic concepts. Sometimes efficiency is expressed in terms of the relative virtues of government intervention and the operation of a free market in promoting societal welfare. Government action may be called for when the market economy cannot adequately protect the public's well-being, for example, from air pollution or crime. Efficiency is prized in the United States. As Deborah Stone (2002, 61) says, it is "an idea that dominates contemporary American discourse about public policy." Its role reflects the high value Americans place on a smoothly functioning market economy and the promotion of economic well-being.

The logic of efficiency in the allocation of scarce government resources is compelling. From an economist's perspective, fiscal resources must be used to best meet human needs—in other words, to increase the well-being of members of society. If the government spends more on one activity, such as an environmental program, than is needed to gain the benefits of the action—cleaner air or water—it will have fewer resources for other services, such as education and health care. Economists therefore tend to favor policy intervention only when the benefits of action exceed the costs. When the costs are greater than the benefits, the possible alternative uses of the labor, capital, and materials are foregone, depriving society of their value (Patton and Sawicki 1993; Weimer and Vining 1999).

Application of these principles can be difficult. The federal Centers for Disease Control and Prevention released a study in 2002 that found that the job productivity lost because of premature deaths from smoking amounted to $3.73 for every pack of cigarettes sold. The nation's medical costs related to smoking were estimated at $3.45 per pack. The nation's total cost of smoking was said to be $158 billion, or $3,391 annually for every smoker (Associated Press 2002a). Should government do more to restrict smoking to reduce these costs, particularly to reduce the rate of smoking among young people? Or should smokers be allowed to make their own choices? During 2002 many states raised cigarette taxes, but they did so less to discourage smoking than to raise revenue to offset budget deficits. The national average cost for a pack of cigarettes rose to about $5, but in New York City new taxes drove the price higher than $7 a pack.[1]

Calculating these societal benefits and costs is not always easy, particularly when they must be expressed in dollar terms. For example, how do analysts calculate the benefits of a war on terrorism compared to the military costs or to the inevitable deaths and injuries of innocent civilians? Should a nation simply spend whatever it takes to fight such a war or provide for security and be prepared for what the military calls collateral damage? When deciding to impose stiffer sentences on drug users, should analysts and policymakers consider the costs in terms of building and maintaining prisons to hold them? What about the costs and benefits of trying to make the nation's mail delivery safer from bioterrorism? In the end, the anthrax scare of late 2001 sickened only twenty-two people and caused five deaths (Florig 2002). Is the slightly improved safety of the mail worth the high cost of the screening equipment, increased postage, inconvenience, and added delays in mail delivery?

A further constraint is that defenders of the efficiency criterion assume that the benefits and costs are more or less equally distributed among the population. Often, however, the benefits of policies such as agricultural subsidies or subsidized tuition for college students go to particular groups in the population, but all taxpayers bear the costs. For regulatory policies, such as controls on polluting power plants, the larger society receives the benefits, but the corporate owners of the plant and the stockholders bear the costs. Analysts therefore need to inquire into the distribution of benefits and costs as part of any attempt to examine economic efficiency and its acceptability.

In fact, no matter what reservations are expressed about using the efficiency criterion in policy analysis and decision making, political reality dictates that it be addressed in some form. The smart analyst can find ways to do so that are reasonable and fair. Moreover, the great weight placed on policy costs today opens the door for creative ways to get policymakers and the public to think about the consequences of proposals under consideration. Actions that seem justifiable on some grounds might appear far less desirable once the costs of action are taken into account.

## Equity

The term *equity* has at least two different meanings in contemporary policy debates: process equity and outcomes (end-result) equity. The first refers to the decision-making process that is used. Is it voluntary, open, and fair to all participants? If so, analysts and citizens might judge the results to be equitable even if some people ultimately fare better than others by gaining benefits such as higher education, better jobs, greater income, nicer houses, and so forth. This view is often associated with the political philosopher Robert Nozick and his book *Anarchy, State, and Utopia* (1974). Those who hold these views tend to believe strongly in the rights of individuals and the freedom to use and dispose of their resources as they see fit. They resist government efforts to promote equality beyond assuring equal opportunity to participate in society's decisions. As this description suggests, political conservatives identify strongly with the concept of process equity.

John Rawls promoted quite a different conception of equity, particularly in his book *A Theory of Justice* (1971). Rawls argued that equity or fairness refers to just outcomes or the fair distribution of societal goods such as wealth, income, or political power. His reasoning is that political institutions and social structures, such as racism and other forms of discrimination, affect the achievement of such goods. In other words, the acquisition of societal goods is not solely a function of the individual qualities of ambition, talent, and a strong work ethic. People who hold this view are more likely than others to favor government intervention to promote the equitable distribution of society's resources. Political liberals are likely to identify with the concept of outcomes equity.

Equity criteria are likely to be central to any consideration of redistributive policies, such as tax reform, welfare reform, efforts to enhance access to education or health services, and assistance to the poor. They may also crop up in other policy areas where the debate and decisions turn on who gains and who loses as a consequence of policy action. The policy analyst might want to ask who receives the benefits of policy action, who does not, and who pays for the costs of the program. *Who* in this context means not individuals, but different groups or categories of people. They can be wealthy, middle class, or poor; city dwellers or suburbanites; ordinary people or huge corporations. Equity issues are pervasive in policy disputes, from tax reform proposals to actions that might restrict access to higher education—such as raising tuition levels.

In 2002, for example, the Republican-controlled U.S. House of Representatives voted to make permanent a 2001 decision to temporarily repeal the estate tax, a federal tax on property that is imposed when the owner dies and paid by the heirs to the estate. The estate tax, or what conservatives refer to as the "death tax," was repealed as part of the negotiated tax cuts made early in the Bush administration in 2001, but the repeal was slated to expire in 2010. Making the tax repeal permanent will be costly to the federal government, and by some standards its effect can be considered inequitable.

Democratic analysts, for example, said the repeal would cost the U.S. Treasury about $740 billion from 2010 to 2020, with most of the benefits going to the very wealthy at a time when the government will need additional resources to provide for health care and retirement benefits to the baby boom generation. They criticized the estate tax repeal as fiscally irresponsible and unfair to the average taxpayers who will have to make up the difference in lost revenue. Some of the nation's wealthiest citizens, such as Microsoft founder Bill Gates and other members of a group called Responsible Wealth, supported that view. They argued that the estate tax should remain to avoid the build-up of "heredity wealth," which they believe will harm democracy. Republicans and many conservative analysts argued, in contrast, that there was little sense in having the estate tax reimposed in 2010 after a period of repeal. Why eliminate the tax for only a short period of time, which could confuse estate planning and lead to unfair impacts on different groups in the population? Supporters of the repeal also defended it in terms of the benefits for the heirs to family farms and small businesses who find themselves capital-rich but cash-poor.

Those favoring action on the estate tax short of its full repeal, such as raising the exemption amount, could find some comfort in Internal Revenue Services (IRS) studies. IRS data indicate that only about 2 percent of estates were subject to the tax in 1999 when the exemption was only $650,000. Moreover, half of the estate taxes collected in 1999 came from only 3,300 estates, or 0.16 percent of the total. One economist who examined the impact of the estate tax in recent years concluded that the widely circulated stories of "family farms and businesses broken up to pay the estate tax are basically rural legends; hardly any real examples have been found, despite diligent searching" (Krugman 2002, 77). With the level of estates to be subject to the tax set to rise to $1 million in 2003, even fewer estates would face any tax at all.[2] Many members of Congress argued that the $1 million limit could be raised to deal with the burdens the estate tax places on families with farms or small businesses. Those who favored outright repeal of the estate tax, however, showed little interest in such a compromise. What is fair or equitable in this case? Is it more fair to repeal the estate tax or to leave it in place? Would raising the limit on estates that are subject to the tax represent a reasonable compromise between the competing arguments?

## Ethics and Other Criteria

In a classic essay on the role of principles in policy analysis, political theorist Charles Anderson (1979, 173) argued that there are "certain fundamental considerations that must be accounted for in any policy evaluation." This "repertoire of basic concepts" includes "authority, the public interest, rights, justice, equality and efficiency." They are, Anderson said, not simply an analyst's preferences but "*obligatory* criteria of political judgment."

In the practical world of policy analysis, some of Anderson's requisite criteria or standards of policy judgment are likely to be ignored. Indeed, some political scientists argue that it is unnecessary or even improper for policy analysts to include **ethical**, or **normative**, **dimensions** in their work. They say this in part because they think ethics and normative values, such as liberty or equality, are beyond the bounds of rational analysis. Or it may be that they believe analysts are incapable of objective analysis because they inevitably inject their personal biases into any such assessment. Some also argue that analysis of normative values is unnecessary because the political process exists to address and resolve ethical and value disputes (Amy 1984). An easy rejoinder to the last argument is that explicit analysis of ethics and values could greatly enhance the quality of argument and debate in policymaking bodies. No doubt, it is easier for analysts to stress criteria such as effectiveness and efficiency where an assessment can be based on hard data such as measurable costs and benefits. Normative issues, however, deserve serious consideration. As Anderson (1979) argues, analysis that ignores basic issues such as the role of government authority, individual rights, or the public interest is incomplete and inadequate.

Policy debates over privacy, property rights, copyright laws, research on human stem cells derived from embryos, and many other contemporary issues clearly require an assessment in terms of normative and legal criteria, not just economics. Even for a seemingly technical subject such as nuclear waste disposal, it is both possible and necessary to analyze the ethical issues of the effect on future generations, voluntarism in the selection of sites for waste repositories, public involvement in decision making, and fairness to "host" communities in terms of benefits that can be provided (Kraft 2000; Shrader-Frechette 1993; Weiss 1990).

As this review of evaluative criteria indicates, there are many different bases on which to analyze policy. Students of public policy need to be aware of the range of standards that are applied and alert to their strengths and limits and the tradeoffs between them. Sometimes, promoting the public's welfare, for example, through food safety or environmental protection policies, imposes a cost on individuals and corporations. Restrictions on their freedom or liberty may be justified by the public's gains. Conversely, at times, the protection of individual rights and liberties is so important that society is willing to tolerate activity that many find abhorrent. Thus, Internet pornography is protected because of the First Amendment's free speech guarantees, and the Constitution extends elaborate protections to those accused of criminal behavior, even for horrific crimes such as serial murder or terrorism.

Shoppers at the Disney Store on West 42nd Street in New York browse the merchandise on display. The Disney Corporation has fought to retain the copyright on its animated characters, including Mickey Mouse, Dumbo, and Donald Duck, and the lucrative businesses that they support. In 1998, after a long, behind-the-scenes lobbying campaign on Capitol Hill, Disney won approval of a copyright term extension bill that effectively preserves its rights to the characters for an additional twenty years. Previously, corporations were allowed to hold copyright for seventy-five years. While Disney hailed the passage of the new law, it was sharply criticized by groups representing consumers and libraries concerned about high prices for videotapes, DVDs, and other products.

The use of diverse evaluative criteria can help in another way. Too often policymakers, analysts, and commentators make statements that reflect their strong ideological beliefs when they discuss pending policy choices. Liberals know what they like and dislike and apply those philosophical standards to the full range of contemporary policies, and conservatives do the same, although both sides would no doubt profit from dispassionate assessments of current government programs and proposed policies. An objective analysis of this kind could be grounded in one or more of the evaluative criteria described in this chapter. Doing so does not mean that citizens and policymakers need to abandon their convictions about what government should or should not be doing; rather, it means that they ought to be sure they have the facts about a given issue, be it school vouchers, gun control, or health care alternatives, and that they think about a range of considerations in addition to their personal values and policy beliefs. They will have an easier time defending the position they take, and the policy positions they endorse will stand a better chance of success.

## USING THE METHODS OF POLICY ANALYSIS

This section surveys the most frequently used methods of policy analysis and highlights their strengths and most significant weaknesses. The suggested reading list at the end of the chapter provides substantial coverage of analytic methods. Those wishing to read further will find this list a good place to start. The leading methods of policy analysis draw heavily from economics and focus on the evaluative criterion of efficiency, particularly for cost-benefit and **cost-effectiveness analyses** (Weimer and Vining 1999; Dunn 1994). The ideas found in these and related methods are useful even for nontechnical analysis. The methods are tools for critical thinking about public policy.

By now, however, it should be clear that public policy evaluation is about more than economics; it is also about effectiveness, equity, liberty, and, fundamentally, about politics. As stated earlier, analytic methods can be used to clarify problems and policy choices, but decisions about which policies to adopt or maintain are up to policymakers and, ultimately, up to the public that chooses the policymakers.

### Cost-Benefit Analysis

Most readers are already familiar with cost-benefit analysis, also called benefit-cost analysis, and they use the techniques, even if they do not use the terms. When a high school senior decides which college to attend, he or she probably makes a list of the advantages and disadvantages of each important option. One college offers a stronger program in the student's area of interest, but it is expensive. Another is affordable but falls a little short on the number of courses in the anticipated major. In addition, the student considers the differences in the range of campus activities, housing, sports facilities, and other qualities of college life. How to make this decision? The student, probably with the help of a counselor and parents, weighs the advantages and disadvantages of each, perhaps writing them down in several columns to compare the choices. Cost-benefit analysis is simply a more systematic method for doing the same thing.

One economist described cost-benefit analysis as follows:

It seeks to determine if the aggregate of the gains that accrue to those made better off is greater than the aggregate of losses to those made worse off by the policy choice. The gains and losses are both measured in dollars, and are defined as the sums of each individual's willingness to pay to receive the gains or to prevent the policy-imposed losses. If the gains exceed the losses, the policy should be accepted according to the logic of benefit-cost analysis (Freeman 2000, 192).

He added that in some respects cost-benefit analysis is "nothing more than organized common sense," even if the term usually refers to a more narrowly defined and technical calculation.

The usefulness of thinking in terms of what public policies and programs cost and what society gets from them should be clear enough. But consider this example. The B-2 stealth bomber is a marvel of high technology capable of delivering precision bombs to distant targets, but has been problem-prone from its beginning. In addition to costing $2.2 billion each, it is among the most expensive planes to maintain. The U.S. Air Force has been spending $150 million per year in maintenance costs on *each* of the bombers. It employs a thousand workers to keep the fleet of twenty-one bombers ready for service. Despite this huge investment, the average B-2 bomber has been available for combat duty only about 30 percent of the time, well short of the Air Force target of 60 percent availability (Dao 2002).[3] Is the B-2 bomber a good use of defense dollars? Could the money be better spent on other aircraft or different defense programs? Many supporters of the military argue strongly in favor of the B-2 because of its unique and essential capabilities, and they do not dwell on the aircraft's cost or reliability problems. Critics of the B-2 focus on the costs and its poor reliability and tend to ignore its distinctive military advantages. Which one of the two groups makes the stronger argument?

Conducting a cost-benefit analysis is relatively straightforward in theory. The analyst identifies all the important long-term and short-term costs and benefits; measures the tangible costs and benefits in monetary terms; uses a discount rate, which adjusts for changes in value over time, to ensure that all are expressed in commensurable terms; estimates the intangible or qualitative considerations; and aggregates, or totals, the costs and benefits. This total is expressed in one of two ways, as the net benefit (benefits minus costs) or as the ratio of benefits to costs (the benefits divided by the costs). The box "Steps to Analysis: Conducting a Cost-Benefit Analysis" indicates how it is done. Public policy students might try to apply these methods to a particular problem, perhaps a campus issue that is receiving attention, such as expanding campus parking lots or building a new sports center.

Some of the limitations of cost-benefit analysis are evident even in the brief summary provided here and in the fuel-tax example used in the box. Determination of what costs and benefits are important enough to be included is in part a judgment call. Measuring them in monetary terms is easier for some costs and benefits than others. The analyst may emphasize costs because they are more identifiable and measurable. What the benefits turn out to be is less certain and may be realized only after a period of time. Economists often try to estimate **opportunity costs**, which refer to the value of opportunities that are foregone when time or resources are spent on a given activity. For example, being stuck in traffic imposes an opportunity cost on drivers because they could be doing something more

## CONDUCTING A COST-BENEFIT ANALYSIS

Conducting a cost-benefit analysis can be fairly simple or quite complicated, depending on the issue. In general, an analyst tries to identify all of the important costs and benefits, measure those that can be expressed in dollar terms and either estimate or acknowledge those that cannot be measured easily, adjust the measurements for changes in value over time, and sum up and compare all the benefits and costs.

For example, consider the U.S. federal gasoline tax, which is the lowest among the world's industrialized nations. Those who support raising it contend that doing so would yield many tangible benefits, among them lowering the country's dependence on imported oil. It would reduce urban air pollution and improve public health; reduce carbon dioxide emissions and the risk of climate change; cut back on traffic congestion and drive time; and reduce traffic accidents, thereby saving lives and preventing injuries. A higher gas tax could yield all of these benefits and substantially increase government tax revenues by internalizing the social costs of driving and providing an incentive to people to drive fewer miles or seek alternative forms of transportation. Raising the gas tax, however, imposes direct costs on drivers and on a variety of services that depend on transportation, and it can have a particularly adverse impact on low- and moderate-income citizens who have few alternatives to using automobiles, and on those who live in sparsely populated areas where they are obliged to drive.

Because a complete cost-benefit analysis of raising the gasoline tax can become

exceedingly complicated, let us consider a recent study that took on only part of the challenge. In a paper prepared for Resources for the Future (RFF), Ian Parry and Kenneth Small examined many of these costs in an effort to determine the "optimal" level for a gasoline tax in the United States. Although economists cannot easily measure all of the benefits noted, they have estimated that the pollution damages amount to about 40 cents a gallon, the carbon dioxide emissions 6 cents a gallon (estimates vary widely here), traffic congestion about 70 cents a gallon on average, and traffic accidents at 60 cents a gallon, for a total of $1.76 a gallon. To take into account that gasoline taxes actually tax the fuel purchased as opposed to the distance that is traveled and some of the negative economic effects of raising fuel taxes, the analysts lowered this amount to about $1.00 per gallon (Parry 2002).

The study reached its conclusion about an optimal level of taxation without considering the economic costs of dependence on foreign oil, which another study estimated to be around 12 cents a gallon, the military costs of defending access to Middle East oil fields, or the damage caused by the production, transportation, and use of gasoline—such as oil spills and leaking storage tanks. Some environmental groups have tried to estimate all of those effects and, not surprisingly, come out with a much higher total. Still, according to the RFF analysis, the $1.00 per gallon optimal tax that would internalize the major social costs is more than twice the average com-

*(continues)*

---

**CONDUCTING A COST-BENEFIT ANALYSIS**
*(continued)*

**STEPS TO ANALYSIS**

bined federal and state taxes on gasoline in the United States, which in 2002 totaled about 40 cents per gallon.

Would you change any of the major social costs considered in this analysis? Are there other costs and benefits that should be considered if the gasoline tax is to be raised?

Do you think that economists can fairly estimate the dollar value of things like improved public health because of reduced air pollution or the value of time lost by those stuck in traffic? Does the conclusion of the study present a cogent argument for raising gasoline taxes?

---

productive with their time. Federal regulations that require companies to spend more than necessary on safety or environmental regulations impose an opportunity cost because this money might have been invested in additional research, plant modernization, enhanced employee benefits, and so forth.

Using a **discount rate** allows analysts to determine the value of future benefits today, but the choice of the rate, essentially an estimate of inflation over time, clearly has a profound impact on the results. For example, consider the present value of $100 earned a hundred years from now with varying assumptions of a discount rate. At a 1 percent discount rate, that $100 is worth $36.97; at 2 percent, $13.80; at 3 percent $5.20; and at 5 percent, only $0.76. As these calculations illustrate, distant benefits may be of minimal value in current dollars, and a cost-benefit analysis can therefore yield wildly different results depending on the rate selected.

Because the choice of a discount rate has a tremendous effect on how one appraises policy options, that choice underlies innumerable conflicts over government policy decisions. The question of climate change is instructive. The benefits to slowing or halting global climate change are clear, but they will occur so far in the future that discounting the benefits to today's values tends to minimize them in a cost-benefit calculation. In contrast, the costs of acting on climate change are quite large because environmentalists are calling for steps to be taken quickly, meaning they will be paid for in today's dollars. These complications lead economic analysts to suggest other methods for discounting in a responsible way that consider long-term costs and benefits.[4]

Another vulnerable part of the process is the estimate of intangible human costs and benefits, such as well-being, aesthetic preferences, or even the value of a life. Some analysts choose not to include them at all in a cost-benefit analysis and instead highlight that omission in reporting the results. Others prefer to use available economic methods to estimate intangible or nonmarket values and then include them in the cost-benefit analysis. For example, economists use techniques known as **contingent valuation methods**, which are essentially interviews with individuals or questionnaires, designed to allow an estimate of the dollar value of the time spent stuck in traffic or the preservation of lakes or forests. If done well, such methods can provide a useful estimate of the value people attach to certain intangibles. The use of **sensitivity analysis** can minimize to some extent the weaknesses inherent in cost-benefit analysis. When the calculations are "sensitive" to a basic assumption such as the chosen discount rate, the analyst can report on several different rates, and the reader can choose the assumptions that seem most reasonable.

Even with its obvious limitations, cost-benefit analysis is a powerful tool that is widely used in government decision making. It forces analysts and policymakers to define what they expect government action to do (produce benefits) and to consider the costs associated with that action. If done properly, cost-benefit analysis can help justify public policy that might otherwise be ignored or challenged. Consider this example. During the 1980s the EPA asked for a reduction in the amount of lead allowed in gasoline from 1.1 grams per gallon to 0.1 grams. The benefits of controlling lead in the environment include a reduction in adverse health and cognitive problems in children, a lower level of high blood pressure and cardiovascular disease in adults, and reduced automobile maintenance costs. Not all of those benefits could be measured, but counting those that could be produced a benefit-cost ratio of 10 to 1 (Freeman 2000, 194). That calculation helped gain approval for eliminating lead in gasoline despite opposition from auto companies and oil refineries and the Reagan administration's concerns about the action.

Critics of cost-benefit analysis claim that the method can be abused if only some costs and benefits are considered and inappropriate measures are used to estimate their value (Stone 2002; Tong 1986). Their concerns are genuine, even though in the real world of policy debate, it is likely that analysts on both sides of the policy question will carefully scrutinize any cost-benefit analysis. Moreover, the Office of Management and Budget (OMB) has set out elaborate guidelines that federal government agencies are expected to follow for the conduct of such studies.

OMB's Office of Information and Regulatory Affairs (OIRA) has been in charge of this process since President Ronald Reagan's 1981 executive order mandating that economic analysis be used to justify proposed regulations. Each successive president has established a similar review process, albeit with differing guidelines and expectations, and the agencies have improved their ability to conduct them. Under legislation approved in 2000, OIRA is also charged with establishing guidelines for how agencies ensure the accuracy of the data on which regulations are based.[5] Despite these expectations and procedures, the public policy student should always ask about the underlying assumptions in a cost-benefit analysis and how the costs and benefits were estimated. As noted in several other examples, such as the ergonomics rule, estimates of a new government regulation's future costs often reveal very wide ranges, indicating that the analysts used quite different assumptions and calculations.

Cost-benefit analysis is used less in areas of public policy where such measurements are not readily available. Even in these areas, however, one could carry out a kind of qualitative cost-benefit analysis in which the important benefits and costs are listed and considered, but without an attempt to place a dollar value on them. Such an exercise might allow citizens, analysts, and policymakers to think comprehensively about the pros and cons of government policies for which they have either no dollar estimates of costs or only partial information.

## Cost-Effectiveness Analysis

Sometimes the concerns about the ability to measure the benefits of a policy action are so significant that cost-benefit analysis is not useful. For example, many policies, such as health regulations, highway safety, or medical research, may prevent disease or devastating injury or save lives. But how do analysts place a dollar value on human lives and health? Government agency officials and analysts, along with insurance companies, have methods for estimating how much a life is worth, even though many critics object in principle to making such calculations (Tong 1986). The advantage of cost-effectiveness analysis is that it requires no measurements of the value of intangible benefits such as human lives; it simply compares different policy alternatives that can produce these benefits in terms of their relative costs. That is, analysts are asking which actions can save the most human lives given a fixed dollar cost, or which dollar investments produce the greatest benefits.

For example, in the early 1990s Oregon created a prioritized list as part of the Oregon Health Plan, which chiefly serves the state's Medicaid beneficiaries. The plan ranked 709 medical procedures "according to their benefit to the entire population being served." Coverage was to be provided for all conditions that fell above a threshold on the list, and the state legislature was to determine the cut-off points each year on the basis of estimates for health care services and budget constraints. The state used a cost-benefit methodology to establish the list, consulting fifty physician panels and surveying the Oregon public. The choices were based on factors such as the likelihood that treatment would reduce suffering or prevent death, the cost of treatment, and the duration of benefits. In effect, the state was trying to determine how to get the greatest benefit to society from the limited resources available for health care. As might be expected, the state's innovative approach was highly controversial, and the federal government initially rejected it, but later approved a modified form (Conviser 1996). Is such a cost-effective approach to state health care benefits a good idea? What are its strengths and weaknesses?

Similar comparisons are also common in safety and environmental regulation, where the cost of the regulations in terms of lives that would be saved is often ten, one hundred, or even one thousand times greater than other actions that could be taken. In these circumstances, critics of regulation cite the wide disparities in costs to argue against the adoption of measures aimed at, for example, improving workplace safety or eliminating toxic chemicals from the environment. Or they suggest that the same benefits might be achieved by taking other, sometimes far cheaper, action (Huber 1999).

Should government always choose the cheapest way to gain benefits? Consider the cost of producing electricity. If the government's goal is to minimize the cost of electricity, policymakers could favor all actions that keep these costs down, including extensive use of nuclear power and coal. Citizens, however, might find the consequences less desirable than cheap electricity. For example, in 2002 the Bush administration favored a change in government regulations that would permit coal companies in West Virginia to fill valleys and streams with rock and dirt from mountaintop mining because that is the cheapest method of slag removal. An alternative method is to haul away the debris and bring it back later to restore the mountain when the mining is finished. The companies defended their proposal as a way to reduce the cost of producing electricity in the region. Many local residents objected strenuously, even though the proposal would help provide jobs in a state that has long been among the nation's poorest. The new jobs would result from lowering coal mining costs, making West Virginia more competitive with other mining states.

## Risk Assessment

Risk assessment is a close relative of cost-benefit analysis. Its purpose is to identify, estimate, and evaluate the magnitude of the risk to citizens from exposure to various situations. Reducing risks conveys a benefit to the public, and this benefit can be part of the calculation in a cost-benefit analysis. The risks vary widely. They are associated with driving a car, flying in an airplane, consuming a certain diet, smoking cigarettes, drinking alcohol, skiing down a mountain, or suffering from a terrorist act, among others. Everyday life is filled with risks, but most are minor and not especially alarming, although people worry about technological risks, such as nuclear waste, hazardous waste, toxic chemicals, and radiation.

Consider this example. In late 2002 the Federal Aviation Administration (FAA) proposed a new regulation that would require airlines to build safer seats to reduce the risk of severe injury or death in the event of an accident. Under the proposal, the airlines would have fourteen years to develop and install the new seats, at an estimated cost of $519 million dollars. The seats would have better belts, improved headrests, and stronger anchors to hold them to the aircraft floor under the stress of an accident. The FAA's risk assessment indicated that the new seats would prevent an estimated 114 deaths and 133 serious injuries in the twenty years after the regulation took effect.[6] Was the FAA's risk assessment reasonable? Is it possible to project accident rates, injuries, and deaths over twenty years when the technology of aircraft design and other elements in aviation safety, not just the seat design, are also likely to change?

Risk assessments of this kind are used widely today in part because of public fears of technological risks and the adoption of public policies to control or reduce these risks. Workplace safety and food safety are two examples. Risk assessments are also prepared to estimate and respond to national security risks, such as terrorist attacks or other threats to the United States. Based on such assessments, the CIA director testified before Congress in late 2002 that, despite the expenditure of vast sums of money and a greatly expanded government effort to combat terrorism, the risk of another domestic attack was as serious as it was before the September 11 aircraft hijackings.[7] Throughout the cold war period, from the late 1940s to about 1990, defense and security analysts regularly made assessments of the risk of nuclear war and other security threats. They continue to conduct similar studies today.

Risk is usually defined as the magnitude of adverse consequences of an event or exposure. The event may be an earthquake, a car accident, a nuclear power plant mishap, or a terrorist attack, and an exposure could come through contaminated food, water, or air, or being in or near a building or other structure under attack (Andrews 2003; Lowrance 1976). The public's concern about risk has deepened in recent years as the media has increased its coverage of these situations. Books on this topic seem to sell well, another indicator of public concern.[8]

Risk is a product of the probability that the event or exposure will occur and the consequences that follow if it does. It can be expressed in the equation $R = P \times C$. The higher the probability of the event or exposure ($P$), or the higher the consequences ($C$), the higher the risk. Some risks, such as an airplane crash, have a low probability of occurring but high consequences if they do. Others, such as a broken leg from a skiing accident, have a higher probability, but lower consequences. People tend to fear high consequence events even if their probability is very low. Partly for this reason, there is often a substantial difference between experts and the lay public in the perception of risks. Public fear of nuclear power and nuclear waste is a good example (Slovic 1987).

The tendency of people to misjudge probability is evident in the purchase of lottery tickets. When the Powerball jackpot rose to about $175 million at one point in 1998, people turned out in droves to buy tickets, even though Powerball hopefuls were forty times more likely to die from falling out of bed than to win even a portion of the lottery jackpot. The odds of winning the full amount were 80 million to 1, while the risk of dying by falling out of bed was 2 million to 1. The risk of dying in an automobile accident was enormous in comparison, at 5,000 to 1.[9]

If risk assessment is the use of different methods to identify risks and estimate their probability and severity of harm, risk evaluation is a determination of the acceptability of the risks or a decision about what level of safety is desired. Typically, higher levels of safety, or lower risk, cost more to achieve. **Risk management** describes what governments or other organizations do to deal with risks, such as adopting public policies to regulate them (Presidential/Congressional Commission on Risk Assessment and Risk Management 1997).

Analysts use many different methods to conduct risk assessments, and they range from estimating the likelihood of industrial accidents to calculating how much radioactivity is likely to leak from a nuclear waste repository over ten thousand years. For some assessments, such as the risk of auto accidents or the likely injury to children from deployment of air bags during an accident, the task is relatively easy because plenty of data exist on the actual experience of drivers, vehicles, and airbag deployment. As a result, insurance companies can figure out how much to charge for car insurance once they know the age of the driver, what kind of car it is, and where

and how far it is driven each day. For other estimates, the lack of experience means that analysts must depend on mathematical modeling and computer projections, for example, to project the risk of climate change and the consequences for society if average temperatures rise, rainfall patterns shift, or severe storms occur more frequently.

As with cost-benefit analysis, conservatives and business interests strongly favor the use of risk assessment methods for domestic policy conflicts. They tend to believe that many risks that government regulates are exaggerated and that further study will show they are not worth the often considerable cost to society (Wildavsky 1988; Huber 1999). It is equally likely, however, that risk assessments will identify genuine and serious risks to public health and welfare that merit public policy action.

In July 2002, Congress approved legislation allowing pilots of U.S. commercial aircraft to carry guns on a voluntary basis in an effort to secure the cockpit and provide an additional barrier to hijackings. The pilots shown here are taking part in a federal firearms training course at the Federal Law Enforcement Training Center in Glynco, Georgia, in April 2003. Those who successfully complete such a course may be sworn in as federal law enforcement officers and can begin carrying weapons on flights. Analysts have questioned whether these and other actions to combat terrorism will be effective or if they will only create additional problems. Newly recognized risks such as expanded terrorist activity or the 2003 SARS (severe acute respiratory syndrome) virus scare can cause great public alarm, but assessing the actual magnitude of the threat they pose is difficult because of lack of information and other variables.

Many risks also involve a difficult balancing act when it comes to government intervention or even personal choice. An issue that rose to prominence after the September 11 terrorist attacks was the risk of bioterrorism, particularly in light of the anthrax scare of late 2001. Experts knew that, even though smallpox had been eradicated from the world as a communicable disease, small stocks of the smallpox virus still existed and might fall into the hands of terrorists. Under this scenario, would it be a good idea to vaccinate the U.S. public against smallpox, without evidence that such an attack is likely to occur? Does the small risk of exposure warrant mass vaccinations, or should the nation wait until there is at least one verified case of smallpox before initiating a huge medical campaign? The cost of the vaccinations is not the only issue here; another is the concern about unnecessarily alarming the U.S. public and subjecting people to the risk of the vaccine's serious side effects. When smallpox vaccinations were still mandatory in the United States (prior to 1972), the vaccine killed several children each year and left others with brain damage (Kolata 2002). Recent estimates suggest that if the entire nation were vaccinated, between two hundred and five hundred people would die from the vaccine, and thousands more would become severely ill.[10]

What should policymakers and citizens do about the smallpox risk and the vaccination question? In 2002 public health scientists recommended that the health care and emergency workers most at risk of exposure to the virus—the so-called early responders in the case of a suspected smallpox case—be vaccinated. The general public would be vaccinated only if an outbreak occurred. The idea was to minimize the public's risk of an adverse reaction to the vaccine, but the public would remain unprotected, at least initially. Is this proposal a good idea? What are its limitations and its benefits?[11]

## Decision Analysis

**Decision analysis** is a formal way to structure possible decisions under conditions of uncertainty. Two or more alternatives can be sketched out in what is called a "decision tree." Each branch of the tree portrays the consequences of choosing one of the alternatives, and each decision is associated with some degree of uncertainty and risk. Policymakers need to ask themselves whether they should choose the option with the least risk, even if the outcomes might be less attractive, or an option that carries greater risk of failure, but more favorable outcomes.

Decision analysis combines some of the features of the methods already discussed, particularly an assessment of costs and benefits, but it uses a graphic portrayal of the available options to allow analysts to follow the consequences of each. Basically, it is another way to consolidate and display the information. This approach is useful because it provides a method to structure analysts' thinking about the problems they are facing and the available alternatives. Figure 6-1 shows a decision tree for some of the options to increase local government revenues to pay for a special project, the renovation of a professional sports stadium. If it refuses to fund the renovation, the city might lose the sports franchise and the income the facility generates. The renovation will be expensive, but it will keep that income flowing. Moreover, the renovated stadium may increase the city's prestige and the team's reputation, improving tourism. What options does the city have? It can raise property taxes, raise the sales tax, charge higher fees for those

**FIGURE 6-1**  Decision Options for Renovating a Sports Stadium

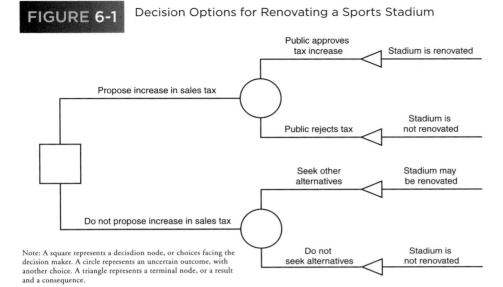

Note: A square represents a decisdion node, or choices facing the decision maker. A circle represents an uncertain outcome, with another choice. A triangle represents a terminal node, or a result and a consequence.

who use the facility, or issue a special revenue bond to borrow part of the money. Each of these options carries some cost. A significant cost is the resentment of citizens who would pay the higher taxes but have no interest in renovating the sports stadium. Which choice is the best?

In their text on quick analysis, which presents an array of decision analysis illustrations, Robert Behn and James Vaupel (1982) argue persuasively that most decision makers are too busy to digest the large amount of analytic detail found in many policy studies. They need quick, simple, but still objective, methods to understand the policy choices they face. Decision analysis is based on the assumption that most people are not very good at making complex decisions without assistance. The sports stadium example suggests how decision analysis could allow city officials to break down the dilemma into its component parts so that they can better understand the costs and benefits of each decision and the possible outcomes.

Decision analysis can also help policymakers think about unintended consequences of the choices they make. For example, in 1990 the United States banned the sale of chlorine, among many other products, to Iraq, largely because of its possible use in manufacturing chlorine gas, an ingredient in chemical weapons. A year later the Pentagon warned Congress that the ban would cause epidemics of waterborne diseases in Iraq because chlorine is used to disinfect drinking water supplies. If the water is not disinfected, it carries a much higher risk of illness and death. By 2002 reports suggested that a hundred thousand Iraqis may have died of such diseases after the ban was approved.[12] Would the decision to ban chlorine have been different had the effects been known in advance? Should U.S. decision makers have been more alert to the possibility of these consequences, given the widespread use of chlorine for disinfecting drinking water?

It is easier ten years later to look back and say it was made on narrow grounds that ignored the consequences. Even if policymakers had been fully alert to the toll the embargoed goods would have on Iraqi citizens, they might have believed that the action was justified nonetheless as part of the U.S. effort to end the Persian Gulf War and to try to remove Iraqi leader Saddam Hussein from power. Decisions made during times of war sometimes pose the greatest ethical dilemmas of this kind.

## Forecasting

Chapter 5 discussed the logic of forecasting in terms of understanding how present problems might change over time. Forecasting can be defined as "a procedure for producing factual information about future states of society on the basis of prior information about policy problems" (Dunn 1994, 190). That is, forecasting methods allow analysts to anticipate what the future is likely to hold based on their understanding of current conditions and how they expect them to change over time. This information can be exceptionally valuable because public problems are dynamic, not static. In other words, when policymakers aim at public problems, they face a moving target.

For example, the population of the United States was 290 million in 2003, but what will it be in twenty-five or fifty years? The U.S. Census Bureau (www.census.gov) has a population clock that reports continuously on the changing U.S. and global populations. It also offers several different projections of the nation's future population. All of those projections depend on a series of assumptions about the average number of children each woman is likely to have, the rate of immigration, and other factors. The bureau offers three different scenarios, with alternate assumptions. The medium projection is most widely cited, and it indicates that the United States has been growing by about 1 percent a year. At that rate, the bureau estimates a U.S. population of 346 million in 2025 and 420 million in 2050 (Kent and Mather 2002). Cities and states (Arizona, California, Florida, and Nevada) that are growing more rapidly than the nation as a whole find their specific forecasts helpful in determining how to cope with the anticipated demand for public services.

Projections of what is usually called geometric or exponential growth, such as population growth, are fairly easy once one knows the rate of growth. It is the same equation used to determine compound interest: $A_n = P (1 + i)^n$, where $A$ is the amount being projected, $n$ is the number of years, $P$ is the initial amount, and $i$ is the rate of growth. The formula is quite handy for determining how much a given amount will grow in one, five, or ten years. A savings account deposit of $100 ($P$) that grows at 3 percent a year will be worth $103 after one year, $116 at the end of five years, and $134 after ten years. To consider a different example, to determine how much a house that is now valued at $200,000 will cost in ten years, one needs only decide what the rate of annual increase is likely to be (3 percent? 5 percent? 8 percent?) and the formula will provide an answer. At a 5 percent annual rate of increase, the house will cost $326,000 in ten years. As these examples illustrate, even a small rate of annual increase can produce great changes over time.[13]

Most forecasting is more involved than the examples, but the principles are the same. Forecasting can include a variety of quantitative methods, such as econometric models for estimating future economic growth and job creation. **Qualitative**, or **intuitive**, **methods** are also widely used. These include brainstorming, the so-called Delphi method of asking experts to estimate future conditions, scenario development, and even simple monitoring of trends that looks for signs of change (Patton and Sawicki 1993; Starling 1988).

As one might guess, whether quantitative or qualitative, forecasting methods are necessarily limited by available data, the validity of the basic assumptions made in projecting the future from present conditions, and how far out the projection goes. A look backward to earlier forecasts is sobering (Solomon 1999). Quite often the futurists have been dead wrong in their projections, sometimes spectacularly so. Population biologist Paul Ehrlich in his 1968 book *The Population Bomb* forecast global famine and exhaustion of natural resources if uncontrolled population growth continued. Other examples abound. During the 1970s, electric power companies believed that energy demand would grow indefinitely at 6 percent to 7 percent a year. They planned for and built power plants that turned out not to be needed, in some cases driving the power companies into bankruptcy. In a strikingly wrong, but telling, statement about the future, in 1899 the head of the U.S. Patent Office suggested that everything important had already been invented.

Lest we think that forecasts about technological change are inevitably better today, it is worth noting that even as late as 1990, few analysts anticipated the explosive demand for home personal computers. Development of the Internet throughout the 1990s was a major reason for that rapid growth, as were falling computer prices and the development of easy-to-use Web browsers. Even in the business community, where the ability to make such forecasts is essential for a company's success, hundreds of major firms and thousands of start-up companies greatly overestimated the demand for Internet business services, and many of them did not survive the dot-com implosion of the late 1990s. To compensate for these kinds of egregious forecasting errors, most analysts recommend using a number of forecasting methods, in the hope that a few of them will come up with comparable findings and increase confidence in the results. Even with the qualifications that should always accompany forecasting studies, being able to anticipate societal changes and prepare for them is a far better strategy than being surprised when problems develop.

## Impact Assessment

During the highly contentious debate in 2002 over oil and gas drilling in the Arctic National Wildlife Refuge, proponents of drilling repeatedly cited a 1990 economic study suggesting that opening the refuge for commercial oil production would create some 735,000 jobs. Independent economists said that number was suspect because the assumptions on which it was based were probably no longer valid. Indeed, a separate study prepared for the Department of Energy in 1992 indicated that approximately 222,000 jobs would result, and that many only when ANWR reached peak production; the jobs would be chiefly in construction and manufacturing. Environmentalists argued that the correct number was lower still, perhaps 50,000 jobs. The wide variation in estimates of job creation may seem to indicate that analysts are unable to forecast economic impacts very well, but the real lesson is probably that studies of this kind may be seriously flawed because of the fanciful assumptions they make. The use of studies ten years after their completion may be equally faulted, because policy advocates may pay little attention to whether the initial assumptions are still valid. Instead, they are probably more interested in scoring political points in a highly contentious debate than they are in arriving at a sound estimate of these jobs.

The jobs impact study is one kind of **impact assessment**. Others include technology impact analysis, environmental impact analysis, and social impact analysis. They are similar in that analysts share an interest in trying to project or predict the consequences of adopting a policy proposal or taking some other form of action. Robert Bartlett (1989, 1) describes the approach this way: "Impact assessment constitutes a general strategy of policy making and administration—a strategy of influencing decisions and actions by a priori analysis of predictable impacts. A simple, even simplistic, notion when stated briefly, making policy through impact assessment is in fact an approach of great power, complexity, and subtlety."

Much like forecasting, the purpose of an impact assessment is to see if analysts can systematically examine the effects that may occur from taking a certain action. That action may be drilling for oil in ANWR, introducing or expanding the use of new Internet technologies, creating gated residential communities for security-conscious home buyers, or deploying a national missile defense system. No matter what the subject, the analyst tries to identify possible impacts and the likelihood they will occur.

Impact assessments are not new. Federal law has required environmental impact analyses since the National Environmental Policy Act (NEPA) was passed in 1969. The logic was simple and powerful. Before governments undertake major projects that are likely to have significant effects on the environment, policymakers ought to identify and measure those impacts, and they also ought to consider alternatives that may avoid the undesirable effects. The law's strength is in its requirement that the impact assessments be made public, which creates an opportunity for environmental groups and others to influence agency decision making. The agency in turn is forced to deal with a concerned public and to respond to the information produced by the impact assessment. The hope was that the combination of information and political forces would "make bureaucracies think" and dissuade them from making poor decisions that harm the environment. Evaluations of NEPA indicate that it has been quite successful on the whole (Caldwell 1998).

## Political Feasibility Analysis

Political feasibility, a criterion for evaluating suggested policy changes, is the extent to which elected officials and other policy actors support the change. No formula is available for estimating political feasibility. Even experienced and thoughtful observers of politics acknowledge how difficult it is to determine the level of support that might be forthcoming for a proposal in local or state government, or at the national level. It may be easier to recognize the actions that are unlikely to fly politically. For example, a steep rise in the federal gasoline tax would seem to lack feasibility given public resentment of tax increases and sensitivity to gasoline prices. Imposing strong restrictions on gun ownership would bring a formidable challenge by the National Rifle Association. Significantly curtailing Social Security benefits, or substantially raising the age at which people qualify for benefits, would likely lack feasibility because senior citizens are superbly organized and would resist such changes. At the margins of policy debate, however, it may be possible to anticipate how slight changes in proposed legislation or regulations, or an alteration in the political or economic environment, can create a majority in favor of action. Sometimes a shift on the part of a few legislators makes the difference in the success or failure of a policy proposal.

Some simple determinations, however, can provide a good idea of political feasibility. Analysts could begin by identifying the policy actors who will likely play a significant role in the decision. These actors may be members of a city council or a state legislature or members of Congress. To the formal policymakers, analysts would add other players, such as representatives of major interest groups and administrative officials, for example, the mayor, the governor, and top officials in a pertinent bureaucracy. For each of the major policy actors, analysts try to determine their positions on the issues, perhaps by investigating their previous stances. Sometimes, it is possible to estimate their positions based on their party affiliation, general political attitudes, and where they stand on comparable issues. Finally, an estimate can be made of their level of interest in the particular decision (how salient it is to them), and the intensity of their views or their motivation to get involved in the decision. These factors are likely to be shaped by the level of interest and preferences of the constituencies they represent, which in turn are influenced by how much the media cover the controversy and how the issues are presented. All of this information can be pulled together to estimate political feasibility.

Analysts need to bear in mind that not all policy actors are equal in influencing feasibility. Relatively small groups with intensely held views on a subject are often capable of defeating proposals that have the broad support of the U.S. public. Gun control is a policy area where this has long been the case. For a great many public policy disputes, especially those that do not rise to the highest levels of visibility, political feasibility is likely to depend on the views of a small number of people and organizations.

## Ethical Analysis

As noted in this chapter, many policy analysts view ethical analysis as problematic. Because they are not quite sure how to do it and sometimes fear that entering the quagmire of ethics compromises the objectivity of their analysis, they leave ethical issues to the policy advocacy community. Ethical issues most definitely are raised as part of policy debate, but they may not receive the kind of careful analysis that we have come to expect for economic issues (Tong 1986).

Two examples illustrate the need for ethical analysis. The first involves family planning programs. The Bush administration, much like other Republican administrations since the mid-1980s, was under pressure from antiabortion groups to curtail U.S. contributions to the UN Population Fund. The fund supports family planning programs around the world, but some people accuse it of condoning abortions. It has repeatedly denied those charges and has assured the U.S. government that none of the nation's funds would be used in support of abortion, which U.S. law forbids anyway. Responding to political pressure from the antiabortion lobby, in 2002 Bush withheld $34 million from the UN program, which amounted to 13 percent of the agency's total budget. According to an agency spokesman, the effect of a $34 million cut "could mean 2 million unwanted pregnancies, 800,000 induced abortions, 4,700 maternal deaths, and 77,000 infant and child deaths" (Crossette 2002).[14] Note the qualification of "could mean" in this statement. It is difficult to project the consequences of the budget cut because other groups might make up some of the difference of the funds withheld. For example, the Population Fund and other organizations concerned about family planning services could ask their members for increased donations for this purpose. Even so, one could ask how likely the Bush administration's action was to achieve its goal of reducing abortions? If the consequences were even close to what the UN official indicates, was the administration's action largely symbolic and political, but one with detrimental consequences for public health? Can the decision be justified in terms of moral or ethical criteria?

The second example concerns the dramatically altered circumstances of airline travel in the aftermath of September 11. Federal law now requires random searches of individuals and carry-on luggage both at the initial security checkpoint and upon boarding each flight during a trip. Federal officials were concerned that if they adopted a system of passenger profiling based on demographic characteristics—that is, groups of people who might require special screening, such as Arab men—they would violate principles of civil liberties. Civil libertarians argue that racial or ethnic profiling should be unacceptable in a free society that values diversity, and many find that view persuasive. The federal government opted for a system of random checks without profiling, but many experts say that while such a system has little chance of preventing hijacking, it imposes high costs and inconvenience on travelers. What is the most acceptable way to promote airline security? Does profiling travelers violate their civil liberties? Even if it did, is this practice a justifiable use of government authority to protect the country?

Other contemporary policy issues, such as human cloning and embryonic stem cell research, raise similar ethical and value concerns. By mid-2001, two dozen states had adopted laws to govern research on embryos and fetuses, and nine of them chose to ban any experiments involving human embryos. Was this position reasonable? Opponents of these laws argue that they could seriously impede important medical research (Stolberg 2001). Indeed, in 2002 California enacted legislation to explicitly allow research on stem cells that are obtained from fetal and embryonic tissue, a direct repudiation of federal limits on such research imposed by the Bush administration in 2001. When he signed the law, Gov. Gray Davis was joined by actor Christopher Reeve, who became a booster of stem cell research after a riding accident left him paralyzed in 1995. Antiabortion groups and the Roman Catholic Church opposed California's action (Associated Press 2002b). If reputable policy analysts cannot provide guidance to the public and policymakers, debate over issues like embryonic stem cell research can deteriorate into emotional name-calling. Equally important, as Reeve and other supporters of the California initiative argued, the ban keeps U.S. health researchers from making discoveries that could pay significant dividends in the improved treatment of disease.

Michael J. Fox (left) and Mary Tyler Moore (right) were among those who spoke before the Senate Appropriations Committee's subcommittee on Labor, Health and Human Services, and Education in September 2000. Fox, who was diagnosed with Parkinson's disease in 1991, and Moore, who has lived with Type 1 (juvenile) diabetes since the 1960s, addressed the controversial issue of federal funding for stem cell research. Both urged Congress to increase spending for such research, which many medical scientists believe holds great promise for treating life-threatening conditions. Stem cells are often obtained from fetal or embryonic tissue, however, and opponents cite the ethical implications of destroying life to save other life. Adding fuel to the political debate, California's governor Gray Davis approved a 2002 bill that allows such tissue to be used in research conducted within the state—directly repudiating the Bush administration's efforts to impose federal restrictions on this area.

## Implementation Analysis and Program Evaluation

The discussion of **implementation analysis** and the related program evaluation is brief because these methods are covered more thoroughly in the chapters that follow. The methods draw far more from the disciplines of political science and public administration than is true for most of the others reviewed here. Implementation occurs after policy adoption, and it deals with how an administrative agency interprets a policy and puts it into effect. Policies are almost never self-implementing, and many circumstances affect success: the difficulty of the problem being addressed, the statute's objectives and legal mandates, and multiple political and institutional factors. These factors include an agency's resources, the commitment and skills of its leadership, the degree of public and political support, and influence from external constituencies (Goggin et al. 1990; Mazmanian and Sabatier 1983).

Implementation analysis is based on the assumption that it is possible to identify the particular circumstances either in advance of a policy's adoption or after it is implemented. In the first case, the analysis can help in the design of the policy to ensure that it can be implemented well. In the second, the analysis can document how well implementation has gone and the aspects of the policy or the parts of the implementing agency that are responsible for any success or failure. Policies can then be modified as needed.

Program evaluation focuses more on policy results or outcomes than on the process of implementation. Analysts use a number of methods to identify a program's goals and objectives, measure them, gather data on what the program is doing, and reach some conclusions about the extent of its success. As with other policy analyses, the intent is to complete those tasks in a systematic way that fosters confidence in the accuracy of the results (Rossi, Freeman, and Lipsky 1999). The studies sometimes make a real difference. For example, analysis revealed that, after years of increased funding, the nation's most popular program to discourage drug use among schoolchildren was ineffective. As a result, the U.S. Department of Education announced that its funds could no longer be used on the Drug Abuse Resistance Education or DARE program, which had paid for police officers to visit schools to convey an antidrug message (Zernike 2001).

## CONCLUSIONS

This chapter introduces and describes the leading evaluative criteria in the study of public policy, with special emphasis on effectiveness, efficiency, and equity concerns. It also briefly reviews the major kinds of policy analysis and their strengths, weaknesses, and potential contributions to the policymaking process. Students of public policy should understand that analysts select from these criteria and methods, with significant implications for the breadth and utility of their findings. They should also be alert to the assumptions and choices made in such studies and ask how they affect the validity of the conclusions reached.

The chapter makes clear that policy analysis is both a craft and an art. The craft comes in knowing the methods of policy analysis and how to apply them in specific situations. The art lies in selecting suitable criteria for policy assessments, in recognizing the limitations of the available methods, and in drawing and reporting on appropriate conclusions. An artful policy analyst recognizes and is sensitive to the public mood and the political and institutional context in which the analysis is conducted and reported. He or she may also find ways to use policy analysis to empower citizens and motivate them to participate in the democratic process (deLeon 1997; Ingram and Smith 1993).

Some critics of policy analysis complain that analysts tend to view politics—that is, public opinion, interest group activity, and the actions of policymakers—as an obstacle to adopting the fruits of their labors, which they believe represent a rational, and therefore superior, assessment of the situation (Stone 2002). It is possible, however, to view the relationship of policy analysis and politics in a different light. Analysis and politics are not incompatible as long as it is understood that analysis by itself does not and should not determine public policy. Rather, its purpose is to inform the public and policymakers so that they can make better decisions. A democratic political process offers the best way to assure that policy decisions further the public interest (Lindblom and Woodhouse 1993).

## DISCUSSION QUESTIONS

Which of the many evaluative criteria are the most important, and why? Are some criteria more important for some kinds of policy questions than for others?

How would you go about applying cost-benefit analysis to one of the following policy issues: (1) instituting a campus program for recycling paper, aluminum cans, and similar items; (2) getting a city to build bicycle lanes on selected streets to promote safety for cyclists; (3) increasing the number of crossing guards at roadway intersections close to elementary schools? What steps would you go through and what kinds of data would you need to conduct such an analysis?

Choose one of the following examples relating to the use of ethical analysis: budgets for family planning programs, restrictions on using embryonic stem cells for medical research, or profiling in airport security screening. How would you apply ethical analysis to clarify the policy choices involved in that case?

If you had to forecast changing student demand for programs of study at a college or university for the next ten to twenty years, how would you do that?

What are the most important factors to consider in conducting a political feasibility analysis? Take a specific example, such as raising gasoline taxes to reduce reliance on imported oil, cutting mandatory prison sentences to lower the cost of keeping nonviolent offenders in prison, or capping student tuition payments to permit greater access to higher education.

## SUGGESTED READINGS

Eugene Bardach, *A Practical Guide for Policy Analysis: The Eightfold Path to More Effective Prblem Solving* (New York: Chatham House, 2000). A concise and helpful handbook on the basics of conducting and presenting policy analysis in the real world.

Kenneth N. Bickers and John T. Williams, *Public Policy Analysis: A Political Economy Approach* (Boston: Houghton Mifflin, 2001). A brief text on policy analysis using the perspective of political economy, or how individual preferences and values are translated into collective policy choices.

Brian W. Hogwood and Lewis A. Gunn, *Policy Analysis for the Real World* (Oxford, U.K.: Oxford University Press, 1984). An older text with good advice about how to conduct and use practical policy studies.

David L. Weimer and Aidan R. Vining, *Policy Analysis: Concepts and Practice,* 3d ed. (Upper Saddle River, N.J.: Prentice Hall, 1999). One of the leading policy analysis texts, drawing heavily from economics.

## SUGGESTED WEB SITES

**http://apsapolicysection.org/index.html.** Public policy section of the American Political Science Association, with extensive links to public policy organizations, journals, and research sites.

**www.appam.org/index.shtml.** Association for Public Policy and Management guides to public policy education.

**www.omb.gov.html.** Office of Management and Budget site that includes guidelines for conducting cost-benefit analyses and risk assessments.

**www.opm.gov/qualifications/sec-iv/a/gs-policy.htm.** The U.S. Office of Personnel Management Web page, offering a description of policy analysis positions in government.

**www.rff.org/methods/cost_benefit.htm.** Selected cost-benefit analyses done at Resources for the Future.

**www.sra.org.** Society for Risk Analysis, with links to risk-related sites.

**www.wfs.org.** World Future Society, with links to publications on future studies such as *Futurist* magazine.

## KEYWORDS

contingent valuation methods   163
cost-effectiveness analysis   160
decision analysis   168
discount rate   163
ethical dimension   158
impact assessment   171

implementation analysis   175
intuitive methods   170
opportunity costs   161
qualitative methods   170
risk management   167
sensitivity analysis   163

CHAPTER

# 7

# ECONOMIC AND BUDGETARY POLICY

THE FOLLOWING INFORMATION APPEARED IN *USA TODAY* IN July 2000: congressional budget analysts announced that federal budget surpluses will total $2.2 trillion over the next ten years, more than double a previous forecast. The revised projection is sure to escalate the election-year debate over how best to use the money—on tax cuts or new programs. The Congressional Budget Office's (CBO) estimate is a recognition that tax revenue is far higher than analysts had expected, thanks to a strong economy that continues to boost incomes. The new estimate is $300 billion larger than the White House's budget office projected June 26, 2000. And it is far larger than the $893 billion, ten-year surplus the CBO predicted as recently as April.[1]

When this story was written, budget surpluses were the order of the day and were forecast well into the future. The good news was that budget surpluses of more than $2 trillion were projected for the next ten years, and they were widely expected to translate into positive economic results for the nation. The deficits that had plagued the country for years had vanished. The national debt was going down as well, albeit slowly. Partisan calls for greater fiscal austerity and government efficiency should have all but disappeared.

Things did not turn out that way, however. As everyone is now aware, those rosy economic scenarios no longer represent reality. In a relatively short time, the surplus turned back into a deficit. Likewise, the debates surrounding these quite different budgetary issues changed as well. According to a recent CBO analysis (and they change often), the United States is projected to have a $246 billion deficit in 2003. A host of forces played havoc with the budget: the economic slowdown, a major tax cut in 2001 pushed through by the Bush administration, the terrorist attacks of September 11, 2001, and the subsequent policies designed to address these events. (The war with Iraq was handled in a separate budget request that put the nation even deeper in the red.) The $300 billion surplus disappeared with an ease that any magician would envy. These budgetary events demonstrate how quickly the public policy landscape can change. They are also perfect examples of how inexact the science of economic projections can be.[2]

In the good old days, when most policymakers were predicting large surpluses for the foreseeable future, one would think that elected officials would be so happy with these

San Francisco-based Quokka Sports opens its doors one last time in July 2001 for an auction preview of the bankrupt dot-com's equipment. The dot-com explosion helped foster strong economic growth during the 1990s, which contributed, in turn, to federal budget surpluses where deficits had long been the rule. Yet control of the economy and predictions of its future are rarely easy. The economic downturn in 2001 caused many dot-coms to go belly up—their assets often sold off at rock bottom prices. In 2003 the sour economy combined with the war on terrorism, a major defense buildup, and the war in Iraq to create record high deficits. Once again U.S. policymakers began to debate how best to deal with budget deficits and stimulate economic growth.

circumstances that they could easily reach agreements. That is not what happened; instead, partisan squabbles continued, and for some issues took on a more bitter tone than during deficit years. Why? One of the fallouts of the deficit was that little money was available either to propose new programs or to institute tax cuts, and partisan arguments over how best to use federal revenues were necessarily constrained. When money appeared to be available once again, the ideological differences between the parties and presidential candidates sharpened over how to spend the surplus. Now, as deficit spending is once again the norm, debate and finger pointing regarding budget austerity has started anew: What happened to the surplus, and who was responsible for its loss? Was the Bush tax cut too large? Has the economy been mismanaged, and if so, what might government do to fix it?

   This chapter explores how economic policy attempts to address such questions and others equally difficult. It assesses economic policy in the United States through a broad review of the powers of government to influence the economy, including the role of the budget. The chapter concentrates on the major goals that policymakers attempt to promote while coping with the inevitable value conflicts and policy choices. The tools and approaches of policy analysis are as appropriate to assessing economic policy as they are to the other policy areas covered in the next chapters.

## BACKGROUND

Managing national deficits and debt is only one of the economic and budgetary tasks to which the federal government must attend on a continuous basis. For more than twenty years, the federal deficit dominated discussions regarding economic policy, and it clearly had major impacts on the nation's capacity to support other policy actions. Indeed, massive tax cuts at the beginning of President Ronald Reagan's administration in 1981 and the subsequent decline in government revenues greatly constrained spending by the U.S. Congress across a range of public programs. In addition, the U.S. national debt soared during the 1980s.

   Economic policy is critical to all other government functions, but most people probably do not recognize it as readily as they do other substantive policy areas such as the environment, education, or welfare. One reason is that the general public does not connect actions such as tax cuts with attempts to influence economic growth or unemployment. In addition, so much attention is given to the Federal Reserve Board's **monetary policy** and its impact on the economy that the public tends to forget that the government's **fiscal policies**, its taxing and spending decisions, have major impacts on the economy. A cut in tax rates or a decision to spend more money on highway constructions, both forms of fiscal policy, can have significant impact on the nation's economy.

   Economic policymaking is crucial to almost everything the government does. In a narrow sense, economic policy is the development of particular programs and policies that are intended to affect economic conditions in the nation, such as reducing unemployment or increasing economic growth. Public policy students should be aware, however, that the development and implementation of other public policies also have substantial effects on the economy and subsequently on the economic policies that the government pursues. For example, conservatives argue that too much government regulation to protect the environment retards economic growth. Because one of government's major economic goals is to encourage such growth, conflict between the two policy goals is likely. For this reason, as well as others, environmentalists emphasize the idea of sustainable development, which they believe can help to reconcile economic and environmental goals that may be at odds.

During the 1980s and into the early 1990s, the United States was burdened by a growing federal deficit. In 1992 it topped out at $290 billion, meaning that the government planned to spend $290 billion more than it was bringing into the Treasury that fiscal year (U.S. Congressional Budget Office 2002). While many economists were debating the potential impacts of the deficits, it was clear that politicians were already aware of the consequences and, knowing that little money was available, limited their policy initiatives. This budget austerity constrained proposal of any grand ideas about what the government should be doing. For example, one of the reasons President Bill Clinton's health care reform ideas failed (see Chapter 8) was a widespread perception that the plan might make the deficit even worse (Dionne 2000). But things change quickly in the world of economic policy. During the 1990s an unprecedented eight years of strong, sustained economic growth replaced budget deficits with projections of budget surpluses. In 2001 the nation struggled with an economic recession, and in 2002, growth slowly returned, but with less confidence that the United States would see the robust and sustained growth of the 1990s anytime soon.

From the Great Depression of the 1930s to the present, government has been intimately involved in trying to control, or at least influence, the economy. Policymakers have moved away from the free-market, "hands-off" approach to the economy endorsed by Adam Smith. Since the Great Depression, the public and government officials have shown little tolerance for wide swings in the economy, which historically had cycled through periods of economic boom and recession as market forces dictated. In recent years, policymakers have adopted a "hands-on" approach to managing the economy that avoids wild fluctuations and produces steady economic growth.

To achieve these and other goals, the government uses fiscal policy—the sum of all taxation and spending policies—as well as the Fed's monetary policy tools to influence the U.S. economy. It does so with varying degrees of success. In addition, government regulation of business has become prevalent since the depression. Business regulation also increased in the 1960s and 1970s, as citizens demanded more government assurances that health, safety, and the environment would be protected. These regulations have major effects on the budget and economic goals of the United States. The looming deficits in the late twentieth century worried public officials and introduced another major goal for them to consider as they developed economic policy.

When the traditional indicators of economic growth suggested a healthy economy during the 1990s, policymakers were eager to find ways to maintain that strength. With the economic downturn of 2000 through 2002 and a plummeting stock market, policymakers were just as concerned with making policy choices that could return the nation to economic good times, particularly with the consideration of tax cuts and government spending to stimulate economic growth. Both options could have significant impact on the deficit over the next several years and on the still-projected (albeit smaller) surpluses after 2008.

Chairman of the Federal Reserve Board Alan Greenspan is shown here speaking at the National Summit on Retirement Savings in February 2002. Economic policy goals are achieved through a combination of tools often characterized as either fiscal or monetary policy. Monetary policy lies within the jurisdiction of the Federal Reserve Board (the Fed), an independent organization responsible for ensuring a stable monetary and financial system. Directed by a seven-member board of governors, the Fed has been chaired by Greenspan since 1987. The chair has a great deal of authority for setting U.S. monetary policy, and some have argued this individual is even more important in economic policy decisions than the president.

## GOALS OF ECONOMIC POLICY

Policymakers try to promote various goals and objectives in relation to economic policy. Government officials in Congress, the White House, and the Treasury Department, and those who sit on the independent Federal Reserve Board, or the Fed, as it is popularly called, have a number of tools to use in pursuing these goals. What is taking place at the federal level is paralleled in states and localities, as their public officials attempt to promote certain economic goals, such as the growth of local and regional businesses. State and local governments also regulate business practices related to health, safety, the environment, and consumer protection, much as the federal government does. They may impose costs on businesses, influence economic competition, and affect a range of other economic values. In some circumstances, the different goals conflict with each other. The major economic goals that government attempts to promote are growth, low levels of unemployment, low levels of inflation, a positive balance of trade, and management of deficits and debt.

### Economic Growth

Economic growth means an increase in the production of goods and services each year, and it is expressed in terms of a rising gross domestic product (GDP). Such growth usually means that, on average, people's incomes increase from year to year. Many benefits flow from economic growth. First, a strong economy is likely to add to the government's tax revenues. One of the major contributing causes of the budget surpluses of the late 1990s was strong economic growth and the tax revenues it generated. Many state governments similarly benefited from economic growth and enjoyed budget surpluses. By 2002, however, those states saw the opposite effect as their economies slowed and state tax revenues declined, prompting budget cuts in many programs, including higher education.

Second, economic growth may make redistributive programs palatable because people are more likely to accept policies that redirect some of their money to others if they have experienced an increase in their own wealth. Economic growth also allows more people to receive benefits or increases in existing benefits from government programs. For a simple explanation, imagine the government is dealing with four areas of expenditures in a given year. If in the following year the economy grows, the budget pie becomes larger. From a budgeting perspective, this means that each of the four areas also can become larger. But if the economy grows only a little, either no program gains or, for one program to get larger, it must take from one or more of the other three programs, which will likely cause political conflict.

From 1996 to 2000 the GDP increased from one year to the next by at least 3.6 percent, and consumer incomes also increased (U.S. Department of Commerce 2000). Such vigorous economic growth and the resulting tax revenues, while obviously welcome news, also send up warning flags. If the economy grows too fast, it could lead to damaging levels of inflation, which the government seeks to avoid. Theoretically, high levels of growth cause wages to go up, and, if people have more money, they can spend more on houses, cars, and other goods. Higher prices usually follow strong consumer demand, particularly for products or services in scarce supply.

Another policy question is what the government should do with the additional revenue coming into the Treasury, if there is a surplus. Should some or all of the money be spent on specific government programs, such as environmental protection, health care, or education? Should a portion go to reducing the federal debt that went up so sharply after 1980? Or should policymakers cut taxes and return part of the money to taxpayers? Just a few years ago, policymakers faced these questions and others. They were among the major issues of the 2000 presidential election, as Vice President Al Gore and Gov. George W. Bush of Texas debated the merits of sharply different scenarios for federal spending and tax reduction.

## Low Levels of Unemployment

Low unemployment, or **full employment**, has obvious benefits to the economy as well as to individuals. In the United States, jobs and people's ability to help themselves are regarded as better alternatives to government social programs to assist the poor. Americans are more comfortable helping individuals find jobs and use their abilities to improve their standard of living than providing public assistance and therefore have chosen low levels of unemployment as a policy goal.

Unemployment not only harms the people without jobs but also has two deleterious effects on the economy and the government's budget. First, the more people who are unemployed, the fewer people are paying income or Social Security taxes, so that means less revenue is coming into the Treasury to pay for government programs. Second, the unemployed may be eligible for a number of government programs geared toward low-income people, such as Medicaid, food stamps, or welfare payments. So the government needs to pay out more money when unemployment levels rise. Most of these programs are entitlements, meaning that the government is required to pay all those who are eligible. If this number is higher than expected, budget estimates will be thrown off.

In recent years, the United States has succeeded in keeping unemployment levels at a rea-sonable rate. Unemployment in the United States dropped from more than 7.5 percent in 1993 to around 4 percent by 2000 (U.S. Department of Labor 2000). In fact, during much of this period some states—Wisconsin, for example—had unemployment rates so low that many businesses could not find qualified employees. For a recent college graduate that is good news; jobs are plentiful and opportunities abound. But low unemployment levels can be problematic for local or state economies because businesses cannot expand without an avail-able labor supply, and that constrains economic development. Businesses may be forced to offer generous incentives to attract and keep their most valued employees. In turn, the busi-nesses may demand that local and state policymakers reduce their tax burdens or provide some other financial benefits.

Although the overall unemployment rate has been low in recent years, the rate is not dis-tributed evenly across the population. For example, African Americans and young people con-tinue to have much higher rates of unemployment than the national average. The rate for African Americans has been about twice as high as the national average (around 8 percent in 1999), and the rate for people sixteen to twenty-four years old has hovered around 10 percent. The Bureau of Labor Statistics compiles this kind of information for the Labor Department. See the box "Steps to Analysis: Employment and Unemployment Statistics."

Another aspect of employment that influences public policy is the changing character of jobs in the U.S. economy and in other advanced industrialized nations. During most of the twentieth century, many of the best jobs for those without a college education were in manu-facturing, but a shift from this traditional sector to the service economy has occurred, and, in

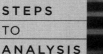

## STEPS TO ANALYSIS  EMPLOYMENT AND UNEMPLOYMENT STATISTICS

The Labor Department's Bureau of Labor Sta-tistics is the primary agency responsible for col-lecting data on employment and unemploy-ment. You already know that the rates vary by geography and demographics. To see these dis-tinctions, go to the following Web site: www.bls.gov/cps/home.htm. The opening page provides current statistics regarding employ-ment and unemployment. What is the current unemployment rate in the United States?

Now look at some of the more detailed sta-tistics and see what differences you can find based on gender, age, race, and other categories. Click on Most Requested Statistics and select the appropriate choices to see differences between demographic categories. For example, "Unemp. Rate-Civilian Labor Force 16-19 yrs" will give you statistics on youth unemployment. How do the statistics on youth unemployment compare to the overall rate? What differences in the unemployment rate do you see with the younger population? What about with the female population?

general, jobs in the service sector do not pay as much as factory jobs. Workers at fast food restaurants or sales personnel in retail may earn the minimum wage or just a little more. Many workers who had jobs that paid quite well, often supported by unions, now see fewer positions of this kind, as competition from abroad and greater efficiencies in production have reduced the need for skilled labor. Some of these workers have been forced to move to the service sector to find employment.

The past several decades have witnessed a significant increase in the two-income family. Several reasons can be cited for this change. First, many families need the income that two wage earners bring home to maintain their lifestyle, to pay for their children's education, or to provide other benefits to their families. Second, more women than in the past are entering the workforce because they want careers and have greater job opportunities than before. Even with the large influx of women into the workforce over the past thirty to forty years (see table 7-1), the number of jobs available continues to grow for people with the right qualifications. The expanding labor force and job opportunities result from a healthy economy.

## Low Levels of Inflation

A simple definition of inflation is an increase in the cost of goods and services. Inflation is an inevitable part of the U.S. economy, but policymakers try to keep it under control—that is, no more than about 3 percent a year. If wages are increasing at the same rate, the rising prices of goods and services are of little concern to most people. They would be of greater concern, understandably, for those on fixed incomes. If inflation continues and grows worse, however, it eventually affects all citizens, which is probably why government policymakers often seem more concerned with inflation than unemployment. To demonstrate

| TABLE 7-1 | Labor Force Participation for Females, 1950–2000 | |
|---|---|---|
| | Year | Rate |
| | 1950 | 33.8% |
| | 1960 | 38.0% |
| | 1970 | 43.5% |
| | 1980 | 51.5% |
| | 1990 | 57.5% |
| | 1995 | 59.0% |
| | 2000 | 60.0% |

Source: Department of Labor Bureau of Labor Statistics, Current Population Survey, www.bls.gov/cps/home.htm#data.

this tendency, one has only to check the various government responses and political rhetoric during the summer of 2000 when gasoline prices rose dramatically. Many state policymakers proposed suspending their state gasoline taxes, and even members of Congress suggested that the federal government partially suspend its excise taxes. These actions were in
direct response to the public outcry about the rising price and the potential political fallout
of not doing anything about it.

In the recent past, the United States had a good record on inflation. During most of the
1990s, inflation, as measured by the **Consumer Price Index** (CPI), was between 2 percent
and 4 percent. This is a level that most government policymakers can accept as tolerable.
What is interesting is that many believe that even this small number may overstate the actual
level of inflation because of the way the CPI is calculated. A commission headed by Michael
Boskin, who served as the first President Bush's chief economic adviser, found that the CPI
overstates inflation by about 1.1 percent (Uchitelle 1997). Why should this seemingly small
discrepancy matter? Many government programs such as Social Security are tied directly to
the CPI as the official measure of inflation. Increases in Social Security benefits are based on
the calculated CPI. If these inflation estimates are reduced by 1 percent, it would save the
government a substantial amount of money in cost-of-living adjustments over a sustained
period. The box "Working with Sources: The Consumer Price Index" explains how the CPI
is calculated.

## Positive Balance of Trade

A positive **balance of trade** is an economic goal related to the role of the United States in an
international economy. Many argue that the goal should be for the nation to export more
than it imports, which would be a positive balance of trade. Another way of thinking about
this is to say that the United States would prefer to sell more goods to other nations than it is
purchasing from them (in terms of the total dollars). For a number of decades, the nation has
failed to meet this goal; in fact, it has had a large negative balance of trade. Among the many
reasons for this state of affairs are the large amounts of oil imported into the United States
(more than half of what the nation uses in gasoline and other oil-based products), the desire
of consumers to purchase foreign products such as Japanese or German electronics, and the
relative weakness in other countries' economies that translates into their inability to purchase
U.S. goods. In addition, labor is cheaper in many parts of the world than it is in the United
States, which has led to what critics maintain is an export of jobs to nations that produce the
clothing, toys, and many other consumer goods that Americans buy at home. This situation
would seem to be problematic, but others question that conclusion, asking whether it matters
that the United States has a negative balance of trade.

Those concerned about negative trade balances, often referred to as protectionists, answer
with a number of reasons why the United States should attempt to rectify the situation. First,
they see the negative balance as evidence that U.S. goods are not as competitive as foreign
goods. If this assertion is correct, a number of U.S. industries and jobs may be at risk. Second,
certain industries are crucial to the nation's security and economic well-being. For example,

# WORKING WITH SOURCES

## THE CONSUMER PRICE INDEX

The Consumer Price Index (CPI) is the statistic most frequently used to measure inflation in the United States. It represents the average change in price over time of a market basket of consumer goods and services. The Bureau of Labor Statistics makes this calculation by collecting data on goods and services from across the country. They can be consolidated into eight major categories, shown below with examples.

| Category of Goods | Examples |
| --- | --- |
| Food and beverages | breakfast cereal, milk, coffee, chicken, wine, full service meals and snacks |
| Housing | rent of primary residence, owners' equivalent rent, fuel oil, bedroom furniture |
| Apparel | men's shirts and sweaters, women's dresses, jewelry |
| Transportation | new vehicles, airline fares, gasoline, motor vehicle insurance |
| Medical care | prescription drugs and medical supplies, physicians' services, eyeglasses and eye care, hospital services |
| Recreation | televisions, cable television, pets and pet products, sports equipment, admission fees to national parks |
| Education and communication | college tuition, postage, telephone services, computer software and accessories |
| Other goods and services | tobacco and smoking products, haircuts and other personal services, funeral expenses |

Source: Consumer Prices Indexes: Frequently Asked Questions. Department of Labor, Bureau of Labor Statistics, at www.bls.gov/cpi/cpifaq.htm#Question%206.

steel manufacture may be seen as critical for national security because steel is essential to support the military. Third are the equity considerations with regard to trade. Some countries place prohibitive tariffs or quotas on U.S. goods that prevent American companies from competing on an equal footing. Protectionists say that in fairness to domestic industries the United States should impose similar trade restrictions. On the political side, policymakers need to support industries (and unions) where jobs may be threatened by trade imbalances.

Some analysts argue, however, that negative balances are not necessarily a problem for the United States. They believe that if it makes economic sense for a country to import more than it exports, the government should not intervene; after all, if the countries involved in the trade relationships do not see mutual benefits, they will not make the trades. Economists often use the theory of comparative advantage versus comparative disadvantage when analyzing international trade issues. Countries that produce a good particularly well and have the comparative advantage should over-produce that good and export the excess to a country that does not produce the same good very well. By the same token, a country should import goods that it does not produce as well (comparative disadvantage). For example, the United States is a prime producer of wheat and should therefore take advantage of this capacity by over-producing and selling the excess to countries, such as Saudi Arabia, that do not produce wheat very well or at all. The United States does not produce oil very efficiently and therefore should be importing this product from another country because it is cheaper to do so. This argument is just one that free-traders cite to promote their point of view.


## Managing Deficits and Debt


Despite the budget surpluses of the late 1990s, the United States still has a large **national debt** that it continues to pay off. The national debt is the accumulation of all of the deficits the nation has run, and recently it was considerably more than $6 trillion (U.S. Department of Treasury 2002). Like any other borrower, the United States must pay interest on its debt. In 2001 this interest amounted to almost $360 billion, and at approximately 12 percent of the federal budget, it constituted one of the year's largest single expenditures (U.S. Department of Treasury 2003). This expenditure was interest only; no principal was repaid. The problem for the nation is the same as a credit card holder paying only the minimum amount billed every month. When the interest due is added, the payment the following month will be very close to the original amount. Most policymakers believed the federal government should have used at least part of the surplus to begin paying down the national debt, even if they disagreed over how much of a commitment to make to this goal.

Limiting the occurrences of federal deficits and the amount of the national debt are serious goals for the United States because they show fiscal responsibility. In other words, they demonstrate the ability to live within one's means, an important political goal. The jury is still out about the economic impact of having deficits and debt. Deficits require the government to borrow from private investors, which makes less money available for private investment. Finally, the interest the government is paying on the national debt is money that cannot be spent on other government programs. It is money that in a sense is paying for nothing. Once the debt is reduced or eliminated, more money becomes available for other government programs or tax reductions. Years of deficit spending did not, however, seem to harm the nation's overall economic situation, so it is fair to ask whether ensuring balanced budgets is an important goal. In early 2003 most Republican lawmakers supported the Bush administration's proposals to cut taxes further and increase defense spending, which would significantly increase the deficit and the national debt. Their stance on fiscal policy was unusual for conservatives, who more often than not argue against deficit spending.

U.S. economic policy in regard to deficits and debt appeared to be moving in the direction of decreasing debt, but as more recent events have shown, the real question is whether the government can sustain this goal. Will strong economic growth return or will the nation continue to have slower rates of growth or even enter another recession? What happens if demands on entitlement programs continue to grow? It is clear that rosy forecasts about budget surpluses and debt reduction can change dramatically and plunge the nation back into a situation where deficit policy—alternatives for how to decrease the deficit—once again takes on a dominant role in government policymaking.

## Interrelationships of Economic Goals

It is difficult to discuss major economic policy goals without also considering how they interact. The relationship between inflation and full employment is a frequent subject of debate. For many years, economists assumed these two goals were in conflict because they believed a certain level of unemployment would keep inflation under control. This theory made economic sense: when a larger number of people are out of work, the demand for products should go down, and with a decrease in demand should come a decrease in prices. The opposite effect should occur when unemployment is low; more people with money to spend fuels the demand for products, and prices go up. The economic problems of the 1970s changed this view when the United States experienced high levels of both unemployment and inflation.

Another often-discussed relationship is that of economic growth and inflation. This connection is of particular interest to the Fed, which is responsible for monetary policy in the United States. The Fed traditionally is concerned with inflation in the economy, and it often implements monetary policy to control it. In general, most policymakers (and citizens) saw the recent economic expansion in the United States as positive, but the Fed looks at the potential of higher prices as a possible negative consequence. If the economy is growing too fast, the Fed argues, people have more disposable income to spend, and the demand for products increases and leads to an increase in prices—inflation. The Fed therefore uses its powers to attempt to slow down the economy, for example, by raising the interest rate, to keep inflation in check.

The third relationship is between federal deficits (and debt) and the other economic indicators. With high deficits or debt, less money is available for private investment, which limits economic growth and perhaps exacerbates unemployment. The discussion here does not exhaust the relationships between these economic goals, but should make clear that the government cannot conduct its economic policies in a vacuum; rather, it must take many factors into consideration before choosing to pursue a particular economic goal.

## TOOLS OF ECONOMIC POLICY

Governments have a variety of policy tools to help them achieve their goals and deal with economic issues. Fiscal policy is a term that describes taxing and spending tools, but governments have other mechanisms, such as regulations or subsidies, that can also be effective. In addition, monetary policy is the Fed's responsibility. The Fed tends to receive more media attention than other economic policymakers in the federal government, but it is only part of the picture. This section examines the various tools used to influence the economy and some of the consequences invariably associated with these choices.

### Fiscal Policy

The president and Congress conduct fiscal policy when they make decisions concerning taxing and spending. At the federal level, major changes in fiscal policy often start with a presidential initiative. The president cannot act alone in this area, but must work with Congress to make any major change. The primary tool of fiscal policy is the budget process that the government goes through every year. During this process, policymakers decide how much money should be spent on government programs ranging from highway building and maintenance to national defense to education. Policymakers frequently reconsider provisions of the tax code, reducing some taxes and raising others. Tax changes and government expenditures are the major tools of fiscal policy, and policymakers use them to achieve certain economic and other public policy goals.

In a recession, for example, government policymakers would attempt to stimulate economic growth. To do this, the president and Congress have two basic choices: cut taxes or increase spending. Reducing the federal income tax puts more money into citizens' pockets, and, with that extra cash, people will likely buy more goods. The demand for products in turn requires companies to increase their production, which means hiring additional employees, driving down unemployment and giving people paychecks so they can make purchases. Theoretically, these activities should promote economic growth and pull the nation out of recession. A boost in government spending would have a similar impact. The increase in spending, for example, to build new highways, creates jobs, and these new workers are able to buy goods and services. Thus, the cycle begins again. When the economy in running "too hot," government can use the opposite tactics to help temper the situation. Raising taxes takes disposable income away from individuals and limits their purchasing power. The subsequent decrease in demand should reduce the level of inflation.

Although using fiscal policy makes sense from an economic perspective and appears to be a logical way to manage or control swings in the economy, elected officials may see the matter differently. A politician campaigning for office finds it easy to support lower taxes "to get the economy moving again," but what happens to a politician who campaigns on a platform of controlling inflation by *raising taxes?* The individual will probably face a hostile public and lose the election, even if the economic policy decision is sound in terms of its impact on the nation's economy.

The Reagan administration introduced a different form of fiscal policy in 1981. Officials argued that a shortage of investment in the United States was causing the sluggish economy and rising deficits and that the way to deal with it was through **supply-side economics**. According to this theory, the government could increase economic growth by cutting taxes, especially for the richest individuals. The largest tax cuts went to the wealthy because, the administration assumed, they would use the additional resources to invest in the economy— building or expanding businesses, hiring more employees, and so forth, which would stimulate the economy, decrease unemployment, and increase the tax revenue collected.

## Monetary Policy

**Monetary policy** is a pivotal component of economic policy in the United States. Indeed, the chairman of the Federal Reserve Board (Alan Greenspan has held the position for years) is widely considered to be among the most powerful people in the nation's capital because of his influence on economic policymaking. Monetary policy differs from fiscal policy in several ways. First, it tries to deal with economic fluctuations by controlling the amount of money in circulation, also referred to as the money supply. Second, the Fed implements the policy itself rather than responding to initiatives from the president and Congress. In other words, the Fed is relatively independent of the government's political institutions. Its independence is deliberate and intended to remove politics from these kinds of economic decisions. Third, the Fed's mechanisms typically affect the economy more quickly than the tools of fiscal policy. Fourth, unlike the decision-making process that occurs in Congress or the executive branch, most of the Fed's deliberations take place behind closed doors. This practice is controversial, given the American political culture of open decision making and political accountability (Rowe 1999).

When trying to influence the economy, the Federal Reserve will either increase or decrease the amount of money in circulation. If the economy is in a recession, the Fed can make money available to stimulate growth. During times of inflation, the Fed may cut back the money supply. In general, the Fed tends to be an inflation hawk and will take action to curtail it even at the risk of hindering strong economic growth. The Federal Reserve has three primary tools at its disposal to try to influence the economy: open-market operations, changing the discount (interest) rate, and changing the reserve requirements. Table 7-2 shows how the Fed uses these tools under different economic circumstances.

Open-market operations occur when the Fed decides to buy or sell U.S. Treasury bonds. The discount rate is the rate the Fed charges member banks to borrow money from the Federal Reserve bank. Changes to this rate subsequently have an impact on the interest that banks charge their borrowers. The reserve requirement is the amount of money (a percentage of its deposits) that member banks must keep on reserve; in other words, the banks cannot use this

| TABLE 7-2 | Tools of Monetary Policy | |
|---|---|---|
| Economic Condition | Federal Reserve Tools | Projected Results |
| If the economy is overheated, inflation is too high, or similar expectations exist. | The Fed can decrease the money supply by: Selling government securities to the general public. | People will buy bonds and have less disposable income with which to buy products. |
| | Increasing the discount rate to member banks. | Member banks have to increase their interest rates, making it more expensive to borrow money. |
| | Increasing the reserve requirement that banks must deposit. | Banks have less money to lend. The decrease in the supply of money available to loan will likely increase interest rates, making it more expensive to borrow. |
| | All of these activities will result in taking money from consumers, reducing the demand for products, slowing the economy, and reducing inflation. | |
| If the economy is sluggish, low levels of economic growth prevail or high levels of unemployment exist. | The Fed can increase the money supply by: Buying government securities from the general public. | The Fed buys securities from the general public using funds from its reserves. This puts money in the sellers' pockets, and they can buy more products. |
| | Decreasing the discount rate to member banks. | Banks drop their interest rates, making it cheaper to borrow money and stimulating new spending and growth. |
| | Decreasing the reserve requirement that bank must deposit. | Member banks are provided with an additional "supply" of money that they can lend to consumers; this reduces the interest rate and stimulates spending and growth. |
| | All of these activities result in giving more money to consumers, increasing the demand for products, and increasing economic growth. | |

money for any other purpose. Changes to the reserve requirement affect how much money banks can lend out and therefore either stimulate or suppress economic growth.

## Regulation

Government regulation is rarely used explicitly to achieve economic goals, but it is a tool that can affect these goals. For example, many conservatives asserted in the 1970s that excessive environmental regulation and health and safety regulation were responsible for holding back economic growth. The logic here is that businesses have to spend money to comply with environmental requirements, making fewer dollars available to them for investment and expansion (Freeman 2000). These kinds of claims fostered many of the economic policies that President Reagan adopted when he took office in 1981.

The primary goals of this kind of social or protective regulation are not usually based on economics; rather, they are enacted to benefit society by providing clean air and water, a safe workplace, and safe consumer products (Harris and Milkis 1996). An unintended consequence may be an increase in the cost of doing business, which in turn may lead to price increases (inflation), unemployment, or a diminished ability to compete with other nations in the global economy. For these reasons, many analysts and policymakers, as noted in chapter 6, favor the use of cost-benefit analysis or another type of economic analysis to help policymakers understand the consequences of regulatory policies.

Chapter 3 defined regulation as any government decree that forces or prevents a particular activity, but other types of government mandates can also directly or indirectly affect economic policy. For example, the United States has a minimum wage law that requires employers to pay at least a certain amount to their employees. The policy exists for good reasons, but it clearly has economic policy ramifications. When the minimum wage goes up, employers may decide either to hire fewer people or to lay off a part of their workforce. If enough employers take these actions, the rate of unemployment goes up. On the other hand, higher wages will provide individuals with more income, spur economic growth, and perhaps lead to inflation. These results are not stated goals of minimum wage policy, but they could be the consequences. Another example is the implementation of security changes following the September 11 terrorist attacks. Additional security measures were required at airports, aboard airplanes, and elsewhere. A new tax on airline tickets helped to pay for the enhanced security requirements. The additional costs probably will not cause people to rethink their decisions to fly, as terrorism might, but the new tax shows how an unrelated policy can have economic impacts.

## Incentives, Subsidies, and Support

In addition to fiscal policy, monetary policy, and regulation, governments have other tools to achieve economic goals. These tools may be applied to a particular industry or individual businesses to promote that industry or favor a particular location. State and local governments trying to encourage regional economic development and growth might provide a tax break to a company willing to locate in their area. They do this because they believe the additional jobs created by a new industry will make up for any loss in their tax base. Sometimes this projection is correct, and sometimes it is not.

At the federal level, Congress provides what is often called "corporate welfare" to large corporations to promote an industry. This assistance comes in the form of subsidies and tax incentives, sometimes called **tax expenditures**. According to a study conducted by the Cato Institute, the 2001 fiscal year budget contained more than $87 billion in corporate welfare expenditures (Slivinski 2001). In an earlier report, Cato cited the Forest Service as spending more than $140 million to build roads in national forests for the primary purpose of helping the timber industry to log and remove trees (Moore and Stansel 1995). Some would also point to the 2002 agriculture bill. It provided $190 billion in subsidies, most of which benefited major corporations.

These kinds of support programs influence economic policy in a number of specific ways. First, government expenditures have a direct effect on the size of the budget and potentially affect deficit and debt policy. Second, tax incentives or breaks reduce the revenue the government collects, thereby limiting what it can spend. Third, if the policies are adopted to improve an industry's performance, they should lead to growth in a particular business or industry and to subsequent economic growth and higher employment rates. In the area of international trade, such programs may allow domestic companies to be more competitive abroad and perhaps improve the nation's balance of trade. Although many of these programs benefit certain businesses and industries, they also constitute another tool government has for managing the economy.

## Tax Policy

Nothing generates as much political debate and consequences as discussions about raising taxes. Given their preferences, politicians would like to avoid the topic altogether, and the Internal Revenue Service (IRS), the agency responsible for collecting the federal income tax, rarely receives high marks in public opinion polls. Indeed, as discussed in Chapter 5, public resentment of the IRS runs so high that Congress forced it to adopt a more friendly posture in its dealings with taxpayers, both individuals and corporations. Still, compared to people in other developed nations, Americans are taxed at a lower rate. According to the Organization for Economic Cooperation and Development (OECD), the total taxes in the United States, expressed as a percentage of GDP, is about 29 percent, while in France it is 45 percent, and in the United Kingdom and Canada it is 37 percent (Public Agenda 2002b).

On its face, the goals of tax policy are quite simple. The government (at whatever level) wants to collect enough revenue to meet its expenditure demands. The problems arise when governments try to decide *how* to tax citizens and corporations. Governments have several different ways to raise revenue, such as income taxes, property taxes, and sales taxes. They might be able to collect similar amounts of revenue using different tax methods, but, because other factors need to be considered, governments turn to policy analysis for help. Tax policy is highly susceptible to policy analysis because the criteria discussed throughout the book—effectiveness, efficiency, equity, political and administrative feasibility, and others—can clarify the effects of adopting one kind of taxation relative to another. What kind of taxes are the most politically acceptable? Which are the most equitable in spreading the burden of taxation among different groups of citizens? Will any given tax generate enough revenue, a measure of effectiveness? Will it be administratively simple to collect? The box "Steps to Analysis: Variables in Making Tax Policy" defines the different factors policymakers need to consider when selecting an appropriate tax policy.

Another question that analysts might ask is whether a proposed tax is regressive or progressive. A **regressive tax** applies the same rate of taxation to all individuals regardless of their income or socioeconomic standing. A **progressive tax** is based on the philosophy that higher earners should pay higher taxes both in terms of actual dollars and as a percentage of income. Most sales taxes are regressive in nature because they treat all income the same. A low-income person buying $50 worth of items pays the same amount in sales tax as a millionaire buying $50 of goods. Payroll deductions such as Social Security and Medicare taxes are also regressive in that the rates of taxation do not vary by tax bracket, and these taxes in particular have

## STEPS TO ANALYSIS

## VARIABLES IN MAKING TAX POLICY

The government has a number of ways to raise $1 million through taxes, but which way is best? Policymakers must think about this question when designing tax policy, and many variables may affect the ultimate decision. B. Guy Peters (2000) notes five major characteristics of taxation: collectibility, fiscal neutrality, buoyancy, distributive effects, and visibility. To these we can add the ideals of horizontal and vertical equity.

**Collectibility:** the ease of collecting the tax and its ability to generate the needed revenue.

**Fiscal neutrality:** whether the system gives preference to one kind of revenue or expenditure without good reason. Think of a tax loophole as something that is not fiscally neutral.

**Buoyancy:** the ability of the tax to keep up with inflation and economic growth.

**Distributive effects:** the impact of the tax on different groups in the population. Who is most affected by the tax, for example, low-income or high-income households?

**Visibility:** the extent to which the tax is visible or acceptable to the general public.

**Horizontal and vertical equity:** the degree to which the tax system is fair or equitable. Horizontal equity means that people who make the same amount of money pay the same amount in taxes. Vertical equity means that people with different income levels pay different amounts in taxes.

These variables reflect different ways of examining tax policy and focus on different analytical issues. For example, the visibility criterion focuses on the political feasibility of implementing a tax, while distributive effects and horizontal/vertical equity refer to issue of fairness.

Think of some of the different kinds of taxes you currently pay or proposals you have heard about. How do they stack up against these criteria? Some examples follow:

The current federal income tax structure or proposals for a "flat tax" system

Local property taxes

Federal and state gasoline taxes

General sales taxes

Cigarettes and alcohol taxes

State income taxes

major effects on take-home pay. Income taxes, on the other hand, tend to be progressive. As income increases, the wage earner not only pays more actual dollars in taxes, but may also graduate to a higher tax bracket and pay taxes on a higher percentage of income. Recent changes in the tax system lowered the tax brackets and reduced their number as well, making the system less progressive than it used to be.

## THE BUDGET PROCESS AND ITS EFFECT ON ECONOMIC POLICY

The budget process is sufficiently complex that even a book-length treatment of how it works would not exhaust the topic. The short introduction to the process provided here is intended to make the public policy student aware of the multitude of decisions that are made each year during the budget process and their implications. The federal government's fiscal year begins

**FIGURE 7-1** The Federal Budgetary Process

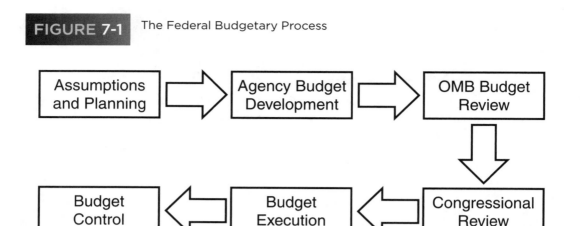

on October 1 and ends on September 30 of the following year, but at any given time policy-makers and government staff may be working on two or three different budgets for various years. Figure 7-1 provides a sketch of the major sequences of decisions in this process.

## Assumptions and Planning

The first major step in developing a budget occurs many months before the government implements the actual plan. During this stage, economic analysts in the executive branch and high-level policymakers begin the process of setting the budget's major taxing and spending goals. In addition, they develop assumptions about the economic conditions of the country, such as the growth rate and unemployment levels. These assumptions are necessary to sketch out a budget that will be implemented more than a year later. The problem with making assumptions is that conditions change and the assumptions may turn out to be wrong once the budget is implemented. For example, if policymakers assume that unemployment will be 4 percent and instead it is 6 percent, that difference has a major impact on the budget. Less revenue will be collected, and expenditures will likely rise to pay benefits to the unemployed. Another critical assumption is whether the economy will grow and by how much, which affects the anticipated revenues from income taxes. Eventually, however, the analysts develop their estimates of the total budget, and this information is communicated to the federal agencies so they can develop their individual budgets.

## Agency Budget Development

Most of the specific work in budget development occurs at the agency level. Each agency is responsible for preparing the estimates for funding in the coming year based on its current programs as well as any new initiatives it would like to implement. Most agencies consist of bureaus or subagencies, and budget preparation begins with them and then is sent up the hierarchical chain until it reaches the highest level of the agency. Because agencies are enthusiastic about their programs, they will likely attempt to increase their budgets from year to year, a process often referred to as incrementalism. They also recognize that they are part of a presidential team, and some will win and others will lose in the budget process. Once the agency has signed off on the budget proposal, it proceeds to the next step.

## OMB Budget Review

The Office of Management and Budget (OMB) is a presidential line agency that has the primary responsibility for reviewing all agency budgets and ensuring that they conform to the administration's policies and agenda. Inevitably, the agency budget request will be higher than the amount the OMB initially planned to provide it. At that point, OMB and the agency begin negotiations to settle on an amount. The OMB holds hearings in which each agency must defend its budget and provide a rationale for its programs and funding. The OMB director receives the final report of these hearings and negotiations and makes changes before delivering the entire package to the president for his review. If agency heads are unhappy with the way OMB treated their submissions, they may attempt to make their case with the president.

The executive budget not only provides the financial information for and about the government and its programs but also sends a strong signal to Congress regarding what the president's priorities are for the coming year. For example, if the presidential budget includes an increase in environmental spending or a cut in defense spending, Congress can expect to see a number of substantive policy changes in these areas. Once the president and his advisers complete their review, the presidential budget is delivered to Congress for the next stage of the process.

## Congressional Review

The president initiates the budgetary process, but Congress's role in budget development is equally, if not more, important. Congress uses a two-step process for considering the president's budget recommendations. In the first step the House and Senate Budget Committees formulate what is called a concurrent budget resolution that sets out the total amount of spending, total revenues, and the expected surplus or deficit for the coming fiscal year. Part of this resolution specifies the total spending in twenty categories, such as national defense, agriculture, and energy, with spending levels for each. This budget blueprint for the year is to guide the House and Senate Appropriations Committees as they formulate more detailed bills that specify how much money the government can spend on specific programs (Davidson and Oleszek 2002). Usually, these committees rely on the president's budget as a baseline for starting the budget discussion, but sometimes a president's budget is declared DOA—dead on arrival. The two Appropriations Committees work primarily through their subcommittees that are set up to mirror the functional units of government, such as defense, energy and water development, agriculture, and education. The members of

Congress who serve on the Appropriations Committees typically gain substantial expertise in their areas of specialization and with this information can influence budget and spending decisions. The subcommittees hold hearings on the budget proposals and mark up their respective budget areas. Upon completion of the subcommittee work, the appropriations bills, like other legislation, move to the full Appropriations Committee and then to the full House or Senate.

What Congress and the president contribute to budget development, in terms of which institution has the primary responsibility, has shifted back and forth throughout U.S. history based on the ebb and flow of power between these branches of government. Major changes occurred in 1974 with the passage of the Congressional Budget and Impoundment Control Act. Congress enacted this legislation to recapture some of the budget authority it had lost to the White House in previous years. The act had a number of noteworthy provisions. First, it created congressional Budget Committees to facilitate the coordination of budget development within the legislative branch. These committees are responsible for setting overall taxing and spending levels (Thurber and Durst 1993). Second, it created the Congressional Budget Office (CBO), a legislative agency responsible for providing Congress with economic and budget information. In the past, Congress often had to rely on the president's OMB estimates and assumptions, and some members were concerned about the potential for political manipulation of the process. The CBO is a nonpartisan organization that most neutral observers believe provides the more accurate assessments of economic and budget issues. If nothing else, Congress now has its own independent assessment of economic assumptions and budget forecasts.

Once Congress passes the budget, the bill goes to the president for his signature or veto in thirteen separate appropriations bills that reflect the functional divisions in government. At this point, the president's options in regard to the budget are limited. He can accept and sign the appropriations bills or veto one or more of them. Many presidents have asked for **line-item veto** authority, a budgeting tool that would allow the president to delete specific items from an appropriations bill without rejecting the whole bill. Many state governors have this power.

The Republican Congress in 1996 provided President Clinton with a version of the line-item veto, sometimes referred to as enhanced rescission authority, that he used a number of times in subsequent years. The Supreme Court, however, in *Clinton v. City of New York* (1998), struck down the line-item veto law as unconstitutional. Specifically, the Court said that the law violated the constitutional provision requiring all legislation to be passed in the same form by both houses of Congress and sent to the president in its entirety for his signature or veto. The Court said by vetoing part of a bill, the president was changing its form.[3]

In recent history, particularly under divided government, partisan politics have made enactment of the budget an excruciating task. The president favors his version of federal spending priorities, and Congress may disagree strongly. If a president is prepared to exercise his veto option, he can force Congress to negotiate with him or risk being held accountable for a breakdown in the budget process. If a budget is not passed by October 1, then technically the government must shut down.

A dramatic example of what can happen if both sides dig in their heels occurred in 1995 when Congress, completely in Republican hands for the first time in forty years, attempted to use the budget to push its agenda. Congress sent its budget to President Clinton for his signature, and he used it as an opportunity to confront the Republicans on what he believed was the wrong direction for the country. He refused to sign the budget, and the result was that the government officially closed—on two separate occasions. In the past when such quarrels occurred, the government shut down for only a few days, with only minor ramifications. In this situation, however, the stalemate between President Clinton and the Republican Congress lasted for almost a month (Thurber 1996b). The other trend in budget politics is for Congress to pass large omnibus bills, often pork-laden, that include many programs the president supports and some he may not. Presidents find it almost impossible to veto these bills.

Typically, however, the president and Congress are able to reach agreement on a budget, even if neither is completely satisfied with the outcome. Sometimes Congress enacts continuing resolutions that allow government agencies to operate while the budget negotiations carry on. When the president signs the final appropriations bills, the budget they represent becomes law, and the next step of the process begins.

## Budget Execution and Control

Once Congress and the president approve a budget, the various government agencies execute it by spending the money to implement the programs receiving budget support. This spending goes for items such as personnel, day-to-day supplies, and providing services and payments to those who qualify under the agency's programs, such as farm price supports or Social Security. Each agency typically decides what mechanisms to use to spend its allotted budget.

The final step in the process, and one that most people pay little attention to, is budget control. After the fiscal year is over, the General Accounting Office (GAO) is responsible for ensuring that the money was spent legally and properly. In many ways this amounts to an audit of the entire government. The GAO reports its findings to Congress, and the members may use the results to reward an agency or hold its metaphorical feet to the fire.

## ECONOMIC POLICY: SUCCESSES AND FAILURES

In the past few decades a number of economic policies have been proposed and implemented. These policies have enjoyed varying degrees of success in achieving their stated goals. Some of them also have unintended consequences, that is, impacts that were neither planned nor foreseen when the policies were designed and implemented. This section considers several of the most significant of these economic policy actions.

## Ronald Reagan's Tax Cuts

When President Reagan took office in 1981, he faced an economy that by many measures was in a recession. Economic growth was low; both inflation and unemployment were high; the deficit was rising; and the country's morale was low. Reagan championed supply-side eco-nomics, which its adherents claimed would encourage investment and economic growth. The political problem for the president was how to sell the idea to a dubious Democratic House of Representatives.

Reagan's electoral mandate—he won 489 electoral votes to President Jimmy Carter's 49—was a major reason for his ability to secure passage of the Economic Recovery Tax Act of 1981. The $162 billion tax cut included a 23 percent reduction in personal income taxes, cuts in the highest tax rate, and major cuts in business taxes (Peterson and Rom 1988). The result was more money in the pockets of individuals, especially the wealthy. The hope of the supply-siders was that this new money would be used to invest in and expand the economy. After a recession in the early 1980s, the U.S. economy indeed began to grow in 1983. Unemploy-ment decreased, and inflation was held in check, so the tax cut and other Reagan economic policies achieved in part many of the administration's economic goals.

One criticism, however, lingers to this day. The president's policies, usually called Reaganomics, created unprecedented increases in the nation's deficit and debt. The national debt went from about $1 trillion in 1981 to well over $5 trillion by the late 1990s. The Reagan administration had hoped that the additional tax revenue generated through economic growth would pay for his spending priorities, including the rise in defense spending. This did not happen. Higher interest rates imposed by the Fed's monetary policy during the 1980s took back part of the money Reagan's fiscal policy had provided. In addition, domestic spend-ing did not slow down enough to offset the potential loss in revenue created by the massive tax cuts. Although the Reagan administration redefined tax policy in many ways, it also helped to create a different problem in terms of economic goals. In fact, it was during this period that policymakers learned to pay more attention than ever before to deficit and debt management in economic policy. Many proposals and policies were offered to address the deficit problem generated by the Reagan policies.

## Gramm-Rudman-Hollings Act

One of the consequences of the Reagan tax cuts was a tremendous growth in the federal budget deficit. Fixing a deficit problem is theoretically a relatively simple matter: either increase taxes or decrease government spending so that revenues are more in line with expenditures. Politi-cally, however, these two policy choices can be difficult. In this particular case, President Reagan was still in office and holding the line against any significant tax increases. Democrats, on the other hand, were unwilling to go along with any additional cuts in the programs they supported. In essence, the political will to decrease the deficit was weak at best. In an effort to deal with the situation, in 1985 Congress enacted the Balanced Budget and Emergency Deficit Control Act, otherwise known as Gramm-Rudman-Hollings (GRH) for the three sen-ators who co-sponsored the legislation.

The idea behind GRH was to require progressive reductions in the deficit over five years to ensure a balanced budget by 1991. Supporters hoped that requiring relatively small reduc-tions in the deficit (about $30 to $40 billion a year) might prove politically feasible. The real innovation with the legislation, however, was an enforcement mechanism that cut spending if

Congress and the president failed to make reductions through the budget process. This mechanism, referred to as sequestration, required automatic spending cuts to ensure achievement of the deficit target in any given year. The spending cuts were to be split evenly between defense and domestic spending.[4] The General Accounting Office was to implement sequestration, but in *Bowsher v. Synar* (1986) the Supreme Court ruled this part of the legislation unconstitutional. This decision led to the enactment of Gramm-Rudman-Hollings II, which gave the sequestration function to the Office of Management and Budget and extended the deficit targets.

The primary goal of GRH and GRH II was to restrain congressional spending and ultimately to achieve a balanced budget. Did it succeed? By almost all accounts, the answer is no. According to GRH, deficits were supposed to decrease by a set amount between 1986 and 1991 until a balanced budget was achieved. In reality, the deficit almost doubled by 1992. Many believed that sequestration would enforce discipline in the budget process because members of Congress or the administration would not want to see forced cuts in their programs. But sequestration was not the "gorilla in the closet" that many thought it would be, and it had little effect on budgetary discipline. The law provided too many loopholes to avoid sequestration. In addition, many legislators saw that forced percentage cuts in their favorite programs were better than targeted cuts that could be larger (Thurber 1996b).

## Budget Enforcement Act

When it became clear that GRH was not going to provide the deficit reductions required, in 1990 Congress and President Bush formulated a new budget plan called the Budget Enforcement Act (BEA). The BEA was similar to GRH in that it attempted to impose discipline on the budget process and to work toward reducing the federal deficit, which was approaching $200 billion by then. The BEA established a deficit reduction target of close to $500 billion over five years. Among the law's most important reforms was a "pay-as-you-go" provision that required all tax and spending legislation to be deficit neutral. In other words, if new legislation increased expenditures for a particular program, the new spending had to be offset either by subsequent increases in revenue or decreases in expenditures in another program. The BEA also established spending ceilings for each discretionary spending category (defense, domestic, and international). If spending went higher, the sequestration process would be applied only to the category of the offending area. Sequestration could occur only by changes to legislation, not by changes in economic conditions (Thurber and Durst 1993).[5]

The effectiveness of the BEA in reducing the deficit has been the subject of serious debate. On the one hand, the deficit was reduced during the late 1990s and the Treasury had a surplus. Some credit the BEA and President Clinton's extension of its components through 1998 as the reason for the country's economic turnaround. On the other hand, others argue that credit for the deficit reduction should go to the nation's economic growth during this time. The reality is that a combination of both factors (and others) improved the country's deficit situation for a few years. Politically, many have been able to take credit for the economic prosperity at the turn of the century. Perhaps the only person who directly experienced negative political ramifications as a result of the BEA was the first President Bush, who broke his "read my lips, no new taxes" pledge when he signed the law. One aspect of the BEA that has become more important over time is the definition of what constitutes an exemption under the law. The BEA always provided for exemptions, situations in which a budget ceiling could be exceeded. For most of the 1990s these situations were limited to true natural or economic disasters. Since then, according to the deputy director of the CBO, "the definition was discarded and any semblance of discipline abandoned" (U.S. Congressional Budget Office 2002). By expanding the definition of what constitutes an emergency, policymakers are able to spend well beyond the limits of the original budget.[6]

## George W. Bush's Tax Cuts

Taking office in 2001, President Bush also had a vision for tax policy in the United States. As part of his campaign, Bush supported an across-the-board tax cut. A significant portion of this cut would go the richest in the nation, which Bush did not see as a problem because the rich pay a significant amount of the taxes. As president, Bush was able to work with the Republican-controlled Congress to enact tax legislation that not only lowered tax brackets but also provided a rebate check of $300 or $600 to many taxpayers during the summer of 2001. The weakening economy helped persuade Congress to approve the bill. It is almost always politically popular to cut taxes, and from an economic standpoint it is an effective way to spur economic growth.

As already noted, however, the tax cut had implications beyond the attempt to stimulate the economy. What were its effects? Was it a fair policy to give large benefits to the rich, especially in light of a growing gap between the rich and the poor (Johnston 1999)? How does the tax cut affect the nation's ability to deal with other public policy issues such as Social Security or Homeland Security following the terrorist attacks of September 11? These will be the crucial questions for the coming years. What do you think?

## FUTURE ECONOMIC ISSUES AND CHALLENGES

Looking at economic policy is always interesting because of the new or renewed challenges that must be faced from year to year. The bear market on Wall Street that started in 2001 and continued into 2002 is ample evidence of this. What might the near term hold in regard to economic challenges and issues for the United States? In addition to the changing nature of budgetary politics, where surpluses can become deficits in a matter of months, there are many other issues to consider.

## Maintaining Economic Growth

America's years of strong, sustained economic growth produced many positive benefits: tax receipts were up; unemployment was and continues to be low; the deficit was eliminated; and there were decreases in the national debt. People across the nation saw the benefits of a strong economy as their wages rose and opportunities for personal advancement expanded. It is clear, however, that this kind of sustained growth could not go on forever.

Growth is a cornerstone of not only a strong economy but also a satisfied electorate, which can translate to a stable political system. The economic growth of the 1990s facilitated action on many of the nation's problems such as the deficit. The strong economy also made possible the action on welfare reform in 1996 and the related policies. Many analysts point out that states were able to meet the caseload reduction requirements of the law because of the strong economy and its effect on employment. When jobs are plentiful people can move off the welfare rolls. The strong economy also allowed Congress to spend money on highway construction and maintenance, budget items that had been deferred because of deficits. These expenditures not only help local communities but also allow members of Congress to score political points with their constituents.

The real challenge for the United States and its economy is what to do when economic growth begins to lose momentum. The 2001 slowdown demonstrated that it is not realistic to expect a high level of growth to continue indefinitely. Will some of the changes in public policy since the late 1990s need to be revisited if the economy continues to be relatively stagnant? These decisions will likely be more difficult for policymakers than trying to figure out how to spend a budget surplus. The box "Working with Sources: Views on Economics and Budgeting" provides some additional sources of information from a variety of organizations interested in budget and economic policy.

## Growth of Entitlements

It is almost impossible these days to pick up a newspaper and not see a story that deals with entitlement programs in the United States. An entitlement program is one with payment

### WORKING WITH SOURCES

#### VIEWS ON ECONOMICS AND BUDGETING

Many of the economic and budget sites available on the Web represent various partisan and ideological perspectives. Some focus on macrobudget issues, while others are concerned with the budget's effects on specific programs and policy areas. Explore the sites and try to identify the partisan or ideological orientation of the organization that sponsors each of them. How evident are the differences in political orientation? What kind of information tells you most reliably what each organization's political leanings are?

**www.nber.org.** National Bureau of Economic Research.
**www.taxfoundation.org.** The Tax Foundation
**www.concordcoalition.org.** The Concord Coalition
**www.whitehouse.gov/cea/index.html.** Council of Economic Advisors
**www.cbpp.org.** Center on Budget and Policy Priorities

obligations determined by the law that created it, not by the budget associated with that program. Under an entitlement program, any person who meets the eligibility requirements is entitled to receive benefits from the program. The clearest example of an entitlement program is Social Security. When people reach a certain age, they are eligible to receive Social Security payments. A major difference between an entitlement program and other government programs is how it is funded. The usual budget process does not apply; in other words, Social Security administrators do not determine their annual budgets as other agencies do. To change the amount of money spent on an entitlement program, Congress has to amend the authorizing law.

By most estimates, entitlement programs account for more than 50 percent of the federal budget. Unless policymakers decide to change the substance of the law, more than half the federal budget is out of their hands at the start. Moreover, entitlements have grown tremendously. In 1968 entitlements made up approximately 28 percent of the budget, but they were at 54 percent in Bush's proposed budget for fiscal year 2003. That is a very large increase in just thirty-five years, and the programs are expected to grow. One of the major concerns with the ever-expanding entitlement programs is that they crowd out other budget expenditures. These other programs must go through the typical budget process and may take the brunt of any cuts because of their more precarious position. So-called discretionary spending, which includes funding for defense, environmental programs, national parks, and upgrading air traffic control systems, among other programs, has decreased significantly as a percentage of the budget in part because of the growing entitlement expenses. How likely is it that the government can get entitlements under control? Economically, it makes sense to do this because policymakers would probably want more authority over government spending. From an equity perspective, it seems only right that no government expenditures receive special treatment in the budget process. The real issue is political. Why did policymakers decide to make programs such as Social Security and Medicare entitlements in the first place? The answer to this question explains why it is so difficult to make changes now.

## Financial Scandals

The year 2002 was something of a landmark for corporate financial scandals. Enron, Arthur Andersen, WorldCom, AOL Time Warner, Halliburton, and scores of other large companies were plagued by discoveries that in several cases left the companies in ruin. Even Martha Stewart and her corporation came under investigation. Stories of CEOs and other top-level managers walking away with millions of dollars, while their employees lost their jobs or retirement benefits, raised the question of what the government should be doing to prevent such abuses. As stock averages plunged, public outrage over the scandals and loss of confidence in the financial markets made the headlines throughout the year.

Both political parties called for action, perhaps starting with the vigorous prosecution of those responsible. In mid-2002 Congress passed and President Bush signed legislation imposing new accounting regulations on publicly traded companies.[7] But further government regulation of business may be needed to prevent fraudulent accounting practices and other misdeeds.

The deregulation of the financial industry during the 1990s was partly responsible for the scandals of 2001 and 2002. Individuals and companies took advantage of looser regulation to inflate earnings in order to deceive shareholders and the public and drive up stock prices, which translated into higher earnings for corporate executives. How closely can government regulate business without undermining the operations of a free market? Policymakers and corporate executives disagree on the issue, and the debate is certain to continue. Some companies argue that excessive regulation could prevent them from making reasonable corporate decisions without fear of prosecution. Moreover, the corporate scandals also served as a reminder that it is difficult for government to regulate the financial ethics of individuals. Ultimately, public and shareholder pressure on businesses to operate openly and fairly may have a greater effect than legislative restrictions.

## Challenges for State Governments

State governments also face challenges, some old and some new. The states have always been obliged to keep their fiscal houses in order, and this task became more problematic during President Reagan's devolution movement, which led to more responsibilities for the states, but not necessarily to more funding to carry them out. The 1980s also saw an increase in the number of unfunded mandates imposed on states. As noted in Chapter 2, unfunded mandates are federal requirements (often regulatory) placed upon the states without federal funding to pay for them. The result was that many states had to either cut services in other areas or raise their own taxes to ensure compliance. Unfunded mandates were alleviated to some extent with passage of the Unfunded Mandates Reform Act in 1995.

States found relief from their financial woes during the the strong economic growth period of the late 1990s, which also helped the federal government deal with its deficit. Many states were running budget surpluses, providing tax relief to their citizens, and expanding services. The passage of welfare reform in 1996 (see Chapter 9), while transferring still more responsibilities to the state governments, came with federal money attached. In many states, the strong economy allowed public officials to reduce their welfare caseloads while using only a fraction of their allotted federal dollars. Many states, in fact, began to use the money for experimental programs such as subsidized day care.

Because states typically may not run deficits, the economic bust that followed was harder on state governments than on the federal government, which can spend money it does not have. The economic slowdown had detrimental impacts on state tax revenues, and deficit projections quickly became the rule for many states. According to the National Association of State Budget Officers, by the end of fiscal year 2002, forty states had budget shortfalls totaling more than $40 billion. The shortfalls forced many states to reduce spending, lay off employees, or use rainy-day funds (National Association of State Budget Officers 2002). Some states even used money from their share of the states' settlement with the U.S. tobacco companies, which was supposed to be earmarked for smoking reduction programs, to balance their budgets. The increase in entitlement programs also affects the states. The Medicaid program especially has stressed, and will continue to stress, state budgets. These pressures will require state policymakers to use all the fiscal tools at their disposal to ensure budgetary integrity in the years ahead.

The past several years have seen many states struggle with financial problems and deficits attributable in large part to a slow economy. State funding for a variety of programs has had to be reduced, and states and communities have been forced to adopt controversial approaches to generate additional revenue. The Temecula Valley Unified School District (shown above), for example, began charging students fees to use school buses in 2001 as a way to deal with budgetary concerns. The imposition of fees is sometimes more politically acceptable than tax increases because the fees only affect those using the service. States have imposed similar fee increases for hunting and fishing licenses.

## FOCUSED DISCUSSION: SURPLUSES AS FAR AS THE EYE CAN SEE . . . TOO BAD WE NEED GLASSES NOW

For a while it seemed that the numbers would keep getting larger. During 2000 each estimated surplus number stating what the surplus would be for the next ten years was greater than the last. In February the Clinton White House projected $746 billion; then in June the figure rose to $1.87 trillion. By July the nonpartisan CBO projected the highest level yet, with the ten-year surplus estimated to reach $2.2 trillion. A number of facts backed up these rosy scenarios, including a strong economy, higher tax revenues, and prudent fiscal policies during the 1990s. But, as has been stressed throughout the chapter, the picture can change quickly with regard to surpluses and deficits, and, despite the return of deficits, it should be clear that this situation can change again with the expansion of economic growth. Long-term projections show that the United States will once again experience surpluses. In that case, what should policymakers do with the money? This focused discussion explores a few of the most frequently suggested alternatives, including the proposals advanced by presidential candidates in the 2000 election, when the surplus was quite large.

The choices available for what to do with a surplus are relatively straightforward and not necessarily mutually exclusive. In fact, many argue that the money should be used to meet more than one of the following objectives:

- pay down the national debt;
- increase the solvency of entitlement programs such as Social Security or Medicare;
- increase spending in the discretionary area;
- provide either an across-the-board or targeted tax cut.

The argument to use surplus funds to pay off the national debt is related to concerns over controlling the federal deficit. It is a way of showing that the nation's financial house is in order, with no debt to worry about. Those who support using the money to improve the solvency of entitlements argue that it needs to be done when funds are available and before the huge baby boom generation retires and funding for these programs could be threatened. Supporters of using the surplus to increase discretionary spending believe that these programs suffered during times of fiscal austerity and need sufficient funds to achieve their established goals. Tax cut advocates say that the government should not collect more revenue than it needs and should give the money back to the people who paid it.

All of these choices involve complex economic relationships that need to be better understood in order to comprehend the arguments put forth and the consequences of each choice. This section examines some of the economic, political, and ethical issues associated with each.

## Economic Issues

The economic issues associated with how to spend a federal budget surplus may be a bit different from those of the other public policy areas discussed in the next chapters. Here, the discussion does not necessarily attempt to address a problem of a market failure, such as a negative externality, but the budget has obvious economic implications that should be understood when looking at the alternatives provided.

Many economists and the Fed chairman continue to support using a surplus to pay down and eventually eliminate the national debt. As long as the United States has to pay interest on the national debt, it cannot use the money for government programs or a tax cut. Many people believe that the general economic situation would improve if the national debt were eliminated. Paying off the debt or even part of it should also lower interest rates and make money available for borrowers who would no longer have to compete for it with the government. Such a development should then spur economic growth, depending on other economic conditions. The money not used for interest payments could spur economic growth in one of two ways. If a tax cut is provided, then people have more money to spend or invest in the economy. If it is used for additional federal spending programs, then it could create jobs that would also stimulate economic growth.

The major arguments for using surplus funds to guarantee entitlement programs are more politically and equity based than the national debt arguments. The pool of people eligible for entitlement programs continues to grow, and the programs will face a crisis when the first baby boomers reach retirement age. The economic argument for using the surplus to ensure the solvency of these programs is the potential impact on the budget if money is not supplied to them. If the government is to continue the programs at the current levels, the money will have to be taken from other budget sources. It is projected that by 2017 the costs of Social Security will be greater than the revenue generated, and that, based on current trends, the trust fund will be exhausted by 2041 (U.S. Social Security Administration 2002c). At that point, money will have to come from general tax revenues to finance the Social Security program, which means either an increase in income taxes or a decrease in federal spending in other areas (or a combination of the two).[8]

The arguments in support of using the surplus to increase discretionary expenditures are either political or related to equity concerns. In some situations, one could say that the amount budgeted for an activity is insufficient to alleviate the existing market failure. For example, perhaps the amount budgeted for environmental protection is inadequate to address the negative externalities associated with the production of goods and services. Another example may be that the funds to ensure a capable military are currently insufficient and that it is the government's responsibility to provide this pure public good. In terms of how the surplus could affect economic growth, the government, by spending the money, can encourage growth by creating new employment opportunities. A good example would be financing infrastructure projects such as urban renewal or building or renovating schools.

The last choice is use the surplus to provide a tax cut. This option can also have major economic impacts depending on the type of tax cut adopted. An across-the-board cut on income taxes puts more money into people's pockets, allowing them to spend and invest more, which should stimulate economic growth. Targeted tax cuts for certain individuals can have similar effects, because whoever benefits from a tax cut will have additional money in their pockets. A targeted tax cut can also be used to address a market failure. For example, a program that allows college students or their parents to deduct tuition costs from their taxes provides a targeted tax break for higher education, which has positive externalities that potentially benefit everyone with a better educated society.

## Political Issues

To say that politics drives most of the debate surrounding the budget surplus alternatives would be a vast understatement. When the nation was suffering from huge deficits, budget austerity masked the ideological differences between the parties because the lack of funds made any discussion of new ideas or programs futile. The surplus brought out ideas on how to spend the money and prompted debate between the political parties and candidates with strong ideological differences over spending priorities.

The proposals of the major party presidential candidates for 2000 are a preview of future conflict if and when surpluses return. The Republican candidate, Governor Bush of Texas, asserted that the money should be returned to the taxpayers. He said he would use a quarter of the federal budget surplus to provide a broad tax cut to all Americans. The Democratic candidate, Vice President Al Gore, offered a broader range of alternatives on how to use the surplus, with the focus on the solvency of Social Security. He also stressed other programs, such as a prescription drug plan for Medicare recipients and paying down the national debt. The partisan differences were clear, and they highlighted the inevitable political debates over such economic policy choices. After President Bush's election, Congress approved a major tax cut that significantly shrank the budget surplus.

Using surplus funds to pay down the national debt is a far less controversial proposal that generates little political debate. Most people support the idea of having a smaller debt as a way of showing fiscal responsibility. President Clinton also seemed to focus on debt reduction during the final months of his presidency, claiming that the national debt would be eliminated by 2013. What is interesting about this option is that as long as the money is not earmarked for a specific project, the surplus automatically goes toward debt reduction. In other words, if no proposals are implemented, the entire amount would go to paying off the debt. So, although major partisan disagreements still surface over how best to spend the surplus, if the parties cannot agree, then the funds are automatically directed toward the national debt.

Promoting a policy that uses the surplus to improve the solvency of the government's entitlement programs has many political implications. In general, those who back this option point out that Social Security and Medicare need additional funds to remain solvent when the baby boomers begin to retire. Not surprisingly, organizations that represent the elderly, such as the AARP, favor this option, but the general population supports it as well. According to a CBS News/*NY Times* poll conducted in May 2000, 54 percent of the respondents believe that the surplus should be used to preserve programs like Social Security and Medicare rather than for tax cuts or to pay down the national debt (Berke and Elder 2000). This strong support likely reflects the belief that everyone expects to benefit from these programs in the future, and politicians find it difficult to argue against using the surplus this way. Few policymakers want to go against one of the strongest interest groups in the country or such clear public support for a policy option. So the debate regarding this economic policy alternative has shifted from the use of the surplus to ways to reform the programs that may be politically popular.

For example, when he was governor, Bush expressed support for a partial privatization of Social Security that would allow people to invest a portion of their payroll deductions in the stock market, with the expectation that this option would generate higher returns than the traditional Social Security program. This idea is appealing because the stock market traditionally returns a higher percentage on investments than the government bonds the Social Security system has to buy. It also garners support from younger workers who want to maximize their retirement benefits and who are concerned about whether Social Security will be there for them in the future. Gore proposed keeping the current Social Security program intact and creating a separate retirement savings plan to put more money into people's accounts by matching their savings with federal dollars. Politically, this plan was popular because it claimed to ensure some level of benefits for everyone ("keeping Social Security secure") while also attempting to provide additional benefits to middle- and low-wage earners by helping them to save more for their retirement.

The third option—to use the surplus to increase spending for new or current programs—

sparks the most heated political debates. Republicans claim that such proposals are nothing more than big government operating as usual. As soon as the money comes in, it is spent on a program. They label those promoting the option (typically Democrats) as "tax and spend" politicians, making decisions on how best to spend "your money." Nevertheless, it is clear that many discretionary programs experienced little, if any, growth during the 1990s because of partisan disagreement over the goals of certain programs. New spending, such as adding prescription drug benefits to the Medicare program, also can raise intriguing political debates. Supporters claim it is a necessity in the current environment of sharply rising medical care costs (see Chapter 8), but opponents are concerned about the expense of such a program and the implications for the private market. For example, will government support cause prices to go up or will the government attempt to impose price controls on drug companies?

The last option, providing a tax cut, is an issue that Republicans traditionally exploit in policy debates. Both parties understand that no one enjoys paying taxes and that, if the opportunity arises to provide tax relief, it usually benefits the party offering to do it. Moreover, Republicans tend to favor reducing tax revenues as a way of depriving the government of the ability to pay for programs that Democrats favor. What is interesting to note, however, was the limited public support for tax relief during the 2000 presidential race. Based on the May 2000 CBS/NY Times survey, only a small percentage of respondents supported the tax cut option as the way to spend the budget surplus. At the time, it appeared that Americans were not overly concerned about their tax rates. Some Democrats have been able to point to this lack of support as evidence that the money could best be used somewhere else. In addition, some have argued that a tax cut could lead to higher interest rates, which in turn have significant implications for the economy.

Given the size of the surplus in 2000–2001, many policymakers who did not initially support tax cuts began to see the political advantages of doing so, at least for a portion of the surplus. The major difference between the parties and different proposals was in the type of tax cut provided. Targeted tax cuts for certain income classes or for certain policy areas, such as child care or tuition for higher education, typically generate more support than cutting the general tax rates. Politically, those who support targeted tax cuts can expect to garner support from those who benefit. When Bush's proposals for across-the-board tax cuts and tax rebates came to Congress, however, both political parties supported them, especially because of the concerns about the economy and the need to spur economic growth. The Bush administration's later round of tax cut proposals, which continued to favor the wealthy, met with more skepticism. The ever-increasing deficit, additional expenditures for homeland security and the war in Iraq, and continued concerns regarding equity have caused many members of Congress, from both parties, to question further tax cuts focused primarily on the rich.

## Equity and Other Ethical Issues

As is often the case with ethical issues, people have different ideas of what is fair or moral. For example, is it fair to take in more revenue than is necessary to cover expenditures? Is it moral to retreat from a promise made years ago? When the question is what the government should have done with the surplus or what it should do with a future surplus, equity and ethics can inform the discussion.

It may be difficult to conceive of moral or fairness arguments for using the surplus to pay down or eliminate the national debt, but those who favor this step offer two reasons why it is the right thing to do. First, living within one's means is valued in American society, and, if doing so is expected of individuals, why not of the government? Second, many believe that it is unfair to burden future generations with a debt that accumulated because of policies over which they had no control. This concern is usually termed *intergenerational equity.*

Others say that the moral argument is strongest for using the surplus to ensure the solvency of entitlement programs, especially Social Security and Medicare. They argue that Social Security is a promise to the American public or a contract the government has with workers: if

Based in a south Denver suburb, Canadian Meds USA is the brainchild of accountant Don Bozarth, who conceived the idea in 2002 while looking for cheaper prescription drugs for his mother-in-law. Bozarth and his wife Jo-Ann (pictured above on the right) ordered several prescriptions through an online pharmacy in Winnipeg, Manitoba, and saved $225 on a three-month supply. Today the company acts as an intermediary between several Canadian pharmacies and U.S. clients, many elderly and living on limited incomes. Some have argued that should the United States once again enjoy a budget surplus, a portion of the money ought to be used to shore up or enhance entitlement programs such as Social Security and Medicare. For example, the surplus could provide prescription drug benefits to Medicare recipients so that senior citizens would not be forced to purchase drugs from Canada or Mexico.

employees contribute during their working lives, the program will pay benefits upon retirement or disability. If the funds are not available because too many people have become eligible, has the government broken its word? Is its action unfair or immoral? Why would anyone want to finance a program that will not provide the promised benefits? As Chapter 9 discusses, many Americans see Social Security as one of the government's most successful programs, and many policymakers and other interested parties therefore consider its stability a priority.

Fairness arguments for using the surplus to increase discretionary spending or to initiate new program spending reflect a different perspective. For years these programs have suffered from budget austerity. Proponents argue that the time to make up for their financial neglect is during a period of budget surplus. The nation's infrastructure is in serious disrepair; education spending is not keeping pace with inflation; and, some argue, military spending and preparedness have suffered. If a surplus were available, it might be possible to alleviate some of these shortcomings. Moreover, these are programs that benefit many people, and they are not limited by eligibility requirements, which some may also see as a more equitable use of government resources.

Many people claim that using the surplus to fund a tax cut is the fairest policy because the money belongs to the people and should be returned to them. The appropriate criterion here is personal freedom and the desire to limit government actions that threaten it. Typically, those supporting limited government also push for citizens to be taxed at the lowest possible level and, in this particular case, they believe that it is immoral for the government to retain excess revenue. It is easy to champion this choice because it plays to many people's fears of an overzealous government that taxes too much and may intrude excessively into citizens' lives through a variety of public policies.

Clearly, all four of the major alternatives for spending a budget surplus have merit, and it is difficult to know which is the best. From a political standpoint, policymakers are likely to advocate using a surplus for many different programs that would not only benefit the country but also bring policymakers the greatest support from the public and specific constituencies. It also must be recognized that much of the budget surplus discussion and what to do with excess money may be moot and likely to remain so for years.

The surplus estimates policymakers have been discussing are based on economic assumptions that may or may not prove to be reasonable. According to the Congressional Budget Office, a one-half of one percentage point decrease in the economic growth projections for 2010 would wipe out a multi-billion dollar surplus. In addition, one of the projections is based on government spending that increases only at the rate of inflation. Many would say that assumption is politically unrealistic given the pressures on policymakers to support popular programs. Even more critical are the changes in the country's situation. The September 11 terrorists attacks and the subsequent policies in response, both military and domestic, were enormously expensive. The war in Iraq that began in March 2003 promised to be costly as well, and analysts expect that the task of rebuilding Iraq following the confrontation will also cost billions. Estimates of the accumulated expenditure as of 2003 were as high as $100 billion. These additional expenditures come at a time when the nation is already facing deficits over $200 billion. Yet many policymakers exhibit little concern for the consequences of such deficit spending.

## CONCLUSIONS

This chapter is the first in the text to consider a substantive public policy issue and its purpose is to demonstrate the different ways to examine problems, alternatives, and policies related to economic policy and budgeting. In other words, it shows how to apply the tools of policy analysis to real issues and the decisions policymakers reach.

Economic policymaking is a bit different from most of the other substantive areas the next chapters discuss. It is almost always a starting point for other policy areas because money or the lack of it influences so much of what government policymakers do at all levels. The best solutions to deal with issues such as prescription drugs for the elderly, terrorism within U.S. borders, or the disposal of nuclear waste can not be adopted and implemented without adequate funding. This chapter shows that budget data and projections change frequently and this information affects how policymakers address a particular problem or fail to do so.

Policy analysis can help policymakers make informed decisions about how to use a limited budget with a number of competing goals. It can also help citizens to better understand how and why these decisions are made. Why, for example, did Congress enact one of the largest agricultural subsidy programs in U.S. history at a time when the nation was again experiencing deficits? How can local leaders justify to their community an increase in a sales tax to build a new professional sports stadium? How did a $200 billion surplus turn into a deficit in a matter of months? Policy analysis of economic and budget matters can help people appreciate the difficulties of these kinds of questions and understand the policies proposed to address them. In the chapters that follow, students will find similar arguments about the importance of thinking critically and creatively about possible solutions to challenges in a range of policy areas.

## DISCUSSION QUESTIONS

The Federal Reserve Board is somewhat independent of political and citizen control in the making of monetary policy. Why do you think the system was set up in this way? Is the independence of the Fed a problem or a strength?

Has your state or local government ever experienced difficulty approving a budget? How did the policymakers handle the situation? What consequences, if any, were associated with the inability to agree on a budget?

Economic policy, as shown in this chapter, depends heavily on projections of future developments, for example, of economic growth and tax revenues. What questions would you ask about any such forecast to determine its reliability?

Why do you think entitlement programs have grown so large in the United States?

Policymakers often use the term "emergency situations" to justify breaking a budget agreement. What would you consider to be an emergency?

## SUGGESTED READINGS

Jeffrey H. Birnbaum and Alan S. Murray, *Showdown at Gucci Gulch: Lawmakers, Lobbyists, and the Unlikely Triumph of Tax Reform* (New York: Vintage, 1987). A journalistic account of the politics of tax reform and how interest groups try to get their most important goals enacted.

Jeffrey E. Cohen, *Politics and Economic Policy in the United States,* 2d ed. (Boston: Houghton Mifflin, 2000). A comprehensive and understandable overview of economic policy, organized around the theme of equity versus efficiency in economic decisions.

Marc Allen Eisner, Jeff Worsham, and Evan J. Ringquist, *Contemporary Regulatory Policy* (Boulder: Lynne Rienner, 2000). One of the few books on regulatory policy. It focuses on the idea of regulatory change and why it occurs. Has chapters on substantive regulatory policies, such as environmental protection, telecommunication, workplace safety, and consumer product safety.

John M. Rothgeb Jr., *U.S. Trade Policy: Balancing Economic Dreams and Political Realities* (Washington, D.C.: CQ Press, 2001). A concise text covering international trade, the political tensions related to it, and its historical roots.

Aaron Wildavsky, *The New Politics of the Budgetary Process* (New York: HarperCollins, 1992). A classic in the field of budget politics and development. The book promotes incrementalism as a way of government budget development—that is, agencies make very small adjustments (typically increases) in their budgets from one year to the next. The book discusses the politics of budgeting as well as many of the institutions and processes responsible for development of the federal budget.

## SUGGESTED WEB SITES

**http://epinet.org.** The Economic Policy Institute is a nonpartisan think tank that examines strategies to promote a fair and prosperous economy. The site contains reports relating to economic and budget issues as well as other substantive policies and how they affect economic issues.

**http://w3.access.gpo.gov/usbudget.** This Government Printing Office site lists Office of Management and Budget documents providing information regarding the current presidential budget proposal submitted to Congress. In addition, you can access past years' budget information, as well as "A Citizen's Guide to the Federal Budget."

**www.cbo.gov.** The Congressional Budget Office provides analysis of economic and budget issues. This site has a variety of data, projections, reports, and analyses on economic issues. This is also the place to get specific budget analysis publications on a range of government issues.

**www.federalreserve.gov.** The main web site for the Federal Reserve Board provides a variety of information on monetary policy, how the Fed works, and how it uses its tools to affect the economy.

**www.treas.gov.** U.S. Department of Treasury site provides general information on economic issues such as taxes, financial markets, and current events. The Public Debt Online link can be accessed to get information on the public debt, including what the debt is at a specific moment.

**www.whitehouse.gov/fsbr/esbr.html.** The Economic Statistics Briefing Room provides current economic indicator information such as unemployment rates and income averages.

## MAJOR LEGISLATION

## KEYWORDS

CHAPTER 8

# HEALTH CARE POLICY

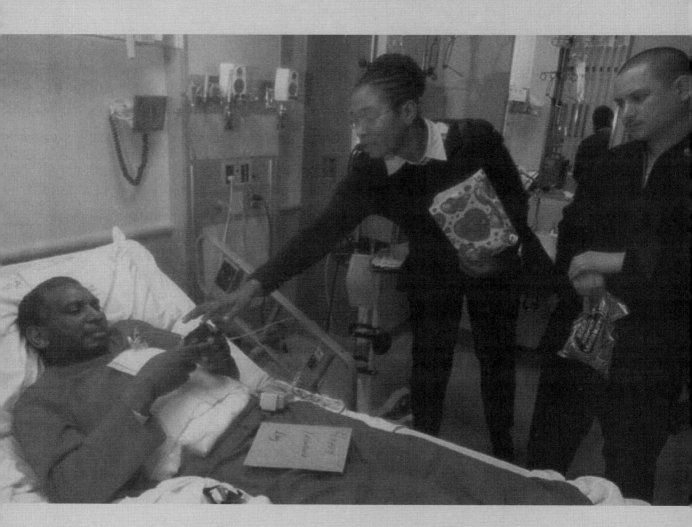

AFTER SEVERAL YEARS OF MODERATE INCREASES, SPENDING ON HEALTH care in the United States soared by nearly 7 percent in 2000 and rose another 8.7 percent in 2001. As a result, health care costs once again moved to the center of the policy agenda. In 2001 insurance premiums for employers went up an average of 11 percent, with little relief in sight. The situation of the California Public Employees' Retirement System, the country's second largest purchaser of health care after the federal government, is an example of what employers face. For 2003 the California system was anticipating a 25 percent rise for its basic **health maintenance organization** (HMO) contracts, and a 19 percent to 22 percent rise for its **preferred provider organization** (PPO) alternative. The steep increases were attributed primarily to hospital services, such as higher wages for nurses and other staff in short supply, and surging prescription drug costs. Spending for prescription drugs in the United States tripled between 1990 and 2000, reaching more than $140 billion per year, and the trend is expected to continue.

Serving its 1.3 million employees and retirees will put enormous strains on the California system, but the state is not alone. Almost every other employer in the nation faces the same kind of challenge as they struggle to deal with rising costs without sacrificing high quality but still affordable health care for their employees. Nevertheless, most employees will almost certainly pay more for health insurance, receive reduced benefits, and face increased pressure to think more carefully about how best to balance the benefits and costs of health care. The days of unlimited and almost free health care are over.[1]

No other area of public policy reaches so deeply into the personal lives of Americans as health care and how to pay for it. Most people rely on employer-provided health care insurance, for which they pay a portion of the cost, or on government programs to meet essential heath care needs. Federal and state health care policies also affect the uninsured and those who pay for their own insurance. Government policies influence access to and the quality of health services across the country, the pace of development and approval of new drugs and medical technologies, and the extent of health research that could lead to new life-saving treatments. Whether the concern is regular check-ups for babies or coping with a life-threatening illness, health care policy decisions eventually affect everyone.

Airmen Robin Cross and Michael Matui give former soldier Ben Freeman a Valentine's Day card and candy as they pass out cards and treats to patients at the Baltimore Veterans Affairs Medical Center. The Department of Veterans Affairs operates over 170 hospitals, 400 outpatient clinics, and 130 nursing homes nationwide. In total, these facilities provide services to some 2.6 million veterans annually. Congress has been relatively generous in funding health care services for the nation's veterans. Yet, as with other federally funded health care programs, scarce budgetary resources do translate into a reduction in the amount and quality of care available to patients such as Mr. Freeman.

This chapter examines some of the problems associated with health care services and the public policies designed to ensure that citizens have access to them. As with other areas of public policy, disagreement exists over the degree of government involvement and how much should be left to the private sector, which includes physicians, insurance companies, and pharmaceutical houses. In addition, among the major controversies in health care are how best to deal with escalating costs, how to ensure sufficient access to health services, and how to maintain the quality of health care services while containing costs. The discussion begins with background information about the evolution of major public policies, such as Medicare and Medicaid, and some of the leading policy disputes: the role of managed care, patients' rights, the high cost of prescription drugs, and the potential of preventive health care and other strategies to keep people healthy and save money. Particular attention is paid, as always, to the effectiveness of current public policies and to economic efficiency and equity issues.

## BACKGROUND

Health care policy includes the actions that governments take to influence the provision of health care services and the various government activities that affect or attempt to affect public health and well-being. Health care policy can be viewed narrowly to mean the design and implementation of federal and state programs that affect the provision of health care services, such as Medicare and Medicaid. It also can be defined more broadly by recognizing that government engages in other activities that influence both public and private health care decision making. For example, the government funds health science research and public health departments and agencies; subsidizes medical education and hospital construction; regulates food, drugs, and medical devices; regulates health-damaging environmental pollution; and allows tax deductions for some health care expenditures.

As a government activity, health care policy is relatively recent, even though governments at every level long ago established public health agencies to counter the threat of infectious diseases and related problems. They also dealt with drinking water supplies, sanitation, and waste removal. Those agencies continue such work today, and, particularly at the federal level, some of the bureaucracies and the programs they manage are sizable by any measure. A brief mention of three of the leading agencies, the Food and Drug Administration (FDA), the National Institutes of Health (NIH), and the Centers for Disease Control and Prevention (CDC), helps to put direct health care service programs into perspective. The box "Working with Sources: Health Care Policy Information" lists some useful Web sites to begin a policy investigation.

Since 1862, when it employed a single chemist and was housed in the U.S. Department of Agriculture (USDA), the Food and Drug Administration has overseen the development of new drugs and medical devices as well as the nation's food supply, other than meat and poultry, which the USDA regulates. The modern FDA dates from 1906, when it was authorized by the Federal Food and Drugs Act and regulatory functions were added to the agency's scientific mission. The agency is now part of the Department of Health and Human Services (HHS). In 2001 the FDA employed about 9,100 people and had a budget of $1.3 billion. In addition to food and drugs, the agency is responsible for regulating biologics (vaccines and blood products); the label-

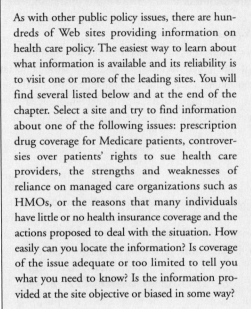

## WORKING WITH SOURCES

### HEALTH CARE POLICY INFORMATION

As with other public policy issues, there are hundreds of Web sites providing information on health care policy. The easiest way to learn about what information is available and its reliability is to visit one or more of the leading sites. You will find several listed below and at the end of the chapter. Select a site and try to find information about one of the following issues: prescription drug coverage for Medicare patients, controversies over patients' rights to sue health care providers, the strengths and weaknesses of reliance on managed care organizations such as HMOs, or the reasons that many individuals have little or no health insurance coverage and the actions proposed to deal with the situation. How easily can you locate the information? Is coverage of the issue adequate or too limited to tell you what you need to know? Is the information provided at the site objective or biased in some way?

**www.aahp.org.** The American Association of Health Plans site, a leading industry trade association. It has broad and excellent coverage of and links to the full range of health care policy issues.

**www.hpolicy.duke.edu/cyberexchange.** Duke University's Health Policy CyberExchange, with exhaustive information on health care and health care policy, and extensive links to health care policy study centers, government agencies, media sources, and other organizations.

**www.iom.edu.** The Institute of Medicine, a component of the National Academies and a major source for reliable health care studies. Also includes links to related sites for health care studies and reports.

**www.kaisernetwork.org.** One of the premier online resources for coverage of health policy news and debate.

**www.nytimes.com/pages/health/index.html.** *New York Times* health news page.

**www.policyalmanac.org/health/index.shtml.** The Almanac of Policy Issues health care page, with many useful links to news, organizations, government agencies, health care statistics, and a range of health policy issues.

ing and safety of cosmetics once they come to market; medical devices, including contact lenses; and radiation in consumer products such as microwave ovens and cell phones.

The federal government is actively engaged in health science research and has been for years. Generous budgets allowed the government to expand its research into the causes of various diseases and possible treatments. The National Institutes of Health, the primary vehicle for federal health science research, was founded in 1887, and consists of twenty-seven separate institutes and centers. NIH is one of eight health agencies of the U.S. Public Health Service, itself a component of HHS. After doubling from 1998 to 2003, NIH's annual budget was in excess of $27 billion, which supports health research across the nation at colleges and universities, medical research centers, and on the NIH main campus in Bethesda, Maryland. The agency took on a national security role following the anthrax scares of October 2001.

The federal Centers for Disease Control and Prevention has been part of the Public Health Service of HHS since 1973. The CDC was established in 1946 as the Communicable Disease Center. It focuses on the development and application of disease prevention and control, environmental health, and health promotion and education. The CDC has long been involved in programs dealing with immunization, the prevention and control of AIDS and other infectious diseases, chronic disease prevention, birth defects and developmental disabilities, occupational safety and health, and the compilation of a treasure trove of national health statistics. After the anthrax scare, the CDC took on expanded responsibilities for threats of bioterrorism and emergency operations. The CDC works through eleven institutes, centers, and offices, and it has a workforce of 8,500 employees and a budget of nearly $8 billion.

As this brief look at the three agencies makes clear, the federal government has been involved in public health, if not the actual provision of health care services, for a considerable period of time. The same is true of state and local governments. Government involvement in health care services, on the other hand, is relatively recent, and in many ways, despite expenditures of more than $600 billion a year, it is still a limited form of intervention into the private sector.

## Evolution of Health Care Policy

What is considered the core of health care policy developed in the United States only after the 1930s, with the idea of health insurance. Individuals could take out an insurance policy, much as they did for their lives, houses, or cars, that would defray the cost of health care should an illness develop or an injury occur. Health insurance works the same way now, but instead of individual policies, most people are insured through their jobs. Employer-sponsored health insurance became popular in the 1950s after the Internal Revenue Service ruled that its cost was a tax-deductible business expense. By the early 1960s the push was on for federal health insurance policies, primarily to aid the poor and the elderly, two segments of the population that normally would not benefit from employer-provided health plans. It is clear that equity concerns in access to health care services were important as health care policy developed. Those efforts culminated in the enactment of the federal Medicare and Medicaid programs in 1965 (Marmor 1999).

Even with adoption of these two programs, the U.S. health care system still falls well short of other industrialized nations, where national health insurance, also known as single-payer (the government) insurance, is the norm. Campaigns to adopt national health insurance in the United States date back to 1948, when the Democratic Party platform endorsed the idea. Members of Congress began to introduce bills to create such a program, but they were unsuccessful, except for the decision in 1965 to establish insurance programs for the poor and the elderly.

The most recent effort to create a national health insurance program occurred in 1993 when President Bill Clinton submitted the National Health Security Act to Congress after extensive analysis by a presidential health care task force headed by his wife, Hillary Rodham Clinton. The plan would have guaranteed health insurance to every American, including the thirty-four million who were uninsured at the time. It proposed doing so through a system of health care alliances that would function much like current managed care organizations. The plan called for individuals to pay about $1,800 a year for coverage, and families about $4,200; both amounts are less than private insurance rates for most of the population. Most employers would have been required to cover their employees under the plan, with subsidies for small businesses that otherwise could not afford to pay.

Republicans in Congress argued that the Clinton plan was too expensive, bureaucratic, and intrusive. The health insurance industry also criticized the plan. The insurance companies lobbied intensely against it and mounted a costly television advertising campaign designed to turn the public against the plan. In the end the Clinton recommendations failed to win congressional approval, as did the many alternatives that members of Congress proposed (Hacker 1997; Rushefsky and Patel 1998). The failure was a classic story of the kind of policy gridlock described in Chapter 2. Divided government cannot be blamed for the result because Democrats controlled both the White House and both houses of Congress. The president was unable to persuade his party members to support him, even though several states, Hawaii, Massachusetts, and Minnesota, had set an example by establishing comprehensive health care programs that combine public and private insurance and by developing innovative approaches to controlling health care costs (Peters 2000).

## A Hybrid System of Public and Private Health Care

Another way to think about the history of health care in the United States and the nation's present health care system is that it continues to rely largely on the private market and individual choice to reach health care goals. The U.S. government plays a smaller role in health care than the governments of Great Britain or Canada, nations which have national health insurance programs that provide comprehensive health services. Their systems are often criticized for the lack of timeliness and quality of care, however, because the demand for health care usually exceeds the supply of available services. In contrast to government-run systems, most health care services in the United States are provided by doctors and other medical staff who work in clinics and hospitals that are privately run, even if some are nonprofit. Indeed, the United States has the smallest amount of public insurance or provision of public health services of any developed nation in the world (Patel and Rushefsky 2000). The result is a health care system that is something of a hybrid. It is neither completely private nor fully public. It does, however, reflect the unique political culture of the nation first discussed in Chapter 1. Americans place great emphasis on individual rights, limited government power, and a relatively unrestrained market system. Those who favor a larger government role to reduce the current inequities in access to health care services are in effect suggesting that health care should be considered a so-called **merit good** to which people are entitled. In short, they tend to believe that normal market forces should not be the determining factor in the way society allocates such a good.

The majority of U.S. adults under the age of sixty-five (about 75 percent) have employer-sponsored, private health insurance; and others purchase similar insurance through individual policies. The average annual premium costs for a healthy, nonsmoking fifty-five-year old woman in 2002 was $4,934, and $2,459 for a twenty-five-year-old, but prices vary widely by state.[2] These policies cover a substantial portion of health care costs incurred, but not all. Some services, such as elective cosmetic surgery, are not covered, and partial payment may apply to others. The federal government can specify particular services that must be included in private insurance plans. There are major gaps in coverage, such as assistance with expensive prescription drugs and provision of long-term care in nursing homes and similar facilities that may follow a disabling injury or illness, or simply aging. People are living longer, and the demand for these services is expected to rise dramatically. Most policies also have a lifetime cap that could be exceeded in the event of serious medical conditions.

## The Perils of Being Uninsured

The number of individuals and families without any insurance coverage has risen significantly since 1990. In 2002, 41 million individuals or 14.6 percent of the population had no health insurance. About 30 million of them were working-age adults, and half of them made less than $35,000 per year. The percentage of people without health insurance varies widely from state to state, from only 7.6 percent in Wisconsin and Rhode Island in recent years to 24 percent in Texas. Arizona, California, Louisiana, and New Mexico also had relatively high proportions of residents without insurance.[3]

As the cost of medical care continues to grow, what happens to the uninsured? The consequences for them can be devastating—a higher life-long risk of serious medical problems and premature death. A recent review of the health consequences for uninsured working-age Americans found that they are more likely than the insured to receive too little medical care and to receive it too late and to be sicker and die sooner. Indeed, they are 25 percent more likely to die than those with insurance coverage. That difference translates into about eighteen thousand deaths per year that can be attributed to being uninsured, an astonishingly high figure. The uninsured also are more likely than the insured to receive less adequate care when they are in a hospital, even for acute care, such as injuries in an automobile accident. They are more likely to go without cancer screening tests, such as mammograms, clinical breast exams, Pap tests, and colorectal screenings, and therefore delay diagnosis and treatment. That finding helps to explain why uninsured women with breast cancer have a 30 percent to 50 percent higher risk of dying than women with private health insurance (Institute of Medicine 2002).

In addition, the uninsured do not receive the care recommended for chronic diseases such as diabetes, HIV infection, end-stage renal (kidney) disease, mental illness, and high blood pressure, and they have worse clinical outcomes than patients with insurance. "The fact is that the quality and length of life are distinctly different for insured and uninsured populations," the report said. It added that if this group obtained coverage, the health and longevity of working-age Americans would improve (Institute of Medicine 2002).

Policymakers are aware of some of these risks and the inequities they present to the U.S. public. As the failure of the Clinton health policy initiative shows, however, reaching agreement on extending insurance coverage to the entire population is not easy. What should the government do about the uninsured? Should it consider health care to be a merit good and put it beyond the market? If so, how should the nation pay for extending services to the uninsured?

## Strengths and Weakness of the U.S. Health Care System

No one doubts that the United States has one of the finest health care systems in the world by any of the conventionally used indicators, such as the number of physicians per capita, the number of state-of-the-art hospitals and clinics, or the number of health care specialists. The United States also has a large percentage of the world's major pharmaceutical research centers and biotechnology companies, which increases the availability of cutting-edge medical treatments.

Despite the U.S. health care system's many strengths, patients and physicians alike frequently complain about it. In addition, some widely used gauges, such as infant mortality rates, put the United States well below the level of other developed nations, particularly for minority populations, even though the nation overall spends about $1.3 trillion each year on health care. For example, according to the World Health Organization, the United States is thirty-seventh among the world's healthiest countries.[4] Such findings reflect the highly unequal access of the population to critical health care services, from prenatal care to preventive screening for chronic illnesses. The poor, elderly, minorities, and those living in rural areas generally receive less frequent and less adequate medical care than white middle class residents who live in urban and suburban areas (Peters 2000).

So, if the United States is spending more on health care per capita than any other nation, are its citizens receiving the benefits that such expenditures should provide? How well are current programs working and how equitable are they? How might they be modified to improve their effectiveness, efficiency, and equity? Plenty of controversy surrounds each of these questions.

## A Pluralistic Health Care System

It may be helpful to have an overview of the U.S. health care system before turning to particular programs and an assessment of how well they are working. The individual health care programs are complicated enough to confuse even the experts, but they do not represent the totality of government activities that affect the health and welfare of the U.S. public. A broad conception of health care policy suggests that many other actions be included as well. Table 8-1 presents a look at the collection of agencies and policies at the federal, state, and local levels.

Especially noteworthy in the table's list is the diversity of departments and agencies involved in health-related services. As is often the case with U.S. public policies, authority is diffused rather than concentrated and is shared among all levels of government. The programs most frequently in the public eye, such as Medicare and Medicaid, are only part of what governments do to promote the public's health. Many activities, such as those sponsored by state departments of public health and federal medical research, are far less visible to the average citizen. Others, such as environmental protection, are not always thought of in terms of their public health orientation.

The broader view of government health care activities suggests that solutions to U.S. health problems are not to be found solely in expanding and modifying the established Medicare, Medicaid, and Veterans Healthcare System programs. In particular, emphasis could be shifted to preventive measures through various avenues, including greater personal responsibility for health care, improved nutrition and health education, medical research,

| TABLE 8-1 | Major Government Health-Related Programs |
|---|---|

| Level of Government | Agency and Function |
|---|---|
| Federal | Department of Agriculture<br>  Food safety inspection (meat and poultry)<br>  Food stamp and child nutrition programs<br>  Consumer education<br>Department of Health and Human Services<br>  Food and Drug Administration<br>  Agency for Healthcare Research and Quality<br>  Centers for Medicare and Medicaid Services<br>  Health Resources and Services Administration (health resources for underserved populations)<br>  Indian Health Service<br>  Substance abuse programs<br>  Health education<br>  U.S. Public Health Service (including the Surgeon General's office, the National Institutes of Health, and the Centers for Disease Control and Prevention)<br>Department of Labor<br>  Occupational Safety and Health Administration (regulation of workplace safety and health)<br>Department of Veterans Affairs<br>  Veterans Health Administration (VA hospitals and programs)<br>Environmental Protection Agency (regulation of clean air and water, drinking water, pesticides, and toxic chemicals) |
| State | Medicaid and Children's Health Insurance Program (CHIP)<br>State hospitals<br>State mental hospitals<br>Support of state medical schools<br>State departments of health<br>Health education<br>State departments of agriculture and consumer protection<br>State environmental protection programs |
| Local | City and county hospitals and clinics<br>Public health departments and sanitation<br>Emergency services<br>City and county health and human services programs |

environmental protection, and a host of public and private programs to improve mental and physical health.

## MAJOR GOVERNMENT HEALTH CARE PROGRAMS

The next sections describe the major federal and state programs that deal directly with health care services. In addition to the programs' goals and provisions, the discussion addresses their effectiveness, efficiency, and equity. Public policy students who want a fuller account and assessment of the programs can find additional information at government agency Web sites and others such as those listed at the end of the chapter. Of particular value for the two most prominent federal programs is the site for the Centers for Medicare and Medicaid Services (www.cms.gov).

## Medicare

The federal Medicare program began in 1965, following authorization by that year's amendments to the Social Security Act of 1935. It was intended to help senior citizens, defined as those age sixty-five and older, to meet basic health care needs. It now includes people under age sixty-five with permanent disabilities and those with diabetes or end-stage renal disease, for example, patients who need dialysis treatment or a kidney transplant. Medicare has about forty million beneficiaries.

*Medicare Program Provisions.* The Medicare program has two parts, one standard and the other optional. Medicare Part A is the core plan, which pays partially for hospital charges, with individuals responsible for a deductible and co-payments that can be substantial. The program is paid for by Medicare trust funds, which most employees pay through a payroll deduction, much like the Social Security tax, which employers match. Part A also covers up to one hundred days in a nursing care facility following release from the hospital, but again with co-payments. Part A of Medicare covers people who are eligible for the federal Social Security system or Railroad Retirement benefits.

The optional part of the Medicare program, Part B, is supplemental insurance for coverage of health care expenses other than hospital stays. These include physician charges, diagnostic tests, and hospital outpatient services. The cost of Part B insurance is shared by individuals who choose to enroll in it (they paid $54 per month for it in 2002) and by the government, which covers about three-fourths of the cost from general federal revenues. Part B also has both deductibles and co-payments, but it does not cover routine physical examinations by a physician. Even with its limitations, about 95 percent of eligible recipients opt for coverage under Part B of Medicare. Under the Balanced Budget Act of 1997, Congress included additional services for Medicare recipients, particularly preventive diagnostic tests to detect major health problems such as diabetes, breast and colon cancer, and osteoporosis, but payment schedules have been lower than health care providers believe to be essential.

Medicare uses a fee schedule of "reasonable" costs that specifies what physicians, hospitals, nursing homes, and home services should charge for a given procedure, and the government pays 80 percent of that amount. Individuals are responsible for the difference, which can be a significant expense for people living on modest retirement incomes. Physicians are free to charge more than this "reasonable" amount, passing along the higher costs to patients. Some physicians choose not to participate in the Medicare system because they believe the fee schedule is too low and their options for raising patient fees unrealistic.

Equally important is that the regular Medicare program does not cover many other medical expenses, including prescription drugs used outside of the hospital, dental care, and eyeglasses. It also pays for only the first ninety days of a hospital stay and limited nursing home

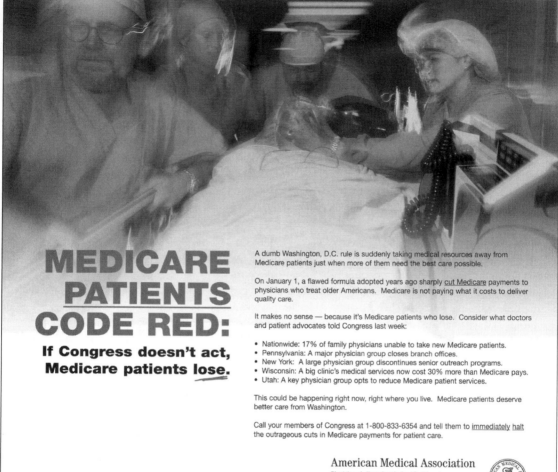

**MEDICARE PATIENTS CODE RED:**

**If Congress doesn't act, Medicare patients lose.**

A dumb Washington, D.C. rule is suddenly taking medical resources away from Medicare patients just when more of them need the best care possible.

On January 1, a flawed formula adopted years ago sharply cut Medicare payments to physicians who treat older Americans. Medicare is not paying what it costs to deliver quality care.

It makes no sense — because it's Medicare patients who lose. Consider what doctors and patient advocates told Congress last week:

- Nationwide: 17% of family physicians unable to take new Medicare patients.
- Pennsylvania: A major physician group closes branch offices.
- New York: A large physician group discontinues senior outreach programs.
- Wisconsin: A big clinic's medical services now cost 30% more than Medicare pays.
- Utah: A key physician group opts to reduce Medicare patient services.

This could be happening right now, right where you live. Medicare patients deserve better care from Washington.

Call your members of Congress at 1-800-833-6354 and tell them to immediately halt the outrageous cuts in Medicare payments for patient care.

**American Medical Association**
Physicians dedicated to the health of America

For more information, go to www.ama-assn.org/grassroots

Physicians and other health care personnel often complain about government rules and regulations that affect the way they provide services. In this advertisement, the American Medical Association sharply criticizes a "dumb Washington, D.C. rule" that limits the fees physicians can charge for treating Medicare patients. The AMA argues that such fee limitations often result in a loss of critical services to older citizens as many physicians and clinics choose not to accept Medicare patients rather than to treat them under the payment plan approved by the government. Federal Medicare officials say that they have little choice but to reduce physician and hospital payments because the Balanced Budget Act of 1997 mandated large cuts to Medicare providers in an attempt to control the rapidly rising costs of the program.

care. Because of these restrictions and the deductibles and co-payment charges, Medicare covers only about two-thirds of the health care costs for the elderly. Individuals must therefore pay for the rest of the costs, or purchase supplementary private insurance policies to cover the gaps in Medicare. Many of the **Medigap** insurance policies are expensive, and few of them offer prescription drug coverage. Low-income elderly also may be eligible for state Medicaid programs, which cover some of these costs. Despite the many restrictions, Medicare is a bargain for the elderly, who would have to pay higher fees for a full private insurance policy, especially because of the chronic and serious health problems they are likely to face.

The costs of health care in general, including Medicare, continue to rise, posing major challenges to the solvency of the Medicare trust fund as the population ages and the ranks of Medicare recipients swell. In an effort to reduce health care expenses, since 1985 Medicare has encouraged its participants to join HMOs, PPOs, and similar managed care plans rather than to rely on the traditional fee-for-service arrangement. In 1997 Congress created Medicare + Choice, Part C of the program, to facilitate this change.

**Medicare + Choice** is the only Medicare program that offers a prescription drug benefit. In addition, the program exemplifies the value of disease prevention, disease management, and "personal nurse" programs that are intended to improve patient compliance with medical advice. In conventional treatment many patients fail to comply with a physician's orders. Fewer than 20 percent of Medicare recipients have enrolled in the Medicare + Choice program, in part because it is not available everywhere in the country, especially smaller cities and rural areas. Surveys indicate, however, that enrollees appear to be very satisfied.

Several problems have surfaced with Medicare + Choice, the main one being a shortage of money. Congress funds the program as a percentage of traditional Medicare, and the insufficient funding is keeping the program from being as successful as it could be. Another problem is that the program attracts the sicker populations in need of greater services, while the healthier population sticks with the less-expensive Medicare Part A. Medicare + Choice, however, may be the best option for low-income and minority populations who suffer the effects of a lifetime of poor access to health care. Unfortunately, many health maintenance organizations (HMOs) found the program unprofitable and pulled out. They argued that government payments under Medicare were too low to compensate them adequately, and that shortfall was exacerbated by the Balanced Budget Act.[5]

***Fraud and Abuse under Medicare.*** Another perennial problem is fraud and abuse committed under Medicare. Less-than-scrupulous health care providers charge the government for services that were not performed or order tests and procedures that may be unnecessary, but for which the health care provider knows Medicare will pay. The Centers for Medicare and Medicaid Services estimates that such fraud accounts for more than $100 billion annually. In a commentary about a 1998 HHS investigation into abuses by community mental health centers, Donna Shalala, then secretary of the department, noted there was "extensive evidence of providers who are not qualified, patients who are not eligible, and services billed to Medicare that are not appropriate," including services "that weren't covered, weren't provided or weren't needed."[6]

In response, the federal government has begun to devote substantial resources to criminal and civil actions against health care fraud. Health care centers have responded to charges of fraud and abuse by saying the government's billing procedures are so complex that it is difficult to avoid making errors. They also say they worry about the government creating a climate of fear in the health care industry that would be detrimental to patient care (Steinhauer 2001). Federal agents who investigate Medicare fraud are not persuaded by such arguments. They charge that health care providers intentionally put services into a higher paying category or "up code" their billing and engage in other illegal practices to increase profits.

***Medicare's Future.*** Given the projections of an aging population, the cost of the Medicare program represents one of the most important issues in health care policy. Unfortunately, little agreement exists on how to modify the program to expand its benefits and to improve its effectiveness. Bipartisan cooperation on health care policy has been noticeably lacking because of intense ideological disagreements about the role of government in health care and the different constituencies to which each of the major parties tries to appeal.

One of the major points of contention is the cost of enhancing benefits for a program that the government already finds difficult to fund and for which the future is bleak because of the new demands facing it. The focused discussion in this chapter lays out one concern, the provision of prescription drug coverage. Information about this and other issues associated with Medicare can be found at www.medicare.gov and at many of the Web sites listed at the end of the chapter.

Based on this description of the Medicare program, do you think it provides sufficient coverage to be termed an effective and efficient health insurance program for senior citizens? Is it equitable? What else could done to improve the program's coverage and operation?

## Medicaid

Medicaid is the other major program of the U.S. health care policy system. Like Medicare, it was established in 1965, as Title XIX of the Social Security Act. It is designed to assist the poor and disabled through a federal-state program of health insurance. It differs from Medicare in one critical way. Medicare serves all citizens once they reach age sixty-five, regardless of income and is therefore a form of national health insurance for seniors, but Medicaid is a specialized health care program for the poor and disabled.

***Medicaid Provisions and Controversies.*** Under Medicaid the federal government establishes standards for hospital services, outpatient services, physician services, and laboratory testing, and it pays about half of the cost. States pay the remainder and set standards for eligibility and overall benefit levels, which vary significantly from state to state. If a state chooses to have a Medicaid program, and nearly all do, it must also extend benefits to welfare recipients and to those receiving Supplemental Security Income because of age, blindness, or disability. Medicaid provides coverage for about 44 million people, including one-fifth of all children, and pays for about two-thirds of nursing home residents in the United States (Pear 2002).

In some respects, the Medicaid programs are more generous than Medicare. The federal government requires states to cover hospitalization, nursing home services, physician services, diagnostic and screening tests, and X-rays. States may opt to cover prescription drug and other expenses. States are also required to cover children under the age of eighteen, if the family income falls below the poverty level. States may set limits on the health care services that are provided, and most offer the minimum level stipulated by federal law.

Much like Medicare expenses, Medicaid costs continue to rise at a rapid pace, and states are constantly at odds with the federal government over the imposition of additional burdens. Except for education, Medicaid is the largest program in most state budgets. As states and counties spend more on Medicaid, they must cut back on the program's optional services, reduce the rate of reimbursement for physician and other services, and curtail funding elsewhere. Education, welfare, and other programs may suffer as Medicaid costs continue to rise (Pear 2002). As with Medicare, Medicaid recipients have been encouraged to join HMOs and other managed care organizations as one way to deal with those rising costs. Indeed, the states are allowed to require Medicaid recipients to join managed care organizations to reduce the cost of the program. By the late 1990s, about half of Medicaid recipients had joined managed care groups, with wide variation among the states.

As part of the Balanced Budget Act of 1997, a new title XXI was added to the Social Security Act to create the state **Children's Health Insurance Program** (CHIP or S-CHIP) that helps to ensure that children living in poverty have medical coverage. The federal government provides funds to the states, which the states match. The states are free to set the eligibility levels, which can include families that earn up to three times the poverty level. Some two million children are covered under CHIP who would not be eligible under Medicaid, but the states vary in their ability to enroll children in the program (Rushefsky 2002).

*Issues of Medicaid Fraud and Abuse.* The Medicaid program, like Medicare, suffers from fraud and abuse by service providers, such as the filing of inaccurate claims for reimbursement. Some estimates suggest that such abuse accounts for up to 7 percent of the overall federal outlay for Medicaid (Peters 2000). The federal government and the states spent $202 billion on Medicaid programs in 2000, and approximately $14 billion of that was wasted through fraud and abuse. Although the money lost to fraud is less than in the Medicare program, the costs are nevertheless substantial. The service providers defend themselves by arguing that they are the victims of an excessively complicated system of eligibility requirements and reimbursement procedures. What should the government do to reduce the incidence of Medicaid fraud and abuse?

## Veterans Health Care

With all the attention paid to Medicare and Medicaid, policymakers and journalists sometimes forget that one of the oldest programs of federal health care service is similar to the national insurance programs that are the rule in Canada and Great Britain, but this one is for veterans only. The **Veterans Healthcare System** is designed to serve the needs of American veterans by providing primary medical care, specialized care, and other medical and social services, such as rehabilitation. The Veterans Health Administration operates veterans hospitals and clinics across the nation and provides extensive coverage for veterans with service-related disabilities and disease and more limited coverage for other veterans, particularly those with no private health care insurance. It also engages in extensive and diverse medical research.

Congress expanded the existing veterans health programs by enacting the Veterans Health Care Eligibility Reform Act of 1996. That legislation created a medical benefits package, an enhanced health benefits plan, that is available to enrolled veterans. The health care plan emphasizes preventive and primary care, but also offers a full range of services, including inpatient and outpatient medical, surgical, and mental health services; prescription and over-the-counter drugs and medical and surgical supplies; emergency care; comprehensive rehabilitative services; and even payment of travel expenses associated with care for eligible veterans. The VA benefits extend to preventive care and include periodic physical examinations, health and nutrition education, drug use education and drug monitoring, and mental health and substance abuse preventive services. Medical needs attributable to service-related injuries and disease typically are free of individual deductibles and co-payments. The VA uses a priority group structure and a financial means test to set co-payment charges for other veterans (see www.va.gov).

At the request of senior military leaders, in 2000 Congress approved another health care program for career military personnel. It expands the military's health plan, known as **TriCare,** to include retirees with at least twenty years of service once they become eligible for Medicare. TriCare pays for most of the costs for medical treatment that are not covered by Medicare, except for $3,000 per year in out-of-pocket expenses. The plan also includes generous prescription drug coverage. One health care policy analyst, Henry Aaron of the Brookings Institution, summed up what many would conclude about this action. "It's interesting that Congress recognizes that for this one group the Medicare benefit package isn't adequate," he said. "One might well ask that if [Medicare] isn't good enough for men and women who served in the armed forces, why is it good enough for men and women who spent a lifetime paying federal payroll taxes?" (Becker 2000). The answer would seem to be that Congress thought this initiative was politically attractive in an election year, but also recognized that providing comparable benefits for the entire nation would be extremely costly and far more difficult.

## OTHER HEALTH CARE POLICY ISSUES

Several major health care policy issues do not directly involve government insurance programs such as Medicare, Medicaid, and the Veterans Healthcare Services, but instead the way private medical insurance operates and the legal rights of policyholders. Two issues merit special attention: the portability of insurance as individuals leave one job for another and the rights of patients to seek legal recourse for decisions made by a managed care or other health organization.

### Portability

Given the large number of people whose health care services are provided under employer-sponsored insurance plans, the possible loss of benefits when an employee switches jobs was a persistent concern. One employer's plan might not be the same as another's in cost or quality. People with preexisting medical conditions, such as heart disease, hypertension, or cancer, might find that a new employer's insurance company is unwilling to cover them at all or will charge higher premiums. To address some of these problems, in 1996 Congress approved the Health Insurance and Portability Accountability Act (HIPAA). The law guaranteed that employees who changed jobs would have the right to insurance coverage, even if that coverage comes at a higher cost. And they would not have to endure a waiting period that policies often imposed to limit coverage of preexisting conditions.

Each state establishes the arrangements for providing these guaranteed-issue individual insurance policies. Typically, an individual must first use all benefits provided under yet another federal policy from the mid-1980s, the Consolidated Omnibus Budget Reconciliation Act (COBRA). This program allows individuals who leave their jobs to remain on the employer's health insurance policy for as long as eighteen months, but the employee is responsible for the premiums. The time period is thirty-six months in the case of spousal rights following divorce or death and twenty-nine months for a disability severe enough to qualify for the Social Security disability program. About forty states have adopted mini-COBRA laws that give employees similar rights. The main problem with the policies purchased under HIPAA or COBRA, even though they are guaranteed, is their cost.

## Patients' Rights

One of the most common complaints about managed care health systems, such as HMOs, is the inappropriate denial of care. More than 150 million Americans rely on HMOs and similar health care plans, which are designed to save money by providing affordable high-quality health care through a consolidated organization of physicians and other professionals. Critics claim that HMOs are so devoted to the goal of cost reduction that they deny patients needed medical care. Dissatisfaction with what seems like the HMOs' callous behavior led to the movement to guarantee patients' rights. Patients who are denied the right to see a specialist or to have medical treatment argue that they should be able to inquire into the financial arrangements that may affect referrals to specialists and a right to sue the health care provider either to gain those services or be compensated for their loss.

The Employee Retirement Income Security Act of 1974 (ERISA) allows individuals to sue health insurance companies for such decisions, but only in federal court. ERISA says that federal regulations supersede state laws that govern employee health plans and that no punitive damages may be sought beyond compensation for actual medical expenses. This provision exempts many health plans from state laws, and millions of patients can sue for damages only in federal court, which is difficult, and not for punitive damages. Advocates of expanding patients' right to sue want to extend this right to state courts and allow for punitive damages (Adams 2001b). Democrats tend to favor expanding patients' rights in this way, and Republicans resist the efforts. Employers argue that extending the right to sue would greatly increase their costs and force them to cut back on insurance coverage. HMOs also resist the proposals and lobby intensely against them for similar reasons. Their arguments have been better received as health care costs have risen sharply.

Nevertheless, everyone agrees that health care plans should be held accountable for decisions that deny patients needed medical care. The disagreement comes over when patients should be allowed to sue and the appropriate damages. Despite the prolonged debate on Capitol Hill, neither party has shown much willingness to compromise on patients' rights (Cary 2002; Jost 1999). In June 2002, however, the Supreme Court got into the act. It ruled 5 to 4 in *Rush Prudential H.M.O. Inc. v. Moran* that states may protect patients' rights in disputes with managed care companies. The Court ruled that when an HMO denies treatments recommended by a patient's primary care physician, the HMO must have an independent review procedure available to resolve the dispute. Rush Prudential argued that an Illinois state law to that effect was preempted by ERISA and was therefore unenforceable. The Supreme Court disagreed. Patients' rights advocates applauded the decision, but also said it did not eliminate the need for Congress to act because similar state laws exclude millions of people who would gain their rights only through federal protection.[7]

What is the equitable solution to the patients' rights dispute? Should HMOs and other managed care organizations be able to deny coverage they deem unnecessary? Should patients be allowed to challenge such decisions in court if no other dispute resolution process is provided? What impact do you think the extension of such patients' rights will have on health care costs?

## RISING HEALTH CARE COSTS

As this chapter has emphasized so far, one of the most difficult issues in health care policy disputes is the cost. What is more, the cost of providing health care services is rising inexorably. Health care is costly enough that individuals whose employers do not provide full coverage can easily find themselves unable to pay for private insurance or for all the medical services they need. The result can be financially devastating should a major medical emergency arise from an acute illness or an accident. Even people with relatively generous health care insurance policies can find themselves facing enormous medical bills because of required deductible expenses and co-payment fees, for example, for prescription drugs.

The data in Table 8-2 show the trend in health care costs. The table lists total U.S. health care expenditures for four years between 1980 and 2000, as well as per capita expenditures. It

| TABLE 8-2 | National Health Expenditures, 1980–2000 | | | |
|---|---|---|---|---|
| ITEM | 1980 | 1990 | 1995 | 2000 |
| Total national health care expenditures (in billions) | $245.8 | $696.0 | $990.3 | $1,299.5 |
| Private | 140.9 | 413.5 | 534.1 | 712.3 |
| Public | 104.8 | 282.5 | 456.2 | 587.2 |
| Per capita health care expenditures | $1,067 | $2,738 | $3,698 | $4,637 |
| Health care expenditures as percentage of GDP | 8.8% | 12.0% | 13.4% | 13.2% |

Source: Drawn from data on the Centers for Medicare and Medicaid Services, Office of the Actuary Web site (www.cms.gov), June 14, 2002: National Health Statistics Group, and from the U.S. Department of Commerce, Bureau of Economic Analysis, and the U.S. Bureau of the Census.

also indicates the relative roles of private and public payment mechanisms in meeting those costs. The data show that health care costs rose substantially over this period. Moreover, after some years of relatively moderate growth during the 1990s, spending accelerated once again in 2001, when it climbed 8.7 percent, on top of a 6.9 percent increase in 2000 and a 5.7 percent rise in 1999. These spikes occurred at a time when annual inflation rates were as low as 2 percent to 3 percent. As a result of the escalating costs, private health insurance premiums in 2000 rose by 8.4 percent, putting pressure on employers and employees alike. Health care expenditures as a percentage of the gross domestic product (GDP) have been more stable in recent years, but in 2000 they stood at 13.2 percent, about the same as in 1992. Expenditures per person rose to a record high $4,637.

As might be expected, soaring costs deeply affect the leading federal health care programs. Medicare expenditures in 2000 totaled $224 billion, or 38 percent of public spending on health care and 17 percent of overall health spending. Federal and state Medicaid spending in 2000, not counting the state CHIP, totaled $202 billion, or about 15.5 percent of overall health spending. Private health care insurance contributed 34 percent of the total, and individual out-of-pocket expenses were 15 percent.

Among the largest increases in recent years is the spending for prescription drugs, which rose from $69 billion in 1995 to $141 billion by 2000. Drug costs went up 17.3 percent in 2000 alone, and rose another 15.7 percent in 2001. So called **third-party payers**, that is, insurance companies, employers, governments, or other parties that pay for the care are now responsible for a much greater share of drug costs than in 1990. This practice contributes to increasing demand that is expected to rise further as the population ages and as new therapies are introduced. As many television viewers have noted, pharmaceutical manufacturers have changed their marketing strategies and now advertise directly to consumers, instead of to health professionals only. Viewers are urged to ask their doctors for the new medications. The practice has been a success for the pharmaceutical companies, as the public demand for expensive new prescription drugs grew, even though many of them are only marginally more effective than cheaper, over-the-counter medications and generic versions of similar drugs. The issue of prescription drugs is the subject of the focused discussion at the end of the chapter.

What is the future of health care costs? The Centers for Medicare and Medicaid Services projections for U.S. health care costs through 2011 show no change in the trend.[8] Total health care expenditures are expected to rise from $1.3 trillion in 2000 to $2.8 trillion in 2011, per capita expenditures from $4,637 to $9,216, and expenditures as a percentage of GDP from 13.2 percent to 17.0 percent. The government projects that pressure will increase on both public and private payers to cover accelerating health care costs, and anticipates additional need to reconsider health care priorities in the years ahead.

A graphic presentation of health care costs can help to put them into perspective. The data in Figure 8-1 are drawn from the federal Health Care Financing Administration and show the sources for the nation's health dollar and where the money is spent. The funds come chiefly from private insurance and from Medicare and Medicaid, and they are spent largely for hospitals, physician services, and other health care professionals in addition to nursing home care, prescription drugs, and over-the-counter medications.

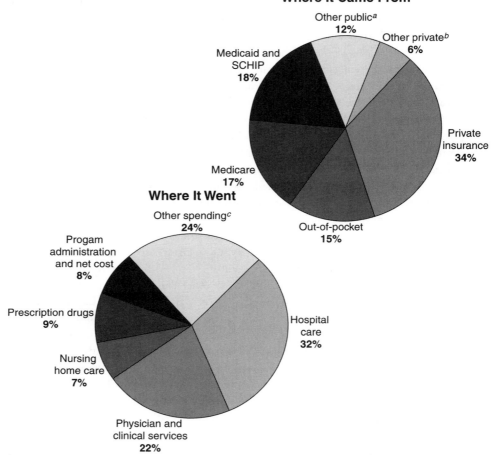

**FIGURE 8-1**   The Nation's Health Care Dollar, 2000

**Where It Came From**

- Other public[a] 12%
- Other private[b] 6%
- Private insurance 34%
- Out-of-pocket 15%
- Medicare 17%
- Medicaid and SCHIP 18%

**Where It Went**

- Other spending[c] 24%
- Hospital care 32%
- Physician and clinical services 22%
- Nursing home care 7%
- Prescription drugs 9%
- Progam administration and net cost 8%

[1]"Other Public" includes programs such as workers' compensation, public health activity, Department of Defense, Department of Veterans Affairs, Indian Health Service, state and local hospital subsidies, and school health.

[2]"Other Private" includes industrial in-plant, privately funded construction, and non-patient revenues, including philanthropy.

[3]"Other Spending" includes dental services, other professional services, home health care, durable medical products, over-the-counter medicine and sundries, public health activities, research, and construction.

Source: Health Care Financing Administration (HCFA) Web site, June 14, 2002. HCFA's data now come from the Centers for Medicare and Medicaid Services, Office of the Actuary, National Health Statistics Group.

## State Policy Innovations

The federal government is not the only policy actor trying to contain health care costs; the states also have a role, and some states have adopted innovative public policies. For example, as Chapter 6 pointed out, Oregon approved a state health plan that offers Medicaid recipients and others universal access to basic and effective health care. Based on a public-private partnership, the plan includes state-run insurance pools, insurance reforms, and a federal waiver allowing for the expansion of Medicaid. The system features rationing of services based on a ranking of medical procedures that the state and its residents believe to be cost effective. Other states, such as California, have engaged in aggressive antismoking media campaigns and raised tobacco taxes in an effort to get people to stop smoking. The goal is to reduce the number of people needing expensive medical services in the future. By all accounts, the effort has been successful, and the state will likely face a declining rate of lung cancer and other serious illnesses as a result. States have also taken measures to deal with rising rates of obesity, such as limiting access to calorie-laden fast food in public schools.

Another state policy innovation deals with the problem of medical errors. In a response to a national report on the subject, New York State revised its reporting system to permit data on medical errors to be posted on the Internet when the state decides to take action against a hospital. Suggesting how effective such information disclosure policies can be, several major corporations, including General Electric and General Motors, vowed to steer their employees toward the hospitals that make the fewest errors.

What should states do to try to improve public health and reduce the long-term costs of health care? Examine one or more of the Web sites listed in the box "Working with Sources: Health Care Policy Information" and at the end of the chapter to see some of the innovative policies states are trying and how well they are working.

## REGULATION OF NEW DRUG APPROVAL

STEPS TO ANALYSIS

The Food and Drug Administration (FDA) requires pharmaceutical and biotechnology companies to conduct elaborate, lengthy, and costly testing of new drugs before they can be approved for patient use. The justification for this process is to ensure the safety and effectiveness of new drugs prior to marketing. Drug manufacturers often complain that the FDA procedures are too demanding and delay the availability of new treatments, prevent some of them from reaching the market at all, and contribute to the high cost of new drug development (Worsnop 1999). They also report that a new drug may take as long as ten to fifteen years to develop, with research and development costs reaching $800 million or more. At the same time, some treatments, such as use of dietary and herbal supplements, are not subject to regulation since passage of a law in 1994.

Has the United States struck an acceptable balance between the need for a speedy approval process and the necessity to ensure drug safety and efficacy? Is the FDA too cautious? Should the FDA use a special expedited procedure to approve so-called breakthrough drugs that offer great promise for serious illnesses, such as cancer and heart disease? What about drugs that might be used to combat bioterrorism? To explore these questions, go to several of the Web sites listed at the end of the chapter to review both sets of arguments. For example, try the FDA site (www.fda.gov), the Pharmaceutical Research and Manufacturers of America or PhRMA site (www.pharma.org), and the Public Citizen site at www.citizen.org/hrg. How do their arguments about the balance between drug safety and the speed of the approval process differ?

### Regulation of Prescription Drugs

Given the already high and rapidly rising cost of prescription drugs, another way to control health care costs is to change the way the federal government and drug manufacturers develop and approve new medicines. The current process of drug development is long and expensive, forcing drug manufacturers to charge high prices to cover their cost of research and development. Is there a way to reduce such costs without jeopardizing the public's health? Or is it more important to maintain a rigorous and demanding drug approval process regardless of the time and costs it imposes? The box "Steps to Analysis: Regulation of New Drug Approval" summarizes these arguments, poses some additional questions to consider, and suggests several pertinent Web sites to visit for different sides of the argument.

## MANAGED CARE ORGANIZATIONS

Managed care, which is now a fixture of modern health care services and policy, was proposed as one way to contain rising health care costs that had soared under the old, unrestrained **fee-for-service** system, in which the patient or an insurance company pays for the medical service rendered. Over the past several decades, the United States has shifted from fee-for-service to a system dominated by managed care, typically with the costs borne by third-party payers. By most measurements, the transition has been successful, particularly in holding down health care costs and promoting preventive health care.

Managed care organizations provide health care by forming networks of doctors, other health care providers, and hospitals associated with a given plan; monitoring their treatment activities; and limiting access to specialists and costly procedures. The best-known managed care organizations are the health maintenance organizations (HMOs). Along with other managed care companies, such as preferred provider organizations (PPOs), they promote health services that are the most cost-effective, such as regular physicals and certain medical screening tests, limit access to costly services and specialists, and negotiate lower fees with health care providers. PPOs differ from HMOs in that enrollees have a financial incentive to use physicians on the preferred list, but they may opt to see other health professionals at a higher cost. By most accounts, HMOs and PPOs save the nation billions of dollars a year in health care costs, an important achievement. By the late 1990s the number of workers in managed care health plans dwarfed those in traditional fee-for-service plans. The ratio was about six to one, with the fee-for-service plans declining steadily throughout the 1990s.

If managed care now dominates the health care system, it is not without its critics, whether justified or not. Surveys in 2001 of the U.S. public indicate a widespread belief that HMOs and other managed care plans have cut the time that doctors spend with patients, made it more difficult to see medical specialists, and decreased the quality of care for those who are ill. These three points of view were reported by between 54 percent and 67 percent of the survey respondents. Only 39 percent of the public believes that managed care makes it easier to get preventive services such as immunizations and health screenings, which should be one of the system's strengths. Thirty-nine percent also say that managed care plans do a "bad job" of serving consumers, double the number reported in a similar 1997 survey; only oil companies earned a lower rating in consumer confidence. Not surprisingly, the survey found that the vast majority of the U.S. public, 81 percent, favored a comprehensive patients' bill of rights to give people the right to appeal decisions denying them certain kinds of care and to sue the insurance companies that run the plans. Only 12 percent opposed the patients' bill of rights. The percentage in favor declines markedly, however, if respondents are told that a patients' bill of rights might lead to a rise in health insurance of $20 or more a month or if employers might find it harder to offer health plans to their employees.[9]

It is not entirely clear why managed care meets with so many complaints despite what is by most indications a highly successful design that balances quality health care service with the concern over how to constrain costs. For example, recent studies indicate that on eighteen of twenty-four quality indicators, the quality of care provided by HMOs was as good or better than care provided in other settings.[10] Moreover, in general, HMO members are more likely to have early diagnosis and treatment for illnesses such as breast cancer, cervical cancer, melanoma, and colon cancer and to receive mammograms. HMOs also have been in the forefront of preventive heath care, the expansion of prenatal care, and management of chronic diseases such as diabetes, emphysema, and heart failure. So why do HMOs have such a poor reputation? Has the press treated HMOs unfairly by singling out unrepresentative cases that make for good reporting? Has Hollywood done the same in films and television programs? For example, in the film As Good as It Gets, one of the leading characters, a single mother, denounces HMOs for having denied a simple allergy test that eventually cures her chronically ill son; audiences around the country erupted in applause at the line.

Criticism of HMOs also focuses on limits placed on patients' stays in hospitals—routinely, only twenty-four hours following childbirth—and denial of or limiting coverage for certain procedures. HMOs counter that they are trying to ensure that limited health care dollars are spent efficiently and fairly and that patients be provided with only safe and proven treatments. They fear that expanding patients' rights might lead to the use of unnecessary and possibly dangerous procedures, resulting in higher insurance fees and injuries to patients. They also argue that laws guaranteeing patients the power to select physicians and to sue their health care plans will raise premium costs and leave more people uninsured and vulnerable to health risks.

Following patient complaints and adverse publicity, however, managed care companies changed some of their policies to become more accommodating than in the past. The evidence suggests they are not denying care in many cases, even though the occasional horror story to that effect pops up in a movie or on television. Indeed, some states, including Connecticut, New Jersey, and New York, require managed care plans to report incidents of care denial and how they were resolved. In these states, plan administrators seem to be reluctant to second-guess physicians, but the plans still deny access to physicians outside of their networks and nonessential or experimental treatments. Economists concerned about rising health care costs think that HMOs and other plans need to be much tougher in overseeing physician decisions to minimize the use of needless and risky surgery and unnecessary and expensive diagnostic tests (Bettelheim 1999). What data would you use to appraise the performance of HMOs?

## REDUCING HEALTH CARE COSTS: BEYOND HMOs

If managed care cannot succeed sufficiently in restraining the rise in health care costs, other strategies may emerge to reach that goal. Four of these merit brief mention: (1) passing on additional costs to health care consumers; (2) setting up personal health accounts; (3) managing disease more effectively; and (4) using preventive health care.

Everyone complains about the cost of health care, but the fact is that few people ever see the full price tag because insurance plans take care of most of it. According to one recent survey, the average person paid just $355 in total out-of-pocket expenses and less than $100 in prescription drug costs in 2001.[11] Yet even simple surgeries can cost thousands of dollars, and many prescription drugs, such as newer antibiotics, can run to hundreds of dollars per month. If employees had to cover more of the costs now paid by their employers' insurance policies, they might have an incentive to reduce their demand for health services that are not essential, such as visiting a hospital emergency room for a nonemergency situation, demanding exotic new drugs when less-expensive alternatives exist, or requesting expensive diagnostic tests that a physician believes are unnecessary. Raising the policyholder's share of the cost with higher deductibles and higher levels of co-payments would inject "market discipline" into health care coverage.

A variation on this theme is that individuals who use health services more frequently than average should pay more of the cost, for example, through higher insurance premiums. In other words, the sicker should pay more, just as those with more driving citations or accidents pay higher auto insurance premiums and those with safe driving records get a break. Is this proposal fair? It might be if the health care consumers brought on their conditions through poor choices over which they had reasonable control. But what about individuals with inherited diseases, or accident victims, or those who simply have the misfortune of suffering from a rare (and expensive) illness? Is it ethical to pass the costs of treatment along to them and their families?

Many employers seeking ways to cope with rising premium costs are setting up personal health accounts for their workers. The employers deposit money into an account that is used to pay for each employee's health expenses that the regular insurance does not cover. The money can be used for prescription drugs, physician visits, dental work, and other health-related bills. Employees make their own decisions about how best to spend the limited funds. Once the money is gone, the employee is responsible for any additional charges that year. These plans typically come with a very high deductible, making them essentially catastrophic insurance policies; that is, the employee is better off using the plan for a highly unusual major medical need, not routine services. Those who make poor choices, or who are unlucky and suffer from a serious injury, or need continuing medical care, may be worse off under such a plan. Is this kind of plan likely to be effective as a compromise to control costs and still cover catastrophic illness or injury?

Disease management programs focus on a few chronic diseases associated with high costs. The programs promise to reduce employers' costs by bringing employee diseases under control more effectively than is likely through conventional medical treatment. Managed care organizations have led the way in developing these kinds of programs. Surveys indicate that a majority of them have implemented programs for managing conditions such as asthma, diabetes, heart disease, end-stage renal disease, cancer, and depression. Their goal is to train patients to take better care of themselves by monitoring their diseases, watching their diets, and seeking appropriate and timely medical care. Some critics are concerned that by singling out employees with chronic conditions for the training the programs may pose a threat to them. Even some insurance programs believe that disease management of this kind raises difficult ethical issues involving medical privacy and employee-employer relationships. But few question that such programs make many individuals healthier and also reduce heath care costs. How would you weigh the ethical issues of disease management?

The incidence of obesity in America is rising at about 1 percent a year, and the causes are not in much dispute. Most of them are evident here: high-calorie, high-fat snack foods, sugar-laden sodas, and a sedentary lifestyle. Simply put, Americans eat too much bad food and exercise too little. Obesity carries numerous health risks, including higher rates of diabetes, heart disease, hypertension, arthritis, pulmonary disorders, and cancer. It increases the likelihood of death from all causes by about 20 percent, with the risk rising dramatically as the level of obesity increases. The cost of treating obesity-related illness in the United States has been estimated to be as much as $200 billion per year. Recent studies suggest that it may account for 300,000 deaths annually, making it the second leading cause of preventable death after smoking.

The logic of preventive care is compelling. If people take good care of themselves throughout their lives, they are likely to be healthier and need less medical care than those who do not. Preventive care health plans usually allow regular physical examinations and diagnostic tests; education and training in diet, exercise, and stress management; and smoking cessation programs. Some employers emphasize preventive care, while others seem to give it little thought, even though the potential to reduce long-term health care costs is substantial. Moreover, most HMO and PPO plans fully cover preventive health care, including educational programs on health and wellness, prenatal care, nutrition, and smoking cessation. Do you think most employees would take advantage of preventive health care if it were offered?

## QUALITY OF CARE

The issue of quality in medical care is easy to understand. At a minimum, every patient should expect to receive professional and competent care that is consistent with good medical practice. The physician or other health care professional should be well trained, up-to-date on new research and treatments, and be able to spend sufficient time with a patient to properly diagnose and treat medical conditions that arise. These expectations are particularly reasonable in the United States, given the vast amounts of money invested by government, insurance companies, and individuals in one of the best medical care systems in the world.

The evidence suggests, however, that quality care is not as routine as many would like to believe. Patients do complain about poor quality care, and even the American Medical Association concedes that errors in diagnosis and treatment occur at a significant rate. In addition, studies indicate that many physicians rely excessively on costly medical technology and drugs, in part to increase revenues for physician offices and hospitals and in part as "defensive medicine," to guard against liability in malpractice claims. Indeed, a 1991 study puts the cost of defensive medicine in the United States at $25 billion per year.[12] Another study in 2002 by the Juran Institute, a group representing large employers, found that $390 billion a year is wasted on outmoded and inefficient medical procedures. The authors argued that poor quality in health care costs the average employer some $1,700 to $2,000 for each covered employee each year (Freudenheim 2002).

Physicians and state medical associations find it difficult to discipline incompetent colleagues who may be guilty of malpractice. Despite the federal law requiring HMOs and hospitals to report any disciplinary action taken against doctors for incompetence or misconduct, few incidents are reported.[13] California and other states, however, have succeeded in reforming medical liability laws without compromising quality patient care. These reforms suggest what can be done if the public and policymakers take the issue of quality health care seriously. For example, as early as the 1970s California chose to limit noneconomic (pain and suffering) awards to $250,000, an approach that apparently has kept malpractice insurance in the state lower than in many others.

If, as patients in HMOs complain, doctors spend less time with them and access to specialists is limited, are these problems evidence of lower-quality care? It might be if physicians and other health care professionals are too busy to properly diagnose and treat their patients. It is true that, to cope with rising patient demand and compensate for lower rates of reimbursement, medical professionals must see greater numbers of patients per day than they did in the past. Still, it is difficult to measure the quality of medical care.[14] The issue is not likely to go away because the amount of care and patients' perceptions of its quality are closely tied to the factors that escalate health care costs, such as seeing physicians more frequently, gaining access to specialists, benefiting from new medical technology and treatments, and using the latest prescription drugs.

## Medical Errors

One element of the concern about the quality of medical care is more concrete and disturbing—the incidence of medical errors. A widely circulated and influential report released in 1999 by the Institute of Medicine (IOM), which is part of the National Academy of Sciences, estimated that between 44,000 and 98,000 patients die each year as a result of medical errors made in hospitals. The errors include operating on the wrong patient or the wrong side of a patient, incorrect drug prescriptions or administration of the wrong dosages, malfunctioning mechanical equipment, and nursing and other staff errors. The study did *not* include medical errors in other health care settings, such as physician offices, clinics, pharmacies, nursing homes, and urgent care facilities, which presumably would add considerably to the overall numbers.

To put the IOM study into perspective, using the lower number of 44,000 deaths per year would make medical errors in hospitals the eighth leading cause of death in the United States, higher than motor vehicle accidents (about 43,000 per year), breast cancer (about 42,000 per year), or AIDS (about 16,000 per year).[15] Aside from the dire consequences for the patients, including injuries as well as death, medical errors are expensive. The IOM study estimated that they cost the nation $37.6 billion each year, about $17 billion of which is associated with preventable errors. Generally, the preventable medical errors are not attributable simply to individual negligence or misconduct, but rather to the health care delivery system, such as the way patient and drug information is handled.

The IOM called for a new federal law to require hospitals to report all such mistakes that cause serious injury or death to patients, just as they are supposed to report disciplinary actions against doctors, but federal health officials have been unwilling to back such a proposal without further study.[16] It is not clear that a reporting system would reduce the number of errors, but much depends on how the system is designed and how well it is funded. That seems to be the lesson from the twenty-two states that already have laws intended to identify and deal with medical errors (Serafini 2000).

## Boutique Health Care

Another aspect of health care quality is noteworthy, if only because of the sharp contrast it provides to the situation affecting those without health insurance or those who find the standard services of HMOs wanting. What is becoming known as **boutique health care** are the upscale and often expensive health care options provided to the wealthy. These options include luxury suites in hospitals, spa-like stress reduction services, and certain cosmetic surgeries and treatments, such as botox injections to reduce facial wrinkles. Insurance companies rarely cover such services if they are medically unnecessary or exceed the specified minimal hospital and other charges they would normally pay, but those who want these services and can afford them do not worry about the expense (Connolly 2002).

Some providers of boutique health care offer special care to patients willing to pay a retainer of several thousand dollars a year. They promise their patients twenty-four-hour availability seven days a week and no waiting to see a physician. Doctors with boutique practices can increase earnings that have been constrained by government policies and managed care rules and regulations. In addition, some doctors say they are tired of the mandates imposed by managed care, which often dictate that they see more patients per day than they believe is compatible with quality care. They genuinely want to spend more time with patients than otherwise possible.

Boutique health care is a reminder that the nation has long had a multi-tier health care system in which those with sufficient money can buy almost any health services they desire, from a comprehensive physical exam at the Mayo Clinic to a visit to a plastic surgeon to receive a breast enhancement. People of limited means are forced to settle for basic care or even less than what is minimally necessary. Policy analysts differ in their appraisals of boutique health care. Conservative analysts, such as those at the Cato Institute, tend to argue that "people should be able to get as much [heath care] as they can pay for." In contrast, liberal analysts are just as likely to criticize what they call "wealth-care" services as inequitable and inappropriate.[17] Which argument is more persuasive?

## LEADING CAUSES OF DEATH AND PREVENTIVE HEALTH CARE

Another way to evaluate the quality of health care is, perversely, to consider the leading causes of death in the United States and ask what can be done to reduce deaths from these conditions. For example, can preventive health care, through routine physical exams, better diagnostic procedures, and improved health care education add years to Americans' lives? Can chronic diseases be better managed, not only to increase longevity and the quality of life but also to reduce health care costs?

Table 8-3 lists the leading causes of death in the United States. As the data make clear, heart disease and cancer dominate the list, followed by cerebrovascular disease (stroke), and

| TABLE 8-3 | Percentage of U.S. Deaths Attributed to the Fifteen Leading Causes, 1999 | | |
|---|---|---|---|
| Rank | Causes of Death | Number of Deaths | Percentage of Total Deaths |
| | All causes | 2,391,399 | 100% |
| 1 | Heart disease | 725,192 | 30.3 |
| 2 | Cancer | 549,838 | 23.0 |
| 3 | Stroke (cerebrovascular diseases) | 167,366 | 7.0 |
| 4 | Lung disease (such as emphysema) | 124,181 | 5.2 |
| 5 | Accidents (including car accidents) | 97,860 | 4.1 |
| 6 | Diabetes | 68,399 | 2.9 |
| 7 | Influenza and pneumonia | 63,730 | 2.7 |
| 8 | Alzheimer's disease | 44,536 | 1.9 |
| 9 | Kidney disease | 35,525 | 1.5 |
| 10 | Septicemia (blood poisoning) | 30,680 | 1.3 |
| 11 | Suicide | 29,199 | 1.2 |
| 12 | Chronic liver disease and cirrhosis | 26,259 | 1.1 |
| 13 | Hypertension (high blood pressure) | 16,968 | 0.7 |
| 14 | Assault (homicide) | 16,889 | 0.7 |
| 15 | Aortic aneurysm | 15,807 | 0.7 |

Source: The data are drawn from the "National Vital Statistics Report," Vol. 49, No. 8, September 21, 2001, Table C, p. 6, (Washington, D.C.: National Center for Health Statistics, Centers for Disease Control and Prevention, online version). Death rates vary by age, and similar statistics are available for different age groups.

chronic respiratory diseases such as emphysema. Among the leading contributing factors in all of these cases are diet, smoking, lack of exercise, stress, and exposure to environmental pollutants. Smoking is the single most preventable cause of premature death in the United States, accounting for more than 440,000 deaths and about $150 billion in health-related economic loses each year, according to the CDC. Secondhand smoke takes an additional health toll, particularly in children. Although the percentage of smokers in the population is declining, in 2002 about 22 percent of adults were still smoking. Roughly half of those who smoke die prematurely from cancer, heart disease, emphysema, and other smoking-related diseases.[18] Do these statistics present a compelling case for government intervention to reduce smoking and therefore smoking-related disease? Or should government not take steps to reduce smoking on the grounds that doing so interferes with individuals' right to choose how to live?

## LIFESTYLE CHOICES AND WELLNESS ACTIVITIES

As the list of the leading causes of death suggests, public health might be improved through changes in personal lifestyles. That is, ill-health and premature death are not merely functions of genetics or exposure to disease-causing microbes or environmental pollutants over which individuals have little control. They also reflect choices people make. If smoking is a major problem, another is being overweight. Americans are becoming fatter, and weight is a major factor in heart and circulatory diseases. The U.S. surgeon general, for example, stated in a December 2001 report that, left unabated, "overweight and obesity may soon cause as much preventable disease and death as cigarette smoking."[19]

Recent studies indicate that about 35 percent of the adult population is overweight and another 30 percent obese. Moreover, the trend is up: the number of people categorized as overweight increased by 61 percent from 1991 to 2000 alone, and the percentage categorized as obese increased by 65 percent during the same period. The CDC reports that many children are severely overweight, and it has launched a research program to study the causes of a seeming epidemic in weight gain (Montgomery 2001).[20] The American diet is a strong contributing factor, with increasing reliance on prepared foods high in calories, fat, and cholesterol. Some critics single out the $800 billion per year food industry for blame, saying it undermines good nutrition by strongly promoting sales of unhealthy food (Nestle 2002).

By most accounts, Americans also fall well short of the recommended levels of physical exercise and fitness wherever they live. In addition, Americans drink too much alcohol. Both habits contribute to poor health. About one in ten adults reports consuming alcohol excessively, with higher percentages among the younger adults. Despite these habits, life expectancy in the United States reached an all-time high of 77.2 years in 2001 (74.4 for men an 79.8 for women).[21]

Lifestyle choices have a substantial impact on individuals' health and longevity. A change in the pattern of unhealthy lifestyles could reduce the incidence of disease and lower health care costs. A major investment in preventive health care, including health education programs, would probably pay substantial dividends, financially and in terms of improved health and well-being. Think of it this way. A young man could conduct his life with little regard for his health, hoping that a pill or other treatment later on will solve whatever health problems develop, preferably at someone else's expense. Or he could be more conscious of the choices he makes throughout his life and the impacts on his long-term health. Does government have a role to play in such choices? Should the federal and state governments, or public schools, try to do more to improve the public's knowledge of healthy lifestyles and to encourage healthy behavior? What about employer investment in so-called wellness programs at work, from physical exercise facilities to stress reduction? Do the rising costs of health care justify such action? The box "Working with Sources: Ethical Issues in Health Care" suggests further topics for exploration.

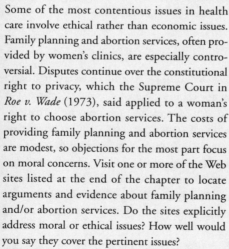

## WORKING WITH SOURCES

## ETHICAL ISSUES IN HEALTH CARE

Some of the most contentious issues in health care involve ethical rather than economic issues. Family planning and abortion services, often provided by women's clinics, are especially controversial. Disputes continue over the constitutional right to privacy, which the Supreme Court in *Roe v. Wade* (1973), said applied to a woman's right to choose abortion services. The costs of providing family planning and abortion services are modest, so objections for the most part focus on moral concerns. Visit one or more of the Web sites listed at the end of the chapter to locate arguments and evidence about family planning and/or abortion services. Do the sites explicitly address moral or ethical issues? How well would you say they cover the pertinent issues?

A newer topic of controversy is embryonic stem cell research. It has provoked considerable debate, even when its purpose is to discover the causes of and possible treatments for life-threatening disease. Conservative religious groups are critical because some researchers use tissue from aborted fetuses. They successfully lobbied the Bush White House to set stringent limits on the use of stem cells in medical research. Was their position justified? Look at the arguments about stem cell research at www.stemcellresearchnews.com or www.nih.gov/news/stemcell. The first is a private site that covers research from around the world, the second is sponsored by the federal government's National Institutes of Health, and it covers presidential and congressional statements, actions on stem cell research, and issues in federal guidelines for research in this area.

Many other ethical issues arise in health care policy. Among some of the most visible are the right to privacy of health records, justifications for rationing health care, the propriety of health insurance companies denying coverage for experimental medicines and procedures, and a variety of equity issues related to the high cost of health care. You can explore the ethical issues through the Web sites listed in the box "Working with Sources: Health Care Policy Information" or at the end of the chapter.

## FOCUSED DISCUSSION: WHAT IS THE BEST POLICY TO COVER PRESCRIPTION DRUG COSTS?

The high cost of prescription drugs and what, if anything, government might do to contain the costs are major topics of debate in Congress and living rooms all over the United States. The high cost of prescription drugs is a particularly acute problem for Medicare beneficiaries because the program currently offers no coverage for them except in the Medicare + Choice program. Moreover, the supplementary insurance policies many elderly rely on offer only limited and unreliable drug coverage.

The debate over what to do about prescription drugs reflects the larger struggle over the health care policy issues addressed throughout the chapter. Should the government pay for drug coverage in the regular Medicare program, or should it regulate the price of drugs to keep costs down? If government does act to control drug costs, what effect will that have on the willingness and ability of drug and biotechnology companies to invest in new drug development, which improves available treatments? In addition, should HMOs incorporate prescription drug coverage into their policies, especially Medicare beneficiaries' policies? How are individuals to cope with the rising cost of drugs, particularly as the population ages and as advances in medical technology push drug prices ever higher?

One might begin to think about these questions by asking yet another: Do Americans have a right to subsidized health care, including prescription drug coverage? Some would answer that a wealthy nation like the United States should provide this coverage to all citizens. Others disagree, citing both philosophical and economic reasons. If people are to rely more on individual choice and the private market, how might they be encouraged to assume greater responsibility for their health and well-being and be more cost-conscious in seeking appropriate medications?

The difficulty of finding sensible answers goes a long way toward explaining Congress's inability to overcome policy gridlock and act on the challenge of prescription drug coverage for the elderly. The political parties are deeply divided on the issue, as are HMOs, drug manufacturers, and senior citizen groups, all of which lobby furiously to get their messages across to policymakers, who have the unenviable task of finding a compromise solution acceptable to all policy actors. The focused discussion provides public policy students with the basic facts in the dispute and possible alternative courses of action in terms of the economic, political, and ethical issues in prescription drug coverage.

## Economic Issues

As has been stressed throughout the chapter, economic issues are at the forefront of health care policy. One of the most contentious issues is how to pay for prescription drugs, and for obvious reasons. Prescription drugs are the fastest growing heath care expenditure, with costs doubling between 1995 and 2000. The average Medicare recipient spent $813 out of pocket on prescription drugs in 2000, $908 in 2001, and an estimated $1,051 in 2002 (Toner 2002). That is only part of the expense. The Congressional Budget Office estimated that the average

Medicare beneficiary used $1,756 worth of prescription medicines in 2002, but about 10 percent of beneficiaries used $4,000 or more. The costs are likely to be much higher in the future.

For the fifty drugs the elderly are most likely to use, the cost rose by an average of 7.8 percent in 2001, about three times the rate of inflation. The average annual cost for a drug on this select list was more than $1,000. Commonly used (and heavily advertised) medications such as Celebrex, Prilosec, Prevacid, Zocor, and Plavix each cost more than $1,400 per year, and it is by no means clear they are to be preferred over cheaper products.[22] For example, according to the Kaiser Family Foundation, Americans in 2000 paid for 45 million prescriptions for the anti-inflammatory drugs Celebrex and Vioxx, at a cost of $3.7 billion, even though most patients could be treated about as well with cheap, over-the-counter ibuprofen. So why all the extra, and probably unnecessary, cost? The answer seems to be the determined efforts by drug manufacturers to maximize profits. They eagerly court physicians and the public with glowing accounts of the wondrous benefits of the new drugs, which creates an artificial demand for them. Patients want the new drugs, and doctors prescribe them. The pharmaceutical companies also spend more than nearly any other U.S. industry directly lobbying policymakers and even more for indirect lobbying via mass media advertising campaigns. So far, they have succeeded in blocking a drug coverage plan for the elderly, which they fear will lead to price controls (Gerth and Stolberg 2000).

The pharmaceutical industry argues that government intervention would harm the development of innovative new drugs and deprive citizens of improved medical care. The biotechnology industry often cites that argument. Drug development costs can be sky high, making the prescription drugs that result incredibly expensive. For example, the arthritis drug Embrel, developed by the Immunex Corporation, costs a patient $12,000 to $13,000 a year. New drugs that stave off AIDS cost even more, as do some cancer therapies. In defense of their pricing policies, the drug companies note that, for every successful product, dozens of others never make it to the market despite millions of dollars in development costs. Moreover, even drugs that are approved have patent protection against generic competition for only about eleven years. Drug coverage by Medicare, industry says, would ultimately have detrimental effects, although such coverage would also expand the market for prescription drugs. Is the industry's position convincing? What kinds of policy action might help to get prices under control without harming new drug development? For example, should drug advertising to consumers be limited?

The economic questions about government coverage of prescription drugs come down to policy preferences. Robert Reischauer, president of the Urban Institute and a health policy expert, put the matter this way. "Is it affordable?" he asked. "No. But we can't have low taxes, growing defense spending, increased resources devoted to education and other domestic priorities and a more adequate Medicare benefit package" (Toner 2002). Even without additional drug benefits, Medicare costs are projected to rise more than 90 percent between 2002 and 2012, from $252 billion to $490 billion a year.

## Political Issues

The political response to the challenge of prescription drug coverage focuses largely on Medicare. Pressured by senior citizen groups, such as the powerful AARP, to offer such coverage, policymakers have developed several different proposals to try to meet the demands. As might be expected, Democrats and Republicans differ dramatically in the kinds of policy alternatives they are prepared to support. The two approaches reflect ideological differences as well as efforts to appease distinctive party constituencies. Recent surveys indicate that about

two-thirds of the U.S. public thinks the Medicare program should include prescription drug coverage, and about the same percentage supports rolling back the 2001 tax cut to provide the funds for it under Medicare.[23]

This kind of broad support for prescription drug coverage helps to explain policy actions in Congress in recent years. In 2002, for example, Democrats and Republicans introduced competing bills to add prescription drug coverage to the Medicare program, with both sides making election-year gambits to impress the parties' core constituencies. If adopted, such a plan would represent the largest increase in the history of the Medicare program. Most political analysts anticipate, however, continued gridlock rather than compromise until one of the parties has a clear majority in Congress.

The Democratic plan of 2002 was the more generous of the two. Enrollees would pay a monthly $25 premium and face a modest $100 annual deductible. The government would pick up 80 percent of drug costs until enrollees paid $2,000, after which 100 percent of the cost would be covered. The measure was estimated to cost the government $800 billion over ten years. The Democratic plan essentially extends a classic, government-managed insurance program, loaded with detailed regulations

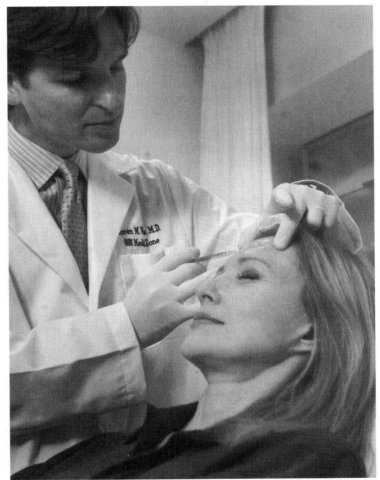

Dr. Soren White injects Lynn Krominga with Botox, a muscle paralyzer, during an April 2002 visit to the SkinKlinic on New York's 5th Avenue. The drug has rapidly gained popularity as a wrinkle reducer, particularly among affluent patients. Botox injections and other kinds of boutique health care services vividly illustrate the reality of unequal access to health care in the United States. While most public policy debates focus on how to meet the basic health care needs of countless insured and uninsured Americans, many other individuals can afford to spend thousands of dollars on elective cosmetic surgery. Legislative battles rage over how to provide affordable prescription drug coverage for the elderly and how best to control the escalating costs of Medicare, Medicaid, and other government heath care programs, yet the demand for procedures such as breast enhancements, liposuction, and face-lifts remains strong.

and reimbursement rules. Despite its popularity, it is not the kind of program conservatives generally support.

The Republican plan turned from government regulation to the free market. It would provide financial incentives to the insurance industry to encourage them to offer "drug-only" coverage to Medicare recipients, although experts in health insurance are skeptical that such policies could be offered at an affordable price. Enrollees would pay a monthly premium of about $35 and face a $250 annual deductible. Insurers would cover 80 percent of drug costs between $250 and $1,000, and 50 percent of the next $1,000. But plan participants would pay all of their costs from $2,000 to $3,700, and Medicare would cover drug costs only after that level of expenditure was reached. This plan was estimated to cost $320 billion over ten years. The proposal also barred the federal government from setting drug prices. Drug manufacturers have supported the Republican approach in part because they fear that adding drug coverage to Medicare will eventually result in federal efforts to impose price controls on drugs, which they say will discourage the research and development needed to produce new drugs.[24]

Which of the two approaches seems to be the best choice? Are there others ideas that would be more effective, efficient, and fair? For example, what about including drug coverage in Medicare Part A and raising premiums to cover the cost? What about encouraging more retirees to select Medicare + Choice managed care programs (HMOs or PPOs), which already offer prescription drug coverage?

## Equity and Ethical Issues

Most attention in the drug coverage debate focuses on the economic costs and the differences between Democratic and Republican policy proposals, but the ethical issues, such as what is right or fair in the treatment of senior citizens, abound, and for good reason. The elderly are far more likely to need prescription drugs than other segments of the population. They use more of them and in general can afford them less. So is a new taxpayer subsidy of retirees both necessary and fair? Many would say it is, but, depending on how drug coverage is paid for, it might not be. For example, a younger, working-age population may have to foot this bill in addition to the substantial burdens already placed on them by Social Security and current Medicare taxes. Chapter 9 points out that those taxes are paid at a fixed percentage rate on income, which makes them regressive. Raising Medicare taxes, therefore, could constitute a kind of generational inequity. Another aspect of this debate is whether the expansion of Medicare benefits should be means-tested; in other words, reserved for less-affluent senior citizens and not extend to people who can afford to pay for their prescriptions.

The fate of drug manufacturers and biotechnology companies that invest millions of dollars in developing potential new pharmaceuticals is another equity issue. If government drug coverage comes with stringent price controls that change the rules of the drug development game, is that fair to the companies and investors? How should analysts and policymakers balance the legitimate interests of drug manufacturers against the public's need for reasonably priced drugs?

Lifestyle choices and wellness activities are also part of the equity question. Would the provision of generous prescription drug coverage encourage some people to ignore sensible lifestyle advice regarding diet, weight, exercise, and smoking in hopes that medical science will be able to treat any resulting illness with little or no cost to them? Some would answer that any expansion of prescription drug coverage should provide sufficient incentives for individuals to take responsibility for the way they live. The incentives could be significant co-payment charges in addition to serious efforts to promote preventive health care education and diagnostic services for all age groups. Preventing disease or at least discovering and treating it at an early stage makes good economic sense and is more justifiable on ethical grounds than not doing so.

How would you design a prescription drug coverage program to deal with these kinds of ethical concerns? Are policymakers and analysts addressing ethical issues in prescription drug coverage sufficiently?

## CONCLUSIONS

This chapter traces the evolution of government health care policies and examines the leading programs. It emphasizes issues of cost, access, and quality and the diverse ways government activities affect the public's health and well-being. The present array of health care programs, from Medicare and Medicaid to innovative state preventive health measures, may seem complex and confusing to many. It strikes health care professionals the same way. Students of public policy, using the criteria discussed in the text, can evaluate all of these programs against standards of effectiveness in delivering quality health care services, the efficiency of present expenditures in terms of the benefits received, and equity in access to and payments for those services. Many analysts, policymakers, health care professionals, and patients alike find strengths and weaknesses in this system in terms of all three criteria. The strengths merit applause, but the weaknesses need to be addressed as well.

Rising costs alone, however, suggest the imperative of change. Even without prescription drug coverage, the costs threaten to bankrupt the Medicare system as the baby boom generation ages. Employers and individuals face similar hurdles in meeting the anticipated increases in insurance policy premiums and almost certainly higher deductibles and co-payments. Health care policy therefore would profit greatly from critical assessments that point to better ways of providing affordable and high quality health care to the U.S. public in the future. The questions posed throughout the chapter encourage such assessments, from how best to reform Medicare and Medicaid to the effectiveness of many state efforts to constrain costs to the promotion of health education and wellness training. Fortunately, information on health care policy is widely available on the Internet through government and independent sites to begin addressing the questions of how to design a more appropriate set of heath care policies and institutions.

## DISCUSSION QUESTIONS

How can the increasing cost of health care services be contained? Try to think of several alternatives and weigh them against the criteria of effectiveness, costs, and equity.

Who should pay for the most of the cost of health care services? Employers, individuals, or government, meaning taxpayers? Is one approach superior in terms of equity?

Should all citizens be covered by government-funded health insurance if they or their employers cannot afford private insurance coverage? What are the advantages and disadvantages of doing so?

Health maintenance organizations play an important role in health care. What do you see as their major strengths? Their most significant weaknesses?

Should Medicare recipients be given broad coverage for prescription drugs? Is the high cost to taxpayers justifiable? What kind of drug coverage plan seems to best balance costs and provision of needed services to the elderly and disabled?

What kinds of public policies might be designed to give individuals more incentives to remain healthy and reduce demand for costly health care services?

## SUGGESTED READINGS

Thomas S. Bodenheimer and Kevin Grumbach, *Understanding Health Policy,* 3d ed. (New York: McGraw Hill, 2001). A broad introduction to the field of health care policy.

Jacob S. Hacker, *The Road to Nowhere: The Genesis of President Clinton's Plan for Health Security* (Princeton: Princeton University Press, 1997). A review of the failure of Clinton's national health care plan of 1993.

Theodore R. Marmor, *The Politics of Medicare,* 2d ed. (Hawthorne, N.Y.: Aldine de Gruyter, 1999). An insightful assessment of Medicare's history and success.

Jack A. Meyer and Elliot K. Wicks, eds. *Covering America: Real Remedies for the Uninsured* (Washington, D.C.: Economic and Social Research Institute, 2001). Full text available online at www.esresearch.org/RWJ11PDF/full_document.pdf. Includes an array of leading analysts specializing in health care policy.

Kant Patel and Mark E. Rushefsky, *Health Care Politics and Policy in America,* 2d ed. (Armonk, N.Y.: M. E. Sharpe, 2000). A major text in health care policy that covers the full spectrum of issues.

## SUGGESTED WEB SITES

**http://cms.hhs.gov.** HHS site for Centers for Medicare and Medicaid Services, formerly HCFA, with valuable links to federal and state health care programs.

**http://movingideas.org/links/healthlinks.html.** Policy Action Network's health care policy page, with links to national and state health care policy, foundations, journals, and research centers. The network is affiliated with the liberal *American Prospect* magazine.

**www.aahp.org.** American Association of Health Plans, a leading industry trade association, with excellent coverage of and links to the full range of health care policy issues.

**www.achoo.com/main.asp.** *Achoo,* a Web magazine, with good coverage of health care news and issues. Also has links to organizations, business and finance, journals and periodicals, health care statistics, and reference works.

**www.citizen.org/hrg.** Public Citizen's Health Research Group site, with extensive links to policy issues and citizen activism.

**www.hiaa.org.** Health Insurance Association of America, a major trade association for the nation's health insurance industry, with links to health policy research and reports on issues such as cost trends, health care fraud, and long-term care insurance.

**www.kaisernetwork.org.** One of the best sites for timely, in-depth coverage of health care news and policy debates, with extensive links to policy organizations, research, public opinion, and advocacy.

**www.kff.org.** Kaiser Family Foundation, respected by both liberals and conservatives for its health care studies and reports. Written for the general public.

**www.milbank.org/quarterly/links.html.** Health care policy journals.

**www.rwjf.org/index.jsp.** Robert Wood Johnson Foundation Web site. Research and policy analysis on health care issues, with a progressive leaning.

## MAJOR LEGISLATION

## KEYWORDS

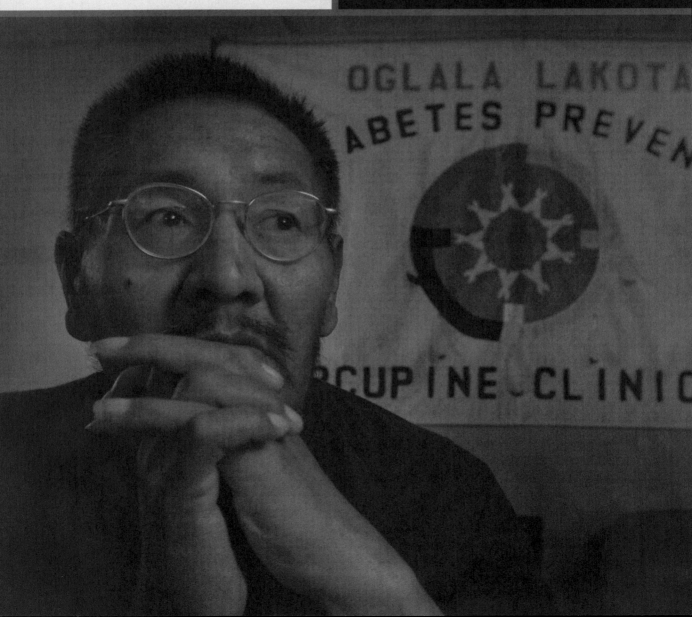

CHAPTER 9

WELFARE AND
SOCIAL SECURITY
POLICY

IN 2001 THE BUSH ADMINISTRATION'S SOCIAL SECURITY COMMISSION provided recommendations for overhauling the retirement system. As the report was being discussed and developed, it was already drawing partisan criticism. The criticism began with the initial outline and grew louder as it headed toward a detailed plan to put the program on a sound financial footing. *New York Times* reporter Richard Stevenson wrote, "Despite opposition from Democrats in Congress, organized labor and other groups, the commission adopted a report saying that Social Security faced demographic pressures that would ultimately overwhelm its ability to pay full benefits if no changes were made. The commission's members, all appointed by President Bush, said any solution should include Mr. Bush's proposal to create personal investment accounts with the system" (Stevenson 2001).

At that point, the administration seemed to lose interest, even though the plan that was ultimately released included proposals the president supported. The *CQ Weekly* reported, "When the commission released its long-awaited recommendations December 11, Bush let the moment pass without comment. For lawmakers and groups who supported Bush's call for action last spring, the commission's report was a missed opportunity. They believe Bush had a narrow window of opportunity at the start of his presidency. . . to build support for an overhaul and get Congress to move on it. Next year is out because of the mid-term elections. With control of Congress at stake, lawmakers are unlikely to act on anything so politically volatile" (Nather and McQueen 2001).

Everyone else, however, is still talking about Social Security's future and financial health. Media accounts suggest that the question of the program's financial solvency is always just below the surface, as the Social Security system moves closer to the point where program benefits exceed the revenues. Even when these signs are quite clear and beyond debate, politics enters the discussion. Policymakers from both parties are unwilling to propose major changes to a program that Americans wholeheartedly support, so Social Security continues to be a major political football that presidential and congressional candidates toss around to garner support for themselves or attack their opponents. Both of the major party presidential candidates in the 2000 campaign, George W. Bush and Al Gore, had plans for reforming Social Security, and much the same is expected of the candidates in 2004.

Demographics have considerable influence on how poverty affects Americans. For example, poverty tends to be more pronounced in rural areas and higher among minority groups. Among other social problems, it affects housing, food quality and quantity, retirement security, and medical care. Shown here, Norm Underbaggage, an Oglala Lakota, awaits dialysis treatment at the Porcupine Clinic on South Dakota's Pine Ridge Indian Reservation. Three times a week, Underbaggage must travel to the clinic to undergo the procedure. The poor can sometimes find it more difficult than others to access medical services because of financial constraints and limitations on public health programs. In 2002, the Native American population had a poverty rate of about 24.5 percent compared to 11.7 percent for the general population.

## BACKGROUND

Social Security is one of a number of federal programs designed to help individuals maintain a minimal level of income after retirement or if they are unable to continue working before they reach retirement age. The other major program is the welfare system, currently administered under the Personal Responsibility and Work Opportunity Reconciliation Act of 1996 (PRWORA). This law was a major reform of the old Aid to Families with Dependent Children (AFDC), and it provides support to low-income individuals. These two programs are the chief components of social welfare in the United States, and they are designed largely to help combat poverty. The two programs differ on a number of levels, however, including their acceptance by the general public, their source of financing, and the potential challenges they face in the future.

To better understand the social welfare programs, one first needs to know something about poverty in the United States. During times of tremendous economic growth and the subsequent increasing number of people in upper income levels, it is sometimes difficult to believe that a substantial number of Americans live in poverty today. The fact is that poverty exists and needs to be addressed. This chapter begins with some information about poverty in the United States and then discusses Social Security and welfare programs.

### Poverty

There are a number of different ways to examine poverty in the United States, starting with the official definition. The Census Bureau places a family of four below the poverty line if its annual income is less than $18,556 (based on 2002 data). The Census Bureau adjusts this number for factors such as the number of people in a family, the composition of a family, and inflation from year to year. Others look at poverty from an income distribution perspective: the more unequal the distribution of income, the greater the potential poverty problem. Still others examine poverty in terms of demographic characteristics such as race, gender, and age.

As an issue, poverty in the United States came to a head during the mid-1960s when President Lyndon Johnson declared a "war on poverty." The government initiated a number of programs to deal with the problem. Between 1965 and 1973 the poverty rate fell from 17.3 percent to 11.1 percent (Haveman 1999), and it appeared the nation was winning the war (see Figure 9-1). Unfortunately, the United States has not achieved a poverty rate this low since 1973. The rate has improved significantly in certain demographic categories; for example, the elderly and intact minority families have made definite advances. Single mothers, children, and poorly educated young people, however, still have a hard time rising out of poverty (Haveman 1999).

Some statistics concerning children in poverty help to drive this point home. In 1998 close to 19 percent of all children were poor. Children make up only 26 percent of the population, but 39 percent of the nation's poor (Delaker 1998). Moreover, minority populations in the United States also experience higher rates of poverty than whites (Delaker 1998), which may indicate something about the weaknesses of government programs to reduce poverty as well as those aimed at improving the status of minorities. Figure 9-1 shows the United States poverty rate by age over the past forty years.

Many look at poverty as an income distribution problem. In other words, a large number of people are living on limited resources, while a smaller percentage of people earn a large proportion of the nation's combined income. Economists often use the **Gini coefficient** (Figure 9-2) as a way of demonstrating a nation's income equality/inequality. Income equality is represented by a forty-five degree line, on which each percentage of the population is making the same percentage of the income. As a curve deviates away from the forty-five degree line, it shows an increase in income inequality. The implicit interpretation of the curve is that if a few people are making a large percentage of the income, more people are put at risk of poverty.

Based on 2000 data from the Census Bureau, the richest 20 percent of the population make close to 50 percent of all of the income in the United States, and the poorest 20 percent of the population make only 3.7 percent of the income. Another way to state this is that the top quintile is making as much income as the other 80 percent of the population (see Table 9-1).

**FIGURE 9-1**   U.S. Poverty Rates by Age, 1959–2000

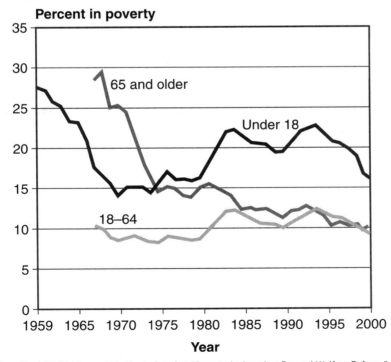

Source: From Daniel T. Lichter and Martha L. Crowley, "Poverty in America: Beyond Welfare Reform," *Population Bulletin* 57, no. 2 (June 2002), 5.

| TABLE 9-1 | Income Distribution in the United States, 2000 |

| Income Quintiles | Percentage of Income | Cumulated Percentage |
|---|---|---|
| Lowest | 3.6% | 3.6% |
| Second | 8.9 | 12.5 |
| Third | 14.9 | 27.4 |
| Fourth | 23 | 50.4 |
| Highest[a] | 49.7 | 100 |

Source: U.S. Census Bureau, Current Population Report, P60-213, *Money Income in the United States: 2000* (Washington, D.C.: U.S. Government Printing Office, 2001).

[a]The distribution of income in the United States is even more unequal than the data in the table suggest. If one examines the gain in income over the past thirty years of the top 10 percent of Americans, one discovers that most of the gain went to the top 1 percent of taxpayers, and 60 percent of the gains of the top 1 percent went to the top 0.1 percent. The disparity between the very rich and the average American has been growing significantly in recent years. For a commentary about the erosion of equality in income distribution, see Paul Krugman, "For Richer: How the Permissive Capitalism of the Boom Destroyed American Equality," *New York Times Magazine,* October 20, 2002, 62–67, 76–77, 141–142.

| FIGURE 9-2 | Gini Coefficient for U.S. Income Distribution, 2000 |

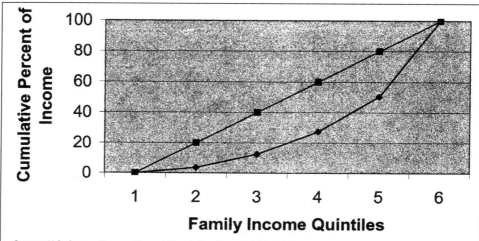

Source: U.S. Census Bureau, Current Population Report, P60-213, *Money Income in the United States: 2000* (Washington, D.C.: U.S. Government Printing Office, 2001).

Some analysts and policymakers have begun to look at the poverty problem in a new way, which they believe will change the debate on the issue. Although levels of poverty, as defined by the Census Bureau, have decreased, other data sources indicate real problems for the poor. For example, the U.S. Conference of Mayors reported in 2002 that instances of hunger and homelessness had increased dramatically over the previous year, citing a 23 percent increase in emergency food assistance.[1] The Census Bureau has considered revising its definition of poverty. Based on information provided in 1999, the bureau's analysis would have raised the income threshold to $19,500 for a nonfarm family of four. This revision would place 46 million individuals, or 17 percent of the population, below the poverty line. Such changes in the poverty-line calculations may be necessary because the original poverty line is based on a number of assumptions made in the mid-1960s that may no longer be accurate. In addition, the poverty level is the same for the lower forty-eight states and does not take into consideration cost-of-living differentials across the country. Discussions continue on this effort, but if poverty is redefined, it would be the first major adjustment, not counting inflation, in how poverty is calculated since creation of the formula (Uchitelle 1999). It is probably safe to say that even the proposed increase in the income threshold and the resulting additional assistance may not be sufficient to cover a family's expenses— housing, food, clothing, child and medical care, and everything else.

Another way to examine poverty is from an ideological perspective. Liberals and conservatives have different ideas about why poverty occurs and consequently make different proposals for addressing it. Conservatives see poverty in part as a personal choice; they believe that little poverty exists in the United States that is involuntary. They may also believe in the "**culture of poverty**," meaning that those brought up in poverty learn how to be poor and work the current system to their benefit, and they remain poor as adults. In addition, conservatives tend to blame government programs for encouraging people to remain poor, in part by not requiring any kind of responsibility in exchange for received benefits. Liberals, on the other hand, see poverty as a problem brought on by economic and social conditions over which individuals have little or no control. Liberals recognize that not everyone has the same opportunity for quality education or job training, and they favor government intervention to help equalize the playing field. They also believe that the high number of minorities who are poor indicates that discrimination also contributes to poverty.

As Chapter 6 discussed, equity is one of the criteria used to analyze problems or policies, but the word can have multiple meanings. In the case of poverty, should the concern be that the process is fair regarding resource distribution? This view is perhaps more ideologically conservative. Or, from the more liberal perspective, does equity mean looking toward a more equal distribution of resources? By now, the public policy student knows that, depending on how one sees the causes of the problem and defines the evaluating criteria, the various alternatives to address it will seem more or less appealing.

Many of the social programs developed throughout U.S. history have attempted to deal with the poverty issue from different perspectives. Social Security, for example, was developed specifically to address poverty among the elderly. By this measure, the program has been somewhat successful. According to the Social Security Administration (2000), 39 percent of the elderly population was kept out of poverty specifically because of their Social Security benefits. Programs such as AFDC or the newer TANF (Temporary Assistance for Needy Families) attempt to deal with the poverty of all individuals who happen to fall below a certain income level (or have no income at all).

## SOCIAL SECURITY

**Social Security** is the single largest federal government program today, providing money for retired workers, their beneficiaries, and disabled workers. The presidential budget request for Social Security for fiscal year 2002 was $490 billion (U.S. Social Security Administration 2002a), which provides some idea of the size and budgetary impact of the program. Social Security was enacted in 1935 during the New Deal period as a way to ensure that certain segments of society were guaranteed an income after their working years. The perception of Social Security both at its birth and today is that it is a social insurance program. Other examples of social insurance programs are unemployment insurance and workers' compensation. With these programs, citizens pay into a fund from which they expect to receive money back when they are eligible. Because of this designation, the public has always looked upon Social Security as more acceptable than other government welfare programs. Social Security is not seen to be a government handout, but as money returned based on an individual's contribution or investment. It should be noted, however, that in most cases, a Social Security recipient eventually receives more money than he or she contributed as a worker.

Social Security is typically classified as a redistributive policy program. In this case, however, money is being redistributed across generations—that is, from workers to nonworkers or young to old—rather than between economic classes. Many people believe that their personal contributions are going into a benefits account to be paid out upon retirement, but that is a misconception. Social Security is a pay-as-you-go program. Someone's current contributions are paying for someone else's current benefits. The program is also considered an entitlement. That is, if a person meets any of the eligibility requirements for Social Security, he or she is entitled to its benefits. The program is typically associated with payments to the elderly, and in fact this is the system's largest outlay, but other people are eligible as well.

Who is entitled to Social Security? Qualifying for the program is based partially on the number of years one has worked and contributed to the program. As individuals work, they earn "credits" toward Social Security. They can earn a maximum of four credits a year, and most people need forty credits to be eligible for benefits. Benefits fall into five major categories.

- Retirement: full benefits currently provided at age sixty-five plus a few months. The minimum age will gradually increase to sixty-seven in future years.
- Disability: benefits are provided to people who have enough credits and have a physical or mental condition that prevents them from doing "substantial" work for a year or more.
- Family benefits: if an individual is receiving benefits, certain family members such as a spouse or children may also be eligible for benefits.
- Survivor: when individuals who have accumulated enough credits die, certain family members, for example, a spouse sixty years or older, may be eligible for benefits.

- Medicare: Part A (hospital insurance) is paid through part of the Social Security tax. Typically, if individuals are eligible for Social Security, they also qualify for Medicare.

The Social Security Administration also administers the Supplementary Security Income Benefits program for low-income individuals who are at least sixty-five years old or disabled. The program is not financed through Social Security taxes.

The Social Security program has two major goals, and in some ways these goals conflict with each other. First, the level of benefits individuals receive is related to the amount they put into the system. In other words, the greater their contributions, the higher their benefits. Second, the program was supposed to ensure that lower-income individuals had at least minimal financial protection (Light 1995; Derthick 1979). Both goals are included in the benefit formula, and, although the rich receive higher total benefits, the amounts are not proportionally higher. The poor on the other hand, get a much greater return on their investment.

Most of Social Security is financed by a specific tax on income. The rate of this tax has remained stable since 1990, with no significant increases since 1985. Currently, the government taxes individuals and employers 7.65 percent of their income. Theoretically, this tax is earmarked, meaning the money collected goes specifically toward the benefits; these taxes also are the only source for these benefits. In reality, the federal government collects more revenue through Social Security taxes than it is currently spending to pay benefits. The government uses the excess dollars for various purposes—most commonly to reduce the size of the federal deficit.

The Social Security tax is capped at an annual income of $87,000 (the 2003 amount, which normally increases each year based on inflation) for a maximum contribution total of $6,655 per year. If an individual's income is greater than $87,000, he or she pays the maximum tax and no more for that year. In other words, a person making $1 million or $10 million pays the same amount of Social Security taxes as someone making $87,000. And everyone is paying the same rate of tax; as discussed in Chapter 7, this formula makes the Social Security tax regressive. Is the Social Security tax fair in light of some of the considerations on tax policy introduced in Chapter 7? Keep in mind that there are also limits imposed on the amount of money that each person can receive each month from the program.

Social Security is often referred to as the "political third rail" because of the potential danger associated with attempts to reform it. Whenever policymakers suggest changes, intense debate arises, and the proposals often anger the people who are currently benefiting from the program or expect to in the near future. From a political standpoint, there are two closely related reasons for the controversial nature of any proposal to change the Social Security system. First, the majority of the recipients are the elderly, who are demographically the most likely voters in the United States. Politicians are necessarily wary about crossing such a politically active group. Second, the work of the AARP, the major interest group representing the concerns of the elderly, is formidable. The AARP claims a membership of more than 33 million people, and it is one of the most influential in the nation. The group also has a large professional staff involved in lobbying public policy. With these political resources, it should be clear why efforts to make major reforms to Social Security can be challenging. The box "Steps to Analysis: The AARP as an Advocacy Group" suggests some ways to become familiar with the group's activities.

STEPS
TO
ANALYSIS

THE AARP AS AN ADVOCACY GROUP

The AARP, formerly called the American Association of Retired Persons, is an advocacy organization adept at developing and using policy
analysis to promote its positions on issues such
as Social Security reform and health care for the
elderly. Visit the AARP's Web site at
www.aarp.org and select the policy and research
page. Here, you will find a number of reports
and responses to reports on many issues of

interest to older people, including long-term
health care, economic security, and prescription
drug coverage. Examine a report in one of these
areas to determine what the AARP's position is
on the issue. How does the organization support its case, for example, on prescription drug
coverage? According to the AARP, should prescription drug coverage be part of Medicare?
Why? What evidence does the group provide?

## Social Security's Changing Demographics

The Social Security program and the number of people eligible for it have changed dramatically since its inception in 1935. In 1945 the program had fewer than five million beneficiaries, but by 2002 the number had grown to approximately fifty million (U.S. Social Security
Administration 2002b). The reason for this increase is simple: life expectancy is higher today
than it was fifty years ago. As more people live beyond the age of sixty-five, larger numbers are
entitled to Social Security benefits. What this has meant is that Social Security, as a program,
has grown enormously since the New Deal years, and, by all estimates, it will continue to
grow well into the future. Analysts are especially worried about the impending retirement of
the baby boom generation. The first wave of Americans born between 1946 and 1964 will
start retiring in 2011.

Social Security is obviously larger now in terms of total dollars. But it is also a larger percentage of government expenditures; it grew from about 14 percent of the federal budget in
1969 to almost 23 percent in 2002 (U.S. Office of Management and Budget 2002). More
problematic for Social Security is that while the number of beneficiaries is growing larger, the
number of workers contributing to the program is becoming smaller, leaving fewer workers
per beneficiary. In fiscal year 2000 the ratio of workers to retiree was approximately 3.4:1; that
is, 3.4 workers were supporting each recipient. Compare this to 1960 when the ratio was
5.1:1, or to 1950 when the ratio was 16.5:1, and the problem becomes apparent. Projected
estimates indicate that with no change to Social Security, by 2045, each recipient will by supported by only two workers (U.S. Social Security Administration 2000), when the typical
2004 college graduate will be only in mid-career. Projections suggest that the amount of revenue coming into the Social Security system will finance only 75 percent of the benefits. For
younger workers today to receive full benefits it might be necessary to increase the withholding tax. This issue will affect people not only in the long term upon their retirement, but also
in the short term if Social Security taxes go up. Would these moves be fair and equitable? If

**FIGURE 9-3** Fewer Workers per Retiree

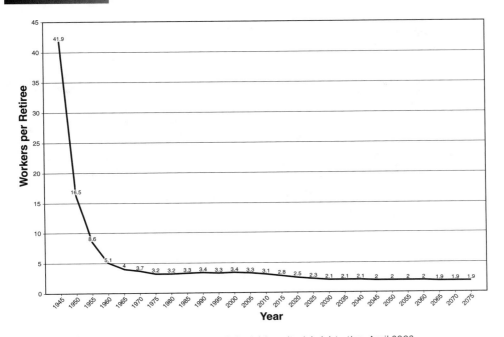

Source: "Income for the Aged Chartbook 2000," U.S. Social Security Administration, April 2002.

not, what are the alternatives to increasing the Social Security tax? Figure 9-3 shows the ratio of workers to Social Security beneficiaries since 1945 and the dramatic decrease in that ratio.

## Problems with Social Security

Beneficiaries and policymakers have acknowledged for years that Social Security, as it currently exists, has a number of problems, even though the government has addressed some of them. In 2000 Congress and the president changed the rule regarding the employment of retired workers and how it affects their Social Security benefits. Under the old rules, beneficiaries who chose to work to supplement their income would lose part of their Social Security benefits if they made more than a certain amount of money during the year. Workers under age sixty-five would lose $1 of benefits for every $2 they earned above $10,048 a year. Workers between the ages of sixty-five and seventy lost $1 of benefits for every $3 earned above $17,000 a year. Now everyone sixty-five and over can earn as much as they want without forfeiting part of their Social Security benefits. Naturally, this change in the law benefits only those senior citizens who continue to work.

"REMEMBER HOW YOU WISHED CONGRESS WOULD DO SOMETHING TO HELP US WITH THE HIGH COST OF PRESCRIPTIONS AND HEATING FUEL?"

The elderly often have to worry more than other people about personal finances, especially about how to pay for goods and services on small, fixed incomes. For years, seniors who chose to work during their retirements were forced to pay a Social Security earnings penalty. Seniors would actually begin to lose benefits if they earned "too much" money. Now that life expectancies are increasing and the health of senior citizens continues to improve, this penalty has become problematic because an increasing number of seniors stay in the work force either by choice or necessity. In 2000, Congress passed and President Clinton signed the Senior Citizens Freedom to Work Act, a law that allows seniors to work without losing Social Security benefits. But as this cartoon shows, while that tax relief may be welcome, that seniors must continue to work well into their older years means that many will continue to face a precarious future financially.

Another Social Security issue the government addressed is the fixed retirement age. Historically, the official age for collecting Social Security benefits was sixty-five, but changes to the law will gradually raise the age of eligibility to sixty-seven in recognition of the population's longer life expectancy and people's tendency to continue to work. Raising the age provides two major benefits for Social Security's solvency. First, if people cannot receive full benefits until sixty-seven, they will not receive as much money over their lifetimes. Second, if they continue to work, they will also continue to contribute to the program.

Increasing the retirement age raises other issues, however, such as equity. Is it fair to the current generation to demand that they work until age sixty-seven when their parents or grandparents could retire at sixty-five? What about quality of life? If people cannot retire until relatively late in life, they may be less able to enjoy their retirement years because of illness or physical limitations. Some social commentators have already raised concerns about the amount of time people spend working in American society, compared to most European countries. In addition, a policy that encourages later retirement may exacerbate problems to family life and employment opportunities for younger people.

A third major problem with Social Security is the potential gender inequity built into the system. When Social Security was enacted, few married women worked outside the home, but now about 60 percent of married women are currently in the workforce (U.S. General Accounting Office 1996). Why is this a concern? Under the current Social Security system, a married woman who does not work receives half of her husband's Social Security benefits (on top of what the husband receives) when she reaches age sixty-five. A working woman will receive her full benefits upon reaching this age, but the nonworking woman (or spouse) will be receiving a significant entitlement without paying anything to the system. Depending on the Social Security contributions of the working person, the nonworking spouse could get a larger payment than a working person. Women in the workforce could conceivably receive less money than a spouse who never worked. The issue has equity implications because working women may not be receiving a fair return on their investment in Social Security.

For unmarried women, the issue is that women do not earn as much as men. In 2000 women's annual median earnings reached a peak of 76 percent of men's annual earnings (U.S. Department of Labor 2001). Women, whether married or single, are also more likely to take extended periods off from work because of family obligations. The result is that, in general, women will be contributing less to Social Security and subsequently will receive lower payments than men upon retirement.

## Financing Social Security

Obviously, the biggest problem with Social Security and the one that gets the most attention is the financing of the program and the projections showing the system running out of money. The strong economy during the 1990s partially improved the situation of Social Security by increasing its solvency. Recent projections by the Social Security Administration, however, show that by 2017 the benefits that must be paid out will exceed the program's revenue from current workers. By 2041 the trust funds, which are in reality a promise to pay, will be depleted and the revenue coming into the program will pay only about 72 percent of the benefits that are due to retirees and other recipients (U.S. Social Security Administration 2002c). These kinds of numbers spark concern among many younger Americans who say they do not believe that Social Security will be around when they are eligible to collect it after they paid a lifetime of taxes into the system.

Solutions to financing Social Security are particularly problematic from a political perspective. Like any other budget problem, the "simple" solution to deal with the coming deficit in Social Security would be to increase revenues flowing into the program or to cut expenditures. In the context of Social Security, how might that be done? To bring in more money, policymakers could increase the tax on individuals and employers by raising either the withholding percentage or the maximum income that can be taxed or both. If, however, the government makes a subsequent change in the benefits to which retirees are entitled, then the additional revenues would be partially offset. As discussed in other chapters, Congress always finds it politically difficult to raise taxes even to protect a popular program such as Social Security.

The other course of action is to reduce expenditures, which can be done in a number of ways. The age of eligibility for benefits has already gone up, which postpones the outlay of funds for a number of years. Another idea, which has been used in the past, is to delay the **cost of living adjustment** (COLA). Social Security benefits go up annually, and the amount is linked to changes in inflation, as measured by the Consumer Price Index (CPI). By not implementing the COLA for a period of time, the Social Security Administration could save billions of dollars. Another solution would be to decrease the COLA outright. In other words, it might only be a partial, not a full, inflationary adjustment.

The reasons for exploring the COLA option are worth considering. First, many workers in the United States do not receive inflationary adjustments in their wages. Is it fair that retirees get regular increases in their income while those who are working do not? Second, as discussed in Chapter 7, many policy analysts believe the government's current indicators, such as the CPI, overstate inflation. This means that the COLAs are actually higher than the true rate of inflation. For sake of illustration, if Social Security pays out $400 billion in benefits this year and the inflation rate is determined to be 3 percent, that would mean an automatic increase in benefit payments the following year (disregarding new beneficiaries or deaths) to $412 billion. Delaying the payment of the COLA increase for six months would save $6 billion a year. Adjusting the COLA down by 1 percent would save $4 billion a year. If either of these proposals were adopted for a number of years, significant savings in the program would materialize.

Privatization is another approach to Social Security financing. The idea here is that individuals would be allowed to invest some of their withholding tax in mutual funds of their choosing, or the government might be permitted to invest Social Security funds in the stock market or other investment to generate a higher rate of return than now possible. Currently, the money collected for Social Security is invested in government bonds with a relatively low yield (albeit with little risk). Many people believe that a partially privatized system would increase the return and extend the financial life of the system. The focused discussion at the end of the chapter explores more fully this option for dealing with Social Security. Clearly, the Social Security system has no shortage of issues. Many of them are directly related to the demographics that will exacerbate the problems in the future. The politics of Social Security also makes reform difficult to discuss and enact, but a growing number of policy analysts and policymakers believe it is imperative that the nation address these concerns before it is too late. The longer the country waits, they argue, the more painful the proposed solutions will be.

## WELFARE

Welfare policies, as most Americans think about them, concern **means-tested programs**. To qualify for a means-tested program, a potential recipient usually must meet an income test—perhaps better described as a lack-of-income test. These programs include food stamps, job training, housing benefits, and direct cash payments to the poor. Means-tested programs differ from social insurance programs such as Social Security. Eligibility for these programs is based on need rather than contributions made to the program.

| TABLE 9-2 | Spending on the Poor, by Category | | |
|---|---|---|---|
| Category | Total | Federal Share | State Share |
| Medical benefits | $196.4 billion | 58% | 42% |
| Cash aid | 94.6 | 78 | 22 |
| Food benefits | 35.5 | 94 | 6 |
| Housing benefits | 29.5 | 91 | 9 |
| Education benefits | 18.1 | 94 | 6 |
| Other services[a] | 12.5 | 58 | 42 |
| Jobs/training | 3.9 | 98 | 2 |
| Energy aid | 1.3 | 95 | 5 |

Source: Mark Murray, Marilyn Webber Serafini, and Megan Twohey, "Untested Safety Net," *National Journal,* March 10, 2001, 684–693.

[a]Includes child care and development block grant.

Because of this distinction, welfare programs do not engender the same level of public support as Social Security. Most people do not see welfare as a social insurance program, but as a government handout or charity, which has different connotations for many in the population. These programs are also redistributive, but in this case funds are being transferred to the poor from those who are paying taxes. Table 9-2 shows how the money allocated to the poor is spent.

## Food Stamps

One of the largest federal programs for the poor is the food stamp program administered by the Department of Agriculture (USDA). The plan provides low-income households with coupons that are used to purchase food to ensure that their nutritional requirements are met. Eligible recipients are allotted a dollar amount based on the size of their household. In 2000 the food stamp program served approximately seventeen million people at a cost of about $20 billion. One of the changes made to the welfare program is that food stamp recipients are expected to register for work and take available employment.

The food stamp program has been controversial throughout its history. One concern was fraud such as food stamp counterfeiting and theft. As a result, the system now distributes benefits electronically, rather than using paper coupons. Clients and others have criticized the program for being overly bureaucratic and making potential recipients jump through hoops to receive benefits. For example, applicants must produce eleven pieces of eligibility verification and may have to recertify several times during the year (Koch 2000). These requirements have convinced many potential applicants that the benefits are not worth the effort. Many eligible people, therefore, may forgo benefits they are entitled to receive, and either they do not get adequate nutrition or turn to other sources for help.[2]

The food stamp program is only one of many public programs geared to meet the nutritional requirements of individuals. The USDA also administers the federally assisted national school lunch and school breakfast programs, which provide well-balanced, nutritional meals at either no cost or reduced cost to low-income children. The school lunch program was first aimed at assisting schools to purchase food for nutritious lunches. The passage of the National School Lunch Act in 1946 gave the program a permanent funding basis and stipulated how funds would be apportioned to the states. The purpose of the law was to ensure the "safety and well-being of the nation's children" through a program that encouraged consumption of nutritious commodities and assisted states to provide such food and necessary facilities.[3] The program, as it is currently conceived, started in 1971, when subsidized meals were tied directly to the poverty guidelines. Today, children in a family of four can receive a free meal if the family's income is less than $453 per week, based on benefits that started July 1, 2002. More than twenty-seven million children benefit from these programs.[4] This program is clearly directed at children living below or near the poverty line, but it is also part of the government's larger effort to provide valuable nutrition education to all Americans. Providing information and education is one tool policymakers use to address public problems. The federal government has even set up a centralized Web site (www.nutrition.gov) where anyone can access nutrition information.

## Aid to Families with Dependent Children

For years, the nation's major means-tested program was Aid to Families with Dependent Children, which was what most people referred to as welfare. AFDC was intended to provide financial aid to low-income mothers and children. The program benefited about fourteen million people in its last year in existence and cost about $14 billion annually (Peters 2000).

Until the government replaced the AFDC program in 1996, critics had denigrated it for years on numerous grounds. First, AFDC provided funds to individuals but expected little in return. Welfare programs are not popular with voters in the first place, because they believe the recipients are getting something for nothing. Widespread media accounts of people taking advantage of the system in various ways made the public angry. Among the stories were allegations that some women had additional children as a way of increasing their benefits. Although little systematic evidence existed to prove that these practices were common, the stories persisted and helped lead to the program's elimination. Other critics disapproved of several of the program's practices. In particular, they said the AFDC program stigmatized the beneficiaries by requiring them to respond to personal questions, home inspections, and other administrative intrusions to qualify for the benefits (Cochran et al. 1999; Peters 2000).

Another frequently raised issue was that the AFDC program seemed to provide a disincentive to work. Under AFDC, beneficiaries could work only so many hours a month. If they earned more than the specified amount, they would lose a part of their benefits. The incentive therefore was to work only up to the point of losing benefits. A related problem was that attempts to move off welfare by taking a job were not necessarily a rational solution for beneficiaries. By the time individuals paid for child care, transportation, and perhaps health care, they often had little money left, especially if they were being paid minimum wage. The smart financial decision, therefore, was to remain in the government welfare program.

Staying on public assistance may have been a rational decision for individuals, but it did not mean that the money provided was adequate. Even those who supported public assistance pointed out that the amount of financial aid was not enough to move people out of poverty.

Statistics showed that the purchasing power of AFDC payments and food stamps had declined over time. During the 1980s and 1990s, the gap between the government poverty line and the welfare benefits provided grew wider (Cochran et al. 1999).

## Welfare Reform Options

The concerns with the AFDC program led to calls for reform from many ideological perspectives. Liberals saw the program as inadequate to provide enough benefits to ensure an adequate standard of living and protect the children who were supposed to be the primary beneficiaries. Conservatives, on the other hand, were more interested in correcting the disincentives for adult beneficiaries to work and try to become self-sufficient. R. Kent Weaver (2000) discusses this conflict as the "duel clientele trap" associated with calls for welfare reform:

> Policymakers usually cannot take the politically popular step of helping poor children without the politically unpopular step of helping their custodial parents; they cannot take the politically popular steps such as increasing penalties for refusal to work or for out-of-wedlock childbearing that may hurt parents without also risking the politically unpopular result that poor children will be made worse off. (p. 45)

Attempts to reform the welfare system in general, and the AFDC program in particular, occurred numerous times. During the 1990s, however, major forces came together to get welfare reform onto the government agenda, and the result was a new policy. As Randall Ripley and Grace Franklin (1986) state, in the U.S. system of government, presidential leadership is often needed to propose any major changes to redistributive programs. The election of President Bill Clinton in 1992 and the subsequent Republican victories in the 1994 congressional elections set the stage for change. Clinton had campaigned as a "New Democrat," meaning he was more centrist than many of his colleagues. On the issue of public support for the poor, Clinton said he wanted to "end welfare as we know it" (Clinton and Gore 1992). His ideas to require work to receive benefits and "demand responsibility" (p. 164) were in some ways more in line with the Republicans than with traditional Democratic constituencies. The Republicans had made welfare reform a tenet of their Contract With America, a set of proposals that formed the basis of their campaign. Their version of welfare reform emphasized work even more firmly than the Clinton proposals (Weaver 2000). The ideological changes in Congress likely also forced some movement in Clinton's position. The eventual outcome, after much negotiation, political posturing, and strong opposition by many liberal interest groups, was the Personal Responsibility and Work Opportunity Reconciliation Act of 1996.

## Welfare Reform Law

The PRWORA ended the old AFDC program, replacing it with a block grant program, Temporary Assistance for Needy Families (TANF), which provided state governments with additional flexibility to run their welfare programs. The law also imposed work requirements for beneficiaries and put lifetime limits on receiving benefits (Weaver 2000). Among the new rules were the following:

- Teenage parents were required to live with their parents or in an adult-supervised setting.
- States were required to ensure people were moving off the welfare rolls and into work. For example, 50 percent of the families were to be working thirty hours a week by 2002. States not meeting the requirements would be penalized by reductions in their TANF block grant funds.
- Adult recipients were limited to a total of five years of receiving federal TANF funds, and states could either impose additional limits or use their own money to fund recipients beyond the five-year period.
- The entitlement structure was changed from one in which individuals who met the eligibility requirements were entitled to AFDC funds to a system in which the states receive the entitlement based on a federal block grant formula (Weaver 2000).

The box "Working with Sources: State Flexibility and Initiatives in Welfare Reform" offers suggestions for investigating the states' welfare activities.

## WORKING WITH SOURCES

### STATE FLEXIBILITY AND INITIATIVES IN WELFARE REFORM

As part of the Personal Responsibility and Work Opportunity Reconciliation Act, the federal government granted the states a larger measure of flexibility to administer their cases and welfare rolls than in the past. The states now have the opportunity to develop solutions to reduce the welfare rolls that they believe work best for their residents. Some examples follow:

- Washington State implemented "Washington Works," a program to "encourage active employer involvement in the creation of opportunities." As part of the program, the state developed a twelve-week job training program for low-income women emphasizing personal effectiveness, skill training, and job readiness. Washington Works serves as a job broker to help match employers and employees.

- Delaware implemented its "Stay in School/ Return to School" program as part of its Temporary Assistance for Needy Families proposals. The program provides at-risk teens with a broad range of academic, counseling, employment, and life skills services to aid them in getting their high school degree or vocational training.

- Many states established transportation programs that help low-income individuals with the purchase or lease of a car or provide subsidized public transportation so that people can get to jobs.

Other initiatives are under way throughout the United States to assist people in welfare programs. If you are curious about what your state is doing in this area, or which states are implementing certain kinds of changes, for example, child care subsidies, go to www.welfareinfo.org.

## Analysis of the Welfare Reform Law

The new welfare reform policy incorporated a number of components of interest to public policy students. In terms of economic efficiency, the Congressional Budget Office estimated that the new law would save $54 billion dollars by fiscal year 2002 (U.S. Congressional Budget Office 1996), with most of the savings coming from reductions in benefits to legal immigrants and other changes to existing programs such as food stamps (Weaver 2000). These savings obviously pleased many in the Washington community, especially conservatives who wanted to cut funding for welfare programs. It is also interesting to note, however, that many of the suggestions for reforming welfare, such as providing job training, child care benefits, or medical care to ensure that adults could work, would actually be more expensive to implement in the short run than the previous AFDC program. Kent Weaver calls this problem the "money trap." Former governor Tommy Thompson of Wisconsin made similar assertions about the changes in his state's welfare programs. According to Thompson, states that are serious about welfare reform needed to spend more money on health care, child care, transportation, and training (Dionne 1997). The PRWORA, however, did not fully endorse many of the high-cost provisions being pushed by advocates of the work requirement.

Politically, the public supported changes to the welfare program. Remember, most of the general public is wary of a program that gives benefits with no strings attached. Public opinion supported a work requirement and providing people with the skills they need to become self-sufficient. In addition, the public wanted something to be done to discourage out-of-wedlock births, another element of the new law (Weaver 2000). On the other side of the fence, many individuals and groups worried about the welfare reforms. Liberal politicians and interest groups, especially child advocacy groups, expressed concerns that the reforms could lead to higher levels of poverty for the affected populations. The supporters of welfare reform, however, constituted a much larger coalition that included nearly all Republicans and conservative and moderate Democrats. Moreover, the Clinton administration was feeling pressured to follow through on one of its major policy proposals, especially as the president was running for a second term.

Looking at the law from the point of view of individual freedom, it is clear that in some ways the welfare reforms impinged on a measure of the beneficiaries' freedom. In fact, many parts of the law reflected what has been called "new paternalism," whose adherents had found the permissiveness in the welfare state appalling (Mead 1986). Requiring work to receive benefits not only takes away part of an individual's freedom but also imposes a different set of values—the government's values—over how people should live. On the other hand, taxpayers prefer a program that has clear guidelines and requirements for what it takes to receive benefits. Ethically, the question that inevitably arises is what happens to the children under this program if parents do not meet their obligations or if they exceed their time limits for receiving benefits? Is the nation willing to cut off benefits to this vulnerable population?

Ultimately, one of the most important questions about the PRWORA is whether it has been (or eventually will be) effective in moving people off the welfare rolls. It is still too early to answer that question with full confidence. The initial numbers showed a dramatic decrease in the welfare caseloads since the enactment of the law in 1996. By the end of 1998, for example, caseloads had decreased by 38 percent, and many states experienced caseload reductions higher than 50 percent (U.S. Department of Health and Human Services 2000).

These positive numbers led many to announce that welfare reform was a major success. The GAO cautioned against making such grand assessments at this stage. According to the GAO (1998), the success documented by their studies might be a factor of the positive economic conditions that prevailed during the mid- to late-1990s. In addition, the first group of beneficiaries who moved from welfare to work were likely to have been the easiest people to place.

Moreover, much "remains unknown about how families fare after leaving welfare with respect to economic stability and child and family well-being" (U.S. General Accounting Office 1998, 8). For example, according to the group Families USA, "nearly a million low-income parents have lost Medicaid coverage and have probably become uninsured" since the welfare system was overhauled (Pear 2000). Another GAO report (1999) found that people were indeed getting jobs after being on the welfare rolls, but the jobs paid so little that the families were still relying on other forms of aid, such as food stamps and the earned income tax credit, to maintain a semblance of economic stability. One analyst at the Urban Institute describes the situation as follows:

> Figuring out whether welfare reform is a success means looking beyond how families that recently left welfare are faring today. For those families that have left welfare and joined the workforce, success will depend on whether they move into jobs with higher wages and benefits so that they can be not just better off than when they were on welfare but move further toward self-sufficiency. (Loprest 1999)

It goes without saying that evaluation of the PRWORA will continue for some time. As is often the case in determining the impact of public policies (Sabatier and Jenkins-Smith 1993), sufficient time must pass before analysts can accurately assess how well the welfare reform act is working. A major test of the law will likely occur when the country's economic growth begins to slow or the nation enters a recession. During 2001 and 2002, for example, the unemployment rate inched upward, and advocates for the poor were concerned that this would cause problems with the TANF program and its beneficiaries. According to the Center on Budget and Policy Priorities, for example, by 2002, thirty-three states had already experienced an increase in the number of cash assistance caseloads during that recessionary period.[5] Will the states be able to weather a surge in people needing cash assistance as jobs decrease in an economic slowdown? Many states have used their TANF funds to provide services to people who moved off the welfare rolls into work. These funds support services such as child care or medical care and have helped former recipients move into jobs. For example, Baltimore transferred $90 million of its federal TANF money to child care and other family support services.[6] If more people need cash assistance because jobs are scarce, will these services be reduced? Another issue that merits serious thought is the time limit imposed on beneficiaries. What kind of impact will the limit have on individuals? What will the public response be to entirely cutting off benefits to children? The next several years should be telling in this regard.

When the PRWORA came up for reauthorization in 2002, one of the topics under discussion was the use of federal dollars to encourage marriage. Supporters claimed that marriage helps people to get off welfare and provides a better standard of living. Statistics back them up. Welfare dependence appears to be greater for unmarried people. Children are more likely to be in poverty if they come from single-parent homes. Opponents raised several issues. Should the government be in the business of promoting these kinds of family policies? Or should that job be in the hands of religious institutions? Critics also question the causal relationships between marriage and poverty. Does promoting marriage make the government too paternalistic? How would the policy affect individual freedom?

As one can imagine, the discussions and debate over the law—not just the promotion of marriage—were highly partisan, with each person using a different study to promote his or her perspective. For example, debate in the Senate Finance Committee revealed diverse opinions about the success of welfare reform. Sen. Max Baucus, D-Mont., pointed to a study in his state that found only 10 percent of families leaving the welfare rolls were earning enough to be self-sufficient, but Sen. Charles Grassley, R-Iowa, said that in his state, families leaving welfare had more money and greater self-esteem (McQueen 2001). Everyone seems to agree that the direction welfare reform took in 1996 was the correct one. Welfare caseloads are down significantly from the early 1990s, and more people are working for their benefits. But are these changes the best way to evaluate success? Remember that the purpose of these programs was to lift people out of poverty. Did that happen? A large number of people, even those that have found work as a result of welfare reform, still remain impoverished. In addition, what remains unclear is how well the families that left welfare are doing economically.

One interesting aspect of the PRWORA is that the original law had no requirements to track these families, a serious matter from the perspective of policy design and evaluation. Instead, the only available data come from the states, and only from the states that choose to

## WORKING WITH SOURCES

### EVALUATING WELFARE REFORM

Many studies and abundant data are available on the 1996 welfare reform law, and more analysis comes on-line almost daily. A great deal of new work was published in 2002 because of deadlines written into the law on caseload reduction requirements and time limits for receiving welfare benefits. You can find information regarding welfare reform and its success or failure at the following Web sites:

**www.urban.org/content/IssuesInFocus/ WelfareReform/Reports/Reports.htm.** The Urban Institute is a nonpartisan think tank that examines social and economic issues. It tends to be somewhat liberal ideologically.

**www.heritage.org/issues/welfare.** The Heritage Foundation is a think tank that formulates and supports conservative policies.

**www.gao.gov.** The General Accounting Office has issued a number of reports regarding welfare reform and its effectiveness. The GAO is widely regarded as a professional office that has no ideological leanings.

**www.mathematica-mpr.com/welfare.htm.** A research firm that conducts studies on a variety of topics for government policymakers. This site contains a number of studies on welfare and the impact of welfare reform.

provide data, which may present only snapshots of welfare recipients and their condition (McQueen 2001). The data continue to come in, but, if the information is inadequate, how will policymakers know what changes to make in welfare programs? Are former welfare recipients better off or worse off? What has been the effect on family lives? Should work requirements be increased?

On the positive side, think tanks and other nonprofit groups are also collecting and analyzing data on all these problems. The box "Working with Sources: Evaluating Welfare Reform" presents a sample of these.

## FOCUSED DISCUSSION: REFORMING SOCIAL SECURITY THROUGH PRIVATIZATION

The precarious state of the Social Security system raises many questions. One is whether the system can remain solvent so that all who contribute to it will receive benefits upon eligibility. Another concerns the rate of return Social Security receives on its investment. Policymakers, analysts, and many others engaged in the search for solutions to these looming problems have come up with several answers. At the most basic level, to increase the solvency of Social Security, only two choices are possible: reduce benefits or increase revenues. Benefits could be reduced by raising the retirement age for eligibility, cutting back the cost of living adjustment, taxing benefits at a higher rate, or all three. Revenue can be increased by raising the payroll tax or eliminating the contribution ceiling. Another way to bring in more revenue is to realize a better rate of return on Social Security investments. This suggestion focuses the discussion on some of the more dramatic changes suggested for Social Security reform.

Proponents of privatizing the Social Security system claim it will increase the rate of return. Privatization has taken on a few different meanings. Some have suggested that Social Security dollars should be invested in the stock market to receive higher returns. Currently, the money is invested in government treasury bills that earn only about 2 percent. If stock market returns are indeed higher, the trust fund would grow faster and protect the solvency of the program. Many people, however, are uncomfortable with the government investing everyone's Social Security dollars in the stock market or some other private system. So, this specific form of privatization has not been seriously considered.

A more popular idea is to allow individuals to put a portion of their Social Security withholdings into investments of their choosing. This proposal partially changes the structure of Social Security from a pay-as-you-go plan to one that is more akin to a 401K plan; it sets up a private account for each person from which he or she can draw upon retirement. Many analysts and public officials endorse this proposal. For example, candidate George W. Bush spoke favorably about it during the 2000 presidential race. The Social Security Advisory Council (1997) included it as one of its proposals, although not all of the committee members supported it. In addition, the National Commission on Retirement Policy (1999), which addressed a number of issues on how to fund retirement, also included a plan to allow for private investment of a portion of withholding tax. Much of the Bush plan was based on the commission's proposal, which would direct approximately one quarter (or two percentage points) of the current 7.65 payroll tax into individual savings accounts for which people could make choices about investment strategies for their money.

The most important question facing policymakers is whether private investment is the best way to preserve Social Security for future generations. The political environment makes it difficult to suggest even modest reforms to the Social Security system, let alone major initiatives. This section analyzes a number of issues concerning the moving of Social Security toward a partially privatized system.

## Economic Issues

From its inception during the New Deal, Social Security's purpose has been to ensure that the elderly receive a minimal level of income, primarily to help alleviate poverty. The current Social Security system provides benefits to eligible people, but is it sufficient to keep them out of poverty? Most people also have pensions, savings, and other sources of income, and they do not rely exclusively on Social Security for their retirement. For a majority of beneficiaries, however, Social Security provides more than half of their total income, and it is the largest share of income for the aged (see Figure 9-4). So the question of the adequacy of Social Security benefits is important. As it currently works, the program invests its funds in safe government securities that provide a small but assured return. Because an individual's benefits are based on the amount of money he or she put into the system, not on the rate of

**FIGURE 9-4** Shares of Aggregate Income by Source, 2000

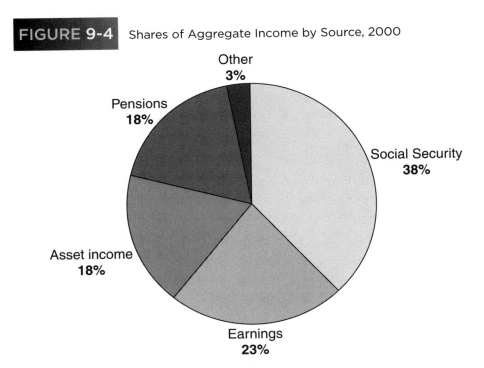

Source: Taken from the Public Agenda Web site, www.publicagenda.com/issues/factfiles_detail.cfm?issue_type=SS&list=5.

return on the investment, most people do not care if the government receives only a small return. As long as the funds are available to pay out the promised benefits, the current pay-as-you-go system is fine.

A system that permits individual retirement accounts and siphons off a portion of the Social Security withholding tax changes the investment picture. These accounts would be specifically earmarked for the individual retiree. In other words, the 2 percent withheld plus interest is dedicated directly to each worker, who will want to get the largest return possible on these investments. Doing so would likely mean investing outside of government securities, particularly in the stock market. Is this a good idea? Policymakers are assessing the proposal in terms of its potential economic effects, both positive and negative.

On the positive side, if individuals make good investment choices, they will receive a higher rate of return from Social Security and subsequently a higher standard of living upon retirement. If their investments generate more money than they would have received through the traditional Social Security system, they will likely spend more money, which in turn can spark additional economic growth. This kind of investment activity may also encourage people to save or invest part of their wages in addition to their Social Security account. Savings and investments have a positive impact on the overall economy by providing money for businesses to invest in growth opportunities.

The negative effects are equally obvious, and the most important of these is the impact on financial markets of a prolonged economic downturn. For example, in 2001 and 2002 the markets suffered some of the steepest losses seen in decades when the economy soured in the United States and abroad. The losses demonstrated the high degree of risk associated with many kinds of investment, particularly in the stock market. This situation raises new questions. Will people be able to manage their investments? How many will make poor choices on where to invest their money? Will financial advisers pressure people to make unwise decisions? If this proposal becomes law, the investment part of people's Social Security donations will not be protected, and they could receive less money than under the current plan. Would society be willing to redirect money into programs to ensure that people can make ends meet? Will action be taken to provide any protection for these self-invested funds? If the answer is yes to either of these questions, it may require so much money from the federal budget that the purpose of the legislation is defeated.

The proposal raises another major economic issue. In the absence of other policy changes, and with 2 percent of the withholding going into individual accounts, the solvency of the current Social Security funds becomes even more fragile. The funds would be depleted earlier than under current projections. The Center on Budget and Policy Priorities estimates that such a change would deplete the reserves in 2023 rather than 2037 (Orszag 2000).

Several reports go into further detail on the potential economic impacts of the private investment plan. According to Henry Aaron and his colleagues at the Social Security Network, adopting a plan that allows for an individual to invest 2 percent privately will cut Social Security benefits for younger workers by about 50 percent, and the individual accounts will only make up a portion of this decrease (Aaron et al 2000). Another report by Barry Bosworth and Gary Burtless (2000) suggests that workers who plan to retire within the next thirty to forty years would get a higher return by maintaining the current Social Security benefits and financing the system through tax increases. It is only in the very long term—forty years and beyond—that a private investment plan would increase savings and lead to higher benefits for workers.

Contrary reports assert that privatizing the Social Security system will not only lead to greater wealth for individuals but also help the general economy by promoting savings (Tanner 2000). These studies point out that even under some of the worse economic and market scenarios, individuals will still generate more money using private investments than relying on the current system. In addition, they look to other countries, such as Chile, that have moved in this direction. For Chile, not only have individual savings increased dramatically, but so too has the total economic growth of the nation (Melville 1996).

The Concord Coalition (2000) suggests a number of potential positives and negatives associated with the individual accounts plan Bush suggested during the presidential campaign. On the positive side, the Concord Coalition points to the higher returns for retirees and greater national savings. In addition, it says the plan would ensure that Social Security dollars are used only for Social Security. On the negative side, the group sees the transition from one plan to another as a problem. If 2 percent of the funds are earmarked for individual accounts, does that threaten Social Security's solvency? Where will the revenue come from to deal with the shortfall? If, as has been suggested, the Social Security fund is depleted faster than predicted, how will the government pay those already drawing benefits? What about the workers who are close to retirement and will not have the time to take advantage of private investments? These authors also address the potential problem of relying on high rates of return to make up for smaller benefit payments. Are such rates sustainable?

## Political Issues

Beyond the economic questions, the politics of Social Security reform merits attention. Social Security is known as the political "third rail" because politicians foolish enough to touch it by suggesting reforms will likely find themselves voted out of office—in other words, "fried." During campaigns, candidates like to accuse each other of trying to harm Social Security and its beneficiaries. The elderly are an attractive target for politicians because, as a group, senior citizens turn out to vote in large numbers. Not surprisingly, the elderly and the interest groups representing them, such as the AARP, have been wary of Social Security reform efforts that may decrease their benefits.

According to the AARP, its members should be concerned about privatization reform plans because of the potential uncertainty associated with the stock market and people's ability to make good investment decisions. These plans could erode the "guaranteed income" that Social Security has come to represent and impose significant costs as people begin managing private investments (AARP 2000). It seems clear that any reform option that includes a form of privatization would need to proceed cautiously and attempt to alleviate the doubts that current beneficiaries and people close to retirement have about whether their benefits will continue at the same rate.

Younger people are concerned about whether Social Security will be available to them at all. They hear reports about the financial problems with the program and how the current fund will not be able to meet expenditures in thirty to forty years. These reports put Social Security on the radar screen for the young because they do not want to put money into a pro-

Protesters from the American Federation of State, County, and Municipal Employees (AFSCME) take part in a June 2001 demonstration in New York City against President Bush's plan to add private investment accounts to Social Security. A partial privatization of the Social Security program is one option being promoted by the Bush administration as a way to ensure the financial solvency of the nation's largest federal program. Groups representing the elderly typically lead the opposition to privatization plans, but other advocates—including the AFSCME and the AFL-CIO—have also raised concerns about the efficacy of such a plan and whether it will provide the guaranteed benefits that many have come to expect from Social Security.

gram that will not pay them back when they retire. During the 2000 presidential campaign Bush made it a point to aim the private investment plan at younger voters. Privatization programs tend to be more popular with younger voters who have the time to take advantage of these investments, are more likely to invest in the market, and are concerned about the current pay-as-you-go system and its future solvency.

When the nation was experiencing surpluses, some argued that the time and political situation might be right to reform Social Security. The budget surpluses accumulated in the late 1990s provided the necessary financial cushion. Moreover, a growing percentage of the population, especially young workers, had lost confidence in the current Social Security program (Bowman 1999). Yet even with the planets aligned, the Social Security system resisted reform. The elderly and the AARP make a powerful team that supports the present system. The program itself is often held up as a significant achievement in public policy, which adds to the difficulty of making major changes in it. In addition, politicians often use the program as a wedge issue in their campaigns against their opponents, which makes sensible discussions for reform difficult, even after the elections are over and the winners are somewhat less constrained in thinking about policy options. They know the next election is never that far away.

## Ethics and Equity Issues

The future of Social Security, and particularly the proposals for privatization, come with heavy burdens of ethics and equity. After all, ethical concerns about the elderly living in poverty motivated the adoption of the Social Security program in the first place. In fact, it is not uncommon to hear policymakers talk about how Social Security is a promise made to our seniors that must be kept. Many see reforms that can potentially violate this trust as a broken promise. But what is ethical about a program that takes taxes from a worker's paycheck for a retirement program that may run out of money before that worker is eligible? From a personal freedom perspective, one might argue that individual accounts allow people to invest money the way they want rather than relying on government intervention.

One of the biggest questions regarding fairness or equity issues is who does better or worse under such a system. It is accepted that under the current Social Security system, low-wage earners get a higher rate of return on their investments than high-wage earners. The reason goes back to the belief that Social Security should provide an adequate income for all workers, even low-wage earners. Switching to a system that uses a part of the with-holding tax for individual accounts would change this dynamic. High-wage earners would likely receive a higher rate of return under such a system because they would have more funds to invest. From the perspective of personal freedom, these individuals would have greater control over what to do with their retirement funds. Low-wage earners, on the other hand, may not do as well under this system. First, their government benefits would likely be lower because of the reduced amount contributed to that part of the system. Second, they make less money, so the amount they could contribute to the individual accounts would also be smaller than high wage earners' contributions. Third, low-wage earners may not have the same ability to make investment decisions, or the same access to investment knowledge as high earners; therefore, their rates of return for their individual accounts would likely be less. Fourth, any draw down of their accounts from stock market reversals would have a more devastating effect on low-income workers than on the wealthy. How serious are these concerns about the adequacy of benefits for low-wage earners? Would other programs be needed to further ensure people remain above the poverty line? The answers are unclear at this point.

Another fairness issue concerns women in the workforce because Social Security is set up to pay significant benefits to nonworking spouses. Setting up individual accounts may be fairer to working women than the traditional system. Because this kind of program has an individual-based component to it, everyone would benefit from their contributions to their own accounts. On the other hand, some people suggest that a privatized system would be unfair to women because of gender pay inequities and because women tend to be more conservative when making investment decisions. In addition, women generally live longer than men, so their monthly benefit for life would be lower even if a man and a woman entered retirement with equal amounts in their accounts (U.S. GAO 1997).

Each of the numerous and conflicting perspectives on proposals to privatize Social Security has plenty of supporting data and reports, but the debate is not only about personal retirement and investment but also, and perhaps more important, how the program will continue to survive for future generations. Social Security has been, and will continue to be, a highly politicized issue, which makes major reforms exceedingly difficult. Any reform effort also has multiple economic implications for individuals and for the nation as a whole. In addition, the perceived success of the program in providing for the elderly and those who cannot work raises important equity issues. All of these issues will become even more significant both to individuals and to the nation as the baby boom generation nears retirement.

## CONCLUSIONS

This chapter examines the challenge of poverty and some of the major programs designed to address it. These programs aim to ensure an adequate income to make ends meet, and they have enjoyed different levels of support from the general public. Social Security is often heralded as a prime example of successful government intervention to deal with a public problem. While most agree that the nation needs to maintain a guaranteed income for the elderly based on their previous working lives, they would also agree that the current Social Security program has some deficiencies and faces serious problems. Welfare programs, on the other hand, have not experienced the same level of public support, and this attitude is apparent in the debates over welfare programs and subsequent changes in how the program is administered.

Poverty continues in the United States, despite the programs aimed at relieving it and getting people into the workforce. The welfare rolls are smaller, but it remains unclear whether fewer people are living in poverty. With Social Security, the debate continues regarding its financing and how to ensure its solvency in the future. Every student of public policy needs to understand the issues and know how to find and assess the available data to make informed decisions about these programs.

## DISCUSSION QUESTIONS

Why is there such a difference of opinion regarding programs such as Social Security and welfare programs? Is there really a difference between the two programs?

What explains the demographic discrepancies in poverty rates across the nation, for example, among racial and ethnic groups? How else might the United States address issues of poverty other than through its means-tested programs?

The level of individual income subject to the Social Security tax was capped at $87,000 in 2003. Should the income level be raised to help address anticipated shortfalls in the Social Security trust fund? Would doing so constitute an unfair taxation on current workers? Would it be more equitable to meet anticipated future demand for Social Security by reducing the level of benefits?

One purpose of the welfare reform law was to provide more flexibility to states in the administration of their programs. What kinds of policies has your state adopted? What can you say about their effectiveness? Political support? Fairness?

## SUGGESTED READINGS

Adriel Bettelheim, "Saving Social Security," in *Issues for Debate in American Public Policy*, ed. Sandra L. Stencel (Washington, D.C.: CQ Press, 1999). An article from the *CQ Researcher* that examines selected proposals for dealing with the financial issues of Social Security and the debate over the proposals.

Sarah Glazer, "Welfare Reform," *CQ Researcher,* August 3, 2001. Examines welfare reform a few years after passage of the welfare reform law, with special attention to issues likely to be faced in the future and the effectiveness of the reform effort.

Kathy Koch, "Child Poverty: Did Welfare Reform Help Poor Children?" *CQ Researcher,* April 7, 2000, 281–304. This article examines the specific issue of child poverty in the context of the welfare reform proposal.

Paul Light, *Still Artful Work,* 2d ed. (New York: McGraw-Hill, 1995). Examines the 1983 Social Security reforms to put the system on sounder footing. The book focuses on the politics involved in these policy changes and assesses more recent concerns about financial issues.

National Commission on Retirement Policy, *The 21st Century Retirement Security Plan: Final Report of the National Commission on Retirement Policy* (Washington, D.C.: U.S. Government Printing Office, March 1999). This U.S. government commission report looks at the issues of Social Security and offers some alternatives for addressing the financial issue.

R. Kent Weaver, *Ending Welfare as We Know It* (Washington, D.C.: Brookings Institution, 2000). Examines the welfare reform movement and the politics affecting it, including innovations developed and used by state governments.

## SUGGESTED WEB SITES

**www.aarp.org.** The AARP is an advocacy group for seniors. The site contains data and research on a variety of issues of concern to this constituency.

**www.acf.dhhs.gov.** HHS site for the Administration for Children and Families, with links data and information on welfare issues.

**www.concordcoalition.org.** The Concord Coalition is a nonpartisan think tank advocating fiscal responsibility for programs such as Social Security and Medicare. The site contains data and analysis concerning Social Security and reform options.

**www.socsec.org.** The Social Security Network provides a large number of reports and analyses on Social Security; provides a link to other Web sites with Social Security information.

**www.ssa.gov.** U.S. Social Security Administration site, with a wide range of information on the Social Security program and its history; also reports and data on projections for the future.

**www.urban.org.** The Urban Institute is a policy research organization. The site contains analyses of Social Security and welfare issues.

**www.welfareinfo.org.** The Welfare Information Network is a clearinghouse of data and analyses on a wide range of welfare and welfare reform issues.

## MAJOR LEGISLATION

Aid to Families with Dependent Children (AFDC)   254
Personal Responsibility and Work Opportunity Reconciliation Act of 1996   254
Temporary Assistance for Needy Families (TANF)   258

## KEYWORDS

cost of living adjustment (COLA)   264
culture of poverty   257

Gini coefficient   255
means-tested programs   264

JUST BEFORE THE BEGINNING OF THE 1999 SCHOOL TERM, THE FOLLOWING story about a Cleveland, Ohio, mother appeared in the *New York Times*. Maria Silaghi did not sleep last night. She scrubbed other people's floors until after midnight. And then she lay in bed and agonized over whether her ten-year-old son, Anthony, might have to leave his Roman Catholic grammar school. People like Ms. Silaghi have been fretfully weighing their options since a federal judge here on Tuesday suspended a four-year-old voucher program that allowed poor children to attend private and parochial schools at taxpayer expense. "Please don't take this away from us," said Ms. Silaghi, "My son needs this."[1]

Because the ruling came so late, parents were frantically trying to determine whether it would end their government education subsidies and require them to take their children out of the private schools they could no longer afford. The judge's ruling was based on his interpretation of one of America's most fundamental beliefs—that government does not advance religion. Most Americans support this position, but consider the children who were benefiting from a program that used public funds to subsidize their education at a parochial school. Would their parents feel more strongly about the constitutional issues or their children's welfare and education? What about the people who assert that public money should be used only for public schools?

Concerned about the inadequacies of public school education, a number of communities have adopted school voucher programs, which provide money to parents to send their children to private schools, whether secular or parochial. Proponents argue that these programs will improve education across the board, a goal that everyone supports. Opponents are dubious about such assertions and believe the programs misdirect funds away from the public schools that desperately need them. Critics also raise constitutional issues, and a number of programs have been challenged in court specifically on these grounds. Educators, parents, and others followed the progress of the Cleveland school voucher case, which eventually reached the Supreme Court. In June 2002 a 5–4 Court ruled that the program did not violate the First Amendment's prohibition on government establishment of religion. Writing for the Court in *Zelman v. Simmons-Harris,* Chief Justice William Rehnquist stated that the program was

U.S. education policy has a storied past. As this 1960 cartoon shows, education has long been considered an important aspect of citizenship and the production of democratic values in the United States since it helps ensure that citizens have the ability to participate in the democratic experiment. It is also important because education has served as a partial substitute for a formal social welfare program. By providing everyone with an education, federal and state governments have attempted to give citizens the necessary tools to improve themselves economically, which means less need for government support. In a land with relatively little long-term history and a populace that is increasingly made up of immigrants, public education also provides a means to inculcate American ideals, philosophies, and values. Ideally, a public education program enables anyone to grow up to become president.

"neutral in all respects toward religion" and that parents exercised "genuine choice" regarding the schools in which they placed their children (Greenhouse 2002). School voucher supporters continue to claim the program is an important way to improve the quality of education, which remains a highly salient issue in the United States. The focused discussion section in this chapter shows how policy analysis can clarify school voucher issues.

Education is one of the public services that people take for granted. For some students, it provides the knowledge and skills that enable them to continue their studies in college. For many others, however, receiving a quality education is a difficult, if not impossible, task. Since the release of the federal report "A Nation at Risk" in 1983, concern has been growing about the quality of education in the United States. Although most people living in the United States are products of a public education system that has been in existence for almost as long as the nation itself, critics claim that the system is broken and that students are suffering from its inadequacies. Indeed, statistics suggest that U.S. students are not performing at the same levels as their counterparts in other countries. This chapter explores a number of different issues associated with education in the United States, but returns to the primary issue: the quality of education and what policies can be adopted to improve it for all students.

## BACKGROUND

Education, especially public education, fulfills many of the nation's basic goals and has done so since the country's founding. First, according to the beliefs of Thomas Jefferson, it provides an avenue to ensure the continuation of U.S. democracy (Mayo 1942). How can people be active, engaged participants in democratic processes if they lack the ability to read and understand the issues? Second, education helps to assimilate large numbers of immigrants. Finally, it is the primary mechanism for social mobility in the United States, as the educated are better able to secure jobs that raise their economic and social status. This goal fits nicely with the American ideal of upward mobility and rewarding those who work hard. An educated population has a better chance of being productive and taking care of itself. Such people are less likely to need government assistance.

If one asks why government took it upon itself to provide education, it becomes apparent that the reasons were both moral and political. Morally, education was seen as a way to help individuals and groups in the population to understand the nation's ideals and to give them a chance to better themselves. An old adage illustrates this way of thinking: "Give a man a fish and you feed him for a day; teach him to fish and you feed him for a lifetime." Politically, education not only informed people about the U.S. system of government but also imparted the nation's political culture. In addition, it served the needs of certain political parties and helped those running for office to get elected. As Chapter 1 pointed out, public education also has been a response to market failure in that it is an example of a positive externality. Society benefits from a well-educated population, which justifies the government's involvement and support. The reasons for providing public education that existed years ago are still relevant as government policymakers deal with education policy today.

Traditionally, public education has been in the hands of state and local government. Policymakers at these levels have guarded this responsibility throughout the years and raised concerns whenever the federal government has attempted to interfere in education policy, especially in primary and secondary schools. State governments have the major responsibilities in education policy with respect to curriculum, teacher training and certification, and, to a greater degree than before, funding public schools. And a great deal of education policy remains under local control. Schoolteachers employed by local government comprise the largest category of public workers. There are more than fourteen thousand local school boards across the United States, all shaping education policy to some degree within their districts (Peters 2000).

This is not to say that the federal government has been completely absent from public education, but its involvement is relatively recent. Congress passed its first major education legislation, the Elementary and Secondary Education Act (ESEA), in 1965. The law raised the amount of federal funding for primary and secondary education (Thomas 1975). In 1999, for example, ESEA provided $14 billion in public school funding (Congressional Quarterly 1999). With federal funding came a variety of contentious issues. Among them were whether the federal government would dictate what was taught and whether parochial schools should receive funding. ESEA also signaled the beginning of increased federal interest in public education. In fact, many elected officials and candidates for office from both political parties regard education as a high-priority issue and want to enact programs designed to improve it.

Historically, however, the federal government has demonstrated a greater interest in higher education than in primary or secondary education. Because education is associated with positive externalities, policymakers want to encourage individuals to attend college and to help defray the cost of doing so; in the end, the better-educated population stimulates economic growth. The national government also provides billions of dollars in research grants to universities every year that cover nearly all disciplines. These grants support basic research in the biomedical and other sciences through the National Institutes of Health (NIH) and the National Science Foundation (NSF). Grants from the National Science Foundation and other agencies fund applied research in support of space exploration, national defense, and environmental protection goals.

Among the early programs in support of higher education was the Morrill Act, approved in 1862. It helped to develop the nation's land-grant college system, which in turn contributed significantly to economic development during the nineteenth and twentieth centuries. Land-grant colleges focused initially on practical fields such as agriculture and engineering, but eventually broadened their scope to include the full range of arts and sciences. Institutions such as Cornell University, Rutgers University, the University of Kentucky, and the University of Wisconsin were first established to foster research, development, and training to improve the practice and productivity of agriculture. These schools, and many others with similar backgrounds, have since blossomed into major centers of higher education. In addition, the federal government fully funds the service academies, such as the U.S. Military Academy at West Point, New York, and the U.S. Naval Academy at Annapolis, Maryland. It costs the government more than $50,000 per year for each student attending the academies.[2]

The federal government also assists the general student population and specific categories of individuals by making money available through direct payments and subsidized loans. Programs such as the GI Bill and the Pell Grant provide money directly to eligible students to make attending college more affordable. The GI Bill, originally, the Servicemen's Readjustment Act of 1944, was instrumental in the decision of tens of thousands of veterans to attend college after World War II. Congress continues to update the law to help fund higher education programs for eligible veterans. The Pell Grant program offers awards (not loans) of as much as $3,300 to eligible undergraduates, depending on financial need and the costs of attending college. Many other students benefit from guaranteed student loan programs. With federal guarantees for the loans, private financial institutions agree to lend money to students at a reduced interest rate, thus making college more accessible.

As even this brief introduction indicates, the federal government has been paying more attention to higher education than to elementary and secondary education, which state and local governments traditionally control. In recent years, however, the federal government has begun to respond to the problems in public education. For example, student performance statistics show wide variation in the quality of education from state to state, and the government has attempted to impose higher standards where needed. The federal government's participation has raised not only suspicion on the part of policymakers who oppose it but also questions about equity and freedom. Does increased federal involvement represent a genuine concern about the quality of education for all students? Or is it an unwarranted intrusion by federal policymakers into an area of public policy where state and local government officials are better able to determine public needs?

The federal government's role in primary and secondary education brings up many issues relating to the goals of education policy and the obligations that government has in ensuring an educated public. In today's world, what are, or should be, the goals and objectives of education policy regardless of the level of government with primary responsibility? It would be easy to say that the goals of education policy are to provide a high-quality education to all students, but that statement raises many additional questions, and the most basic is what constitutes "high quality"? The Department of Education, based on the Goals 2000: Educate America Act of 1994, established a list of national educational goals that can be found in the box "Steps to Analysis: Educational Goals, Definition and Evaluation."

## STEPS TO ANALYSIS

### EDUCATIONAL GOALS, DEFINITION AND EVALUATION

Goals are often difficult to define and evaluate. An abbreviated list of the goals associated with the Educate America Act appears below. In addition, you can find the detailed goals for the legislation at the Department of Education site: www.ed.gov/legislation/GOALS2000/TheAct/sec102.html. As you look at this list, think about the steps you would take to determine if a particular goal is being met. How would you measure outcomes to decide if a law has been successful? Do you perceive any biases in the goals?

Goal 1: School Readiness
Goal 2: School Completion
Goal 3: Student Achievement and Citizenship
Goal 4: Teacher Education and Professional Development
Goal 5: Mathematics and Science
Goal 6: Adult Literacy and Lifelong Learning
Goal 7: Safe, Disciplined, and Alcohol- and Drug-Free Schools
Goal 8: Parental Participation

While the goals provided in this report provide some relatively specific ideas about the preferred direction for education, they tend to deal with a broad range of educational issues, including teacher training, not an overriding "theme" of the purpose of education in the United States.

## PROBLEMS FACING EDUCATION

To provide the means for elementary and secondary schools to do the best they can for each student, policy analysts and policymakers need to address a number of problems and issues. Among them are funding for public schools, the separation of church and state, the quality of education, school vouchers, and the merit of a host of proposals, such as teacher standards and testing requirements, for improving the performance of public schools.

### Funding

Traditionally, a significant portion of funding for public schools in the United States comes from local property taxes. In fact, it is this characteristic of education policy that has ensured that state and local governments maintain a large measure of control over school curriculums in their jurisdictions. This form of financing, however, has run into problems. First, in general, the property tax does not keep pace with the inflationary costs of providing an education, or, to use a tax policy term, it is not *buoyant*. So, while teacher salaries, textbooks, school supplies, and other costs continue to increase, the amount of money provided through property taxes remains unchanged. In essence, schools find themselves having to provide more services with fewer resources. For example, the passage of Proposition 13 in California in 1978 required a two-thirds majority of the legislature to approve new property tax measures. This decision had the effect of shifting primary responsibility for financing schools to the state, which may be more vulnerable to economic swings. School budgets were drastically cut and only recently have been restored in a meaningful way. Even so, California spends less than the national average on its public schools (Purdum 2000).

The second problem is equity. Property tax revenue directed to public schools varies considerably among the fifty states and within states. For example, in 1998 and 1999 New Jersey spent approximately $9,703 per student on public education, while Utah spent only about $3,807 (Llanos 2000). Yuba County, California, spent $7,800 per student, but another county in the state, San Joaquin, spent only $4,800 (California Department of Education 2000). The result is that students from poor areas may be receiving a lower-quality education. Many believe that financing education with local property taxes is inequitable and should be replaced with a system of state or federal funding to ensure greater equality. Education funding is a topic ripe for policy analysis. The box "Steps to Analysis: Education Funding" provides some guidance for engaging in this topic.

In response to political and legal pressures, some states have begun to change the way they finance their public schools. Michigan, for example, adopted a statewide sales tax that is to be distributed to the state's school districts according to need. Other states continue to use the

STEPS

TO

ANALYSIS

## EDUCATION FUNDING

The discussion of how states fund their public education systems suggests the importance of the different evaluative criteria discussed throughout the book. Questions of equity, political feasibility, economics, and effectiveness are particularly pertinent to this discussion. Which criteria do you think are the most important in examining education funding? Is one criterion typically the "driving force" in making decisions regarding funding sources? Using the criteria discussed throughout the text, examine different mechanisms of education funding, for example, property taxes, state support, and lotteries.

property tax to fund schools, but have worked out a system of redistributing a portion of the revenue to poorer districts within the state. This egalitarian approach puts some politicians on the defensive. They have to explain why their constituents' property taxes are being used to finance another child's education elsewhere in the state. When this issue arose in Vermont, its state supreme court ruled that an equal educational opportunity is a right that must be guaranteed by the state. Following the ruling, the state legislature passed Act 60, which uses a portion of the tax money from richer communities to help fund the schools in poorer districts. Some of the "gold towns" objected and for a while refused to provide their designated amounts to the state (Associated Press 1998). The squabble over tax money in Vermont is just one symptom of a more serious nationwide concern, which is the wide discrepancies between districts and the many school districts that are not adequately funded. State courts have decided that these differences are illegal and have sought solutions. Some have even suggested that state governments take on a greater role in the funding of public education to ensure greater equity.[3]

School funding has a direct bearing on the quality of education. School districts have to deal with growing costs and flat budget resources; some have to face the low end of unequal funding. Without adequate resources, schools are unable to hire well-qualified teachers and other staff, provide the needed books and supplies, make use of computers and other technological resources, or even give students a clean, safe building in which to learn.

## Separation of Church and State

The First Amendment to the U.S. Constitution provides, among other strictures, "Congress shall make no law respecting an establishment of religion, or prohibiting the free exercise thereof." These two clauses dealing with freedom of religion, the **Establishment Clause** and the **Free Exercise Clause,** established the concept that church and state are separate in the United States. Certain policies have come into conflict with these First Amendment clauses, and the conflicts continue to this day. Prayer in public schools and government funding of religious institutions of learning are the two leading areas of education policy that have caused disagreements that have led to Supreme Court cases.

The issue of prayer in public schools relates to both religion clauses. Opponents to school prayer argue that it represents an establishment of religion by government. If a public school or an official of the school, such as a teacher or principal, requires prayer in the classroom, then, according to judicial interpretations, the practice is state sponsorship of religion and a violation of the Establishment Clause. Even though a majority of the public supports some form of prayer in the schools, since the Supreme Court case *Engel v. Vitale* (1962), the courts have consistently ruled against any kind of school-sponsored prayer. The prohibition extends to student-led prayer in an officially sanctioned event such as a football game, as the Court ruled in *Santa Fe Independent School District v. Doe* (2000). The courts also have dealt with the so-called "moment of silence" or a "moment of reflection," and whether this practice also violates the Constitution's Establishment Clause. Politically, the moment of silence may be more acceptable because it involves no established prayer that could violate an individual's religious freedoms. It should also protect an individual's rights for the same reasons. Is there any reason to be opposed to school use of a moment of silence? Are the issues similar to school requirement of a prayer?

But what about school prayer and the Free Exercise Clause, which states that the government cannot prohibit the practice of religion? In theory, students who choose to pray on their own should have that right; that is, the school cannot prohibit students from engaging in prayer. In the *Santa Fe* case, the school district argued that preventing students from expressing their views amounted to an unconstitutional censorship of their speech. The Court did not agree with the argument, saying that the practice not only constituted an endorsement of religion but also was coercive in that it forced students who wished to attend school-sponsored activities, such as football games, to conform to a state-sponsored religious activity.

Public funding of religious schools is the other major issue related to the separation of church and state in education, and here the courts have been more lenient than on school prayer, despite some contradictory rulings. In general, if the public money is being used for a secular purpose and the money is being provided to students rather than to the religious institutions that run the schools, the courts have ruled public funding allowable. This issue took on added importance because of the growing popularity of school vouchers. The voucher program provides parents with public funds in the form of vouchers that they can use to send their children to private schools. Proponents of the voucher movement see it as a way to introduce competition into education and improve the quality of education across the board (Chubb and Moe 1990). The constitutional question is whether parents can use these publicly funded vouchers to send their children to parochial schools. The Supreme Court said yes, they could, when it upheld the Cleveland voucher system, which the Court said did not violate the First Amendment.

It should be clear that even a constitutional issue, such as the separation of church and state, relates to concerns about educational quality, especially the public funding for parochial schools. Parents who believe their children are trapped in a poor public school have a strong incentive to look for alternative ways to improve their education and opportunities for the future.

## Quality

Statistics support the concern about the quality of education in the United States. According to the National Science Foundation, U.S. students scored below the international average in math and science. For example, the study showed that U.S. students scored 461 out of 800 in math (the average score was 500). Countries that did better than the United States included Slovenia (512), the Czech Republic (466), and the Russian Federation (471). With a score of 560, the leading country was the Netherlands (Public Agenda Online 2002a). In addition, SAT scores, often used as a measure of college preparedness, went down for a number of years during the 1980s, but rebounded slightly during the 1990s. Although these statistics may be questioned in terms of the validity of the measurements used, they do correspond with qualitative accounts of public education's failings in the United States. Does the information in the box "Steps to Analysis: Don't Know Much about History" prove that the lack of competence extends to social studies?

One problem is that defining what a quality education means is not so easy, but, as public policy students have learned, it is necessary. The way a public problem is defined affects the appraisal of it, the alternatives that are considered, and the policies that might be adopted to deal with it. In that regard, education is no different from any other policy area. Education traditionalists suggest that quality is decreasing because schools are not emphasizing the basics such as math, English literature, reading, writing, and science, in their teaching. By offering flexibility and electives, especially for secondary school students, the traditionalists say that the education system has moved away from its responsibilities of teaching the fundamental skills and subject matter and allowed quality to slip. Others argue that students need to be

**STEPS TO ANALYSIS**

**DON'T KNOW MUCH ABOUT HISTORY**

The standards movement may be a direct result of national surveys of academic material that educators (and others) believe everyone in the population should know. In 2000 the American Council of Trustees and Alumni conducted a poll of seniors on issues of history in the United States at what *U.S. News & World Report* names as the fifty-five top colleges. The results were not very promising. Eighty-one percent of the seniors received a D or an F. They could not identify Valley Forge and the principles of the Constitution. Here are several specific results:

- Less than a quarter could identify James Madison as the father of the Constitution;

- Only 22 percent were able to identify the line "Government of the people, for the people and by the people" as part of the Gettysburg Address;
- More than a third did not know that the Constitution provides for a division of power in the United States.

How important is this kind of knowledge? Do the results suggest that college seniors are not prepared to exercise their roles as citizens?

Source: American Council of Trustees and Alumni, "Losing America's Memory: Historical Illiteracy in the 21st Century," 2000. Available at www.goacta.org/Reports/acta_american_memory.pdf.

encouraged to learn and provided with opportunities to pursue their interests. The abilities to access, understand, and judge information and to work with others are more important than simply memorizing geometric theorems, chemical formulas, and the steps for how a bill becomes a law. These kinds of skills, proponents argue, create life-long learners and will ultimately be of greater value to society. Unfortunately, such goals are much more difficult to measure and typically are not "tested" through the traditional quality measures.

So, is the quality of education in the United States better or worse than in the past? This question may get a different answer, depending on what the respondent believes are the ultimate goals of the education system. But if one assumes that education quality *is* a problem compared to the past, why is this so? What variables might be explored to improve the education system? What can be changed to help students learn more effectively?

One area of exploration is **teacher quality**. Some analysts assert that current teachers have less skill and knowledge than teachers did in the past. A study conducted by the American Council on Education, for example, found that more than half of the students in grades seven through twelve have unqualified teachers for the physical sciences (American Council on Education 1999). Another study by the Education Trust found that a quarter of all high school classes are taught by out-of-field instructors—teachers who did not major or minor in the subject area—and the rate increases dramatically for schools in poorer areas. In fact, the study also found that no progress had been made on this score since the 1993–1994 academic year and that the problem is worse in middle schools than in high schools, with 44 percent of the classes taught by out-of-field instructors (Jerald 2002).

If the quality of teachers is lower today, what are the reasons? Another study provided a different perspective. It showed that one in five teachers leaves the profession after only three years and those who leave are more likely to have been in the top of their education classes when they graduated (Cooper 2000b). A common explanation is that teachers are paid far less than those in other professions with comparable educational requirements. From an economic standpoint, why should good students become teachers and earn a starting salary in the midtwenties when they can choose another field and make substantially more? Another reason may be the level of respect for the teaching profession. An old adage states that "those who can, do; those who can't, teach," suggesting that people become teachers by default, that they cannot succeed in other professions. Outsiders may see teaching as an easy job because teachers get the summers off. What they do not see is that teachers are on nine-month contracts and get paid accordingly. Moreover, teachers may become discouraged about their jobs. The classroom atmosphere is different from the way it was thirty or forty years ago. School violence, crowded classrooms, and pupils' unstable family situations have made it more difficult for students to learn, and fewer of them are inspired to become teachers than in the past.

Another explanation for the disappointing quality of education centers on the students themselves. Teachers who have been in the field for some time often compare the present situation to how things "used to be." Students today spend more time watching television, working, or playing video games and less time reading and focusing on schoolwork.[4] In addition, the increase in one-parent families, those in which both parents work, and other changes in home life have likely hindered the ability of students to learn.

In response to poor quality education, states and the federal government have called for the implementation of **competency testing** or standards that must be met before students can move to the next grade or graduate from high school. At the beginning of 2002, as part of the reauthorization of ESEA, President Bush signed into law a major education bill that involved the federal government more directly in the education of the nation's children than in the past. The No Child Left Behind Act of 2001, which had strong bipartisan support, will require student testing as one mechanism to try to close the education gap. The law requires states and school districts to be accountable for student performance. Under its provisions, all states will administer a single test, the **National Assessment of Education Progress**, to determine if the schools are meeting the appropriate standards. Schools that fail to improve for two years in a row could receive more federal funds, but if improvement still does not occur, the money could be used to provide tutoring or to move students to different schools. One goal of the standards movement is to prevent "social promotions." According to the testing proponents, the requirements ensure that students are promoted based on their understanding of

---

**STEPS TO ANALYSIS**

## WISCONSIN MODEL EDUCATION STANDARDS

The Wisconsin school system developed standards to test the proficiency of students in grades four, eight, and twelve for a number of subjects. Below are several examples of performance standards that students are expected to meet in social studies, in this case political science and citizenship. Do you think you would meet the standards? Are they the appropriate standards to use?

By the end of **grade four,** students will:

C.4.2 Identify the documents, such as the Declaration of Independence, the Constitution, and the Bill of Rights, in which the rights of citizens in our country are guaranteed.

C.4.4 Explain the basic purpose of government in American society, recognizing the three levels of government.

By the end of **grade eight,** students will:

C.8.1 Identify and explain democracy's basic principles, including individual rights, responsibility for the common good, equal opportunity, equal protection of the laws, freedom of speech, justice, and majority rule with protection for minority rights.

C.8.4 Describe and explain how the federal system separates the powers of federal, state, and local governments in the United States, and how legislative, executive, and judicial powers are balanced at the federal level.

C.8.8 Identify ways in which advocates participate in public policy debates.

By the end of **grade twelve,** students will:

C.12.6 Identify and analyze significant political benefits, problems, and solutions to problems related to federalism and the separation of powers.

C.12.7 Describe how past and present American political parties and interest groups have gained or lost influence on political decision making and voting behavior.

C.12.8 Locate, organize, analyze, and use information from various sources to understand an issue of public concern, take a position, and communicate the position.

C.12.10 Evaluate the ways in which public opinion can be used to influence and shape public policy.

Source: Wisconsin Department of Public Instruction, Wisconsin Model Academic Standards For Social Studies, Standard C (Political Science and Citizenship) www.dpi.state.wi.us/standards/ssstanc.html.

the material. The box "Steps to Analysis: Wisconsin Model Education Standards" looks at one state's standards for primary and secondary school students to illustrate the challenge of developing testing requirements on a national basis.

President Bush defended testing as an important way to ensure that students are getting the education they need, and without tests, how can one be sure that they are? Not everyone agrees, however, that testing, or perhaps the issue is overtesting, is the right policy choice. Will the increase in testing lead to less classroom instruction? Will teachers "teach to the test" to be sure the children will pass? As Figure 10-1 shows, parents and teachers disagree on this issue. Another issue causing discord is the threat of losing federal aid. Should the government stop

**FIGURE 10-1** Is There Too Much Testing?

### Parents

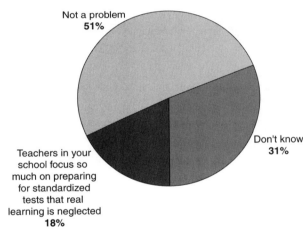

Not a problem
**51%**

Don't know
**31%**

Teachers in your school focus so much on preparing for standardized tests that real learning is neglected
**18%**

### Teachers

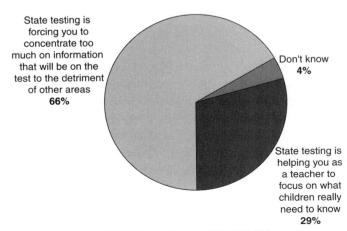

State testing is forcing you to concentrate too much on information that will be on the test to the detriment of other areas
**66%**

Don't know
**4%**

State testing is helping you as a teacher to focus on what children really need to know
**29%**

Source: Kenneth Jost, "Testing in Schools," *CQ Researcher,* April 20, 2001, 327.

Mandatory standardized testing is a hotly contested issue at all levels of government. Standard-ized exams are supposed to measure student competencies in critical areas such as math, Eng-lish, social studies, and science, and proponents argue that they ensure that students master the material and thus qualify for promotion to the next grade. Supporters also believe that school districts should be held accountable for poor results. Critics, however, are concerned that teach-ers "teach to the test" rather than emphasize essential material, and that testing will only lead to a reduction of creative thinking by students. In addition, they question the validity of the exams themselves and worry about the stress such tests place on students.

funding schools that do not improve? What additional issues will be raised by a policy of cutting aid to schools as a way to ensure compliance with the standards?

Standardized testing creates its own problems. First, the way the exams are written and graded may introduce racial or cultural bias. Second, is the imposition of such standards an infringement on state and local education? Third, the testing is expensive. Could the resources be put to better use in the classroom? The new federal requirements also have encouraged states to reassess their existing standards or issue new ones that students must meet in specific subject areas. Given that these state standards may differ considerably from one another, is it wise to allow such variation, given that people frequently move to pursue employment opportunities and for other reasons?[5]

Many other issues affect the quality of education. Inadequate facilities, increases in student violence, and high student-faculty ratios are just a few of the many variables frequently associ-ated with school quality. All are fruitful areas for investigation and public policy analysis.

## HIGHER EDUCATION ISSUES

Unlike primary and secondary education, attending college is not required; rather, it is a student's personal choice. Governments do, however, get involved by encouraging students in many ways to continue their education. From the point of view of public policy, two of the major issues in higher education are affirmative action in admissions and the costs of going to college.

## Affirmative Action

For years, many colleges and universities, in the name of promoting diversity in their student bodies, have given admissions preferences to certain demographic groups such as African Americans or Hispanic Americans. Administrators and faculty members argued that a more diverse student body adds value to the education of all the students at a college or university. For that reason, they believed it was justifiable, indeed essential, to admit some students whose academic work or test scores may not have been at the same level as others but whose other qualities enriched the campus community.

Recently, a number of states, most notably California and Texas, have moved to eliminate these kinds of preference programs from their state institutions. Administrators at other institutions, such as former University of Michigan president Lee Bollinger, believe that racial diversity is critical to the goals of education (Jost 2001). At most schools, the effect of eliminating these programs is likely to be minor. It is at the more selective institutions—the elite schools—where they currently have the greatest effect. For example, the 2000 admission figures show that at the University of California at Berkeley, the number of African American, Hispanic, and Native American students admitted dropped to 1,169; in 1997 the figure was 1,778 (Whitaker 2000). Is such a decline in minority admissions a significant problem? Some worry about fostering even greater inequalities between elite and non-elite universities than has existed for some time. Those who favor the abolition of affirmative action programs, however, see non-affirmative action admissions practice as more equitable to all the applicants. The students who score lower on SATs and other admission criteria are not being denied a higher education, but they may have to choose a less-competitive institution. This result seems to be what happened in the University of California system, where admissions for minorities at some of the less-competitive campuses have increased since 1997 (Whitaker 2000).

From a policy analysis perspective, how might one examine the issue of affirmative action programs in higher education? There are obvious ethical and fairness issues associated with affirmative action, but naturally, proponents and opponents of affirmative action programs both defend their positions in terms of equity. Proponents of affirmative action might point out that in the past minorities were excluded from many institutions of higher learning. In addition, many minorities have faced discrimination and inadequate preparation to attend elite schools, and affirmative action programs help to level the playing field. Opponents argue that it is unfair to give preferences just because of racial characteristics. They strongly defend the position that admission to college should be based on individual abilities rather than demographic characteristics. Any other method, they say, is unfair.

Have affirmative action programs been effective? That depends on one's definition of the problem. More minorities are attending college than ever before, and these increases are across the board in terms of the quality of institution. A study by William Bowen and Derek Bok (1998) found that affirmative action programs in highly selective institutions have been successful in educating and promoting the students who benefited from the admissions policy. This particular study, however, is somewhat limited because it concentrates on selective institutions rather than a broader range of schools. Many institutions assert that affirmative action programs are effective because they reach the goal of diversified student bodies. But are the programs effective if they also deny admission to qualified students?

College admissions are partially a zero-sum game. In any given year or program, each university has only so many openings, and competition can be fierce for the highly selective schools. One person's admission results in another's denial. It is interesting to note that, in light of the continuing debate over affirmative action programs in higher education, recent lawsuits challenging these policies have focused entirely on the best state universities. Elite private colleges have been spared legal challenges (Cooper 2000a). Why do such legal disparities exist? The cases involving the University of Michigan and its law school may soon clarify the situation (Jost 2001). After the Sixth Circuit Court of Appeals upheld the law school's race-conscious admission policy, the Supreme Court heard the case in April 2003. A large number of colleges and universities from around the country submitted amicus briefs supporting Michigan's admissions system. In June 2003, the Court ruled on the two University of Michigan cases in split decisions, stating that minorities could be given an edge for admissions, but limiting the extent that race can play as a factor in selecting students.

## Cost of Higher Education

Most readers of this text need no reminder that the costs of college education are substantial and continue to go up. For much of the past several decades, they have been rising faster than the rate of inflation. Because a college education is regarded as essential for a competitive and productive workforce and for maintaining economic growth, the ever-higher price tag for a college degree is alarming. The cost of attending a private college or university can be prohibitive. For example, at Harvard University the 2002–2003 comprehensive fee (tuition, room and board) was a little over $37,000, although, as with other private institutions, scholarships often bring the cost down. Many students who might have considered private institutions have turned instead to public colleges and universities that almost always cost less. Attending the University of Wisconsin in 2002, for example, cost a little over $12,000 for tuition and room and board for in-state residents, and around $23,000 for out-of-state residents.

Given the costs, one of the most important issues in higher education is the level of state support provided to students. Students may consider such support to be unexceptional, much as they expect the public to pay for the cost of elementary and secondary education, but public support for higher education raises important questions of equity. Should state governments be providing such subsidies for individuals to attend college? Or should individuals be responsible for paying their own college costs on the grounds that they are getting the benefits of the enhanced social and economic status that a college education usually provides? If some amount of subsidy is warranted, how much is justifiable? Equity questions like these arise because public subsidies for higher education involve a transfer of income from those who do not attend college to those who do; that is, state residents pay the taxes that support higher education, but not all the residents or members of their families attend college. To be sure, everyone benefits from having a well-educated population, but, even taking that point into account, inequities exist.

Even though the subsidies continue, in almost every state they cover a smaller percentage of the college and university operating budgets than they used to. State support for higher education has gone down over the past twenty years as competition for funding has increased, particularly from the prison systems and state support for Medicaid and other social service programs. Colleges and universities therefore raised tuition to make up for the shortfall. According to the Mortenson Research Seminar (2002), between fiscal years 1978 and 2002, almost every state had cut its appropriations to higher education from 1.6 percent to as much as 54.1 percent. The average cut across all states was 27 percent.[6] For public institutions to continue to operate at the same level as in previous years, one must expect future increases in tuition. According to the authors of the study, if this trend continues, state funding for higher education will reach zero by the year 2036, a frightening possibility.

Some state and federal programs have helped to ameliorate the impact of these rising costs. Georgia, for example, offers Hope Scholarships to seniors graduating with better than a B average. President Bill Clinton signed into law a similar policy that provides a tax credit for part of the costs of the first two years of attending college. Other federal financial programs have also been put into place to help alleviate the costs of higher education. These kinds of

---

## STEPS TO ANALYSIS

### WHERE ARE THE GUYS?

The Mortenson Research Seminar has observed a disturbing trend in higher education today, other than the increasing costs. The Mortenson seminar documents the decreasing percentage of men going to college and receiving degrees. In 1950 more than 76 percent of the bachelor's degrees were awarded to men. In 1996 this percentage fell to just under 45 percent, and it is projected to shrink to 42 percent by 2007.

The good news is that women are taking advantage of opportunities for higher education, but one must wonder why the rate for men is falling. The trends for college attendance are evident across a variety of demographic characteristics and academic disciplines. Although the traditionally male-dominated academic fields, such as engineering and business, continue to have a higher percentage of men, the gender gap is disappearing. For example, in 1970 men received more than 91 percent of the business degrees, but in 1996 nearly equal numbers of men and women received business degrees.

If these statistics have not alarmed you, try this one: if the current trend continues (which is highly unlikely), all of the graduates in 2068 will be women. The trend also raises important social and family issues. If all women college graduates choose to marry after college, 66 percent of them will not marry a male college graduate. Christina Hoff Sommers of the American Enterprise Institute asks, "What does it mean in the long run that we have females who are significantly more literate, significantly more educated than their male counterparts? It is likely to create a lot of social problems" (Fletcher 2002).

How can the public policy student find out what is causing the shift in male and female college attendance rates? Does the situation constitute a problem that merits government concern?

Source: Mortenson Research Seminar on Public Policy Analysis of Opportunity for Postsecondary Education, "Where Are the Guys?" *Postsecondary Education Opportunity* 76 (October 1998).

programs raise the same equity concerns as the state-supported plans because such policies involve a redistribution of income. In addition, which students are more likely to achieve a B average or higher and thus qualify for the Hope Scholarship program? Middle-class or upper-middle class students or those from a working-class or blue-collar background? Those from cash-strapped inner-city schools or those from well-supported suburban high schools? Can such programs be justified on the basis of equity or fairness?

Although higher education costs provoke considerable debate, the value of a college education cannot be underestimated. On average, students with a bachelor's degree or higher earn substantially more than those who only complete high school. Based on 2000 data, males aged twenty-five to thirty-four with a bachelor's degree or a higher degree earn on average 60 percent more than those without a college degree. Young females with a college degree see an even greater rate of return—95 percent higher than women who only finished high school (U.S. Department of Education 2002). Although it seems apparent that a college education is highly valued, the box " Steps to Analysis: Where Are the Guys?" points out that one group of potential students is becoming smaller.

It is also evident that many students place a high value on attending some of the most prestigious colleges and universities despite what other people believe are exorbitant costs. Clearly, they think their investment in such a college degree will prove to be well worth it over time. Much the same is true of students who pay high tuition costs to attend professional graduate programs in law, medicine, or business administration. They expect to recoup their investment many times over once they graduate and begin work.

## EDUCATION POLICY REFORMS

It is not surprising that many of the education reforms that policymakers and others have proposed, debated, and implemented originated as a response to their concern over the quality of education. This section assesses some of these ideas for reform and their potential impact.

### Merit Pay

One of the most divisive issues concerning education and quality is the system most public schools use to pay their teachers. In general, teachers get raises based on their years of service. Although there may be good reasons to provide raises based on longevity, critics say that teachers have little incentive to change their methods to improve their teaching. Many workers in the United States get raises based on performance, but teachers, regardless of the quality of their work, generally are not held to such a standard. To correct what they see as a flaw in the system, some reformers have promoted the idea of tying teacher salary increases to merit. **Merit pay**, according to those who support this plan, should lead to better education as teachers improve themselves to be eligible for the greatest raises or promotions possible. Some states have implemented merit pay systems in their school districts with varying success. Lamar Alexander, a former governor of Tennessee and former U.S. secretary of education, stated that merit pay systems in Tennessee increased morale among teachers and raised the level of quality of the education in the state (Alexander 1992). On the negative side, a study of a merit pay system in Fairfax County, Virginia, found that teacher morale suffered from the competitive atmosphere created in the work environment (Geiger 1992).

Opponents raise several issues about linking pay increases to performance. First, no objective or agreed-upon measurement has yet been formulated for what constitutes an effective or quality teacher. Using student performance as an indicator of quality disregards other factors that may affect how students perform in the classroom. In addition, tying merit pay to student performance may produce some possibly undesirable incentives in the education system as the pressure mounts on schools to ensure high scores or for teachers to receive bonuses. A *Newsweek* article spotlighted a number of situations in which teachers cheated by providing answers to students during standardized tests or by teaching to the exam (Kantrowitz and McGinn 2000). According to a related *Newsweek* article, students reported that a principal told them, "You might want to look at this one again," and held up a map and pointed to the country students were being asked about (Thomas and Wingert 2000). Without some agreement as to what makes a quality teacher, bias and inequity could taint the assessments. Second, many argue that until teacher salaries are competitive with other occupations, merit pay will not succeed in attracting and retaining highly qualified people. Third, opponents point out that merit pay does not achieve the stated goal. A report from the California State University Institute for Education Reform (1997) found that merit pay systems reward a small percentage of the teachers as individuals (in contrast to recognizing the value of team-based activities) without addressing the overall problems of education quality. In addition, the study reported that funding for such programs is not maintained, resulting in "pervasive cynicism among teachers about new pay schemes" (p. 9).

The American Federation of Teachers (AFT) has promoted a related proposal that would provide significant salary increases to those who become board certified by the National Board for Professional Teaching Standards. This nonprofit organization has set standards for teacher excellence and is analogous to boards that certify doctors (American Federation of Teachers 2000). By having specific standards that teachers must meet and demonstrate, this process is not only objective but also offers a monetary incentive for teachers to pursue excellence in the classroom. It also adds an element of professional status that sometimes is lacking in the education field. For more information regarding the standards, access the organization's Web site at www.nbpts.org.

## Teacher Standards

Related to merit pay are proposals for teachers to meet certain standards to become and remain certified in the profession. Requiring a uniform level of competency for teaching should ensure a better quality education for the students. For example, the standards would end the practice of assigning teachers to courses in fields that are not their specialties.

Requiring a **competency test** for teachers is not without its problems. The validity of any kind of standardized test, for example, can be questioned. One can also ask which kind of expertise is more important, knowledge of the content (substance) or the ability to transmit that knowledge (pedagogy)? The quick answer is that they are equally important. But the reality is that the nation already suffers from a teacher shortage, and the imposition of additional requirements may intensify the problem. Rather than using a test to certify teaching competence, states such as Indiana and Connecticut have focused on programs that help current teachers improve their skills. The development of more stringent standards can be part of this process. Indiana, for example, adopted a rigorous set of standards developed by the National Board for Professional Teaching Standards as part of its licensing system. Connecticut adopted similar standards that teachers must meet within three years; if they fail to meet the expectations the state can dismiss them (Billitteri 1997). School districts need to maintain a balance because if the standards become too onerous, the schools may not have enough qualified teachers, at least in the short term. A teacher shortage is not all bad news, however. Over time it would likely cause teacher salaries to rise, which in turn might make the profession more attractive to those who would not otherwise consider it.

## Teacher Salaries

Few would dispute the importance of ensuring that the nation's children receive a quality education and develop a capacity to participate actively in the economy and government, and few doubt that the majority of U.S. residents strongly support a better education system. Even so, teacher salaries continue to seriously lag behind what other professions earn. Table 10-1 shows starting salaries for selected undergraduate majors in 2001. Proponents of higher teacher salaries argue that if teachers are professionals, their school districts must pay them as such.

The pay scale has likely contributed to a mismatch between the great demand for teachers, especially in urban school districts, and the supply of individuals willing to accept such positions. According to the report *The Urban Teacher Challenge* (Fideler et al. 2000), most of the major city school districts reported teacher shortages in special education, math, and science. The study also estimated that approximately 700,000 new teachers would be needed in major urban school districts in the coming decade. Without pay raises, the teacher shortage problem will likely continue. The right salaries, however, can turn the situation around quickly. In 2002 New York City was able to nearly eliminate its teacher shortage by offering attractive financial incentives to recruit

**TABLE 10-1** Average Starting Salaries of Selected Majors

| Major | Average Starting Salary |
|---|---|
| Computer science | $52,723 |
| Electrical engineers | 51,910 |
| Chemical engineers | 51,073 |
| Accounting | 39,397 |
| Geology and geological science | 35,568 |
| Teaching | 27,989 |

Source: U.S. Bureau of Labor Statistics, *Occupational Outlook Handbook*. The 2002-2003 edition is available at http://stats.bls.gov/oco/home.htm.

new teachers despite the difficult working conditions that exist in many parts of the city. By offering higher salaries, New York City was able to draw qualified people from other teaching jobs and individuals in other professions who were willing to change careers.[7]

## School Vouchers, School Choice, and Charter Schools

Local school boards typically draw district lines that determine which school each student attends. Unless parents decide to send their children to a private school, students go to the school closest to where they live in the district. One way to look at the students in a particular school district is that they are a captive market because a single provider (a monopoly) supplies their public school education. Americans traditionally mistrust business monopolies, believing that they can increase prices indiscriminately or offer lower quality goods and services, but consumers have little or no choice. Monopolies are seen as inefficient in a market system, and such companies have no incentive to improve on quality if consumers have nowhere else to turn. Some analysts see the same lack of competition in education (Chubb and Moe 1990). Schools do not need to improve their product because they have a guaranteed market. In essence, public schools are a government-sponsored monopoly.

Many have argued that to break up the public school monopoly, society needs to reform the system in a way that gives parents options about where to send their children to school. Among the suggested reforms are school choice, school vouchers, and charter schools. Supporters argue that when parents can exercise choice, the schools will compete for students by providing higher quality education, and the competition will raise the level of quality for everyone. The focused discussion in the next section analyzes vouchers, but, first, a general explanation of the policy alternatives may prove useful.

**School choice** programs allow parents to send their children to any public school in a particular area. The competition is among public schools only, not between public and private schools, but these programs do foster competition. With school choice programs, school selection is no longer based on school districts, but where the child might get the kind of education desired. If the chosen school also receives government funding associated with the child, then this arrangement should spur competition. The various schools might try to improve the education they offer to maintain or even increase the size of their student body. It should be noted that many education reformers use the term *school choice* to encompass all reform efforts that provide parents with options about where to send their children, including charter schools and voucher programs.

School vouchers, theoretically, are also intended to improve education by promoting competition between schools. The major difference is that with school vouchers, the government provides a certain dollar amount that parents can then apply to private or parochial school tuition or as part of the full cost of a public school education. The government voucher normally is not enough to cover the full cost of tuition, but it allows parents the choice of sending a child to a private school by relieving the family of part of the financial burden. In this way, the government encourages competition by bringing private schools into the education market.

The **charter school** is another way of introducing choice into education. Charter schools are unique in that they are government supported but independent. A state board of education gives an independent entity the responsibility of establishing a school and delivering education services with limited control by the school board. The state funds these schools, but the regulations that typically govern public schools are significantly reduced to allow the schools to have a particular focus. Some examples of charter schools in Illinois illustrate their variety. The Academy of Communications and Technology seeks to prepare students for careers in communications and computer technology. The Young Women's Leadership Charter School follows the small schools model and focuses on academic achievement. It offers a rigorous career and college preparatory curriculum that emphasizes math, science, and technology; leadership; and personal and social development. Charter schools may choose to pursue certain educational needs or strategies to improve student performance, and they are responsible for meeting the standards they develop. The number of charter schools is growing, with nearly 2,500 opening between 1992 and 2002 (Center for Education Reform 2002). Some see charter schools as just another form of voucher system because the state is paying for these schools while perhaps reducing the funding for traditional public schools.

## FOCUSED DISCUSSION: SCHOOL VOUCHERS AND EDUCATIONAL QUALITY

Many advocates of education reform support the school voucher system because they believe it offers a realistic chance to improve the quality of education. By providing parents with a voucher for a designated dollar amount, the voucher system gives parents additional choices because parents may use the voucher to send a child to a private school. Proponents also argue that the voucher system will improve the quality of all schools; to entice students to enroll, administrators will do everything they can to compete in this open market. The schools that do not improve or offer a high-quality education will lose "customers" and will likely fail just as any other business might fail. Is this an appropriate way to look at education or to improve its quality? This section uses some of the tools of policy analysis to conduct an in-depth examination of the viability of school voucher ideas.

Most school voucher systems currently in place in the United States, including the best-known plans in Cleveland and Milwaukee, are limited voucher systems in that they are aimed at assisting low-income students. For example, to be eligible for a voucher in the Milwaukee program, a family of four must have an income no higher than about $28,000 a year. School voucher purists would support a universal voucher system in which every family would receive a designated amount of money for their children's education.

The school voucher programs became politicized because opponents see them as unconstitutional and took the school boards to court. Opponents assert that the school voucher programs can violate an individual's religious freedom and the principle of separation of church and state. They argue that giving public money to parents to send their children to parochial schools is a clear violation of the First Amendment because, no matter what the religious denomination, the funds are being used to promote religion. According to federal district court judge Soloman Oliver Jr., who ruled the Cleveland program unconstitutional, the program "results in government-sponsored religious indoctrination." More than 82 percent of the schools participating in the voucher program, he said, "are religiously affiliated," and all of the pupils' work is "Christ-centered" (Denniston 1999). The Wisconsin Supreme Court, however, ruled that the Milwaukee program did not violate the state constitution or the U.S. Constitution because "the program's expansion was driven largely by a 'secular purpose'—to expand educational opportunities for poor children." The court also noted "any child attending a parochial school under the program could be excused from religious instruction if his or her parents requested such an exemption" (Koch 1999, 287–288).

The Supreme Court's 2002 ruling in the Ohio case perhaps has clarified the legal environment surrounding school voucher programs. The decision is certain to affect the voucher debate, but it remains unclear exactly what the full effects will be. Voucher opponents had hoped that the constitutional issues would be resolved in their favor. With that option gone, the debate is likely to move into other policymaking arenas, such as state courts, state legislatures, and referendums.[8] Regardless of the legal debate, other aspects of the voucher system and its implications for the quality of education merit study and discussion. The policy analysis framework used throughout the book can be used to explore the major questions in this ongoing debate. What are the economic impacts of these programs? What political issues hamper or promote them? Are vouchers the best way to address the quality issue? Are voucher programs effective in improving education?

## Economic Issues

Traditionally, education, especially public education, has been regarded as a pure public good. As such, most people assumed that having government provide education was the best option to ensure its continued existence. Proponents of school vouchers would likely challenge that assumption and express their beliefs in economic terms: education is a service like any other, subject to poor quality and market mechanisms. The economic aspects of the school voucher debate merit close examination. For example, how much money could be removed from the public schools as a result of voucher programs? If parents choose to use a government voucher to send their child to a private school, the public schools lose that child's portion of the school district's funds. Proponents of vouchers believe that school quality will improve as all schools—public and private—are forced to compete for resources. The question that often comes up, however, is how can a public school improve if it is losing the resources necessary to make improvements? One answer is that these schools are also losing students as well, and it is likely that the value of the voucher is less than the average cost of educating these students. So, while a school may lose money as a student takes his or her voucher dollars elsewhere, it is still left with the residual dollars associated with the average cost of educating that student, and therefore be somewhat ahead on a dollar per student basis, at least for that school year. A related concern is whether the public schools will lose their best students because the parents of these students may want to provide a greater challenge for them. This would have a secondary effect of potentially causing test scores to fall at the abandoned school.

Within a competitive market, if a business is not able to hold its own, it closes down. Theoretically, this situation could apply to schools as well. A school that loses too many students may not be able to stay open if it suffers from the inefficiencies associated with having too few customers. Such a possible outcome raises serious questions about what Americans expect from public education, some of them economic and others more political and ethical. For example, should people think about public schools the same way they do about private businesses? Should schools be subject to closures because of lack of revenue? If so, what impact would that have on students who depend on these schools? Given the new competitive forces unleashed by voucher programs, can state and local governments still ensure that approved educational objectives will be achieved, even in the private schools?

One economic factor that also raises concerns about equity or fairness is the eligibility standard for school vouchers. To date, most school voucher programs are for low-income families. Some proponents of voucher programs favor a more expansive approach that would make vouchers available to every family with school-age children. Such a universal program would be substantially more expensive. It also poses a greater threat to the public school system. Other people support limited voucher programs and question whether they should be open to all. For example, Howard Fuller, the former superintendent of Milwaukee's schools and a staunch supporter of the current voucher program, said, "I'll fight it. I don't support universal vouchers. I didn't get into this to get money for people who already have it" (Koch 1999). Others see these limited voucher programs as not taking full advantage of the market mechanisms to ensure that schools will actually improve. They also raise issues of fairness in that taxpayer dollars are being redistributed to low-income families. Redistribution is almost always politically controversial.

One last economic issue is the possibility of higher private school tuition. If parents are provided with public funds, private schools might choose to raise their tuition because the schools know how much money the voucher is worth and that families can probably afford to pay more. The schools also have less incentive to try to keep costs down. In addition, parents are more likely to demand more private school education. Increased demand for most goods and services typically leads to higher prices.

## Political Issues

Despite the urgent economic issues, the major controversies over school voucher plans are mainly political. Voucher opponents see the program as an attack on public schools. They believe the voucher system will eventually cripple public school systems by taking money away from them. Opponents point to the lack of needed resources in public schools and argue that more competition is not what will make schools succeed. In their minds, the money being proposed for school voucher systems needs to be funneled into public schools so that they have sufficient resources to improve the quality of education.

This position is consistent with the view of the two largest teacher's organizations: the AFT and the National Education Association (NEA). Specifically, these two organizations maintain that funds should be used for all concerned and not just for a select few who receive vouchers. Voucher opponents also raise concerns about separation of church and state, accountability, and equitable access. These are the hot button issues that opponents use to generate public sympathy for their position or to convince policymakers not to adopt voucher programs.

On the other side of the issue, voucher supporters attempt to make equally compelling arguments, the strongest being that vouchers will improve all schools through competition.

Many also see vouchers as a way to reintroduce moral teachings into the school curriculum. If parents feel strongly about this aspect of education, they can choose to send their child to a private school, most likely a religious school, that emphasizes such teachings. Supporters also raise the "fairness" issue by stating that vouchers provide additional educational opportunities to low-income families not previously available to them. In other words, why should only the rich be able to send their children to private school? It is unlikely, however, that vouchers will permit the average child with average income parents to attend the better private schools without scholarship money.

On the ideological and partisan fronts, the positions on school vouchers are clear. In general, liberals tend to favor public school education as it has traditionally been provided in the United States, and they see vouchers

A group of Cleveland parents and students say the pledge of allegiance following the press conference celebrating the Supreme Court's decision on school vouchers in June 2002. One proposal to improve the school quality is to provide vouchers to parents so they can afford to send their children to private schools if they choose. Many private schools in the United States are parochial schools, however, meaning that they may teach religion. This has made vouchers a major area of policy conflict: Do such vouchers represent a violation of the First Amendment's Establishment Clause, the prohibition of government sponsorship of religion?

as the wrong fix for education problems. Democrats often receive endorsements and campaign funding from teacher organizations and are more likely than Republicans to oppose voucher programs. Conservatives tend to favor limited government and the greater use of market mechanisms and individual choice; they find voucher programs entirely consistent with these principles. In addition, conservative religious groups and their followers, such as those associated with the Christian Coalition, tend to support voucher systems as a way of promoting moral and religious education. These voucher supporters are primary constituencies of the Republican Party.

The politics of vouchers gets a bit more complicated when one looks at some of the traditional supporters of the two major parties. For example, suburban voters who generally support the Republican Party typically do not favor vouchers because their suburban public schools perform quite well. These voters have little to gain from voucher systems and see no reason to institute them. On the other hand, many inner-city African American parents support vouchers because they see them as a way of ensuring a better education for their children. This constituency is usually associated with the Democratic Party.

Politically, support for voucher programs increases when they are linked to low-income families. In this way, the traditional voucher supporters may be able to form coalitions with organizations that champion the causes of the needy, which are usually more liberal or Democratic.

Even firm supporters of public schools may want the opportunity for an alternative if the schools are failing their children. The Clinton administration supported a range of innovations in education, including use of charter schools as a way to offer educational choices. The administration firmly opposed school vouchers, preferring instead to put additional money into the public school systems. One of the major reasons for this opposition is the relatively small number of students that private schools can currently handle, which is around six million. In comparison, public schools enroll about forty-six million students (Koch 1999). The Bush administration, however, supported the use of school vouchers and defended them as a viable way to improve the education of America's children. Florida, under the leadership of President Bush's brother, Gov. Jeb Bush, has one of the more ambitious voucher programs in the country.[9] Despite the president's general support for vouchers, he has not made the issue a central one. For example, in signing the No Child Left Behind Act of 2001, Bush dropped references to vouchers and focused his remarks instead on education standards.

On the right side of the ideological spectrum, groups such as the Heritage Foundation assert that the evidence is mounting that school choice is working and not creating the multitude of problems that opponents predicted. Their reports find that students are not abandoning the public schools and that the student body demographics in private systems and public systems with vouchers in place are similar (Shokrail Rees 2000). In addition, a number of reports have suggested that public opinion may be changing on this issue as more people begin to look for alternatives to the public school system and its perceived problems. Voucher supporters can use such evidence to push their own agenda much in the same way opponents can.

Nevertheless, voucher supporters have a number of major political hurdles to navigate to increase the use of such programs around the country. State support for vouchers is by no means assured. In the past, state debates over vouchers have been somewhat tempered, in part because neither Democrats nor Republicans dominated the state governments. When the voucher issue is placed on state ballots, however, the support is not there. For example, in referendums held in California and Michigan voters defeated state voucher programs.[10] As these programs continue to be challenged within the federal court systems, and education continues to be a major concern of the general public, one can expect to see lively debate at all levels of government.

## Equity and Ethical Issues

One of the main equity issues of school vouchers is who should be eligible to receive them. Should they be restricted to low-income families or open to all? Limiting the program to low-income families runs the risk of the political fall-out associated with redistributing taxpayer money, but that is the way most of the current voucher programs operate. Proponents say that reserving the vouchers for low-income families makes the educational system fairer by providing additional opportunities to those who might not otherwise have them. It might also be argued that restricting the vouchers is unfair because it denies the benefit to others in a system funded by everyone's tax dollars. Would voucher programs be more equitable if they were open to all in a given school district?

Another issue is whether the government is ignoring civil liberties as they relate to education. Specifically, do the voucher programs violate the Establishment Clause? Does the provision of public funds to families who can use them to send children to parochial school equate with government sponsorship of religion? Earlier Supreme Court decisions made it clear that as long as any financial aid from the government benefits the student rather than the religious institution, the First Amendment is not violated. As noted, in 2002 the Supreme Court ruled that the Cleveland voucher program is constitutional, so now these debates will likely return to the state courts and move into the political arena.

## Effectiveness

Ultimately, voucher programs must be judged on their effectiveness of improving education, but this evaluation is going to be difficult. First, a number of questions can be asked about judging effectiveness. Is the program's goal to improve the education of the children using the vouchers? Or is it to improve education generally, with the voucher program serving as a mechanism to promote competition among schools and stimulate change? Or is the goal to provide options for parents? Another major difficulty is interpreting the conflicting evidence on the success of voucher programs. Organizations are adept at using information and analysis in ways that promote their favored positions, and evidence suggests that this has been the case in the school voucher debate.

Opponents cite a number of studies suggesting that voucher programs have minimum effects at best in improving education programs. In addition, they state that the financial resources can be better used in other programs that could help all public school students. The NEA provides a list of studies suggesting either zero or minimum positive effects of voucher programs (see www.nea.org/issues/vouchers/index.html). By citing studies of the existing voucher programs that support their position, they hope to use supposedly unbiased analysis to sway the voucher debate. Studies by John Witte et al. (1995, 1997, 2000), Cecilia Rouse (1997), and Kim Metcalf et al. (1998) all support the NEA contention that voucher programs are not as effective as proponents claim and that other, more accessible programs, can provide better results. Witte's most recent study of the Milwaukee voucher program found that, in relation to student outcomes, "There is no consistent and reliable evidence that the Choice students differed in achievement from randomly selected Milwaukee Public School students" (Witte 2000, 143). The NEA even cites a study by known voucher supporters to point out its methodological limitations and claim further support for the organization's assertions that vouchers are ineffective in promoting educational achievement (Greene, Peterson, and Du 1996). According to this collection of studies, therefore, the current school voucher programs have had somewhat limited results. In most cases, educational gains are modest or nonexistent. As new data become available, these and other conclusions may well be reexamined.

Naturally, supporters of school voucher programs point to their own set of studies, or even parts of the same studies, that contradict the arguments of their opponents. The Heritage Foundation, for example, cites studies by Kim Metcalf (1999) and Paul Peterson, William Howell, and Jay Green (1999) that found positive benefits associated with voucher programs. According to Heritage, the Metcalf study found that "Cleveland scholarship students show a small but statistically significant improvement in achievement scores in language and science," and Peterson claims that parents are more satisfied with many aspects of the school they chose (Shokrail Rees 2000). Heritage also cites Witte's 2000 study as evidence to support choice by stating that the author—whose reports are often used to argue against voucher programs—claims that choice is a "useful tool to aid low-income families" (Shokrail Rees 2000). What the study actually states, however, is that "choice *can be* (emphasis added) a useful tool," which is not quite as definite.[11] A study by Cecilia Rouse (1998), using data from the Milwaukee school choice program similar to that used by Witte, found a positive effect on math scores for students participating in the choice program. Finally, a major study conducted by William Howell and Paul Peterson (2002) found that the use of vouchers had a significant impact on the success of African American students. Using this measure of effectiveness, that is, whether the program improves educational success for a particular demographic group, is another way researchers can present their results and voucher proponents can claim success.

One explanation for the contradictions in these studies and the policy arguments based on them clearly relates to using different ways to define effectiveness. Some of the studies correctly argue that the students in the voucher programs are improving and therefore the program is effective based on this definition. If the goal is to improve the performance of all students, including those in the traditional public schools, however, the measurement used is not adequate. Rouse (1998) makes this point by stating that, although the Milwaukee program improved math achievement, "It cannot shed light on whether vouchers provide an incentive for the public schools to improve and therefore increase the quality of education provided to all low-income children" (p. 594). Parent satisfaction is another variable measured to gauge effectiveness. This is a traditional market measurement, but parents may be more satisfied because they were given a choice to begin with. Analysts need to take all of these issues, which many of the studies recognize, into consideration when they try to evaluate the effectiveness of the program. Unfortunately, organizations with a particular bias will take advantage of some of these nuances when making their claims in support of or opposition to the voucher programs.

As with any other public problem, analyzing education quality and the likely effects of the voucher program requires careful assessment from a number of angles. Each perspective affords a somewhat different way of thinking about the purposes of voucher programs and

Children at a Denver charter school practice powers of observation during "discovery" time. Throughout the United States, individuals are turning to charter schools in response to the poor performance of public schools in their communities. Charter schools are public schools that are typically allowed more autonomy in return for greater accountability for ensuring positive academic results and for their adherence to the charter contract each school develops. Their curriculums are often focused on specific academic areas such as science, computer science, or language arts, and parents tend to feel that they provide a higher quality of education for students in a more personal, academic atmosphere.

judging their success or acceptability. Even this brief review of conflicting studies makes it clear that students of public policy need to evaluate the differing perspectives and the studies used to support them with a critical eye to sort out legitimate conclusions from partisan and political arguments that lack a solid foundation in the facts. Only in this way can the careful analyst fairly evaluate the issues raised and the alternatives that are put forth.

## CONCLUSIONS

This chapter examines education policy and a number of associated issues. The heart of the debate is this question: What is the best way to improve the quality of education in the nation's schools? Whether it is raising standards for students and/or teachers, increasing teacher pay, or providing additional choices for parents, all of the alternatives address what is perceived to be a problem of less-than-adequate quality.

Traditionally, education issues are the responsibility of state and local governments, but today federal policymakers are also taking an interest in education. Their rhetoric on the subject reflects differing partisan and ideological views, and the conflicts over education policy show little sign of dissipating. Given the high level of public concern over education, this response by federal officials is not surprising, but state and local government officials continue to be guarded about the federal role in education policy. They welcome any increase in federal dollars flowing their way, but they remain wary of national programs and the possible threat they pose to their long-standing control over education policy. They would much prefer federal funds that they can use at their own discretion.

Given the partisan and ideological differences over education policy goals and growing federal involvement, policy change will depend on which party controls the White House and Congress. The bipartisan effort that led to the new federal law on education standards could continue. The law represents a major departure in education policy, particularly in federal-state relations. But partisan differences remain. Interest groups will also contribute to this debate, particularly groups such as the National Education Association. If the conflicts make the future of education policy somewhat unpredictable, it is nevertheless certain that policymakers and the public will continue to seek more effective ways to reach education goals, and very likely with an eye toward efficient use of scarce resources and the promotion of equity in education programs.

## DISCUSSION QUESTIONS

Should education policy remain primarily a state and local government concern, or should the federal government be involved? What advantages and disadvantages are associated with each level of government?

Should government continue to support higher education and students who attend college? What factors should be considered when making such a policy decision? What are the arguments for and against such government support?

Should school districts change the usual expectations for teacher training to recruit a sufficient number of applicants? What is the best way to reconcile these two competing goals?

What are the major advantages and disadvantages of adopting a school voucher program? How would you design such a program so that it can address most of the criticisms?

What are the implications of raising the standards for student promotion and graduation in elementary and secondary schools? What is the relationship between such standards and the criteria of effectiveness, efficiency, and equity?

## SUGGESTED READINGS

Thomas J. Billitteri, "Teacher Education," in *Issues for Debate in American Public Policy,* ed. Sandra L. Stencel (Washington, D.C.: CQ Press, 1997). An article on teacher quality and what should be done to improve it from the *CQ Researcher.* Discusses the history, issues, and debate on the issue.

William G. Bowen and Derek C. Bok, *The Shape of the River: Long-Term Consequences of Considering Race in College and University Admissions* (Princeton: Princeton University Press, 1998). Explores affirmative action policies in some of the nation's selective institutions; states that the policies had a positive effect on the lives of the benefited students.

John E. Chubb and Terry M. Moe, *Politics, Markets, and America's Schools* (Washington: D.C.: Brookings Institution, 1990). One of the first scholarly books to discuss the issues of the nation's public school systems and how these monopolies could be improved by the introduction of school choice and voucher programs.

R. Kenneth Godwin and Frank R. Kemerer, *School Choice Tradeoffs: Liberty, Equity, and Diversity* (Austin: University of Texas Press, 2002). An overview and appraisal of school choice examining a number of issues related to this education policy alternative and the tradeoffs associated with it, such as equality of opportunity and religious freedoms.

William G. Howell and Paul Peterson, with Patrick J. Wolf and David E. Campbell, *The Education Gap: Vouchers and Urban Schools* (Washington, D.C.: Brookings Institution, 2002). A comprehensive analysis of different school voucher programs around the country. The study finds, among other things, that voucher programs have a consistent positive benefit on African-American students who participate in such programs.

John F. Witte, *The Market Approach to Education* (Princeton: Princeton University Press, 2000). Examines the school voucher issue—primarily the Milwaukee system—and begins the process of evaluating the success or failure of the program.

## SUGGESTED WEB SITES

**http://edreform.com.** Nonprofit organization founded to support teachers, parents, and communities trying to bring reform to the public schools. Information available on education issues, reports, current news and updates, and links to other organizations.

**http://nces.ed.gov.** The National Center for Education Statistics is part of the U.S. Department of Education. A wide range of information is available at this site.

**www.acenet.org.** The site for the American Council of Education, which is the coordinating organization for higher education. It also conducts research on issues of higher education and provides a clearinghouse for news related to higher education.

**www.aft.org.** Site of the American Federation of Teachers, an advocacy group that conducts research and publishes studies on a range of education issues.

**www.ed.gov.** U.S. federal government site for the Department of Education, with links to resources, news, policies, statistics. Users can also access information about the "No Child Left Behind" law signed into law in 2002.

**www.edtrust.org/edtrusthome.htm.** Nonprofit organization that focuses on schools in low-income areas and schools with high numbers of minority students. Reports, data, and news on these issues are provided on this site.

**www.heritage.org/library/education.html.** Heritage Foundation's portal to its reports and information regarding its ideas on education policy.

**www.nbpts.org/nbpts.** National Board for Professional Teaching Standards site. Provides information regarding professional standards for the teaching profession.

**www.nea.org.** Major organization representing teachers and supporting public education. Reports and information available on a number of education issues.

**www.pta.org/index.stm.** National organization for the Parent-Teacher Association, a child advocacy organization that promotes engagement in the school system as a way to help children. Resources, news, and links to other organizations available.

**www.publicagenda.org/issues/frontdoor.cfm?issue_type=education.** General public policy site that provides resources, options, data, and links regarding issues of education.

## MAJOR LEGISLATION

## KEYWORDS

IN JUNE 2002 THE BUSH ADMINISTRATION COMPLETED A report on U.S. climate action to send to the United Nations as part of the country's compliance with the 1992 Framework Convention on Climate Change. The United States signed that agreement at the Earth Summit in Rio de Janeiro in 1992, but the government has struggled since then to create politically acceptable and economically feasible policies consistent with it. The report was quietly submitted to the UN without the customary press release or announcement. As the news of the report spread, however, the president was subjected to what the press termed "intense criticism from conservatives" to downplay it. President George W. Bush then disavowed his administration's study: "I read the report put out by the bureaucracy," he said, clearly implying it did not reflect his administration's policy. He added that he remained opposed to the Kyoto protocol on climate change, the international agreement calling for mandatory reduction of greenhouse gases by industrialized countries, which the UN adopted in 1997. In a striking departure from Clinton administration policies, in early 2001 the Bush White House had rejected the Kyoto treaty as "fatally flawed." It placed unfair burdens on the U.S. economy, Bush said at the time, by not requiring developing nations to control their emissions (Seelye 2002). Despite pleas from leaders of other developed nations, Bush would not change his mind.

The reason for the administration's cautious position, and the outrage from conservatives, was the report's conclusion that climate change would have far-reaching consequences for the U.S. environment. These effects included an increase in stifling heat waves; threats to alpine meadows, coral reefs, and other vulnerable ecosystems; and public health threats from heat stress, air pollution, extreme weather, and diseases that spread easily in a warm climate. The report laid the blame for these dire environmental and health effects squarely on human activities, especially the burning of fossil fuels such as coal, oil, and natural gas.[1] This position was sharply at odds with the Bush administration's argument that the science of climate change is inexact and cannot make such forecasts with any precision. The focus on fossil fuels may have been particularly unwelcome to the White House. The president's national energy policy, submitted to Congress in 2001, emphasized the need to *increase* use of fossil fuels, in direct opposition to the arguments of environmentalists and most Democrats that the United States

An Alyeska Pipeline Service spill response worker, dressed in an environmental protection suit, checks a pump used to drain oil that spilled onto the tundra from a bullet hole in the Trans-Alaska pipeline. Built in the mid-1970s, the oil pipeline runs eight hundred miles from Prudhoe Bay, Alaska, to the southern ice-free port of Valdez and carries about one million barrels a day, or 17 percent of the nation's oil production. Proposals to drill for oil and natural gas in the coastal zone of the Arctic National Wildlife Refuge, not far from the Prudhoe Bay oil fields in Alaska's North Slope, have sharply divided the American public and Congress in recent years. Concern over the environmental impacts of oil drilling is likely to persist.

needed to improve energy efficiency and conservation. Was the Bush White House correct in distancing itself from what it viewed as an inappropriate climate change report? Or did those who criticized the president's policy have the more justifiable position?

Like so many scientific studies and bureaucratic reports of the past decade, the 2002 climate change study raised numerous questions about public policy. The study also underscored the strong relationship between energy and environmental policy; that is, the amount of energy Americans use and its sources, especially fossil fuels and nuclear energy, have profound environmental impacts, including increased urban air pollution, the production of toxic chemicals, and damage to ecosystems. By the same token, environmental policy, such as clean air and water regulation, affects the production and use of energy.

This chapter describes and evaluates U.S. environmental and energy policies. It discusses their evolution in some detail because this history, especially since the 1970s, is necessary to understand the conflicts and struggles to rebuild and redirect environmental policy for the twenty-first century. These conflicts center on the impacts of regulatory policies adopted during the 1970s and 1980s, the cost of those policies, the burdens they impose on industry, the promise of alternative policies, and the potential for integrating economic and environmental goals through sustainable development in the United States and globally. The chapter gives special consideration to the effectiveness of current policies and to economic and equity issues in evaluating policy ideas and proposals.

## BACKGROUND

Environmental policy is not easy to define. As is the case with health care policy, its scope is much broader than one might see at first glance. Many people believe the environment, and therefore environmental policy, refers only to humans' relationship to nature—which they see as wilderness and wildlife, parks, open space, recreation, and natural resources such as forests. Defining the issues that way often makes it easy for industry and public officials to assert that where conflicts exist between the economy and the environment, the latter must give way to meet human needs. For example, in the early 1990s a controversy developed over protecting the threatened northern spotted owl in the Pacific Northwest. The timber industry and its allies argued that maintaining jobs should take priority over the protection of a species, despite the provisions of the Endangered Species Act (ESA) of 1973. Enforcement of the act would have greatly limited logging in the owl's natural habitat of old growth forests. President George H. W. Bush agreed with the timber industry; as he said during a 1992 campaign trip to the Northwest, "It's time to put people ahead of owls."

Environmental scientists argue that a better way to understand the environment is to see it as a set of natural systems that interact in complex ways to supply humans and other species with the necessities of life, such as breathable air, clean water, food, fiber, energy, and the recycling of waste. To put it another way, humans are intimately dependent on environmental systems to meet their essential needs. People cannot survive without these systems but often fail to recognize their functions or to place a reasonable value on the natural services that everyone takes for granted (Daily 1997). In a striking example of how important it is to recognize these natural services, New York City avoided construction of a $6 billion water filtration plant by deciding to invest $1 billion over ten years in better land management practices around an upstate watershed that supplies 90 percent of the city's water.[2]

Numerous scientific reports in recent years also make it clear that human beings are now so numerous and use nature to such an extent to meet their needs that they threaten to disrupt these natural systems and lose the services on which life depends. Jane Lubchenco, a biologist and former president of the American Association for the Advancement of Science, observed that "humans have emerged as a new force of nature." She argued that people are "modifying physical, chemical, and biological systems in new ways, at faster rates, and over larger spatial scales than ever recorded on Earth." The result of these modifications is that humans have "unwittingly embarked upon a grand experiment with our planet" with "profound implications for all of life on Earth" (Lubchenco 1998, 492).

At the 1992 Earth Summit, delegates from 179 nations developed an elaborate agenda of action for the twenty-first century called Agenda 21 (United Nations 1993). It addresses environmental concerns by emphasizing sustainable development, or economic growth that is compatible with natural environmental systems and social goals. The objective of sustainable development is "meeting the needs of the present without compromising the ability of future generations to meet their own needs" (World Commission on Environment and Development 1987, 43). Given the continued growth of the human population and the economic expansion that must occur to provide for the roughly nine billion people who will inhabit the planet during this century, that will be no easy task. In September 2002, the tenth anniversary of the Earth Summit, a new **World Summit on Sustainable Development** was held in Johannesburg, South Africa, and continued to define that challenge. The box "Steps to Analysis: The World Summit on Sustainable Development" suggests some ways to study and evaluate the success of the World Summit.

## THE WORLD SUMMIT ON SUSTAINABLE DEVELOPMENT

## STEPS TO ANALYSIS

Visit the Web page for the 2002 World Summit (www.johannesburgsummit.org) to review its agenda and actions. The site contains a vast amount of information on implementation of Agenda 21 from the 1992 Earth Summit, efforts to pursue sustainable development, and documents on international environmental policy goals, achievements, and challenges. Many questions might be asked.

What were the major issues addressed at the summit, and how did they relate to the long-term goal of sustainable development?

What positions did the world's nations endorse at the summit, and how do they compare to the positions advocated by environmental groups? By business organizations?

What justifications were offered for these positions, and how persuasive do you find them to be?

What role did the United States play at the summit, and how does the U.S. position reflect domestic policy and politics?

Put in this broader context, environmental policy can be defined as all government actions that affect or attempt to affect environmental quality and the use of natural resources. The policy actions may take place at the local, state, regional, national, or international level. Traditionally, environmental policy was considered to involve the conservation or protection of natural resources such as public lands and waters, wilderness, and wildlife. Since the late 1960s, however, the term has also been used to refer to governments' environmental protection efforts that are motivated by public health concerns, such as controlling air and water pollution. In the future, environmental policy will be tightly integrated with the comprehensive agenda of sustainable development at all levels of government. Environmental policy will extend to government actions affecting human health and safety, energy use, transportation and urban design, agriculture and food production, population growth, and the protection of vital global ecological, chemical, and geophysical systems (Flavin et al. 2002; Vig and Kraft 2003). Environmental policy is going to have a pervasive and growing impact on modern human affairs.

To address these challenges effectively, however, policy analysts, policymakers, and the public need to think in fresh ways about environmental and energy policies and redesign them where needed. Many existing policies were developed more than three decades ago, and criticism of their effectiveness, efficiency, and equity abound. Naturally, some criticism comes from the business community. These objections are understandable because stringent laws dealing with clean air, clean water, toxic chemicals, and hazardous wastes have a direct effect on business. But others are just as likely to find fault, including state and local governments that must handle much of the routine implementation of federal laws and pay a sizable part of the costs. Critical assessments come as well from independent policy analysts who see a mismatch between what the policies are intended to accomplish and the strategies and tools on which they rely (Davies and Mazurek 1998; National Academy of Public Administration 2000; Sexton et al. 1999). Finally, groups concerned about **environmental justice** object to the inequitable burden placed on poor and minority communities that often bear the worst pollution risks, and they argue for reform (Ringquist 2003).

For more than two decades, environmental policy has been bitterly contested with no clear resolution, and energy policy has been similarly disputed. Piecemeal and incremental policy changes have improved some existing programs, such as pesticide regulation and provision of safe drinking water, but what remains is a fragmented, costly, often inefficient, and somewhat ineffective set of environmental and energy policies. During the 1990s President Bill Clinton's Environmental Protection Agency (EPA) tried to "reinvent" environmental regulation to make it more efficient and more acceptable to the business community. For example, it experimented with streamlined rulemaking and more **collaborative decision making**, in which industry and other stakeholders worked cooperatively with government officials. The experiments were only moderately successful. His successor likewise proposed a "new era" of more flexible and efficient regulation and a greater role for the states, but few experts thought Bush's efforts would be more effective than Clinton's. Clinton and Bush preferred different kinds of reforms of the major environmental laws to make them more appropriate for the twenty-first century, but political constraints prevented them from realizing their goals (Vig and Kraft 2003).

Environmental policy has reached an important crossroads, as have energy policies, particularly as they relate to the use of fossil fuels and climate change. More than ever before, policymakers and analysts need to figure out what works and what does not and to remake environmental policy for the emerging era of sustainable development. How Congress, the states, and local governments will change environmental and energy policy in the years ahead remains unclear. Much depends on the way leading policy actors define the issues and how the media cover them, the state of the economy, the relative influence of opposing interest groups, and whether political leadership can help to forge a national consensus. Concerned citizens have a role to play as well. Until policy breakthroughs occur, however, today's pluralistic, and only partially effective, environmental and energy policies are likely to continue. But some of the most innovative policy actions are taking place at the regional, state, and local levels, and they provide a glimpse of what might eventually be endorsed at higher levels of government (Mazmanian and Kraft 1999; Rabe 2003).

## THE EVOLUTION OF ENVIRONMENTAL AND ENERGY POLICY

Modern environmental policy was developed during the 1960s and shortly thereafter became firmly established on the political agenda in the United States and other developed nations. During the so-called environmental decade of the 1970s, the U.S. Congress enacted most of the major environmental statutes in effect today. Actions in states and localities paralleled these developments, as did policy evolution at the international level (Kraft 2004; McCormick 1989; Vig and Axelrod 1999). Energy policy experienced a somewhat different history, but here too it has been considered in a comprehensive and serious way only since the 1970s.

### Early Environmental and Energy Policies

Although formal environmental policy in the United States is a relatively recent development, concern about the environment and the value of natural resources can be traced back to the early seventeenth century when New England colonists first adopted local ordinances to protect forest land (Andrews 1999). In the late nineteenth and early twentieth centuries, conservation policies advanced to deal with the excesses of economic development in the West, and new federal and state agencies emerged to assume responsibility for their implementation, including the National Forest Service (1905) and the National Park Service (1916). In 1892 Congress set aside two million acres in Wyoming, Montana, and Idaho to create Yellowstone National Park, the first of a series of national parks. Many of the prominent conservation organizations also formed during this period. Naturalist John Muir founded the Sierra Club in 1892 as the first broad-based environmental organization, and others followed in the ensuing decades.

None of these developments seriously challenged prevailing U.S. values relating to the sanctity of private property, individual rights, a limited role for government, and the primacy of economic growth—all of which impose important cultural constraints on environmental policy. They did, however, signal the emergence of new social forces that eventually collided with these long-standing values and by the late twentieth century led to the government's strong role in environmental protection and resource management. The early policy actions and creation of new bureaucracies established the important principle that resources in the public domain, such as the national forests, should be used for the benefit of all citizens. In the late nineteenth century, cities began to recognize the importance of establishing urban services such as providing clean water, waste management, and wastewater treatment. Consistent with these activities to promote urban public health, the first air pollution statutes, dating from the 1880s, were adopted to control smoke and soot from furnaces and locomotives.

Following a number of natural disasters, most memorably the Dust Bowl of the 1930s, President Franklin Roosevelt expanded conservation policies to deal with flood control and soil conservation as part of his New Deal. Congress created the Tennessee Valley Authority (TVA) in 1933 to stimulate economic growth by providing electric power development in that region. The TVA demonstrated a critical policy belief: that government land use planning could further the public interest. Other measures followed, including the Taylor Grazing Act of 1934, which was intended to end the overgrazing of valuable rangelands and watersheds in the West, and the creation of the Bureau of Land Management in 1946 to manage vast public lands in the West.

Prior to the 1970s, energy policy was not a major or sustained concern of government. For the most part it consisted of federal and state regulation of coal, natural gas, and oil, particularly of the prices charged and competition in the private sector. The goal was to stabilize markets and ensure both profits and continuing energy supplies. The most notable exception was substantial federal support for the commercialization of nuclear power. Beginning in the late 1940s, Congress shielded the nascent industry from public scrutiny, spent lavishly on research and development, and promoted the rapid advancement of civilian nuclear power plants through the Atomic Energy Commission and its successor agencies, the Nuclear Regulatory Commission and the Department of Energy (DOE). The Price-Anderson Act of 1957 greatly restricted the industry's liability and allowed it to flourish (Duffy 1997).

## The Modern Environmental Movement and Policy Developments

By the 1960s the modern environmental movement was taking shape in response to changing social values. The major stimulus was the huge spurt in economic development that followed World War II (1941–1945). During the 1950s and 1960s the nation benefited further from the rise in consumerism. An affluent, comfortable, and well-educated public began to place a greater emphasis on the quality of life, and environmental quality was a part of it. Social scientists characterize this period as a shift from an industrial to a postindustrial society. In this context, it is easy to understand a new level of public concern for natural resources and environmental protection. Scientific discoveries also helped. New studies, often well publicized in the popular press, alerted people to the effects of pesticides and other synthetic chemicals. Rachel Carson's influential book *Silent Spring*, which documented the devastating effects that such chemicals had on song bird populations, was published in 1962, and for many it was an eye opener.

The initial public policy response to these new values and concerns focused on natural resources. Congress approved the Wilderness Act of 1964 to preserve some national forest lands in their natural condition. The Land and Water Conservation Fund Act, also adopted in 1964, facilitated local, state, and federal acquisition and development of land for parks and open spaces. In 1968 Congress enacted the National Wild and Scenic Rivers System to preserve certain rivers with "outstandingly remarkable" scenic, recreational, ecological, historical, and cultural values.

Action by the federal government on pollution control issues lagged in comparison to resource conservation, largely because Congress deferred to state and local governments on these matters. Congress approved the first modest federal water and air pollution statutes in 1948 and 1955, respectively. Only in the late 1960s and 1970s did it expand and strengthen them significantly. International environmental issues began to attract attention in the 1960s. In his 1965 State of the Union message, President Lyndon Johnson called for federal programs to deal with "the explosion in world population and the growing scarcity in world resources." The following year Congress authorized the first funds to support family planning programs in other nations (Kraft 1994).

These early policy developments were a prelude to a wholesale shift in the political mood of the nation that led to the present array of environmental protection, natural resource, and energy policies. Public opinion was the driving force in most of this policy advancement. Membership in environmental organizations such as the Sierra Club and Audubon Society surged during the 1960s, reflecting a growing public concern about these issues. By the early 1970s newer groups, such as the Natural Resources Defense Council, were established, and almost all of them saw their budgets, staffs, and political influence soar. As a result, policymakers became aware of a concerned public that demanded action, and they were eager to respond and take political credit (Dunlap 1995).

Congress approved most of the major federal environmental laws now in effect between 1969 and 1976 in a stunning outpouring of legislation not repeated since then. Policymakers were convinced that the public favored new federal regulatory measures that would be strong enough to force offending industries to clean up. In many respects, this development illustrates the kind of market failure discussed in Chapter 1. The public and policymakers demanded that the federal government intervene to stop rampant pollution by industry that constituted a market externality. Most of the states also were constrained from taking action. As Chapter 2 noted, the states either lacked the necessary policy capacity at that time, or they chose not to act because of pressure from local industry. Eventually, Congress decided that only national policy action would suffice (Davies and Davies 1975). The development of environmental and resource policies during the 1960s and 1970s, therefore, grew out of the same factors that led to other public policies: market failures, a belief that government action was the right thing to do (ethical reasons), and the eagerness of elected officials to respond to strong public demand (political reasons). Table 11-1 lists the most important of the federal environmental laws enacted between 1964 and 2002. Comparable policy developments took place at the state level and abroad (Rabe 2003; Vig and Axelrod 1999).

| TABLE 11-1 | Major U.S. Environmental Laws: 1964 to 2002 |
| --- | --- |

| Year Enacted | Legislation |
| --- | --- |
| 1964 | Wilderness Act, PL 88-577 |
| 1968 | Wild and Scenic Rivers Act, PL 90-542 |
| 1969 | National Environmental Policy Act (NEPA), PL 91-190 |
| 1970 | Clean Air Act Amendments, PL 91-604 |
| 1972 | Federal Water Pollution Control Act Amendments (Clean Water Act), PL 92-500 |
| | Federal Environmental Pesticides Control Act of 1972 (amended the Federal Insecticide, Fungicide and Rodenticide Act (FIFRA) of 1947), PL 92-516 |
| | Marine Protection, Research and Sanctuaries Act of 1972, PL 92-532 |
| | Marine Mammal Protection Act, PL 92-522 |
| | Coastal Zone Management Act, PL 92-583 |
| | Noise Control Act, PL 92-574 |
| 1973 | Endangered Species Act, PL 93-205 |
| 1974 | Safe Drinking Water Act, PL 93-523 |
| 1976 | Resource Conservation and Recovery Act (RCRA), PL 94-580 |
| | Toxic Substances Control Act, PL 94-469 |
| | Federal Land Policy and Management Act, PL 94-579 |
| | National Forest Management Act, PL 94-588 |
| 1977 | Clean Air Act Amendments, PL 95-95 |
| | Clean Water Act (CWA), PL 95-217 |
| | Surface Mining Control and Reclamation Act, PL 95-87 |
| 1980 | Comprehensive Environmental Response, Compensation and Liability Act (Superfund), PL 96-510 |
| 1982 | Nuclear Waste Policy Act, PL 97-425 (amended in 1987 by the Nuclear Waste Policy Amendments Act, PL 100-203) |
| 1984 | Hazardous and Solid Waste Amendments (RCRA amendments), PL 98-616 |
| 1986 | Safe Drinking Water Act Amendments, PL 99-339 |
| | Superfund Amendments and Reauthorization Act (SARA), PL 99-499 |
| 1987 | Water Quality Act (CWA amendments), PL 100-4 |
| 1988 | Ocean Dumping Act, PL 100-688 |
| 1990 | Clean Air Act Amendments, PL 101-549 |
| | Oil Pollution Act, PL 101-380 |
| | Pollution Prevention Act, PL 101-508 |
| 1991 | Intermodal Surface Transportation Efficiency Act (ISTEA) PL 102-240 |
| 1992 | Energy Policy Act, PL 102-486 |
| | The Omnibus Water Act, PL 102-575 |
| 1996 | Food Quality Protection Act (amended FIFRA), PL 104-120 |
| | Safe Drinking Water Act Amendments, PL 104-182 |
| 1998 | Transportation Equity Act for the 21st Century (also called ISTEA II or TEA 21), PL 105-178 |
| 2002 | Small Business Liability Relief and Brownfields Revitalization Act, PL 107-118 |

Note: A more complete list, with a summary description of major features of each act, can be found in *Environmental Policy*, 5th ed., ed. Norman J. Vig and Michael E. Kraft (Washington, D.C.: CQ Press, 2003), Appendix 1; and in Michael E. Kraft, *Environmental Policy and Politics*, 3d ed. (New York: Longman, 2004), 123, 188–189.

Policymakers also appeared to believe at the time that pollution problems and their remedies were simple. Today, few would make such assumptions because they understand the complexity of environmental problems and the difficulty of solving them. But in the 1960s and 1970s policymakers and the public had more confidence that the chosen solutions would work. They thought that application of technological or engineering know-how would do the trick and that no change would be required in human behavior, for example, in using personal automobiles in urban areas or in creating far-flung suburbs. These policy beliefs dominated legislative debates, although it was evident to some even then that the necessary technical knowledge did not always exist and that government agencies sometimes lacked the necessary resources and skills to take on the many new responsibilities mandated by these laws (Jones 1975; Mazmanian and Sabatier 1983).

On the one hand, these policy actions are a remarkable testimony to the capacity of government institutions to move quickly to approve major legislation when public and partisan consensus demands a policy such as pollution control. On the other hand, this history of policy development suggests why so many of these environmental laws later came under intense criticism from business groups, and conservatives, and why economists worried about the cost they imposed on society and their limited success in reaching the ambitious policy goals they embodied.

Some thoughtful environmental philosophers offer a different perspective, which is more closely attuned to current concepts of sustainable development. They argue that environmental policies can never succeed as long as human population growth and material consumption continue and society's institutions remain unchallenged. Mere reformist policies of pollution control and ecological management, they say, are doomed to failure because they do little to alter human attitudes and behavior or to confront the economic and political systems that contribute to environmental degradation in the first place (Ophuls and Boyan 1992). Chapter 4 referred to one of the dilemmas facing policy analysts—whether to deal with fundamental or root causes of public problems or to focus on the more manageable proximate causes. Environmental policies for the most part dealt with the latter.

## FROM CONSENSUS TO CONFLICT IN ENVIRONMENTAL POLICY

If consensus on environmental policy was the norm during the 1970s, by the 1980s political conflict became the new standard in policymaking. The shift in perspective had many causes, but chief among them were the conservatives' growing concern about the strong role of government and its implications for the private sector, increasing doubts among policy analysts about the effectiveness and efficiency of the dominant command-and-control regulation, and the business community's resentment over the burdens and costs of the new policies. Industry representatives frequently argued that the costs could not be justified by what they saw as the limited benefits produced in improved public health or environmental quality.

### Reagan and Bush Administration Policies

These new ideas about environmental policy rose to prominence during Ronald Reagan's presidency (1981–1989), when environmental agencies suffered deep budget cuts, lost experienced professional staff members, and saw their program activities slow down. Reagan's agenda was largely one of providing temporary relief to the business community and to western resource development interests, such as mining, logging, and ranching. His administration demonstrated little interest in genuine reforms of environmental programs to make them more effective and efficient (Vig and Kraft 1984). That goal would have been much tougher. To work toward it would have meant rewriting the basic environmental laws, and that in turn required broad agreement among the major policy actors, which did not exist.

Ultimately, the Reagan administration was ineffective in rolling back environmental policy, primarily because the U.S. public continued to favor strong environmental protection, and, in response to public opinion, Congress blocked many of the president's efforts (Dunlap 1995). The result, perversely, was a *strengthening* of the major environmental laws and adherence to the same command-and-control policy strategy that policy analysts and other critics were questioning. That reaction was particularly evident in the 1984 amendments to the Resource Conservation and Recovery Act, which established demanding standards and detailed requirements for the handling of hazardous wastes.

This pattern of policy enhancement continued through 1990, as George Bush, who served as Reagan's vice president for eight years, worked closely with Congress to enact the Clean Air Act Amendments of 1990. That law was a major expansion of the original act and set out an elaborate and exacting plan to bring all urban areas into compliance with national air quality standards over a twenty-year period. It also toughened regulation of toxic air pollutions (listing 189 specific toxic chemicals the EPA was to regulate) and for the first time extended the act's reach to include sulfur dioxide and nitrogen oxides, the precursors of acid rain, emitted largely by coal-burning power plants. Environmentalists cheered their success in keeping the policies and programs of the 1970s intact and in some instances expanding them. But policy analysts continued to argue that reform of those policies was essential to make them more effective and to control their substantial and rising costs (Davies and Mazurek 1998; Portney and Stavins 2000).

## Partisan Conflict over Environmental Policy

Partisan conflict had much to do with the inability to focus seriously on the real reform agenda and to chart new environmental policy directions for the future. The two major political parties grew further apart over environmental policy, even though they had worked together in the 1970s to advance environmental protection. President Richard Nixon, for example, created the Environmental Protection Agency at the end of 1970 through an executive order that consolidated government agencies and expanded their role. He also cooperated with a Democratic Congress in enacting the Clean Air Act Amendments of 1970, although the lawmakers had to pass the 1972 Clean Water Act over his veto. By the 1990s a widening gulf divided the parties on fundamental issues such as the legitimacy of government regulation to protect the public's welfare, private property rights, and even how serious the environmental problems were.[3]

These differences were evident in congressional voting on all major environmental protection and natural resource issues. An analysis of voting records in Congress shows that the gap between the parties grew from the early 1970s through the late 1990s. On average the parties have differed by nearly 25 points on a 100-point scale, and the differences increased during the 1980s and 1990s (Shipan and Lowry 2001). Scores compiled by the League of Conservation Voters for the first session of the 107th Congress (2001–2002) were typical of recent

## STEPS TO ANALYSIS

## VOTING RECORDS ON THE ENVIRONMENT

The League of Conservation Voters is a leading environmental organization. For three decades it has kept tabs on how members of Congress vote on the environment. Each year the group compiles the National Environmental Scorecard, which records members' choices on ten to fourteen key votes. Go to the league's Web site (www.lcv.org) to see a recent scorecard. The entire report can be viewed as a pdf file, or the scores of individual members or state delegations can be viewed as html files. Look up the voting records for one or more members in the House of Representatives and Senate from your state or a state you find interesting. If using the full report, you can see how these votes compare to the average for the member's party and for the House or Senate as a whole. These averages are listed at the beginning of the report. Why do you think the member has the score he or she does? Does it reflect the nature of the constituency, the locally active environmental or business groups, or the member's own political philosophy or ideology?

The LCV scores reported on the site represent how often a member of Congress voted in accordance with the position taken by the league and the coalition of environmental group leaders on which it relies to select an annual list of key environmental votes. Look at the votes the LCV selected in a particular year and the way it compiles the environmental voting score. These are described at the beginning of the full report. Do you think the score fairly represents the voting record of members of Congress on environmental and energy issues? Compare the voting records of Democrats and Republicans, either nationwide or within your own state. Why do you think Republicans consistently have much lower LCV scores than Democrats? Does it represent a bias in the way the scores are calculated? The nature of the constituencies within each of the major parties? Another factor?

years. Senate Democrats averaged 82 percent support for the positions the league and the environmental community favored. Senate Republicans averaged 9 percent. In the House, Democrats averaged 81 percent, and Republicans 16 percent. Clearly, the parties no longer saw eye to eye on environmental issues. The box "Steps to Analysis: Voting Records on the Environment" explains how these scores are compiled and points to the Web site where students can find the environmental voting record of any member of Congress.

The differences between the two parties on environmental votes were especially evident in the latter half of the 1990s, as the Republicans gained control of both houses of Congress and aggressively sought to curtail environmental policy actions, much as the Reagan administration had done. Once again, Congress cut agency budgets and tried to rein in what they described as regulatory bureaucracies run amok. The EPA was a prime target. As was the case during the 1980s under Reagan, however, the anti-environmental agenda won too few converts to succeed. The U.S. public continued to demonstrate strong support for environmental protection, the Clinton White House fought hard to defend existing programs, and lobbying by environmental groups such as the Sierra Club and NRDC prevented enactment of the most severe measures considered by Congress. The most common result during the 1990s was policy gridlock, as the opponents of environmental policy could not muster the votes to repeal or significantly change the established policies and programs. But this outcome also meant that Congress could not enact the much needed reforms of the Clean Air Act, the Clean Water Act, the Superfund program for cleaning up hazardous waste sites, and the Endangered Species Act, among others (Kraft 2003).

## Environmental Policy under George W. Bush

Heated battles over the direction of environmental policy continued after the 2000 election of George W. Bush. This time, however, the efforts to weaken environmental policy came at least as much from the White House as from congressional conservatives. Democrats in Congress strongly opposed the president's initiatives, including substantial budget cuts for environmental programs. They successfully blocked many of them, most notably his proposed national energy policy that centered on oil and gas drilling in the Arctic National Wildlife Refuge (ANWR).

Like his father, who had served as president a decade earlier, Bush acknowledged popular support for environmental protection and resource conservation, but, as a conservative Republican, he could not ignore his party's ideological and financial base in the business community, particularly industrial corporations and timber, mining, agriculture, and oil interests. In fact, Bush drew heavily from those constituencies, as well as conservative ideological groups, to staff the EPA and the Interior, Agriculture, and Energy Departments. In addition, he sought to deregulate environmental protection through what he termed a new era of voluntary, flexible, and cooperative programs and to transfer more responsibility for enforcement of federal laws to the states (Jehl 2003; Vig 2003). Environmentalists criticized the president's approach as unlikely to be effective and far too generous to the business community.

## MAJOR FEDERAL ENVIRONMENTAL POLICIES

Environmental policy consists of the many different statutes enacted during the 1960s and 1970s and their amendments, but there is no single consolidated policy on the environment that describes the nation's goals and the strategies needed to reach them. Nor is environmental policy concentrated in one executive department or agency; rather, at the national level, responsibility for the environment is divided among eleven cabinet departments and the EPA, the Nuclear Regulatory Commission, and other agencies. The EPA has the lion's share of responsibility, but it must work with other departments and agencies, especially the Departments of Interior, Agriculture, and Energy, to carry out its mission.

Because so many agencies contribute to U.S. environmental policy, the best way to survey the subject is to highlight the major elements within each of three areas: environmental protection policy or pollution control, natural resources policy, and energy policy. Only one statute, the National Environmental Policy Act, cuts across these categories. For each of the three categories, this chapter emphasizes the broad goals that policymakers have adopted and the policy strategies or means they use to achieve them. It also evaluates selected policy achievements and considers policy options for the future. Students who want a more complete description of the major environmental or energy policies should consult the suggested readings listed at the end of the chapter or visit the Web sites of the implementing agencies, where summary descriptions as well as the full statutes are usually available. The box "Working with Sources: Executive Agencies with Environmental Responsibilities" lists the Web sites for the leading executive agencies with environmental responsibilities.

The focus here is on national environmental and resource policies, even though, as noted earlier, some states, especially California, Minnesota, New Jersey, Oregon, Vermont, and Wisconsin, are at the forefront of policy innovation. One of the best ways to compare state environmental policies is to visit the Web site for the Council of State Governments

## WORKING WITH SOURCES

### EXECUTIVE AGENCIES WITH ENVIRONMENTAL RESPONSIBILITIES

Visit the Web pages of the leading federal environmental and natural resource departments and agencies to learn more about their missions, the laws they administer, the agencies and programs under their jurisdiction, and program achievements or shortcomings. The Department of the Interior, for example, includes the U.S. Geological Survey, Fish and Wildlife Service, National Park Service, and Bureau of Land Management. The U.S. Forest Service and the Natural Resources Conservation Service are parts of the Department of Agriculture. The Department of Energy sponsors a large number of energy research and development programs and has broad responsibilities for cleaning up former defense installations, including heavily contaminated nuclear weapons production facilities. The DOE is also in charge of the nuclear waste disposal program slated for Yucca Mountain, Nevada.

All of the agency Web sites have links to current programs and issues, studies and reports, internal organization issues, related programs at other departments and agencies, or White House positions on the issues. In interpreting information at these sites on program accomplishments, you should bear in mind that government agencies almost always offer a positive assessment of their activities and say little about their weaknesses or failures.

Parallel agencies work at the state level. To find your state agency, visit the Web site for the Council of State Governments (www.csg.org) and look for the link to state pages, where all fifty state governments are listed. Once on the state government home page, look for agencies dealing with the environment, natural resources, or energy.

**www.epa.gov** (U.S. Environmental Protection Agency)

**www.doi.gov** (U.S. Department of the Interior)

**www.energy.gov** (U.S. Department of Energy)

**www.usda.gov** (U.S. Department of Agriculture)

**www.nrc.gov** (U.S. Nuclear Regulatory Commission)

**www.whitehouse.gov/ceq** (Council on Environmental Quality) (www.csg.org) for links to all the state home pages. Those pages in turn describe environmental policy within the state. Another source for state environmental policy is the Web site for the Environmental Council of the States, a national nonpartisan association of state environmental commissioners that reports on a range of issues concerning state environmental policy activities and federal-state relations (at www.sso.org/ecos).

## The National Environmental Policy Act

One law that might appear to constitute a coherent national policy on environmental issues is NEPA, the National Environmental Policy Act of 1969, a brief (six-page) statute. The enactment of this law signified the beginning of the modern era in environmental policy. NEPA acknowledged the "profound impact of man's activities on the interrelations of all components of the natural environment" and the "critical importance of restoring and maintaining environmental quality" for human welfare. The instrument for achieving these goals, however, is procedural rather than substantive: the preparation of an **environmental impact statement** (EIS), which is then used in government agency planning and decision making. Such statements are required for major federal actions "significantly affecting the quality of the human environment." They are intended to offer a detailed and systematic assessment of the environmental effects of a proposed action, such as building a highway, and alternatives to the action that might be considered. In effect, NEPA mandates that agencies engage in policy analysis before they make decisions. Its real effect, however, comes less from the preparation of these impact statements than from a requirement that they be made public. Doing so means that agencies have to give serious consideration to the consequences of their decisions and anticipate how critics of those decisions might respond.

NEPA requires only that such EISs be prepared and be subject to public review; it does not prevent an agency from making an environmentally harmful decision. Nevertheless, most evaluations of the policy find that it has had a substantial impact on decision making by government agencies such as the U.S. Forest Service, the Federal Highway Administration, and the Army Corps of Engineers (Bartlett 1989; Caldwell 1998). In a way, NEPA symbolized environmental policy action during the late 1960s and 1970s by establishing new decision-making procedures that opened the policy process to public scrutiny and assured widespread consultation with affected parties, including environmental groups and local governments. The old subgovernments, long dominant in many areas of natural resource management, such as logging, mining, and ranching, were forever changed as a result of these procedural requirements.

NEPA also created a presidential advisory body for environmental issues called the Council on Environmental Quality. The CEQ is charged with supervising the EIS process, and it works with executive agencies to define their responsibilities under the act. As might be expected, not all agencies adapted quickly to the new requirements for impact statements and public review, but over time most have significantly altered their decision making. Still, about a hundred court challenges to agency decisions under NEPA are filed every year. The most common complaints are that no EIS was prepared when one should have been or that the EIS was inadequate. For more information on how NEPA works, visit the CEQ Web site (www.whitehouse.gov/ceq).

## Environmental Protection Statutes and the EPA

The U.S. Congress has enacted and, over time, strengthened with amendments seven major environmental protection, or pollution control, statutes: the Clean Air Act; Clean Water Act; Safe Drinking Water Act; Resource Conservation and Recovery Act; Toxic Substances Control Act; Federal Insecticide, Fungicide, and Rodenticide Act; and Comprehensive Environmental Response, Compensation, and Liability Act. This is a diverse set of public policies, but with much in common. The EPA develops regulations that affect the current and future use and release of chemicals and pollutants that pose a significant risk to public health or the environment.

The Clean Air Act Amendments of 1970 (CAA) required for the first time the development of national ambient air quality standards that were to be uniform across the country, with enforcement shared by the federal and state governments. These standards were to "provide an adequate margin of safety" to protect human health, and cost was not to be a consideration. The CAA also set emissions standards for cars, trucks, and buses, the mobile sources of pollution, and it regulated fuels and toxic and hazardous air pollutants. In addition, it set emissions limits on stationary sources of pollution such as power plants, oil refineries, chemical companies, and other industrial facilities. The extensive 1990 amendments added acid rain controls and set new deadlines for improving urban air quality and controlling toxic air pollutants.

The Clean Water Act of 1972 (CWA) is the major federal program regulating surface water quality. Like the Clean Air Act, the CWA set a national policy for water pollution control. It set 1985 as the deadline for stopping the discharge of pollutants into navigable waters (a stipulation that allows federal jurisdiction) and sought to make all surface water "fishable and swimmable" by 1983. The act encouraged technological innovation and comprehensive regional planning for attaining water quality. And like the Clean Air Act, the CWA gave the states primary responsibility for implementation as long as they followed federal standards and guidelines. Essentially, these involve water quality standards and effluent limits set by a permit system that specifies how much each facility is allowed to discharge and the control technologies to be used. For years the CWA also provided substantial subsidies and loans to the states to help construct new wastewater treatment plants.

The Safe Drinking Water Act of 1974 was designed to ensure the quality and safety of drinking water by specifying minimum health standards for public water supplies. The EPA sets the standards for chemical and microbiological contaminants for tap water. The act required regular monitoring of water supplies to ensure that pollutants stay below safe levels, and it regulated state programs for protecting groundwater supplies that many areas use for drinking water. To assist states and localities in meeting these goals, the act provided loans and grants to defray the costs. A 1996 amendment established a more flexible approach to regulating water contaminants based on their risk to public health and allowed consideration of the costs and benefits of proposed regulations. It also added a "right-to-know" provision that

Despite over thirty years' worth of laws that regulate the release of toxic chemicals, including the Clean Water Act of 1972 and other statutes, contamination of many bodies of water around the nation continues. Here, warning signs are posted along the entire drainage system of the Quicksilver Mine on the shores of Almaden Lake in San Jose, California. Mining wastes have contaminated local rivers and lakes, and scientists have concluded that the old Santa Clara County mine is the biggest source of mercury in the San Francisco Bay.

requires water systems to provide customers once a year with a report of any contaminants in the local water supply.

The Resource Conservation and Recovery Act of 1976 (RCRA) is the nation's main hazardous waste control policy. The law was intended to regulate existing hazardous waste disposal practices and promote the conservation and recovery of resources through comprehensive management of solid waste. It required the EPA to develop criteria "necessary to protect human health and the environment" for the safe disposal of solid waste and to set standards for the treatment, storage, and disposal of hazardous wastes. The 1984 amendments to RCRA made the act even more demanding and set tight new deadlines, largely because the EPA had made insufficient progress toward the goals that Congress initially set.

The Toxic Substances Control Act, also approved in 1976, gave the EPA comprehensive authority to identify, evaluate, and regulate risks associated with commercial chemicals. The idea was to help develop a national database of chemicals posing an "unreasonable risk of injury to health or the environment," but without unduly burdening industry or impeding technological innovation. Policymakers combined these two competing goals and saddled the EPA with a difficult and time-consuming set of procedural requirements that greatly limited the act's effectiveness.

The Federal Insecticide, Fungicide, and Rodenticide Act of 1972 (FIFRA) was similarly ambitious and limited. It required the EPA to register the pesticides used commercially in the United States. It also required that the pesticides not pose "any unreasonable risk to man or the environment," but allowed consideration of the economic and social costs and benefits of pesticide use. The EPA had to balance the benefits of using pesticides against their impact on public health, and the government had the burden of proof to show harm if it attempted to ban an existing pesticide. FIFRA was modified significantly by the Food Quality Protection Act of 1996, which required the EPA to apply a new, uniform "reasonable risk" approach to regulating pesticides used on food, fiber, and other crops. The new standard is more stringent than the old one. In addition, the agency is required to give special consideration to the impact of pesticide residues on children and to set higher standards for these residues. The law gives the EPA greater authority to suspend a pesticide believed to pose a public health hazard, and the agency must review all pesticide registrations at least once every fifteen years.

The last of the seven statutes, the Comprehensive Environmental Response, Compensation, and Liability Act of 1980, also known as Superfund, is perhaps the most criticized of the lot. It was enacted after the public became alarmed about toxic waste dumps, such as the one at Love Canal in New York. Superfund is directed at the thousands of abandoned or uncontrolled hazardous waste sites in the nation. Congress gave the EPA responsibility to respond to the problem by identifying, assessing, and cleaning up these sites. If necessary, the EPA can draw from a special fund for that purpose, which is how the program got its nickname. The fund originally was financed through a tax on the petrochemical industry and other chemical manufacturers, which Congress declined to renew after 1995. One of the central principles of Superfund is that polluters should pay the costs of cleanup, and the act's financial liability provisions have caused controversy for years.[4] In 1986 Congress strengthened the act, put more money into the fund, and added an entirely new provision on the public's right-to-know about toxic chemicals made by, stored within, or released by local businesses. The Toxics Release Inventory, or TRI, is published each year and can be accessed on the EPA's Web site and elsewhere in map form that pinpoints and describes toxic releases in communities across the country.

***Common Themes in Environmental Protection Policy.*** Separately and collectively these seven policies created diverse regulatory actions that touch virtually every industrial and commercial enterprise in the nation. They also affect ordinary citizens by regulating air, food, and water quality, and the cars and other consumer products everyone buys. In other words, almost every aspect of daily life is affected by the way these statutes were written and how the EPA and the states implement them. It should not be surprising, therefore, that routine implementation of the policies and their periodic renewal in Congress usually spark contentious debates. People argue over the extent of the risks citizens face, the appropriate standards for protecting public health and the environment, the mechanisms used to achieve these standards, and how the benefits of these policies should be weighed against the costs of compliance and other social and economic values. The box "Working with Sources: Environmental Policy Advocacy" lists some of the environmental and industry groups that have been active in these policy debates. Their Web sites are included as well.

These disagreements put the EPA, whether fairly or not, at the center of fractious political fights. The agency is a frequent target of criticism by members of Congress, the business community, and environmental groups, all of whom often fault its scientific research and regulatory decision making. The EPA is an independent executive agency, but its administrator reports directly to the president, and its decision making tends to reflect White House priorities. The agency is the largest of the federal regulatory agencies, with a staff of nearly eighteen thousand and a budget in 2002 of about $8 billion. More than half of the employees are assigned to the ten regional offices where they work closely with their state counterparts as one component of the federal-state joint implementation of environmental policy (Scheberle 1997). By most accounts the EPA handles its job fairly well and is among the most professional of the federal environmental agencies. Policy analysts have long observed, however, that the EPA's resources are insufficient to handle its vast responsibilities. They have also concluded that to succeed at its demanding tasks, the agency must adopt new policy approaches and work with Congress to ensure that it has the authority and tools it needs (National Academy of Public Administration 1995, 2000; Rosenbaum 2003).

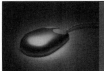

**WORKING WITH SOURCES**

## ENVIRONMENTAL POLICY ADVOCACY

Many organizations play an active role in shaping environmental policy in Congress, federal executive agencies, federal courts, and state and local governments. To learn more about what positions they take and what they do, visit some of the following Web sites. We list environmental groups first and then several groups that normally oppose the environmentalist position. Comparable groups are involved at state, local, and regional levels.

### ENVIRONMENTAL GROUPS

**www.nrdc.org** (Natural Resources Defense Council)

**www.sierraclub.org** (Sierra Club)

**www.environmentaldefense.org** (Environmental Defense)

**www.nwf.org** (National Wildlife Federation)

**www.greenpeace.org** (Greenpeace)

### INDUSTRY GROUPS

**www.uschamber.com** (U.S. Chamber of Commerce)

**www.nam.org** (National Association of Manufacturers)

**www.nfib.com** (National Federation of Independent Businesses)

The core environmental protection policies have over time produced substantial and well-documented environmental and health benefits, which are especially evident in dramatically improved urban air quality and control of point sources of water pollution. Not every policy has been equally effective, however, and those dealing with control of toxic chemicals and hazardous wastes have been the least successful. Moreover, existing policies barely touch some substantial environmental risks, such as indoor air pollution, even though the cost of these policies has been relatively high. The U.S. General Accounting Office (1992) estimated that between 1972 and 1992 the cumulative expenditures for pollution control exceeded $1 trillion. By the late 1990s, the EPA put the continuing cost to both government and the private sector at more than $170 billion per year, and, by most estimates, more than half of that cost is paid by the private sector, which no doubt passes it along to consumers as higher product prices. Is the cost too high? Are the benefits worth it? Might the costs be reduced through adoption of different policies?

The seven major environmental protection statutes share a common approach to problem solving. All rely on a regulatory policy strategy, or what critics call a command-and-control system; economists would call it a system of **direct regulation.** What this means is that **environmental quality standards** are set and enforced according to the language of each statute, and each specifies how the agency makes its decisions. Generally, Congress gives the EPA discretion to set standards that are consistent with the law, and the EPA is expected to base its decisions on the best available science. Invariably, however, setting environmental quality standards involves an uncertain mix of science and policy judgment about how much risk is acceptable to society. The cost of implementing the standard is usually considered also. These kinds of judgments are necessary whether the issue is the amount of pesticide residues allowed on food, the level of lead or arsenic in drinking water, or how much ground-level ozone in the air is acceptable. That is, the laws do not aim for the elimination of risks to public health or the environment; instead, they seek to reduce the level of risk to a point that is reasonable in light of the costs.

Because the science is almost never complete or definitive, agency officials must make policy or political judgments about how stringent a standard ought to be. These kinds of decisions are never easy, and they invariably cause disagreements. Business groups criticize the standards for being too strong, and environmental and health groups say they are too weak. One side or the other in a dispute, and sometimes both, may decide to challenge the standard in court. As might be expected, EPA decision making operates under somewhat different expectations in Democratic and Republican administrations. For example, Clinton's EPA was more likely than Bush's EPA to adopt tough environmental standards (Vig and Kraft 2003). Once a standard is set, the EPA and the states take various actions, through issuing rules and regulations, to ensure that it is met. For example, the EPA required the auto industry to adopt catalytic converters to limit exhaust emissions. Various industries have been forced to use new technologies to reduce air and water pollution.

The elaborate laws and regulations for environmental protection actions might lead one to believe that the government is protecting the public against the most significant risks out there. Unfortunately, that is not always the case. Several **comparative environmental risk** studies, which weigh the risks to the public against EPA program priorities, have shown that the agency tends to focus on highly visible risks that the public is concerned about, rather than on the most dangerous to the public's health. For example, people worry about hazardous wastes and abandoned waste sites, and Congress has told the EPA to deal with these problems. According to the professionals' rankings of environmental risks, however, hazardous wastes are not as dangerous as the public believes, while other risks that the public barely recognizes, are near the top of the list. Among these problems are indoor air pollution from radon and second-hand (passive) smoke and ecological concerns, such as climate change, stratospheric ozone depletion, habitat alteration, and species extinction and loss of biological diversity (U.S. EPA 1990).[5]

To put the matter in slightly different terms, the way people perceive environmental risks is often at odds with how professionals see them (Slovic 1987). Public perceptions tend to drive the policymaking process, which sometimes results in distorted priorities that do not adequately protect the public's health. The solution to this dilemma may lie in educating the public better on environmental and health risks and involving the public in environmental decision making at all levels of government. Many analysts also argue that Congress needs to rewrite environmental laws to give the EPA more discretion to act on the most important risks to public and environmental health (Davies 1996; National Academy of Public Administration 2000).

***How Well Do Environmental Protection Programs Work?*** With all the criticism that has been directed at environmental protection policy and command-and-control regulation, one would think the programs have been dismal failures. But that would be a tough argument to make. The evidence suggests they have been quite successful on the whole.

People often misjudge the seriousness of different environmental problems. They tend to worry a great deal about some risks that are covered prominently in the mass media, such as pesticide residues on food, contaminated drinking water, hazardous wastes, and air pollution. Yet they often are complacent about some risks that environmental scientists and public health officials consider to be equally, if not more, important. These include indoor air pollution, which can be far more dangerous than most people recognize. Among the most serious indoor air pollutants are second-hand smoke from cigarettes and radon, an extremely toxic but odorless and colorless radioactive gas that occurs naturally in many parts of the country. The EPA estimates that radon in indoor air causes between 15,000 and 22,000 lung cancer deaths each year in the United States.

Granted, environmental policies are difficult to evaluate, in part because they entail long-term commitments to broad social values and goals that are not easily quantified. Short-term and highly visible costs tend to attract more attention than long-term gains in public and environmental health—another source of debate over the value of environmental programs.

Some environmental conditions, such as air and water quality, are regularly monitored, but it is still difficult to assess how well present programs are achieving other objectives. For many critical natural resource concerns, such as protection of biological diversity, accurate measures are still being developed and national inventories are not yet available. The uncertainties over environmental trends means that scientists and policy advocates frequently debate whether the environment is deteriorating or improving. Many state-of-the-environment reports address such conditions and trends, and they can be found on Web sites for government agencies and environmental research institutes. The box "Working with Sources: Evaluating Environmental Policy" lists some of the most useful sources of such data and analysis of what the information means. Visit some of these sites to better appreciate what is involved in assessing how well environmental and resource programs are working.

Fairly good information is available for air and water quality and for hazardous waste sites. On air quality the EPA estimates that, between 1970 and 2001, total emissions of the six principal air pollutants regulated by the Clean Air Act decreased by 25 percent, even though the nation's population grew by 39 percent, the gross domestic product rose by 161 percent, and vehicle miles traveled increased by 149 percent. For a more recent period for which the data are better, between 1982 and 2001 the nation experienced a reduction in ambient levels (concentration in the air) of 94 percent for lead, 62 percent for carbon monoxide, 52 percent for sulfur dioxide, 14 percent for particulate matter (covering only 1992–2001), 24 percent for nitrogen dioxide, and 11 percent for ozone (using the more stringent eight-hour standard).

Despite these impressive gains in air quality, however, in 2001 the EPA reported that more than 170 million tons of pollutants were emitted into the air each year. Moreover, about 133 million people lived in counties that failed to meet at least one of the national air quality standards for these six major pollutants. Approximately 110 million people resided in counties where pollution levels in 2001 exceeded federal standards for ozone, the chief ingredient of urban smog.[6] What conclusions do these data suggest? Are the declines in air pollution over the past three decades a good indicator that the Clean Air Act is working well? Or does the continuation of significant air pollution suggest the opposite?

Although progress in improving the nation's water quality has come more slowly and has been more uneven across the country, some success is also evident. EPA's 2000 biennial **National Water Quality Inventory**, the latest available, showed that 61 percent of the river and stream miles the states assessed fully supported all water uses set by states and tribes. The remaining 39 percent were impaired to some degree, meaning that the bodies of water did not meet or fully meet the national minimum water quality criteria for swimming, fishing, drinking-water supply, and support of aquatic life. About 45 percent of lakes, ponds, and reservoirs were also found to be impaired. These numbers indicate not only a measure of improvement over previous years but also that many problems remain. EPA data suggest that the major sources of remaining water quality problems are agricultural and urban runoff and municipal sewage treatment plants, rather than industry. Some people would consider the prevention of further degradation of water quality in times of economic and population growth an important achievement, while others would say that water quality clearly falls short of the goals of the Clean Water Act.[7] Which conclusion do you think is more defensible?

As a final example, consider the Superfund program. Critics assert that too few sites on the program's **National Priorities List** (NPL), which compiles the worst sites in the nation, have been cleaned up. They also allege that the cleaned-up sites cost too much; historically, the sites have averaged about $30 million each, although the cost has been coming down. The EPA reported that, as of September 2000, 757 Superfund sites had been fully cleaned up and construction (remediation or removal of material) was taking place at another 417 sites. Remediation study or design was under way at most of the remaining fifteen hundred sites on the NPL.[8] Assessment and remediation of such sites is complex and time consuming, often taking ten to fifteen years. Disputes over a given site and which companies or cities are liable for the

## WORKING WITH SOURCES

### EVALUATING ENVIRONMENTAL POLICY

As stated throughout the text, it is important to evaluate how well policies have worked and what they have achieved. The organizations and Web sites listed here offer such information from many different perspectives. Government Web sites usually have official reports and databases, such as the annual EPA report on air pollution. The General Accounting Office conducts independent evaluations of executive agencies and programs for Congress. Many other groups evaluate environmental and resource programs in terms of economic costs, efficiency, and effectiveness (Resources for the Future); the role of government and regulatory burdens (Cato, Heritage Foundation, and the Competitive Enterprise Institute); and environmental science and advocacy (Environmental Defense, Natural Resources Defense Council, and the Union of Concerned Scientists); or some combination of these criteria.

**www.epa.gov** (Environmental Protection Agency)

**www.doi.gov** (Department of the Interior)

**www.gao.gov** (General Accounting Office)

**www.rff.org** (Resources for the Future)

**www.environmentaldefense.org** (Environmental Defense)

**www.nrdc.org** (Natural Resources Defense Council)

**www.sierraclub.org** (Sierra Club)

**www.ucsusa.org** (Union of Concerned Scientists)

**www.heritage.org** (Heritage Foundation)

**www.cato.org** (Cato Institute)

**www.cei.org** (Competitive Enterprise Institute)

Go to one of these Web sites to find an evaluation of a specific federal environmental program, such as the Clean Air Act, Clean Water Act, Superfund, or the Endangered Species Act. For example, at the Competitive Enterprise Institute Web site, select the link for Research an Issue, and then look under the heading for Environment. One of the listings is for environmental education programs, and here CEI offers articles that are highly critical of the EPA's support of what CEI considers to be "biased and politicized" education programs. Compare this evaluation to statements found on the EPA's own Web page that describes federal support for environmental education: www.epa.gov/enviroed/eedefined.html. On the same page you will find assessments of the EPA environmental education program as well as the practice of environmental education in the nation.

For this example or another, what position does the organization take on the policy's success or failure? On the performance of the agency charged with its implementation? To what extent do the arguments and evidence you find at the site support the evaluation offered? Can you find any significant weaknesses in the arguments advanced or the data used to support the evaluation? For example, are selective and misleading data used to criticize or laud an agency's performance?

cleanup costs can add years to the schedules and millions of dollars to the costs. So, are the program's achievements an indicator of good progress? Or should the EPA have completed more cleanups by now? Which conclusion is fair?

***Policy Options for the Future.*** What kinds of policy alternatives should be considered for the future to replace or, more likely, to supplement environmental regulation? Critics of regulation frequently mention the greater use of market incentives or market-based approaches, more reliance on public information disclosure, more flexible and cooperative approaches to regulation, and further decentralization of power to the states (Davies and Mazurek 1998; National Academy of Public Administration 2000; Sexton et al. 1999). Such alternatives may be especially appropriate where conventional regulation works poorly. Two examples are reducing indoor air pollution and cleaning up nonpoint water pollution, which cannot be traced to a single source. Either there are too many sources to regulate, or regulation simply is impractical; for example, no government can regulate indoor air quality in every U.S. dwelling. What might work instead are subsidies, public education campaigns, and tax credits, which are a form of market incentive. The federal government and the states have experimented with such policy options. For example, Wisconsin has used a combination of educational outreach programs directed at changing farming practices, providing technical assistance, and partially subsidizing the cost of new nonpoint source controls to improve water quality.

The 1990 Clean Air Act revision incorporated market incentives by allowing marketable permits for emissions of sulfur dioxide. The idea behind the permits is that some companies will find it cheaper than others to make needed changes to reduce emissions, and they can then sell the "extra" permits to other companies. The program operates in two ways: the market incentives improve economic efficiency by reducing the overall cost of environmental improvement, and the government reduces the number of permits over time to ensure that the goal of lower emissions is reached. Although the federal program is thought to have worked well, a similar effort in the Los Angeles metropolitan area through a regional air quality management system has not entirely lived up to expectations. Nevertheless, environmental economists have high hopes for these efforts because they provide important economic incentives for industry to work toward environmental goals, even to go "beyond compliance" to make greater improvements than the law requires (Portney and Stavins 2000). Is their assessment persuasive?

As a policy strategy, information disclosure is a useful supplement to regulation. The nation uses this strategy by compiling the Toxics Release Inventory, by publishing auto fuel efficiency standards, which are also attached to the windows of new cars, and in other ways.[9] The hope here is that individuals and organizations will use the information to press industry and government to move more aggressively on environmental improvements than they might otherwise be inclined to do. Or, acting proactively to avoid embarrassment, those same parties might undertake initiatives, such as reducing pollution or improving fuel efficiency, to avoid criticism.

The use of **flexible regulatory approaches** and **collaborative regulatory approaches** was a hallmark of the Clinton administration's EPA, and the Bush administration also favors these techniques (Vig and Kraft 2003). The general idea is to reduce conflict between regulators and those being regulated and to work cooperatively to develop appropriate environmental standards, regulations, and action programs. The intention is to move from the contentious, legalistic system of regulation to one in which the various stakeholders work together to seek solutions. Environmentalists are sometimes skeptical of these arrangements, fearful that they will endanger what has been achieved in environmental quality, but business interests, state and local governments, and many policy analysts think highly of the promise of flexible regulations and collaborative decision making. What is the case for relying on such collaborative approaches rather than always using regulation to achieve environmental quality goals?

Further decentralization of environmental responsibilities to the states is also controversial. Over the past two decades, a major transfer of environmental authority from the federal government to the states has taken place. How much more is desirable and what the likely effects will be are questions yet to be answered. Policymakers in both parties favor increased decentralization, but many analysts are skeptical about whether giving additional powers to the states will improve policy effectiveness. They also raise questions of equity. Many states have a greater capacity for environmental policy than they did three decades ago, but the performance from state to state is uneven. As noted, California, Minnesota, New Jersey, Oregon, and Wisconsin are leaders in environmental policy innovation and enforcement, but others lag behind and may be subjecting their citizens to preventable health risks. The tendency of states to compete with one another economically could constrain enforcement of environmental laws. In addition, many environmental problems—including acid rain, toxic air pollutants, and water pollution—cross state lines, suggesting that a national or regional approach might be both more effective and more equitable than leaving the solution to the states. Ultimately, what is needed is a sorting out of which environmental functions are best suited for state and local governments and which require national, or even international, management (Rabe 2003).

## Natural Resource Policies

Many of the same kinds of concerns that arise in pollution control also pertain to natural resource policies that govern the management of public lands, forests, and parks, and the efforts to protect species and biological diversity. Public policies for the management of natural resources developed in response to concerns over their abuse. After more than a century of policies that encouraged exploitation of resources in the vast federal lands of the West, the twentieth century brought a new ethic of **environmental stewardship**, the protection of resources for the future. That change has taken effect only slowly, however, and the resource development interests, such as timber, ranching, agriculture, mining, and oil and gas drilling, almost always disagree with conservation interests over what policies best promote the public interest. Indeed, some of the strongest opposition to environmentalists over the past several decades has come from development interests and their supporters in the so-called Wise Use, County Supremacy, and property rights movements (Switzer 1997).

Most of the current federal natural resource policies are grounded in the principle of **multiple use**, which Congress intended to help balance competing national objectives of economic development and environmental preservation. Should old growth forests in the Northwest be cut for timber or preserved as wildlife habitat? To what extent should mining for gold, silver, and other minerals, which can cause extensive environmental damage, be permitted on public lands—and how much should developers pay the Treasury for the right to do it? Should the government protect the Arctic National Wildlife Refuge, and other similar land, from oil and gas development, or is expansion of energy sources a more important priority? Using the guidance found in the various natural resource laws, the officials in federal resource agencies, mostly in the Interior and Agriculture Departments, are charged with deciding these questions.

One of the major federal policies that governs these kinds of debates is the National Environmental Policy Act, which began this discussion. Through the environmental impact statement process this legislation mandates, agencies are forced to consider a broader set of issues and to open decision making to a wider group of stakeholders than before. As was noted, NEPA helped to break up some of the subgovernments and diminish the influence that, for example, the mining industry had long exercised in federal decisions on mineral leasing and the timber industry in decisions on federal forest management.

Two other major statutes, the Federal Land Policy and Management Act of 1976 (FLPMA) and the National Forest Management Act of 1976 (NFMA), had comparable effects in changing the way the government makes natural resource decisions. These acts set out new procedures for government planning and management of resources, including extensive public participation, and they established a mission for long-term stewardship of public resources. In effect, these policies required government officials to consider diverse values in managing resources, not just the highest dollar return (Clarke and McCool 1996; Davis 2001). For example, the NFMA helped to shift the U.S. Forest Service away from an emphasis on timber production. The law requires the Forest Service to prepare long-term, comprehensive plans for the national forests and to involve the public in its decision making through meetings and hearings. The FLPMA gives the Bureau of Land Management greater authority to administer federal land under a broad multiple-use mandate that leans toward environmental values and away from its previous practice of favoring grazing as the dominate use.

These two policies did not end the disputes over public lands and forests, however. Environmentalists continue to battle with timber, ranching, mining, and oil and gas interests, and the winners often depend on which party is in the White House. Republican administrations tend to side more often with the forces of development, and Democratic administrations are usually more favorably inclined toward land preservation. For example, President Clinton used his executive authority under the Antiquities Act of 1906 to establish nineteen new national monuments and enlarge three others. In all, he protected more than six million acres of public land in this way. In addition, just before he left office, Clinton issued an executive order protecting nearly sixty million acres of roadless areas in the national forests from future development. President Bush challenged many of Clinton's policies and has been far more receptive to development interests than to conservation (Vig 2003). Indeed, a comprehensive examination of his natural resource policies after more than a year in office found that Bush was "aggressively encouraging more drilling, mining, and logging on much of the seven hundred million acres controlled by the Interior Department and the Forest Service."[10]

One of the most controversial of the natural resource policies is also one of the toughest Congress approved in the early 1970s. The Endangered Species Act of 1973 (ESA) in many ways symbolizes the nation's commitment to resource conservation goals, and, perhaps for that reason, it has become a lightning rod for anti-environmentalists. The ESA broadened federal authority to protect threatened and endangered species and established procedures to ensure the recovery of all species threatened with extinction. It prohibited the "taking" of such species by fishing, hunting, or habitat alteration or destruction whether the species inhabited state, federal, or private land. The U.S. Fish and Wildlife Service (FWS) administers the ESA for land-based species, and the agency has struggled to achieve its goals amidst frequent congressional criticism and perennially inadequate budgets. Despite condemnation from conservatives who see the ESA as a threat to property rights, most decisions under the act have been made without much controversy, and the act has prevented few development projects from going forward. More recently, the FWS has made good use of collaborative decision making in developing habitat conservation plans to avoid such confrontations.

***Evaluating Success.*** As with pollution control policies, evaluating the success of natural resource policies is not easy. The kinds of measurements available, such as the number of acres of protected lands set aside in national monuments and parks, are not good indicators of what really matters. Still, these laws have brought about considerable achievements. Since 1964 Congress has set aside 103 million areas of wilderness; the national wildlife refuge system occupies three times the land it did in 1970; and the national park system has more than tripled in land area from 1970 to 2000, with twice the number of park units. By 2000, twenty-seven years after passage of the ESA, more than twelve hundred U.S. species had been listed as either endangered or threatened. Administrators have designated scores of critical habitats, and a number of recovery plans are under way. State and local governments have also set aside large amounts of open space for parks and recreational purposes, some of it funded through the federal Land and Water Conservation Fund Act of 1964.

Still, the true measurement of success or failure is the status of ecosystem functioning or health, but even ecologists cannot agree on what it means to call an ecosystem healthy or sustainable or on what indicators to use. Ecologists are attempting to develop such standards so that communities across the nation can determine whether, or to what extent, a lake, river, bay, or land area should be preserved or restored to a healthy condition. Many communities are already trying to make those kinds of decisions. Massive federal and state efforts to restore damaged ecosystems such as the Great Lakes, the Florida Everglades, and the Chesapeake Bay testify to the need for accurate ecological indicators.

The box "Working with Sources: Evaluating Environmental Policy" lists Web sites that are especially helpful for evaluating environmental policies, and the box "Working with Sources: Executive Agencies with Environmental Responsibilities" lists agency Web sites that provide much of the data needed to judge how well policies and programs are working. Look back at those boxes and explore some of the sites to reach your own conclusions about the success or failure of these programs and agencies.

***Policy Options for the Future.*** Even without the most accurate indicators to judge the success of natural resource policies, suggestions abound for reforming the policies to make them more effective, efficient, and fair. Among the most frequently proposed are reduction or elimination of subsidies for resource development or exploitation; the imposition of **user fees**, which is a form of market incentive; devolution of resource decisions to the state, county, or local level; the use of ecosystem management; and greater reliance on collaborative decision making and collaborative planning.

Natural resource policies have long incorporated generous **resource subsidies** to users—the ranchers and mining and timber companies. Often, the user pays the government far less in fees than the cost to taxpayers of providing services to these businesses. For example, for years the Forest Service realized less money from timber sales than it cost the agency to build and maintain access roads for loggers. Because of the Mining Law of 1872 (little has changed since its adoption), the mining industry has paid only nominal sums for the right to mine public lands and has paid no royalty on the minerals extracted from them. Critics argue that the government should reduce or end resource subsidies. These subsidies are hard to defend on equity or efficiency grounds, and often they contribute to environmental degradation. Environmentalists say that development interests should pay the full cost of access to public resources through user fees. Although the argument seems reasonable, the developers stoutly defend their long-standing subsidies, arguing that changing the rules at this time would be unfair to them and the industries they represent and would harm the economy in many rural areas of the West. Clinton's secretary of the interior, Bruce Babbitt, fought to impose user fees during the 1990s, largely without success. The development interests had strong support in Congress to maintain the historic subsidies, and Babbitt was never able to arouse enough public concern about grazing and mining fees to alter the political formula.

The idea of imposing user fees extends to charges for entering national parks and other federal lands. Historically, visitors paid a small fee that was well below what they would pay for comparable recreation on private land, and hardly sufficient to cover the costs of park maintenance. Fees have gone up, but is this fair? Some argue that people already pay for the national parks with their federal taxes. Should they have to pay again when they enter a park? From the perspective of equity, the answer might be yes, those who use public services should pay a premium for them. Otherwise, taxpayers who do not use the parks are subsidizing those who do. What is fair in this case?

Devolution proposals, as noted in regard to pollution control policies, call for decentralization of resource decision making to state and local governments. The assumption is that these governments are more alert to the needs of their populations and more capable of taking appropriate action. Critics charge that state and local governments are likely to favor development interests within the state and would not necessarily represent the interests of the nation. How the states would use their additional power will no doubt vary. Some may be inclined to support development interests more than the federal government does at present. Given the level of public concern over the environment, it is also likely that conflict over natural resources will continue, but perhaps more at the state and local levels of government than at the federal level (Lowry 2003).

As a policy, **ecosystem management** means a shift in emphasis toward principles of protect-

Two local boys hold abnormal leopard frogs found near St. Albans Bay of Lake Champlain in St. Albans, Vermont. Frogs with missing, deformed, or extra legs were first discovered in Vermont in 1996, and biologists are unsure if parasites, pollution, ultraviolet radiation, or something else entirely is to blame. Environmental scientists are concerned that such deformities, found increasingly among amphibians nationwide, may be a sign of the adverse effects a growing human population is having on other species, and ultimately, on its own environment. As industrial activity increases and residential areas expand, humans are altering the complex natural processes that sustain ecosystems and the organisms they contain.

ing habitat and maintaining biological diversity. Among its supporters are natural scientists, particularly biologists and ecologists who are concerned about the loss of biodiversity and the fragmentation of ecosystems that do not coincide with the boundaries of national parks and wilderness areas. Essentially, ecosystem management is a long-term comprehensive approach to natural resource management, with a priority on ecosystem functioning rather than human use (Cortner and Moote 1999). Protection of old growth forests in the Pacific Northwest is one example. Others include the restoration of the Florida Everglades and the Chesapeake Bay. Critics of ecosystem management include economic development interests that predict less access to natural resources and conservatives who question the wisdom of increasing government agencies' authority over public and private lands. A skeptical Congress has thwarted efforts to advance ecosystem management. For example, Congress objected to a Clinton administration proposal to establish a new biological service to survey U.S. biodiversity and instead shifted a modified program to the U.S. Geological Survey.

Collaborative decision making and planning aspires to resolve conflicts over local and regional natural resource issues. It brings the various stakeholders together in an ad hoc and voluntary process characterized by cooperation and consensus building. Policymakers have used it to develop successful habitat conservation plans, protect and restore damaged ecosystems, and plan for the future of river basins, among many other activities (Weber 2003; Wondolleck and Yaffee 2000). The parties have an incentive to cooperate because collaboration may speed up the decision-making process and allow them to avoid costly litigation. Although the principle is generally applauded, critics of collaboration argue that not all interests are necessarily represented and that the most powerful interests may dominate the process. Nevertheless, such collaboration holds considerable promise for the future, and its use is likely to continue.

## ENERGY POLICIES

Energy policy is part environmental protection and part natural resources policy, but most analysts would probably agree that the United States has no real energy policy. They can discern no comprehensive or coherent energy policy comparable to those for protecting the environment and natural resources. Instead, individual and corporate decisions in the marketplace largely determine energy use, with each sector of energy influenced to some extent by a variety of government subsidies and regulations. For example, since the 1940s nuclear power has benefited substantially from government subsidies; indeed, the financial aid made its commercial development possible. Other subsidies have promoted coal, natural gas, and oil, often in ways that those outside the industries barely recognize.

To the extent that the United States had a clear energy policy goal before the 1970s, it was to maintain a supply of cheap, abundant, and reliable energy, preferably from domestic sources, to support a growing economy and to ensure a reasonable profit for producers. Critics of this system would add that it fostered the development of large, centralized energy sources, primarily fossil fuels and nuclear power, and made the nation heavily dependent on imported oil. The critical questions for energy policy today are the extent to which this historical bias should be altered to create a more diversified set of energy sources and whether and how to reduce dependence on imported oil and other fossil fuels in light of concerns about climate change. Governments can use a variety of tools, including regulation, public education or persuasion, tax credits or allowances, and subsidies for research and development, to increase energy supply, decrease demand, or alter the mix of fuels used. Some of these tools are more likely than others to be effective, efficient, and fair in moving the nation toward a sensible energy policy.

Energy policy is something of an anomaly compared to the collection of broadly supported environmental policies listed in Table 11-1. For energy, the prevailing pattern has been gridlock since the 1970s. Presidents Richard Nixon, Gerald Ford, and Jimmy Carter all attempted to formulate national energy policies to promote energy independence by increasing domestic supplies, primarily fossil fuels. Following the oil embargo imposed by the **Organization of Petroleum Exporting Countries (OPEC)** in 1973 and the subsequent sharp increases in the cost of oil, Carter, who was elected in 1976, undertook the most sustained and comprehensive of these presidential policy efforts, but for the most part they failed. The reasons were Carter's inability to overcome public disinterest in energy issues, the combined force of organized group opposition to policy action, and his poor relations with Congress on energy (and other) issues (Kraft 1981). Congress did create the Department of Energy in 1977 to consolidate previously independent energy agencies, but the DOE's chief mission was national defense (nuclear weapons development), not energy.

The other major outcomes from the 1970s-era energy policy debates were enhanced federal research support for energy conservation and efficiency and automobile fuel efficiency requirements. The **corporate average fuel economy (CAFE) standards** require passenger cars to average 27.5 miles per gallon, but those in the light truck category, which includes vans and SUVs, need to average only 20.7 miles per gallon. After an initial improvement in fuel economy, the average mileage rating for all vehicles sold in the United States declined during the 1990s, as buyers came to favor SUVs, which now account for more than 50 percent of passenger vehicles sales. Drivers might have an incentive to buy vehicles with greater fuel efficiency if the cost of gasoline were higher, but, adjusted for inflation, gas was cheaper in 2002 than it was in the 1950s. Would the government be more effective in reducing gasoline consumption (and oil imports) if it raised gasoline taxes instead of relying on the CAFE standards? The decision represents a classic choice between two of the most common policy options: regulation and the use of market incentives.

The result of the efforts taken during the 1970s was no result: the United States adopted no national energy policy worthy of the name. Nor did the Reagan administration pursue such a policy during the 1980s because President Reagan and his advisers preferred to defer to the free market rather than use government authority to chart a particular energy path. The Bush administration adopted a modest measure, the Energy Policy Act of 1992, that created some new energy conservation programs, aimed chiefly at electric appliances, lighting, plumbing, and heating and cooling systems, and efficiency programs for alternative-fuel fleet vehicles. It did nothing to curtail U.S. reliance on imported oil or on fossil fuels in general (Kraft 2004).

As late as 2002 Congress was still unable to agree on national energy policy, despite the nation's continued dependence on oil imported from the volatile Middle East. The Senate rejected the Bush administration's proposal to drill in ANWR, and the outlook for the near term at least is that this option is off the table. It is a sensitive issue that sharply divides the parties, but the Senate also turned down environmentalists' proposals to raise auto fuel economy standards. According to the

DOE, the United States imports more than 54 percent of the oil it uses, and most of it goes for transportation. The DOE expects that percentage to rise significantly over the next few decades, which has important economic, national security, and environmental implications. About 85 percent of the nation's energy continues to come from fossil fuels—oil, coal, and natural gas, and the rest comes from other sources, primarily hydroelectric and nuclear power. Currently, renewable sources, such as solar, wind, geothermal, and hydrogen-powered fuel cells, produce only a tiny amount. Environmental groups have argued for years that the nation would be better served by investing in renewable sources. Some of these proposals are considered next.

## FOCUSED DISCUSSION: CLIMATE CHANGE AND ENERGY POLICY ALTERNATIVES

Climate change is probably the most important environmental challenge of the twenty-first century, and policymakers are only beginning to deal with it seriously. As the opening vignette

Environmental groups and many Democrats have roundly criticized the national energy policy proposals of the Bush administration for relying too heavily on increased production of fossil fuels and for doing too little to promote energy conservation. The cartoon above focuses on a closely linked issue—the administration's hesitation to endorse actions to reduce the risk of global climate change attributable to the release of greenhouse gases such as carbon dioxide. The Bush White House maintained that the science of climate change was too uncertain to warrant any public policy action beyond additional support for further scientific research.

in this chapter indicated, each new study or report illustrates continuing controversy over the extent of the problem and the possible solutions. Many scientists and environmentalists are convinced that enough is already known about the risks of climate change to justify taking strong measures now to reduce future harm to people and the environment. Skeptics, including the Bush White House, argue that climate science is inadequate to forecast such risks with much precision. They support more research on the subject, but oppose most other policy actions as premature and excessively costly. They also argue that the United States can adapt to climate change once it occurs and need not be overly concerned about preventing it.

Although commentators and public officials do not always make the linkage clear, climate change policy is closely tied to energy policy. Acting on climate change means reducing the world's emissions of greenhouse gases, with attention focused on carbon dioxide. Most experts, including those who work under the auspices of the UN-sponsored **Intergovernmental Panel on Climate Change**, argue that one of the surest ways to slow the rate of climate change and reduce its harm is to cut back on the use of fossil fuels, which produce large amounts of carbon dioxide when burned. If coal, oil, and natural gas remain the dominant energy sources, carbon dioxide emissions will continue. Because about 85 percent of the energy used in the United States comes from fossil fuels, many policymakers are reluctant to endorse a reduction in fossil fuel use for fear that it will significantly harm the economy. They also argue that the nation at this time has no other major fuel sources to substitute for fossil fuels.

Has science supplied enough information about climate change and its effects on public health and the environment for policymakers to take action? What kinds of public policies should be considered, and which of them is likely to be the most effective? The least costly? How can the benefits of taking action be balanced against the costs? What about ethical issues? Is it fair for people today to continue their dependence on fossil fuels and to pass along the risks of climate change to future generations?

## Economic Issues

If policymakers focused just on reducing the use of fossil fuels to cut carbon dioxide emissions, what actions might they suggest? Among the most common policy recommendations are to increase taxes on fossil fuels to reduce their use (a market incentive approach) and to raise energy efficiency standards that apply to motor vehicles (a regulatory approach). Other proposals would probably include government support for alternative energy sources, research and development funds, tax credits for buying energy efficient appliances and cars, and the like. But consider the first two approaches.

Should the federal government, for example, raise gasoline taxes by a substantial amount, perhaps 50 cents to $1.00 per gallon? Gasoline in the United States would still be far cheaper than it is in most other industrialized nations, where it is usually two to three times higher because of government taxes. Raising gasoline taxes has several benefits, including additional revenues for government support of other environmental and energy programs. More important is the impact on consumer behavior. A large increase in the cost of gasoline should be a strong incentive for consumers to change their behavior. They might look for fuel efficient vehicles, use mass transit, and find other ways to reduce the use of their cars. According to recent studies, traffic congestion already costs the nation more than $78 billion a year in wasted fuel and extra travel time, a figure that is expected to soar over the next twenty years as the U.S. population grows and the number of vehicles keeps pace.[11] Reducing the use of motor vehicles could bring many economic benefits as well as improving air quality in urban areas. Would people cut back on their driving in response to a large increase in gasoline taxes? Would you?

What about raising auto fuel efficiency standards? Studies by the National Academy of Sciences conclude that the technology already exists to raise fuel efficiency substantially without sacrificing vehicle performance or safety, for example, by using variable valve timing, variable transmissions, tires with low rolling resistance, and unibody construction to reduce vehicle weight. These results were feasible, the academy said, if automakers had the ten to fifteen years necessary to further develop and refine the technologies. Most automakers, however, are strongly opposed to higher government efficiency standards, and they have successfully lobbied Congress to block them.[12] New hybrid vehicles such as a Honda Civic model and the Toyota Prius get substantially higher mileage, about fifty miles to the gallon, than conventional cars at a modest premium in purchase price. Even hybrid SUVs are expected to reach the market soon, and fuel-cell powered vehicles within a decade. But because most vehicles sold over the next twenty years or so will run on gasoline engines, higher efficiency standards could make a big difference in greenhouse gas emissions. Should the government adopt tougher fuel efficiency standards to force automakers to build vehicles that will use less gasoline? Would you be willing to pay more for a car that got better mileage but otherwise had the same performance and safety features as present cars?

## Political Issues

During the 2002 debate in Congress on President Bush's national energy policy, proposals to raise auto fuel efficiency standards did not fare well. A measure to raise CAFE standards to 36 miles per gallon by 2015 was defeated, and instead the Transportation Department was asked to study the subject further. CAFE standards have not changed since 1985, and the average gas mileage of vehicles sold in the United States continues to drop. Policymakers also show no enthusiasm for raising gasoline taxes by any substantial amount. As noted, auto manufacturers, with the exception of Honda, adamantly oppose higher fuel economy standards as an unwarranted intrusion into the marketplace.[13] Their multimillion dollar lobbying and advertising campaign, in association with autoworkers unions, emphasize the importance of individual choice of vehicle and imply that, if such standards are adopted, people will be forced to drive small cars. Sen. Trent Lott, R-Miss., was the Senate minority leader when he criticized Democratic proposals for higher efficiency standards as "nanny government" that will deprive him of the SUV he uses to drive his three grandchildren. Some of Lott's colleagues said that higher efficiency standards would drastically reduce vehicle size and weight and increase traffic fatalities.[14] Automakers worry that higher economy standards will reduce the sales of SUVs, a big moneymaker for them.

As for gasoline taxes, policymakers fear the voters' wrath over any tax increase, especially a tax that will annoy them every time they fill their gas tanks. Previous legislative debates suggest that a large gasoline tax increase is not politically feasible, but would it be more acceptable if it were clearly linked with a decrease in other taxes, a move known as tax shifting? In other words, if the gas tax had a neutral impact on overall taxation rates, would the public accept it? Would policymakers vote for a higher gas tax under these circumstances?

Democrats have been more supportive of raising fuel efficiency standards than have Republicans, but neither party seems to be willing to back higher gasoline taxes. With energy policy at the national level in gridlock for years, and with no consensus on how to reduce the use of fossil fuels, state legislators have taken on the energy issues themselves and with some success. For example, in 2002 California approved legislation that for the first time would compel automakers to limit emissions of carbon dioxide by building more fuel efficient vehicles. The California Air Resources Board is to develop a plan by 2005 for the "maximum feasible reduction" in emissions of greenhouse gases. The regulations would take effect for the 2009 car models. The auto industry said in response that the measure, which they and the Bush administration challenged, would drive up the cost of cars unacceptably. Cars and light trucks are responsible for fully one-third of the nation's greenhouse gas emissions, but that number rises to 40 percent in California. In 2002 polls indicated that 81 percent of Californians favored requiring automakers to further reduce greenhouse gases as mandated by the new legislation.[15]

In addition to California's unique approach, many other states (and cities) have adopted or are considering policies to reduce greenhouse gas emissions, including offering subsidies for the purchase of alternative-fuel vehicles, such as natural gas cars, gasoline and electric hybrids like the Prius and Civic, and fuel-cell cars. Indeed, one analysis concluded that the states were taking the lead on climate change policies by offering more innovative and serious policies than the federal government (Rabe 2002). Independently, by 2002 the states had enacted more than three dozen laws, most of them in just two years, that established specific strategies, from electricity generation to transportation, forestry, and agriculture, to reduce greenhouse gases. Oregon established a tough standard for carbon dioxide releases from new electric power plants. Massachusetts also set limits on carbon dioxide emissions for many of the state's power plants.

Reflecting this state-level concern about climate change, in July 2002 the attorneys general of eleven states (all Democrats) wrote to President Bush to urge adoption of strong federal measures to limit greenhouse gases. They argued that the Bush administration had created a "regulatory void" that left to the states the task of piecing together a patchwork of varying and conflicting regulations, and they asked for a more coherent national policy.[16] In addition to the poor image created by federal inaction in the face of innovative city and state policies, the United States was the only industrialized nation to reject the Kyoto protocol on climate change. As other nations adopt specific policies to work toward the treaty's goals, the United States is certain to suffer continuing criticism and international political pressure.

## Ethical Issues

The ethical issues of climate change and energy policy concern how the various policy proposals affect different groups of citizens now and in the future. For example, many point out that the gasoline tax is regressive, that it has an adverse effect on the poor. Will raising this tax make driving to work prohibitively expensive? What about people who live in sparsely populated rural areas and need to drive farther to work and for other necessities, or who need to use heavy-duty pick-up trucks and vans that get lower mileage? Will adding new technologies to make cars more fuel efficient push the price of already expensive vehicles beyond the reach of many people?

Some of the most intriguing ethical issues relate to the U.S. role in climate change. The United States, with less than 5 percent of the world's population, uses almost 30 percent of its commercial energy and produces 25 percent of global greenhouse gas emissions. Is its refusal to sign the Kyoto protocol and decision to defer action on climate change justifiable on equity grounds? Environmentalists argue that it is not right for U.S. citizens to use so much energy and contribute so much to global climate change while doing so little about it. Do you agree?

Also to be considered is **intergenerational equity**, or what is fair to future generations. Climate change forecasts suggest that the adverse impacts will be felt most by people fifty to one hundred years in the future. Taking action on climate change, however, would impose economic burdens on those living now. Is it more equitable to defer action on climate change to improve economic well-being today or to take action now to protect future generations from an unreasonable risk of climate change and its effects? What obligations does the present generation have to the future in this regard? A related issue concerns the role of the United States as an international leader. As the wealthiest and most powerful nation in the world, does the United States have an obligation to take a leadership role on climate change and promote sustainable development? What impact does the U.S. role have on the likelihood that other nations will commit themselves to plans to reduce greenhouse gas emissions?

## CONCLUSIONS

This chapter traces the evolution of environmental and natural resource policies to explain how current policies came to be adopted. It surveys the broad range of policies now in force and their strengths and limitations. It highlights an important shift from political consensus during the 1970s to a greater degree of conflict in the 1980s and 1990s. Disagreement about environmental and resource policies continues in the twenty-first century, as shown by congressional challenges to the Bush administration's policy actions. Nevertheless, it is clear that the U.S. public is concerned about environmental and health risks and continues to support strong public policies. When the Gallup Poll in 2000 asked people to name what they thought would be the most important problem facing the United States twenty-five years in the future, more people named the environment than any other issue.

The chapter also emphasizes the need to modernize environmental, resource, and energy policies for the twenty-first century. From many perspectives, including that of policy analysis, the policies are neither as effective nor as economically efficient as they could be. Policymakers need to evaluate them and consider alternative approaches that hold more promise for better performance in the future. Among the changes the U.S. environmental policy system needs is a set of priorities that is more in tune with the reality of risk to public and environmental health, including policies to deal with climate change and the protection of biological diversity. Ultimately, these and other policy changes must also be consistent with the widely recognized, long-term goal of sustainable development.

## DISCUSSION QUESTIONS

What are the strengths and weakness of U.S. environmental policies? What policy elements do you think are most in need of change? For example, should the nation rely more on the use of market incentives rather than regulation? Should more responsibility for environmental policy be devolved to the states?

How successful have environmental protection policies been in achieving their goals? What has contributed to their success or failure? What kinds of policy approaches might make them more successful?

How successful have natural resource policies been? What has made them successful or has limited their success? What kinds of policy options might make them more successful?

If the United States needs a national energy policy, what should it emphasize? On what policy strategies should it be based?

What should the United States do about climate change? How would you compare the benefits of acting on climate change and the costs of doing so?

## SUGGESTED READINGS

David Howard Davis, *Energy Politics,* 4th ed. (New York: St. Martin's, 1993). A survey of energy policies and politics, covering coal, oil, natural gas, electricity, nuclear energy, and alternative sources such as wind and solar.

Michael E. Kraft, *Environmental Policy and Politics,* 3d ed. (New York: Longman, 2004). A short text that focuses on the major environmental problems and their consequences for society, the policymaking process, the evolution of U.S. policies, and current issues and controversies.

Judith A. Layzer, *The Environmental Case: Translating Values into Policy* (Washington, D.C.: CQ Press, 2002). A collection of intriguing case studies in environmental politics and policy that emphasize conflicts in values and how they are resolved in pollution control and natural resources management. Case subjects include clean air and water, hazardous and nuclear wastes, oil development in the Arctic National Wildlife Refuge, and protection of the Florida Everglades.

Paul R. Portney and Robert N. Stavins, eds. *Public Policies for Environmental Protection,* 2d ed. (Washington, D.C.: Resources for the Future, 2000). An excellent collection of studies of air and water pollution control, hazardous wastes and toxic chemicals, climate change, and solid waste policies by leading experts in the field, with an emphasis on economic issues.

Norman E. Vig and Michael E. Kraft, eds., *Environmental Policy: New Directions for the Twenty-First Century,* 5th ed. (Washington, D.C.: CQ Press, 2003). A collection of original studies covering U.S. political institutions and policymaking, the role of the states and local communities, natural resource policies, climate change, environmental justice, global population growth and economic development, and international trade.

## SUGGESTED WEB SITES

**www.cnie.org.** National Council for Science and the Environment, with links to environmental news sites, a national library for the environment, environmental studies by the Congressional Research Service, and other information on the role of science in environmental policy.

**www.energy.gov.** Department of Energy portal, with news links and access to DOE studies and reports on energy and environment, and debates over national energy policy.

**www.epa.gov.** Home page for the U.S. Environmental Protection Agency. Contains the full text of the major laws the EPA administers and associated rules and regulations. Useful links to all major environmental problems and current government activity on them.

**www.interior.gov.** Department of the Interior portal, with news links, and access to the department's agencies such as the National Park Service, U.S. Geological Survey, Fish and Wildlife Service, and Bureau of Land Management.

**www.nam.org.** National Association of Manufacturers, with a page on resources and environmental issues, providing business commentary on a range of current policy disputes.

**www.nrdc.org.** Natural Resources Defense Council site, with an extensive set of links to environmental issues, recent events, news releases, and reports.

## MAJOR LEGISLATION

# KEYWORDS

collaborative decision making   314

collaborative regulatory approaches   333

comparative environmental risk   329

corporate average fuel economy (CAFE)
   standards   339

direct regulation   328

ecosystem management   337

environmental impact statement (EIS)   324

environmental justice   314

environmental quality standards   328

environmental stewardship   334

flexible regulatory approaches   333

intergenerational equity   344

Intergovernmental Panel on Climate
   Change   341

multiple use   334

National Priorities List   331

National Water Quality Inventory   331

National Wild and Scenic Rivers System   317

Organization of Petroleum Exporting
   Countries (OPEC)   339

resource subsidies   336

user fees   336

World Summit on Sustainable
   Development   313

CHAPTER **12**

POLITICS,

ANALYSIS,

AND POLICY CHOICE

IN MAY 2002 VOTERS IN PORTLAND, OREGON, WERE PRESENTED WITH A ballot initiative that would have overturned a three-decades-old regional growth policy that was widely recognized as a national model for controlling urban sprawl. The developers who placed the initiative on the ballot were expressing their frustration at the strict local rules that limit housing developments in the area around the city. State law in Oregon requires larger cities and towns to create an urban growth boundary for the purpose of maintaining free-of-development farmland and forests outside the city. Consistent with these goals, a regional government body called Metro regulates land use and transportation within the Portland metropolitan area. On three previous occasions, voters in Portland turned down efforts to weaken or eliminate their local growth plan.

This time, however, builders, property rights advocates, and even some environmentalists complained that Portland's stringent regulation of new housing construction was leading to lofty home prices and high population density. They wanted to change the plan to allow new development outside the city in the greenbelt. Supporters of the existing land-use plan defended it as essential for allowing Portland to accommodate new housing while protecting the rural character and open spaces at the edge of the city. As a result of the long-standing plan, Portland resembles many European cities, with an efficient and popular mass transit system, compact urban residential neighborhoods, and abundant forests and farms just outside the urban boundary. In part because of these qualities, Portland regularly appears near the top of rankings of the most livable cities in the United States.

In the end, 57 percent of voters in the Portland metropolitan area opposed the ballot initiative, and 43 percent voted in favor. A leader of the pro-development coalition said the result meant that "there was no groundswell of sentiment against how Portland has shaped its urban destiny." A local urban planning professor saw the vote as an endorsement, even during a recession, of the city's growth restriction policy. "There are an awful lot of people who are comfortable with the idea that the planning that's occurring is still making things better rather than worse," she said.[1]

The Portland growth management initiative illustrates several points this concluding chapter addresses. The first is the substance of policy choices and the impact they have on society.

Residents of Portland, Oregon, have long defended their strict urban land use policies in the face of criticism about the impact of these policies on property values and the constraints they place on regional growth. A May 2002 referendum vote reaffirmed the city's commitment to a growth management plan that maintains an abundance of open space around the city, as exemplified by the city's many parks, extensive walking trails, and abundant green space. Even within the city, Portlanders place a high value on compact neighborhoods, scenic vistas, and a robust mass transit system that reduces the need for highway construction. Often ranked among the most livable of U.S. cities, Portland is an example of government policy meeting public desire.

The way policymakers design public policies can make them more or less effective, efficient, and fair. How these policies affect people's lives depends on the choices made about policy goals and the means used to achieve them. The Oregon state law and the Portland land-use plan made a real and important difference in the quality of life for the city's residents. So too do many other federal, state, and local policies, even if they are often unappreciated.

The growth management initiative also illustrates the potential for policy analysis to clarify the problems that citizens face and to help people find and assess the possible solutions to them. Whether applied to contemporary challenges or those expected several decades in the future, analysis can define the issues more sharply, focus public debate, and help find the best solutions.

Finally, the Portland initiative is a clear demonstration of the decision-making processes that go into these kinds of policy choices, especially the opportunities for citizen participation. At all levels of government, citizens can choose to play an active role in decision making, sometimes by the simple act of voting on a ballot initiative and sometimes through deeper involvement in government and civic affairs. Initiatives and referendums offer citizens the chance to vote directly on public policy measures, but many people also choose to be active in countless other ways in their communities and states and on a national basis.

## PUBLIC POLICIES AND THEIR IMPACTS

Chapter 1 defined public policy as what governments and citizens choose to do or not to do about public problems. Such choices are made at every level of government through the kind of policymaking processes outlined in Chapter 3 and elsewhere in the book. General descriptions of policymaking are somewhat abstract, however, and do not convey how important those choices can be, especially the great impact they can have on people's lives. The examples are myriad. Social Security policy has enormous consequences for the ability of senior citizens to live in dignity and meet their most essential needs during what is often a financially difficult period in life. So too do health care policies such as Medicare and Medicaid, which provide insurance coverage when health care is urgently needed, expensive, and often beyond the means of many individuals. Education policies can affect every public school in the country, what children learn, and how well prepared they are for college or employment. Economic and environmental policies that shape human well-being in the short term can also have serious long-term effects, as the discussion of climate change in Chapter 11 indicated. In short, even though many people may not be aware of it, government and public policy matter.

Because policymaking involves a specification of policy goals as well as the means used to achieve them, a natural part of it is disagreement in every policy area. Should the Endangered Species Act continue to require stringent measures to protect threatened species and biological diversity, and, if so, should Congress add provisions to protect the rights of property owners? Should the federal Medicare program include prescription drug benefits; if so, how generous should those benefits be? What regulations might the government adopt to control the rising cost of drugs? As these and countless other examples illustrate, policy design can make a big difference in how much policies cost and how well they work to meet people's needs. Particular statutory or regulatory provisions can have significant effects on the way policies are implemented, how individuals and institutions comply with the law, and the impacts those laws have on society.

## Policy Conflicts and Incremental Decision Making

Conflict arises when policy actors have differing views about the substance of public policies or whether government intervention is justifiable at all. Conservatives favor limits on environmental protection regulations because they believe the public and environmental health risks from toxic chemicals, hazardous wastes, or climate change are not as serious as environmentalists assert they are. They also question whether the benefits of environmental policies can justify the high costs and the adverse impacts on the business community and property owners. Liberals balk at proposals for government regulation of a woman's right to abortion counseling and services or family planning services on the grounds that such intervention violates privacy rights and constrains personal decisions.

Conflicts over the role of government and public policy underscore the political nature of policymaking. Inevitably, policymaking involves choices about social values as well as calculations about policy design. In the heat of public debate, the differences are not always clear, even to those most directly involved. Policymakers and interest groups may disagree intensely about whether government intervention is warranted and about broad policy goals such as environmental protection or equality in the workplace. Forging consensus is more difficult on fundamental goals and values than it is

Michigan resident Eddie Joe Lloyd is freed in August 2002 after serving seventeen years in prison for the rape and murder of a teenage girl. Lloyd is one of more than one hundred individuals nationwide to be exonerated by the technology of DNA testing. As the text notes, public policies are often changed incrementally, even in the face of new technology and new public demands. Policies dealing with the death penalty and criminal justice have been slow to change despite evidence that many prosecutions and judicial proceedings have been based on false or misleading evidence. The availability of DNA testing and the overturning of so many convictions illustrate the social costs associated with obsolete criminal justic policies.

on policy means, such as the use of market incentives, public education, or regulation. The history of policy gridlock in areas as diverse as energy policy and health care reflects the inability of policymakers to resolve some of these deep conflicts, particularly when organized groups on each side subject the policymakers to intense lobbying.

Because political conflict is endemic to policymaking, almost all policies represent a compromise on the goals being sought as well as the means proposed to achieve them. Compromise means that the policies are likely to be only partially effective and that the debate over further changes will continue. Thus, elected officials enact policies to remove agricultural subsidies only to put them back again a few years later when farmers complain that the free market that policymakers anticipated is not working well. Congress approved the Clean Air Act Amendments in 1970 but debated two decades later whether to add acid rain controls to the act's provisions and how to improve its dismal achievements in curbing toxic air pollutants. Such examples show that policymaking is never complete, but an ongoing process in which new problems emerge, old ones are seen in a different light, and arguments are advanced once again about how best to further the public interest (Anderson 2003; Kingdon 1995). These and other characteristics of U.S. politics almost always mean that public policies change in small steps over time.

Incremental policymaking of this kind can be a sensible way to act on public problems. It can provide short-term political stability by minimizing conflict over social values and policy goals. It can forge compromises that help diverse policy actors gain something that they want while delivering needed services to the public. It subjects policy proposals to careful evaluation of their likely effectiveness, costs, and impacts, thus reducing the risk of serious mistakes. It can help to build political legitimacy and confidence in the policymaking processes. Finally, it can encourage policy experimentation and learning, the kind of trial-and-error decision making that allows policymakers, especially at the state level, to try new approaches to see how they work before making an enduring commitment to a particular course of action (Lindblom and Woodhouse 1993). Programs that are successful or broadly supported, such as Head Start, can be expanded over time, and those that fall short can be curtailed or modified in other ways.

## Policy Strategies with No Crystal Ball

Incremental policymaking is the dominant style in the U.S. political system, and, although it is suitable for many public problems and circumstances, it also has its limitations. Some critics suggest that it may be least appropriate when governments face new problems for which they are ill-prepared and where considerable uncertainty exists over the risks, the costs of trying to reduce them, and the likely effectiveness of policy measures (Ophuls and Boyan 1992). Others may be tempted to say that this is precisely when incremental policy change makes more sense than a radical departure from the status quo.

Global climate change offers a context in which to consider the relative advantages of incrementalism and radical change. Climate science is still developing, and forecasts of future climate scenarios are necessarily uncertain. But opting for minimal policy responses while awaiting more definitive scientific evidence on the seriousness of the problem may be catastrophic to societies around the world. Adopting radical changes that could be quite costly, however, poses a different kind of risk to society, that of spending money that could be better used for other purposes. What should governments do in these circumstances?

Luckily, a middle course is available. Many recent proposals in a range of policy areas have emphasized the value of policy flexibility and adaptive management, meaning that policymakers can continue to evaluate the situation while taking incremental policy steps. For climate change, this type of policymaking might mean a real effort to promote energy efficiency and conservation; which are relatively cheap to achieve and for which technologies already exist. Or it might mean funding a research program to develop alternatives to fossil fuels. Whatever policies are adopted could have enough built-in flexibility to allow program changes as new knowledge develops. Administrators might be given the discretion to alter course when conditions justify doing so. Policymakers can always revisit the policy when they have enough evidence to warrant a change in direction.

At the same time, and also pertinent to the example of climate change, some analysts cite the precautionary principle as a guideline. This principle was developed as a way of dealing with uncertain future risks. It states that when an activity raises serious threats of harm to human health or the environment, precautionary measures should be taken even if scientists do not fully understand all of the cause and effect relationships. It also states that the proponents of an activity should bear the burden of proof that little or no harm will result and that action can be taken in the face of uncertainty. In other words, the principle encourages a prudent or conservative response to potentially serious threats, with a bias in favor of protecting human health and the environment rather than advancing proposals for new technologies or economic development activities (Raffensperger and Tickner 1999). It also reflects a belief that ethical standards may be able to inform policy debates that otherwise might center on economic issues.

Another way of thinking about responses to an uncertain future is evident in the example of Portland's land-use plan. Because their policy decisions have long-term effects, city and state governments need methods for making reasonable predictions about the future. They can turn to forecasting methods to determine what the city and state might look like in twenty or fifty years if present trends continue. They can also work with citizens to define what they prefer to see in the future. Once a preferred vision or ideal for the city or state is identified, officials can develop plans and policies to help realize it. Chapters 5 and 6 discussed a similar trend in many localities to shape their futures around the idea of sustainable development or how best to enhance the quality of life for citizens on an enduring basis. The movement toward sustainable communities is a striking testimony to the belief that citizens can affect their futures through cooperation and local action that includes adopting policies that attempt to integrate economic development, environmental protection, and social well-being. Hundreds of communities across the country have tried to chart their futures in this way, and scholars have begun to assess their success and the conditions that foster it (Mazmanian and Kraft 1999; Portney 2003; Paehlke 2003).[2]

In this vein, one of the most frequently observed limits of decision making, including policymaking, is that it tends to focus on events or developments that are closest to people in time and space. Commentators often fault policymakers for having a short-term time horizon, by which they mean that elected officials tend to think about impacts only through the next election, two, four, or six years away. But that bias, even if exaggerated, exists throughout society. Corporations, for example, focus heavily on short-term profits shown in quarterly and annual financial reports. As a result, they may lose sight of long-term goals, which are not highly valued in the marketplace.

A cloned piglet curiously approaches a visitor while his littermates play in the background at the College of Veterinary Medicine at Texas A&M University. In 2001, the Veterinary School and the university's Center for Animal Biotechnology and Genomics (CABG) announced that the university had become the first academic institution to clone three different animal species—successfully reproducing pigs, goats, and cattle. Animal cloning demonstrates how scientific developments can have dramatic effects on politics and public policy. Along with stem cell research, cloning holds enormous potential for medical research and the development of new treatments for human diseases. At the same time, these developments have placed pressure on state and federal policymakers to constrain research in the field out of concern for deeply felt moral and ethical beliefs

As understandable as such a fixation on the short term is, public policy of necessity must look ahead. It must also adopt a broader perspective that includes people and institutions located at some distance, geographically and culturally, from policymakers and citizens. As the nation has learned since the terrorist attacks of September 11, 2001, fighting global terrorism means more than guarding domestic airports or taking military action against specific targets in other countries. It involves trying to understand and respond to cultural and economic forces around the world that breed resentment toward the United States and sympathy and support for terrorists.

The September 2002 World Summit on Sustainable Development, mentioned at the beginning of Chapter 11, is a good example of forward-looking and wide-ranging policymaking. The world's population is expected to climb to nine billion or more by 2050, and the Census Bureau projects a U.S. population of more than 420 million by then. To provide for all these people, nations will have to foster more economic development to meet the demand for energy, food, water, clothing, housing, transportation, jobs, and other essentials. To be sustainable, economic development around the globe would have to be designed to avoid the severe environmental and social strains that would likely come with reliance on conventional growth. The World Summit was arranged to try to identify and build support for this new kind of economic development.

As these examples illustrate, public policy aims at a moving target. Public problems change over time, in part because economic, cultural, social, and political conditions are dynamic. New values and perspectives arise, for example, about welfare and work or the right to health insurance, and policy processes shift accordingly. In the mid-1990s, many Republicans in Congress wanted to abolish the Department of Education, which was created during the Carter administration in part as a way of showing support for teachers, a major Democratic constituency. Yet many of these same Republicans took the lead in supporting additional federal power for education with the passage of the No Child Left Behind Act of 2001 that required national testing of students. What changed? The U.S. public said it was tired of failing public schools, and Republicans became interested in broadening their party's base. They were now prepared to back a stronger federal role in education.

Policies also change in response to the development of new technologies, such as cellular phones and information databases on the Internet. These developments in turn stimulate new public demands for government intervention, as illustrated by cities and states trying to regulate the use of cell phones by drivers or protect individual privacy rights on the Internet. The federal government is forced to define its position on human cloning and use of embryonic stem cells as medical science advances and new technologies in that field raise ethical concerns.

Because the targets of public policy are always shifting, analysts, policymakers, and citizens need to be alert to changing situations and consider new policy ideas. As the substantive policy chapters showed, too often old policies continue in place long after they are outdated. If the nation truly values effective and efficient public policies, it must be open to evaluating those policies and changing them as needed. The same argument applies to addressing new concerns about the equity of public policies, whether the concern is over environmental justice for poor communities or equal access to opportunities in education.

## POLICY ANALYSIS AND POLICY CHOICES

Making public policies more effective, efficient, and equitable raises once again the subject of policy analysis and its role in policymaking. As Chapters 4 through 6 discussed, policy analysis has the potential to bring greater clarity to public problems and their solutions than might otherwise be the case. Analysts acknowledge the political character of the policymaking process, but also believe that objective knowledge can reveal the nature of problems and their causes and help guide the search for public policies that promise a measure of success. If nothing else, policy analysis can clarify the issues and sharpen political debates. The potential for using policy analysis in state and local problem solving may be even greater than at the national level because state and local governments often lack the same level of expertise seen in the federal government.

Oregon's land-use case indicates that potential. In deciding whether to continue or alter the thirty-year-old growth management policy, voters benefited from reliable knowledge of what the policy had achieved to date and a fair assessment of how changing the policy would affect the quality of life in the metropolitan area. For example, how would additional residential development outside of the city affect highway travel, congestion, and air pollution? Would businesses migrate from the central city to suburban shopping malls, as they have done in most other urban areas around the country? How would development in the current greenbelt around the city affect recreational opportunities? Would farmers sell their land to developers? In this case and many others like it, local officials and the citizens who vote on the ballot initiative would benefit from unbiased information that addresses such questions.

## Evaluating Public Policy

Among other evaluative criteria, this book has placed special emphasis on three: effectiveness, efficiency, and equity. Effectiveness, or how well a policy works or might work, is always difficult to address, but it is obviously an important consideration at a time when many critics doubt the capacity of government to solve any problem. At the earliest stages of the policy process, when policy alternatives are proposed, effectiveness is necessarily based on various assumptions and projections of the future that may or may not come to pass.

Consider the issue of high-level nuclear waste, which is now stored at or near the nation's civilian nuclear power plants. Which is the more effective policy, to leave the waste where it is or to move it to the centralized repository planned for Yucca Mountain, Nevada? How would analysts determine effectiveness? Most discussions of nuclear waste try to compare the relative costs, benefits, and risks of the two policy choices. That is a reasonable way to decide, but making the comparisons will never be straightforward given the number of issues that must be addressed, including the risk of terrorist attacks on nuclear power plants and shipments of radioactive wastes and the possibility of water contamination of the waste site and leakage to the outside environment over the ten-thousand-year period that federal regulations specify. The complexity of determining effectiveness is a strong reason to draw from policy studies to try to determine which of the policy alternatives will work best. Policymakers and citizens would be foolish to rely solely on off-the-cuff judgments about the policy alternatives for nuclear waste when repository costs will run to $60 billion or more and where risks to public health and the environment can be substantial.

At periodic stages of the policy process, effectiveness is the criterion analysts use to determine how well a policy has lived up to expectations. Did it succeed in producing the desired results? Even after a reasonable period of time, it is not easy to identify and measure a policy's impacts and compare them to the initial policy goals. Policymakers and independent analysts in and out of government conduct such evaluation studies, which have great value, despite their limitations. Whether school vouchers are effective in improving educational outcomes, for example, depends on what one measures. Should analysts consider parental support, improvement by participating students, or if all students are doing better? The difficulty in measuring success means that students of public policy need to think critically about such studies and their findings.

Efficiency is probably the criterion most likely to receive attention in contemporary policymaking as policy alternatives and existing programs are assessed. The reasons are clear. Government budgets are almost always under tight constraints, and it is a rare politician or taxpayer who favors tax increases, so policymakers want to ensure a good return on the money spent. They will want to know how much proposed programs cost and where the money will come from to pay for them. They will almost certainly demand a cost-benefit analysis. They may even compare different programs according to which are most efficient in producing good results for the same dollar amount invested. Policy analysis can contribute to answering those questions. While this is all well and good, public policy students already know that measuring and comparing costs and benefits are rarely simple. Not all costs and benefits can be identified and measured, and it is difficult to compare costs and benefits over time. Policymakers and the public need to exercise care in the way they use such studies and pay attention to the assumptions and methods that are used so that they understand the studies' limitations.

Equity issues are addressed less frequently than effectiveness and efficiency, but they are no less important in public policy. Equity can be defined in several different ways, and therefore it may include concerns that range from protecting individual freedom to how policy costs and benefits are distributed among groups in a population. The issue of individual (or corporate) freedom arises frequently when a new program is proposed or an old one expanded. For example, federal health care policies offer benefits to Medicare and Medicaid recipients, but impose constraints on health insurance companies and health professionals. Federal and state environmental regulations can help to protect the public's health, but at some cost to the rights of corporations to make decisions about the technologies they use and the kinds of products they make. Policy analysis can facilitate policy choices by clarifying these kinds of tradeoffs. Analysis can be similarly useful in describing the way many programs, such as Social Security, welfare, and education, either redistribute wealth in society or try to promote equity in some other ways.

## Improving Policy Capacity

Policy analysis also can help improve the performance of government and its responsiveness to citizen concerns. Now might be as good a time as any to consider how to improve the policy capacity of government. Public trust and confidence in government institutions fell almost steadily from the 1960s to the late 1990s, with a small upward trend only in the fall of 2001, following the terrorist attacks and the U.S. response to them. It is not yet clear whether that short-term shift will last or the longer-term decline in confidence will return (Mackenzie and Labiner 2002).

Objective evidence does not confirm the verdict that government has failed to perform well, but there is little doubt from public commentary and political rhetoric that many people believe that is the case (Bok 2001). In response to this skeptical public mood, policymakers at all levels of government have struggled with how to improve public policies and programs and better meet citizen needs. Various efforts to "reinvent" government and to improve its efficiency were tried during the 1990s, and they continue today. It might be advisable for government to include a broader policy capacity to define and respond effectively to public problems, both present and future.

What can policy analysis contribute to improving the policy capacity of government? One way is through the analysis of proposed institutional reforms, such as changes in the electoral process, campaign finance, term limits for legislators, and opportunities for citizens to participate in decision making. This is a task at which political scientists excel. Yet too often their analyses fail to reach the public or even policymakers, who then must act without benefit of what the analysis has uncovered. The box "Steps to Analysis: Money in Politics" illustrates these needs. It highlights a Web site that allows analysis of the role of money in politics and underscores some of the concerns that motivate campaign finance reform efforts.

Other chapters have suggested that policy capacity can also be improved through better evaluation of the agencies charged with implementing policies and programs. Thanks to the Government Performance and Results Act of 1993, the federal government is likely to conduct more evaluations of this kind than in the past. But think tanks and other independent bodies carrying out external evaluations may be better able to identify institutional strengths and weaknesses and to suggest meaningful paths to reform. For example, Chapter 11 noted that a series of studies by the National Academy of Public Administration (1995, 2000) identified many elements of the U.S. environmental protection system that could be changed to improve the effectiveness and efficiency of the Environmental Protection Agency (EPA) and other agencies. Studies by Resources for the Future have reached similar conclusions (Davies and Mazurek 1998).

Sometimes evaluations of government institutions and processes come from citizen groups such as Public Citizen and Common Cause, which favor reforming laws on campaign finance and lobbying. Policy entrepreneurs such as Ralph Nader and John Gardiner, longtime repre-

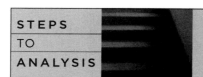

## STEPS TO ANALYSIS

### MONEY IN POLITICS

No other aspect of politics may be as well documented as the role of money. The Center for Responsive Politics allows you as a citizen to examine the data to see how money is donated and spent to influence the policymaking process. The center's Web site, www.opensecrets.org, lists the amounts of money donated to campaigns, dollars spent on lobbying activity, and soft money contributions. This kind of information can give voters a great deal of insight into the politics of policymaking. The center believes that turning the "sunshine" on these activities will get policymakers thinking about how they go about making decisions and just who is supplying not only the money but also the information they use to make them.

The Web site also provides research and reports on political issues, and you can make your own assessments of the information. For example, during 2001 and 2002, lawyers and law firms contributed more than $9.9 million to candidates through their political action committees (PACs). Go to the site and find your member of Congress or a senator and see how much he or she received and spent during the last election. What percentage of the money came from PACs? Which corporate, union, or other PACs gave the money? Look at the donations for your entire state. The data presented here allow citizens to see how much money different organizations spend to lobby public officials, but interpreting the information is never easy. What impact do you think such contributions have on policymaking? Do they merely buy "access," or does such money influence how policymakers decide where they stand on issues?

sentatives of those two groups, helped to get these issues on the political agenda, attract media coverage of reform proposals, and pressure Congress to act. The organizations scored a major victory in 2002 with enactment of the Bipartisan Campaign Finance Reform Act of 2002, which imposed new restrictions on contributions of funds to political parties and campaigns.

One of the central tasks in improving policy capacity in government is in the hands of the people. If citizens lack interest in public affairs and fail to educate themselves on the issues, government will continue to respond to organized groups and special interests. What citizens see as faulty performance in government sometimes reflects the influence of organized groups that work to ensure that policies affecting their operations are *not* effective or that they inflict minimum constraints on their activities. A well-known example of the late 1990s was the influence of corporations in weakening government oversight of their financial operations. The weaker financial regulations provided the opportunity for corporate abuses at companies such as Enron and WorldCom that shocked and disgusted the public in 2002. The best way to counter such self-serving actions by special interests is for citizens to get involved.

## CITIZEN PARTICIPATION IN DECISION MAKING

The final point this chapter emphasizes is the politics of policymaking, that is, how policy choices are made. The decision-making process affects what kinds of decisions are made and, ultimately, what impacts they have on society. The policy outcomes reflect who participates in the process, who does not, and the different resources that each policy actor brings to the decision-making arena. In a democracy one would expect public policies to be consistent with public preferences and to meet the needs of citizens. As noted, however, policymakers are often more responsive to organized interests—agriculture, the mining industry, the oil industry, health insurance companies, or the music recording industry—than they are to the general public. The discussion of subgovernments, elites, and the role of interest groups in Chapters 2 and 3 highlighted these patterns.

### Citizen Capacity and Policy Engagement

How might that situation be changed? One way is to strengthen citizen capacity to participate in policymaking processes. The level of public participation in policy processes, whether voting in elections or taking an active role in civic affairs, has declined over the past several decades (Putnam 2000; Skocpol and Fiorina 1999). Of all the age groups, the youngest, including college students, have the lowest level of interest in politics and policymaking and active participation in these processes. However, some contrary indicators of citizen interest in public affairs, especially in their local communities, have been noted. The movement toward sustainable communities and recent surveys by the Pew Partnership for Civic Change indicate that Americans have a "profound sense of connectivity to their communities and neighbors" and are willing to work with others to solve problems.[3] Nevertheless, it remains clear that citizen participation has a long way to go to be truly effective.

There is no shortage of analyses about why the U.S. public has been so disengaged from politics and civic affairs. At least part of the explanation is the disconnect between the policy process and people's daily lives. That is, most citizens either do not see how government actions affect their lives or they do not believe they can do much to change what government does. Yet public policies unquestionably have a great impact on people's lives. Workers have Social Security taxes withheld from their paychecks without knowing whether the full benefits will be available to them when they retire. The cost of attending a state college or university reflects competing demands on the state budget. Will high quality and affordable health care services be available to all citizens? Public policy decisions will determine what happens in all these policy areas.

In addition to making the connection between policy choices and individual lives clearer, improving the public's access to government information might encourage more people to participate. Consider the activities of the public interest group Environmental Working Group (EWG), which in 2002 became heavily involved in congressional debates over agricultural subsidies. Frustrated by the lack of public attention to what it believed were inequitable payments to wealthy farmers, the group secured access to the raw data for the government's farm subsidy

## STEPS TO ANALYSIS

### USING WEB SITES TO INFLUENCE PUBLIC OPINION AND POLICY DEBATE

The groups Public Citizen and Government Accountability Project analyzed the U.S. Department of Agriculture's (USDA) testing records for Salmonella bacteria found at ground-beef processing plants. They acquired the data with a Freedom of Information Act request. The groups' 2002 report cited many plants that failed the tests, some repeatedly, because of lax USDA enforcement. They placed the list of failing plants on the Public Citizen Web site (www.citizen.org).

Go to the Web site to reach your own conclusions about how serious the threat to public health is and whether the two groups were fair in their reaction to the USDA's efforts to protect the public's well-being. Locate your state on the site and see if any plants in the state were identified as failing the USDA test. What does the information suggest about the plants' operation? Do you believe you have enough information to make that judgment?

It should be said that the majority of the nation's meatpacking plants operate in accordance with new USDA standards for Salmonella testing, and such contamination has declined in recent years. One further problem, however, is that Congress has refused to give the agency adequate powers of enforcement, leaving it with few options to deal with failing plants (Perl 2000). Under these circumstances, what do you think is the best way to bring all plants up to acceptable standards for meat processing?

According to the U.S. Centers for Disease Control and Prevention, improperly handled ground beef and other food contaminated with pathogens such as Salmonella, Listeria, and E. coli bacteria are implicated in 14 million illnesses, 60,000 hospitalizations, and about 1,500 deaths in the United States every year. Illness and death are particularly high among newborns, the elderly, and those with weakened immune systems. The information is on the CDC Web site: www.cdc.gov/ncidod/eid/vol5no5/mead.htm#Figure%201.

payments and placed the information on its Web site (www.ewg.org). Members of Congress frequently cited the data and the EWG Web site when considering the bill, probably because they had heard from their constituents on the subject. Particularly important was the revelation that hundreds of farmers and absentee landlords were receiving millions of dollars in subsidies.[4]

Later in the year, as Congress began debating whether to approve construction of the Yucca Mountain nuclear waste repository, the same group put information about possible nuclear waste shipment routes on its site. It included an interactive map that allowed citizens to determine how close the shipments would come to their communities. The site also provided data on the amount of nuclear waste in each state, the likely number of shipments of waste by truck and rail through the state, the number of people who live within one mile of a transportation route, and similar information. Once again the Web site attracted a great deal of media coverage, along with plenty of criticism. Critics said the information was misleading because the government has yet to approve any transportation routes for the nuclear waste shipments and that the maps therefore were speculative. Whether one thinks that the group's efforts were praiseworthy or not, its strategy suggests the potential political power of Web-based citizen education and lobbying. The box "Steps to Analysis: Using Web Sites to Influence Public Opinion and Policy Debate" illustrates yet another group effort to shape public opinion and policy debate.

## New Forms of Citizen Participation

Public participation in the policy process can go well beyond voting, writing letters or e-mail messages to policymakers, and talking with others about policy issues. Historically, only a small percentage of the public is even this active. But the percentage could rise as technology makes public involvement easier and as policymakers become more interested in having a higher level of public participation in government.

Some government agencies already make a concerted effort to promote the use of their Web sites, to offer information and public services through "e-government," and to invite the public to engage the issues. For example, in 2001 the EPA completed an online national dialogue on how to improve public involvement in EPA decision making.[5] The opportunities to become involved in policymaking are even greater at the state and local levels. In addition to inviting people to public meetings and hearings and asking the public to submit comments on proposed government actions, policymakers also ask citizens to serve on advisory panels and assist them in making often difficult choices.

The nearly universal access to the Internet should make it easier for citizens to become active in public affairs. But, like public policy students, every citizen also must be alert to bias in Internet-based information. Each person must learn to ask about the source of the data and how reliable it is. Despite the difficulties, there are reasons to be optimistic about the potential of the Internet and citizen access to information about government and public policy.

Policy analysts have long recognized different social goals furthered by public involvement in policymaking and the criteria by which participation can be evaluated. Thomas Beierle and Jerry Cayford (2002) identify five goals: (1) incorporating public values into decisions (a fundamental expectation in a democracy); (2) improving the substantive quality of those decisions (for example, by suggesting alternatives and finding errors of inappropriate assumptions underlying policy proposals); (3) resolving conflict among the various competing interests (by emphasizing collaborative rather than adversarial decision making); (4) building trust in institutions and processes (thereby improving their ability to solve public problems); and (5) educating and informing the public (raising public understanding of the issues and building a shared perspective on possible solutions). The last of these goals can be thought of as enhancing public capacity for participation in policy processes, an example of what Anne Schneider and Helen Ingram (1997) refer to as the capacity-building tools that governments possess.

Government agencies and public officials are often unclear about what they expect public participation to accomplish, and citizens might be puzzled as well. Some agencies feign interest in public involvement to appear to be doing the "right thing" and to comply with legal mandates. But they greatly limit the degree to which citizens can affect decision making. Responding to that common practice, some analysts have suggested that there are four quite different models of citizen involvement, with increasing degrees of public influence on decision making. The first is the commentary model, in which agencies and proponents dominate; second, the social learning model, in which citizens learn about policy proposals and provide advice on them; third, the joint planning model, in which citizens engage in a dialogue with policymakers and planners and work collaboratively with them; and fourth, the consent and consensus model, in which citizens share authority with government and work together to solve problems.[6] Which model makes the most sense? Are citizens well enough informed on the issues to share authority with government officials? If they are not well informed, how might their knowledge be increased enough to permit such a sharing of authority?

## CONCLUSIONS

Throughout this book, we have emphasized an integrated approach to the study of public policy rather than focusing on policy history and program details. Although this kind of information is clearly important, policy and program particulars change quickly, and the knowledge learned may be of limited use over time. In the long run, the perspectives and approaches of policy analysis are more helpful in understanding how the nation's policies evolved into their present state and considering what alternatives might work better. The book has stressed how to think about policy issues, where to find pertinent information, and how to interpret it. It also underscored the need to develop a robust capacity for critical and creative thinking about public problems and their solutions.

This last chapter revisits some of these points in the context of the policy challenges governments face as they try to make difficult decisions about the future. It focuses on the way policy decisions can affect people's lives, how policy analysis can clarify public problems and possible solutions, and the role of citizens in the policymaking process. Despite a prevailing sense of cynicism toward government and politics, we believe that the present is a time of exceptional opportunity for citizens to get involved in public affairs. New technologies, particularly the Internet, greatly facilitate access to a vast range of policy information. Governments at all levels are welcoming citizen involvement, giving new vitality to the promise of American democracy. We urge you to take advantage of those opportunities and play an active role in designing and choosing public policies for the future.

## SUGGESTED READINGS

Derek Bok, *The Trouble with Government* (Cambridge: Harvard University Press, 2001). A perceptive assessment of government and civic shortcomings, with thoughtful recommendations for greater citizen participation in public affairs.

Michael J. Kryzanek, *Angry, Bored, Confused: A Citizen Handbook of American Politics* (Boulder: Westview Press, 1999). A short, refreshing introduction to U.S. government and politics that adopts the perspective of an anxious consumer who seeks to understand and improve government, politics, and public policy.

Paul Loeb, *Soul of the Citizen: Living with Conviction in a Cynical Time* (New York: St. Martin's Press, 1999). Describes how ordinary citizens can make their voices heard and take action in a time of widespread cynicism and despair.

Robert D. Putnam, *Bowling Alone: The Collapse and Revival of American Community* (New York: Simon and Schuster, 2000). A best-selling data-filled treatment of civic disengagement in the United States, the reasons for it, and possible solutions.

William A. Shutkin, *The Land That Could Be: Environmentalism and Democracy in the Twenty-First Century* (Cambridge: MIT Press, 2000). Describes a new kind of environmental and social activism in the nation that joins environmental interests to civic health and sustainable local economies. Sees this civic environmentalism as a new form of public discourse.

## SUGGESTED WEB SITES

**www.apsanet.org/CENnet.** American Political Science Association's Civic Education Network, with links to civic and political education organizations, centers and institutes, teaching and research resources, and links to service learning programs.

**www.citizen.org.** Public Citizen home page, with many links to policy issues and activism.

**www.civiced.org/index.html.** Center for Civic Education, with links to Internet resources, national and state programs.

**www.excelgov.org.** Council for Excellence in Government, a nonprofit organization working to improve government at all levels and to encourage greater citizen involvement. Links to other resources and sites, including the Center for Democracy and Citizenship.

**www.firstgov.gov/Citizen/Citizen_Gateway.shtml.** FirstGov's citizen portal, with links to e-government services and public action.

**www.ipi.org.** Institute for Policy Innovation, a research organization that believes in individual liberty and limited government; research and papers on policy options.

## CHAPTER 1 PUBLIC POLICY AND POLITICS

1. For a discussion of the public demand for organic food and the development of the new labeling requirements, see Candy Sagon, "An Organic Standard," *Washington Post National Weekly Edition,* October 14–20, 2002, 31. The USDA Web site contains the complete text of the new regulations. The gist of the new standard is that, to warrant the term *organic,* a food must have been produced without pesticides, hormones, antibiotics, irradiation, or the use of bioengineering. In addition, organic farmers are required to conserve water and soil (important to protect environmental quality) and treat their animals humanely.
2. See Eric Schmitt, "Tobacco Lobby Tries to Keep Pentagon Cigarette Subsidy," *New York Times,* October 20, 1996, 1, 12. The Pentagon's analysts estimated that the tobacco subsidy cost the Defense Department $384 million a year in health expenses and $346 million a year in lost productivity.
3. See Mary Dalrymple, "Many Divisions Yield Gloomy Forecast for Upcoming Appropriations Season," *CQ Weekly,* May 18, 2002, 1294–1297. The volatile economy in 2002 made budget projections of this kind more difficult than usual.
4. The fiscal 2003 projections for mandatory spending come from the budget President Bush submitted to Congress in early 2002. See www.whitehouse.gov/omb/budget/index.html.

## CHAPTER 2 GOVERNMENT INSTITUTIONS AND POLICY ACTORS

1. Donald G. McNeil Jr., "Upstate Waste Site May Endanger Lives," *New York Times,* August 2, 1978, A1.
2. The Bush reorganization left the CIA and FBI largely unaffected. This decision was somewhat surprising because criticism of the two agencies' failure to share their knowledge of terrorist activities prior to the attacks of September 11, 2001, was the impetus for the president's plan. For a description of the reorganization proposal, see Adriel Bettelheim and Jill Barshay, "Bush's Swift, Sweeping Plan Is Work Order for Congress," *CQ Weekly,* June 8, 2002, 1498–1504.
3. For many policy activities, Indian tribes constitute sovereign entities that deal directly with the federal government rather than with the states where tribal land is located.
4. In March 2003 New York joined the list of states that ban smoking in restaurants. Many localities in the state already had done so.
5. Antismoking campaigns illustrate the wide variation in policy action from state to state. One study found that only six states spent even the minimum amount on programs designed to prevent or stop smoking, as recommended by the Centers for Disease Control and Prevention. Most states spent less than one-half the recommended level, and two supported no antismoking programs at all with their portion of the $206 billion national settlement against U.S. tobacco companies. See Greg Winter, "State Officials Are Faulted on Anti-Tobacco Programs," *New York Times,* January 11, 2000, A20.
6. In addition to the 435 members, the House of Representatives has four delegates and a resident commissioner, bringing the total to 440. These five positions were created by statute. Puerto Rico elects a commissioner, and Congress has approved nonvoting delegates for the District of Columbia, Guam, the Virgin Islands, and American Samoa. See Roger H. Davidson and Walter J. Oleszek, *Congress and Its Members,* 8th ed. (Washington, D.C.: CQ Press, 2002).
7. See Rick Weiss, "Political Science: HHS Panels Are Made Over in Bush's Image," *Washington Post National Weekly Edition,* September 23–29, 2002, 29. See also Sheryl Gay Stolberg, "Bush's Science Advisers Drawing Criticism," *New York Times,* October 10, 2002, A28.
8. A sign of their success may be found in a proposal by the Bush administration to sharply limit an expected rise in the budget for the Securities and Exchange Commission. The budget increase was to help the SEC implement the new corporate antifraud legislation, the Sarbanes-Oxley Act, which the president signed in mid-2002. See Stephen Labaton, "Bush Seeks to Cut Back on Raise for S.E.C.'s Corporate Cleanup," *New York Times,* October 19, 2002, 1, B14. In early 2003 the SEC staff recommended a softening of the proposed rules for regulating lawyers and accountants. The staff's recommendations came on the heels of intense lobbying by prominent law firms, bar associations, and leading accounting firms and trade groups. See Stephen Labaton and Jonathan D. Glater, "Staff of S.E.C. Is Said to Dilute Rule Changes," *New York Times,* January 22, 2001, C1, 11.

9. Measuring the size of government is not easy. Should it include only government employees or also count those in the private sector who produce goods and services for the government under contract? For an assessment of government size, see Paul Light, *The True Size of Government* (Washington, D.C.: Brookings Institution, 1999).

## CHAPTER 3  UNDERSTANDING THE POLITICS OF PUBLIC POLICY

1. See Lori Nitschke and Wendy Boudreau, "Provisions of the Tax Law," *CQ Weekly,* June 9, 2001, 1390–1394, for an objective summary of the provisions of the tax cut legislation.
2. The Congressional Budget Office has one of the best economic forecasting reports for estimating government revenue and spending over the next decade. It is available at www.cbo.gov.
3. In addition to the implications for U.S. programs and budgets, the massive farm bill had a serious global impact. By increasing price guarantees for corn, wheat, soybeans, and other crops, the policy significantly raised production levels of those crops and thereby depressed global prices. Lower prices hurt nations desperately struggling to develop economically and repay loans. See Elizabeth Becker, "Raising Farm Subsidies, U.S. Widens International Rift," *New York Times,* June 15, 2002, A3.
4. The policy process model is not without its critics. Some argue that it should be replaced by a more accurate and genuinely causal model of policy activities that lends itself to empirical testing and to the incorporation of a broader variety of policy actors and behavior. See Paul A. Sabatier and Hank C. Jenkins-Smith, eds. *Policy Change and Learning: An Advocacy Coalition Approach* (Boulder: Westview Press, 1993); and Paul A. Sabatier, ed. *Theories of the Policy Process* (Boulder: Westview Press, 1999). We disagree with much of this critique. The policy cycle model can be useful for describing the diversified players in the policy game and for alerting observers to pertinent actions that contribute to understanding public policy and politics. One should not, however, treat the stages in the model as anything more than helpful constructs.
5. On the subject of nonissues and decisions to keep issues off the agenda, see Peter Bachrach and Morton S. Baratz, *Power and Poverty: Theory and Practice* (New York: Oxford University Press, 1970). We think the agenda-setting theories of John Kingdon and Frank Baumgartner and Bryan Jones offer equally if not more useful insights on the process. See John W. Kingdon, *Agendas, Alternatives, and Public Policies,* 2d ed. (New York: HarperCollins College, 1995); and Frank R. Baumgartner and Bryan D. Jones, *Agendas and Instability in American Politics* (Chicago: University of Chicago Press, 1993).

## CHAPTER 4  POLICY ANALYSIS: AN INTRODUCTION

1. See Gina Kolata, "Accidents Much More Likely When Drivers Hold a Phone," *New York Times,* February 13, 1997, 1, A14. The estimated equivalence to driving under the influence of alcohol came from a study published in the *New England Journal of Medicine* that analyzed some 27,000 cell phone calls.
2. Governor Pataki's quotes are from an Associated Press release, "New York Cell Phone Ban Signed into Law," June 28, 2001.
3. Danny Hakim, "Ban on Drivers' Cell Phones Cuts Use, Study Finds," *New York Times,* August 19, 2002, A14.
4. Practical policy analysis is also sometimes referred to as "quick analysis," or "quickly applied basic methods," but the intent is to offer an analytical and objective assessment of the issues, even when policymakers must make decisions quickly. See Robert D. Behn and James W. Vaupel, *Quick Analysis for Busy Decision Makers* (New York: Basic Books, 1982). and Carl V. Patton and David S. Sawicki, *Basic Methods of Policy Analysis and Planning,* 2d ed. (Englewood Cliffs, N.J.: Prentice Hall, 1993).
5. For example, many organizations and think tanks on the right end of the political spectrum have received substantial funding from foundations supportive of conservative causes and publications. Among the most notable of these are the John M. Olin Foundation, Scaife Family Foundation, Koch Family foundations, Lynde and Harry Bradley Foundation, and the Adolph Coors Foundation. For an assessment of how such conservative foundations have affected public policy debate, see the report by People for the American Way, "Buying a Movement," available at the organization's Web site: www.pfaw.org. For an assessment of how industry-funded think tank studies, including those supported by Koch Industries, influence environmental policy debates, see Curtis Moore, "Rethinking the Think Tanks," *Sierra,* July-August 2002, 56–59, 73.
6. See "Homeless in America: A Statistical Profile," *New York Times,* December 12, 1999, Week in Review Section, 3. The *Times* report relied on statistics supplied by the Department of Housing and Urban Development, which came from surveys and interviews conducted in 1995 and 1996 with adults who used services for the homeless, such as shelters. This database indicated that 32 percent of the homeless were female and 68 percent male. Some

12 percent of the homeless were between seventeen and twenty-four years of age, and 80 percent were between the ages of twenty-five and fifty-four, but no data were available in this survey on homeless children.

7. Michael M. Weinstein, "The Aid Debate: Helping Hand, or Hardly Helping? *New York Times,* May 26, 2002, Week in Review Section, 3. The many successful projects were highlighted in a 2002 tour of sub-Saharan Africa by Secretary of the Treasury Paul H. O'Neill and rock star Bono of U2. Bono has been an active proponent of economic assistance to poor nations. Some of the economic studies on the consequences of aid programs can be found in Joseph Kahn and Tim Weiner, "World Leaders Rethinking Strategy on Aid to Poor," *New York Times,* March 18, 2002, A3.

## CHAPTER 5  PUBLIC PROBLEMS AND POLICY ALTERNATIVES

1. See David Cay Johnston, "Investigations Uncover Little Harassment by I.R.S.," *New York Times,* August 15, 2000, 1, C13.
2. David Cay Johnston, "Hunting Tax Cheats, I.R.S. Vows to Focus More Effort on the Rich," *New York Times,* September 13, 2002, 1, C3. See also Johnston, "Departing Chief Says the I.R.S. Is Losing Its War on Tax Cheats," *New York Times,* November 5, 2002, 1, C2; Johnston, "A Smaller I.R.S. Gives Up on Billions in Back Taxes," *New York Times,* April 13, 2001, 1, C2; and Alan K. Ota, "Cost of IRS Overhaul Has Former Backers Wary," *CQ Weekly,* September 2, 2017–2019.
3. For an overview of the effects of budget cuts on the IRS and the implications for taxpayers, see Albert B. Crenshaw and Stephen Barr, "Taxing Times at the IRS," *Washington Post National Weekly Edition,* March 20, 2000, 6–7.
4. See Matthew L. Wald, "Urging Young to Buckle Up, Officials Try Switch in Tactics," *New York Times,* May 20, 2002, A18. Wald cites a study stating that 52 percent of teenagers killed in auto accidents were not wearing seat belts. This rate is twice that of all people killed in auto accidents.
5. See Louis Uchitelle, "How to Define Poverty? Let Us Count the Ways," *New York Times,* May 26, 2001, A15, A17.
6. "Diane Rehm Show," National Public Radio, February 18, 2003.
7. Ironically, the longer sentences and the increase in the prison population are not deterring people from committing crimes. The recidivism rate is rising in part because, to save money, state governments cut back on rehabilitation programs such as drug treatment, vocational education, and classes that help to prepare convicted criminals to return to society. See Fox Butterfield, "Study Shows Building Prisons Did Not Prevent Repeat Crimes," *New York Times,* June 3, 2002, A11.
8. For an overview of methods that can be used to obtain policy information, see Carl V. Patton and David S. Sawicki, *Basic Methods of Policy Analysis and Planning,* 2d ed. (Englewood Cliffs, N.J.: Prentice Hall, 1993), particularly chapter 3; and Allen D. Putt and J. Fred Springer, *Policy Research: Concepts, Methods, and Applications* (Englewood Cliffs, N.J.: Prentice Hall, 1989). Patton and Sawicki offer a helpful guide for arranging and conducting interviews with policymakers. Any recent social science methods text will discuss how to construct and use questionnaires as well as how to conduct interviews. See, for example, Earl Babbie, *The Practice of Social Research,* 9th ed. (Belmont, Calif.: Wadsworth, 2000).
9. See James C. Benton, "Washington's Repetitive Stress over Ergonomics Rules," *CQ Weekly,* February 26, 2000, 401–405. The article cites the following industries as most affected by musculoskeletal disorders: airline, airport and terminal services; buses, commuter rail lines, and taxis; trucking and warehousing firms; hospitals, clinics, doctors' offices, and nursing homes; car, truck, aircraft, boat, and railroad car makers; and meatpackers, dairies, grain mills, bakeries, and packaged food makers.
10. See Timothy Egan, "Once Braced for a Power Shortage, California Now Finds Itself with a Surplus," *New York Times,* November 4, 2001, A17.
11. See Crenshaw and Barr, "Taxing Times at the IRS," and David Cay Johnston, "I.R.S. Is Bolstering Efforts to Make Cheaters Pay Up," *New York Times,* February 13, 2000, 1, 28.
12. *New State Ice Co. v. Liebmann,* 285 U.S. 262, 311 (1932).
13. Quoted in a *Science* magazine editorial by Donald Kennedy, March 22, 2002, 2177.

## CHAPTER 6  ASSESSING POLICY ALTERNATIVES

1. Laura Mansnerus, "Northeast Sets Smokers Gasping from More Than the Habit," *New York Times,* June 25, 2002, A24.

2. See Carl Hulse, "House Supports Permanent End to Estate Tax," *New York Times,* June 7, 2002, 1, A17.
3. Other military aircraft are exceedingly expensive as well. The Air Force F-22 fighter cost $200 million per plane in 2000, and the tilt-rotor Osprey aircraft, a kind of combination helicopter and plane, cost $83 million each—and was plagued with operating problems. See Tim Weiner, "How to Build Weapons When Money Is No Object," *New York Times,* April 16, 2000, Week in Review, 3.
4. See Paul R. Portney, "Time and Money: Discounting's Problematic Allure," *Resources* 136 (summer 1999): 8–9. See also Paul R. Portney and John P. Weyant, eds., *Discounting and Intergenerational Equity* (Washington, D.C.: Resources for the Future, 1999).
5. The new guidelines for agency scientific data were pushed through Congress as a rider attached to a fiscal 2001 appropriations bill in late 2000, largely at the request of business and industry groups, and signed by President Bill Clinton. Business groups have long maintained that many government regulations are based on faulty data and the new law will make it easier for them to challenge regulations they view as burdensome. See Rebecca Adams, "OIRA Directs Guidelines on Data Quality," *CQ Weekly,* March 23, 2002, 827.
6. The proposal can be found at the FAA Web site (www.faa.gov).
7. See David Johnston, "C.I.A. Puts Risk of Terror Strike at 9/11 Levels," *New York Times,* October 18, 2002, 1, A12.
8. For example, a book published a year after the September 11 terrorist attacks discusses public anxiety over unfamiliar and highly publicized risks and attempts to assess the true risk: David Ropeik and George Gray, *Risk: A Practical Guide for Deciding What's Really Safe and What's Really Dangerous in the World Around You* (Boston: Houghton Mifflin, 2002). The book sold briskly at Amazon.com and Barnes and Noble's online site.
9. The odds are taken from Larry Laudan, *The Book of Risks: Fascinating Facts About the Chances We Take Everyday.* (New York: John Wiley and Sons, 1994), as cited in a CNN news story, May 20, 1998.
10. The estimates were reported by Susan Okie, in "The Smallpox Tradeoff," *Washington Post National Weekly Edition,* May 13–19, 2002.
11. The options that were being considered in 2002 are discussed in a National Center for Infectious Diseases newsletter: www1.umn.edu/cidrap/content/bt/smallpox/news/acipupdate.html. In July 2002 the federal government decided to vaccinate about a half-million health care and emergency personnel rather than the fifteen thousand it originally believed necessary. See William J. Broad, "U.S. Expands Plan for Administering Smallpox Vaccine," *New York Times,* July 7, 2002, 1, 16.
12. Many different sources are available for these estimates, but for an account of the case and the general use of such economic sanctions, see Joy Gordon, "Cool War: Economic Sanctions as a Weapon of Mass Destruction," *Harper's,* November 2002, 43–49.
13. A compound interest calculator is available on the Web at http://javascript.internet.com/calculators/compound-interest.html. To use it, enter an amount of money, an interest rate, and the number of years the money will be invested and immediately see how much the initial amount changes over this time period.
14. Similar calculations are made regularly by the Alan Guttmacher Institute, the policy analysis arm of Planned Parenthood. Their studies can be found at www.agi-usa.org.

## CHAPTER 7 ECONOMIC AND BUDGETARY POLICY

1. William M. Welch, "Budget Surplus Forecast Doubles," *USA Today,* July 18, 2000.
2. For a review of budget forecasting accuracy and related issues, see Julie Kosterlitz, "Colored by Numbers," *National Journal,* March 31, 2001, 932–939.
3. For a brief discussion of the line-item veto law, see http://rs9.loc.gov/home/line_item_veto.html.
4. Although the spending cuts were split between defense and domestic spending, a large portion of the budget was considered off-limits in regards to sequestration. This part of the budget included most entitlement programs, such as Social Security, and interest payments on the debt (Thurber 1996b). The result was that sequestration had an even larger effect on those programs that could be sequestered.
5. In other words, if the law was changed to provide for greater benefits for a particular program, it could trigger sequestration. But if the economy soured and as a result there was an increase in unemployment and a subsequent increase in the number of people eligible to receive benefits, that would not trigger sequestration.
6. For example, in fiscal year 1999, the total emergency appropriation was just over $34 billion and was the largest since 1991, the year of Desert Storm. See U.S. Congressional Budget Office, "Emergency Spending Under the Budget Enforcement Act: An Update" (1999), www.cbo.gov/showdoc.cfm?index=1327&sequence=0.
7. See Keith Perine, "Regulation is Back in Vogue," *CQ Weekly,* July 27, 2002, 2018–2020.
8. These assumptions are based on no other changes being made to the existing program, such as an increase in the eligibility age or an increase in the Social Security withholding tax.

## CHAPTER 8 HEALTH CARE POLICY

1. The figures for the California case come from Consumer Reports, "The Unraveling of Health Insurance," part one of a two-part series, in *Consumer Reports,* July 2002, 48–53.
2. Ceci Connolly, "A Drop in the Bucket? Bush Health Plan Called Inadequate," *Washington Post National Weekly Edition,* May 20–26, 2002, 12.
3. The numbers come from a Census Bureau estimate for 2001. See Robert Pear, "After Decline, the Number of Uninsured Rose in 2001," *New York Times,* September 30, 2002.
4. See Keith Epstein, "The Quest to Keep Americans Healthy," *CQ Weekly,* July 20, 2002, 1976–1987. A long-term monitoring project on U.S. health goals also finds mixed results in improving public health. From 1979 to 1999 the rates of heart disease and stroke declined, as did infant mortality rates and deaths from breast cancer. However, physical activity declined, obesity increased, and childhood asthma hospitalizations increased. Rates vary significantly among ethnic groups, with African Americans and Hispanics generally scoring lower on health. See Philip J. Hilts, "Nation Is Falling Short of Health Goals for 2000," *New York Times,* June 11, 1999, A24.
5. See Marilyn Werber Serafini, "Medicare's Challenge," *National Journal,* May 20, 2000, 1602–1606.
6. Robert Pear, "Cost of Rampant Mental Health Care Fraud Soars in Medicare," *New York Times,* September 30, 1998, A12.
7. See Linda Greenhouse, "Court, 5–4, Upholds Authority of States to Protect Patients," *New York Times,* June 21, 2000, A15.
8. The data are available at the Center for Medicare and Medicaid Services, www.cms.gov. The projections are based on data released in January 2002 and use intermediate demographic and economic assumptions, that is, the most reasonable of the assumptions made in projections of this kind.
9. For example, see the "Kaiser/Harvard National Survey of Americans' Views on Managed Care" from November 1997, published by the Henry J. Kaiser Family Foundation. An updated survey from 2001 is available at the foundation's Web site, and others may be published in the future: www.kff.org.
10. R. H. Miller and H. S. Luft, "Does Managed Care Lead to Better or Worse Quality of Care?" *Health Affairs* 16 (September/October 1997): 7–25.
11. Cited in "The Unraveling of Health Insurance," *Consumer Reports,* July 2002, 48–53.
12. See Richard E. Anderson, "The High Cost of Defensive Medicine," posted on the Web page of the Health Care Liability Alliance: http://64.177.60.131/html/hcla061498.htm.
13. Robert Pear, "Inept Physicians Are Rarely Listed as Law Requires," *New York Times,* May 29, 2001, 1, A12.
14. For research on health care quality and discussions of national commitment to quality health care, see the Web site for the Agency for Healthcare Research and Quality at www.ahcpr.gov/qual/measurix.htm.
15. See Linda T. Kohn, Janet M. Corrigan, and Molla S. Donaldson, eds., *To Err Is Human: Building a Safer Health System* (Washington, D.C.: National Academy Press, Institute of Medicine, 2000). A summary is available online at: http://books.nap.edu/books/0309068371/html/index.html. The high numbers of deaths reported in these studies represent an extrapolation from several state level studies, including analysis of deaths in hospitals in New York, Colorado, and Utah. Some critics charge that the estimates are too high, and others believe they may be too low.
16. Robert Pear, "U.S. Health Officials Reject Plan to Report Medical Mistakes," *New York Times,* January 24, 2000, A14.
17. The quotations come from Jim Avela, "Boutique Medical Practices on Rise," reported on the MSNBC Web site, April 3, 2002.
18. The figures come from the CDC, which reports regularly on smoking-related deaths and economic losses. See www.cdc.gov/tobacco.
19. Quoted in a review of Marion Nestle's *Food Politics: How the Food Industry Influences Nutrition and Health* (Berkeley: University of California Press, 2002), by Ben Geman, *National Journal,* June 22, 2002, 1899.
20. A summary of recent data from the CDC and the trends in obesity since 1960 can be found in Sally Squires, "We're Fat and Getting Fatter," *Washington Post National Weekly Edition,* October 14–20, 2002, 34. A significant proportion of Americans can be classified as obese or overweight. Obesity is defined as having a body mass index (BMI) of 30 or greater, and being overweight is defined as having a BMI of 25 or higher.
21. These statistics on health measures come from the National Center for Health Statistics, which reports on an annual survey by the Centers for Disease Control and Prevention and other data: www.cdc.gov/nchs/releases. The 2001 figures were reported in April 2003.
22. Robert Pear, "Study Finds Top Drugs for Aged Easily Outpace Inflation," *New York Times,* June 25, 2002, A21.
23. Harvard University conducted the survey for the Kaiser Family Foundation. It is available at the foundation Web site: www.kff.org.
24. Robert Pear, "Air of Inevitability: Despite the Impasse on Medicare, the Elderly Will Still Get Something," *New York Times,* June 29, 2002, A12; Mary Agnes Cary, "Much Variety, Little Traction in Medicare Drug Plans," *CQ Weekly,* July 13, 2002, 1848–1856.

## CHAPTER 9 WELFARE AND SOCIAL SECURITY POLICY

1. For additional information on poverty, other measures related to the poor, and potential problems of the current estimate of poverty, see Deepak Bhargava and Joan Kuriansky, "Drawing the Line on Poverty," *Washington Post National Weekly Edition,* September 23–29, 2002, 23.
2. For more information on hunger and the food stamp program, see Kathy Koch, "Hunger in America," *CQ Researcher,* December 22, 2000.
3. This information comes from the U.S. Department of Agriculture's National School Lunch Program Web site, available at www.fns.usda.gov/cnd/Lunch/AboutLunch/ProgramHistory.htm.
4. This information and more is from the U.S. Department of Agriculture Web site: www.fns.usda.gov/cnd/Translations/English/English.htm.
5. This information comes from a report by Zoe Neuberger, Sharon Parrott, and Wendell Primus, "Funding Issues in TANF Reauthorization," Center on Budget and Policy Priorities, February 5, 2002. Available at www.centeronbudget.org/1-22-02tanf5.htm.
6. For a full discussion of the potential of a recession's impact on the nation's programs designed to help the poor, see Mark Murray, Marylyn Werber Serafini, and Megan Twohey, "Untested Safety Net," *National Journal,* March 10, 2001.

## CHAPTER 10 EDUCATION POLICY

1. Dirk Johnson, "Many Cleveland Parents Frantic After Ruling Limits School Vouchers," *New York Times,* August 26, 1999.
2. This figure is based on the institutions' entire budget for the year divided by the number of students attending. The U.S. Naval Academy in Annapolis, for example, has a budget of $219,223,214 and serves 4,020 students. According to the Department of Education, the per student subsidy was $54,533.
3. An increase in state support would require a dramatic shift in how many states currently fund their public education systems and likely cause states to raise taxes. For more information, see William C. Symonds, "Closing the School Gap," *Business Week,* October 14, 2002, 124.
4. According to an anti-TV advocacy group, the average American spends three hours and forty six minutes per day watching television. Children between the ages of two and eleven spend about twenty hours a week watching television (TV-Free America 2000).
5. Kenneth Jost discusses many of the issues regarding standardized testing in, "Testing in Schools," *CQ Researcher,* April 20, 2001.
6. These percentages are based on the amount of state tax funds for operating expenses of higher education per $1,000 of personal income.
7. See Richard Rothstein, "Teacher Shortages Vanish When the Price Is Right," *New York Times,* September 25, 2002, A16.
8. For additional information regarding the role of state constitutions, their legal environments, and the effect on school vouchers, see Kenneth R. Godwin and Frank R. Kemerer, *School Choice Tradeoffs: Liberty, Equity, and Diversity* (Austin: University of Texas Press, 2002).
9. Nine thousand Florida students were eligible; 542 took advantage of the program in 2002 by attending private schools, and another 900 switched to different public schools. See Cynthia L. Webb, "Results Disputed in Florida School Voucher Plan," *Boston Globe,* March 4, 2002.
10. The National Education Association's Web site, www.nea.org/issues/vouchers/index.html, contains a variety of resources regarding school vouchers. The site provides the referendum results of previous voucher programs, which show that the voters in these states do not support the programs. Indeed, the voting is quite one-sided against vouchers.
11. See www.heritage.org/library/keyissues/education/schoolchoice.html.

## CHAPTER 11 ENVIRONMENTAL AND ENERGY POLICY

1. The report is summarized by Andrew C. Revkin, in "Climate Changing, U.S. Says in Report," *New York Times,* June 3, 2002, 1, A11, and it can be found in full at the EPA Web site: www.epa.gov/globalwarming/publications/car/index.html. The climate report was consistent with other recent reports on the subject, including studies by the U.S. National Academy of Sciences and the Intergovernmental Panel on Climate Change: www.ipcc.ch.

2. See Kirk Johnson, "City's Water-Quality Plan Working So Far, U.S. Finds," *New York Times,* June 1, 2002, A14.

3. For a good introduction to conservative views of environmental issues, see Peter Huber, *Hard Green: Saving the Environment from Environmentalists, a Conservative Manifesto* (New York: Basic Books, 1999).

4. In 2002 the Bush administration announced it would not seek reauthorization of the Superfund tax. It would sharply curtail the number of Superfund sites to be cleaned up and cover the costs through general Treasury funds. In an op ed article, former Clinton EPA administrator Carol Browner called the Bush action "an enormous windfall for the oil and chemical companies." See "Polluters Should Have to Pay," *New York Times,* March 1, 2002, A23.

5. For a direct comparison of the EPA risk ranking to public concerns drawn from poll data, see Leslie Roberts, "Counting on Science at EPA," *Science* 249 (August 1990): 616.

6. The air pollution figures in these paragraphs are taken from U.S. EPA, *Latest Findings on National Air Quality: 2001 Status and Trends* (Research Triangle Park, N.C.: Office of Air Quality Planning and Standards, September 2002), available online at www.epa.gov/oar/aqtrnd01.

7. EPA, *National Water Quality Inventory: 2000 Report to Congress* (Washington, D.C.: Office of Water, August 2002), at www.epa.gov/305b/2000report.

8. EPA, "Superfund Cleanup Figures," at www.epa.gov/superfund/action/process/mgmtrpt.htm, January 17, 2002. The fund was nearly out of money by mid-2002.

9. See Mary Graham and Catherine Miller, "Disclosure of Toxic Releases in the United States," *Environment* 43 (October 2001): 8–20; and Mary Graham, "Regulation by Shaming," *Atlantic Monthly,* April 2000, available online at www.theatlantic.com.

10. See Margaret Kriz, "Working the Land: Bush Aggressively Opens Doors to New Mining, Drilling, and Logging on Federal Lands, as Green Activists Despair of Even Keeping Track," *National Journal,* February 23, 2002, 532–539.

11. See Mark Murray, "Road Test," *National Journal,* May 25, 2002, 1548–1553.

12. John Lancaster, "Debate on Fuel Economy Turns Emotional," *Washington Post,* March 10, 2002, A12. The National Academy of Sciences report is *Effectiveness and Impact of Corporate Average Fuel Economy (CAFE) Standards* (Washington, D.C.: National Academy Press, 2002).

13. Honda's unique role in supporting higher fuel economy standards, even for SUVs, is detailed by Danny Hakim in "Honda Takes Up Case in U.S. for Green Energy," *New York Times,* June 2, 2002, C1, C4.

14. Lancaster, "Debate on Fuel Economy Turns Emotional," and David Rosenbaum, "Senate Deletes Higher Mileage Standard in Energy Bill," *New York Times,* March 14, 2002, A26.

15. See Danny Hakim, "At the Front on Air Policy: California Is Moving to Set U.S. Standard," *New York Times,* July 3, 2002, 1, A12.

16. The letter was reported by James Sterngold in, "State Officials Ask Bush to Act on Global Warming," *New York Times,* July 17, 2002, online version.

## CHAPTER 12 POLITICS, ANALYSIS, AND POLICY CHOICE

1. Timothy Egan, "Portland Voters Endorse Curbs on City Growth," *New York Times,* May 23, 2002, A25.

2. In *Taking Sustainable Cities Seriously: Economic Development, the Environment, and Quality of Life in American Cities* (Cambridge: MIT Press, 2003), Kent E. Portney examined major cities that have "started to take the idea of sustainability seriously as a matter of public policy." These included Portland, Seattle, San Francisco, Boston, Santa Monica, Boulder, Tucson, Austin, and others. Beyond his own analysis, Portney suggests the value of more systematic analysis that can reveal why cities undertake such efforts and the factors that make some of them more successful than others.

3. The Pew study, "Ready, Willing and Able: Citizens Working for Change," is available at www.pew-partnership.org. The site also has similar studies and recommendations for civic engagement.

4. Elizabeth Becker, "Accord Reached on a Bill Raising Farm Subsidies," *New York Times,* April 27, 2002, 1, A11.

5. The EPA dialogue can be found at www.network-democracy.org/epa-pip/welcome.shtml.

6. See Hardy Stevenson Associates, "How to Conduct National Level Consultations," in the company newsletter, *Social and Environmental Assessment Bulletin* (Toronto, Ontario: Hardy Stevenson Associates, spring 2002).

# REFERENCES

1994–1996 Advisory Council on Social Security. 1997. *Report of the 1994–1996 Advisory Council on Social Security, Vol. 1: Findings and Recommendations.* Washington, D.C. Available at www.ssa.gov/history/reports/adcouncil/report/toc.htm.

Aaron, Henry, Alan Binder, Alicia Munnell, and Peter Orszag. 2000. *Governor Bush's Individual Account Proposal: Implications for Retirement Benefits.* Available at www.socsec.org/facts/Issue_Briefs/PDF_versions/11issbrf.pdf.

AARP. *AARP on the Issues: Social Security.* Available at www.aarp.org/ontheissues/issuesocsec.html.

Adams, Rebecca. 2001a. "Intense Lobbying Gets Under Way over Whether to Block Ergonomics Rules." *CQ Weekly,* February 10, 328–329.

———. 2001b. "House Sends Patients' Rights on to Last Critical Test." *CQ Weekly,* August 4, 1900–1905.

———. 2002. "Politics Stokes Energy Debate." *CQ Weekly,* January 12, 109.

Alexander, Lamar. 1992. "Merit Pay Programs Would Improve Teacher Performance." In *Education in America: Opposing Viewpoints.* Edited by Charles P. Cozic. San Diego: Greenhaven Press.

American Council of Education. 1999. "To Touch the Future: Transforming the Way Teachers Are Taught. Available at www.acenet.edu/resources/presnet/report.cfm.

American Federation of Teachers. 2000. "Where We Stand: True Merit Pay." (March). Available at www.aft.org/stand/previous/2000/0300.html.

Ammons, David N. 2002. *Tools for Decision Making: A Practical Guide for Local Government.* Washington, D.C.: CQ Press.

Amy, Douglas J. 1984. "Why Policy Analysis and Ethics Are Incompatible." *Journal of Policy Analysis and Management* 3: 573–591.

Anderson, Charles W. 1979. "The Place of Principles in Policy Analysis." *American Political Science Review* 73: 711–723.

Anderson, James E. 2003. *Public Policymaking.* 5th ed. Boston: Houghton Mifflin.

Andrews, Richard N. L. 1999. *Managing the Environment, Managing Ourselves: A History of American Environmental Policy.* New Haven: Yale University Press.

———. "Risk–Based Decision Making." In *Environmental Policy.* 5th ed. Edited by Norman J. Vig and Michael E. Kraft. Washington, D.C.: CQ Press.

Asher, Herbert. 2001. *Polling and the Public: What Every Citizen Should Know.* 5th ed. Washington, D.C.: CQ Press.

Associated Press. 1998. "Vermont Town May Blink in Dispute with State." *Boston Globe,* December 20.

———. 2002a. "Cigarettes Cost U.S. $7 per Pack Sold, Study Says." *New York Times,* April 12, A20.

———. 2002b. "California Law Permits Stem Cell Research." *New York Times,* September 23.

Bardach, Eugene. 2000. *A Practical Guide for Policy Analysis: The Eightfold Path to More Effective Problem Solving.* New York: Chatham House.

Bartlett, Robert, ed. 1989. *Policy Through Impact Assessment: Institutionalized Analysis as a Policy Strategy.* New York: Greenwood Press.

Baumgartner, Frank R., and Beth L. Leech. 1998. *Basic Interests: The Importance of Groups in Politics and Political Science.* Princeton: Princeton University Press.

Baumgartner, Frank R., and Bryan D. Jones. 1993. *Agendas and Instability in American Politics.* Chicago: University of Chicago Press.

Becker, Elizabeth. 2000. "Congress Approves Plan to Insure Military Retirees." *New York Times,* October 13, A16.

———. 2002. "Bill Defines Irradiated Meat as 'Pasteurized.' " *New York Times,* March 5, A18.

Behn, Robert D., and James W. Vaupel. 1982. *Quick Analysis for Busy Decision Makers.* New York: Basic Books.

Beierle, Thomas C., and Jerry Cayford. 2002. *Democracy in Practice: Public Participation in Environmental Decisions.* Washington, D.C.: Resources for the Future.

Berman, Evan. 2002. *Essential Statistics for Public Managers and Policy Analysts.* Washington, D.C.: CQ Press.

Berry, Jeffrey M. 1997. *The Interest Group Society.* 3d ed. New York: Longman.

———. 1999. *The New Liberalism: The Rising Power of Citizen Groups.* Washington, D.C.: Brookings Institution.

Berry, Jeffrey M., Kent E. Portney, and Ken Thomson. 1993. *The Rebirth of Urban Democracy.* Washington, D.C.: Brookings Institution.

Bettelheim, Adriel. 1999. "Managing Managed Care." *CQ Outlook,* May 1, 8–28.

Billitteri, Thomas J. 1997. "Teacher Education." In *Issues for Debate in American Public Policy.* Edited by Sandra L. Stencel. Washington, D.C.: CQ Press.

Birkland, Thomas A. 1997. *After Disaster: Agenda Setting, Public Policy, and Focusing Events.* Washington, D.C.: Georgetown University Press.

Bok, Derek. 2001. *The Trouble with Government.* Cambridge: Harvard University Press.

Bond, Jon R., and Richard Fleisher, eds. 2000. *Polarized Politics: Congress and the President in a Partisan Era.* Washington, D.C.: CQ Press.

Borins, Sandford. 1998. *Innovating with Integrity: How Local Heroes Are Transforming American Government.* Washington, D.C.: Georgetown University Press.

Bosso, Christopher J., and Deborah Lynn Guber. 2003. "The Boundaries and Contours of American Environmental Activism." In *Environmental Policy.* 5th ed. Edited by Norman J. Vig and Michael E. Kraft. Washington, D.C.: CQ Press.

Bosworth, Barry, and Gary Burtless. 2000. "The Effects of Social Security Reform on Saving, Investment and the Level and Distribution of Worker Well-Being." Center for Retirement Research at Boston College. Available at www.bc.edu/bc_org/avp/csom/executive/crr/papers/wp_2000–02.pdf.

Bowen, William G., and Derek C. Bok. 1998. *The Shape of the River: Long-Term Consequences of Considering Race in College and University Admissions.* Princeton: Princeton University Press.

Bowman, Ann O'M., and Richard C. Kearney. 1999. *State and Local Government.* 4th ed. Boston: Houghton Mifflin.

Bowman, James S., and Frederick A. Elliston, eds. 1988. *Ethics, Government, and Public Policy.* Westport, Conn.: Greenwood Press.

Bowman, Karlyn. 1999. "Social Security: A Report on Current Polls." American Enterprise Institute for Public Policy Research. (April).

Brennan, Timothy J. 2001. *The California Electricity Experience, 2000–2001: Education or Diversion?* Washington, D.C.: Resources for the Future, November 14.

Brody, Jane E. 2002. "Cellphone: A Convenience, a Hazard, or Both?" *New York Times,* October 1, D7.

Caldwell, Lynton Keith. 1998. *The National Environmental Policy Act: An Agenda for the Future.* Bloomington: Indiana University Press.

California Department of Education. *Ed-Data District Profiles and Reports.* Available at www.eddata.k12.ca.us/dev/District.asp.

California State University Institute for Education Reform. 1997. *Paying for What You Need: Knowledge- and Skill-Based Approaches to Teacher Compensation.* (September).

Cannon, Carl M. 1998. "America: All Locked Up." *National Journal,* August 15, 1906–1915.

Cary, Mary Agnes. 2002. "With No Patients' Rights Agreement in Sight, Daschle Prepares to Name Conferees." *CQ Weekly,* May 25, 1394–1395.

Center for Education Reform. 2002. Available at http://edreform.com.

Chubb, John E., and Paul E. Peterson, eds. 1989. *Can the Government Govern?* Washington, D.C.: Brookings Institution.

Chubb, John E., and Terry M. Moe. 1990. *Politics, Markets, and America's Schools.* Washington, D.C.: Brookings Institution.

Cigler, Allan J., and Burdett A. Loomis, eds. 2002. *Interest Group Politics.* 6th ed. Washington, D.C.: CQ Press.

Clarke, Jeanne Nienaber, and Daniel McCool. 1996. *Staking Out the Terrain: Power and Performance Among Natural Resource Agencies.* 2d ed. Albany: State University of New York Press.

Clines, Francis X. 2001. "Deaths Spur Laws Against Drivers on Cell Phones." *New York Times,* February 18, 1, 18.

Clinton, Bill, and Al Gore. 1992. *Putting People First.* New York: Times Books.

Cobb, Clifford, Ted Halsted, and Jonathan Rowe. 1995. "If the GDP Is Up, Why Is America Down?" *Atlantic Monthly,* October, 59–78.

Cobb, Roger W, and Charles D. Elder, 1983. *Participation in American Politics: The Dynamics of Agenda Building.* 2d ed. Baltimore: Johns Hopkins University Press.

Cochran, Clark E., Lawrence C. Mayer, T. R. Carr, and N. Joseph Cayer. 1999. *American Public Policy: An Introduction.* 6th ed. New York: Worth.

Concord Coalition. "Issue Brief: Social Security Reform." Available at www.concordcoalition.org/socialsecurity/000628issuebriefsocsecrefgorebush.pdf.

Congressional Quarterly. 1999. "ESEA Title I Reauthorization." *CQ Weekly,* November 27.

Connolly, Ceci. 2002. "The Best Care Money Can Buy." *Washington Post National Weekly Edition,* June 3–9, 8.

Connolly, William. E., ed. 1969. *The Bias of Pluralism.* New York: Atherton.

Conviser, Richard. 1996. "A Brief History of the Oregon Health Plan and Its Features." Available at www.ohppr.state.or.us/docs/pdf/histofplan.pdf.

Cooper, Kenneth J. 2000. "A Campus Diversity Experiment." *Washington Post National Weekly Edition,* April 10.

———. 2000. " 'Best and Brightest' Leave Teaching Early, Study Says." *Washington Post,* January 13.

Cortner, Hanna J., and Margaret A. Moote. 1999. *The Politics of Ecosystem Management.* Washington, D.C.: Island Press.

Cronin, Thomas E. 1989. *Direct Democracy: The Politics of Initiative, Referendum, and Recall.* Cambridge: Harvard University Press.

Crossette, Barbara. 2002. "U.N. Agency on Population Blames U.S. for Cutbacks." *New York Times,* April 7, A11.

Dahl, Robert A. 1966. *Who Governs? Democracy and Power in an American City.* New Haven: Yale University Press.

Daily, Gretchen, ed. 1997. *Nature's Services: Societal Dependence on Natural Ecosystems.* Washington, D.C.: Island Press.

Dao, James. 2001. "Amid Applause, Caution Urged on Missile Defense." *New York Times,* July 16, A8.

———. 2002. "16 of 21 B-2's Have Cracks Near Exhaust, Officials Say." *New York Times,* March 20, A19.

Davidson, Roger H., and Walter J. Oleszek. 2002. *Congress and Its Members.* 8th ed. Washington, D.C.: CQ Press.

Davies, J. Clarence, ed. 1996. *Comparing Environmental Risks: Tools for Setting Government Priorities.* Washington, D.C.: Resources for the Future.

Davies, J. Clarence III, and Barbara S. Davies. 1975. *The Politics of Pollution.* 2d ed. Indianapolis: Bobbs-Merrill.

Davies, J. Clarence, and Jan Mazurek. 1998. *Pollution Control in the United States: Evaluating the System.* Washington, D.C.: Resources for the Future.

Davis, Charles, ed. 2001. *Western Public Lands and Environmental Politics.* Boulder: Westview Press.

Delaker, Joseph. 1998. U.S. Census Bureau, Current Population Reports, Series P60–207, *Poverty in the United States: 1998.* Washington, D.C.: U.S. Government Printing Office.

deLeon, Peter. 1997. *Democracy and the Policy Sciences.* Albany: State University of New York Press.

Denniston, Lyle. 1999. "Federal Court Judge Strikes Down Cleveland School Voucher Program," *Baltimore Sun,* December 21.

Derthick, Martha. 1979. *Policymaking for Social Security.* Washington, D.C.: Brookings Institution.

———. 2002. *Up In Smoke: From Legislation to Litigation in Tobacco Politics.* Washington, D.C.: CQ Press.

Dionne, E. J., 1997. *"Welfare Reform: The Clues Are in Wisconsin."* Washington Post, September 23.

———. 2000. "Why Americans Hate Politics." *Brookings Review* 18, no. 1 (winter).

Donahue, John D. 1997. *Disunited States.* New York: Basic Books.

Duffy, Robert J. 1997. *Nuclear Politics in America: A History and Theory of Government Regulation.* Lawrence: University Press of Kansas.

Dunlap, Riley E. 1995. "Public Opinion and Environmental Policy." In *Environmental Politics and Policy.* Edited by James P. Lester. Durham: Duke University Press.

Dunlap, Riley E., Michael E. Kraft, and Eugene A. Rosa, eds. 1993. *Public Reactions to Nuclear Waste: Citizens' Views of Repository Siting.* Durham: Duke University Press.

Dunn, William J. 1994. *Public Policy Analysis: An Introduction.* 2d ed. Englewood Cliffs, N.J.: Prentice Hall.

Dye, Thomas R. 2001. *Top Down Policymaking.* New York: Chatham House.

Dye, Thomas R., and L. Harmon Zeigler. 2003. *The Irony of Democracy.* 12th ed. Monterey, Calif.: Brooks/Cole.

Easton, David. 1965. *A Systems Analysis of Political Life.* New York: Wiley.

Eberstadt, Nicholas. 1995. *The Tyranny of Numbers: Mismeasurement and Misrule.* Washington, D.C.: AEI Press.

Edelman, Murray. 1964. *The Symbolic Uses of Politics.* Urbana: University of Illinois Press.

Ehrlich, Paul R. 1968. *The Population Bomb.* New York: Ballantine.

Eisner, Marc Allen, Jeff Worsham, and Evan J. Ringquist. 2000. *Contemporary Regulatory Policy.* Boulder: Lynne Rienner.

Elazar, Daniel J. 1984. *American Federalism: A View from the States.* 3d ed. New York: Harper and Row.

Ellis, Richard J. 2002. *Democratic Delusions: The Initiative Process in America.* Lawrence: University Press of Kansas.

Eulau, Heinz, and Kenneth Prewitt. 1973. *Labyrinths of Democracy.* Indianapolis: Bobbs-Merrill.

Fideler, Elizabeth F., Elizabeth D. Foster, and Shirley Schwartz. 2000. *The Urban Teacher Challenge.* Urban Teacher Collaborative. (January). Available at www.cgcs.org/pdfs/utc.pdf.

Figlio, David N. 1995. "The Effect of Drinking Age Laws and Alcohol-Related Crashes: Time Series Evidence from Wisconsin." *Journal of Policy Analysis and Management* 14: 555–566.

Fischer, Frank. 1995. *Evaluating Public Policy.* Chicago: Nelson-Hall Publishers.

Flavin, Christopher, Hilary French, Gary Gardner, et al. 2002. *State of the World 2002.* Washington, D.C.: Worldwatch Institute.

Fletcher, Michael A. 2002. "A Cap and Gown Gender Gap." *Washington Post National Weekly Edition,* July 1–14. 30.

Florig, H. Keith. 2002. "Is Safe Mail Worth the Price?" *Science* 295: 1467–1468.

Foerstel, Karen. 2002. "Moderation on Endangered List as Safe Seats Breed Rigidity." *CQ Weekly,* May 18, 2002, 1282.

Freeman, A. Myrick III. 2000. "Economics, Incentives, and Environmental Regulation." In *Environmental Policy.* 4th ed. Edited by Norman J. Vig and Michael E. Kraft. Washington, D.C.: CQ Press.

———. 2003. "Economics, Incentives, and Environmental Policy." In *Environmental Policy.* 5th ed. Edited by Norman J.Vig and Michael F. Kraft. Washington: D.C.: CQ Press.

Freeman, J. Leiper. 1965. *The Political Process: Executive Bureau-Legislative Committee Relations.* Rev. ed. New York: Random House.

Freudenheim, Milt. 2002. "Study Finds Inefficiency in Health Care." *New York Times,* June 11, C12.

Fritschler, A. Lee, with James M. Hoefler. 1995. *Smoking and Politics: Policy Making and the Federal Bureaucracy.* 5th ed. Englewood Cliffs. N.J.: Prentice Hall.

Geiger, Keith. 1992. "Merit Pay Programs Do Not Improve Teacher Performance." In *Education in America: Opposing Viewpoints.* Edited by Charles P. Cozic. San Diego: Greenhaven Press.

Georgia Student Finance Commission. 1999. "Hope Scholarship Program." Available at www.gsfc.org/hope.

Gerth, Jeff, and Sheryl Gay Stolberg. 2000. "Drug Industry Nurses Ties to Wide Range of Groups." *New York Times,* October 5, 1, A23.

Gilmore, John B. 1995. *Strategic Disagreement: Stalemate in American Politics.* Pittsburgh: University of Pittsburg Press.

Goggin, Malcolm L., Ann O'M. Bowman, James P. Lester, and Laurence J. O'Toole Jr. 1990. *Implementation Theory and Practice: Toward a Third Generation.* Glenview, Ill.: Scott Foresman/Little Brown.

Goldenberg, Jacob, David Mazursky, and Sorin Solomon. 1999. "Creative Sparks." *Science,* September 3: 1495–1496.

Gormley, William T., Jr. 1987. "Institutional Policy Analysis: A Critical Review." *Journal of Policy Analysis and Management* 6 (March): 153–169.

Graham, Mary. 2002. *Democracy by Disclosure: The Rise of Technopopulism.* Washington, D.C.: Brookings Institution.

Graham, Mary, and Catherine Miller. 2001. "Disclosure of Toxic Releases in the United States." *Environment* 43 (October): 6–20.

Green, Donald P., and Ian Shapiro. 1994. *Pathologies of Rational Choice Theory: A Critique of Applications in Political Science.* New Haven: Yale University Press.

Greene, Jay, Paul Peterson, Jiangtao Du. 1996 *The Effectiveness of School Choice in Milwaukee: A Secondary Analysis of Data from the Program's Evaluation.* Cambridge: Harvard University.

Greenhouse, Linda. 2002. "Supreme Court Upholds Voucher System that Pays Religious Schools' Tuition." *New York Times,* June 28, A1.

Greenhouse, Steven. 2001. "Ergonomics Report Cites Job Injuries." *New York Times,* January 18, C6.

———. 2002. "Bush Plan to Avert Work Injuries Seeks Voluntary Steps by Industry." *New York Times,* April 6, A1–A12.

Hacker, Jacob S. 1997. *The Road to Nowhere: The Genesis of President Clinton's Plan for Health Security.* Princeton: Princeton University Press.

Hadden, Susan G. 1989. *A Citizen's Right to Know: Risk Communication and Public Policy.* Boulder: Westview Press.

Harris, Richard A., and Stanley M. Milkis. 1996. *The Politics of Regulatory Change: A Tale of Two Agencies.* 2d ed. New York: Oxford University Press.

Haveman, Robert. 1999. "The Poverty Problem After a Forty-Year War: Reflections and a Look to the Future." *The LaFollette Policy Report* 10, no. 2 (fall).

Heclo, Hugh. 1978. "Issue Networks and the Executive Establishment." In *The New American Political System.* Edited by Anthony King. Washington, D.C.: American Enterprise Institute.

Hedge, David M. 1998. *Governance and the Changing American States.* Boulder: Westview Press.

Hibbing, John R., and Elizabeth Theiss-Morse. 1995. *Congress as Public Enemy: Public Attitudes Toward American Political Institutions.* New York: Cambridge University Press.

——— 2002. *Stealth Democracy: America's Beliefs about How Government Should Work.* New York: Cambridge University Press.

Hill, Stuart. 1992. *Democratic Values and Technological Choices.* Stanford: Stanford University Press.

Hogwood, Brian W., and Lewis A. Gunn. 1984. *Policy Analysis for the Real World.* Oxford, U.K.: Oxford University Press.

Homer-Dixon, Thomas. 1999. *Environment, Scarcity, and Violence.* Princeton: Princeton University Press.

Howell, William G., and Paul E. Peterson. 2002. *The Education Gap: Vouchers and Urban Schools.* Washington, D.C.: Brookings Institution.

Huber, Peter. 1999. *Hard Green: Saving the Environment from the Environmentalists (A Conservative Manifesto).* New York: Basic Books.

Illinois State Board of Education. 2001. "Where Are the Illinois Charter Schools?" Available at www.isbe.state.il.us/charter/charterschoolsinbrief.htm.

Ingram, Helen, and Steven Rathgeb Smith, eds. 1993. *Public Policy for Democracy.* Washington, D.C.: Brookings Institution.

Institute of Medicine. 2002. *Care Without Coverage: Too Little, Too Late.* Washington, D.C.: National Academy Press.

Jehl, Douglas. 2002. "Atlanta's Growing Thirst Creates Water War." *New York Times,* May 27, 1, A9.

———. 2003. "On Environmental Rules, Bush Sees a Balance, Critics a Threat." *New York Times,* February 23, 1, 22.

Jenkins-Smith, Hank C. 1990. *Democratic Politics and Policy Analysis.* Pacific Grove, Calif.: Brooks/Cole.

Jerald, Craig D. 2002. "No Action: Putting an End to Out-of-Field Teaching." The Education Trust (August). Available at www.edtrust.org/main/documents/AllTalk.pdf.

John, Dewitt, and Marian Mlay. 1999. "Community-Based Environmental Protection: Encouraging Civic Environmentalism." In *Better Environmental Decisions: Strategies for Governments, Businesses, and Communities.* Edited by Ken Sexton, Alfred A. Marcus, K. William Easter, and Timothy D. Burkhardt. Washington, D.C.: Island Press.

Johnston, David Cay. 1999. "Gap Between Rich and Poor Found Substantially Wider." *New York Times,* September 5, 14.

Jones, Charles O. 1975. *Clean Air: The Policies and Politics of Pollution Control.* Pittsburgh: University of Pittsburgh Press.

———. 1984. *An Introduction to the Study of Public Policy.* 3d ed. Monterey, Calif.: Brooks/Cole.

———. 1999. *Separate but Equal Branches: Congress and the Presidency.* 2d ed. New York: Chatham House Publishers.

Jost, Kenneth. 1999. "Patients' Rights." In *Issues for Debate in American Public Policy.* Edited by Sandra L. Stencel. Washington, D.C.: CQ Press.

———. 2001. "Affirmative Action." *CQ Researcher,* September 21, 737–760.

Kantrowitz, Barbara, and Daniel McGinn. 2000. "When Teachers Are Cheaters." *Newsweek,* June 19.

Kelman, Steven. 1980. "Occupational Safety and Health Administration." In *The Politics of Regulation.* Edited by James Q. Wilson. New York: Basic Books.

Kent, Mary M, and Mark Mather. 2002. "What Drives U.S. Population Growth." *Population Bulletin* 57 (December): 1–40.

Kerwin, Cornelius M. 1999. *Rulemaking: How Government Agencies Write Law and Make Policy.* 2d ed. Washington, D.C.: CQ Press.

Kessler, Glenn. 2000. "Analysis: Real Surplus May Be in Promises." *Washington Post,* July 19.

Kingdon, John W. 1995. *Agendas, Alternatives, and Public Policies.* 2d ed. New York: HarperCollins College.

Kitfield, James. 2000. "The Ultimate Bomb Shelter." *National Journal,* July 8, 2212–2223.

Koch, Kathy. 1999. "School Vouchers." *CQ Researcher,* April 9, 281–304.

———. 2000. "Hunger in America," *CQ Researcher,* December 22, 1033–1056.

Kolata, Gina. 2002. "With Vaccine Available, Smallpox Debate Shifts." *New York Times,* March 30, A8.

Kraft, Michael E. 1981. "Congress and National Energy Policy: Assessing the Policy Process." In *Environment, Energy, Public Policy: Toward a Rational Future.* Edited by Regina S. Axelrod. Lexington, Mass.: Lexington Books.

———. 1992. "Technology, Analysis, and Policy Leadership: Congress and Radioactive Waste." In *Science, Technology, and Politics,* Edited by Gary C. Bryner. Boulder: Westview Press.

———. 1994. "Population Policy." In *Encyclopedia of Policy Studies.* 2d ed. Edited by Stuart S. Nagel. New York: Marcel Dekker.

———. 2000. "Policy Design and the Acceptability of Environmental Risks: Nuclear Waste Disposal in Canada and the United States." *Policy Studies Journal* 28 (1): 206–218.

———. 2003. "Environmental Policy in Congress: From Consensus to Gridlock." In *Environmental Policy.* 5th ed. Edited by Norman J. Vig and Michael E. Kraft. Washington, D.C.: CQ Press.

———. 2004. *Environmental Policy and Politics.* 3d ed. New York: Addison Wesley Longman.

Kriz, Margaret. 2001. "Hot Rod Targets." *National Journal,* December 15, 3838–3840.

Krugman, Paul. 2002. "For Richer: How the Permissive Capitalism of the Boom Destroyed American Equality." *New York Times magazine,* October 20, 62–67, 76–77, 141–142.

Lasswell, Harold D. 1958. *Politics: Who Gets What, When, How.* New York: Meridian Books. Originally published in 1936 by McGraw-Hill.

Lewin, Tamar. 2000. "Now a Majority: Families with 2 Parents Who Work." *New York Times,* October 24, A14.

Lieske, Joel. 1993. "Regional Subcultures of the United States." *Journal of Politics* 55 (4): 888–913.

Light, Paul. 1995. *Still Artful Work.* 2d ed. New York: McGraw-Hill.

Lindblom, Charles E. 1972. "Integration of Economics and the Other Social Sciences Through Policy Analysis." In *Integration of the Social Sciences through Policy Analysis.* Edited by James C. Charlesworth. Philadelphia: American Academy of Political and Social Science.

Lindblom, Charles E., and David K. Cohen. 1979. *Usable Knowledge: Social Science and Social Problem Solving.* New Haven: Yale University Press.

Lindblom, Charles E., and Edward J. Woodhouse. 1993. *The Policy-Making Process.* 3d ed. Upper Saddle River, N.J.: Prentice Hall.

Llanos, Miguel. 2000. "States Get C- on Teacher Quality." MSNBC, at www.msnbc.com/news/356550.asp?cp1=1.

Loprest, Pamela. 1999. "Long Ride from Welfare to Work." *Washington Post.* August 30.

Lowi, Theodore J. 1964. "American Business, Public Policy, Case Studies, and Political Theory." *World Politics* 16 (July): 667–715.

———. 1979. *The End of Liberalism.* 2d ed. New York: W. W. Norton.

Lowrance, William W. 1976. *Of Acceptable Risk: Science and the Determination of Safety.* Los Altos, Calif.: William Kaufman.

Lowry, William R. 2003. "A New Era in Natural Resource Policies?" In *Environmental Policy.* 5th ed. Edited by Norman J. Vig and Michael E. Kraft. Washington, D.C.: CQ Press.

Lubchenco, Jane. 1998. "Entering the Century of the Environment: A New Social Contract for Science." *Science,* January 23, 491–497.

Mackenzie, G. Calvin, and Judith M. Labiner. 2002. "Opportunity Lost: The Rise and Fall of Trust and Confidence in Government After September 11." Washington, D.C.: Brookings Institution, Center for Public Service. Available at www.brook.edu.

MacRae, Duncan, Jr., and Dale Whittington. 1997. *Expert Advice for Policy Choice: Analysis and Discourse.* Washington, D.C.: Georgetown University Press.

MacRae, Duncan, Jr., and James A. Wilde. 1979. *Policy Analysis for Public Decisions.* North Scituate, Mass.: Duxbury.

Manza, Jeff, Fay Lomax Cook, and Benjamin I. Page, eds. 2002. *Navigating Public Opinion: Polls, Policy, and the Future of American Democracy.* New York: Oxford University Press.

Marmor, Theodore R. 1999. *The Politics of Medicare.* 2d ed. Hawthorne, N.Y.: Aldine de Gruyter.

Martinez, Gebe. 2002a. "Playing the Blame Game on Farm-Friendly Politics." *CQ Weekly,* April 20, 1008–1014.

———. 2002b. "Free-Spending Farm Bill a Triumph of Politics." *CQ Weekly,* May 4, 1147–1149.

Mayhew, David R. 1974. *Congress: The Electoral Connection.* New Haven: Yale University Press.

———. 1991. *Divided We Govern: Party Control, Lawmaking, and Investigations 1946–1990.* New Haven: Yale University Press.

Mayo, Bernard, ed. 1942. *Jefferson Himself.* Cambridge: Riverside Press.

Mazmanian, Daniel A., and Michael E. Kraft, eds. 1999. *Toward Sustainable Communities: Transition and Transformations in Environmental Policy.* Cambridge: MIT Press.

Mazmanian, Daniel A., and Paul A. Sabatier. 1983. *Implementation and Public Policy.* Glenview, Ill: Scott Foresman.

McConnell, Grant. 1966. *Private Power and American Democracy.* New York: Random House.

McCool, Daniel C. 1990. "Subgovernments as Determinants of Political Viability." *Political Science Quarterly* 105 (summer): 269–293.

———, ed. 1995. *Public Policy Theories, Models, and Concepts: An Anthology.* Englewood Cliffs, N.J.: Prentice Hall.

McCormick, John. 1989. *Reclaiming Paradise: The Global Environmental Movement.* Bloomington: Indiana University Press.

McQueen, Anjetta. 2001. "Welfare Law's Big Question: Has Success Been Real?" *CQ Weekly,* March 30, 869–870.

Mead, Lawrence M. 1986. *Beyond Entitlement: The Social Obligations of Citizenship.* New York: Free Press.

Meier, Kenneth J. 1993. *Politics and the Bureaucracy: Policymaking in the Fourth Branch of Government.* Pacific Grove, Calif.: Brooks/Cole.

Melville, Keith. 1996. *The National Piggybank: Does Our Retirement System Need Fixing?* National Issues Forums Institute. Dubuque, Iowa: Kendall/Hunt.

Metcalf, Kim K. 1999. "Evaluation of the Cleveland Scholarship Program, 1996–1999." (September). Bloomington: Indiana University, Indiana Center for Evaluation.

Metcalf, Kim, et al. 1998. *A Comparative Evaluation of the Cleveland Scholarship and Tutoring Program and Evaluation of the Cleveland Scholarship Program, Second Year Report, 1997–98.* Bloomington: Indiana University, Indiana Center for Evaluation.

Mezey, Michael L. 1989. *Congress, the President and Public Policy.* Boulder: Westview.

Millikan, Max F. 1959. "Inquiry and Policy: The Relation of Knowledge to Action." In *The Human Meaning of the Social Sciences.* Edited by Daniel Lerner. New York: Meridian Books.

Miringoff, Marc, and Marque-Luisa Miringoff. 1999. *Social Health of the Nation: How America Is Really Doing.* New York: Oxford.

Mitchell, Alison. 2002. "Law's Sponsors Fault Draft of Campaign Finance Rules." *New York Times,* May 31, A16.

Montgomery, Lori. 2001. "Are Our Suburbs Making Us Fat?" *Washington Post National Weekly Edition,* January 29–February 4, 31.

Moore, Stephen, and Dean Stansel. 1995. "Ending Corporate Welfare as We Know It." *Cato Institute Policy Analysis* 225, May 12.

Mortenson Research Seminar on Public Policy Analysis of Opportunity for Postsecondary Education. 1997. "The Rise and Fall of State Investment Effort in Higher Education, 1962–2002," *Postsecondary Education Opportunity* 115. January.

Murray, Mark. 2002. "Road Test." *National Journal,* May 25, 1548–53.

Nather, David, with Anjetta McQueen. 2001. "Social Security Overhaul Panel's Report Lands with a Thud." *CQ Weekly,* December 15, 2982–2983.

National Academy of Public Administration. 1995. *Setting Priorities, Getting Results: A New Direction for EPA.* Washington, D.C.: National Academy of Public Administration.

————. 2000. *Environment.gov: Transforming Environmental Protection for the 21st Century.* Washington, D.C.: National Academy of Public Administration.

National Association of State Budget Officers. 2002. *The Fiscal Survey of States.* Available at www.nasbo.org/Publications/fiscsurv/may2002fiscalsurvey.pdf.

National Commission on Retirement Policy. 1999. *The 21st Century Retirement Security Plan: Final Report of the National Commission on Retirement Policy.* (March). Washington, D.C.: Center for Strategic and International Studies, CSIS Press.

National Education Association. 2002. "Vouchers." Available at www.nea.org/issues/vouchers/index.html.

Nestle, Marion. 2002. *Food Politics: How the Food Industry Influences Nutrition and Health.* Berkeley: University of California Press.

Nieves, Evelyn. 2000. "California Gets Set to Shift on Sentencing Drug Users." *New York Times,* November 10.

Nozick, Robert. 1974. *Anarchy, State and Utopia.* New York: Basic Books.

Nye, Joseph S., Philip D. Zelikov, and David C. King, eds. 1997. *Why People Don't Trust Government.* Cambridge: Harvard University Press.

O'Connor, Karen, and Larry J. Sabato. 2002. *American Government: Continuity and Change.* Boston: Allyn and Bacon.

Office of Personnel Management. 2002. *Federal Civilian Workforce Statistics: The Fact Book, 2002 Edition.* Available at www.opm.gov/feddata/02factbk.pdf.

O'Leary, Rosemary. 2003. "Environmental Policy in the Courts." In *Environmental Policy.* 5th ed. Edited by Norman J. Vig and Michael E. Kraft. Washington, D.C.: CQ Press.

Olson, Mancur. 1971. *The Logic of Collective Action.* Cambridge: Harvard University Press.

Ophuls, William, and A. Stephen Boyan Jr. 1992. *Ecology and the Politics of Scarcity Revisited: The Unraveling of the American Dream.* New York: W. H. Freeman.

Orszag, Peter. 2000. "Impact of 2 Percent Accounts on Social Security Solvency." Center on Budget and Policy Priorities. May 15.

Ostrom, Elinor. 1998. "A Behavioral Approach to the Rational Choice Theory of Collective Action." *American Political Science Review* 92, 1 (March): 1–22.

————. 1999. "Institutional Rational Choice: An Assessment of the Institutional Analysis and Development Framework." In *Theories of the Policy Process.* Edited by Paul A. Sabatier. Boulder: Westview Press.

Paehlke, Robert. 2003. "Environmental Sustainability and Urban Life in America." In *Environmental Policy.* 5th ed. Edited by Norman J. Vig and Michael E. Kraft. Washington, D.C.: CQ Press.

Page, Benjamin I. 1992. *The Rational Public: Fifty Years of Trends in Americans' Policy Preferences.* Chicago: University of Chicago Press.

Parry, Ian W. H. 2002. "Is Gasoline Undertaxed in the United States?" *Resources* (summer), issue 148: 28–33.

Patel, Kant, and Mark E. Rushefsky. 2000. *Health Care Politics and Policy in America.* 2d ed. Armonk, N.Y.: M. E. Sharpe.

Patton, Carl V., and David S. Sawicki. 1993. *Basic Methods of Policy Analysis and Planning.* 2d ed. Englewood Cliffs, N.J.: Prentice Hall.

Pear, Robert. 2000. "A Million Parents Lost Medicaid, Study Says." *New York Times,* June 20.

————. 2002. "Governors Say Medicaid Needs More Federal Help to Control Rising Costs." *New York Times,* February 15, A14.

Perl, Peter. 2000. "Packaged Poison: Why Did Regulators Act So Slowly in a Deadly Case of Food Contamination." *Washington Post National Weekly Edition,* January 24, 6–10.

Peters, B. Guy. 2000. *American Public Policy: Promise and Performance.* 5th ed. New York: Chatham House.

Peterson, Paul E., and Mark Rom. 1988. "Lower Taxes, More Spending, and Budget Deficits." In *The Reagan Legacy: Promise and Performance.* Edited by Charles O. Jones. Chatham, N.J.: Chatham House.

Peterson, Paul E., William G. Howell, and Jay P. Green. 1999. "An Evaluation of the Cleveland Voucher Program After Two Years." (June). Cambridge: Harvard University, Program on Education Policy and Governance.

Pianin, Eric. 2002, "A Yucca Nuclear Showdown." *Washington Post National Weekly Edition,* April 22–28, 30–31.

Pianin, Eric, and John M. Berry. 1999. "Taking the High Ground." *Washington Post National Weekly Edition,* February 8.

Polsby, Nelson W. 1980. *Community Power and Political Theory.* 2d ed. New Haven: Yale University Press.

Portney, Kent E. 2003. *Taking Sustainable Cities Seriously: Economic Development, the Environment, and Quality of Life in American Cities.* Cambridge: MIT Press.

Portney, Paul R., and Robert N. Stavins, eds. 2000. *Public Policies for Environmental Protection.* Washington, D.C.: Resources for the Future.

Presidential/Congressional Commission on Risk Assessment and Risk Management. 1997. *Risk Assessment and Risk Management in Regulatory Decision-Making.* Vol. 2: Final Report. Washington, D.C.: Presidential/Congressional Commission on Risk Assessment and Risk Management. Available at www.riskworld.com.

President's Council on Sustainable Development. 1996. *Sustainable America: A New Consensus for Prosperity, Opportunity, and a Health Environment.* Washington, D.C.: Government Printing Office.

Pressman, Jeffrey L., and Aaron Wildavsky. 1979. *Implementation.* Berkeley: University of California Press.

Public Agenda Online. 2002a. Education Fact Files. Available at www.publicagenda.org/issues/factfiles. cfm?issue_type=education.

———. 2002b. Federal Budget Fact File. Available at www.publicagenda.org/issues/factfiles_ detail.cfm?issue_ type=federal_budget.

Purdum, Todd S. 2000. "Booming Economy Helping California Improve Its Schools." *New York Times,* June 26.

Putnam, Robert D. 1995. "Tuning In, Tuning Out: The Strange Disappearance of Social Capital in America." *PS: Political Science and Politics* 28 (December): 664–683.

———. 2000. *Bowling Alone: The Collapse and Revival of American Community.* New York: Simon and Schuster.

Rabe, Barry G. 2002. "Statehouse and Greenhouse: The States Are Taking the Lead on Climate Change." *Brookings Review* 20, 2 (spring): 11–13.

———. 2003. "Power to the States: The Promise and Pitfalls of Decentralization." In *Environmental Policy.* 5th ed. Edited by Norman J. Vig and Michael E. Kraft. Washington, D.C.: CQ Press.

Raffensperger, Carolyn, and Joel Tickner. 1999. *Protecting Public Health and the Environment: Implementing the Precautionary Principle.* Washington, D.C.: Island Press.

Raney, Rebecca Fairley. 2002. "From Parking to Taxes, a Push to Get Answers Online." *New York Times,* April 4.

Rawls, John. 1971. *A Theory of Justice.* Cambridge: Harvard University Press.

Rein, Martin. 1976. *Social Science and Public Policy.* New York: Penguin Books.

Revkin, Andrew C. 2002. "Dispute Arises Over a Push to Climate Change Panel." *New York Times,* April 2, A10.

Ricci, David M. 1993. *The Transformation of American Politics: The New Washington and the Rise of Think Tanks.* New Haven: Yale University Press.

Ringquist, Evan J. 1993. *Environmental Protection at the State Level: Politics and Progress in Controlling Pollution.* Armonk, N.Y.: M. E. Sharpe.

———. 2003. "Environmental Justice: Normative Concerns, Empirical Evidence, and Governmental Action." In *Environmental Policy.* 5th ed. Edited by Norman J. Vig and Michael E. Kraft. Washington, D.C.: CQ Press.

Ripley, Randall B., and Grace A. Franklin. 1986. *Policy Implementation and Bureaucracy.* 2d ed. Chicago: Dorsey Press.

———. 1991. *Congress, the Bureaucracy, and Public Policy.* 5th ed. Pacific Grove, Calif.: Brooks/Cole.

Rochefort, David A, and Roger W. Cobb, eds. 1994. *The Politics of Problem Definition: Shaping the Policy Agenda.* Lawrence: University Press of Kansas.

Rosenbaum, David E. 2002. "Senate Blocks Drilling in Alaska Wildlife Refuge." *New York Times,* April 19, A6.

Rosenbaum, Walter A. 2003. "Still Reforming After All These Years: George W. Bush's 'New Era' at EPA." In *Environmental Policy.* 5th ed. Edited by Norman J. Vig and Michael E. Kraft. Washington, D.C.: CQ Press.

Rossi, Peter H., Howard E. Freeman, and Mark W. Lipsky. 1999. *Evaluation: A Systematic Approach.* 6th ed. Newbury Park, Calif.: Sage Publications.

Rouse, Cecilia E. 1997. *Private School Vouchers and Student Achievement: An Evaluation of the Milwaukee Parental Choice Program.* Princeton: Princeton University Press.

———. 1998. "Private School Vouchers and Student Achievement: An Evaluation of the Milwaukee Parental Choice Program." *Quarterly Journal of Economics* 113 (May): 553–602.

Rowe, James L., Jr. 1999. "Holding the Purse Strings: Our Money and Our Economic Lives Depend on the Federal Reserve." *Washington Post National Weekly Edition,* June 28, 6–9.

Rushefsky, Mark E. 2002. *Public Policy in the United States.* 3d ed. Armonk, N.Y.: M. E. Sharpe.

Rushefsky, Mark E., and Kant Patel. 1998. *Politics, Power and Policy Making: The Case of Health Care Reform in the 1990s.* Armonk, N.Y.: M. E. Sharpe.

Russell, Milton. 1993. "NAPAP: A Lesson in Science Policy." *Forum for Applied Research and Public Policy* 8: 55–60.

Sabatier, Paul A., and Hank C. Jenkins-Smith, eds. 1993. *Policy Change and Learning: An Advocacy Coalition Approach.* Boulder: Westview Press.

Sanger, David E. 2002. "Bush Was Warned Bin Laden Wanted to Hijack Planes." *New York Times,* May 16.

Savas, E. S. 2000. *Privatization and Public-Private Partnerships.* New York: Chatham House.

Schattschneider, E. E. 1960. *The Semisovereign People: A Realist's View of Democracy in America.* New York: Holt, Rinehart, and Winston.

Scheberle, Denise. 1997. *Federalism and Environmental Policy: Trust and the Politics of Implementation.* Washington, D.C.: Georgetown University Press.

Schneider, Anne L., and Helen Ingram. 1997. *Policy Design for Democracy.* Lawrence: University Press of Kansas.

Seelye, Katharine Q. 2002. "President Distances Himself from Global Warming Report." *New York Times,* June 15, 2002, A19.

Serafini, Marilyn Werber. 2000. "First, Do No Harm." *National Journal,* February 19, 542–545.

Sexton, Ken, Alfred A. Marcus, K. William Easter, and Timothy D. Burkhardt, eds. 1999. *Better Environmental Decisions: Strategies for Governments, Businesses, and Communities.* Washington, D.C.: Island Press.

Shepsle, Kenneth A., and Mark S. Bonchek. 1997. *Analyzing Politics: Rationality, Behavior, and Institutions.* New York: W. W. Norton.

Shipan, Charles R., and William R. Lowry. 2001. "Environmental Policy and Party Divergence in Congress." *Political Research Quarterly* 54 (June): 245–263.

Shokrail Rees, Nina. 2000. "School Choice 2000: Annual Report." *The Heritage Foundation Backgrounder,* no. 1354, March 30. Online version available at www.heritage.org/Research/Education/loader.cfm?url=/commonspot/security/getfile.cfm&PageID=10973.

Shrader-Frechette, K. S. 1993. *Burying Uncertainty: Risk and the Case Against Geological Disposal of Nuclear Waste.* Berkeley: University of California Press.

Sinclair, Barbara. 2000. *Unorthodox Lawmaking: New Legislative Processes in the U.S. Congress.* 2d ed. Washington, D.C.: CQ Press.

Skocpol, Theda. 1995. *Social Policy in the United States: Future Possibilities in Historical Perspective.* Princeton, N.J.: Princeton University Press.

Skocpol, Theda, and Morris P. Fiorina, eds. 1999. *Civic Engagement in American Democracy.* Washington, D.C.: Brookings Institution.

Slivinski, Stephen. 2001. "The Corporate Welfare Budget: Bigger than Ever." *Cato Institute Policy Analysis,* no. 415, October 10.

Slovic, Paul. 1987. "Perception of Risk." *Science,* 280–285.

Social Security Administration. 1999. www.ssa.gov/statistics/Supplement/1998/Tables/PDF/t2f2.pdf (June 4).

Solomon, Burt. 1999. "False Prophets." *National Journal,* December 11.

Spinner, Jackie. 2002. "Don't Mess with Accountants." *Washington Post National Weekly Edition,* May 20–26, 20.

Starling, Grover, *Strategies for Policy Making.* Chicago: Dorsey Press, 1988.

Steinhauer, Jennifer. 2001. "Chasing Health Care Fraud Quietly Becomes Profitable." *New York Times,* January 23, A1, A17.

Stevenson, Richard W. 1999. "Missile System Passes a Test as a Target Is Destroyed." *New York Times,* October 4, A18.

———. 2001. "Social Security's Fate Hinges on Investing Plan, Panel Says." *New York Times,* July 25, A14.

Stolberg, Sheryl Gay. 2001. "Washington Not Alone in Cell Debate." *New York Times,* July 23, A12.

Stone, Deborah. 2002. *Policy Paradox: The Art of Political Decision Making.* New York: W. W. Norton.

Sundquist, James L. 1986. *Constitutional Reform and Effective Government.* Washington, D.C.: Brookings Institution.

Switzer, Jacqueline Vaughn. 1997. *Green Backlash: The History and Politics of Environmental Opposition in the U.S.* Boulder: Lynne Rienner.

Tanner, Michael. 2000. "Saving Social Security is Not Enough." *The Cato Project on Social Security Privatization,* May 25.

Thomas, Evan, and Pat Wingert. 2000. "Bitter Lessons." *Newsweek,* June 19.

Thomas, Norman C. 1975. *Educational Policy in National Politics.* New York: David McKay.

Thurber, James A. 1991. *Divided Democracy: Cooperation and Conflict Between the President and Congress.* Washington, D.C.: CQ Press.

———, ed. 1996a. *Rivals for Power: Presidential-Congressional Relations.* Washington, D.C.: CQ Press.

———. 1996b. "Congressional-Presidential Battles to Balance the Budget." In *Rivals for Power: Presidential-Congressional Relations.* Edited by James A. Thurber. Washington, D.C.:CQ Press.

Thurber, James A., and Samantha L. Durst. 1993. "The 1990 Budget Enforcement Act: The Decline of Congressional Accountability." In *Congress Reconsidered.* 5th ed. Edited by Lawrence C. Dodd and Bruce I. Oppenheimer. Washington, D.C.: CQ Press.

Toner, Robin. 2002. "Why the Elderly Wait . . . and Wait." *New York Times,* Week in Review section, June 23, 1, 14.

Tong, Rosemarie. 1986. *Ethics in Policy Analysis.* Englewood Cliffs, N.J.: Prentice Hall.

Tyson, Laura D'Andrea. 2001. "Bush's Tax Cut: Nickels and Dimes for the Working Poor." *Business Week,* July 2. Available at www.businessweek.com.

Uchitelli, Louis. 1997. "Economist's Survey Supports Theory That Inflation Is Overstated." *New York Times,* February 13.

United Nations. 1993. *Agenda 21: The United Nations Programme of Action from Rio.* New York: United Nations.

U.S. Congressional Budget Office. 1996. *Federal Budget Implications of H.R. 3734, The Personal Responsibility and Work Opportunity Reconciliation Act of 1996,* August 9, 1996.

———. 2002. "CBO Testimony: Budgetary Discipline." Available at www.house.gov/budget/hearings/anderson02.pdf.

U.S. Department of Commerce. 2000. "Gross Domestic Product: Fourth Quarter 1999 (Final) Revised Estimates, 1929–1999." Available at www.bea.doc.gov/bea/newsrel/gdp499f.pdf.

U.S. Department of Education. 1995. *Education Programs that Work: National Goals for Education.* Available at www.ed.gov/pubs/EPTW/eptwgoal.html.

———. 1999. "Annual Earnings of Young Adults, by Educational Attainment." Washington, D.C.: Department of Education, National Center for Education Statistics. Available at www.nces.ed.gov/pubs99/1999009.pdf.

———. 2001. "Digest of Education Statistics, 2001." Washington, D.C. Available at http://nces.ed.gov/pubs2002/digest2001/tables/dt168.asp.

———. 2002. "The Condition of Education." Washington, D.C. Available at http://nces.ed.gov/pubsearch/pubsinfo.asp?pubid=2002025.

U.S. Department of Health and Human Services. 2000. "Annual Report to Congress. Washington, D.C.: Administration for Children and Families, August. Available at www.acf.dhhs.gov/programs/opre/annual3.pdf.

U.S. Department of Labor, Bureau of Labor Statistics. 2000. Occupational Employment Statistics. 1998. *National Employment and Wage Data from the Occupational Employment Statistics.* (May). Available at http://stats.bls.gov/news.release/ocwage.t01.htm.

———. 2001. "Highlights of Women's Earnings in 2000." (August). Available at www.bls.gov/cps/cpswom2000.pdf.

U.S. Department of Treasury. 2002. "The Public Debt to the Penny." Available at www.publicdebt.treas.gov/opd/opdpenny.htm.

———. 2003. "Interest Expense on Public Debt Outstanding." Available at www.publicdebt.treas.gov/opd/opdint.htm.

U.S. Environmental Protection Agency. 1990. *Reducing Risk: Setting Priorities and Strategies for Environmental Protection.* Washington, D.C.: EPA, Science Advisory Board.

U.S. General Accounting Office. 1992. *Environmental Protection Issues, Transition Series.* Washington, D.C.: U.S. Government Printing Office.

———. 1996. *Social Security: Issues Involving Benefit Equity for Working Women.* (April). Washington, D.C.: U.S. Government Printing Office.

———. 1997. *Social Security Reform: Implications for Women's Retirement Income.* (December). Washington, D.C.: U.S. Government Printing Office.

———. 1998. *Welfare Reform: States Are Restructuring Programs to Reduce Welfare Dependence.* Washington, D.C.: U.S. Government Printing Office, June 17.

———. 1999. *Welfare Reform: Information on Former Recipients' Status.* Washington, D.C.: U.S. Government Printing Office, April 28.

U.S. Office of Management and Budget. 2002. *Budget of the United States Government: Fiscal Year 2003.* Available at www.whitehouse.gov/omb/budget/index.html

U.S. Social Security Administration. 2000. "Income of the Aged Chartbook 1998." (June).

———. 2002a. "The President's Budget for FY 2002." Available at www.ssa.gov/budget/#Summary.

———. 2002b. "Facts and Figures About Social Security." Available at www.ssa.gov/statistics/fast_facts/2002/index.html#toc.

———. 2002c. "The 2002 OASDI Trustees Report." At www.ssa.gov/OACT/TR/TR02/index.html.

Van Natta, Don, Jr., and Neela Banerjee. 2002. "Review Shows Energy Industry's Recommendations to Bush Ended Up Being National Policy." *New York Times,* March 28, A16.

Van Natta, Don, Jr., and David Johnston. 2002. "Wary of Risk, Slow to Adapt, F.B.I. Stumbles in Terror War." *New York Times,* June 2, 1, 24–25.

Vig, Norman J. 2003. "Presidential Leadership and the Environment." In *Environmental Policy.* 5th ed. Edited by Norman J. Vig and Michael E. Kraft. Washington, D.C.: CQ Press.

Vig, Norman J., and Regina S. Axelrod, eds. 1999. *The Global Environment: Institutions, Law, and Policy.* Washington, D.C.: CQ Press.

Vig, Norman J., and Michael E. Kraft, eds. 1984. *Environmental Policy in the 1980s: Reagan's New Agenda.* Washington, D.C.: CQ Press.

———. 2003. *Environmental Policy: New Directions for the Twenty-First Century.* 5th ed. Washington, D.C.: CQ Press.

Wald, Matthew L. 2001. "Low Seat Belt Use Linked to Teenage Death Rates." *New York Times,* May 21, A12.

———. 2002. "Bury the Nation's Nuclear Waste in Nevada, Bush Says." *New York Times,* February 16.

Walker, Jack L. 1977. "Setting the Agenda in the U.S. Senate: A Theory of Problem Selection." *British Journal of Political Science* 7: 423–445.

Weaver, R. Kent. 2000. *Ending Welfare as We Know It.* Washington, D.C.: Brookings Institution Press.

Weber, Edward P. 2003. *Bringing Society Back In: Grassroots Ecosystem Management, Accountability, and Sustainable Communities.* Cambridge: MIT Press.

Weimer, David L., and Aidan R. Vining. 1999. *Policy Analysis: Concepts and Practice*. 3d ed. Upper Saddle River, N.J.: Prentice Hall.

Weiss, Carol H. 1978. "Improving the Linkage Between Social Research and Public Policy." In *Knowledge and Policy: The Uncertain Connection*. Edited by Laurence E. Lynn Jr. Washington, D.C.: National Academy of Sciences.

———, ed. 1992. *Organizations for Policy Analysis: Helping Government Think*. Newbury Park, Calif.: Sage Publications.

Weiss, Edith Brown. 1990. "In Fairness to Future Generations." *Environment* 32, 3: 7–11, 30–31.

Whitaker, Barbara. 2000. "Minority Rolls Rebound at University of California." *New York Times,* April 4.

White, John K. 2002. *The Values Divide: American Politics and Culture in Transition*. New York: Chatham House.

Whiteman, David. 1995. *Communication in Congress: Members, Staff, and the Search for Information*. Lawrence: University Press of Kansas.

Wildavsky, Aaron, 1979. *Speaking Truth to Power: The Art and Craft of Policy Analysis*. Boston: Little, Brown.

———. 1988. *Searching for Safety.* New Brunswick, N.J.: Transaction Books.

Williams, Juan. 1987. *Eyes on the Prize: America's Civil Rights Years 1954–1965*. New York: Penguin Books.

Wilson, Edward O. 1998. *Consilience: The Unity of Knowledge*. New York: Knopf.

Wilson, James Q. 1977. *Thinking about Crime* New York: Vintage Books.

———, ed. 1980. *The Politics of Regulation*. New York: Basic Books.

Witte, John F. 2000. *The Market Approach to Education*. Princeton: Princeton University Press.

Witte, John, et al. 1995. *Fifth Year Report: Milwaukee Parental Choice Program,* University of Wisconsin-Madison.

———. 1997.*Achievement Effects of the Milwaukee Voucher Program,* University of Wisconsin-Madison.

Wolpe, Bruce C., and Bertram J. Levine. 1998. *Lobbying Congress: How the System Works*. Washington, D.C.: CQ Press.

Wondolleck, Julia M., and Steven L. Yaffee. 2000. *Making Collaboration Work: Lessons from Innovation in Natural Resources Management*. Washington, D.C.: Island Press.

World Commission on Environment and Development. 1987. *Our Common Future*. New York: Oxford University Press.

Worsnop, Richard L. 1999. "Reforming the FDA." In *Issues for Debate in American Public Policy.* Edited by Sandra L. Stencel. Washington, D.C.: CQ Press.

Zernike, Kate. 2001. "Antidrug Program Says It Will Adopt a New Strategy." *New York Times,* February 15, A1–A23.

# INDEX

# PHOTO CREDITS

**Frontispiece:** Courtesy of the National Archives

**Chapter 1:** 2 AP/Wide World Photos. 7 Thanks to Minnesota Prevention Resource Center, and a coalition of prevention partners. www.emprc.org. 18 AP/Wide World Photos.

**Chapter 2:** 32 AP/Wide World Photos. 40 Governor's Office of Arkansas. 48 AP/Wide World Photos. 54 AP/Wide World Photos.

**Chapter 3:** 68 AP/Wide World Photos. 72 Larry Downing/Reuters. 73 AP/Wide World Photos. 91 AP/Wide World Photos. 93 A/Wide World Photos.

**Chapter 4:** 100 AP/Wide World Photos. 120 Las Vegas Review-Journal, Craig L. Muran.

**Chapter 5:** 126 Photo courtesy of Amtrak. 131 TriMet, Portland, Oregon. 147 AP/Wide World Photos.

**Chapter 6:** 150 Courtesy of Unocal Alaska. 159 Mike Segar/Reuters. 167 Rick Fowler-STR/Reuters. 174 Win McNamee/Reuters.

**Chapter 7:** 178 AP/Wide World Photos. 182 UPI. 206 Courtesy of North County Times, Steven Thornton. 211 AP/Wide World Photos.

**Chapter 8:** 216 Courtesy of Soundoff! 226 Courtesy American Medical Association. 239 Getty Images. 247 Peter Morgan/Reuters.

**Chapter 9:** 252 Andy Clark/Reuters. 276 Peter Morgan/Reuters.

**Chapter 10:** 280 Courtesy of the Library of Congress. 303 Mike Levy © 2002 The Plain Dealer. All rights reserved. Reprinted with permission. 306 Denver Post, Lyn Alweis.

**Chapter 11:** 310 AP/Wide World Photos. 326 AP/Wide World Photos. 337 AP/Wide World Photos.

**Chapter 12:** 348 Bureau of Planning, Portland, OR. 351 Rebecca Cook/Reuters. 354 STR/Reuters.

# ABOUT THE AUTHORS

**MICHAEL E. KRAFT**

**SCOTT R. FURLONG**

**Michael E. Kraft** is professor of political science and public affairs and Herbert Fisk Johnson Professor of Environmental Studies at the University of Wisconsin, Green Bay. He is the author of numerous works, including *Environmental Policy and Politics,* 3d ed. (2003) and *Environmental Policy: New Directions in the 21$^{st}$ Century,* 5th ed. (2002). In addition, he cowrote *Toward Sustainable Communities: Transition and Transformations in Environmental Policy* with Daniel A. Mazmanian and *Technology and Politics* with Norman J. Vig and coedited *Public Reactions to Nuclear Waste* with Riley E. Dunlap and Eugene A. Rosa.

**Scott R. Furlong** is associate professor of political science and public affairs at the University of Wisconsin, Green Bay. His areas of expertise are regulatory policy and interest group participation in the executive branch, and he has taught public policy for ten years. His articles have appeared in such journals as *Public Administration Review, Journal of Public Administration, Research and Theory, Administrative Studies Quarterly,* and *Policy Studies Journal.*